SAP PRESS e-books

Print or e-book, Kindle or iPad, workplace or airplane: Choose
where and how to read your SAP PRESS books! You can now get
all our titles as e-books, too:

▶ By download and online access
▶ For all popular devices
▶ And, of course, DRM-free

Convinced? Then go to **www.sap-press.com** and get your
e-book today.

Pricing and the Condition Technique in SAP ERP®

 PRESS

SAP PRESS is a joint initiative of SAP and Rheinwerk Publishing. The know-how offered by SAP specialists combined with the expertise of Rheinwerk Publishing offers the reader expert books in the field. SAP PRESS features first-hand information and expert advice, and provides useful skills for professional decision-making.

SAP PRESS offers a variety of books on technical and business-related topics for the SAP user. For further information, please visit our website: *www.sap-press.com*.

Martin Murray, Jawad Akhtar
Materials Management with SAP ERP: Functionality and Technical
Configuration (4th edition)
2016, 739 pages, hardcover and e-book
www.sap-press.com/4062

Ricardo Lopez, Ashish Mohapatra
Configuring Sales and Distribution in SAP ERP (2nd edition)
2016, 526 pages, hardcover and e-book
www.sap-press.com/3903

Uwe Blumöhr, Manfred Münch, Marin Ukalovic
Variant Configuration with SAP (2nd edition)
2012, 694 pages, hardcover and e-book
www.sap-press.com/2889

Faisal Mahboob
Integrating Materials Management with Financial Accounting in SAP
(2nd edition)
2012, 508 pages, hardcover and e-book
www.sap-press.com/3125

Ursula Becker, Werner Herhuth, Manfred Hirn

Pricing and the Condition Technique in SAP ERP®

Rheinwerk®
Publishing

Bonn • Boston

Editor Meagan White
Acquisitions Editor Emily Nicholls
Translation Werner Herhuth, Ursula Becker
Copyeditor Kezia Endsley
Cover Design Graham Geary
Photo Credit Shutterstock.com/138706697/© sevenke
Layout Design Vera Brauner
Production Marissa Fritz
Typesetting SatzPro, Krefeld (Germany)
Printed and bound in the United States of America, on paper from sustainable sources

ISBN 978-1-4932-1421-1
© 2017 by Rheinwerk Publishing, Inc., Boston (MA)
1st edition 2017

Contents at a Glance

Dear Reader,

Having recently revisited my cable and internet bill with a beleaguered customer service representative, I can say the following in unequivocal terms: From a consumer's standpoint, pricing is complicated business.

From service packages (up to three TVs!) to bundled products (premium channels!); from temporary discounts (30% off, this week only!) to price hikes (surprise renewal charge!); and from special deals (router delivered at no charge!) to promotions ($15 rebate!), everything seems so…conditional.

So how does a seller set, track, modify, and enforce so many variables? For businesses that run SAP ERP, the key is the condition technique. Between these pages, expert authors Werner Herhuth, Ursula Becker, and Manfred Hirn cover pricing and the condition technique in SAP ERP from the ground up. Their book will help you both understand and modify your pricing landscape—letting you dig into the "why" and "how" of pricing. Whether you learn best by diving into nitty-gritty details or through practical examples, you're sure to find what you need to demystify pricing and set the best terms.

As always, your comments and suggestions are the most useful tools to help us make our books the best they can be. Let us know what you thought about *Pricing and the Condition Technique in SAP ERP*! Please feel free to contact me and share any praise or criticism you may have.

Thank you for purchasing a book from SAP PRESS!

Meagan White
Editor, SAP PRESS

Rheinwerk Publishing
Boston, MA

meaganw@rheinwerk-publishing.com
www.sap-press.com

Contents

PART II Standard Configuration

PART III   Advanced Techniques, Tips, and Tricks

11 System Adaptation Using Requirements, Formulas, and User Exits 385

Preface by Manfred Hirn

In 1984, after my first job in the IT department of a brewery, I had the opportunity to join SAP. I had gained some experience with the SAP R/2 software during a training session at SAP and I was impressed by its flexibility. During that session, I also obtained some insight as to the working environment of a developer of standard software and found it very exciting. As a software developer at SAP at that time, you were involved in all phases of the software development—from acquisition, design, implementation, support, and creating customer modifications, to training.

When, in 1987, SAP decided to address the specific demands of the consumer goods industry, I was given the task, together with some interested customers and a small team of colleagues, of enhancing the sales module of the SAP R/2 software accordingly. The solutions we developed were first implemented as customer modifications.

The greatest demands came from pricing. Despite their flexibility, the existing capabilities of the standard SAP system did not, by far, match the needs. The main challenge was to store the pricing information on any level of the customer or product hierarchy. The new solution's goal was to be able to handle any hierarchical structures and to cover the already existing SAP R/2 pricing, which consisted of product prices, price lists, and customer-specific prices.

The central component of this solution occurred to me during a train ride to Düsseldorf for a project meeting at the local SAP office. I called it the *access sequence*. This component opened up a new dimension of flexibility. Once the newly created *condition technique* was ready for the pricing component after a series of optimization steps, it was used to solve other determination processes, such as the material determination and the material listing.

Customer interest in the new pricing increased fast, and so I flew with a small magnetic tape to the United States, where I implemented and presented the software to a large chemical company. Everything went excellently. A little later, we adopted the solution into the standard SAP R/2 system.

Another milestone in the history of the pricing and condition technique was when the solution was transferred to the emerging SAP R/3 system. On this occasion, some significant improvements were made, in particular for the benefit of the flexibility. A particularly exciting aspect was our attempt to convince as many other departments as possible to use the Sales and Distribution pricing and condition technique for their areas, a campaign that was quite successful. In the following years, further optimization steps have been made, which ultimately led to the currently available functionality in the SAP ERP system—a functionality that is still unequaled today.

In all these exciting times, my motto has always been, "Nothing is impossible!" And after reading this book, you will find out that you can competently tackle new challenges in the condition technique and pricing.

Östringen,
Manfred Hirn

Preface by Werner Herhuth

In 1994, I worked on my first SAP R/3 implementation project (then on the customer side) and had my first contact with the pricing and with the condition technique. I was immediately impressed by the possibilities offered by the special nature of the configuration. However, I quickly came to my limits, as I could not program a special requirement that I considered necessary in order to achieve a particular behavior in pricing. After experimenting, I decided to create a support request describing my problem. A few days later, my phone rang. It was Manfred Hirn from SAP, who explained to me that my desired requirement must be set up as a condition value formula instead of as a requirement. Thus, the problem was solved. Because of my lack of detailed knowledge and experience, I had tried to find the solution for that specific problem in the wrong place.

This book is about the complexity of the pricing and the condition technique, which can be very difficult for beginners to deal with. When first starting out, you can handle many demands using the standard configuration (Customizing), after a fundamental introduction; however, this will not always be true.

As with so many areas of life, experience matters here—and experience is acquired faster if you have a mentor who can give you advice. We hope that this book will be such a mentor for you. Besides presenting the standard Customizing configuration, we also provide the detailed technical knowledge that you need to make customer-specific adaptations that are stable, performant, and of high quality (with the assumption that you meet some preconditions, such as a basic ABAP knowledge). There are always new demands on pricing from daily business dealings that you must meet.

Presenting this detailed knowledge in such a comprehensive way has only been possible because I convinced Manfred Hirn—the inventor and developer of the condition technique—to collaborate on this book.

In retrospect, I do not really know why I did not ask him much earlier. The time was right for this book, and I am confident that it will be an important source of information and a frequently used reference book for all who deal with the pricing and condition technique.

Mannheim,
Werner Herhuth

Preface by Ursula Becker

My journey with SAP began in 1998 in the Development Support department, where I worked on customer tickets in the area of the pricing and condition technique. In addition to the occasional genuine programming errors that were to be corrected, the majority of the support tickets dealt with inquiries in which the questioner just lacked the right knowledge about the possibilities and (perhaps) the pitfalls of pricing. Initially, I often went into the office of Manfred Hirn, who fortunately sat right next to me. I soon learned about the rich functionality and flexibility of the pricing and condition technique and how many requirements can be fulfilled when you have the right knowledge. Actually, there is hardly any requirement that cannot be met.

After two years, I moved out of support and into the Development department and on to other applications. However, pricing never completely let me go, since it is closely linked to so many other areas. Therefore, a few years later, I happily took the opportunity to return to pricing as a development architect.

When the inquiry came if I would be available for a second edition of the German-language book, I agreed immediately. As luck would have it, after years of relative quiet, there were some interesting new developments that—in my opinion— deserve to be presented to a wider audience. In this book, you will learn about configurable parameters and formulas, for example, which increase the flexibility of pricing and bridge the gap between the pricing and condition technique on one side and SAP's Business Rules Framework on the other.

A detailed section on rebate processing has also been included. Although this is not a new application, it lacked a truly comprehensive view before now. This may be due to the fact that rebate processing is so highly dependent on the condition technique and pricing application that a description outside this context is always in danger of remaining superficial. Therefore, this book offers a unique opportunity to introduce rebate processing as the "little brother" of the pricing functionality.

Dossenheim,
Ursula Becker

Introduction

Everything has its price. This is especially true when buying or selling products, whether goods or services. When you create a sales order or a purchase order in the SAP ERP system, for example, the system will always calculate and propose a sales price or purchase price. How does the system actually perform this process and how can you adjust the pricing and calculation so that they meet your demands? After all, there are various ways to determine a price. There are, for example, special wholesale and quantity discounts or time-limited special conditions and freight costs and taxes to be considered. All these price elements need to be stored somewhere in the system so that they can be found and combined by flexible rules to determine the desired final price.

For this purpose, the SAP ERP system provides the pricing and the condition technique that we present in detail in this book. The pricing and condition technique have been around quite a while—since the introduction of the SAP R/3 system. Of course, some enhancements have been added over the years.

History of the Pricing and the Condition Technique

In the early days of SAP R/2, there were three sources for determining the starting price: the price from the material master, the customer-specific price, and the price list. Furthermore, the system provided eight item condition types and eight header condition types with a configurable key structure in order to represent discounts and surcharges. With increasing numbers of customers from various industries, this infrastructure soon reached its limits. In particular, the specific demands of the consumer goods industry exceeded the existing possibilities.

Therefore, in 1987 a development project with four typical customers was launched, in which their additional requirements were evaluated and implemented as a customer solution. The main challenge was to be able to store pricing information on any level of customer or product hierarchy.

The central component of the solution for this demand was the *access sequence*. Using the access sequence, it was possible to handle any hierarchical structures and to cover the already existing SAP R/2 pricing. Another advance was that all value components of a document could be defined and calculated at one single location via the newly introduced *pricing procedure*. This feature applied, for example, to prices, discounts and surcharges, costs, profit margin, credit price (total net value plus taxes), and statistical value, to name just a few. In addition, the *requirements* were introduced in this project development to map situations that are even more complex. In a next step, the flexibility of the new condition technique was used on other basic functions, such as material substitution and material listing.

The project solution was a resounding success and was delivered in advance to certain customers. Most of this project solution was then transferred to the standard SAP R/2 system.

With the development of SAP R/3, this concept was brough over from SAP R/2, but newly coded. Based on the experience with the solution for SAP R/2, *formulas* were introduced to extend the flexibility and customer-specific adaptability, allowing calculations that went beyond the standard Customizing. Another design change was to spread the header conditions to the items. This ensured that, for example, for a partial billing the pro rata values were taken into account correctly; this was an area that was implemented insufficiently in SAP R/2. Generated *condition tables* were now used for data storage of the condition master data.

A number of enhancements led to the currently available functionality in the SAP ERP system, among which in particular was the introduction of the *variable data* of the condition master data.

How Will This Book Help You?

The elements of customizing the condition and technique pricing have become more and more powerful over the years. The result is that many project requirements can be met by creatively using the standard customizing elements of pricing in SAP ERP. However, in practice, diverse demands make customer-specific adaptations inevitable. To ensure a stable and performant operation of those adaptations, a level of detailed technical knowledge is required that was previously only partially and very laborious to acquire, if possible at all.

This book will help you master the challenges in pricing. It not only gives you a comprehensive derivation and description of the standard customizing—we explain, for example, the customizing by a step-by-step solution of a typical practical case—but it also reveals the technical foundations that have not previously been published at this level of detail and transparency.

What Is the Structure of the Book?

We divided the book in four main parts. **Part I: Foundations** is an introduction of the condition technique, which forms the centerpiece of pricing and is used for many other finding processes. This part starts in Chapter 1 with the application areas and with the components of the condition technique, followed by the presentation of the master data of pricing (condition records) in Chapter 2 and its analysis in Chapter 3.

Part II: Standard Configuration is the central part of the book. The components and skills of the standard customizing of pricing are presented in Chapter 4. Chapter 5 focuses on working with condition records and Chapter 6 focuses on creating an insight into the pricing results. Chapter 7 covers special functions in pricing. These issues are explored more deeply in Chapter 8, which deals with selected pricing procedures and condition types.

Part III: Advanced Techniques, Tips, and Tricks is the "expert" part of the book. In this part, you'll find the detailed technical knowledge needed to create customer-specific adaptations in a stable, performant manner and with high-quality results. Chapter 9 starts with the special features of the condition technique for pricing, and Chapter 10 continues with the presentation of the most important programs of pricing. Chapter 11 discusses system adaption using requirements, formulas, and user exits. Chapter 12 then discusses typical practical case requirements for pricing and their solutions. These considerations are extended in Chapter 13 to other areas, such as purchase order and accounting. Part III ends with a treatise about performance and testing in Chapter 14.

In **Part IV: Rebate Processing in Sales**, you will find a comprehensive description of the rebate processing technique, which relies on many features of the pricing and the condition technique. This is the topic of Chapter 15.

The book ends with Appendix A on condition type profiles, which describes in a compact way all the special customizing details that you need to build the specific condition type you are looking for.

Who Is the Target Audience of the Book?

This book addresses a wide circle of persons: it spans from the beginner to the advanced key user and from the junior consultant all the way to the very experienced consultant. This is because the complexity of the condition technique and pricing has multiple layers.

Depending on your personal level of knowledge, there are different ways to work with the book. Of course you can simply start reading from the beginning. But if you are a beginner or a key user and are in a hurry, you can jump start to Part II. Based on a concrete example, Chapter 4 gives you a comprehensive introduction to the configuration (Customizing) of the condition technique and pricing. If you have access to a test system, you can reproduce this example step-by-step in the system. After working through Part II, beginners and key users will be well prepared for most of the everyday questions of the pricing and condition technique.

As a *consultant*, you will most likely navigate using the table of contents and go directly to the topics you are wrestling with. These topics will often—but not exclusively—be located in Part II, and Part IV. However, be warned: For a full understanding of Part III, APAP programming skills are a prerequisite.

The *experienced consultant* will at first also focus on Parts III and IV, as these parts contain topics that, outside of this book, have not been published on before. It is quite possible that, in particular cases, this new knowledge will lead you to review your already implemented solutions, as you will now have knowledge of better solutions and approaches.

Each chapter in itself is worth reading and contains a wealth of information.

Note on the Examples in this Book

All solutions listed in this book are based on SAP ERP 6.0 Enhancement Packages (EHPs) 4 and 7 and were successfully tested by the authors. If you use the ideas in this book on your own adaptations, you must of course consider very carefully your individual demands and your system's landscape. In other words: "All information is supplied without guarantee." You are ultimately responsible for your modifications. However, using the information provided in this book, you will be able to tackle those modifications competently.

PART I
Foundations

The first part of this book introduces the condition technique, which represents the core of pricing. The condition technique was originally developed for pricing. As it evolved, the condition technique was also used for many other determination processes such as output determination. This part includes an introduction to the application areas and elements of the condition technique, the maintenance of the condition master data for pricing, and their evaluations and worklists.

The condition technique is a configurable method that was built to define and access master data. It was developed as a generic solution for determination processes. In this first chapter, essential basic functionalities are presented and we will become familiar with the terms of the condition technique.

1 Application Areas and Elements of the Condition Technique

Every business function requires master data: Customer order management and billing use customer master data and material master data, purchasing needs vendor master data and posting documents need G/L accounts. When designing master data objects, you always ask yourself how the key structure of these objects should look. Should the data depend on the sales organization, the company code, or other organizational elements? This is not always an easy decision, especially because SAP as a vendor of standard software aims to meet not only the known requirements but also as much as possible potential future challenges. This means that a maximal flexibility is needed. SAP's response to this challenge is the *condition technique*.

The basic idea for the condition technique was born during the development of the pricing functionality, but it soon became clear that the underlying construction principles were also perfect for other application areas. The condition technique is also used in all new functionalities where the key structure of the master data objects was not fixed from the start, but instead highly dependent on the customer demands. Examples of this are *material listing*, *material exclusion*, and *material substitution*.

To differentiate between application areas, the term *condition usage* (or simply *usage*) was introduced. Before we look at some examples of this condition usage, we will concentrate on properties of condition master data (condition records) that contrast with other master data.

1.1 Condition Records

First of all, it is important to understand that the key structure of the different condition records is not predefined (of course, there are standards delivered), but instead can be defined by the customer for his SAP installation using a configuration tool.

The Access Key of Condition Records Is Freely Configurable

The fundamental difference between condition records and other master data, such as customer master data or material master data, is that the key structure of a condition record is freely configurable using a customizing transaction.

The information defining the key structure of a master data table for storing condition records, also known as the *condition table*, is saved as metadata in customizing tables. Based on this metadata, Data Dictionary (DDIC) tables are generated. Later, the condition records are stored in these generated tables. The option to freely configure the key structure is obviously a challenge for the master data maintenance programs. Therefore, the necessary maintenance programs and screens (for SAP GUI) are generated for a condition table too. Besides the variable key fields, the validity periods are an essential part of the condition records.

Condition Records Are Date-Dependent

Another important property of condition master data is the date-dependency; that means every condition record is assigned a validity period. Other master data, such as customer master data or material master data, does not have this capability.

In addition to the definition of the variable key fields of a condition table, reading the condition table during processing (e.g., pricing in the customer order) is of particular importance. The access is done using the *access sequence* search strategy.

The Access Sequence Search Strategy

The access sequence makes it possible to freely configure the reading of the condition tables during processing. In particular, it becomes feasible to prioritize the found condition records and process the hierarchical structures.

Together with the use of requirement routines, the access sequence gives the condition technique an exceptional capability, because the resulting flexibility can help you avoid expensive modifications in customer installations of the SAP system.

Let's now look at some selected business functions that use the condition technique and introduce some initial technical terms. The condition technique serves to solve business requirements, but it is a rather technical topic. That is why we need to introduce some technical terms along the way.

1.2   Application Areas (Using Condition Tables)

Table 1.1 gives you an overview of the application areas of the condition technique, that is, those business functions that use the condition technique. In the following discussion, we use the technical terms usage (or *usage of condition tables*) for these application areas. As every usage of condition tables is normally utilized in several business processes (e.g., pricing is used in order management, billing, purchasing, and accounting), the term *application* (or *condition application*) was introduced to better delimit the objects. Large parts of the configuration (customizing) process are dependent on the application, such as field catalog, condition types, and pricing procedures. You will receive an overview of these applications in Section 1.4.

The usage is defined by the single-digit domain KVEWE, whose value range is contained in database table T681V. Usage T (data collection) is not listed, because it isn't implemented in the standard SAP system, but we will discuss this topic in Section 1.3.9.

Usage	Description	Communication Structure	Sample Table	Sample Report	Module Pool
A	Pricing	KOMG	A000	RV13A000	SAPMV13A
B	Output	KOMB	B000	RV13B000	SAPMV13B
C	Account determination	KOMCV	C000		
D	Material determination	KOMGD	D000	RV130000	SAPMV13D

Table 1.1 Usage of the Condition Tables (Transaction SM30, View V_T681V)

Usage	Description	Communica-tion Structure	Sample Table	Sample Report	Module Pool
E	Rebate	KOMG	E000	RV13E000	SAPMV13A
G	Listing and exclusion	KOMGG	G000	RV130000	SAPMV13G
H	Batch determination	KOMGH	H000	RV130000	SAPMV13H
I	Profile determination	KOMI	I000	RV130000	SAPMV13I
M	Portfolio determination	KOMGM	M000	RV13M000	SAPLWPOT
N	Free goods	KOMG	N000	RV130000	SAPMV13N

Table 1.1 Usage of the Condition Tables (Transaction SM30, View V_T681V) (Cont.)

The most important information you should take away from the usage is the following:

- **Communication structure (e.g., KOMG)**
  The communication structure defines the field list of all attribute fields that can be used to generate condition tables. It is also used in the maintenance program for condition records.

- **Sample table (e.g., A000)**
  The sample table serves as a template to generate the specific condition tables and determines whether the usage enables validity periods. The key field VAKEY is replaced by the specific key fields when generating a new condition table.

- **Sample report (e.g., RV13A000)**
  The sample report serves as a template to generate specific selection reports for a condition table. This is necessary because the different condition tables have different key fields.

- **Module pool (e.g., SAPMV13A) of the maintenance program for SAP GUI**
  You can see in Table 1.1 that usage C (account determination) has no module pool assigned. That's because for this simple usage of condition tables, the condition record maintenance is done via a generated maintenance view. This is possible because the condition records of usage C consist exclusively of the condition table itself (no other additional tables) and do not support validity periods.

1.3   Selected Application Areas (Usages)

In this section, we briefly introduce the most important application areas of the condition technique. In the following discussion, we use the technical term *usage* (or *usage of condition tables*) for these application areas.

1.3.1   Usage A: Pricing

Usage A within SAP ERP Sales and Distribution (SD) (application V) and especially the utilization of the condition records in this process are the main topics of this book. Further information concerning pricing in selected applications is contained Chapter 13.

1.3.2   Usage B: Output

Messages are used to trigger further functions for an object. In the condition master data, you define the circumstances under which the messages are output.

The following features are supported in the output determination (usage B):

▶ **Print with the form variants SAPscript, Smart Forms, and PDF**
In addition, the print documents can be stored in an optical archive for auditing purposes.

▶ **Electronic Data Interchange (EDI) output**
Transfer of structured data, by agreed message standards, from one computer system to another without human intervention.

▶ **Special function**
You can trigger subsequent processing for a document by using customer-specific processing programs. This is a popular (and highly recommended) means to make process adjustments without modifications.

▶ **Triggering of a workflow event**
In the sales order, a workflow event is always triggered, but not in the billing process. For example, you can realize this through the output processing.

A special feature of usage B is that it supports different communication structures.

1.3.3   Usage C: Account Determination

The *account determination* usage (C) is used in order processing and billing. The task is to identify general ledger accounts for the interface to accounting. Keep in mind that the condition records do not support a validity period. Within various *applications,* account determination is carried out for the following purposes:

▸ **Application V: Revenue account determination**
The revenue account determination is performed for revenues and sales deductions. For specific statistical condition types, a second account is determined for the posting of accruals. This is required, for example, for deferred income condition types. There, at the time of billing, the expected sales deductions are posted in the P&L (profit and loss) accounting and this reserve account is later cleared with the rebate settlement run.

▸ **Application VB: Reconciliation account determination**
For an invoice, an open item in Accounts Receivable accounting is set up for the customer. The posting to the balance sheet account for receivables is automatically carried out in parallel to this booking. This account receivable is determined from the customer master record. With the reconciliation account determination, a deviating reconciliation account for the receivables can be found in specific situations.

▸ **Application VC: Account determination for cash settlement**
For cash sales, no open item is created with posting to the receivables account. Instead, it is only booked on a special balance sheet account for cash settlement. This account is determined here.

▸ **Application VD: Account determination for payment cards**
When using payment cards, the clearing account for a card type is determined with this account determination.

1.3.4   Usage D: Material Determination

As part of order processing, you may need to replace—permanently or for a certain time period—one product with another. This may be either because the product has run out or because it should be replaced during a sales action (e.g., a holiday special) with another product with a different packaging. The material determination usage (D) makes this possible.

1.3.5 Usage E: Rebate

The rebate usage (E) was introduced for technical reasons as a sub-function of the pricing usage (A). On the surface (in Customizing), this usage does not appear. The difference compared with usage A is that a different sample table (E000) is used, which contains the additional key field KNUMA (number of the agreement). Rebate condition records can only be maintained exclusively within a rebate agreement and are connected via KNUMA with this agreement.

1.3.6 Usage G: Material Listing and Exclusion

During order entry, you can activate a check against listed or excluded items. The condition technique includes this functionality because customers wanted to be able to maintain the listing and exclusion data at any level of a customer hierarchy. Here the prestep condition, which we will discuss in Section 1.13, is particularly important. During order entry, a check is performed at the header level to determine the customer hierarchy node for which listing data exists. Then the listing check is carried out at the lowest hierarchy node containing listing data.

1.3.7 Usage N: Free Goods

In addition to monetary discounts, there is also the possibility of pricing with free goods. In the respective condition records, you can make the following settings:

▶ Scale quantities, from which the free goods should be granted, as well as the free goods proportion of the item quantity.

▶ Inclusive free goods with item generation (buy x of A, pay only y). In this variant, a part of the ordered quantity is free.

▶ Exclusive free goods (buy x of A and receive y of B for free). In this variant, in addition to the quantity ordered, another item is added for free.

▶ Inclusive free goods without item generation (buy x of A, pay only y). As in the first variant, a part of the ordered quantity is free.

The result of the free goods determination (N), which is performed before calling the pricing, leads to either a situation where free sub-items are generated, or where, within the pricing, a special discount condition type is found that represents the value of the free goods.

1.3.8   Usage 3: Campaign Determination

Campaign management is a function of SAP Customer Relationship Management (SAP CRM). There you can create a campaign as a sales promotion for a certain period. An essential component of this campaign is to agree on discounts in the form of immediate discounts, free goods, or subsequent payments. In addition, you define the circle of customers qualified for this campaign. Because of its flexibility, the condition technique was also used here. The condition records for campaign determination (usage 3) and for the discounts are transferred from SAP CRM to the SAP ERP system and they ensure that in SAP CRM and SAP ERP, within the order processing, the same results are provided.

1.3.9   Usage T: Data Collection

When you display the customizing view V_T681V of the usages, you will find the value T DATA COLLECTION. This usage was originally intended to provide a general data collection using the condition technique. Thus, it was intended to enable you to create date-dependent master data attributes, a property that does not apply to most master data in the SAP system. With this usage, therefore, existing fixed master data assignments could be overridden as date-dependent.

> **General Data Collection Using the Condition Technique**
>
> Usage T has not been realized in the standard SAP system, but you can utilize the usage A (pricing) with special condition types precisely to realize this function via user exits. The solution is found in Chapter 12, Section 12.8.

In connection with contracts (e.g., rental or maintenance contracts), you can well imagine that document attributes should also be maintained as date-dependent. These changes should then be applied on the desired date in the periodic invoices (e.g., payment terms). If you then set up the mentioned condition types for data collection with condition tables that use the document number as a key field, you can reach this goal with the aforementioned solution.

1.4   Applications of the Condition Technique

Table 1.2 shows a summary of the application areas where the condition technique is used. For these applications, which are always business processes, we use the term *application* or *condition application*. Technically, those applications are represented by business objects. Such objects are customer order, invoice, purchase order, accounting document, or cost center.

The *application* is defined by the domain KAPPL whose value range is stored in database table T681A. The mapping table T681Z specifies in which *applications* the different *usages of conditions* are utilized. Table 1.2 shows an extract of table T681Z.

Usage	Description	Application	Description	Header	Item	Dynamic
3	Campaign	V	Sales/Distribution	KOMK	KOMP	
A	Pricing	BA	IS-Bank	KOMK	KOMP	KOMPAZD
		CS	Cost Centers	KOMK	KOMP	KOMPAZD
		F	Shipment Costs	KOMK	KOMP	KOMPAZD
		J0	IS-P SD for Publish.	KOMK	KOMP	KOMPAZD
		KA	Orders	KOMK	KOMP	
		KE	Profitability Analysis	KOMK	KOMP	KOMPAZD
		M	Purchasing	KOMK	KOMP	KOMPAZD
		MS	Ext. Services Mgmt.	KOMK	KOMP	KOMPAZD
		P	ICM: Payment	KOMK	KOMP	KOMPAZD
		TX	ICM: Taxes	KOMK	KOMP	KOMPAZD
		V	Sales/Distribution	KOMK	KOMP	KOMPAZD
		W	Merchandise Mgmt.	KOMK	KOMP	KOMPAZD
B	Output	EF	Purchase Order	KOMKBEA	KOMPBEA	
		ME	Inventory Mgmt.	KOMKBME	KOMPBME	
		MR	Invoice Verification	KOMKBMR	KOMPBMR	

Table 1.2 Usages/Applications of the Condition Technique (Transaction SM30, View V_T681Z)

Usage	Description	Application	Description	Header	Item	Dynamic
		V1	Sales	KOMKBV1	KOMPBV1	
		V2	Shipping	KOMKBV2	KOMPBV2	
		V3	Billing	KOMKBV3	KOMPBV3	
		V7	Transport	KOMKBV7		
C	Account determination	M	Purchasing	KOMKCV	KOMPCV	
		V	Sales/ Distribution	KOMKCV	KOMPCV	
		VB	Reconciliation Acct	KOMKCV	KOMPCV	
		VC	Cash Settlement	KOMKCV	KOMPCV	
		VD	Payment cards	KOMKCV	KOMPCV	
D	Material determination	V	Sales/ Distribution	KOMKD	KOMPD	
		VS	Cross-Selling	KOMKD	KOMPD	
G	Listing and Exclusion	V	Sales/ Distribution	KOMKG	KOMPG	
H	Batch determination	CO	Production Orders	KOMKH	KOMPH	
		ME	Inventory Mgmt.	KOMKH	KOMPH	
		V	Sales/ Distribution	KOMKH	KOMPH	
		WM	Warehouse Mgmt.	KOMKH	KOMPH	
N	Free goods	M	Purchasing	KOMK	KOMP	
		V	Sales/ Distribution	KOMK	KOMP	
		VP	Bonus Buy	KOMK	KOMP	

Table 1.2 Usages/Applications of the Condition Technique (Transaction SM30, View V_T681Z) (Cont.)

On the application level, the following attributes are assigned:

▶ **Header (e.g., KOMK)**
The header communication structure is the field catalog formed by a selection of the document fields of the objects in an application. In the case of pricing, all applications must use the same structure: KOMK. This means that this structure contains the sum of all pricing-relevant fields of all involved business objects. This includes all characteristic fields that have a header-like character. "Header-like" means that these fields are either fields in the document header or are identical in most items. We will explain this relationship in more detail in Chapter 9, Section 9.1 and in Chapter 14, Section 14.2.

▶ **Item (e.g., KOMP)**
The item communication structure forms, in addition to the header communication structure, the second part of the field catalog, which consists purely of item fields.

▶ **Structure of dynamic item fields**
This structure is supported only in usage A (pricing) and serves to process variable data fields in condition records. In addition to the VAKEY variable key fields, the vadat variable data fields can be used in pricing conditions. Only the KOMPAZD structure is intended for these purposes.

The communication structures utilized in a usage are identical, except for the output determination, in which each application can have its own communication structure. We want to complete the topic of applications with an overview of the associated business objects:

▶ V: Sales document, delivery, billing document

▶ V1: Sales document

▶ V2: Delivery

▶ V3: Billing document

▶ CS: Cost center

▶ F: Transport

▶ KA: Internal order

▶ M: Purchase order

▶ P: Insurance contract/industry solution insurance

▶ TX: Accounting document

We have now introduced the terms usage (of condition tables) and (condition) application. These terms will appear throughout the course of the book. The discussion will now become more specific and start with the application of the condition technique.

1.5 Elements of the Condition Technique

The condition technique makes it possible to configure the majority of determination in the Customizing of the SAP system. For example, it is the objective of *pricing* to determine prices, discounts, surcharges, freights, and taxes automatically for a sales process via corresponding master data.

Because this process is different for each SAP customer in detail, SAP delivers standard customizing examples that you can use as a template to map your individual processes.

When mapping the customer requirements in the SAP system, the basic elements of the condition technique listed following Figure 1.1. You will likely need to create new manifestations of these elements in the customer namespace, though you can use the standard objects if they fulfill your needs. When we use elements in our examples whose name starts with Z, you will not find them in the standard SAP system because they are in the customer namespace. However, with the information provided, you should be able to recreate all the examples given in the book.

We will explain the technical order in which you need to proceed when setting up the application. The business approach is done in reverse order, especially in pricing. In a business, you first think about the pricing procedure and the condition types used therein, all before you deal with the master data design and the search strategy for the individual condition types. In contrast, the technical order starts with the master data design, with the condition table at the beginning and adjustment of the pricing procedure at the end. We will be working with these elements in Chapter 4 in detail in order to execute a concrete configuration task for pricing.

You find the elements of the condition technique in the relevant configuration section in Customizing. We will look at the simple example of account determination for cash settlement (see Figure 1.1), which can be reached via the menu path: IMG • SALES AND DISTRIBUTION • BASIC FUNCTIONS • ACCOUNT ASSIGNMENT/COST-ING • CASH ACCOUNT DETERMINATION. We selected this usage for entry, because we find all elements of the condition technique under a single Customizing node. Thus, we can work through it step by step.

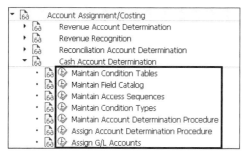

Figure 1.1 Elements of the Condition Technique: Customizing

Specifically, we will be working with the following elements:

▶ **Field catalog and communication structures**
This element maintains the allowed fields that can be used when creating condition tables and access sequences.

▶ **Condition table**
The condition table is a generated DDIC structure for storing the condition master data in the database.

▶ **Access sequence**
The access sequence represents a search strategy for reading the condition master data for a condition type.

▶ **Condition type**
The condition type is a descriptive characteristic and an integral key part of any condition record.

▶ **Condition master data/condition records (e.g., assign G/L accounts)**
A maintenance dialog for condition records is needed. In this example, the master data is located in Customizing because the account determination has customizing characters. In other usages, the master data maintenance is likely to be found in the Application menu.

▸ **Determination procedure (e.g., maintain account determination procedure)**
Contains a list of condition types to be searched for.

▸ **Assignment of the determination procedure (e.g., assign account determination procedure)**
Assignment of the determination procedure to the business transaction.

In the next section, we work mainly in Customizing for pricing via IMG • SALES AND DISTRIBUTION • BASIC FUNCTIONS • PRICING. We will specifically point out any exceptions.

1.6   Field Catalog and Communication Structures

We will now discuss the individual elements of the condition technique and start with the field catalog, which is based on the *communication structures*.

1.6.1   Field Catalog

The foundation of the condition technique is the *field catalog* of allowed fields (the term "characteristics" is also used interchangeably). This field catalog is needed to build condition tables and to access these condition tables via access sequences.

> **Definition: Field Catalog**
>
> The field catalog contains the application-specific subset of the set of all possible fields of a condition usage, which are defined by the communication structures. In the case of pricing, the overall catalog is defined by the structures KOMG, KOMK, KOMP, and KOMPAZD.

The communication structures of a field catalog can be found in Table 1.1 and Table 1.2.

In the field catalog, any fields that were particularly needed to build up the delivered condition tables and access sequences have already been included by SAP. It is a compilation of characteristics used by many SAP customers. Since the standard SAP system cannot cover all future customer requirements, this field catalog can be extended in Customizing (we discuss this topic in detail in Chapter 4).

The field catalog is stored in the cross-client customizing table T681F (see Figure 1.2). As you can see, the field catalog for account determination is quite manageable. In pricing, this looks quite different, of course.

Field Catalog (Accnt Determination Cash Settlement)	
Field	Description
KTGRD	AcctAssgGr
KTGRM	Acct assignment grp
SPART	Division
VKORG	Sales Organization
VTWEG	Distribution Channel
WERKS	Plant

Figure 1.2 Configuration of the Field Catalog for Account Determination (View V_T681F)

1.6.2 Communication Structures

Programs that generate condition tables for the maintenance of the condition master data and that set up the access sequences use DDIC structures as interfaces. The field catalog can only use fields that are contained in these communication structures.

In our simple example, the account determination, the following structures are used (see Table 1.1 and Table 1.2):

▶ KOMKCV and KOMPCV for the access sequences

▶ KOMCV for table generation and master data maintenance

The KOMKx structures contain (document) header-like fields. These are fields that in most line items are typically equal (e.g., customer ID, price date, and customer attributes). The KOMPx structures contain item fields (e.g., product attributes).

Whether a field should be in one structure or another is typically determined by performance. We will discuss this issue in more detail in Chapter 14.

1.7 Condition Tables

The condition table is the main constituent of the condition master data and essentially forms the primary key. Depending on the condition usage, it is complemented by additional DDIC tables that contain application-specific data. Our simple example for account determination, however, requires no such additional information.

> **Definition: Condition Table**
>
> The condition table is a DDIC table and is used to store the condition master data in the database system. It contains essentially the primary key and, in most cases, a pointer to more detailed data.

To maintain and store these condition tables, there is normally a special maintenance program for each usage (see Table 1.1). In simple usages, as in our example (without additional data), master data maintenance is performed via a generated maintenance view.

The variable key of a condition table is formed in the creation dialog by selecting and arranging the desired fields from the field catalog (see Figure 1.3).

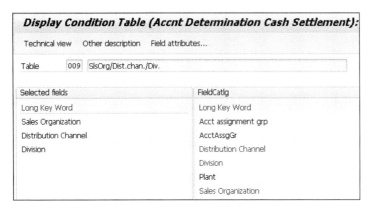

Figure 1.3 Configuration of the Condition Table C009 for Account Determination (Transactions VK03 to VK05)

The table definition is stored in the form of metadata; from that data, the corresponding DDIC table is generated. This metadata is *cross-client* and is stored in the Customizing tables T681 and TMC1*.

From the sequence of the key fields in particular, the generated maintenance screen for master data maintenance is defined. Occasionally, there is a need to evaluate the condition records stored on the database. It is quite useful if you know how these are named. The generated DDIC tables usually have the following naming convention:

▶ First digit: Condition usage

▶ Second to fourth digit: Number of the condition table

In our example of the account determination, the DDIC table is C009 (see Figure 1.4).

Field	Key	Ini...	Data element	Data Type	Length	Deci...	Short Description
MANDT	✓	✓	MANDT	CLNT	3	0	Client
KAPPL	✓	✓	KAPPL	CHAR	2	0	Application
KSCHL	✓	✓	KSCHC	CHAR	4	0	Condition type for account determination
KTOPL	✓	✓	KTOPL	CHAR	4	0	Chart of Accounts
VKORG	✓	✓	VKORG	CHAR	4	0	Sales Organization
VTWEG	✓	✓	VTWEG	CHAR	2	0	Distribution Channel
SPART	✓	✓	SPART	CHAR	2	0	Division
SAKN1	☐	✓	SAKNR	CHAR	10	0	G/L Account Number
SAKN2	☐	✓	SAKNR_ACCR	CHAR	10	0	Number of Provision Account

Figure 1.4 Condition Table C009 for Account Determination: DDIC Structure

Each condition usage has assigned a sample condition table, for example A000 for pricing, B000 for output determination, and C000 for account determination. When generating specific condition tables, the placeholder VAKEY is replaced with the actual characteristic fields (see Figure 1.5).

Field	Key	Ini...	Data element	Data Type	Length	Deci...	Short Description
MANDT	✓	✓	MANDT	CLNT	3	0	Client
KAPPL	✓	✓	KAPPL	CHAR	2	0	Application
KSCHL	✓	✓	KSCHA	CHAR	4	0	Condition type
VAKEY	✓	✓	VAKEY	CHAR	100	0	Variable key 100 bytes
DATBI	✓	✓	KODATBI	DATS	8	0	Validity end date of the condition record
DATAB	☐	✓	KODATAB	DATS	8	0	Validity start date of the condition record
VADAT	☐	☐	VADAT_KO	CHAR	100	0	Variable Data Part
KNUMH	☐	✓	KNUMH	CHAR	10	0	Condition record number

Figure 1.5 Sample Condition Table A000 for Pricing: DDIC Structure

Here, of course, date dependency is essential. In addition to the variable key component VAKEY, you can add variable data fields (non-key components). These are stored similarly to the key fields in the placeholder VADAT. In Chapter 9, Section 9.2, and Chapter 12, Section 12.8, you will learn the many possibilities that are behind date dependency.

When setting up new condition tables, you should note that the sum of all variable fields must not exceed a total length of 100 bytes.

1.8 Access Sequences

We have now set up condition tables and must specify in the next step how to access the data. To do this, we define the access sequence. Understanding access sequences is very important to understanding the condition technique.

Definition: Access Sequence

The *access sequence* is a search strategy that the system uses to search for valid condition master records for a certain condition type in the database.

An access sequence consists of one or several accesses. By the order of the accesses, the priority of the individual condition records is defined, if the order is important.

You can specify whether to stop searching after the first successful access (exclusive access) or whether the next access should also be carried out (additive access). You can also make the execution of an access dependent on whether a requirement is met.

The access sequences are stored cross-client in the Customizing tables T682* (accessible via Transaction VK01 and Transaction V/07).

1.8.1 Access Sequence with Different Condition Tables

To explain the operation of the access sequence, we will use the condition type PR00 (price) from usage pricing with the assigned access sequence PR02, as it's a popular example. This access sequence represents the simple hierarchical structure illustrated in Figure 1.6.

Figure 1.7 shows the accesses levels of the access sequence PR02. Table 1.3 lists the field assignments of the single accesses. You can maintain these field assignments by selecting the level FIELDS in the dialog structure for each access seen in Figure 1.7. For clarity, we chose the tabular presentation, which is helpful because, at a glance, all the information is visible for the entire access sequence.

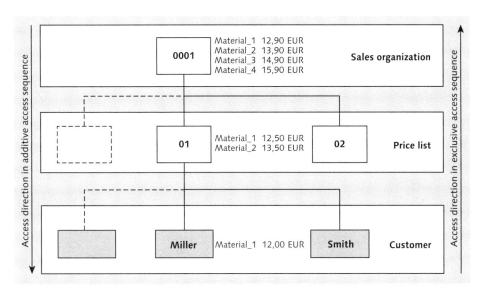

Figure 1.6 Hierarchical Structure Defined by the Condition Tables A304, A305, and A306 and the Access Sequence PR02

Dialog Structure	Access sequence	PR02	Price with Release Status		
▼ ☐ Access sequences					
▼ 🗀 Accesses		Overview Accesses			
• ☐ Fields					

No.	Tab	Description	Requiremnt	Exclusive
10	305	Customer/material with release status		✓
20	306	Price list category/currency/material with release status		✓
30	306	Price list category/currency/material with release status	3	✓
40	304	Material with release status		✓

Figure 1.7 Exclusive Access Sequence of Pricing PR02 (Transaction V/07)

Access	Table	Condition Field		Document Field	
10	A305: Customer specific price	VKORG	= KOMK	VKORG	
		VTWEG	= KOMK	VTWEG	
		KUNNR	= KOMK	KUNNR	
		MATNR	= KOMP	PMATN	

Table 1.3 Access Sequence PR02: Field Assignments (Transaction V/07)

Access	Table	Condition Field		Document Field
20	A306: Price list in document currency	VKORG	= KOMK	VKORG
		VTWEG	= KOMK	VTWEG
		PLTYP	= KOMK	PLTYP
		WAERK	= KOMK	WAERK
		MATNR	= KOMP	PMATN
30	A306: Price list in local currency (requirement 003)	VKORG	= KOMK	VKORG
		VTWEG	= KOMK	VTWEG
		PLTYP	= KOMK	PLTYP
		WAERK	= KOMK	HWAER
		MATNR	= KOMP	PMATN
40	A304: Material price (base price)	VKORG	= KOMK	VKORG
		VTWEG	= KOMK	VTWEG
		MATNR	= KOMP	PMATN

Table 1.3 Access Sequence PR02: Field Assignments (Transaction V/07) (Cont.)

You can translate every access in a simple `select` statement; for example, using access 30 (see Listing 1.1).

```
select * from a306 where kappl = 'V'
                   and kschl = 'PR00'
                   and vkorg = komk-vkorg
                   and vtweg = komk-vtweg
                   and pltyp = komk-pltyp
                   and waerk = komk-hwaer
                   and matnr = komp-pmatn
                   and datbi ge preisdatum
                   and datab le preisdatum.
```
Listing 1.1 Select Statement for an Access of the Access Sequence

Through the access sequence PR02, it is determined that the condition records for condition type PR00 can be stored in the database in the three condition tables A304 (base price per material), A305 (customer specific price), and A306 (price list).

The accesses on the condition records are then executed in pricing as follows:

1. Access 10 on table A305 with characteristics customer/material.

2. Access 20 on table A306 with characteristics price list/document currency/material.

3. Access 30 on table A306 with characteristics price list/local currency/material, but only if the requirement 003 is met, so it is a foreign currency document.

4. Access 40 on table A304 with characteristic material.

Worth mentioning is the handling of the field MATNR (material number) in the field assignments. You will find with most access sequences that an access is not executed with the source field komp-matnr but with the field komp-pmatn. The two fields are generally identical, but it is possible to assign a different material number, especially for pricing in the material master data (assigned in field PRICING REFERENCE MATERIAL).

1.8.2 Access Sequence with a Single Condition Table (Access with Partial Key)

To illustrate the possibilities of the condition technique, we will show, using the example of access sequence Z901 (see Table 1.4), how the same result can be achieved with a single condition table A901 (see Figure 1.9). In addition, you could store a price on a two-level customer hierarchy. This condition table, in conjunction with the access sequence, defines the hierarchical structure shown in Figure 1.8. We at first combined all fields of the condition tables A304, A305, and A306 contained in the access sequence PR02 in a single new condition table A901. In Figure 1.8, we indicated that the prices—in other words the condition records—can be stored at each level of the represented hierarchy, which is modeled by the access sequence Z901. The different hierarchy levels are as follows:

❶ Customer (lowest level)

❷ Customer hierarchy level 1

❸ Customer hierarchy level 2

❹ Price list type

❺ Sales organization (top level)

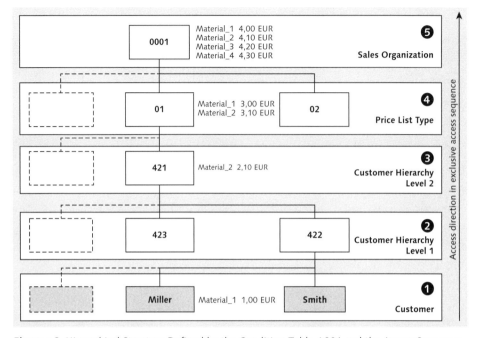

Figure 1.8 Hierarchical Structure Defined by the Condition Table A901 and the Access Sequence Z901

If you have more than two customer hierarchy levels, you only have to add more accesses using the same pattern; up to 15 levels are possible.

Field	Key	Ini...	Data element	Data Type	Length	Deci...	Short Description
MANDT	✓	✓	MANDT	CLNT	3	0	Client
KAPPL	✓	✓	KAPPL	CHAR	2	0	Application
KSCHL	✓	✓	KSCHA	CHAR	4	0	Condition type
VKORG	✓	✓	VKORG	CHAR	4	0	Sales Organization
PLTYP	✓	✓	PLTYP	CHAR	2	0	Price list type
WAERK	✓	✓	WAERK	CUKY	5	0	SD Document Currency
KUNNR	✓	✓	KUNNR_V	CHAR	10	0	Customer number
MATNR	✓	✓	MATNR	CHAR	18	0	Material Number
KFRST	✓	✓	KFRST	CHAR	1	0	Release status
DATBI	✓	✓	KODATBI	DATS	8	0	Validity end date of the condition record
DATAB	☐	✓	KODATAB	DATS	8	0	Validity start date of the condition record
KBSTAT	☐	☐	KBSTAT	CHAR	2	0	Processing status for conditions
KNUMH	☐	✓	KNUMH	CHAR	10	0	Condition record number

Figure 1.9 Condition Table A901 of Pricing: DDIC Structure

Access	Table	Condition Field		Document Field	Initial Value Allowed
10	A901: Customer specific (customer no.)	VKORG	= KOMK	VKORG	
		PLTYP	= KOMK	KDUMMY	X
		WAERK	= KOMK	KDUMMY	X
		KUNNR	= KOMK	KUNNR	
		MATNR	= KOMP	PMATN	
11	A901: Customer hierarchy level 01	VKORG	= KOMK	VKORG	
		PLTYP	= KOMK	KDUMMY	X
		WAERK	= KOMK	KDUMMY	X
		KUNNR	= KOMK	HIENR01	
		MATNR	= KOMP	PMATN	
12	A901: Customer hierarchy level 02	VKORG	= KOMK	VKORG	
		PLTYP	= KOMK	KDUMMY	X
		WAERK	= KOMK	KDUMMY	X
		KUNNR	= KOMK	HIENR02	
		MATNR	= KOMP	PMATN	
20	A901: Price list price in local currency (requirement 003)	VKORG	= KOMK	VKORG	
		PLTYP	= KOMK	PLTYP	
		WAERK	= KOMK	WAERK	
		KUNNR	= KOMK	KDUMMY	X
		MATNR	= KOMP	PMATN	
21	A901: Price list price in document currency	VKORG	= KOMK	VKORG	
		PLTYP	= KOMK	PLTYP	
		WAERK	= KOMK	KDUMMY	X
		KUNNR	= KOMK	KDUMMY	X
		MATNR	= KOMP	PMATN	
30	A901: Material	VKORG	= KOMK	VKORG	
		PLTYP	= KOMK	KDUMMY	X
		WAERK	= KOMK	KDUMMY	X
		KUNNR	= KOMK	KDUMMY	X
		MATNR	= KOMP	PMATN	

Table 1.4 Exclusive Access Sequence Z901 (Transaction V/07)

Condition Maintenance for Condition Type Z901

In Figure 1.13, you can see the maintenance for condition type Z901 (hierarchy condition) that uses the presented access sequence Z901.

In this example, the accesses are exclusively performed on condition table A901 as follows:

1. Access 10 with characteristics customer/material.
2. Access 11 with characteristics customer hierarchy level 01/material.
3. Access 12 with characteristics customer hierarchy level 02/material.
4. Access 20 with characteristics price list type/document currency/material, but only if requirement 003 is met, so it is a foreign currency document (document currency is not equal to local currency).
5. Access 21 with characteristics price list type/material (price list in local currency, that is the currency assigned to the sales organization).
6. Access 30 with characteristic material.

In Table 1.4, you can see that we assign, for the document fields that should not be taken into account during the access, the field KOMK-kdummy (the field is always initial), and at the same time we set the indicator INITIAL VALUE ALLOWED. This specifies that, when maintaining condition records, the condition field can be left blank. You can check this for the sample condition records in Figure 1.13.

The configuration variant for access sequences with the different condition tables is recommended if the individual tables are large, because then the combined condition table becomes too large. The configuration variant with a single condition table makes the master data maintenance more straightforward, as you can maintain the condition records for all allowed key variants in one single maintenance screen. Of course, a combination of methods is possible.

1.8.3   Exclusive or Additive Access

The access sequence PR02 has been designed with exclusive accesses. That is, the priority decreases from top to bottom. When the first condition record is found, the search is terminated and, as result, one single condition record is transferred to pricing.

Price condition types have a special built-in standard logic in their calculation. If several prices are found, only the last price in the pricing procedure is active. A special case is to determine the active price via condition exclusion (e.g., most favorable price). To be able to find the most favorable price, we must use an access sequence that runs the accesses in the exact reverse order of PR02, with the accesses defined as additive. This means that all accesses of the access sequence are always carried out and the decision of which of the various condition records found is the right one is taken in pricing. As a result, we see in the pricing detail screen then all potentially applicable prices (customized price, material price, price list), but only one (generally the last in the pricing procedure) is active. This improves transparency, but at the expense of the storage footprint and performance.

If you use a condition exclusion scenario (see Chapter 7, Section 7.2), where you want only the most favorable records from all found discount condition records, for example, you need to choose the additive version. In all other cases, it's best to use the exclusive version of accesses.

1.8.4 Direct Values

You can also use a direct value in the field assignment instead of a field from the communication structures KOMK* or KOMP*. One application example is the pricing condition type MW15 with the access sequence MWM1. This condition type is configured so that the condition records for condition type MWST are read, but not with the tax classification of the current material; instead, they use the fixed value "1", which is used for identifying goods with a full tax rate. The condition type MW15 will therefore, in the sale of a product with tax classification 2 (half tax), apply the full tax rate for commissions or freight surcharges that are fully taxable separately as a service (e.g., for condition type RL00 [factoring discount], also known as *del credere commission*).

1.8.5 Data Determination During Access

Because of the functionality of the access sequences introduced so far (they already existed in SAP R/2), we have already achieved a high degree of flexibility. However, new customers and new industries bring new demands. One problem was that within the condition technique not all the information required for pricing were provided as part of the SAP master data. In addition, there was the demand to override *date-dependent* relationships that were stored in the standard master data (customer master, material master). To this end, you can include variable data fields in the condition tables in addition to the variable key fields. These can then be transferred within the access sequence in the structure KOMPAZD and then reused in subsequent accesses. We will discuss this feature in more detail in Chapter 9, Section 9.2 and in Chapter 12, Section 12.8.

1.9   Condition Types

As you have already learned, the condition type and access sequence elements are closely linked.

Definition: Condition Type

The *condition type* is an integral part of the key of every condition table. Its purpose is to define and parameterize the associated business transaction.

Condition records are always stored for a condition type. Depending on the condition usage, condition types are referred to as *message types*, *account determination types*, *exclusion types*, etc.

By the optional assignment of an access sequence in the condition type, it is defined if condition records need to be created. If no access sequence is assigned, the determination of values can only be done using formulas (see Chapter 11). We will discuss the attribute parameters of the condition types for pricing in detail in Chapter 4.

The condition types are stored client-specific in the Customizing tables T685* (Transactions VK01 and V/06). Depending on the application, there are additional tables besides the main table T685, where further control parameters are stored.

1.10   Condition Master Data

Using the information from the previous sections, you will be able to create *condition records*, which contain the condition master data, for the condition types we introduced. We will use the two terms synonymously.

The condition master data determines the result of a condition determination (e.g., in pricing). They are stored in the database for a condition type in the condition table(s) determined by the access sequence.

For additional information on the condition records for pricing, see Chapters 2 and 5.

1.10.1 Data Model

As already mentioned, the condition master data is composed at least of the condition table, and, depending on the usage, of additional supplement tables, as shown by the examples of the pricing (see Figure 1.10) and free goods (see Figure 1.11) usages.

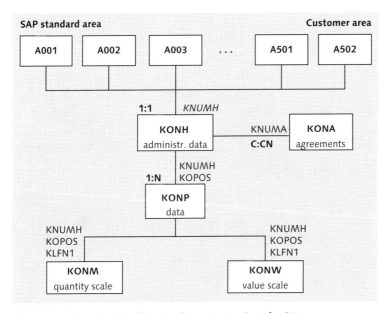

Figure 1.10 Data Model of the Condition Master Data for Pricing

As you can see here, the free goods usage has the different naming convention KOTN*** for the condition tables. At some point in the history of the SAP system, the naming convention for newly developed usages was changed to the prefix KOT plus the usage (e.g., N for free goods).

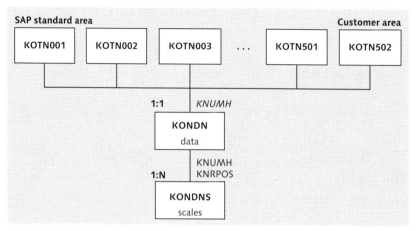

Figure 1.11 Data Model of the Condition Master Data for Free Goods

1.10.2 Maintenance Dialog for Simple Usages (Application Areas)

In Section 1.7, we presented a simple example of the account determination table C009. We now have configured a new account determination type called ZASH with the access sequence of the same name (see Table 1.5). Now we can create and edit the condition records (account determination records) with a generated maintenance view (see Figure 1.12). Since the access sequence is configured to work with partial keys, we can, as seen in the example, leave the fields VTWEG (distribution channel) and SPART (division) blank. Thus, the number of the required condition records is reduced considerably.

Access	Table	Condition Field		Document Field	Initial Value Allowed
10	C009: Division	VKORG	= KOMKCV	VKORG	
		VTWEG	= KOMKCV	VTWEG	
		SPART	= KOMPCV	SPART	
15	C009: Distribution channel	VKORG	= KOMKCV	VKORG	
		VTWEG	= KOMKCV	VTWEG	
		SPART	= KOMKCV	KDUMMY	X
20	C009: Sales organization	VKORG	= KOMKCV	VKORG	
		VTWEG	= KOMKCV	KDUMMY	X
		SPART	= KOMKCV	KDUMMY	X

Table 1.5 Access Sequence ZASH (Masking) for the Condition Zash (Transaction VK01)

A...	CndTy.	ChAc	SOrg.	DChl	Dv	G/L Account	Provision acc.
			SlsOrg/Dist.chan./Div.				
VC	ZASH	INT	0001			100000	
VC	ZASH	INT	0001	10		100101	
VC	ZASH	INT	0001	10	00	100102	

Figure 1.12 Simple Maintenance View for the Cash Account Determination C009: Condition Type ZASH (Transaction OV77)

Just as with the access sequences PR02 and Z901 for pricing that were already presented, the ZASH access sequence represents a hierarchical structure. The hierarchy levels are in this case:

1. Sales organization/distribution channel/division (lowest level).
2. Sales organization/distribution channel.
3. Sales organization (top level).

1.10.3 Maintenance Dialog for Complex Usages

For complex usages such as pricing, there are additional tables along with the actual condition table, as is apparent from the data model in Figure 1.10. These tables are managed by a separate maintenance transaction. These maintenance programs (see Figure 1.13) are generated when you create a new condition table. For our example, we have configured the condition type Z901 (hierarchy condition) with the access sequence of the same name from Table 1.4.

Change Hierarchy Condition Condition (Z901) : Overview

Sales Organization 1000 Germany Frankfurt
Valid On 09.04.2016

Price List	Curr...	Customer	Material	S	Description	P...	Amount	Unit	per	U...	C..	S..	Valid From	Valid to
		2300	HT-1000		Notebook Basic 15		350,00	EUR		1PC	C		09.04.2016	31.12.9999
01			HT-1000		Notebook Basic 15		400,00	EUR		1PC	C		09.04.2016	31.12.9999
01	USD		HT-1000		Notebook Basic 15		420,00	USD		1PC	C		09.04.2016	31.12.9999

Figure 1.13 Condition Maintenance for the Condition Table A901: Condition Type Z901 with Access Sequence Z901 (Transactions VK11 to VK13)

Some settings determine which fields are positioned on the entry screen in the header (for condition type Z901, this is the sales organization) and which fields are positioned on the item level. In addition, the description is displayed for a selected key field (in this example, this is the Material field).

The entry into the maintenance of the condition records can be made via the following:

► The condition type by selecting a condition table of the assigned access sequence (Transactions VK11 to VK14)

► An area menu using the flexible pricing reports (Transactions VK31 to VK34)

We will discuss *condition maintenance* for pricing condition records in detail in Chapter 2.

1.10.4 Validity Periods

For some usages, you can enter a validity period in the condition maintenance. This is the case if the DATAB (valid from date) and DATBI (valid to date) fields are contained in the respective pattern structure (e.g., D000). Only the DATBI field is located in the key part of the table. The DATAB field is positioned in the data part. The respective maintenance programs ensure that there are no overlapping periods for the same variable key.

Prices are generally created with unlimited valid to dates (e.g., 01/01/2016 to 12/31/9999). Price changes—without touching the current values—are made by creating a new condition record with a valid from date in the future (e.g., 07/01/2016 to 12/31/9999). During this maintenance process, the validity period of the existing condition record is automatically reduced ("cut off") (see Table 1.6).

Situation Before Price Change			
VAKEY	**DATBI**	**DATAB**	
HN1080	99991231	20160101	(10.00 USD)
Situation After Price Change			
VAKEY	**DATBI**	**DATAB**	
HN1080	20160630	20160101	(10.00 USD)
HN1080	99991231	20160701	(11.00 USD)

Table 1.6 New Condition Record for the Price from 07/01/2016 (DATAB)

The date is always stored in the database in the form YYYYMMDD. This arrangement ensures that the read access to the database table by specifying a valid date will return a maximum of one condition record. Moreover, the access is performant, even if, due to many changes in prices, many records with different validity periods exist. In special cases, multiple records can be found for a variable key (e.g., for rebate conditions).

Listing 1.2 shows a typical Select statement from the central access module SD_ COND_ACCESS.

```
Select * from (t681-kotab) appending table <cond_tab> up to 1
    rows           where kappl  = se_kappl
           and    kschl  = se_kschl
           and    datbi >= se_date
           and    datab <= se_date
           and    (coding_tab).
```
Listing 1.2 Select Statement for Condition Tables

When you configure your condition table, you decide whether your condition table supports the validity periods. After the generation of the condition tables, a subsequent change is not possible.

1.10.5 Release Status and Processing Status

Within the pricing usage, you have the option to provide newly created condition records with a status that ensures that the existing pricing is not affected. You can check the impact of these inactive condition records in connection with the topic net price list (see Chapter 3, Section 3.3).

For example, you can use this status if price changes should be approved and released by a second person. The release itself is handled by changing the processing status.

1.11 Determination Procedures

We now have created the necessary condition master data and want to process them. Before you activate a condition determination in the context of an operational application (e.g., sales order processing), you must have a determination procedure. In this determination procedure, you have to list all condition types that should be processed. In addition, the search for a condition type can be subject to a requirement. In pricing, the order of condition types in the pricing procedure is important because it determines the calculation algorithm.

> **Definition: Determination Procedure**
>
> The *determination procedure* is the link to the business transaction and it triggers the condition determination. The determination procedure must contain all condition types that are to be processed and their application may be subject to requirements.

Depending on the conditions usage, we speak of a pricing procedure, output determination procedure, account determination procedure, etc. An example of a simple revenue account determination procedure is shown in Figure 1.14.

The determination procedures have to be assigned to the business transactions. This is implemented differently depending on the condition usage and application. In the case of pricing the sales order, the pricing procedure assignment is done using Customizing table T683V. The pricing procedures are stored client-specific in the Customizing tables T683* (Transactions VK01 and V/08).

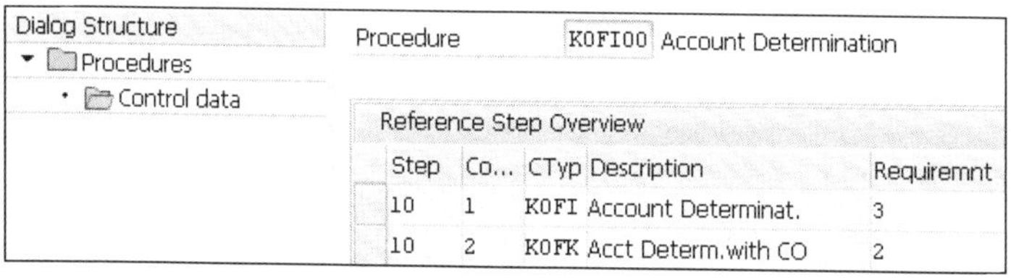

Dialog Structure	Procedure	KOFI00	Account Determination	
▼ ☐ Procedures				
• ☐ Control data	**Reference Step Overview**			
	Step	Co...	CTyp Description	Requiremnt
	10	1	KOFI Account Determinat.	3
	10	2	KOFK Acct Determ.with CO	2

Figure 1.14 Simple Revenue Account Determination Procedure (Transaction VK01)

If you have configured everything correctly, you are finished. If the account determination, pricing, etc., does not provide the desired result, you have to go into determination analysis.

1.12 Determination Analysis

Since the condition technique is a complex method, is often necessary to explain the result of the determination. Therefore, usually in the business transactions, a respective *determination analysis* is provided. In particular, you can determine if requirements are not met and you can check the specific field contents with which the access to the condition tables is made.

The analysis generally does not reproduce the situation as it was given at the time of the original determination task. It works in most usages in such a way that, with the current document state, a new determination is performed and recorded. The result of the original determination might differ from the currently performed determination during analysis. We will look at that topic more closely in Chapter 12, Section 12.2. Figure 1.15 shows the analysis of the revenue account determination for an invoice, accessible via Transaction VF03 and ENVIRONMENT • ACCOUNT DETERM. ANALYSIS.

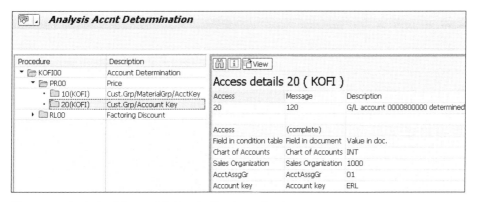

Figure 1.15 Analysis of Account Determination for an Invoice

One possible reason that conditions have not been found may be due to an unfulfilled requirement. This leads us to the last element of the condition technique.

1.13 Requirements

You learned that the execution of an access within an access sequence and the processing of a condition type within the determination procedure could be subject to a requirement. For example, access 30 of pricing access sequence PR02 has assigned the requirement 003. Requirements are created with Transaction VOFM (see Figure 1.16) and consist of an ABAP code. Thus, maximum flexibility is given; however, its use requires ABAP programming skills.

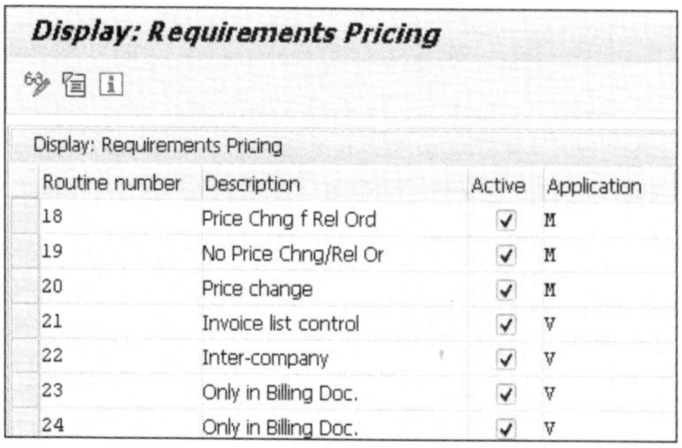

Display: Requirements Pricing

Display: Requirements Pricing

Routine number	Description	Active	Application
18	Price Chng f Rel Ord	✓	M
19	No Price Chng/Rel Or	✓	M
20	Price change	✓	M
21	Invoice list control	✓	V
22	Inter-company	✓	V
23	Only in Billing Doc.	✓	V
24	Only in Billing Doc.	✓	V

Figure 1.16 Requirements for Pricing (Transaction VOFM)

Definition: Requirement

Requirements are ABAP routines that can be assigned to the condition types within a determination procedure and to individual accesses within an access sequence. During the condition determination, this routine is executed. If it returns a negative outcome, the condition type or access will not be processed.

The example given in Figure 1.17 shows the requirement 024. It is used for rebate condition types in the standard pricing procedure RVAA01 and specifies that these condition types will appear only in invoices and will not be determined in the sales order. This provides performance advantages during order processing.

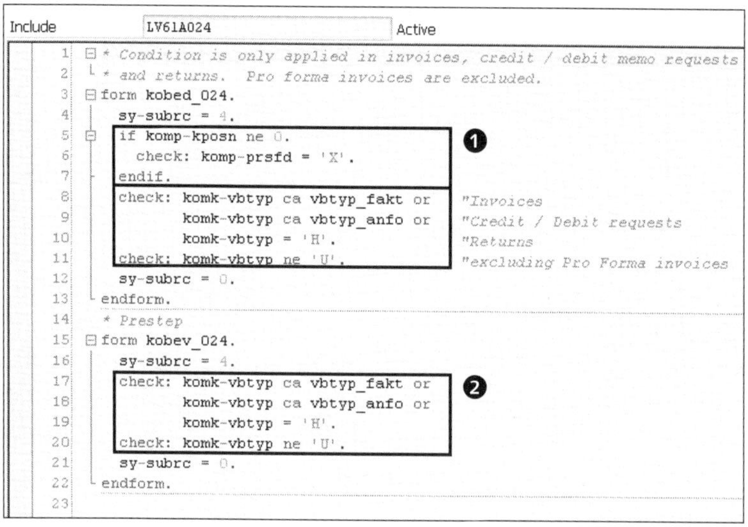

Include LV61A024 Active

```
* Condition is only applied in invoices, credit / debit memo requests
* and returns.  Pro forma invoices are excluded.
form kobed_024.
  sy-subrc = 4.
  if komp-kposn ne 0.
    check: komp-prsfd = 'X'.
  endif.
  check: komk-vbtyp ca vbtyp_fakt or        "Invoices
         komk-vbtyp ca vbtyp_anfo or        "Credit / Debit requests
         komk-vbtyp = 'H'.                  "Returns
  check: komk-vbtyp ne 'U'.                 "excluding Pro Forma invoices
  sy-subrc = 0.
endform.
* Prestep
form kobev_024.
  sy-subrc = 4.
  check: komk-vbtyp ca vbtyp_fakt or
         komk-vbtyp ca vbtyp_anfo or
         komk-vbtyp = 'H'.
  check: komk-vbtyp ne 'U'.
  sy-subrc = 0.
endform.
```


Figure 1.17 Requirement 024 for Pricing (Transaction VOFM)

The requirements consist of two FORM routines—the KOBED part and the KOBEV part (see Listing 1.3).

```
form kobed_nnn.
  .....
endform.
* Prestep
form kobev_nnn.
  .....
endform.
```

Listing 1.3 Structure of a Requirement Routine

In the KOBEV part, the prestep, only fields from the "header-like" communication structures (KOMKx) can be evaluated. Requirements that are already negated bring performance advantages, as they are checked in general only once per document and such condition types or accesses are then no longer considered at an item level. In the KOBED part, which is the final condition check, all fields, including the item-like fields (KOMPx), can be evaluated.

In Transaction VOFM, after selecting a requirement number, you open the ABAP editor and program the routine (see Figure 1.17). You can see by the example of requirement 024 that we have addressed only KOMP fields in the KOBED ❶ and only KOMK fields in the KOBEV ❷.

1.14   The Complete Process at a Glance

The process of condition determination and the interaction of the elements of the condition technique are shown in Figure 1.18, using the example of the usage A (pricing).

The pricing procedure (tables T683 and T683S) is the starting point of the determination process. All condition types listed there are processed from top to bottom. If the condition type (tables T685 and T685A) is configured with an access sequence, we perform the accesses to the condition tables Annn (with additional tables KONP, KONM, and KONW) according to access sequence (tables T682, T682I, and T682Z). The table KONH is not required at this time. Depending on whether an access is configured as *exclusive* or as *additive*, we stop the access sequence after the first record found for a condition type and continue with the next condition type, or we execute all the accesses of the access sequence.

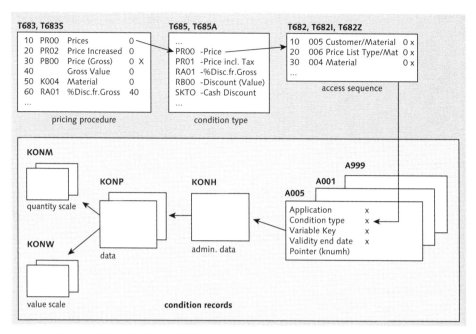

Figure 1.18 Overall View for Usage A (Pricing)

1.15   Summary

The first chapter was meant to familiarize you with the terms of the condition technique. Now you know the basics of all the elements of the condition technique and their interaction. For access sequences, which is the most important component, you have already acquired profound knowledge. We will focus on the other elements intensely in the following chapters, starting with the condition master data.

Together with the condition technique, you need condition master data to automate the respective determination processes. In this chapter, you learn about the maintenance of this master data.

2 Pricing Condition Master Data

Along with customer master data and product master data, the condition master data is the third major pillar for processing sales documents. A range of tools is available for maintenance of these condition records, which we will discuss in this chapter. We will begin by discussing maintaining condition records using condition types in great detail and then take a look at the other maintenance tools. We will also discuss creating pricing condition records in connection with an agreement and take a quick look at the use of price agreements.

2.1 Condition Maintenance via Condition Type

Using the menu path SAP EASY ACCESS • LOGISTICS • SALES AND DISTRIBUTION • MASTER DATA • CONDITIONS • SELECT USING CONDITION TYPE, you will find the standard maintenance transactions for the maintenance of condition master data for usage A (pricing), application V (sales/distribution):

- ▶ VK11 (create)
- ▶ VK12 (change)
- ▶ VK13 (display)
- ▶ VK14 (create with template)

This master data maintenance works with a generated dialog that is ready to use when you configure a customer-specific condition type (this is discussed in detail in Chapter 4, Section 4.4). This means that customer-specific condition types are treated the same way as the condition types in the standard SAP system. The differences are apparent to the user only in the customer namespace of the condition types.

A typical maintenance task, for example, involves creating a price (condition type PR00) for a new product. After calling Transaction VK11 (create condition record), you select the condition type PR00 (price). Since the access sequence for condition type PR00 contains three condition tables (that is, three key combinations), another selection opens up to determine the desired key combination (see Figure 2.1). To create a material price, you select MATERIAL WITH RELEASE STATUS.

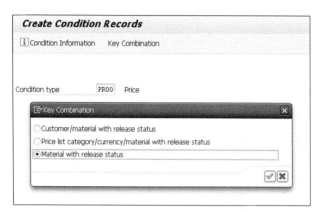

Figure 2.1 Create Condition Records with Transaction VK11

After confirming the selection by pressing ⌷Enter⌷, the fast entry screen opens up (see Figure 2.2). Here it is advisable to press ⌷Enter⌷ after you set each of the key fields SALES ORGANIZATION, DISTRIBUTION CHANNEL, and MATERIAL. As a result, attributes like CURRENCY, QUANTITY UNIT, CALCULATION TYPE, and VALIDITY PERIOD are filled with default values (e.g., from the configuration of the condition type). Thus, it is usually sufficient to enter only the condition amount.

Create Price Condition (PR00) : Fast Entry

| Sales Organization | 1000 | Germany Frankfurt |
| Distribution Channel | 12 | Sold for resale |

Material with release status

Material	S	Description	P..	Amount	Unit	per	U...	C..	S..	Valid From	Valid to
1400-310		CrossFun / 350 cm3			EUR	1PC		C		12.04.2016	31.12.9999

Figure 2.2 Fast Entry Screen

From the CREATE PRICE CONDITION (PROO) screen, you can maintain multiple condition records on one screen. To enable this maintenance, at least one key field must be available at item level when defining the key combinations (condition tables).

By navigating with the icons in the upper part of the fast entry screen (see Figure 2.2), you have the options shown in Table 2.1:

Icon	Details
	Header data
	Details
	Additional data
	Scales
	Condition supplement
	Validity periods
	Free goods
	Status information
	Conversion factors
	Key
	Cumulative values
	Overview of condition records
	Other condition type

Table 2.1 Fast Entry Icons

Let's look at the most important of these additional maintenance screens in the following sections.

2.1.1 Details Functionality

On the DETAILS screen (see Figure 2.3), there are some attributes with which you can influence the processing of the condition record.

In the field group AMOUNTS, we find next to the condition AMOUNT the fields LOWER LIMIT and UPPER LIMIT. If we enter limit values, they are checked during document processing if you manually change the condition value found. A manual entry falling outside the limits is then rejected. These limits are also taken into account in the SCALES screen, which we will describe in the next section.

Figure 2.3 Details Screen

In the field group CONTROL, you can change the scale type proposed from the configuration of the condition type. In addition, you can set an EXCLUSION indicator for the *condition exclusion* here. This also includes the standard SAP system scenario X – NET PRICE. If this EXCLUSION indicator is set in a condition record, if you later find this condition record in a pricing procedure, subsequent discount condition types can be ignored (because the second requirement in the pricing procedure is not fulfilled). A price marked this way thus acts as a net price. For further information about condition exclusion, see Chapter 7.

2.1.2 Additional Data Functionality

On the ADDITIONAL DATA screen (see Figure 2.4), the field group ASSIGNMENTS shows if the condition record has been created as part of a sales deal or if this sales deal was assigned to a promotion. If the SAP ERP system is configured as a retail system, the assignment to a retail promotion can be recorded, too.

In the field group Payment, you can enter a Terms of payment. This option is used with sales document items for which this condition record is found during pricing. Moreover, it is possible to provide a Fixed value date or Additional value days.

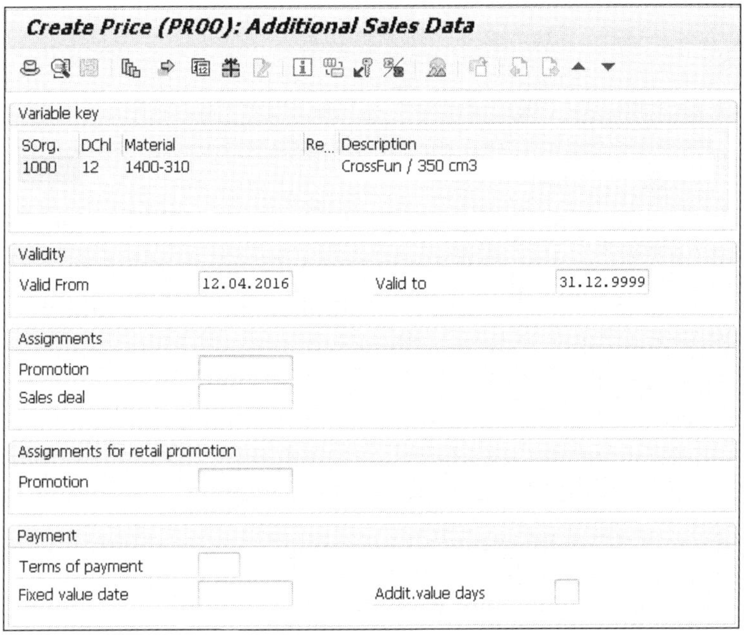

Figure 2.4 Additional Sales Data Screen

Only if the Condition Update attribute is set in the configuration of the condition type will the additional field group called Limits for Pricing be available. We will discuss the functionality of Condition Update in Chapter 7, Section 7.3.

2.1.3 Scales Functionality

On the Scales screen (see Figure 2.5), you can enter scale values for the condition record if needed. The Scale Type is proposed from the configuration of the condition type. If no special scale type is defined, a base scale is proposed and the proposal can be changed to a To scale in the individual condition record.

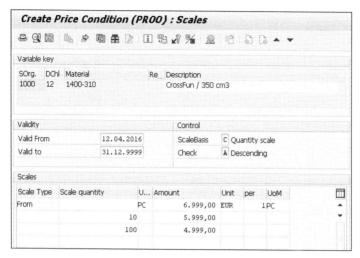

Figure 2.5 Scales Screen

2.1.4 Condition Supplement Functionality

On the CONDITION SUPPLEMENT screen, you can maintain the condition supplements. The prerequisite is that the condition type has assigned an additional determination procedure that defines the set of condition types for condition supplements. You can find more information about the condition supplements in Chapter 4, Section 4.2.3 and Chapter 5, Section 5.3.

2.1.5 Validity Periods Functionality

On the VALIDITY PERIODS screen, the existing validity periods for the condition record are displayed. Here you can monitor how the condition value amounts evolve over time.

2.1.6 Free Goods Functionality

The FREE GOODS screen gives you the ability to jump directly to the maintenance of free goods discounts.

2.1.7 Status Information Functionality

This screen displays the status information for the condition record (e.g., CREATED ON and CREATED BY).

2.1.8 Cumulative Values Functionality

If the CONDITION UPDATE attribute is set in the configuration of the condition type, the values of the condition update will be displayed on the CUMULATIVE VALUES screen. We will discuss the functionality of condition update in Chapter 7, Section 7.3.

2.1.9 Other Condition Type Functionality

The OTHER CONDITION TYPE screen gives you the ability to jump directly to the condition record maintenance of another condition type.

In daily use, you will mostly only need to use the fast entry screen and the SCALES screen. The remaining screens complement the functionality of these two screens, but are rarely used.

2.2 Condition Maintenance via Area Menu

Since SAP R/3 4.6, menu path SAP EASY ACCESS • LOGISTICS • SALES AND DISTRIBUTION • MASTER DATA • CONDITIONS • SELECT USING CONDITION TYPE leads to the following additional maintenance transactions:

- ▸ VK31 (Create)
- ▸ VK32 (Change)
- ▸ VK33 (Display)
- ▸ VK34 (Create with Template)

By default, these transactions use the area menu COND_AV (area menu maintenance is done using Transaction SE43) to enable condition record maintenance that can even be *cross-condition type* and *cross-condition table*, using pricing reports as a filter medium. The possibilities depend on the characteristics of the pricing report you use, as you will see in Chapter 3, Section 3.1.

There are ultimately three ideas—area menu, pricing report, and condition maintenance—that were assembled for an interesting new approach. The construction design becomes clear when you look at a concrete example. After calling up, for example, Transaction VK32, the screen in Figure 2.6 is displayed.

Figure 2.6 Transaction VK32 (Change Condition Records)

The expanded menu structure is the standard defined by the area menu COND_ AV. If you concentrate on the entry MATERIAL PRICE and edit this node on the EDIT AREA MENU COND_AV screen (see Figure 2.7), you'll see that in the node, the call of the pricing report ❶ (MATERIAL PRICE) with variant SAP&PR00 was configured. (We will discuss pricing reports in Chapter 3, Section 3.1.)

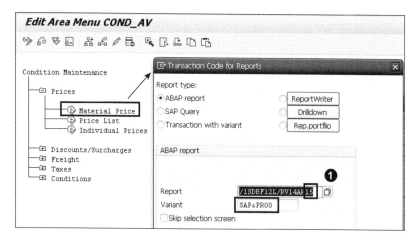

Figure 2.7 Area Menu COND_AV

In this process, the pricing report is used as a filter to select the desired set of condition records.

Definition: Variant

A filled selection screen that has been saved is known in the SAP system as a *variant*. The menu path to create a variant, starting from the current selection screen, is GOTO • VARIANTS • SAVE AS VARIANT.

The variant SAP&PR00 thus constitutes the basis for the default settings of the selection screen when you select the menu item MATERIAL PRICE in Transaction VK32 (see Figure 2.8).

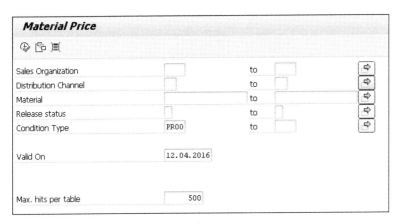

Figure 2.8 Selection Screen for Material Price

Setting different selection fields and confirming with EXECUTE could display, for example, the screen shown in Figure 2.9.

This type of condition maintenance dialog is, by its nature, generic. We no longer have the specific dialog generated for the single condition type, but the information that was divided in the classical condition maintenance on multiple screens is largely gathered in a *central table control* (i.e., a screen element for tabular representation of data). Basically, the same functions are available as in the condition maintenance via condition type. You have to get used to the special operation, however.

Finally, let's consider the function of the DETAIL function. It is used to display information such as scales and validity periods, which cannot be included in the line-oriented table control (see Figure 2.10). Therefore, if you want to display the validity periods for a condition record that is shown in the table control, you must click on the magnifying glass icon at the beginning of the line. This opens at the bottom of the screen a small subscreen with the relevant details on the VALIDITY PERIODS, SCALES, CONDITION TEXTS, and KEY tabs.

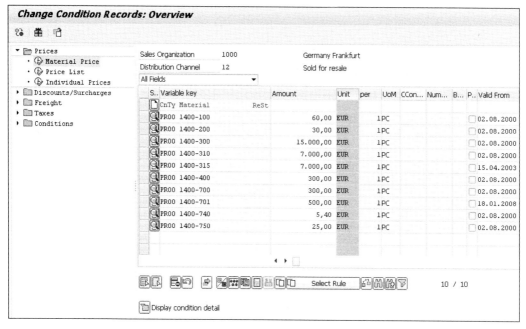

Figure 2.9 Transaction VK32 (Change): Selection Result

We will go into greater detail regarding this form of maintenance in Chapter 5, Section 5.4, as it can provide additional possibilities by providing special area menus. For example, you might think of specific menu nodes like *Corporate Group XY*, behind which you configure a variant of a pricing report with precompleted selection fields that essentially selects the desired condition records by pressing a button.

One disadvantage of this form of maintenance is that a new condition type can be maintained only after it is included in a pricing report and can thus be selected.

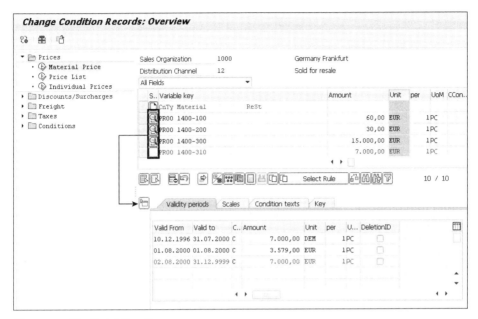

Figure 2.10 The Detail Function

2.3 Condition Maintenance via Index

Another form of the condition maintenance can be accessed via the menu path SAP EASY ACCESS • LOGISTICS • SALES AND DISTRIBUTION • MASTER DATA • CONDITIONS • SELECT USING INDEX. The following transactions are available:

▸ V_I7 (Create Conditions)

▸ V/I5 (Change Conditions)

▸ V/I6 (Display Conditions)

A prerequisit for this form of the condition maintenance is the existence of a condition index. In addition, for each condition type the CONDITION INDEX attribute has to be set so that the condition type takes part in the index writing.

The standard SAP system contains two example indices. Using these indices, regardless of the condition type, all condition records for a certain material (index 001) or to a particular customer (index 002) can be selected. Selecting customer 1174 could provide the information reproduced in Figure 2.11. As you can see, a cross-condition type maintenance is also possible here.

Figure 2.11 Condition Maintenance via Index

Note that the number of indexes to be written affects the system performance when saving (updating) condition records. Keep that in mind when you create and activate indexes.

The configuration settings for condition indexes can be reached under the menu path IMG • Sales and Distribution • Basic Functions • Pricing • Maintain Condition Index.

2.4 Agreements

You can create pricing condition records in connection with an agreement. Generally, we distinguish between two agreement types: *sales deals* and *rebate agreements*.

2.4.1 Sales Deals

To create special conditions in connection with marketing programs, which can later be evaluated, you can create a *promotion*, which defines, among other things, a total validity period. As a second step, you can then allocate sales deals, which contain special prices and/or discounts, to these promotions. The set of allowed condition types is defined in Customizing by a condition type group, which is assigned to the sales deal type. The validity period of these sales deals must be within the validity period of the superordinate promotion. The condition records created within the sales deal contain the key of the corresponding sales deal and possibly the key of the promotion in their master data. If such a condition record is found later in the document pricing, these numbers will be transported to the line item data and can then be collected for evaluation purposes in the statistics.

Let's have a look at two agreements from the standard SAP system—the promotion type 0030 and the sales deal type 0020 using the menu path: SAP EASY ACCESS • LOGISTICS • SALES AND DISTRIBUTION • MASTER DATA • AGREEMENTS • PROMOTION • CREATE (see Figure 2.12).

Create Promotion

Promotion	
Description	Sales Promotion 08/16
External description	MOTOCYCLE FAIR
Default data	
Validity period	01.08.2016
To	30.08.2016
Terms of payment	
Fixed value date	Addit.value days

Figure 2.12 Create Promotion (Transaction VB31)

This promotion does not yet contain condition data. These are only maintained as part of the sales deals. Using the menu path SAP EASY ACCESS • LOGISTICS • SALES AND DISTRIBUTION • MASTER DATA • AGREEMENTS • SALES DEAL • CREATE, we reach Transaction VB21 (see Figure 2.13).

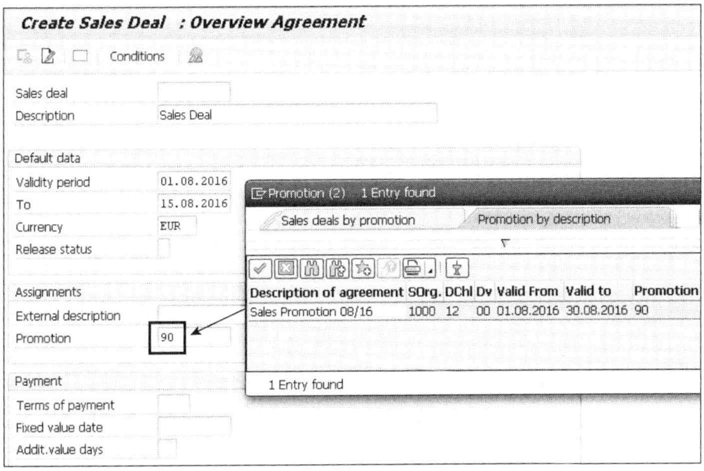

Create Sales Deal   : Overview Agreement

Conditions

Sales deal	
Description	Sales Deal
Default data	
Validity period	01.08.2016
To	15.08.2016
Currency	EUR
Release status	
Assignments	
External description	
Promotion	90
Payment	
Terms of payment	
Fixed value date	
Addit.value days	

Promotion (2)   1 Entry found

Sales deals by promotion   Promotion by description

Description of agreement	SOrg.	DChl	Dv	Valid From	Valid to	Promotion
Sales Promotion 08/16	1000	12	00	01.08.2016	30.08.2016	90

1 Entry found

Figure 2.13 Create Sales Deal (Transaction VB21)

In the sales deal, the reference to the superordinate promotion can now be established. In contrast to the screen where the promotion is created, the CONDITIONS button is available here, which calls the condition maintenance. After selecting the CONDITIONS button, a selection screen is displayed showing the set of available condition types, which is determined by the condition type group that was assigned to sales deal type 0020.

As an example, we want to create two trade fair prices. This is done via the classic fast entry screen (see Figure 2.14) and the validity period is proposed from the sales deal.

Figure 2.14 Create Sales Deal: Overview Price

You can display the superordinate promotion and get the overview screen shown in Figure 2.15, which lists the subordinate sales deals.

Figure 2.15 Display Promotion with Assigned Sales Deals (Transaction VB33)

The configuration settings for pricing agreements can be reached using the menu path IMG • SALES AND DISTRIBUTION • BASIC FUNCTIONS • PRICING • PRICING AGREEMENTS.

Dynamic Determination of Sales Deals

The topic sales deals has experienced an interesting development with the idea of the *price book*. It allows you to dynamically determine a sales deal during pricing in order to incorporate the data in pricing, which is not included in the sales document.

As an example of this functionality, the pricing procedure RVAA02 is part of the standard SAP system. The aim of the price book is to provide a group of customers or individual customers with special prices. However, these prices should be based on a price book whose prices are defined as customer-independent. The needed individualization is achieved because, depending on the customer, a sales deal is determined in which the special arrangements are stored.

These special arrangements are then considered during pricing by special techniques (data determination during access). We will discuss this topic and the necessary technical background in more detail in Chapter 9.

2.4.2 Rebate Agreements

A *rebate* is a retroactively granted discount, which is granted to a rebate recipient based on purchasing a defined sales volume within a certain period. Rebate agreements are created in order to determine the necessary values for a rebate settlement within the duration of the rebate agreement.

A rebate agreement consists of two parts: the rebate agreement itself and the condition records created within the agreement, which are used to calculate the rebate. The rebate condition record in the agreement defines (possibly with scales) the sales target and the corresponding rates of remuneration. In addition, the bonus condition record serves as a "reporting entity" for a turnover update. If a bonus condition record for a billing item is found, this billing is relevant for the accumulation of the rebate basis of the agreement for which the condition record has been created. If specified in the condition record, accruals can be posted during the release of the billing document to accounting.

Rebate agreements are created via the menu path SAP EASY ACCESS • LOGISTICS • SALES AND DISTRIBUTION • MASTER DATA • AGREEMENTS • REBATE AGREEMENT • CREATE (Transaction VBO1).

To configure the rebate condition types (attribute CONDITION CLASS = C – EXPENSE REIMBURSEMENT), you will apply the same design principles as you will for the other pricing condition types in Chapter 4 (except for the reduced number of attributes within the condition type).

The settings in Customizing for the rebate agreements can be reached via the menu path IMG • SALES AND DISTRIBUTION • BILLING • REBATE PROCESSING • REBATE AGREEMENTS (see Chapter 15).

2.5   Price Agreements

With price agreements, you can define contract-specific condition records. Such price agreements are typically used in rental, service, and maintenance contracts. For price agreements, however, not only are values entered in the header or item condition screen, but condition records are also created, having in the key their origin (the transaction number), and which take effect immediately. These condition records can therefore be inherited by an appropriately structured access sequence, for example, when you create a service order with reference to a service contract. In Chapter 6, Section 6.4, we will discuss the use of price agreements in more detail.

2.6   Summary

In most cases, the tool of choice for pricing master data will certainly be the classic condition maintenance via the condition type. The advantage is that you can use all the tools in parallel. A condition record remains a condition record—regardless of how it was created—and can be further processed with all other maintenance tools, if the relevant preconditions such as filtering condition lists for the maintenance via area menus or the activation of the index writing for the maintenance via index are fulfilled.

In larger companies, the number of condition records can easily break the one million mark. Therefore, evaluations and worklists are indispensable for selecting the records of interest from a large amount of condition records. In the next chapter, we deal with the required tools.

Like any other master data, condition records must also be maintained by the respective departments of the company. Efficient tools can select the relevant subset from a large population of condition records to assist in this task.

3   Condition Lists

In addition to the different maintenance transactions, additional tools are provided to maintain condition records and to evaluate them in order to answer different questions. For example, you can use pricing reports or personalized worklists to get an overview of condition records or use price lists for price information.

In the following sections, we will take a look at executing, configuring, and using pricing reports. We will also discuss worklist provided for the internal sales representative role (SAP_BPR_INT_SALES_REP_14 or SAP_SR_INT_SALES_REP_5), the use of the net price list, and the performance-optimized price list.

3.1   Pricing Reports

To get an overview of the condition records in the system, you can use special pricing reports. For example, the condition records can be searched to answer the following questions:

▶ Which customer-specific price agreements exist in my sales organization for specific products?

▶ Which condition records are stored in the system for certain *incoterms*?

▶ What conditions have been created for a specific customer?

In the standard SAP system, there are a number of preconfigured pricing reports, such as pricing report 16 (INDIVIDUAL PRICES). In addition, you can configure further pricing reports by a report generator within Customizing (see Section 3.1.2) to cover any customer requirements. Let us now take a look at how to handle pricing reports.

3.1.1 Execution of Pricing Reports

To call a pricing report, choose the menu path SAP EASY ACCESS • LOGISTICS • SALES AND DISTRIBUTION • MASTER DATA • CONDITIONS • LIST • PRICING REPORT (Transaction V/LD).

Let's look at this tool using the example of pricing report 16 (see Figure 3.1): Initially, after starting a pricing report, a selection screen appears to restrict the query. The number of selection fields can be configured, as you will also see in Section 3.1.2, when creating the pricing report in Customizing. You can also configure the default for the attributes in the field group LIST SCREEN.

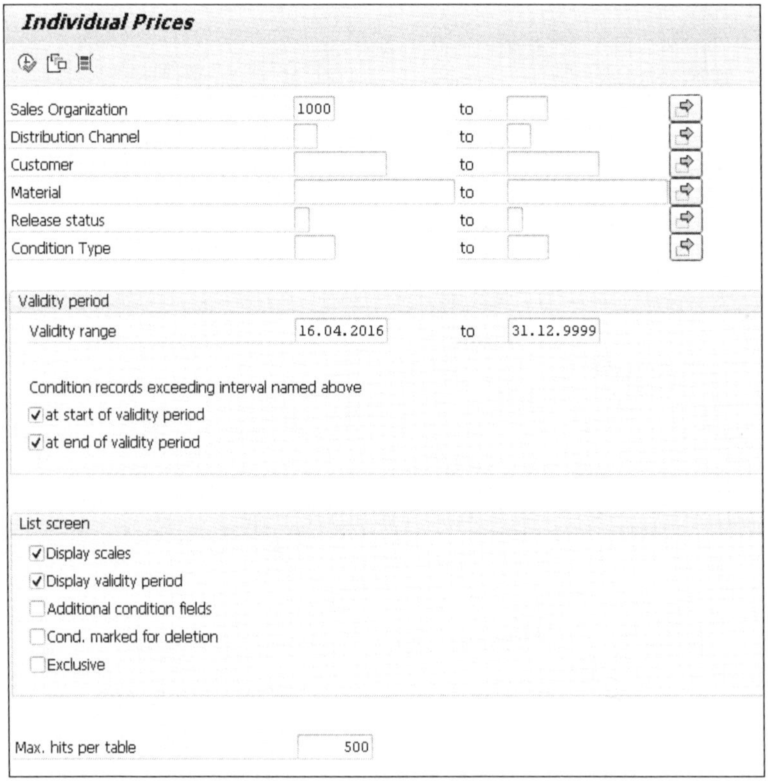

Figure 3.1 Calling the Individual Prices Pricing Report (Transaction V/LD)

After entering the selection criteria, you can start the pricing report by selecting EXECUTE or using F8. The results will displayed (see Figure 3.2). Within the possibilities offered, the appearance of the result list (e.g., positioning a field on the page header, group header, or item level) can be configured in the Customizing of the pricing report.

```
Individual Prices

 I◀  ◀  ▶  ▶I  □  ⌀  ⅋

Sales Org.     1000            Germany Frankfurt
Distr. Channel 10              Final customer sales

Customer
CnTy Material     ReSt S Scale qty UoM   Amount Unit per UoM Valid From Valid to

1234      K.F.W. Berlin
PR00 QS8X35                               0,10   EUR   1   PC   15.11.2000 31.12.9999

1235      K.F.W. London
PR00 QS8X30                               0,10   EUR   1   PC   16.11.2000 31.12.9999
PR00 QS8X35                               0,10   EUR   1   PC   15.11.2000 31.12.9999

1250      LCH Markt
PR00 T-FV100-EM-01                        9,00   EUR   1   KG   30.01.2003 31.12.9999

1410      PILAR am Neckar
PR00 P-109                            3.323,00   EUR   1   PC   26.07.2000 31.12.9999

CUSTOMER00 Becker 00
PR00 P-WO-200                             5,00   EUR   1   PC   20.05.2010 31.12.9999
```

Figure 3.2 Individual Prices: Result List

From the results list, you can branch to the condition maintenance Transactions VK11 (Create), VK12 (Change), and VK13 (Display). In the case of display and change, you jump directly to the condition record marked in the list.

3.1.2 Configuration of a Pricing Report

The configuration of pricing reports cannot be done in the application menu of the end user, but it is part of Customizing. The settings for the pricing reports can be accessed via the menu path IMG • SALES AND DISTRIBUTION • BASIC FUNCTIONS • PRICING • MAINTAIN PRICING REPORT.

To create a new pricing report, you first select a two-digit abbreviation from the customer namespace (these are, by definition, all two-digit combinations that begin with a letter) and a title. In our example report, we will choose the abbreviation X0 and the title CONDITIONS PER CUSTOMER (see Figure 3.3).

Create Pricing Report
Name of List
X0
Title
Conditions per Customer

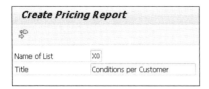

Figure 3.3 Create Pricing Report: Initial Screen

Next, a screen appears with all fields that are part of a condition table in the underlying development system (see Figure 3.4).

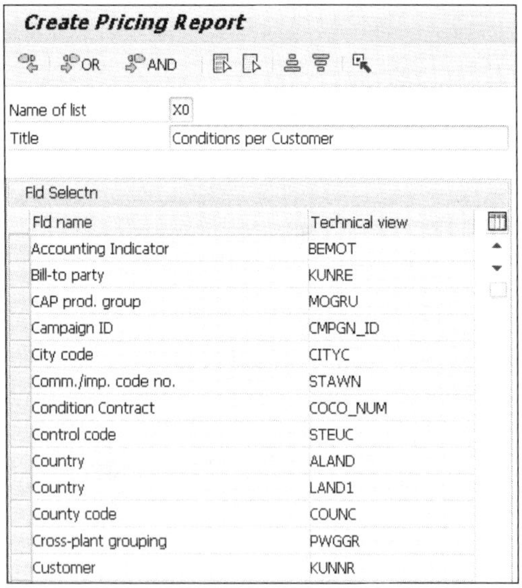

Create Pricing Report
OR
AND
Name of list
X0
Title
Conditions per Customer
Fld Selectn
Fld name
Technical view
Accounting Indicator
BEMOT
Bill-to party
KUNRE
CAP prod. group
MOGRU
Campaign ID
CMPGN_ID
City code
CITYC
Comm./imp. code no.
STAWN
Condition Contract
COCO_NUM
Control code
STEUC
Country
ALAND
Country
LAND1
County code
COUNC
Cross-plant grouping
PWGGR
Customer
KUNNR

Figure 3.4 Create Pricing Report: Field Selection

When selecting the fields, the challenge is to make a preliminary decision: Which condition tables and condition types are to be evaluated in the resulting pricing report? Here, a combination of the fields with AND or with OR is possible. Each option has an impact on the selection of the condition tables. We opt for the CUSTOMER (KUNNR) field. As a result, we receive a listing of all condition tables in which field KUNNR is included, as shown in Figure 3.5.

We select condition tables `005`, `007`, `305`, and `307` and come to the last screen in the generation sequence (see Figure 3.6), where we can influence the selection screen and the appearance of the result list.

Figure 3.5 Create Pricing Report: Selection of Condition Tables

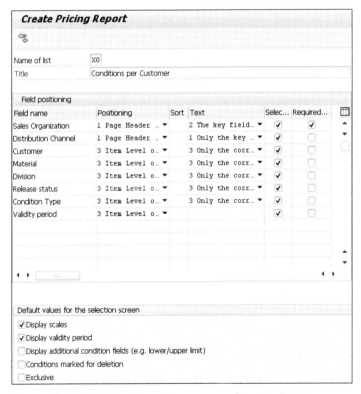

Figure 3.6 Create Pricing Report: Appearance of the Result List

The system offers the key fields of all previously selected condition tables as selection fields. In the Positioning column, you can choose between three options:

▶ 1: Page Header of Pricing Report

▶ 2: Group Header of Pricing Report

▶ 3: Item Level of Pricing Report

In the Sort column, the order of the fields in a level (page header, group header, or item level) can be set. The sort order does not affect the order of the page header, group header, and item level itself.

In the Text column, you also have three options available:

▶ 1: Only the key field is displayed

▶ 2: The key field and the corresponding text are displayed

▶ 3: Only the corresponding text is displayed

These options apply only to the levels of group header and item level. In contrast, in the page header, the field name and description are always displayed. Due to lack of space, either the field name or the associated text should be displayed at the item level.

In the Selection column, you can deselect some of the selection fields as necessary, though we have not done so in our example. In the Required input column, the Sales Organization field has been marked as a required entry field. Click Save to generate the new pricing report X0. A first test run of the new pricing report shows the result displayed in Figure 3.7.

Conditions per Customer

| Sales Org. 1000 | | Germany Frankfurt | | | | | | | | | | |
| Distr. Channel 12 | | Sold for resale | | | | | | | | | | |

Condition type	Dv	Customer		S	Scale qty	UoM	Amount	Unit	per	UoM	Valid From	Valid to
Customer Discount	Cross-division	Motomarkt Stuttgart GmbH					10,000-	%			01.03.2015	31.12.9999

| Sales Org. 1000 | | Germany Frankfurt | | | | | | | | | | |
| Distr. Channel 12 | | Sold for resale | | | | | | | | | | |

CnTy	Customer	Material		ReSt	S	Scale qty	UoM	Amount	Unit	per	UoM	Valid From	Valid to
Price	Motomarkt Stuttgart GmbH	CrossFun / 350 cm3						6.500,00	EUR	1	PC	01.04.2016	31.12.9999

Figure 3.7 Conditions per Customer: First Test Run

Since the appearance of the result list is not completely in line with our expectations, we edit the pricing report again in change mode and replace the attributes in the TEXT column labeled 3 - ONLY THE CORRESPONDING TEXT IS DISPLAYED with the attribute 1 - ONLY THE KEY FIELD IS DISPLAYED. A new call of the pricing report X0 shows the result displayed in Figure 3.8.

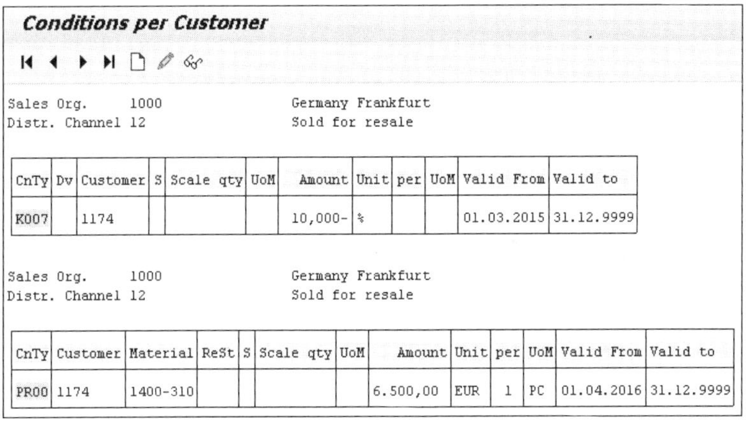

Conditions per Customer

Sales Org.   1000   Germany Frankfurt
Distr. Channel 12   Sold for resale

CnTy	Dv	Customer	S	Scale qty	UoM	Amount	Unit	per	UoM	Valid From	Valid to
K007		1174				10,000-	%			01.03.2015	31.12.9999

Sales Org.   1000   Germany Frankfurt
Distr. Channel 12   Sold for resale

CnTy	Customer	Material	ReSt	S	Scale qty	UoM	Amount	Unit	per	UoM	Valid From	Valid to
PR00	1174	1400-310					6.500,00	EUR	1	PC	01.04.2016	31.12.9999

Figure 3.8 Conditions per Customer: Second Test Run

Usually several change rounds will be necessary to customize the options of the result list according to your needs.

3.1.3 Pricing Report for Condition Maintenance via Area Menu

As described in Chapter 2, the pricing reports play an important role in the condition maintenance via area menus. They act as filters, which are assigned to a node of the area menu in the form of a variant of a pricing report (e.g., in area menu COND_AV).

If you want to use a pricing report as a filter in an area menu, no specific settings are required when generating the report. However, the condition maintenance Transactions VK31 to VK34 provide an adapted selection screen that is controlled by them. Therefore, the selection screen shown in Figure 3.1 of pricing report 16 (INDIVIDUAL PRICES) looks slightly different when used as a filter in the condition maintenance (see Figure 3.9).

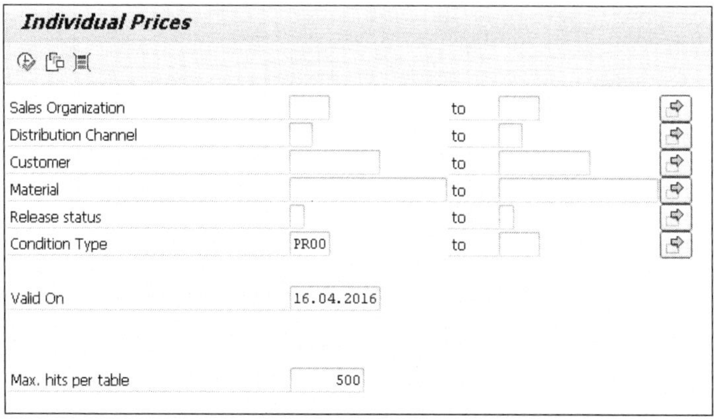

Figure 3.9 Pricing Report as a Filter in the Condition Maintenance

Pricing reports are by themselves very useful and flexible tools made even more valuable by their use as a filter element in the condition maintenance via area menus.

The latest development in condition lists are the *worklists* introduced for the internal sales representative role, which are presented next.

3.2   Worklists for the Internal Sales Representative Role

Since SAP ERP 6.0 EHP 2, the *Internal Sales Representative* business package has been available. To use it, however, you must activate the business function SD_01 (Logistics: S&D Simplification) with Transaction SFW5 (Switch Framework).

In the accompanying supplied sample user role SAP_BPR_INT_SALES_REP_14 (or SAP_SR_INT_SALES_REP_5 later with EHP 5), a personal worklist for condition information is contained. This worklist provides the sales staff with a flexible overview of the different types of conditions as well as extensive search facilities to identify condition master data according to different selection criteria. The individual queries are provided in the form of personal worklists—also called POWLs (personal object worklists). The salesperson receives different lists with the customer-specific agreements such as customer-specific prices, discounts, and free goods. In addition, lists are available with material prices, freight costs, and price lists.

This POWL can be adjusted individually by the user with regard to their use of selection criteria (CHANGE QUERY), the visibility and the name of the queries (PERSONALIZE), and the presentation of the search result (SETTINGS). In addition, users can even create their own queries (DEFINE NEW QUERY).

Initially, the functionality of the internal sales representative role was exclusively available via portal usage. Starting with SAP ERP 6.0 EHP 4, there is also the option to use the role with the SAP Business Client. The functionality relating to the worklist for condition information is identical. Figure 3.10 shows the worklist for condition information after accessing the system with the SAP Business Client and choosing menu node PRICES.

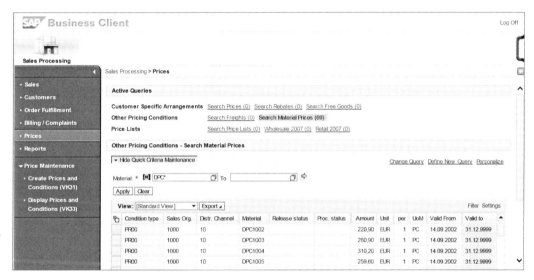

Figure 3.10 Screen of the Internal Sales Representative Role

To ensure that you receive insight into the capabilities of POWL, we will discuss the features of this list in the following sections, using a practical example.

3.2.1 Change Query

The queries in the personal worklist should of course reflect the specific information needs of the user. You can adjust existing queries by using the function CHANGE QUERY (see Figure 3.10). In our example, we select the query SEARCH MATERIAL PRICES in the screen area ACTIVE QUERIES and choose the function

CHANGE QUERY. As a result, a selection screen opens with a large number of possible selection fields, which you can fill in with any combinations (see Figure 3.11).

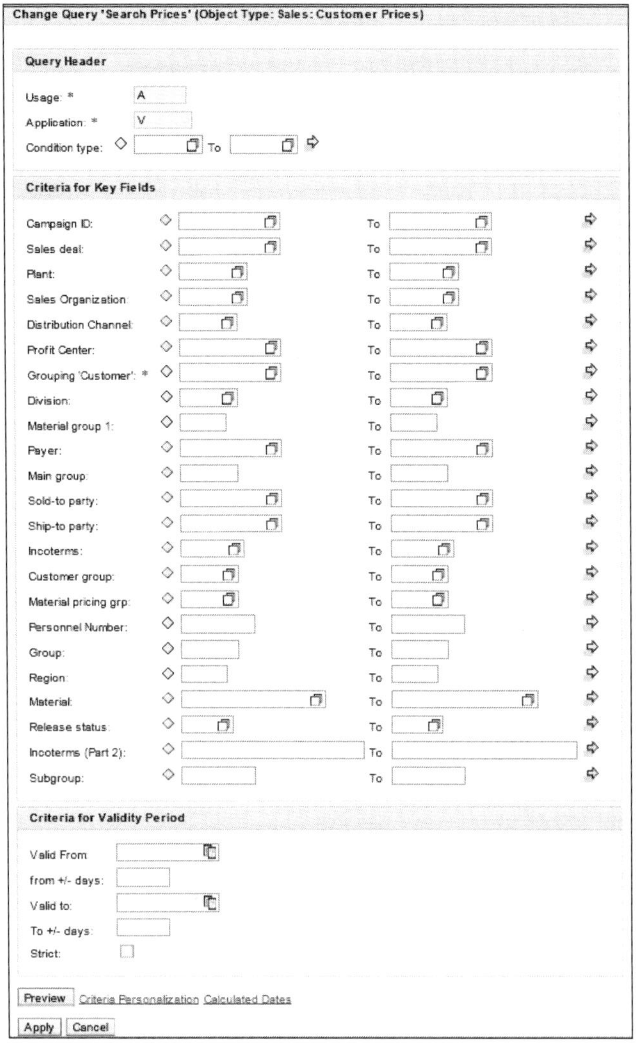

Figure 3.11 Selection Fields of the Search Prices Query

The available selection fields are defined in the configuration of the underlying POWL. This configuration can be reached via the menu path IMG • SALES AND DISTRIBUTION • "INTERNAL SALES REPRESENTATIVE" ROLE • PERSONAL WORKLIST (NEW) • PERSONAL WORKLIST FOR CONDITION INFORMATION.

The main worklist types for sales employees' work areas are predefined and assigned to SAP ERP Sales and Distribution (SD):

▸ SALES: CUSTOMER REBATES

▸ SALES: CUSTOMER FREE GOODS

▸ SALES: CUSTOMER PRICES

▸ SALES: DOCUMENT PRICES

▸ SALES: FREIGHT

▸ SALES: MATERIAL PRICES

▸ SALES: PRICE LIST

Customer-Specific Worklist Types

In addition to the predefined worklist types, customer-specific worklist types can be created. Nevertheless, for this purpose, Business Add-ins (BAdIs) must be programmed!

As you can see on closer inspection in Figure 3.11, the underlying worklist type for the query SEARCH PRICES is the type SALES: CUSTOMER PRICES.

3.2.2 Personalize Query

To personalize a query, select the PERSONALIZE function in the initial screen of the query (see Figure 3.10). This will open the screen shown in Figure 3.12. You can enable or disable the available queries and design your worklist.

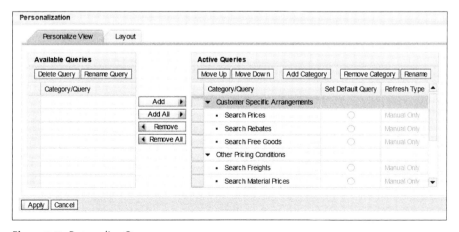

Figure 3.12 Personalize Query

3.2.3   Define New Query

To search condition records according to other aspects, you can create new queries. After selecting the DEFINE NEW QUERY function, a wizard starts that guides the user in three steps through the creation of the new query.

First, select the object type of the query (see Figure 3.13).

Figure 3.13 Define New Query: Step 1

The second step is in the input of the selection criteria (see Figure 3.14). As already mentioned, the selected query type defines these.

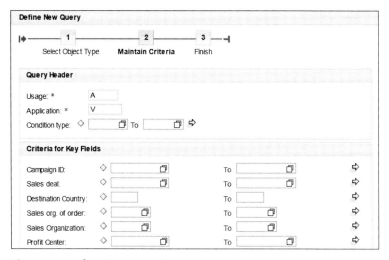

Figure 3.14 Define New Query: Step 2

The third and final step is to specify the description and the category under which the query should appear in the worklist (see Figure 3.15).

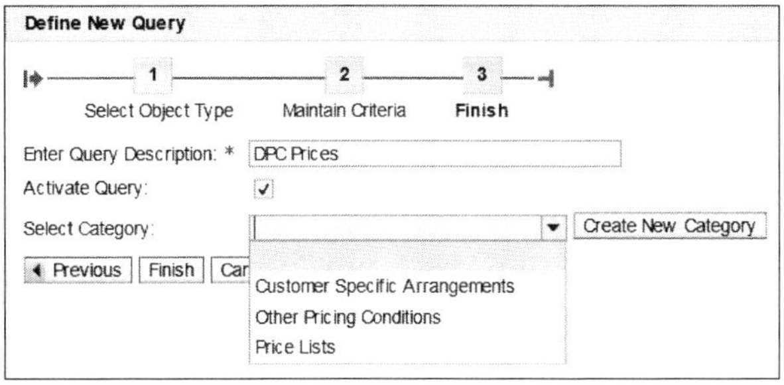

Figure 3.15 Define New Query: Step 3

After you click on the FINISH button, you can use the new query in the worklist (see Figure 3.16).

Figure 3.16 New Query in the Worklist

As you can see, it can be worthwhile to use the Internal Sales Representative business package. In addition to the worklist for price data, it contains many other interesting areas, such as the customer cockpit. For more information on this, we recommend a look at the SAP ERP documentation at *http://help.sap.com*.

3.3   Net Price List

The net price list provides price information on a selected set of products for a specific customer. The net prices cannot simply be read from a master data table, but instead must be calculated. For this purpose, an invoice is simulated (using function module `GN_INVOICE_CREATE`) and a corresponding pricing run is performed. Therefore, in the selection screen of the net price list, all information must be entered that is necessary for a specific pricing procedure determination: sales area, sales document type (from which the DOCUMENT PRICING PROCEDURE field is derived), and the customer (from which the CUSTOMER PRICING PROCEDURE field is derived).

The net price list can be accessed via the menu path SAP EASY ACCESS • LOGISTICS • SALES AND DISTRIBUTION • MASTER DATA • CONDITIONS • LIST • NET PRICE LIST (Transaction V_NL).

A selection screen is displayed (see Figure 3.17), and the previously mentioned selection criteria must be entered for the pricing procedure determination.

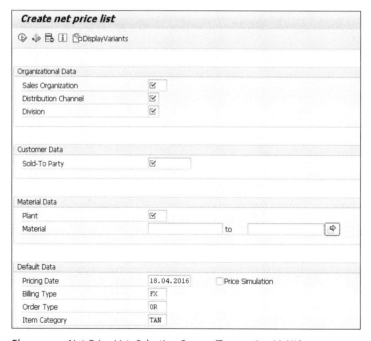

Figure 3.17 Net Price List: Selection Screen (Transaction V_NL)

You also need the PLANT field to identify the country of departure (impact on the tax determination). The PRICE SIMULATION attribute determines whether conditions with release status B – RELEASED FOR PRICE SIMULATION or C - RELEASED FOR PLANNING AND PRICE SIMULATION are to be taken into account.

As a result, an SAP List Viewer (ALV) is displayed with a selected set of fields that can be edited with the usual procedure in the ALVs (menu path Settings • Layout) (see Figure 3.18).

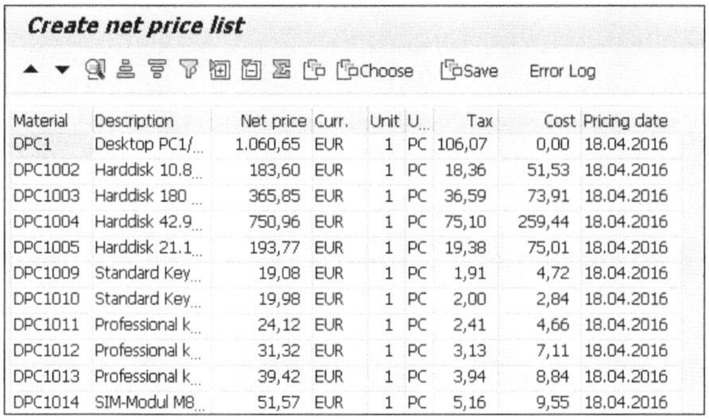

Material	Description	Net price	Curr.	Unit	U...	Tax	Cost	Pricing date
DPC1	Desktop PC1/...	1.060,65	EUR	1	PC	106,07	0,00	18.04.2016
DPC1002	Harddisk 10.8...	183,60	EUR	1	PC	18,36	51,53	18.04.2016
DPC1003	Harddisk 180...	365,85	EUR	1	PC	36,59	73,91	18.04.2016
DPC1004	Harddisk 42.9...	750,96	EUR	1	PC	75,10	259,44	18.04.2016
DPC1005	Harddisk 21.1...	193,77	EUR	1	PC	19,38	75,01	18.04.2016
DPC1009	Standard Key...	19,08	EUR	1	PC	1,91	4,72	18.04.2016
DPC1010	Standard Key...	19,98	EUR	1	PC	2,00	2,84	18.04.2016
DPC1011	Professional k...	24,12	EUR	1	PC	2,41	4,66	18.04.2016
DPC1012	Professional k...	31,32	EUR	1	PC	3,13	7,11	18.04.2016
DPC1013	Professional k...	39,42	EUR	1	PC	3,94	8,84	18.04.2016
DPC1014	SIM-Modul M8...	51,57	EUR	1	PC	5,16	9,55	18.04.2016

Figure 3.18 Net Price List: Result Screen

The net price list, which can also contain information such as transfer prices, is primarily an internal information tool for the department. If such a net price list is forwarded to the customer, of course, that information must be removed from the list. Since it is an ALV, a personalization of the columns displayed is easily possible by choosing menu path Settings • Layout • Current.

3.4   Performance-Optimized Price List

Starting with SAP ERP 6.0 EHP 7, Support Package 3, a performance-optimized price list is offered with business function LOG_SD_PRICE_LIST and enhanced with LOG_SD_PRICE_LIST_2 (Support Package 4). Unlike the original net price list, the performance-optimized price list can handle multiple customers at a time and has, in general, more options. Its purpose is not so much to provide information to the department (although this is of course still possible) but to create lists that, for example, can be sent automatically and on a regular basis to your customers. The technical realization of this new list is quite different and no longer uses any document simulation. We will comment on this later when discussing the various possibilities of customer enhancements in Section 3.4.2, Section 3.4.5, and Section 3.4.6.

Let us begin with the creation of an optimized price list and then have a closer look on the configuration and enhancement possibilities.

3.4.1 Creation of Price Lists

If the relevant business functions are switched on, the optimized price list can be accessed via the menu path SAP EASY ACCESS • LOGISTICS • SALES AND DISTRIBUTION • MASTER DATA • CONDITIONS • LIST • NET PRICE LIST (Transaction V_NLN), thereby replacing the original list that you can still invoke with Transaction V_NL.

At first glance, the upper part of the selection screen in Figure 3.19 looks very similar to the traditional price list from Figure 3.17.

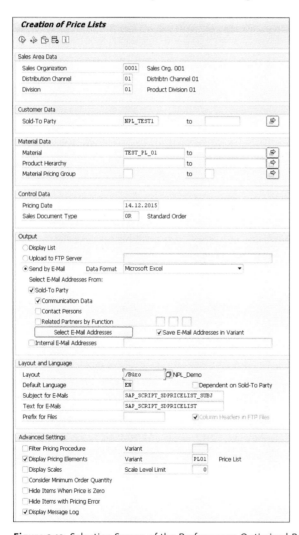

Figure 3.19 Selection Screen of the Performance Optimized Price List

If you look closer, you will see that you can now select several customers at once and that the selection of the products is more flexible. Net prices are calculated for each possible customer/material combination.

The lower part of the selection screen offers several new options. There are three radio buttons in the OUTPUT section of the selection screen, as follows:

▶ DISPLAY LIST

If you choose this button, the prices will be displayed on your screen in the form of one ALV, including all calculated customer/material combinations. You can personalize the list to your needs, create different layouts, filter, etc. You can enter an existing layout in the LAYOUT AND LANGUAGE section. We will describe later how to control and enhance the available fields in the output list. A possible result could look like the one shown in Figure 3.20.

Creation of Price Lists

Pricing date	Customer	Material	Description	Quantity	Sales	Net Value	Doc.
14.12.2015	NPL_TEST1	TEST_PL_01	Folder	1	ST	1,49	EUR
14.12.2015	NPL_TEST1	TEST_PL_02	Loose-leaf Folder	1	ST	0,99	EUR
14.12.2015	NPL_TEST1	TEST_PL_03	Print-out Paper 10	1	PAC	3,99	EUR
14.12.2015	NPL_TEST2	TEST_PL_01	Folder	1	ST	2,09	EUR
14.12.2015	NPL_TEST2	TEST_PL_02	Loose-leaf Folder	1	ST	0,99	EUR
14.12.2015	NPL_TEST2	TEST_PL_03	Print-out Paper 10	1	PAC	3,69	EUR
14.12.2015	NPL_TEST3	TEST_PL_01	Folder	1	ST	2,99	EUR
14.12.2015	NPL_TEST3	TEST_PL_02	Loose-leaf Folder	1	ST	0,99	EUR
14.12.2015	NPL_TEST3	TEST_PL_03	Print-out Paper 10	1	PAC	3,49	EUR

Figure 3.20 Example Output of Performance-Optimized Price List

▶ UPLOAD TO FTP SERVER

Alternatively, you can upload the price list as a CSV file to an FTP server. The server address, user, and password are defined in the Customizing of the price list function (IMG • SALES AND DISTRIBUTION • BASIC FUNCTIONS • PRICING • PRICE LISTS • SELECTION AND RESULT • DEFINE FTP SETTINGS). Price lists for different customers are stored in different files, with the customer number being part of the filename. You may define a prefix for the files in the LAYOUT AND LANGUAGE section of the report. The system will then put the prefix in front of the file-names that are composed as follows: `<Prefix>_<Customer Number>_<Time-stamps>`.

The files can be stored with or without the column headers (checkbox in the LAYOUT AND LANGUAGE section).

► SEND BY E-MAIL

It is also possible to send the price lists via e-mail. The report allows you to select the e-mail addresses from different sources such as, for example, the communication data of the customer or the contact person in the customer master data. You can also set the e-mail addresses manually for each customer (the SELECT E-MAIL ADDRESSES button) and store them in a report's variant, or send all lists to one or several internal e-mail addresses. SAP provides the PRO-CESS_CUSTOMER_EMAIL method in the BAdI BADI_PIQ_SDPRICELIST, where you can program you own logic if necessary.

Price lists can be sent in CSV or Microsoft Excel format. For all output options, the system will take the denoted layout from the LAYOUT AND LANGUAGE section into account and send one list per customer. You can specify a default language for all texts or decide to retrieve the language for each customer separately from the sold-to master data record. You can also create language-dependent SAPscript texts for the e-mail header and body in Transaction SO10 and specify them on the selection screen. The texts can also be filled in using the method PROVIDE_EMAIL_TEXT_NAME of the BAdI BADI_PIQ_SDPRICELIST.

The advanced settings section offers options to influence the result of the price list, as follows:

► FILTER PRICING PROCEDURE

When creating a price list, you may not need all lines of your pricing procedure. Maybe you do not care about the freight cost or you are not interested in the cost conditions. The new price list Customizing offers the definition of *filter variants* for pricing procedures where you mark non-relevant steps. These steps are then ignored or skipped during the price calculation, thus improving performance. You can maintain one or more filters for a pricing procedure here: IMG • SALES AND DISTRIBUTION • BASIC FUNCTIONS • PRICING • PRICE LISTS • SELECTION AND RESULT • DEFINE FILTER FOR PRICING PROCEDURE. Just flag the rows in the procedure that you do not need in the price list calculation (see Figure 3.21).

► DISPLAY PRICING ELEMENTS

The previous net price list provides net price and tax information but no information about individual price elements or subtotal lines, for example the overall discount or a special sales deal. In a similar way to filtering some lines from the pricing procedure, you may define *display variants* where you mark those lines in the procedure that will be available for output in the price list result.

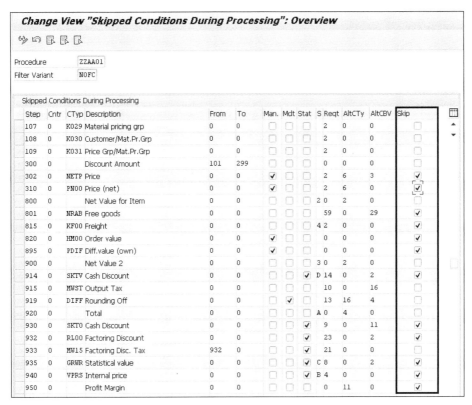

Figure 3.21 Definition of a Filter Variant: Rows in the Pricing Procedure Irrelevant for the Net Price List Result Are Marked to be Skipped

The relevant Customizing is located in IMG • Sales and Distribution • Basic Functions • Pricing • Price Lists • Selection and Result • Define Pricing Elements Display. We will explain the exact setting needed to make the flagged elements part of the output list in Section 3.4.6.

▶ Display Scales

The performance-optimized price list supports the display of scale information in the result. If you flag the Display Scales checkbox, the system will evaluate all scales involved in the calculation of the net price and will deduce the quantities where it expects the effective net price to change. For these quantities, the system recalculates the price and adds corresponding lines to the result (see Figure 3.22). You can thereby inform your customer about the opportunity to get better prices if they purchase higher quantities.

The number of additional quantities can be limited by the SCALE LEVEL LIMIT field. If you leave it empty, the price list will calculate and display all relevant quantities. If you enter "4", for example, you will receive up to four additional lines or five in total.

The net price list supports any mixture of value, quantity, weight, and volume scales and has a from-scale notation in the output; i.e., the listed price is valid from the indicated sales quantity upwards. Graduated scales are not permitted since they result in different prices for each sales quantity. Scale-base formulas may interfere with the calculation of the sales quantities in an unpredictable way and are similarly not allowed. However, BAdI `BADI_PRC_NPL_SCALES` allows you to overrule these restrictions and to give your own set of sales quantities to be calculated.

Creation of Price Lists

Pricing date	Customer	Material	Description	Quantity	Sales	Net price	Doc.	Pricin	Unit
14.12.2015	NPL_TEST1	TEST_PL_01	Folder	1	ST	1,49	EUR	1	ST
14.12.2015	NPL_TEST1	TEST_PL_02	Loose-leaf Folder	1	ST	0,99	EUR	1	ST
14.12.2015	NPL_TEST1	TEST_PL_03	Print-out Paper 100 pc	1	PAC	3,99	EUR	1	PAC
14.12.2015	NPL_TEST1	TEST_PL_03	Print-out Paper 100 pc	10	PAC	3,49	EUR	1	PAC
14.12.2015	NPL_TEST1	TEST_PL_03	Print-out Paper 100 pc	50	PAC	2,99	EUR	1	PAC

Figure 3.22 Output of the Price List with Scales Displayed

▶ CONSIDER MINIMUM ORDER QUANTITY
Usually the price list will calculate the net price and value for the quantity 1 in sales units of measure. If you mark this checkbox, the prices will be calculated for the minimum order quantity instead.

▶ HIDE ITEM WHEN PRICE IS ZERO
Customer/material combinations with a zero net price will be excluded from the result list.

▶ HIDE ITEMS WITH PRICING ERROR
Customer/material combinations with errors in the price calculation will be excluded from the result list.

▶ DISPLAY MESSAGE LOG
We will explain in the next section how the necessary data for the pricing call is gathered. Especially in the setup and test phases, the message log can give you valuable hints if the required Customizing settings for the data retrieval are not complete.

3.4.2 Customizing and Customer Enhancements

We already mentioned that the performance-optimized price list does not use any kind of business document simulation, so user exits, like those found in the sales order or billing document, are not called. Instead, the price list coding analyzes the access sequences, user exits, formulas, and requirements used in the relevant pricing procedures to determine the actual list of required fields for the pricing communication structures KOMK and KOMP. Only the relevant fields are then determined, with as few database accesses as possible.

While the system can identify fields needed in access sequences reliably, this is not possible for fields used in formulas or requirements. That is why this information is stored in a dedicated customizing table. To allow an effective and flexible bundling of database selects, the necessary table accesses for data retrieval are also stored in customizing tables in form of metadata.

If you use customer-specific fields in access sequences, user exits, formulas, or requirements, you need to include the same information (which fields are needed and how they are determined) in the customer areas in Customizing.

> **Note**
>
> We will now explain the necessary settings with an example. In doing so, we have to assume some technical knowledge and need to delve into some details and enhancement concepts described later in the book, especially topics covered in Chapters 9 and 11. If you are more of a novice in pricing, you may want to skip the following sections for now and continue with Chapter 4.

You will find all necessary activities under the node IMG • Sales and Distribution • Basic Functions • Pricing • Price Lists.

3.4.3 Registration of Fields

Let's assume that we have added the fields ZZMVGR1, ZZMVGR2, ZZSIZECAT, and ZZPROMO to the item communication structure of pricing KOMP. ZZM-VGR1 and ZZMVGR2 correspond to the fields MVGR1 (material group 1) and MVGR2 (material group 2) from the sales data in the material master record. ZZSIZECAT is stored in our own table `ZZTSIZECAT` with the material number as the key field. ZZPROMO is derived by some dedicated business logic. We assume that we use ZZMVGR1 in one of our condition accesses, while ZZMVGR2,

ZZSIZECAT, and ZZPROMO are used only in our requirement 999 (see Figure 3.23). ZZPROMO is used inside function module Z_CHECK_RELEVANCE.

```
Include          RV61A999                          Active
     1  ⊟ FORM kobed_999.
     2       DATA lv_subrc TYPE sysubrc.
     3       sy-subrc = 4.
     4  ⊟    IF komp-kposn NE 0.
     5         CHECK: komp-prsfd CA 'BX'.
     6         CHECK: komp-zzmvgr2 NE '001'.
     7         CHECK: komp-zzsizecat NE 'XL'.
     8         CALL FUNCTION 'Z_CHECK_RELEVANCE'
     9           EXPORTING
    10             is_komk  = komk
    11             is_komp  = komp
    12           IMPORTING
    13             ev_subrc = lv_subrc.
    14
    15         CHECK lv_subrc IS INITIAL.
    16       ENDIF.
    17       sy-subrc = 0.
    18  ⊢ ENDFORM.
```

Figure 3.23 Requirement 999 Using Fields ZZMVGR2, ZZSIZECAT, and ZZPROMO

The performance-optimized price list tries to identify all needed fields for a specific price calculation. Therefore, it scans all access sequences of the pricing procedure involved and thus becomes aware of ZZMGR1. However, fields required in the execution of user exits, customer-specific formulas, or requirements must be explicitly published in Customizing. To do so, choose the IMG activity IMG • SALES AND DISTRIBUTION • BASIC FUNCTIONS • PRICING • PRICE LISTS • EDIT FIELDS USED IN PRICING ENHANCEMENTS.

On the entry screen, we restrict the view to the relevant pricing procedure and decide that we want to see only customer-developed enhancements. We navigate to requirement 999. A double-click on include RV61A999 would lead us to the coding, but we double-click the node 999 instead.

We now have the list of fields automatically found by means of a simple code scans: ZZMVGR2 and ZZSIZECAT. However, the field KOMP-ZZPROMO is "hidden" behind a function module call and hence was missed. Therefore, we register it manually by clicking the ADD FIELD MANUAL button and entering the necessary data. You can see the result in Figure 3.24, where the found fields have not yet been confirmed and the ZZPROMO field has been added manually.

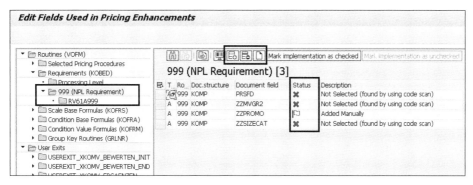

Figure 3.24 Result of the Generic Code Scan for Requirement 999 Searching for Relevant Fields

In the second step, we have to select all fields that must be filled in a price list run (there may be fields that are not relevant) and confirm them explicitly. For this, we select the field(s) and click the SELECT FIELDS button. The status of the fields then changes to SELECTED (Figure 3.25). You can remove fields that are not relevant for the price lists calculation again with the DESELECT button.

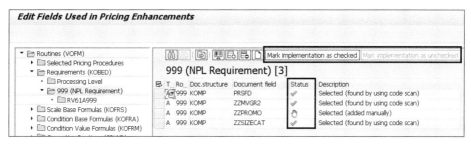

Figure 3.25 Fields Have Been Selected as Relevant

Since the automatic code scan is quite basic, you should always check the system's proposal for your routines and user exits.

After reviewing and completing all entries, you finalize and document your settings by clicking on the MARK IMPLEMENTATION AS CHECKED button. Only now will the net price list take your settings into account.

> **Note**
>
> You can undo your settings any time by clicking the MARK IMPLEMENTATION AS UN-CHECKED button. Manually added fields will automatically be removed.

In addition to specifying which fields are required in your pricing exits, you may also specify a *processing level* for your requirements (Figure 3.26). If, for example, a requirement uses only fields from the header communication structure KOMK (so-called header fields), it is usually sufficient to test it only once per pricing header and buffer the result for the following items.

The available processing levels are HEADER, ITEM, CONDITION TYPE (the hat, list, and coin icons, respectively) and STANDARD PROCESSING LEVEL (the green square icon). The STANDARD PROCESSING LEVEL corresponds to an unmaintained processing level. Here nothing is buffered and the requirement is processed each time it's necessary. In simple cases, this is often faster than writing and reading a buffer. That is why SAP has not maintained any level for many standard requirements.

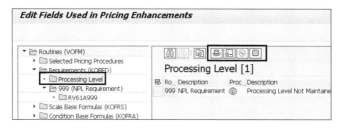

Figure 3.26 Setting the Processing Level of a Requirement

When setting the processing level, you need to be aware that, for performance reasons, the flow logic of pricing is slightly different in the price list processing. The condition accesses are not performed on each item separately in the pricing function module, but for all items together prior to pricing. Consequently, the call of the requirements is brought forward too, and takes place outside of pricing. Hence, if you do more in your requirement than simply check the relevance of a condition, you should assign the standard level or no level at all. By doing so, you ensure that the requirement is called again at the usual place. An example of such a routine is the standard requirement 62, which fills the internal table XKOM-PLOOP.

3.4.4 Define the Data Determination

We have already mentioned that the new price list tries to bundle database accesses. This applies in particular when filling the communication structures in pricing. Thus, in order to enable the system to identify collectable accesses in a generic way, the necessary information is stored in the form of metadata. It is important that you understand how the price list determines its data since you must provide the same information in your own fields. For this purpose, we will have a closer look now at the definition of the table accesses and the corresponding source fields (including customer-specific fields).

Define Table Access

Setting up the metadata consists of two steps. First, you need to specify how a database table will be accessed. This happens in IMG • SALES AND DISTRIBUTION • BASIC FUNCTIONS • PRICING • PRICE LISTS • PRICE INQUIRY • DEFINE TABLE ACCESS.

In Figure 3.27 you will see that for the table containing the sales data of the customer master KNVV, three DB or *table aliases* are defined. For table KNVV, three different aliases are specified: KNVV, KNVV_RG, and KNVV_WE. Each of them accesses the table with different fields.

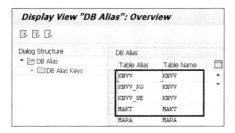

Figure 3.27 Definition of Table Alias

If we navigate to the DB ALIAS KEY node, we realize that the three aliases differ in their access fields. The alias KNVV accesses the table with the contents of the source fields KUNNR, SPAKU, VKORG, and VTWKU, reading data from the sold-to party. The alias KNCC_RG, on the other hand, reads data from the payer, accessing the same table as the KUNRG, SPAKU, VKORG, and VTWKU fields (Figure 3.28). The DB alias thus defines the table and the Where clause of the required Select statement.

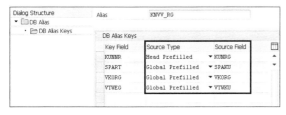

Figure 3.28 The DB Alias KNVV_RG Accesses the Sales Data of the Payer

What does the SOURCE TYPE in Figure 3.28 represent? It defines where the source field comes from, or technically speaking, in what internal structure the field resides. We distinguish the following fields:

▸ GLOBAL PREFILLED data is relevant for the whole price list, such as organizational data or the price date

▸ HEAD PREFILLED data is usually derived from the customer and relevant for all products

▸ ITEM PREFILLED data is usually derived from the material

▸ HEADITEM PREFILLED data depends on customer and material combination

▸ DIRECT VALUE is a constant that can be set in Customizing

Simply put, prefilled data is data whose determination is hard-coded in the price list. It is also possible to preempt your own data via a BAdI implementation. In this case, you have to choose the additional data source types (GLOBAL, HEAD, ITEM, or HEADITEM).

Finally, there is *caller data*. Roughly speaking, this is additional data coming from the outside, especially if the price determination is called outside the net price list via the dedicated function PIQ_CALCULATE. We will come back to this very technical detail in Section 3.4.8. For the moment, it is sufficient to know that the F4 help on the source field will provide you with all possible fields for the selected source type.

To summarize, the DB alias KNVV_RG can be translated into as follows:

```
select <?> from KNVV into <?> where KUNNR = (Head Prefilled)-KUNRG.
```

Maintain Sources for Communication Structures

In IMG • SALES AND DISTRIBUTION • BASIC FUNCTIONS • PRICING • PRICE LISTS • PRICE INQUIRY • SOURCES FOR COMMUNICATION STRUCTURES we define how the fields relevant for pricing are determined in detail. In Figure 3.29 you can see the fields of the header communication structure KOMK. The distribution channel VTWEG is transferred from prefilled data. Other fields like the payment terms ZTERM are determined using a DB alias. Let's have a closer look at the ZTERM field. The line you see in Figure 3.29, together with the definition of the DB alias KNVV_RG, means that the field ZTERM is filled from the field ZTERM from table KNVV using the payer KUNRG to access the table, i.e., the payment terms are read from the sales area data of the payer.

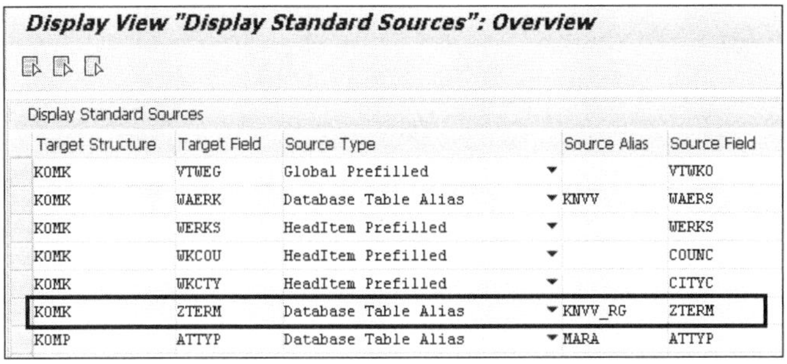

Figure 3.29 Sources of the Fields from the Pricing Communication Structures

Together with the DB alias definition, the following `select` will be performed:

`select ZTERM from KNVV into KOMK-ZTERM where KUNNR = (Head Prefilled)-KUNRG.`

After evaluating all metadata, the price list can optimize the access and read all required fields from a database table together.

> **Available Fields with Standard Sources**
>
> The price list report does not yet support all fields from the communication structure. You can find out which fields are available by displaying the standard sources in the IMG. If the required field is not listed there, you need to add a corresponding entry in the customer section. Customer entries will always overrule standard settings.

Add Customer Fields

It is time to come back to our example. With what you have just learned, you can now enter the necessary data to determine the fields.

ZZMVGR1 and ZZMVGR2 correspond to fields MVGR1 and MVGR2 from table MVKE. We quickly find a suitable DB alias: Alias MVKE reads from table MVKE with material number and organizational data. Therefore, all you need to tell the system is that you want to select material groups 1 and 2 and have them transferred into the fields ZZMVGR1 and ZZMVGR2 (see Figure 3.30).

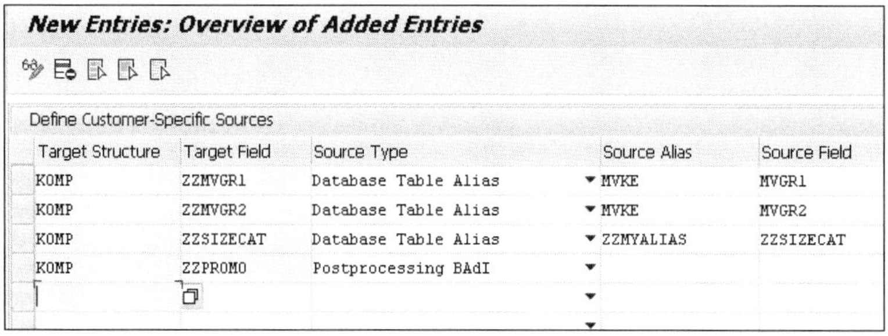

New Entries: Overview of Added Entries

Define Customer-Specific Sources

Target Structure	Target Field	Source Type	Source Alias	Source Field
KOMP	ZZMVGR1	Database Table Alias	▼ MVKE	MVGR1
KOMP	ZZMVGR2	Database Table Alias	▼ MVKE	MVGR2
KOMP	ZZSIZECAT	Database Table Alias	▼ ZZMYALIAS	ZZSIZECAT
KOMP	ZZPROMO	Postprocessing BAdI	▼	
			▼	

Figure 3.30 Define the Sources of Customer Fields

Table Alias

All data derived by the same table alias is selected together. You should therefore always check if you can reuse an existing DB alias to avoid additional, unnecessary database accesses.

We store the field ZZSIZECAT field in our own table so we need to create a new DB alias first. We define that we want to access table ZZTSIZECAT (Figure 3.31) with the prefilled material number (Figure 3.32).

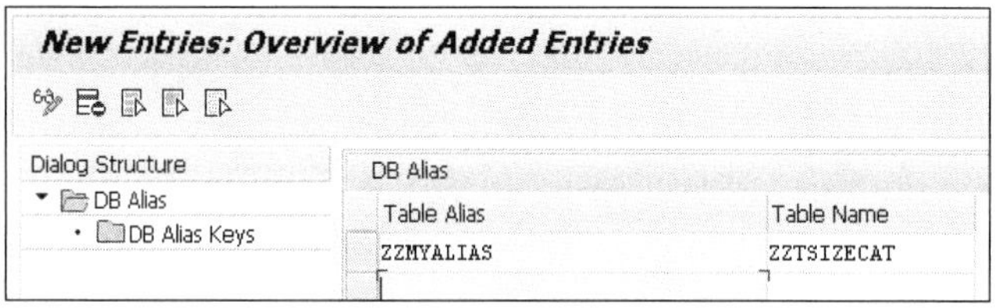

New Entries: Overview of Added Entries

Dialog Structure
▼ 🗁 DB Alias
 • 🗀 DB Alias Keys

DB Alias

Table Alias	Table Name
ZZMYALIAS	ZZTSIZECAT

Figure 3.31 Creating an DB Alias for Accessing Table ZZTSIZECAT

Next, we need to request the selection of field ZZSIZECAT. Go back to the activity IMG • SALES AND DISTRIBUTION • BASIC FUNCTIONS • PRICING • PRICE LISTS • PRICE INQUIRY • DEFINE SOURCES FOR PRICING COMMUNICATION STRUCTURE and enter the third line shown in Figure 3.30.

We have assumed that our last field ZZPROMO cannot be determined using a simple `select`. For such cases, SAP provides the BAdI `BADI_PIQ_PREPARE`, where you can program your own logic. We nevertheless maintain an entry in Customizing for ZZPROMO with the source type POSTPROCESSING BAdI (see Figure 3.30). This will prevent the system from issuing warnings indicating that the source of the field is unknown.

Dialog Structure	Table Alias	ZZMYALIAS		
▼ ☐ DB Alias				
• ☐ DB Alias Keys	DB Alias Keys			
	Key Field	Source Type	Source Field	Dire...
	MATNR	Item Prefilled ▼	MATNR	
		☐	▼	

Figure 3.32 Defining How to Access Table ZZTSIZECAT

You find BAdI BADI_PIQ_PREPARE in IMG • SALES AND DISTRIBUTION • BASIC FUNCTIONS • PRICING • PRICE LISTS • BUSINESS ADD-INS (BADIS) • BADI: PRICE INQUIRY PREPARATION. As mentioned, the underlying *price inquiry* function can run in different scenarios. Each scenario has a specific caller ID (see Figure 3.33) that defines how to access table ZZTSIZECAT.

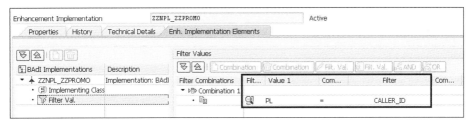

Figure 3.33 BAdI Implementations Need Filter Value PL to be Relevant for Net Price List Calculations

The method ADAPT_KOMK_KOMP_DATA substantially corresponds to the known user exits in the various documents and allows you to change the content of the pricing communication structures. You will find some tips how to reuse your user exit coding in SAP Note 2019242. Looking at the signature of the method, you can see that apart from the header and item table, there is an additional table called CT_KOMP_HEADFIELDS. It contains all fields that simultaneously can depend on the customer and the material. The plant is a prominent example. The plant is therefore empty in CT_KOMK and filled in CT_KOMP_HEADFIELDS instead for each customer/material combination. So, if you have added fields to KOMP or KOMK whose content also depends on header data, you need to add these fields to KOMP_HEAD_FIELDS.

The BAdI interface has a second method called ADAPT_HEAD_ITEM_DATA. You can add fields to the already mentioned source ADDITIONAL DATA here. It is useful if you have fields you want to use in DB aliases because ADAPT_HEAD_ITEM_DATA is processed before the database selects.

Similar to user exits and formulas, you can request the determination of additional fields from KOMK and KOMP for your implementation of method ADAPT_KOMK_KOMP_DATA. To do so, go to IMG • SALES AND DISTRIBUTION • BASIC FUNCTIONS • PRICING • PRICE LISTS • BUSINESS ADD-INS (BADIS) • DEFINE FIELDS USED IN BADI: PRICE INQUIRY PREPARATION and enter the required fields (see Figure 3.34).

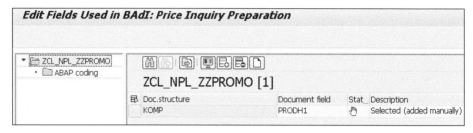

Figure 3.34 Publishing Fields Needed in the Implementation of Method ADAPT_KOMK_KOMP_DATA

The activity works very similarly to EDIT FIELDS USED IN PRICING ENHANCEMENTS; however, there is no code scan. The system will fill the fields requested here, even if the price determination does not need them.

As you can see, the setup of the new price list function requires a certain amount of effort. However, you are usually rewarded with significantly shorter run times.

> **Check Reports**
>
> Currently, two reports exist that allow some control of the settings:
>
> ▸ SD_PRC_MULTI_ITEM_CHECK
> Examines the new bundled access to condition tables, but not the data determination for the KOMK and KOMP fields and is therefore of limited use to the end user. It may be helpful in isolating the cause if the result of the price list is not as expected. It has a very detailed protocol that makes it easy to find inconsistent conditions.
>
> ▸ SDPIQAPICOMPARE
> Compares the price list result with that from an order simulation or the traditional net price list run. The protocol is not as detailed as in SD_PRC_MULTI_ITEM_CHECK.

3.4.5 Enhancements of the Selection Screen

You can extend the selection criteria and the result fields of the price list. Let's assume that we want to use the customer price group KONDA as additional selection criteria. To enhance the selection screen, we will have to enhance the price list report SDPIQPRICELIST using enhancement spot ES_PIQ_SDPRICELIST. In enhancement point ES_PIQ_SDPRICELIST_EXT1, we add the field to the screen. We use enhancement point ES_PIQ_SDPRICELIST_EXT7 to add a field label and enhancement point ES_PIQ_SDPRICELIST_EXT6 to transfer our selection option to the program using ABAP macro transfer_select_option. Listing 3.1 shows the necessary coding.

```
REPORT sdpiqpricelist.
...
ENHANCEMENT-POINT ES_PIQ_SDPRICELIST_EXT1 SPOTS
                            ES_PIQ_SDPRICELIST STATIC .
*$*$-Start: ES_PIQ_SDPRICELIST_EXT1---------------------
ENHANCEMENT 4  ZZ_NPLTEST.    "active version
 Select-OPTIONS: konda for knvv-konda.
ENDENHANCEMENT.
*$*$-End:   ES_PIQ_SDPRICELIST_EXT1---------------------
...
Customer extension: change of selection field texts
ENHANCEMENT-POINT ES_PIQ_SDPRICELIST_EXT7
                            SPOTS ES_PIQ_SDPRICELIST .
*$*$-Start: ES_PIQ_SDPRICELIST_EXT7---------------------
ENHANCEMENT 3  ZZ_NPLTEST.    "active version
  loop at screen.
    if screen-name = '%_KONDA_%_APP_%-TEXT'.
      %_KONDA_%_APP_%-TEXT = 'Customer Price Group'.
      exit.
    endif.
  endloop.
ENDENHANCEMENT.
*$*$-End:   ES_PIQ_SDPRICELIST_EXT7---------------------
...
transfer the search criteria of customer extension fields to price list
 API
ENHANCEMENT-POINT ES_PIQ_SDPRICELIST_EXT6 SPOTS ES_PIQ_SDPRICELIST .
*$*$-Start: ES_PIQ_SDPRICELIST_EXT6---------------------
ENHANCEMENT 2  ZZ_NPLTEST.    "active version
  transfer-select_option 'KNVV' 'KONDA' konda.
ENDENHANCEMENT.
*$*$-End:   ES_PIQ_SDPRICELIST_EXT6---------------------
```

Listing 3.1 Adding the Customer Price Group KONDA as Selection Criteria

Finally we make an entry in IMG • SALES AND DISTRIBUTION • BASIC FUNCTIONS • PRICING • PRICE LISTS • SELECTION AND RESULTS • DEFINE FIELDS because we need to tell the system from which master data table the KONDA value can be derived and how it is connected to the customer or material data (see Figure 3.35).

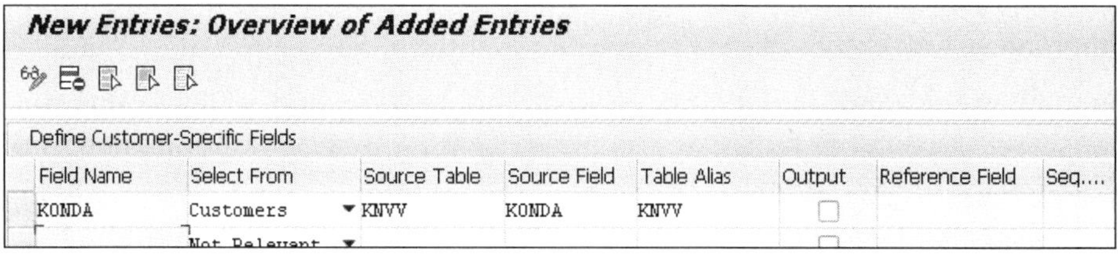

Figure 3.35 Inform the Price List That Field KONDA Can Be Selected from Table KNVV with Alias KNVV

Similar to the data determination for the pricing communication structure, the information for the generic selection of customers and materials is stored in the form of metadata. The table entry in Figure 3.35 tells the system that, while selecting the customer, it can find the relevant customer group information in field KONDA of table KNVV. The table alias KNVV is the DB alias you saw in Figure 3.27.

The KONDA field is now available as selection criteria on the selection screen (see Figure 3.37) of the price list.

Additional Fields for Selection and Output

The price list report uses tables KNVV and MVKE to retrieve all necessary data for selection and output. You can only add fields from related tables such as KNA1 or MARA. The program creates a generic select statement joining all necessary tables during runtime. BAdIs exist for more complex cases.

In a very similar way, you can extend the selection screen by your own input parameter. Let's assume you want to provide the price list currency. In this case, you add the code in Listing 3.2.

```
REPORT sdpiqpricelist.
...
* Customer extension: further criteria in control block
ENHANCEMENT-POINT ES_PIQ_SDPRICELIST_EXT3 SPOTS
                            ES_PIQ_SDPRICELIST STATIC .
*$*$-Start: ES_PIQ_SDPRICELIST_EXT3---------------------
ENHANCEMENT 8  ZZ_NPLTEST.    "active version
PARAMETERS Waerk like komk-waerk OBLIGATORY.
ENDENHANCEMENT.
*$*$-End:   ES_PIQ_SDPRICELIST_EXT3---------------------
SELECTION-SCREEN END  OF BLOCK control.
...
Customer extension: change of selection field texts
```

```
ENHANCEMENT-POINT ES_PIQ_SDPRICELIST_EXT7 SPOTS ES_PIQ_SDPRICELIST .
*$*$-Start: ES_PIQ_SDPRICELIST_EXT7--------------------
ENHANCEMENT 3  ZZ_NPLTEST.     "active version
  loop at screen.
    if screen-name = '%_WAERK_%_APP_%-TEXT'.
      %_WAERK_%_APP_%-TEXT = 'Price List Currency'.
      exit.
    endif.
  endloop.
ENDENHANCEMENT.
*$*$-End:    ES_PIQ_SDPRICELIST_EXT7--------------------
...
transfer the search criteria of customer extension fields to price list
 API
ENHANCEMENT-POINT ES_PIQ_SDPRICELIST_EXT6 SPOTS ES_PIQ_SDPRICELIST .
*$*$-Start: ES_PIQ_SDPRICELIST_EXT6--------------------
ENHANCEMENT 2  ZZ_NPLTEST.     "active version
  add_name_value 'WAERK' WAERK 'KOMK'.
ENDENHANCEMENT.
*$*$-End:    ES_PIQ_SDPRICELIST_EXT6--------------------
```

Listing 3.2 Adding the Document Currency as Control Parameter

To inform the price list that, from now on, it has to read the currency from the caller data and not from the customer master data, you add the entry shown in Figure 3.36 in IMG • Sales and Distribution • Basic Functions • Pricing • Price Lists • Price Inquiry • Sources for Communication Structures.

You might have noticed the addition of OBLIGATORY in Listing 3.2. This is necessary because with the entry from Figure 3.36, the currency is no longer read from the customer master. Therefore, you must require that the user supply a currency on the selection screen. Alternatively, we could fill the currency in method ADAPT_ KOMK_KOMP_DATA of BAdI BADI_PIQ_PREPARE in case it has not been set by the user.

Change View "Define Customer-Specific Sources": Overview

New Entries

Define Customer-Specific Sources

Target Structure	Target Field	Source Type		Source Alias	Source Field	Dire
KOMK	WAERK	Global Caller Data	▼		WAERK	

Figure 3.36 Retrieve the Currency from the Caller Data

You can see the result of these enhancements in Figure 3.37.

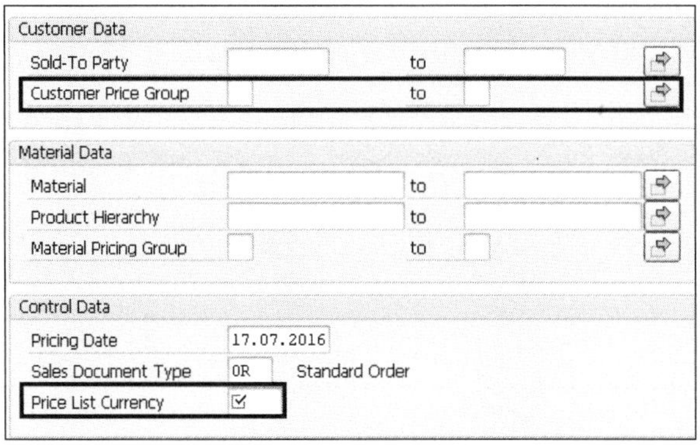

Figure 3.37 Selection Screen Now Enhanced with Customer Price Group and Currency

In addition to the enhancement spot ES_PIQ_SDPRICELIST, SAP provides the BAdI BADI_PIQ_SDPRICELIST to influence the selection of the price list. Here, the methods GET_CUSTOMER_DATA and GET_MATERIAL_DATA are particularly worth mentioning. They allow you to add or remove customers and materials from the price list processing. Method PREPARE_PRICING permits final changes to global, control, head, and item data before the underlying price inquiry API is called.

3.4.6   Enhancements of the Price List Result

You can also adjust the output to your needs. Suppose that in addition to the customer number, we also want to display the customer's name. We know that the customer's name is stored in the field NAME1 of the customer master table KNA1. Selecting the path IMG • SALES AND DISTRIBUTION • BASIC FUNCTIONS • PRICING • PRICE LISTS • SELECTION AND RESULTS • DEFINE TABLE MAPPING, we find that an access to table KNA1 with the customer number is already available as the DB alias KNA1. Since only the tables KNVV and MVKE (sales area data for customer and material) are used for the selection and the output of the price list, we need to tell the system how KNA1 relates to KNVV. The system can then select the data with one access by joining the two tables. We choose the customer section using IMG • SALES AND DISTRIBUTION • BASIC FUNCTIONS • PRICING • PRICE LISTS • SELECTION AND RESULTS • DEFINE TABLE MAPPING and specify that the customer number KUNNR of KNVV must be equal to the customer number KUNNR of KNA1 (see Figure 3.38).

Next, we have to define that the field NAME1 is retrieved from KNA1. We go to Customizing activity IMG • SALES AND DISTRIBUTION • BASIC FUNCTIONS • PRICING •

PRICE LISTS • SELECTION AND RESULTS • DEFINE FIELDS and enter the line shown in Figure 3.39 in the customer section.

Change View "Define Customer-Specific Table Relations": Overview

⬚ New Entries ⬚ ⬚ ⬚ ⬚ ⬚ ⬚

Define Customer-Specific Table Relations

Table Alias	Target Field	Source Table	Source Field	Constant Value	Language to be Con:
KNA1	KUNNR	KNVV	KUNNR		☐

Figure 3.38 Specifying the Relation between Two Tables

Define Customer-Specific Fields

Field Name	Select From	Source Table	Source Field	Table Alias	Output	Reference Field	Seq....
NAME1	Customers ▾	KNA1	NAME1	KNA1	☑		

Figure 3.39 Selecting the Customer Name for Display in the Price List Result

Now the price list will read field NAME1 from table KNA1 with the key field KUNNR being the same as in KNVV. We flag the checkbox OUTPUT to add the field to the output data.

In addition, we want to display a particular discount in the price list. As discussed earlier in the chapter, we need to create a display variant to make the selected lines of the pricing result available.

We create a variant and select the rows in the pricing procedure in IMG Customizing activity IMG • SALES AND DISTRIBUTION • BASIC FUNCTIONS • PRICING • PRICE LISTS • SELECTION AND RESULTS • DEFINE PRICING ELEMENTS DISPLAY (see Figure 3.40).

Change View "Display of Pricing Elements": Overview

⬚ ⬚ ⬚ ⬚ ⬚

Procedure	RVAA01
Display Variant	NPL1

Display of Pricing Elements

Step	Cntr	CTyp	Description	From	To	Man.	Mdt	Stat	S	Reqt	AltCTy	AltCBV	Display
8	0	EK01	Actual Costs	0	0	☑	☐		B	2	0	0	☐
11	0	PR00	Price	0	0	☐	☑			2	0	0	☐
13	0	PB00	Price (Gross)	0	0	☑	☐			2	0	0	☐
20	0	VA00	Variant Price	0	0	☐	☐			2	0	0	☐
100	0		Gross Value	0	0	☐	☐		1	0	2	0	☑
101	0	KA00	Sales deal	0	0	☐	☐			2	0	0	☑
102	0	K032	Price Group/Material	0	0	☐	☐			2	0	0	☐
103	0	K005	Customer/Material	0	0	☐	☐			2	0	0	☐

Figure 3.40 Display Variant: Data from the Gross Price Subtotal Line and the Condition Line KA00 Are Provided for the Result List

Similar to the NAME1 fields, we need entries in the customer-specific fields list to make the pricing element details available in the output. First, we have to realize what fields we need. In our case, we want the condition amount KBETR and its currency WAERS from the KA00 condition that is the second price element in our display variant (see Figure 3.40). Therefore, we add the lines shown in Figure 3.41. Price elements are always read from the price result (item condition details) and the corresponding source table is PIQS_CALCULATE_COND_RESULT (the exception to this rule is the description of a price element or subtotal line, which is stored in PIQS_CALCULATE_STEP_DESCR). Since we need the second line of the variant, we add the SEQUENCE NUMBER 2. To ensure the correct formatting of the amount, we also enter a reference field.

New Entries: Overview of Added Entries

Define Customer-Specific Fields

Field Name	Select From		Source Table	Source Field	Table Al...	Output	Reference Field	Seq....
KBETR2	Read from Pricing Result (Item Condition Detai...	▼	PIQS_CALCULATE_COND_RESULT	KBETR		✓	WAERS2	2
WAERS2	Read from Pricing Result (Item Condition Detai...	▼	PIQS_CALCULATE_COND_RESULT	WAERS		✓		2
REMARK	BAdI	▼	ZZNOTICE	VTEXT		✓		

Figure 3.41 Adding Fields to the Output

Last but not least, we want to add a text field where we can write a short notice. For more complex field determinations, SAP provides the method PROCESS_RESULTS in BAdI BADI_PIQ_SDPRICELIST where you can fill your output fields dependent on other result data. We add the third line from Figure 3.41, indicating that we will fill the fields in the BAdI. Nevertheless, we have to supply a source table and field to define the technical properties of our field.

We decide to add text if the discount exceeds a certain limit (see Listing 3.3).

```
METHOD if_badi_piq_sdpricelist~process_result.
  FIELD-SYMBOLS: <ft_result>    TYPE STANDARD TABLE,
                 <fs_result>    TYPE any,
                 <fv_kbetr>     TYPE kbetr,
                 <fv_remark>    TYPE text30.
  DATA: lv_limit TYPE kbetr VALUE '-25.00'.
  DATA: comp1 TYPE komp_type VALUE 'KBETR2',
        comp2 TYPE komp_type VALUE 'REMARK'.
  ASSIGN cr_result->* TO <ft_result>.

  LOOP AT <ft_result> ASSIGNING <fs_result>.
    ASSIGN COMPONENT comp1 OF STRUCTURE <fs_result> TO
                                     <fv_kbetr>.
```

```
      CHECK <fv_kbetr> IS ASSIGNED.
      IF <fv_kbetr> LE lv_limit.
        ASSIGN COMPONENT comp2 OF STRUCTURE <fs_result>
                                        TO <fv_remark>.
        CHECK <fv_remark> IS ASSIGNED.
        <fv_remark> = 'greatly reduced'.
      ENDIF.
    ENDLOOP.

  ENDMETHOD.
```

Listing 3.3 Adding Text if the Discount Exceeds 25%

Finally, we want to adjust the labels of our new columns. To do so, we go to IMG • Sales and Distribution • Basic Functions • Pricing • Price Lists • Selection and Results • Define Labels of Result Fields and enter suitable descriptions (see Figure 3.42). We can define the labels in general or depending on the particular pricing procedure. However, be aware that procedure-related labels do not appear in the Display List option. This output option can combine several customers in one list and there may be more than one pricing procedure involved. The column label needs to be unique, however.

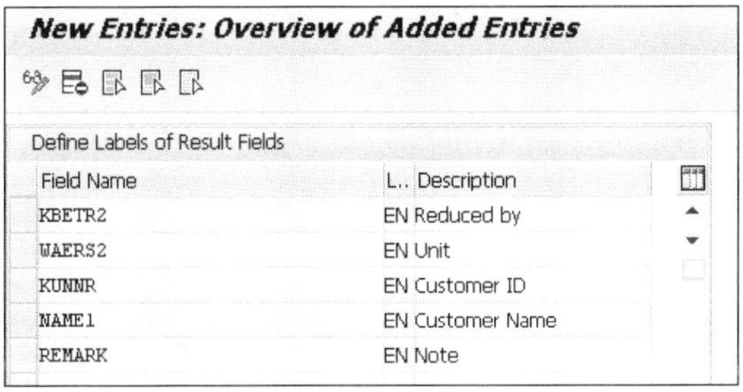

Field Name	L..	Description
KBETR2	EN	Reduced by
WAERS2	EN	Unit
KUNNR	EN	Customer ID
NAME1	EN	Customer Name
REMARK	EN	Note

Figure 3.42 Adjusting the Column Header of the Price List Result

After adjusting the layout of the price list report, the final list will look something like the one shown in Figure 3.43 (Customer Name, Reduced by, and Note have been added).

We do not want to finish this section without pointing out another BAdI. The method PROCESS_OUTPUT of BAdI BADI_PIQ_SDPRICELIST_OUTPUT allows you to program your own output options. You can, for example, decide to store the price list result in a database table for analytical purposes.

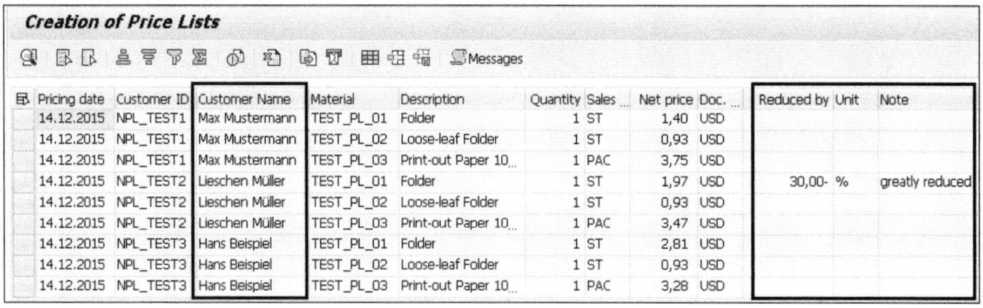

Pricing date	Customer ID	Customer Name	Material	Description	Quantity	Sales ...	Net price	Doc. ...	Reduced by	Unit	Note
14.12.2015	NPL_TEST1	Max Mustermann	TEST_PL_01	Folder	1	ST	1,40	USD			
14.12.2015	NPL_TEST1	Max Mustermann	TEST_PL_02	Loose-leaf Folder	1	ST	0,93	USD			
14.12.2015	NPL_TEST1	Max Mustermann	TEST_PL_03	Print-out Paper 10...	1	PAC	3,75	USD			
14.12.2015	NPL_TEST2	Lieschen Müller	TEST_PL_01	Folder	1	ST	1,97	USD	30,00-	%	greatly reduced
14.12.2015	NPL_TEST2	Lieschen Müller	TEST_PL_02	Loose-leaf Folder	1	ST	0,93	USD			
14.12.2015	NPL_TEST2	Lieschen Müller	TEST_PL_03	Print-out Paper 10...	1	PAC	3,47	USD			
14.12.2015	NPL_TEST3	Hans Beispiel	TEST_PL_01	Folder	1	ST	2,81	USD			
14.12.2015	NPL_TEST3	Hans Beispiel	TEST_PL_02	Loose-leaf Folder	1	ST	0,93	USD			
14.12.2015	NPL_TEST3	Hans Beispiel	TEST_PL_03	Print-out Paper 10...	1	PAC	3,28	USD			

Figure 3.43 The Final ALV Output of Price List Example

SAP Note 1949280 provides some detailed descriptions if you want to engage more deeply in selection and output enhancements.

3.4.7 Customizing Overview

This section serves as a recap and brief overview of the Customizing and Enhancement options of the performance-optimized price list. Figure 3.44 shows the relevant part of the IMG.

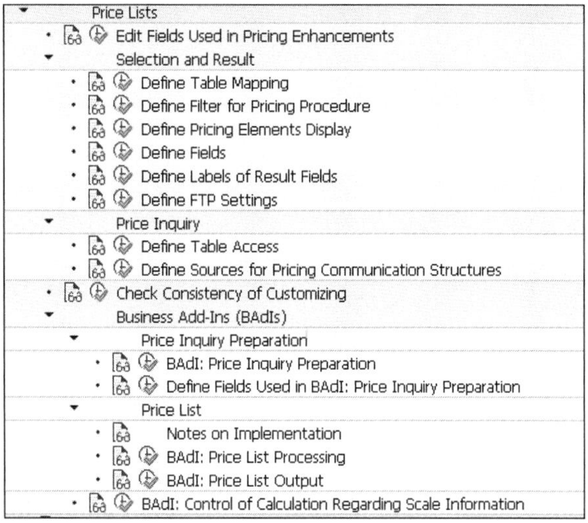

Figure 3.44 IMG Activities for the Performance-Optimized Price List

It helps to understand the structuring, if you know that the price list technically has two layers. The outer one, the *price list layer*, processes the data from the selection screen and builds up the caller data we have seen before. It calls the inner layer, the *price inquiry layer*, and processes the result of the price calculation, for example, by sending the lists to the customers via e-mail. The inner layer is responsible for taking the caller data, deriving from it all necessary information for pricing, performing the call to pricing, and passing the result back to the caller. The price inquiry layer can be called stand-alone and distinguishes its callers by their caller IDs. The price list has the PL caller ID.

The most important activities in the Customizing are as follows:

▶ EDIT FIELDS USED IN PRICING ENHANCEMENTS
In this activity, you register fields you need in formulas, requirements, and user exits. With this information, the price inquiry will identify the relevant fields for the price calculation.

▶ DEFINE TABLE MAPPING
Either display the standard table aliases and relations, or register your own tables for database `select`s. You need to define how they relate to `KNVV` or `MVKE`. `KNVV` and `MVKE` are the core tables for the selection of customers and products for the price list processing. The defined relation allows a `Join` statement to select all necessary data.

▶ DEFINE FILTER FOR PRICING PROCEDURE
In a filter variant, you select lines in a pricing procedure to be skipped during the pricing call. This reduces the runtime of the price list.

▶ DEFINE PRICING ELEMENTS DISPLAY
Lines selected in a display variant are available for output in the price list processing.

▶ DEFINE FIELDS
Display standard fields or register additional fields for selection or output.

▶ DEFINE LABELS OF RESULT FIELDS
Adjust the column labels in the output list.

▶ DEFINE FTP SETTINGS
Register the server address, user, and password for storing the price list result on an FTP server.

▶ DEFINE TABLE ACCESS
Display the DB aliases of standard table accesses or define new ones. DB aliases define how to access a database table.

▶ DEFINE SOURCES FOR PRICING COMMUNICATION STRUCTURE
Display the sources of standard fields or define how your own fields can be determined.

▶ CHECK CONSISTENCY OF CUSTOMIZING
Check the consistency of the Customizing.

▶ BADI: PRICE INQUIRY PREPARATIONS
BAdI to fill fields in the pricing communication structures.

▶ DEFINE FIELDS USED IN BADI
Price Inquiry Preparation: Register fields you need in your BAdI implementation. The system will then provide the necessary information if possible.

▶ BADI: PRICE LIST PROCESSING
Allows influencing parameters for the price inquiry call. Allows influencing the result.

▶ BADI: PRICE LIST OUTPUT
You can program your own output options here.

▶ BADI: CONTROL OF CALCULATION REGARDING SCALE INFORMATION
Influence the standard algorithm and how the relevant quantities are calculated.

3.4.8 Important Programs and Function Modules

Following are the most important programs and function modules of the performance-optimized price list:

▶ SDPIQPRICELIST
This is the standard report for the creation of price lists. It has a dedicated selection screen allowing you to select customers and products and to choose from various options. You can enhance the report's screen by implementing enhancement spot ES_PIQ_SDPRICELIST.

▶ API_PIQ_SDPRICELIST
You can use this function module if you want to access the price list functionality from within another program. The interface corresponds more or less to the selection screen of the price list. SAP Note 1949280 provides a detailed description.

▶ **BAPI_PIQ_SDPRICELIST**

With BAPI_PIQ_SDPRICELIST, you can call the price list functionality remotely. It is very similar to the function module API_PIQ_SDPRICELIST but allows you to disable the consistency check on the input table for performance reasons. In addition, SAP note 1949280 gives a more detailed description of BAPI_PIQ_SDPRICELIST.

▶ **PIQ_CALCULATE**

PIQ_CALCULATE is an RFC-enabled function module and can be useful if you need to calculate prices outside a document simulation with good performance. It requires some control data and a list of customers and materials. It reads metadata from Customizing to optimize the database accesses. Different callers can register different caller IDs in table PIQC_API_CALLER or use the standard ID STD. When using your own caller ID, you need to define the sources for the pricing communication structure for your fields and your new ID in table PIQC_PREP_FLD_C. Unlike the price list APIs, the price inquiry can trigger a group processing for items belonging together.

If you're using PIQ_CALCULATE, keep in mind that it does not create any document simulation. Hence, not all functionality related to pricing is available. Examples are free goods, product substitution, down payment functionality, EAN numbers, batch determination, etc.

3.5 Summary

With the ability to configure pricing reports, you can ensure, for example, as department supervisor, that pricing reports are provided for your departments that are adapted to their specific information needs. Pricing reports can be created without programming by a kind of list generator in Customizing for pricing.

In addition to the traditional pricing reports, which have also been introduced as a filter medium in the condition maintenance via area menus, we have—starting with SAP ERP 6.0 (but subject to the activation of the business function SD_01)—the worklist for price data from the Internal Sales Representative role as a new development.

With the net price list or its successor, the performance-optimized price list, you can give your customers individual price information for a large number of products.

This chapter marks the end of the first part of this book about the condition technique. We now move on to the second and central part of this book, standard pricing configuration.

PART II
Standard Configuration

In this second part of this book, we present the elements and the possibilities of the standard customizing of pricing in detail. In addition, we focus on working with condition records and on presenting and handling the pricing result in different sales document types.

In this chapter we will explain, using a step-by-step example, how you should proceed when implementing a customer-specific pricing scenario.

4   Pricing Configuration

Configuring pricing elements is done in the reverse order from how they are processed during pricing execution. This means that before starting the configuration, you must have a clear picture of the condition records and values that should be determined.

With this objective in mind, we will create the necessary elements in the order of their use, as follows:

1. The *condition table* defines the key fields of the future condition record.

2. The *access sequence* contains the search sequence for reading the condition records.

3. The *condition type* provides the functional properties of the condition record. Thus, in the end, a condition type models a function $f(x)$: Depending on an input value x (10 pieces, 100 kg, etc.), a resulting value $f(x)$ must be found or calculated.

4. The *pricing procedure* defines the sequence of the condition types and the relationships between them.

5. The *pricing procedure determination* specifies the pricing procedure that is used in a specific sales document.

In this chapter, we pass through all steps necessary for a classic configuration using the possibilities of the standard configuration.

4.1 Implementation of an Initial Customer-Specific Scenario

A customer-specific configuration for a given pricing problem is always necessary when there is no adequate solution offered within the standard SAP system.

In our example for this chapter, we need a value-based percentage discount, which should be applied for all orders in a specific sales organization, a specific distribution channel, and a specific customer group. Therefore, we know how our future condition records must look like and can start with the configuration. In the following sections, we will walk through the required steps, from creating a condition table to testing the pricing scenario.

4.1.1 Creating a Condition Table

Condition records are always created and stored using a specific key. The structure of this key is defined by the configuration element condition table. If there is already a condition table available with the needed key combination for the current pricing problem, it can be reused. If you want to find out if such a condition table already exists, you can display the existing condition tables in the implementation guide (see Figure 4.1) using the menu path IMG • SALES AND DISTRIBUTION • BASIC FUNCTIONS • PRICING • PRICING CONTROL • DEFINE CONDITION TABLES • DISPLAY CONDITION TABLES.

However, the short descriptions of the condition tables do not always reflect the complete key structure. Very often, the sales organization and distribution channel are not mentioned here.

We could check all 232 condition tables found in this system to find out if there is already a condition table with the desired key-combination sales organization, distribution channel, and customer group. That would be cumbersome.

Fortunately, there is a little trick to simplify this kind of search. You can let the system do this search via the pricing report toolkit. The trick is that we do not want to create a new pricing report, but we use the respective creation dialog to get the desired information (see Figure 4.2). To do this, choose the menu path IMG • SALES AND DISTRIBUTION • BASIC FUNCTIONS • PRICING • PRICING CONTROL • MAINTAIN PRICING REPORT • CREATE PRICING REPORT.

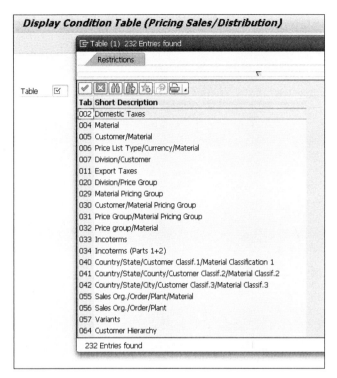

Figure 4.1 Display Condition Table

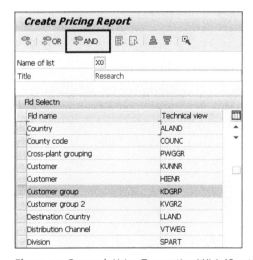

Figure 4.2 Research Using Transaction V/LA (Create Pricing Report)

Transaction V/LA create pricing report determines all of the condition tables containing the desired key fields—here Customer group (see Figure 4.3). Of course, you can also select all three fields and search using AND.

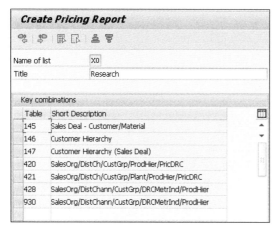

Figure 4.3 Condition Tables Containing the Customer Group Field

As our desired key combination is not contained in the list of found condition tables, we have to create a customer-specific condition table. The customer namespace for a customer-specific condition table is 501 to 999. To create a new condition table, use the menu path IMG • Sales and distribution • Basic Functions • Pricing • Pricing Control • Define Condition Tables • Create Condition Tables.

If we choose table 501 and confirm by pressing Enter, we see the screen shown in Figure 4.4.

We recommend that you flag the With validity period attribute regardless of circumstances. Only then you can later maintain the condition records for condition types built with that condition table with a validity period and, for example, make price changes at a specific date. If you deselect this attribute, you will only be able to have one unique condition record for each key combination with unlimited validity.

The With release status attribute makes it possible to block condition records and prevent them from being considered in document pricing until they are released (we will take a closer look at that in Chapter 5, Section 5.1).

Figure 4.4 Create Condition Table

On the right side of the screen (see Figure 4.4), you will find the FIELD CATALOG. By double-clicking the field names, we can now choose the desired fields: SALES ORGANIZATION, DISTRIBUTION CHANNEL, and CUSTOMER GROUP. The order in which the fields are selected is important, because this will influence the screen layout of the maintenance dialog (see Figure 4.5).

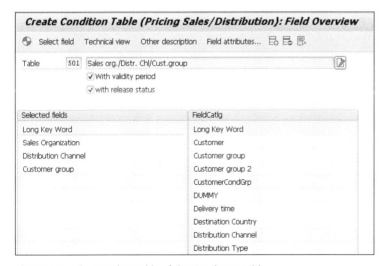

Figure 4.5 Selecting the Fields of the Condition Table

It is interesting to select the TECHNICAL VIEW to look at some technical details (see Figure 4.6). You can see that all three fields we have selected have by default the KEY attribute. By deselecting the KEY attribute of a field, we would create the special case of a *data field in the condition table* (we will take a closer look at that in Chapter 9, Section 9.2).

Create Condition Table (Pricing Sales/Distribution): Technical View

Dictionary elements   Other description   Field attributes...

Table   501   Sales org./Distr. Chl/Cust.group

☑ With validity period
☑ with release status

Selected fields

Short Description	Key	Footer fld	Text field	Field Name	Data element	Domain name
Sales Organization	☑	☐	○	VKORG	VKORG	VKORG
Distribution Channel	☑	☐	○	VTWEG	VTWEG	VTWEG
Customer group	☑	☑	◉	KDGRP	KDGRP	KDGRP

Figure 4.6 Create Condition Table, Technical View

The FOOTER FIELD attribute must be selected as the last key field (here it's CUSTOMER GROUP). This checkbox cannot be deselected, since the maintenance dialog that is automatically generated later needs at least one key field for the tabular display of the condition records. All key fields that are not marked as a FOOTER field are later displayed in the header area of the maintenance screen. We could, for example, mark also the field DISTRIBUTION CHANNEL as a FOOTER field, with the corresponding consequences for the display of the field in the generated maintenance screen. (Curious readers can view the generated maintenance screen in Figure 4.15.)

The TEXT FIELD attribute is represented as a radio button. For example, even if you mark more than one key field as a FOOTER field, you can only select for one field the TEXT FIELD attribute. In the generated maintenance screen for this field, the description is displayed beside the key.

If you have finished the field selection and the attribute assignment, you can proceed by clicking the GENERATE button (highlighted in the upper-left corner of Figure 4.6). Subsequently, the generation log is displayed on the screen (see Figure 4.7), informing us that condition table A501 was created and the reports and screens for table A501 were MARKED FOR GENERATION. This means that they will be compiled at their first usage.

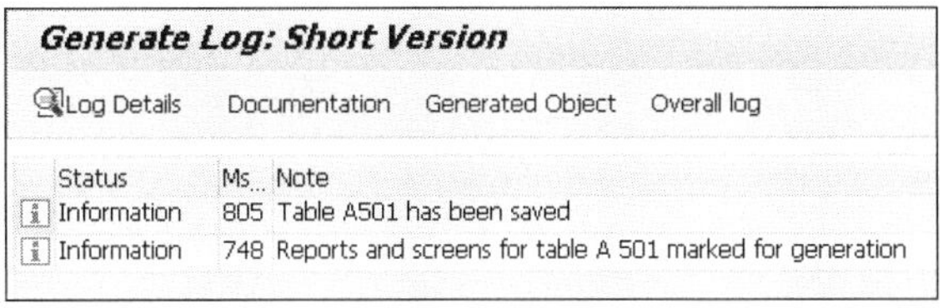

Figure 4.7 Generation Log of Condition Table 501

With this, we have completed the first step in our configuration and can now proceed with the next step—creating our access sequence.

4.1.2 Creating an Access Sequence

Prices, discounts, and surcharges can be defined on different key levels. We have learned about the condition table, which is the configuration element to map those different key levels. But to enable the system to take into account different, and eventually concurring, key levels during pricing, we need another configuration element, the *access sequence*, to specify the condition tables and to define the order of the search sequence. In many cases, the definition of the access sequence will—as in our configuration example—consist of only one access with a single condition table. If an access sequence consists of several accesses using different condition tables, it defines a kind of search strategy. This can be shown, as an example, with standard access sequence PR02, which is assigned to the condition type PR00 price. To view this access sequence, use the menu path IMG • SALES AND DISTRIBUTION • BASIC FUNCTIONS • PRICING • PRICING CONTROL • DEFINE ACCESS SEQUENCES • MAINTAIN ACCESS SEQUENCES.

In this access sequence (see Figure 4.8), the order of the different condition tables in the accesses determines that the system looks first for a condition record on the level sales organization, distribution channel, customer, and material (condition table 305) for a valid price. This means the price agreed individually for a customer and stored in a respective condition record has the first priority.

If such a customer-specific price is not available, the system tries to find a price on a price list assigned to the customer (field PRICE LIST in customer master data). Condition table 306 therefore contains SALES ORGANIZATION, DISTRIBUTION CHANNEL, PRICE LIST, DOCUMENT CURRENCY, and MATERIAL as key fields.

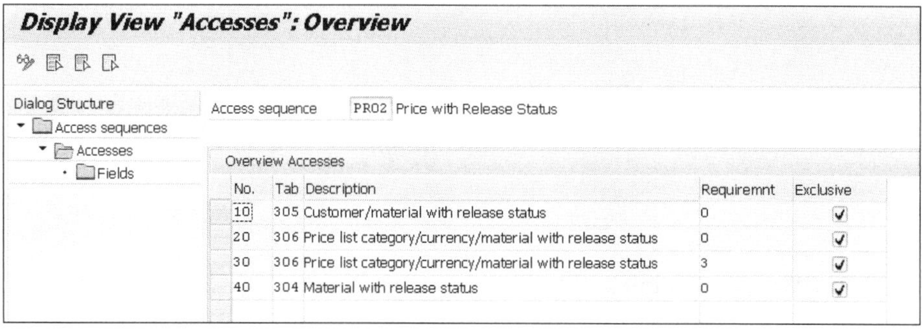

Display View "Accesses": Overview

Dialog Structure					
▼ ☐ Access sequences	Access sequence	PR02	Price with Release Status		
▼ ☐ Accesses					
• ☐ Fields	Overview Accesses				

No.	Tab	Description	Requiremnt	Exclusive
10	305	Customer/material with release status	0	✓
20	306	Price list category/currency/material with release status	0	✓
30	306	Price list category/currency/material with release status	3	✓
40	304	Material with release status	0	✓

Figure 4.8 Access Sequence PR02 (Price with Release Status)

Access number 30 represents another attempt to a find a condition record for condition table 306, if requirement 3 (foreign currency document) is true. If there is no condition record found on the price list level, the search continues with condition table 304 using the key fields SALES ORGANIZATION, DISTRIBUTION CHANNEL, and MATERIAL.

The EXCLUSIVE attribute controls whether the system stops searching for a condition record after the first successful access within an access sequence. By selecting the EXCLUSIVE attribute, you ensure that the system only takes into account the most specific condition record.

Returning to our own configuration, we have only planned one access using our previously defined condition table 501. To create a new access sequence, use the menu path IMG • SALES AND DISTRIBUTION • BASIC FUNCTIONS • PRICING • PRICING CONTROL • DEFINE ACCESS SEQUENCES • MAINTAIN ACCESS SEQUENCES • NEW ENTRIES.

The customer namespace for access sequences starts with Y or Z. We choose key Z501 and description CUSTOMER GROUP (see Figure 4.9).

In the navigation tree of the dialog structure, you choose ACCESSES and this takes you to the next screen (see Figure 4.10). After selecting NEW ENTRIES, the overview screen is ready for input and we can create access 10 using condition table 501. The REQUIREMENT and EXCLUSIVE attributes stay deselected (for a single-level access sequence, the attribute EXCLUSIVE is irrelevant).

New Entries: Overview of Added Entries

Dialog Structure
▼ 📁 Access sequences
   ▼ 📁 Accesses
      • 📁 Fields

Utilities...

Overview Access Sequence

AS	Description	Ty.	Description
Z501	Customer Group		

Figure 4.9 Creation of an Access Sequence

New Entries: Overview of Added Entries

Dialog Structure
▼ 📁 Access sequences
   ▼ 📁 Accesses
      • 📁 Fields

Access sequence   Z501 Customer Group

Overview Accesses

No.	Tab	Description	Requiremnt	Exclusive	
10	501	Sales org./Distr. Chl/Cust.group		☐	
				☐	

Figure 4.10 Definition of the Access by the Condition Table

Select the line with the access and select FIELDS in the dialog structure on the left side to go to the FIELDS level. A warning message appears, stating that the field assignments are not yet done. After confirming the warning by pressing ⌈Enter⌋, the concluding screen displayed in Figure 4.11 appears.

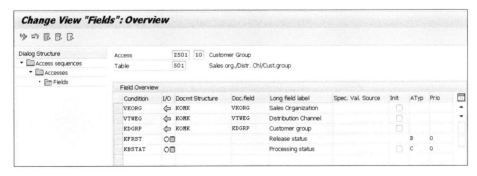

Change View "Fields": Overview

Dialog Structure
▼ 📁 Access sequences
   ▼ 📁 Accesses
      • 📁 Fields

Access   Z501 10 Customer Group
Table   501 Sales org./Distr. Chl/Cust.group

Field Overview

Condition	I/O	Docmt Structure	Doc.field	Long field label	Spec. Val. Source	Init	AType	Prio	
VKORG	⇐	KOMK	VKORG	Sales Organization		☐			
VTWEG	⇐	KOMK	VTWEG	Distribution Channel		☐			
KDGRP	⇐	KOMK	KDGRP	Customer group		☐			
KFRST	○▣			Release status			B	0	
KBSTAT	○▣			Processing status		☐	C	0	

Figure 4.11 Field Level of Access

Missing Field Assignment

If you forget the field assignment step, you will receive during the testing the error message 301 (FIELDS MISSING FOR ACCESS SEQUENCE). You will then need to go back to Customizing and edit the access sequence to complete this step.

As you can see in Figure 4.11, in addition to the key fields of condition table 501, two more fields, FRSTAT and KBSTAT, were added to the access because the WITH RELEASE STATUS attribute was set in condition table 501. These fields are needed if a release status is set in the condition record (we will have a closer look at that in Chapter 5, Section 5.1).

For a common access sequence, no further attributes have to be set here. Additional available attributes are SPEC(ific) VAL(ue) SOURCE, INIT, ATYP, and PRIO. We will discuss the relevance of these attributes later in Section 4.2.2.

We can save access sequence Z501 and it is now ready for use.

4.1.3   Customizing a Condition Type

As previously mentioned, the condition type provides the functional properties of the condition record. Thus, in the end, a condition type models a function (see Figure 4.12). So far we have defined the key structure (condition table 501) and built with it the access sequence Z501. In the next step we must deal with the mapping of such requirements as the percentage discount during configuration. This is the task of the *condition type* pricing element.

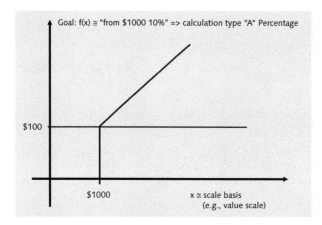

Figure 4.12 Understanding a Condition Type as a Function

As the result of our configuration, we must be able to maintain and later find a specific condition record during pricing. To achieve this result, we will now identify the appropriate attributes within the configuration element condition type.

If we, for example, review the discount condition type KA00 (sales promotion) from the standard SAP system, we get our first glimpse of the Customizing screen for condition types. To view this condition type, use the menu path IMG • SALES AND DISTRIBUTION • BASIC FUNCTIONS • PRICING • PRICING CONTROL • DEFINE CONDITION TYPES • MAINTAIN CONDITION TYPES.

If you mark the line with the entry KA00 and click the DETAILS button, the configuration screen for condition types is displayed (see Figure 4.13). The screen is divided in seven field groups, which we will discuss in more detail in Section 4.2.3:

1. CONTROL DATA 1

2. GROUP CONDITION

3. CHANGES WHICH CAN BE MADE

4. MASTER DATA

5. SCALES

6. CONTROL DATA 2

7. TEXT DETERMINATION

In Figure 4.13 you see the entire set of available attributes. (The ENABLED FOR CPF attribute is only available after activating certain business functions delivered with SAP ERP 6.0 EHP 7. This will be discussed in Section 4.5.) We have framed the main attributes which, in our example, make condition type KA00 a percentage discount.

The following attributes are of particular note:

▶ COND. CLASS
This main switch has the characteristic A – DISCOUNT OR SURCHARGE.

▶ CALCULAT.TYPE
Our function $f(x)$ has the characteristic A – PERCENTAGE.

▶ SCALE BASIS
Our X-axis has the characteristic B – VALUE SCALE.

Figure 4.13 Customizing Screen for Condition Types

▶ PLUS/MINUS
This has the characteristic X – NEGATIVE, which ensures that the discount cannot turn into a surcharge by mistake.

▶ ACCESS SEQ.
Only for a condition type that has assigned an access sequence can you maintain condition records and find them later in document pricing.

Now that you have gained a first impression of the configuration of a condition type, we proceed with our configuration task by creating a condition type with our required characteristics.

4.1.4 Creating a Condition Type

We are now ready to create the respective pricing element condition type in the customer namespace. The customer namespace for condition types starts with Y or Z. We choose the key Z501 and description CUSTOMER GROUP DISCOUNT.

Choose the menu path IMG • SALES AND DISTRIBUTION • BASIC FUNCTIONS • PRICING • PRICING CONTROL • DEFINE CONDITION TYPES • MAINTAIN CONDITION TYPES. On the displayed screen (see Figure 4.14), we mark the line with the entry KA00 and select the COPY AS button 📋. The characteristics of KA00 are displayed as a template and we can change the condition type key to Z501, the description to CUSTOMER GROUP, and the access sequence to Z501 as well. After confirming with ⌨Enter⌨, we can save condition type Z501.

Change View "Conditions: Condition Types": Overview

New Entries

CTyp	Condition Type	Condition class	Calculation type
KA00	Sales Promotion	Discount or surcharge	Percentage
KA02	Promo Discount % 1	Discount or surcharge	Percentage
KA03	Promo Discount % 2	Discount or surcharge	Percentage
KA04	Promo Discount MD 1	Discount or surcharge	Quantity
KA05	Promo Discount MD 2	Discount or surcharge	Quantity
KAD0	Material Costs(VKHM)	Discount or surcharge	Quantity
KAD1	Handling Costs(VKHM)	Discount or surcharge	Quantity
KBM1	Good will/guarantee	Discount or surcharge	Percentage
KF00	Freight	Discount or surcharge	Gross weight
KP00	Pallet Discount	Discount or surcharge	Quantity
KP01	Incomp.Pallet Surch.	Discount or surcharge	Quantity

Figure 4.14 Maintain Condition Types

As the other attributes of the new condition type meet our requirements, this new condition type Z501 (customer group discount) differs from the copying template KA00 only by the deviating key combination defined via access sequence Z501.

To create a condition record, we use the menu path SAP EASY ACCESS • LOGISTICS • SALES AND DISTRIBUTION • MASTER DATA • CONDITIONS • SELECT USING CONDITION TYPE • CREATE and select condition type Z501.

After a small delay for the initial generation of the program, the fast entry screen for condition records appears (see Figure 4.15) and offers the keys SALES ORGANIZATION, DISTRIBUTION CHANNEL, and CUSTOMER GROUP defined previously.

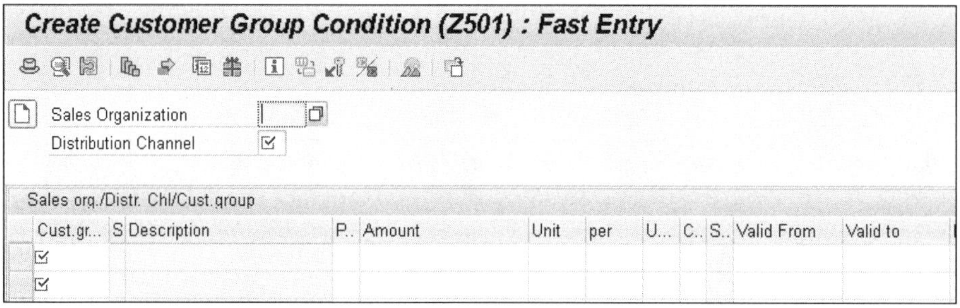

Create Customer Group Condition (Z501) : Fast Entry

| Sales Organization | | | | | | | | | | |
| Distribution Channel | ☑ | | | | | | | | | |

Sales org./Distr. Chl/Cust.group

Cust.gr...	S	Description	P..	Amount	Unit	per	U...	C..	S..	Valid From	Valid to	
☑												
☑												

Figure 4.15 Generated Maintenance Screen

We can now create our first condition record (see Figure 4.16).

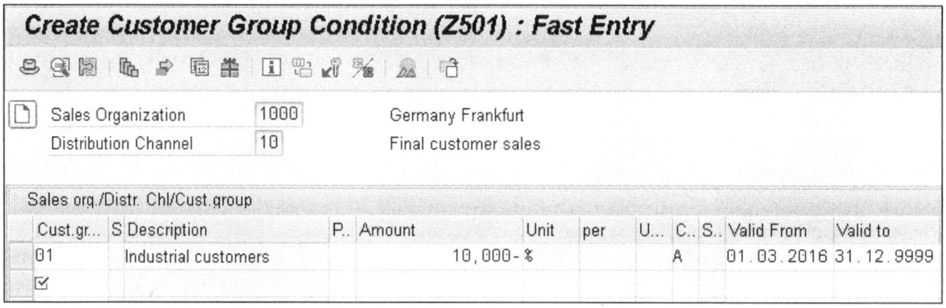

Create Customer Group Condition (Z501) : Fast Entry

| Sales Organization | 1000 | | Germany Frankfurt | | |
| Distribution Channel | 10 | | Final customer sales | | |

Sales org./Distr. Chl/Cust.group

Cust.gr...	S	Description	P..	Amount	Unit	per	U...	C..	S..	Valid From	Valid to
01		Industrial customers		10,000- %				A		01.03.2016	31.12.9999
☑											

Figure 4.16 Creation of a First Condition Record

In order to grant the discount only starting with 1000 EUR, we must switch to the SCALES screen (SCALES icon 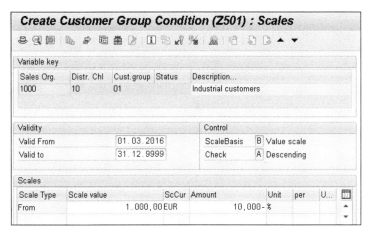) and set the value FROM to 1000 EUR. After that, we can save the condition record (see Figure 4.17).

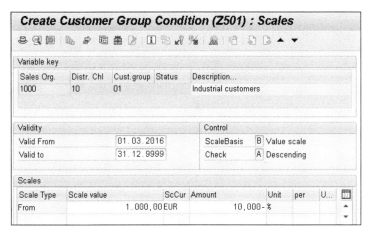

Create Customer Group Condition (Z501) : Scales

Variable key

Sales Org.	Distr. Chl	Cust.group	Status	Description...
1000	10	01		Industrial customers

Validity		Control		
Valid From	01.03.2016	ScaleBasis	B	Value scale
Valid to	31.12.9999	Check	A	Descending

Scales

Scale Type	Scale value	ScCur	Amount	Unit	per	U...	
From	1.000,00	EUR	10,000- %				

Figure 4.17 Condition Maintenance, Scales Screen

4.1.5 Inserting a Condition Type into a Pricing Procedure

To be able to use our new discount within document pricing (e.g., sales order), we have to insert the new condition type into the respective pricing procedure. The standard SAP system contains various examples of pricing procedures that you can use as a template to build your pricing scenarios. A prominent example is pricing procedure RVAA01 (standard). If you want to use this pricing procedure as the basis for your own pricing scenario, you can copy it into the customer namespace starting with Y or Z. We choose Z00001 as the key and COMPANY STANDARD as the description. A message is displayed asking if dependent objects should be copied too. We answer this question by clicking the COPY ALL button. The menu path for maintaining pricing procedures is IMG • SALES AND DISTRIBUTION • BASIC FUNCTIONS • PRICING • PRICING CONTROL • DEFINE AND ASSIGN PRICING PROCEDURES • MAINTAIN PRICING PROCEDURES.

Deleting Unused Condition Types

If you copy a template pricing procedure in practice, you should remove all condition types that are unused in your company. This applies in particular to a variety of discount condition types.

We insert our new condition type Z501 (customer group) at the end of the discount block, in our example, using step 130 (see Figure 4.18). For the attributes of the new pricing procedure entry, we focus on a similar existing discount and set the following attributes:

- PRINT = X (printing at item level)
- REQT (requirement) = 2 (item with pricing)
- ACCKEY (account key) = ERS (sales deductions)

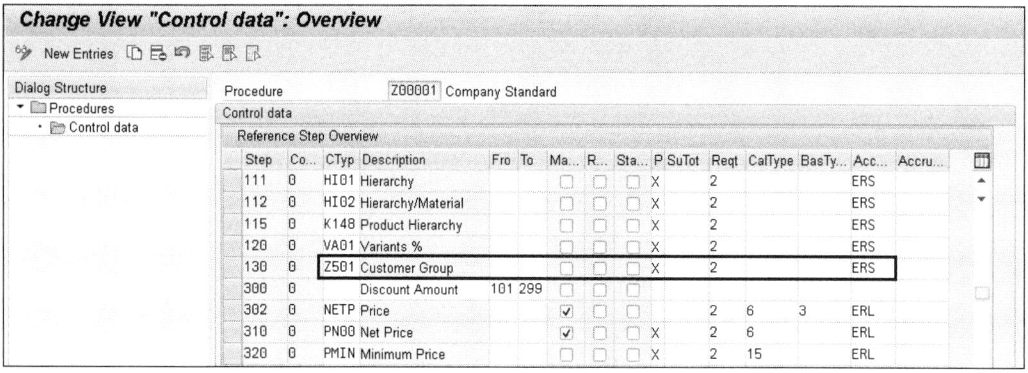

Change View "Control data": Overview

New Entries

Dialog Structure		
▼ 🗀 Procedures	Procedure	Z00001 Company Standard
• 🗀 Control data	Control data	

Reference Step Overview

Step	Co...	CTyp	Description	Fro	To	Ma...	R...	Sta...	P	SuTot	Reqt	CalType	BasTy...	Acc...	Accru...	
111	0	HI01	Hierarchy			☐	☐	☐	X		2			ERS		
112	0	HI02	Hierarchy/Material			☐	☐	☐	X		2			ERS		
115	0	K148	Product Hierarchy			☐	☐	☐	X		2			ERS		
120	0	VA01	Variants %			☐	☐	☐	X		2			ERS		
130	0	Z501	Customer Group			☐	☐	☐	X		2			ERS		
300	0		Discount Amount	101	299	☐	☐	☐								
302	0	NETP	Price			☑	☐	☐			2	6	3	ERL		
310	0	PN00	Net Price			☑	☐	☐	X		2	6		ERL		
320	0	PMIN	Minimum Price			☐	☐	☐	X		2	15		ERL		

Figure 4.18 Adding a Condition Type to a Pricing Procedure

After embedding our condition type into a pricing procedure, we can proceed with the configuration.

4.1.6 Defining the Pricing Procedure Determination

We have now created a new pricing procedure into which we inserted our new condition type but until now no document pricing can use this new pricing procedure. The precondition for this is the existence of an appropriate pricing procedure determination. The menu path for defining the pricing procedure determination is IMG • SALES AND DISTRIBUTION • BASIC FUNCTIONS • PRICING • PRICING CONTROL • DEFINE AND ASSIGN PRICING PROCEDURES • ASSIGN PRICING PROCEDURES.

The determining parameters for pricing procedure determination are:

- Sales organization
- Document pricing procedure key (from the document type)
- Customer pricing procedure key (from the sales area data of the customer master)

For the combination sales area 1000/10/00, document pricing procedure A and customer pricing procedure 1 in our SAP system, until now the pricing procedure RVAA01 is assigned. We change this entry by assigning our own PRIPR. Z00001: COMPANY STANDARD instead of RVAA01 (see Figure 4.19).

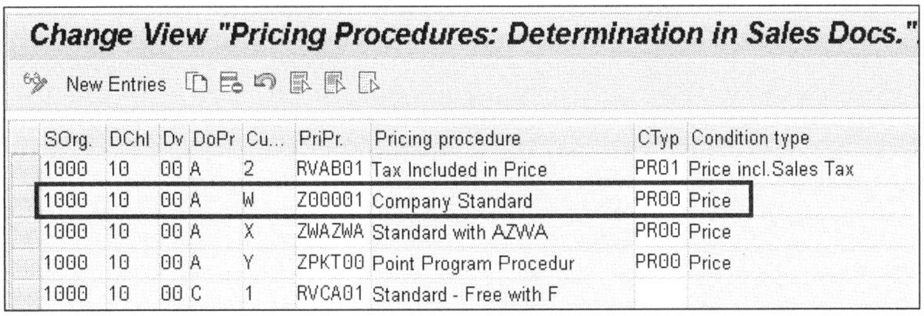

Change View "Pricing Procedures: Determination in Sales Docs."

New Entries

SOrg.	DChl	Dv	DoPr	Cu...	PriPr.	Pricing procedure	CTyp	Condition type
1000	10	00	A	2	RVAB01	Tax Included in Price	PR01	Price incl.Sales Tax
1000	10	00	A	W	Z00001	Company Standard	PR00	Price
1000	10	00	A	X	ZWAZWA	Standard with AZWA	PR00	Price
1000	10	00	A	Y	ZPKT00	Point Program Procedur	PR00	Price
1000	10	00	C	1	RVCA01	Standard - Free with F		

Figure 4.19 Pricing Procedure Determination

After this last step, the configuration is finished and the new condition type can be used in document pricing. With a final test, we want to make sure that all the involved objects that we have created work together flawlessly.

4.1.7 Testing the Pricing Scenario

We create a sales order for a customer assigned to the INDUSTRY customer group and check if the condition record we created earlier will be found during document pricing (see Figure 4.20).

If the test had not been successful, we would use the determination analysis presented in Chapter 1, Section 1.12 to detect the missing link in the pricing chain (e.g., wrongly assigned access sequence), repair the error, and test until we found and corrected all errors.

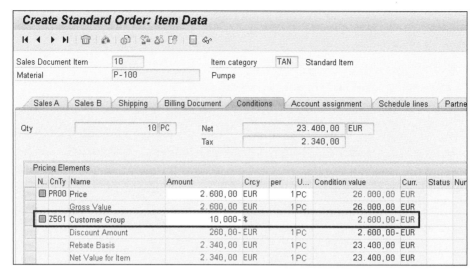

Figure 4.20 The New Condition Type in the Pricing Screen

4.2 Elements of Pricing in Detail

During the implementation of our first customer-specific pricing scenario, we deliberately omitted all further details that were not yet needed in order to focus on the basic considerations. We will now go through an overview of all details and attributes to prepare for future pricing scenario demands.

4.2.1 Condition Table

The main task of a condition table is to define the key fields of a condition record. In addition, the attributes WITH VALIDITY PERIOD and WITH RELEASE STATUS are available. In addition, non-key fields can be added at the end of condition table — as is done in the special case (see Chapter 9, Section 9.2).

Condition table 702 is displayed in Figure 4.21 as an example that uses all available options.

If you use Transaction SE11 to check the structure of the generated database table A702, you can see all the details (see Figure 4.22).

Figure 4.21 Example of a Condition Table Using All Options

Dictionary: Display Table

Transparent Table	A702	Active
Short Description	Sales org./Distr. Chl/Cust.group/CondPrcgDt	

Attributes | Delivery and Maintenance | Fields | Entry help/check | Currency/Quantity Fields

Field	Key	Ini...	Data element	Data Type	Length	Deci...	Short Description
MANDT	✔	✔	MANDT	CLNT	3	0	Client
KAPPL	✔	✔	KAPPL	CHAR	2	0	Application
KSCHL	✔	✔	KSCHA	CHAR	4	0	Condition type
VKORG	✔	✔	VKORG	CHAR	4	0	Sales Organization
VTWEG	✔	✔	VTWEG	CHAR	2	0	Distribution Channel
KDGRP	✔	✔	KDGRP	CHAR	2	0	Customer group
KFRST	✔	✔	KFRST	CHAR	1	0	Release status
DATBI	✔	✔	KODATBI	DATS	8	0	Validity end date of the condition record
DATAB	☐	✔	KODATAB	DATS	8	0	Validity start date of the condition record
KBSTAT	☐	☐	KBSTAT	CHAR	2	0	Processing status for conditions
KDATU	☐	☐	KDATU	DATS	8	0	Condition pricing date
KNUMH	☐	✔	KNUMH	CHAR	10	0	Condition record number

Figure 4.22 Structure of Database Table A702

The set of fields used for creating a condition table is limited by the field catalog available in the creation screen. Fortunately, one fundamental idea of the condition technique is that this field catalog can be extended without modification, if needed. This means that every field that is needed for solving a specific pricing scenario (and even customer specific fields that were not delivered by SAP) can be available for the configuration of condition tables. We discuss this method in Section 4.3.

4.2.2 Access Sequence

We have already seen that an access sequence is configured by using at least one condition table. With access sequence PR02 from Figure 4.8, we also saw how an access sequence can represent a search strategy by using several condition tables. We checked the level of the accesses with the REQUIREMENT and EXCLUSIVE attributes. Let's now have a closer look at the field level using the example of access number 30 (see Figure 4.23).

Access	PR02	30	Price with Release Status				
Table	306		Price list category/currency/material with release status				

Condition	I/O	Docmt Str...	Doc.field	Long field label	Spec. Val. Source	Init	ATyp	Prio
VKORG	⇐	KOMK	VKORG	Sales Organization		☐		
VTWEG	⇐	KOMK	VTWEG	Distribution Channel		☐		
PLTYP	⇐	KOMK	PLTYP	Price List		☐		
WAERK	⇐	KOMK	HWAER	Local Currency		☐		
MATNR	⇐	KOMP	PMATN	Pricing Ref. Matl		☐		
KFRST	O☐			Release status			B	0
KBSTAT	O☐			Processing status		☐	C	0

Figure 4.23 Attributes on Field Level of an Access

As a special case, the document field WAERK (DOCUMENT CURRENCY) copied originally from condition table 306 was replaced with the HWAER (LOCAL CURRENCY) field by clicking the FIELD CATALOG button (not visible in the figure) and selecting the desired source field.

Besides the substitution of fields based on the field catalog, you can modify the access using the SPEC. VAL. SOURCE attribute. You could, for example, fill the field VKORG (sales organization) for the condition record access with a fixed value (e.g., 2000) if this would contribute to the solution of your pricing scenario.

Figure 4.23 also shows the usage of the ATYP (access type) attribute. The RELEASE STATUS field has access type B - KEY FIELD NOT RELEVANT FOR ACCESS and the PROCESSING STATUS field has access type C - DATA FIELD FROM CONDITION TABLE.

The INIT attribute (initial indicator) has two functions within Customizing for accessing sequences. First, it determines that the system does not access the condition if the field in the document header/item is blank or zero. Secondly, during the automatic return transfer of data that was determined in the access, it allows an initial value to be returned.

Attribute INIT Only for Fields Marked as Footer Fields

The INIT attribute only makes sense when the respective field of the condition table was marked as a footer field, because header fields are always mandatory in the generated maintenance dialog and thus cannot be left initial.

4.2.3 Condition Type

You have already seen during the implementation of our first customer-specific scenario that the customizing screen for condition types (see Figure 4.13) is split into seven field groups. If we distinguish the attributes by the frequency of their use, we can form two groups:

▸ Almost always used are:
  ▹ CONTROL DATA 1
  ▹ CHANGES WHICH CAN BE MADE
  ▹ MASTER DATA
  ▹ SCALES
▸ Less frequently used are:
  ▹ GROUP CONDITION
  ▹ CONTROL DATA 2
  ▹ TEXT DETERMINATION

The usage of the attributes contained in the field groups of course depends on the requirements that a condition type must meet. Particularly easy is the definition of a "manual" condition type without an access sequence such as RC00 (QUANTITY DISCOUNT; see Figure 4.24).

In this case only the two field groups—CONTROL DATA 1 and CHANGES WHICH CAN BE MADE—are needed.

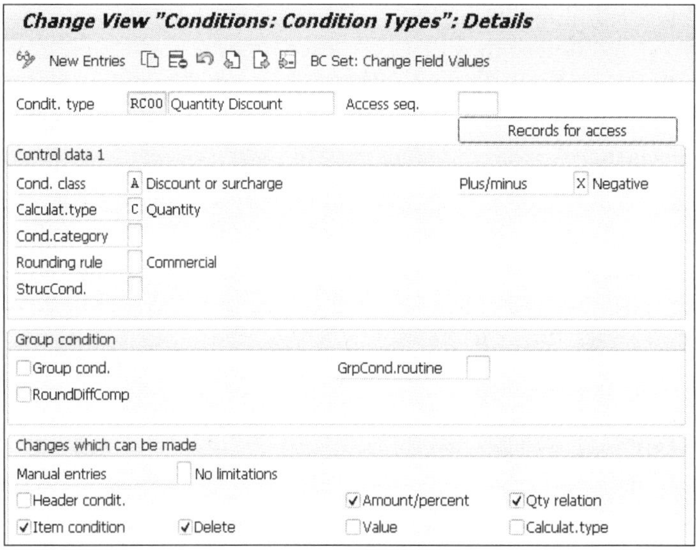

Figure 4.24 Manual Condition Type RC00 (Quantity Discount)

Control Data 1

The CONTROL DATA 1 field group contains six attributes that categorize the condition type.

Condition Class

The main switch COND. CLASS (condition class) represents a preliminary structuring of the condition types for later processing. Some important values of this switch are:

▶ A: DISCOUNT OR SURCHARGE

▶ B: PRICES

▶ C: EXPENSE REIMBURSEMENT

▶ D: TAXES

▶ H: DETERMINING SALES DEAL

Plus/Minus Sign

The PLUS/MINUS flag determines if a condition value can be entered only as a negative value (discount), a positive value (surcharge), or both. This can help to avoid input errors.

Calculation Type for Condition

The CALCULAT.TYPE flag determines how the system calculates prices, discounts, or surcharges in a condition. Some important values of this switch are:

- ▶ A: PERCENTAGE
- ▶ B: FIXED AMOUNT
- ▶ C: QUANTITY
- ▶ D: GROSS WEIGHT
- ▶ E: NET WEIGHT
- ▶ F: VOLUME

The calculation type defines, in accordance to our understanding, the condition type as a function $f(x)$.

Condition Category

The COND.CATEGORY flag classifies conditions according to pre-defined categories (e.g., all conditions that relate to freight costs). Examples are:

- ▶ D: TAX
- ▶ E: CASH DISCOUNT
- ▶ F: FREIGHT

If you, for example, change the incoterms during the ORDER PROCESSING dialog, a message is displayed saying that all freight charges are newly determined. The affected freight condition types are detected by the system via condition category F.

Rounding Rule

The ROUNDING RULE attribute determines how the system rounds condition values during pricing. The last digit will be rounded.

- ▶ _ (blank): COMMERCIAL
- ▶ A: ROUND UP
- ▶ B: ROUND DOWN

Structure Condition

The STRUCCOND. (structure condition) attribute controls whether the condition type should be a duplicated condition or an accumulated condition.

- A: CONDITION TO BE DUPLICATED.
  A duplicated condition is copied into all assigned items.

- B: CUMULATIVE CONDITION.
  An accumulated condition contains the net value of all assigned items.

This control is only helpful when you use bill of materials or configurable materials.

Group Condition

Document pricing is performed on the item level and a *group condition* has a cross-item effect on a certain group of items.

Group Condition

The GROUP COND. (group condition) attribute can have different effects, depending of other attributes of the condition type. Simplifying, we could also say it this way: the attribute GROUP COND. is the instruction to the system to process all related items together.

For example, in the case of an item condition with an access sequence assigned, GROUP COND. indicates that the system calculates the basis for the scale value from all items in the document belonging to a group. You can freely define the group to meet the needs of your pricing scenario. For example, the items could all belong to the same material group.

In the case of a header condition with the calculation type B - FIXED AMOUNT, group condition indicates that the value is distributed proportionally among the items. The system compares the condition value at the header level with the total of the condition values at the item level. A potential rounding difference is then added to the largest item.

Routine Number for Creating a Group Key

In the GRPCOND.ROUTINE attribute, you can specify a routine number for creating a group key. By specifying such a routine, you can have the scale base accumulated only for special items. We take a closer look at that functionality in Chapter 7, Section 7.1.

Rounding Difference Comparison

The ROUNDDIFFCOMP attribute controls whether the rounding difference is set for group conditions with a group key routine. If the indicator is set, the system compares the condition value at the header level with the total of the condition values at the item level. The difference is then added to the largest item.

Changes Which Can Be Made

In the field group called CHANGES WHICH CAN BE MADE, all attributes are displayed that can be used to influence the fields that are ready for input in the CONDITION DETAIL screen of the sales document processing.

Manual Entries

The MANUAL ENTRIES attribute controls the priority within a condition type between a condition entered manually and a condition automatically determined by the system. The following values can be used:

▶ _ (blank): NO LIMITATIONS

▶ B: AUTOMATIC ENTRY HAS PRIORITY (i.e., if a condition record exists, the condition cannot be entered manually)

▶ C: MANUAL ENTRY HAS PRIORITY (i.e., when you enter the condition manually, the system does not check whether a condition record exists)

▶ D: NOT POSSIBLE TO PROCESS MANUALLY

Amount/Percent, Quantity Relation, Value, Calculation Type, Delete

Depending on these attributes, different columns of the CONDITIONS screen (see Figure 4.25) are available for input if manual entries were allowed by the previous attribute. Normally only the AMOUNT/PERCENT and DELETE indicators are marked.

Header Condition and Item Condition

The HEADER CONDIT. and ITEM CONDITION attributes (see Figure 4.24) determine if you can enter the condition type in the HEADER CONDITIONS or ITEM CONDITIONS screens, respectively.

Figure 4.25 Changeability of Fields in the Conditions Screen

Master Data

Within the MASTER DATA field group (see Figure 4.13), specifications are made that influence the master data maintenance.

Valid From

The VALID FROM attribute specifies the beginning validity date that the system automatically proposes when you create a condition record for this condition type.

Valid To

The VALID TO attribute specifies the proposed value for how long a condition should remain valid.

Pricing Procedure (for Condition Supplements)

In the PRICINGPROC field, you can enter the key of a pseudo-pricing procedure that is used to define the allowed condition types that can be maintained as *condition supplements* for this condition type. Only condition types listed in this pricing procedure can be maintained later in the CONDITION SUPPLEMENT screen of the condition record maintenance for this condition type.

> **"Pricing Procedure" for Condition Supplements**
>
> The PRICINGPROC attribute is particularly confusing for beginners of pricing because you would not expect the entry of a "pricing procedure" within the configuration of a condition type, as this contradicts the logic that has been presented before. This pseudo-pricing procedure is only used as a grouping tool to list the condition types allowed as condition supplements for this condition type.

As an example, you will see in the Customizing screen of the condition type PR00 (price) of the standard SAP system the PRICINGPROC attribute filled with PR0000 (see Figure 4.26). This enables the condition type PR00 the maintenance of the listed condition types as condition supplements using the menu path GOTO • CONDITION SUPPLEMENT.

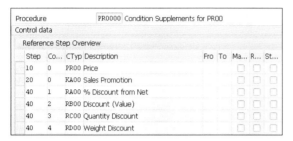

Step	Co...	CTyp	Description	Fro	To	Ma...	R...	St...
10	0	PR00	Price			☐	☐	☐
20	0	KA00	Sales Promotion			☐	☐	☐
40	1	RA00	% Discount from Net			☐	☐	☐
40	2	RB00	Discount (Value)			☐	☐	☐
40	3	RC00	Quantity Discount			☐	☐	☐
40	4	RD00	Weight Discount			☐	☐	☐

Figure 4.26 Condition Supplements for Price PR00

Delete from Database

The DELETE FR. DB attribute controls how the system operates when deleting condition records. The following options exist:

▸ **_ (blank)**
You can set an indicator so that the condition record is no longer used in pricing. The condition record is then archived in the archiving run.

▸ **A**
You can delete the condition records from the database. You then receive a popup, asking whether the condition record should actually be deleted or whether the deletion indicator should simply be set.

▸ **B**
You delete the condition records from the database. You only receive a popup if there are condition supplements available.

Options A and B, introduced with SAP R/3 4.5B, are still little known.

Reference Condition Type and Reference Application

In the REFCONTYPE attribute, a condition type can be specified which can be used as a reference so that you only have to create condition records once for condition types that are very similar. You may need to use different condition types for the same condition. These can differ in the access sequence, the description, the reference stage of the pricing procedure or the calculation type, for example.

For example, condition type MWSI (output tax) only differs with condition type MWST (output tax) in the calculation type. For this purpose, an entry *MWST* is made in REFCONTYPE field for condition type MWSI. Now, condition records only need to be created for condition type MWST and not for MWSI.

The REFAPPLICATION field is used to refer to condition records from other applications.

Condition Index

The CONDITION INDEX attribute specifies whether the system updates one or more condition indices when maintaining condition records. This makes it possible to list or maintain condition records independently of condition type and condition table.

Condition Update

If you mark the CONDIT.UPDATE attribute, the condition records for this condition type will have a kind of *memory*, allowing you to enter a cross-document limit value up to which the condition record can be used. This means that the condition records store and accumulate the respective values every time they are found in the document pricing. If the entered limit is reached for a condition record, it will no longer be taken into account in the next document pricing.

Scales

The attributes combined in field group SCALES define, in accordance with our understanding of the condition type as a function $f(x)$, the X-axis.

Scale Basis

The SCALE BASIS attribute defines the base value the condition type will work with—this means, for example, whether the condition is based on quantity, value, or volume. Some important examples are:

- B: VALUE SCALE
- C: QUANTITY SCALE
- D: GROSS WEIGHT SCALE
- E: NET WEIGHT SCALE
- F: VOLUME SCALE

Check Value

The CHECK VALUE attribute indicates whether the scale rates will optionally be checked if they are entered in ascending or descending order.

Scale type

The SCALE TYPE attribute defines when the scale values are applied:

▶ Starting with a certain quantity or value (base scale)

▶ Up to a certain quantity or value (to scale)

▶ As a graduated-to interval scale: (e.g., when you sell 25 pieces, the first 10 pieces should cost $10, the next 10 pieces $9, and each additional piece $8; this is typical with licenses)

Scale Formula

In the SCALE FORMULA attribute field, you can enter a formula key to specify a special calculation method for the scale base.

Unit of Measure

In the UNIT OF MEASURE attribute, you can specify a unit of measure that the system uses to determine scales when you use group conditions. The system will also propose this unit of measure when you maintain records for group conditions that are either weight- or volume-dependent.

Control Data 2

In the CONTROL DATA 2 field group, attributes are grouped together that are less frequently used and that often are related to a special requirement of pricing that can be mapped with the help of those attributes, as in the case of condition type RL00 (factoring discount), needing the INV.LIST COND attribute. (This condition type is described in Appendix A.)

Currency Conversion

The CURRENCY CONV. attribute controls the currency conversion if the currency used in the condition record deviates from the document currency. To calculate a condition value in a document, the system multiplies the amount that results from the condition record by the item quantity. If you mark the attribute field, the system converts the condition value into the document currency after multiplication. If you leave the field blank, the system converts the condition value into the document currency before multiplication.

Exclusion

In the EXCLUSION attribute field, you can enter a default exclusion indicator for the CONDITION EXCLUSION for CONDITION TYPES AND RECORDS. When you create a condition record for this condition type, the EXCLUSION field will be filled with this indicator by default.

Accruals

The ACCRUALS attribute indicates that the system posts the amounts resulting from this condition to financial accounting as accruals. The condition will appear in the document as a statistical condition. Examples of condition types that use this indicator are the following condition types from Purchasing within SAP ERP Materials Management (MM):

- KAD0: Material costs (sales aid materials)
- KAD1: Handling costs (sales aid materials)

In addition, this attribute is set by the pricing program for all rebate condition types.

Variant Condition and Condition for Intercompany Billing

In releases prior to SAP R/3 4.0, you had to create variant conditions (VA00) with CONDITION CATEGORY = O (variants). But, for example, it was not possible to configure a variant condition as a price for intercompany billing or freight at the same time. For this reason, in SAP R/3 4.0, two indicators were set up in the condition type configuration:

- Variant condition (KVARC)
- Intercompany billing condition (KFKIV)

With the new VARIANT COND. (condition for configuration) attribute, you can now indicate, for example, a freight condition as variant condition.

Conditions for internal costing, for example PI01 and PI02, were defined before SAP R/3 4.0 by COND.CATEGORY = I (price for intercompany billing) and it was also not possible to indicate freight at the same time as price for intercompany billing.

With the new INT-COMBILLCOND (condition for intercompany billing) attribute, you can now indicate, for example, a freight condition as an internal costing condition.

Pricing Date

The PRICING DATE attribute field (see Figure 4.13) specifies the identification code for the date to which a condition of this type is to be calculated in the sales document. If you do not enter an identification code, the pricing date or the date of services rendered is used. Possible identification codes are:

- _ (blank): Standard (komk-prsdt; tax and rebate komk-fbuda)
- A: Date of services rendered (komk-fbuda)
- B: Pricing date (komk-prsdt)
- C: Billing date (komk-fkdat)
- D: Creation date (komk-erdat)
- E: Order date (komk-audat)

Condition for Invoice List

With the INV.LIST COND. attribute, you can mark the condition type as relevant for the processing of invoice lists, as it is done for condition types RL00 (factoring discount) and MW15 (fact. discount tax).

Quantity Conversion

This QTY CONVERSION attribute controls the quantity conversion during determination of the condition basis. The field is only relevant for CALCULATION TYPE = C (quantity) and if the sales quantity unit of measure and the condition quantity unit of measure are identical (and different than the basis quantity unit). The possible settings are:

- **Deactivated**
  The condition basis quantity is converted via the quantity to the stock-keeping unit of measure. This means that the condition quantity is determined for planned factors. As a result, changes to the conversion factors in the delivery or the order are not taken into account. Rounding errors can also occur during quantity conversion.

▶ **Activated**
If the sales quantity unit of measure and the condition quantity unit of measure are identical, the quantity of the document item is used, i.e., the actual quantity.

Relevance for Account Assignment

The REL.ACC.ASSIG attribute controls how the account assignment is performed for conditions of this type. If you leave the field blank, account assignment is performed in the usual way. If you enter the indicator B, the system includes the accounting indicator in the account assignment process. The information from the condition record is forwarded to Controlling (CO) with the classification ACCOUNTING indicator. The system links the condition record to the underlying billing document item to find the accounting indicator that has been assigned to a particular transaction. In the standard system, the condition type KBM1 (goodwill/guarantee) is set up for use in transactions involving an accounting indicator.

Account assignment using an accounting indicator is often used in service management. It enables you to identify how costs incurred by a particular service transaction arose (for example, goodwill, under guarantee).

Service Charge Settlement

The SERVICECHGESE attribute indicates that the trading contract conditions should be calculated using the vendor billing document. The condition type must be assigned to an additional costs type in Customizing for the trading contract.

Budget Condition

The BUDGET COND. attribute indicates that the condition is a budget condition. The condition type ACRN is used to assign the receivables to certain budgets within resource-related billing.

Enabled for CPF

The ENABLED FOR CPF attribute is only visible if the LOG_SD_COMMODITY_02 or LOG_MM_COMMODITY_02 business functions are activated. If you select this indicator, you can assign a configurable parameters and formulas (CPF) to a condition type either in the master data or in a document. During pricing, the condition is then calculated using the assigned CPF. We will take a closer look at that in Section 4.5. Currently this attribute must not be used for group conditions, rebate conditions, and condition types using calculation type Q (commodity price).

Text Determination

The TEXT DETERMINATION field group was added with SAP R/3 4.6C when text determination was also made available for condition records.

Text Determination Procedure

With the TEXTDETPRC attribute, you can specify a text determination procedure. The text types contained in that procedure can then be maintained in the DETAILS screen of the CONDITION MAINTENANCE dialog for this condition type.

Text-ID for Text Edit Control

With the TEXT ID attribute you can specify a text ID that appears by default in the TEXT EDIT CONTROL of the DETAILS screen of the CONDITION MAINTENANCE dialog. For example, in Figure 4.27 shows the INTERNAL COMMENT.

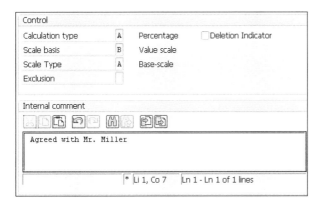

Figure 4.27 Text Maintenance in a Condition Record

The configuration of the vast majority of condition types is done with a relatively small subset of the presented attributes. Typically, a new condition type is created by first looking for a template condition type and then adapting some diverging attributes after copying. It is not necessary that you know all those attributes and their possible values by heart, but hopefully you should now have an understanding of what is possible using this wide range of attributes.

4.2.4 Pricing Procedure

The pricing procedure combines the required condition types in the desired sequence. Thus, the pricing procedure defines the processing sequence of the condition types as an important part of the configuration. A test of our newly created customer group discount Z501 was only possible after we had incorporated it into the respective pricing procedure. The attributes available in the Customizing screen of pricing procedures (see Figure 4.28) will be described next.

Change View "Control data": Overview

New Entries

Dialog Structure	Procedure	Z00001 Company Standard

Procedures · Control data

Control data

Reference Step Overview

Step	Co...	CTyp	Description	Fro	To	Ma...	R...	Sta...	P	SuTot	Reqt	CalType	BasTy...	Acc...	Accru...	
111	0	HI01	Hierarchy			☐	☐	☐	X		2			ERS		
112	0	HI02	Hierarchy/Material			☐	☐	☐	X		2			ERS		
115	0	K148	Product Hierarchy			☐	☐	☐	X		2			ERS		
120	0	VA01	Variants %			☐	☐	☐	X		2			ERS		
130	0	Z501	Customer Group			☐	☐	☐	X		2			ERS		
300	0		Discount Amount	101	299	☐	☐	☐								
302	0		NETP Price			✓	☐	☐			2	6	3	ERL		
310	0	PN00	Net Price			✓	☐	☐	X		2	6		ERL		
320	0	PMIN	Minimum Price			☐	☐	☐	X		2	15		ERL		

Figure 4.28 Adding a Condition Type to a Pricing Procedure

Reference Step and Counter

Reference STEP and COUNTER are key attributes that specify the order of the entries in the pricing procedure. A step number can be referenced within a subsequent entry of the pricing procedure using the FROM or TO attributes.

As a rule, the value of COUNTER is zero, but to be able to define several manual condition types on the same step level, the subkey COUNTER was added. The arrangement of several manual condition types on the same step level is necessary when you want to keep the manual input sequence of those condition types within the processing of the sales document. For a better understanding, Figure 4.29 shows an example that you can test with pricing procedure RVAA01 from the standard SAP system.

Step/Counter

110	1	RA01	% Disc. from Gross
110	2	RA00	% Discount from Net
110	3	RC00	Quantity Discount
110	4	RB00	Discount (Value)
110	5	RD00	Weight Discount

Previous Value:	1000			Previous Value :	1000		
RA00 -10%	-100	900		RB00 -100	-100	900	
RB00 -100	-100			RA00 -10%	-90		
Results in:	800			Results in:	810		

Figure 4.29 Effect of the Counter Attribute Field

Condition Type

The CTYP (condition type) field either specifies the condition type to be processed by the current step of the pricing procedure or—by leaving the field empty—you can define a subtotal. For example, see the DISCOUNT AMOUNT in step 300 in Figure 4.28. In this case, the DESCRIPTION field is ready for input and you can enter the description of your new subtotal.

From-To

The reference attribute field FROM allows you to define an alternative base for calculating the condition value (the default base is the *current value* resulting from processing the previous condition types). An example of this is condition type RA01 (% disc. from gross) in pricing procedure RVAA01.

By entering a FROM-TO range, you can define subtotals like DISCOUNT AMOUNT. The values of the condition lines contained in the FROM-TO range are then automatically summarized and assigned to the respective line in the pricing procedure.

Manual Indicator

Conditions with the MANUAL attribute in the pricing procedure are only included in price determination if they are entered manually during document creation or if they are transferred from an external process, such as costing.

Required Indicator

A condition type that is marked with the REQUIRED attribute must exist in the price determination of the sales document item. If this is not the case, a message is displayed saying: PRICING ERROR: MANDATORY CONDITION XY IS MISSING. If the message is ignored, the sales document is incomplete. This attribute is typically set at least for the basic price condition of the pricing procedure (e.g., for PR00).

Statistics Indicator

A condition type that is marked with the STATISTICS attribute does not alter the net value of the sales document item. Those valued are used for the calculation of statistics data.

Print Indicator for Condition Lines

The PRINT INDICATOR field controls the issuing of condition lines when printing documents such as order confirmations or invoices. There are two sets of logic that can be used: The original logic—which is still today applied in most cases—uses only three values:

▸ _ (blank): Condition line is not printed

▸ X: Condition line is printed at item level

▸ S: Condition line is printed in totals block

A description of the interrelationship of these print indicators can be found via the help menu F1. The basic principles are visualized in Figure 4.30.

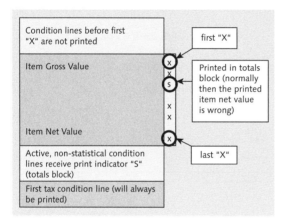

Figure 4.30 Print Indicator

We will discuss this topic in more detail in Chapter 7, Section 7.8, where we will also take a short look at the second available logic.

Subtotal

The SUBTOTAL field controls whether and in which fields condition amounts or subtotals (for example, a customer discount or the cost of a material) are stored.

If the same subtotal indicator is entered in various lines of the pricing procedure (e.g., 1, which is a carryover value to KOMP-KZWI1) the system totals the individual amounts.

Requirement

If a pricing requirement routine number is entered in the REQUIREMENT attribute field, the condition line is only processed if the requirement is fulfilled.

Condition Formula for Alternative Value Calculation

The CALTYPE attribute field offers the possibility of entering an alternative formula to determine the value of the current condition line of the pricing procedure.

Condition Formula for Basis

The BASTYPE attribute field offers the possibility of entering a formula to determine the condition basis as an alternative to the standard.

Account Key

The ACCKEY attribute field enables the system to post amounts to certain types of revenue accounts. For example, the system can post freight charges (generated by the freight pricing condition) to the relevant freight revenue account.

Account Key for Accruals

The ACCRUALS attribute field enables the system to post amounts to certain types of accrual accounts. For example, rebate accruals that are calculated from pricing conditions can be posted to the corresponding account for rebate accruals.

Reversal of Accruals

If accruals are posted, there must always be a process to reverse the accruals. (For the accruals based on rebate conditions, this is the rebate settlement process.)

We became familiar with the pricing procedure as the central controlling element of pricing that establishes the relationship between the condition types. With the presentation of the available attributes, we gained an initial insight into the possibilities of the configuration. In Chapter 8, we will deepen our knowledge about several important pricing procedures from the standard SAP system.

4.3   Customer-Specific Adaptations and Customer Namespaces

Before starting to make customer-specific adaptations within pricing, you should consider if the requirement could be met by a creative use of the possibilities of the standard configuration.

4.3.1   Creative Use of the Standard Configuration

Let's consider here the example of composite functions. There are functional requirements that cannot be mapped to a unique condition type (see Figure 4.31) and therefore it seems at first that there is no solution using the standard configuration possibilities.

The requirements for the function to be created are: "10% (of the base value), but not exceeding $100". There is no such calculation type within the configuration of condition types. After having acquired the respective know-how, you might be tempted to create a solution by creating customer-specific condition formulas. This means a customer-specific adaptation with the respective risk that comes with customer-specific programming. For example, you might forget that such a routine can also run in another business context (e.g., order vs. return).

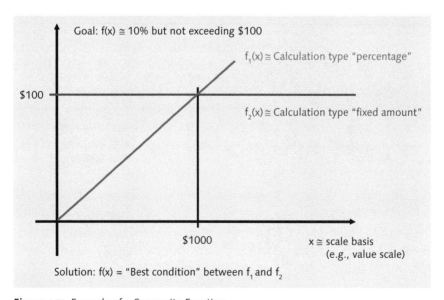

Figure 4.31 Example of a Composite Function

When you concentrate on the final result and understand this requirement as a "competition" between two functions f_1 and f_2, where f_1 is equipped with calculation type PERCENTAGE and f_2 with calculation type FIXED AMOUNT, the problem can be solved by the functionality of the *condition exclusion* for groups of conditions using the CONDITION EXCLUSION PROCEDURE A - BEST CONDITION BETWEEN CONDITION TYPES. This involves only pure standard configuration.

If it is impossible to fulfill the requirements of the pricing scenario by a creative use of the standard configuration, we have still the customer-specific adaptation left. We will briefly discuss the possibilities in the following sections.

4.3.2 New Fields for Pricing

The scope of pricing is initially limited by the catalog of allowed fields for creating condition tables. So it is no surprise that the possibilities for customer-specific adaptations start with the extensibility of this catalog. Find the relevant information using the menu path IMG • SALES AND DISTRIBUTION • SYSTEM MODIFICATIONS • CREATE NEW FIELDS (USING CONDITION TECHNIQUE) • NEW FIELDS FOR PRICING.

Detailed Instructions in the IMG Documentation

The IMG documentation for the step NEW FIELDS FOR PRICING contains a detailed description of what you must do. We are focusing on the essential points here.

Depending on whether the desired new field is a header field or an item field, it must be added in the include KOMKAZ or KOMPAZ, respectively. In addition, the assignment of values for the field has to be done using one of the provided user exits:

- `userexit_pricing_prepare_tkomk` (for header fields)
- `userexit_pricing_prepare_tkomp` (for item fields)

After you execute these two steps, the new field can be used in pricing requirements and pricing formulas.

The new field must be added to the catalog of allowed fields for condition tables first, if the field is also required for creating a new condition table. This registration is done using the menu path IMG • SALES AND DISTRIBUTION • BASIC FUNCTIONS • PRICING • PRICING CONTROL • DEFINE CONDITION TABLES • CONDITIONS: ALLOWED FIELDS.

The field will then be selectable in the creation screen for condition tables (see Figure 4.4) and can be used release-independent, just like the fields of the standard SAP system.

4.3.3 Requirements and Formulas (Routines)

The next level of adaptations consists of customer-specific routines (requirements and formulas) that are integrated in various places within the different pricing elements. These routines are created using Transaction VOFM, which can be found in customizing using the menu path IMG • SALES AND DISTRIBUTION • SYSTEM MODIFICATIONS • ROUTINES.

Figure 4.32 provides the initial overview of the intervention possibilities that exist within the standard configuration of pricing.

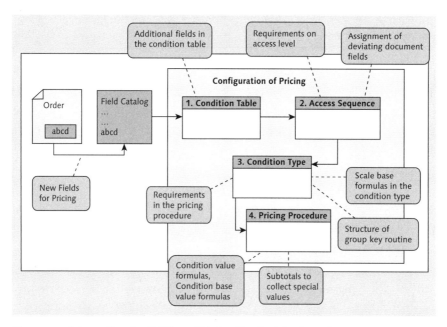

Figure 4.32 Intervention Possibilities within the Standard Configuration

Needless to say, a certain knowledge of ABAP programming language is a prerequisite to create your own routines. However, because this knowledge alone is not sufficient, we have brought together a wealth of information in Chapter 11.

4.3.4 User Exits for Pricing

In addition to the routine's intervention possibilities routines, we have predefined *user exits*, which allow more complex release independent customer-specific adaptations. Based on Figure 4.32, we could try to visualize this concept by illustrating that we can influence the framework conditions under which pricing is processed (see Figure 4.33).

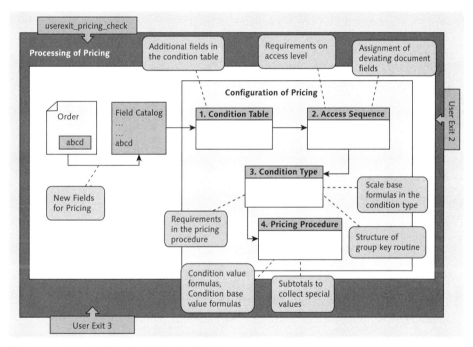

Figure 4.33 User Exits in the Context of Pricing

As an example, we can quote `userexit_pricing_check`. With the help of this user exit, you can install additional checks to the standard checks of condition lines that cannot be done with standard configuration. We will discuss this user exits topic in detail in Chapter 11, Section 11.8.

4.4   Example for the Implementation of Complex Pricing Scenarios

To be able to implement more complex pricing scenarios, it is inevitable that we deal with the technical foundations of pricing. As a starting example we will take a look at the implementation of the MINIMUM ORDER VALUE functionality of the standard SAP system. For this purpose, you can define a threshold value in the form of a condition record for condition type AMIW (minimum sales order value If this threshold is not reached in the order, the differential amount to the achieved net value is added automatically to the order pricing.

In the order example in Figure 4.34, a minimum order value of 500 EUR was determined. As the achieved net value of the order is only 300 EUR, a condition AMIZ (minimum value surcharge) with the amount 200 EUR was automatically calculated.

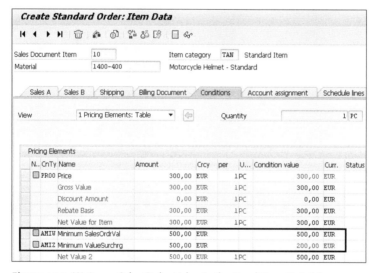

Figure 4.34 Minimum Sales Order Value in the Conditions Detail Screen

In the underlying pricing procedure (here RVAA01), we find the two involved condition types on reference step levels 817 and 818. Condition type AMIW has the STATISTICS attribute. Thus, the found threshold value does not affect the net value of the items. However, the found value is stored in subtotal D (xworkd). The subsequent condition type AMIZ itself has no condition records, as the value is determined by the assigned condition value formula 13 (see Figure 4.35).

| Procedure | | RVAA01 Standard | | | | | | | | | | |

Control data

Reference Step Overview

Step	Co...	CTyp	Description	Fro	To	Ma...	R...	St...	P	SuTot	Reqt	CalTy...	BasT...	Acc...
810	2	HB00	Discount (Value)			✓	☐	☐						ERS
810	3	HD00	Freight			✓	☐	☐		4				ERF
815	0	KF00	Freight			☐	☐	☐		4				ERF
816	0	FK00	Cust. shipment(IDES)			✓	☐	☐						
817	0	AMIW	Minimum SalesOrdrVal			☐	☐	✓	D	2				
818	0	AMIZ	Minimum ValueSurchrg			☐	☐	☐		2	13			ERS
820	0	HM00	Order Value			✓	☐	☐						ERL

Figure 4.35 Minimum Sales Order Value in the Pricing Procedure

The condition value formula 13 (minimum value surcharge) calculates the difference between the minimum order value and the achieved order value, if this value is below the minimum order value (see Figure 4.36).

Interestingly, you can see here that the formula not only contains the respective IF commands that we expect, but also other controlling statements. Looking at the coding of formula 13, you might wonder why, depending of the field komp-shkzg, different logics are performed.

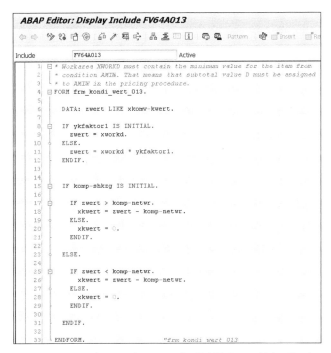

Figure 4.36 Condition Value Formula 13 (Minimum Value Surcharge)

In Part III, we present the advanced technical foundations to become capable to understand the background of this coding. We explicitly discuss the meaning of the komp-shkzg field in Chapter 13, Section 13.1.

4.5   Configurable Parameters and Formulas

CPF is a relatively new development in the pricing area. It was first delivered in SAP ERP 6.0 EHP 7 with the business functions LOG_SD_COMMODITY_02 and LOG_MM_COMMODITY_02 (available for a fee). It was designed to deal with the often complex and individual pricing rules in commodities trading.

In the previous sections, you saw that customer-specific extensions to fields and routines are defined and assigned in Customizing and therefore cannot be easily changed in individual documents. If you want to be able to choose between different modes of calculations in a document, you need to plan for this in the pricing procedure, perhaps by having several condition types with different formulas assigned. This would be cumbersome when many different calculations are possible. A second challenge is that user-defined fields that you might need in the calculation do not appear automatically on the UI to be checked and maintained there. Besides, adding new formulas or fields to the UI generally requires knowledge of ABAP.

The CPF functionality addresses these challenges. Even though you create a *CPF formula* in Customizing as well, it is not assigned directly to any condition type or pricing procedure step but can be added to an individual condition record in the condition record maintenance or even to an individual document condition in a document (e.g., in an order or contract). A CPF formula consists of a set of parameters that you select freely from the parameter catalog and one or more routines or functions to execute specific usage tasks. SAP has provided tasks to influence the condition amount, the condition basis value, and the condition value.

If you assign the formula to a condition record, the corresponding parameters appear automatically on the DETAILS screen and you can maintain their values. Alternatively, parameters can be set up to be determined by the system. Accordingly, these values will be closed for input on the user interfaces. The execution of the usage tasks can be either modeled in SAP's Business Rules Framework Plus (BRFplus) or coded as conventional Business Add-In (BAdI) implementations.

If you assign a CPF formula to a condition record that is found during the condition access within pricing, the formula will be taken over and the tasks executed. Given that the customizing of the condition type allows manual changes, you may add formulas and adjust parameter values directly in the business document. The parameter and calculated results will be stored together with the general pricing result in the database.

We will now show you step-by-step how to set up a simple CPF formula.

4.5.1 Implementing an Initial Scenario with Configurable Parameters and Formulas

For our example, we will use a scenario from commodity trading. Assume that we want to sell copper concentrate. Since the buyer is ultimately interested in the copper, there should be a discount, or penalty, if the copper content of the ore deviates from the content agreed in the contract. In the SAP system, the copper content of a product can, for example, be stored as a *characteristic* in the associated material or batch class. However, we will not go into those details here.

For the discount, we create a condition type ZGEH with the calculation type PER-CENTAGE. Its amount should be calculated as follows:

$$[(Copper\_Content_{agreed} - Copper\_Content_{actual}) \div Increment] \times Base\_Penalty$$

The amount of the base penalty, the agreed copper content, and the increment are negotiable and can be individually stipulated in the contract or order.

To achieve this, we will create a suitable CPF formula and assign it to a condition record. Our CPF formula must include the necessary parameters and an appropriate calculation algorithm. The actual copper content is to be determined by the system, the agreed content, and the base penalty, and the increment must be ready for input in the condition maintenance and contract.

Creating a CPF Formula in Customizing

First we have to determine which parameters we need. In our example, these are:

- Agreed copper content of the copper ore
- Actual copper content of the copper ore

- Increment

- Base penalty

Only parameters defined in the parameter catalog can be used in a CPF formula. We can maintain the parameter catalog following the menu path IMG • SALES AND DISTRIBUTION • BASIC FUNCTIONS • PRICING • CONFIGURABLE PARAMETERS AND FORMULAS IN PRICING • DEFINE ENTRIES FOR PARAMETER CATALOG.

Here, we establish next to the names of the parameters their types or structures. In other words, we define the parameter's meaning. A parameter can either reference an existing data element of the ABAP Data Dictionary or one of the predefined CPF basic structures. These elementary data types of the CPF resemble the elementary data types of the BRFplus and are listed in Table 4.1. The CPFS_ PRICE_RATE type, however, has no equivalent in the BRFplus. It is designed to contain a condition amount of the form X USD/ N PC and consists of an amount (number plus currency) and a quantity (number plus unit of measure).

Name of the Data Type	Description
CPF_NUMBER	Number
CPFS_AMOUNT	Value: Structure consisting of a number and an assigned currency
CPFS_QUANTITY	Quantity: Structure consisting of a number and an assigned unit of measure
CPFS_PRICE_RATE	Rate: Structure consisting of a CPF amount and a CPF quantity to store data such as 5 EUR / 1 PC
CPFS_PRICE_BASE	Base value: Structure consisting of a CPF amount and a CPF quantity. Only for internal use

Table 4.1 The Elementary Data Types of the CPF

As a third possibility, you can combine DDIC data elements and CPF data types into *custom structures* and assign these to a parameter. A custom structure is very similar to a flat DDIC structure, except that it is not defined in the ABAP Dictionary, but only in the customizing of the CPF.

You can reuse all parameters in the catalog at will.

We now create the needed parameters in the parameter catalog. You can see the result in Figure 4.37.

New Entries: Overview of Added Entries

Usage   A

CPF Parameter Catalog

Parameter Name	Descript.	Referenced Data Type	Data Cat.		DataSource	Description Long
MY_AGREED_CONTENT	Agrd.Cont	CPFS_QUANTITY	CPF Elementary Data Type	▼		Agreed Content of Component
MY_ACTUAL_CONTENT	Act.Cont	SAP_QUALITY	CPF Custom Structure	▼	1	Actual Content of Component
MY_INCREMENT	Increment	CPFS_QUANTITY	CPF Elementary Data Type	▼		Increment
MY_BASE_PENALTY	Penalty	CPFS_PRICE_RATE	CPF Elementary Data Type	▼		Base Penalty
☑		☑		▼		

Figure 4.37 Creation of the Parameters in the Parameter Catalog

We named the agreed content MY_AGREED_CONTENT. In this case, it is a percentage. Since the unit % is a unit of measure in the SAP system, we choose one of the elementary data types of the CPF, the structure CPFS_QUANTITY as referenced data type. We plan to enter the parameter manually in the condition record maintenance or the business document. The actual copper content MY_ACTUAL_CONTENT on the other hand is to be picked up automatically from the material master or batch class of the material. Thus we need to be able to specify which commodity content is required. Therefore we choose the structure SAP_QUALITY as the reference data type that is delivered by SAP.

To maintain or display custom structures, follow the menu path IMG • SALES AND DISTRIBUTION • BASIC FUNCTIONS • PRICING • CONFIGURABLE PARAMETERS AND FORMULAS IN PRICING • DEFINE CUSTOM STRUCTURE (see Figure 4.38).

Figure 4.38 The Custom Structure SAP_QUALITY

SAP_QUALITY consists of two components. The first is a text field to enter a characteristic's name from the classification system (referenced data type ATNAM). We can hence reuse the structure for all characteristics. The second component is provided for the characteristic's value and references `CPFS_QUANTITY`. The `MY_ACTUAL_CONTENT` parameter thus consists of a characteristic name and value. To trigger the automatic determination, we assign a *data source* to it in the parameter catalog. The data sources routines are BAdI implementations. The routine numbers serve as filter values. We choose to implement routine 1, the determination of the value from the material or batch class (see Figure 4.37). We will later explain the data acquisition through data sources in more detail. In particular, we will show you how to determine if a routine can be used for a specific parameter.

The increment is a percentage and therefore again references `CPFS_QUANTITY`. The base penalty represents an amount of the form number currency/number quantity unit. For condition amounts or rates, the elementary CPF type `CPFS_PRICE_RATE` is provided.

After maintaining all the necessary parameters in the catalog, we can now start creating the actual CPF formula. The associated menu path is IMG • Sales and Distribution • Basic Functions • Pricing • Configurable Parameters and Formulas in Pricing • Define Formula. Click on the New Entries button and enter a formula ID and a description. Next, specify the required parameters by selecting Assign Formula parameter and then select the required parameter via the F4 Help.

Figure 4.39 shows some additional parameters that we did not enter. These are the result parameters for the individual usage tasks and are labeled as Result.

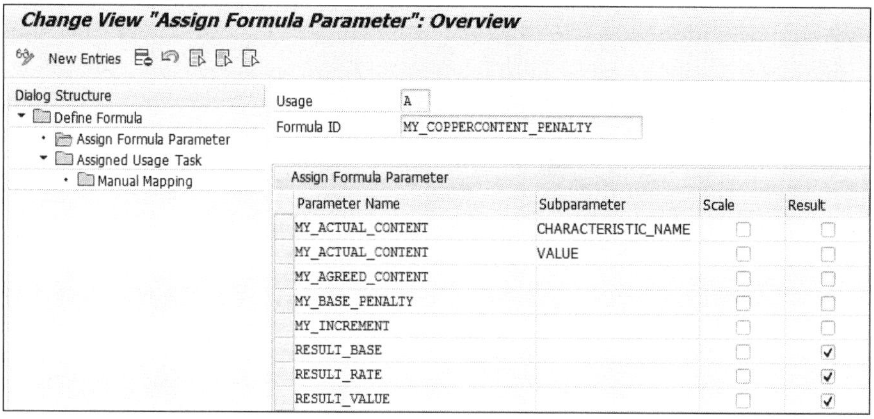

Figure 4.39 Assigning Parameters to a Formula

They are added automatically to every formula and will contain the outcome of the tasks. Since we have usage tasks for the amount, the base value, and the value of a condition, we have the additional parameters RESULT_RATE, RESULT_BASE, and RESULT_VALUE.

You can use the value of these parameters as well as that of all the other parameters in your calculation, but you should keep in mind that it may change during the pricing, depending on whether the corresponding usage task has already been carried out or not.

With all necessary parameters in place, we can implement the necessary calculation algorithm. For this we navigate to the formula's usage tasks (see Figure 4.40).

The usage tasks are technically a set of BAdIs with multiple implementations, each with its own filter value, the CPF routine number. By selecting a specific routine, the underlying implementation is called in the pricing. In our example, we want to calculate the amount of our discount ZGEH. Hence, we only need to enter a routine for the relevant usage task CALCULATE RATE. We could program our own BAdI implementation in ABAP. However, since one of the advantages of the CPF is that it allows a large variety of calculations without ABAP skills, we will model the calculation in a BRFplus function instead. It is beyond the scope of this book to explain the full capabilities of BRFplus. Fortunately, this is not necessary for a basic understanding of the CPF. You can find detailed information on the BRFplus in the book, *BRFplus: Business Rule Management for ABAP Applications* (*www.sap-press.com/2016*) by Carsten Ziegler and Thomas Albrecht (SAP PRESS, 2010).

Change View "Assigned Usage Task": Overview

Usage	A
Formula ID	PENALTY_COPPERCONTENT

Assigned Usage Task

Usage Task	Usage Task Descr.	CPF Routine	BRFplus Function Name
CALCULATE_BASE	Calculate condition base		
CALCULATE_RATE	Calculate condition rate		
CALCULATE_VALUE	Calculate condition value		
DATA_RETRIEVAL	Retrieve parameter values		

Figure 4.40 Usage Tasks in Formula Maintenance

Since we want to use BRFplus, we select the routine number 1 that is delivered by SAP. This routine will execute an assigned BRFplus function. Now we need an appropriate function. We can either use an existing one or create a new one. To assign an existing one, you need to press the chain icon in the top-left corner of Figure 4.40.

However, we click on the red and white circle icon on the far left to create a new one.

On the following popup (see Figure 4.41), we enter the name of a suitable BRFplus application and the function name M<small>Y</small>_C<small>OPPER</small>C<small>ONTENT</small>_P<small>ENALTY</small>. We then click the G<small>ENERATE AND</small> S<small>AVE</small> button.

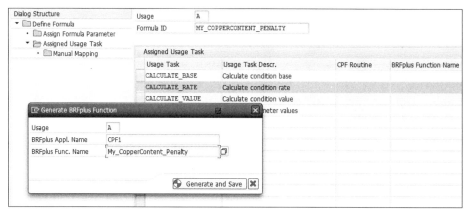

Figure 4.41 Creation of a BRFplus Function

The system now generates the M<small>Y</small>_C<small>OPPER</small>C<small>ONTENT</small>_P<small>ENALTY</small> function in the BRF-plus framework and immediately saves it. The *signature*, i.e., the interface of the BRFplus function, is derived from the parameters of the CPF formula. As the parameters' names on both sides are the same, there is no need for an explicit mapping between CPF parameters and BRFplus components. Such a mapping is possible under the MANUAL MAPPING item and may be necessary if you reuse BRFplus functions. The system will now automatically proceed to the maintenance of the function (see Figure 4.42).

If we take a closer look at the signature of the generated function, we find a component that does not exist in the CPF formula: the component `PRICING_CPF_CON-TEXT`. This structure, which you will find in the Data Dictionary (DDIC) under the name `PRCS_PRICING_CPF_CONTEXT`, is automatically added to the signature of each BRFplus function created out of a CPF formula. It provides some useful data from the context of pricing such as the customer number, the material number, quantities and units, as well as the pricing date. It also contains the most important characteristics of the condition line, on which the formula is executed, e.g., the condition type and the values determined within pricing so far for condition amount, basis, and value.

Figure 4.42 Generated Signature of the BRFplus Function

In addition, you can see that the result object of the function is the same as the result parameter of the corresponding usage task. For the determination of the condition amount, this is the RESULT_RATE parameter.

Now we insert the desired algorithm for calculating the penalty in the formula editor of BRFplus (Figure 4.43). We need to decide whether we want to save the calculated percentage in the AMOUNT or QUANTITY component of the result parameter. (The result parameter is of type CPFS_PRICE_RATE and therefore consists of an amount and a quantity.) Either is possible and is accepted when transferred back to pricing. We select the AMOUNT component because in pricing the percentage is the condition amount. Thus, the subsequent maintenance for the user is more familiar. Unfortunately, this is not entirely consistent with the fact that percent values are regarded as quantities in BRFplus, since the % unit is regarded as unit of measure. However, unless you really need the unit in BRFplus, e.g., for conversions, you can also work with the AMOUNT field.

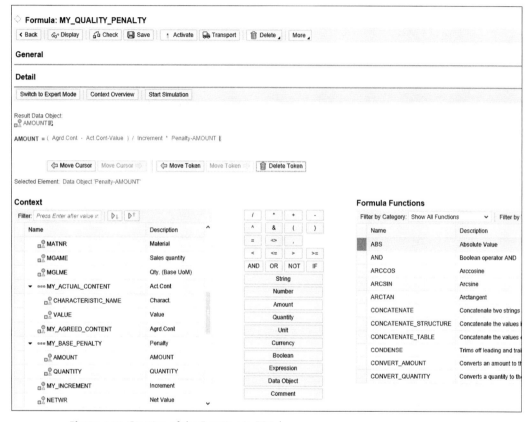

Figure 4.43 Creation of the Function in BRFplus

We save and activate the BRFplus function and return to our CPF formula. The BRFplus function name now appears in the formula (Figure 4.44)

If you click on the name or on the right icon at the top, you can go to the BRFplus function at any time and make changes or additions. You can also remove the BRFplus function and replace it with another one using the open chain icon.

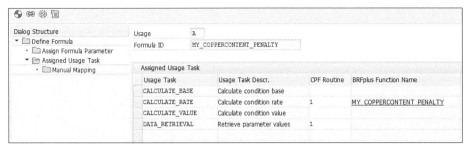

Figure 4.44 Usage Tasks in the CPF Formula after Adding the BRFplus Function

Last but not least, we enter CPF routine 1 for usage task DATA_RETRIEVAL. Thus, the data source routines associated in the catalog will be executed for all parameters. This is important because otherwise our actual copper content would not be determined by the system. We have thus completed the maintenance of the formula and save it.

Assigning a CPF Formula to a Condition Record

We want our pricing formula to be automatically found during the sale of copper concentrate. To achieve this, we have to assign it to a suitable condition record. In order that a condition may use CPF formulas in the first place, we have to set the ENABLED FOR CPF flag in the Customizing for condition types (see Section 4.2.3 and Figure 4.45). Only then can we assign a CPF formula to this condition type in condition record maintenance or in a business document.

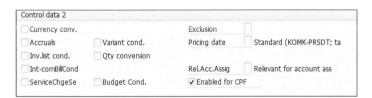

Figure 4.45 Enable a Condition Type for Using CPF Formulas

For our example, we have created condition type ZGEH and have set the ENABLED FOR CPF flag accordingly. We will now create a condition record for copper concentrate (Figure 4.46).

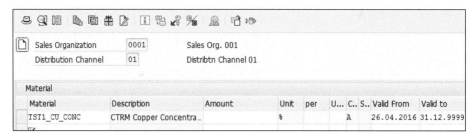

Figure 4.46 Creation of a Condition Record

You associate a CPF formula to a condition record by marking the desired condition line and clicking the small icon on the top right of Figure 4.46. We do so for our condition record. On the next screen (Figure 4.47), we enter our formula My_ CopperContent_Penalty and confirm the input. The system reads the formula from Customizing and offers the formula parameters for maintenance.

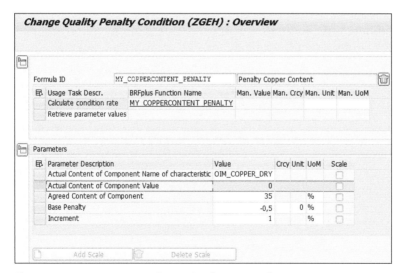

Figure 4.47 Assigning a Formula to a Condition Record

You can now enter for all parameters the values that you want to propose in the document. If you look closely at Figure 4.47, you see that the value of the actual content is not ready for input. The reason is that this value is determined by a data source. A manual value would be overwritten by the data source and therefore is not allowed.

After saving the condition record, we are ready to test our scenario.

Testing the Scenario

We create an order for copper concentrate and look at its pricing result in Figure 4.48.

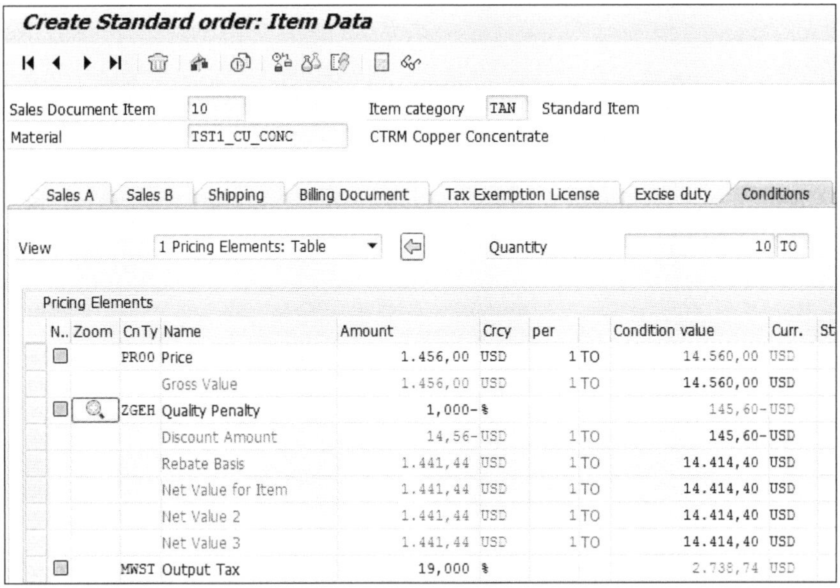
Create Standard order: Item Data
Sales Document Item 10
Item category TAN Standard Item
Material TST1_CU_CONC
CTRM Copper Concentrate
Sales A
Sales B
Shipping
Billing Document
Tax Exemption License
Excise duty
Conditions
View 1 Pricing Elements: Table
Quantity 10 TO
Pricing Elements
N.. Zoom CnTy Name Amount Crcy per Condition value Curr. St
PR00 Price 1.456,00 USD 1 TO 14.560,00 USD
Gross Value 1.456,00 USD 1 TO 14.560,00 USD
ZGEH Quality Penalty 1,000- % 145,60-USD
Discount Amount 14,56-USD 1 TO 145,60-USD
Rebate Basis 1.441,44 USD 1 TO 14.414,40 USD
Net Value for Item 1.441,44 USD 1 TO 14.414,40 USD
Net Value 2 1.441,44 USD 1 TO 14.414,40 USD
Net Value 3 1.441,44 USD 1 TO 14.414,40 USD
MWST Output Tax 19,000 % 2.738,74 USD

Figure 4.48 Pricing Result: You Can Navigate to the CPF Formula by Clicking the Magnifying Glass Icon

Next to the ZGEH condition there is a magnifying glass icon. If you click it, you navigate to the DETAILS view of the assigned CPF formula where you find the overall formula result, the parameters, and their values (see Figure 4.49). The actual copper content was determined as desired by the data source routine and used for the calculation of the discount.

You can adjust the manual parameter values or replace the whole formula if necessary. On the other hand, parameter values that are calculated automatically cannot be overwritten here.

In addition, you can override the results of all active tasks using a manual value (except for RETRIEVE PARAMETER VALUES). The fields are only partly visible on the far right in Figure 4.49. This capability is important, as the CPF would override a manual amount in the overview view of the pricing screen. As you can see in Figure 4.48, the amount field is thus closed. Here ends our example.

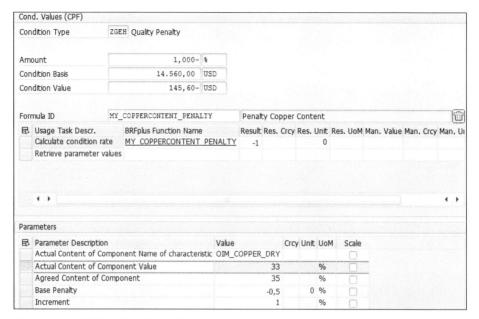

Figure 4.49 CPF Formula in the Business Document

Before we look at the CPF setting options in detail, we will briefly explain where and when CPF formulas are processed in the program flow of the pricing module.

In the step of finding the condition record, a check is performed to determine whether a found condition has a CPF formula assigned. If so, this is copied into the document. While calculating, pricing will always call the data retrieval task, also for copied conditions. Thus, the result is always based on the most current data.

After the classical calculation of the condition basis (but before the execution of a possible base value formula), the usage task for base calculation is processed. This means that you can override the result of the CPF again or hand over parameter values for further calculations in pricing using a price formula.

It may seem surprising that the calculation of the base value takes place before the calculation of the condition amount, since the units of measure of the amount for sure have a direct bearing on the condition base value. However, bringing the amount calculation forward would mean that it takes place prior to the evaluation of the scales, which happens after base calculation. However, this does not make sense, because the amount derived from scales must not overwrite the amount from CPF. SAP has therefore decided to place the CPF amount determination after a potential scale evaluation. Until then, the condition amount corresponds to the one stored in the condition record. If the unit of the condition amount changes inside the CPF formula, the system will recalculate the base value if necessary. You should keep this sequence in mind when you want to use the results of other CPF use tasks in your calculation.

The value calculation of the CPF is also performed after the default calculation, but before a possible value formula.

4.5.2 Elements of CPF in Detail

Having explored an example of the use of CPF in the previous section, we will now deal with the details so that you can later exploit the full possibilities of the CPF. The complete customizing tree in the IMG can be found by navigating to IMG • SALES AND DISTRIBUTION • BASIC FUNCTIONS • PRICING • CONFIGURABLE PARAMETERS AND FORMULAS IN PRICING (Figure 4.50).

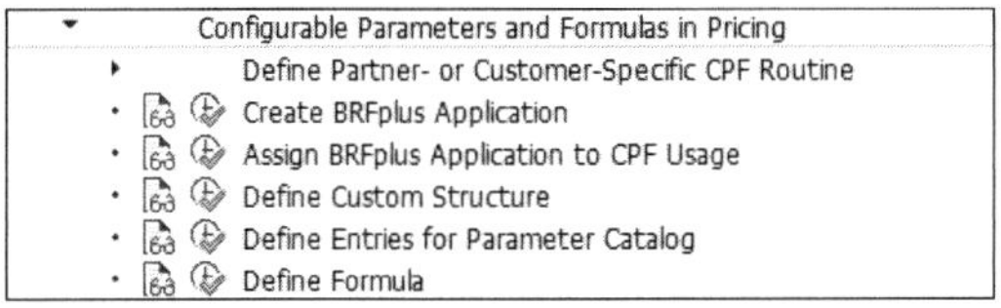

Figure 4.50 Customizing Activities for CPF

Creating a BRFplus Application

If you want to use the BRFplus as part of the CPF, you should create one or more applications in BRFplus, where you can organize and save your functions. To do this, select the corresponding activity in the IMG (Figure 4.50). Select CREATE APPLICATION and enter the name and a suitable description for your application. Save the application in your development class. It is important that the STORAGE TYPE be set to CUSTOMIZING so that the transport behavior of your BRFplus functions corresponds to those of the CPF formulas. You must also enter the class name CL_PR_CPF_BRFPLUS_APPL_EXIT in the application PROPERTIES, field APPLICATION EXIT CLASS. This is necessary to delegate the quantity and currency conversions to pricing and ensure that the information available there, such as the exchange rate or manual conversion factors, is used. If in doubt, look at the delivered application CPF1.

Assigning a BRFplus Application to CPF Usage

Here you can assign your applications to CPF and mark one of them as the default. This one will be proposed as the target application when a BRFplus function is created out of the formula maintenance.

Custom Structure

Now we turn to custom structures. You have already seen one of these structures, namely SAP_QUALITY, in the example. Custom structures are similar to structures in the DDIC, although they are not defined there, but rather in the Customizing of the CPF (and consequently can only be used within the CPF). Parameters that reference custom structures have a well-defined set of *components* or *sub-parameters* that we can rely on, for example, in the programming of a data source routine. We will explain this with the help of a small example.

Let's look at another custom structure delivered by SAP: SAP_REFERENCE_RATE, as shown in Figure 4.51. It enables us to reference the amount of a specific condition line in the pricing result. It thus consists of the components COND_TYPE for the name of the referenced condition, ITEM_NO for the item number, and RATE for the condition amount.

Custom Structure	SAP_REFERENCE_RATE				
Custom Structure Components					
Cust. Structure Comp.	Descr.	Description (long)	Referenced Data Type	Data Cat.	
COND_TYPE	CondType	Condition Type	KSCHL	Data Element	▼
ITEM_NO	ItemNo	Item Number	KPOSN	Data Element	▼
RATE	Price	Rate	CPFS_PRICE_RATE	CPF Elementary Data Type	▼

Figure 4.51 Custom Structure SAP_REFERENCE_RATE

Suppose that you need the amounts of two different conditions for your calculation. Therefore, you establish two parameters, COND1 and COND2, both referencing the custom structure SAP_REFERENCE_RATE and both having the data source routine 2 assigned in the catalog. This routine retrieves the amount of a pricing element specified by condition type and item. The interface of a data source expects one or several flat parameters. In case of a custom structure, the system dissolves the structure and passes the sub-parameters to the routine. Therefore, the routine can handle any parameter of type SAP_REFERENCE_RATE because they all have sub-parameters named COND_TYPE, ITEM_NO, and RATE.

Custom structures also ensure that parameters contain exactly the components that are needed. They are a kind of template for parameters and share the same meaning or address the same kind of entity.

You can create custom structures via the menu path IMG • SALES AND DISTRIBUTION • BASIC FUNCTIONS • PRICING • CONFIGURABLE PARAMETERS AND FORMULAS IN PRICING • DEFINE CUSTOM STRUCTURE. They consist of a name, a description, and a set of components referencing a data element from the DDIC or an elementary data type of the CPF.

Parameter Catalog

Parameters to be available in formulas are defined in the parameter catalog that you maintain from IMG • SALES AND DISTRIBUTION • BASIC FUNCTIONS • PRICING • CONFIGURABLE PARAMETERS AND FORMULAS IN PRICING • DEFINE ENTRIES FOR PARAMETER CATALOG. A parameter consists of its name, a description, its referenced data type and, if necessary, a data source. The referenced data type determines the technical structure of the parameter. You can choose between data elements of the DDIC, elementary data types of the CPF, and custom structures.

If the system determines the value of a parameter or one of its sub-parameters automatically during the pricing call, you need to assign a data source routine here. Data source routines are nothing more than implementations of the BAdI BADI_PR_CPF_DATA_SOURCE, which can be distinguished by filter values. This filter value is also referred to as a *routine number*. If you want to create your own implementations, you can do this from IMG • SALES AND DISTRIBUTION • BASIC FUNCTIONS • PRICING • CONFIGURABLE PARAMETERS AND FORMULAS IN PRICING • DEFINE PARTNER- OR CUSTOM-SPECIFIC CPF ROUTINE • DEFINE DATA SOURCE ROUTINE.

From the same menu path, you provide a list of (sub)parameters expected by your routine and hence a kind of interface. So, when assigning the data source to a parameter in the catalog, the systems can check whether the parameter's structure is compatible with the expected set of fields, or you can find out which parameters a specific routine requires.

A parameter can have only one data source. So if you create very complex parameters, you also might need to provide a dedicated data source routine, which supplies all the necessary sub-parameters.

Maybe you have noticed the reference to a Usage A in Figure 4.37. Similar to the condition technique, the CPF could potentially be used for various purposes because the underlying structures are very common. Currently, however, this is not the case.

Define Formula

You already know about the customizing activity for the creation of CPF formulas (path IMG • Sales and Distribution • Basic Functions • Pricing • Configurable Parameters and Formulas in Pricing • Define Formula) in Section 4.5.1. You learned that a formula is made up of a set of parameters and a set of usage tasks. However, we have not yet gone into detail.

For each required task, you can define your own routine number that corresponds to a BAdI implementation. You can also assign a BRFplus function, if the routine is marked accordingly in the Customizing.

To do so, set the BRFplus Enabl flag in the IMG activity by navigating to IMG • Sales and Distribution • Basic Functions • Pricing • Configurable Parameters and Formulas in Pricing • Define Partner- or Customer-Specific CPF Routine • Define CPF-Routines (see Figure 4.52).

Usage Task	CPF Routine	Description (long)	BRF Enabl.	BAdI Implementation Name	BAdI I...	BAdI S...
CALCULATE_BASE	1	Calculate base by using BRFplus Function	✓	BADI_PR_CPF_BASE_0000001		
CALCULATE_RATE	1	Calculate base by using BRFplus Function	✓	BADI_PR_CPF_RATE_0000001		
CALCULATE_VALUE	1	Calculate base by using BRFplus Function	✓	BADI_PR_CPF_VALUE_0000001		

Figure 4.52 Defining CPF Routines for Usages Tasks

In our example, we created a BRFplus function directly from the CPF formula. But it is also possible to assign an existing function. In this case the components in the BRFplus function might not have the same names as the parameters in the CPF formula. The system will notify you and you will have to define a mapping.

Suppose that alongside the formula MY_COPPERCONTENT_PENALTY from our example, we want to create another formula for gold with the same calculation algorithm. Of course, we could have chosen a slightly more neutral name for our copper formula from the start, but we wanted to make it easy for our users to find the right formula. We therefore create a new formula and this time name the parameters referring to the gold content MY_ACTUAL_GOLD_CONTENT and MY_AGREED_

GOLD_CONTENT. Since we want to reuse our BRFplus function, we must make the mapping entries, as you can see in Figure 4.53.

Dialog Structure							
▼ 🗀 Define Formula	Usage	A					
· 🗀 Assign Formula Param	Formula ID	MY_GOLD_CONTENT_PENALTY					
▼ 🗀 Assigned Usage Task	Usage Task	CALCULATE_RATE					
· 🗀 Manual Mapping							
	Manual Mapping						
	Routine/BRFplus Parameter	Routine/BRFplus Subpa...	Data Type	Parameter Name	Subparameter	Data Type
	MY_BASE_PENALTY		CPFS_PRICE_RATE	MY_BASE_PENALTY		CPFS_PRICE_RATE
	MY_INCREMENT		CPFS_QUANTITY	MY_INCREMENT		CPFS_QUANTITY
	MY_AGREED_CONTENT		CPFS_QUANTITY	MY_AGREED_GOLD_CONTENT		CPFS_QUANTITY
	MY_ACTUAL_CONTENT	CHARACTERISTIC_NAME	ATNAM	MY_ACTUAL_GOLD_CONTENT	CHARACTERISTIC_NAME	ATNAM
	MY_ACTUAL_CONTENT	VALUE	CPFS_QUANTITY	MY_ACTUAL_GOLD_CONTENT	VALUE	CPFS_QUANTITY

Figure 4.53 Mapping Entries

The list of parameters in the mapping table needs to be complete. It thus also contains parameters with the same name on both sides, such as the MY_BASE_PENALTY parameter.

Scales

Another feature that we have not yet presented are the scales in CPF formulas. As you can see in Figure 4.39, the indicator SCALE can be set for each parameter. What this all about can best be explained by an example: assume that in our copper sale, the base penalty increases gradually if the supplied copper content falls below certain limits.

To achieve this, we set the SCALE flag for the MY_BASE_PENALTY parameter in the MY_COPPERCONTENT_PENALTY formula (see Figure 4.54).

Dialog Structure					
▼ 🗀 Define Formula	Usage	A			
· 🗁 Assign Formula Parameter	Formula ID	MY_COPPERCONTENT_PENALTY			
▼ 🗀 Assigned Usage Task					
· 🗀 Manual Mapping	Assign Formula Parameter				
	Parameter Name	Subparameter	Scale	Result
	MY_ACTUAL_CONTENT	CHARACTERISTIC_NAME	☐	☐
	MY_ACTUAL_CONTENT	VALUE	☐	☐
	MY_AGREED_CONTENT		☐	☐
	MY_BASE_PENALTY		☑	☐
	MY_INCREMENT		☐	☐
	RESULT_BASE		☐	☑
	RESULT_RATE		☐	☑
	RESULT_VALUE		☐	☑

Figure 4.54 Enabling a Parameter for Scales

In condition maintenance, we mark the parameter BASE PENALTY and click the ADD SCALE button (see Figure 4.55).

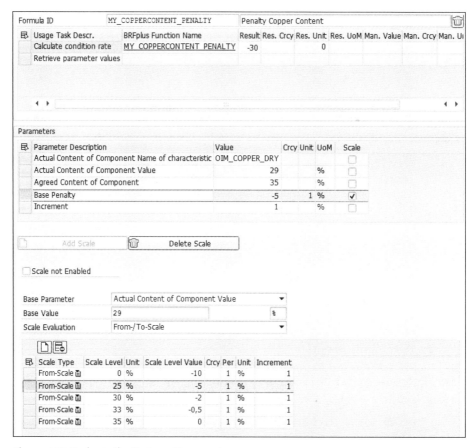

Figure 4.55 Scales in the Business Document

Now we need to specify the parameter that serves as the scale basis. In our case, this is the value of the actual copper content. You also need to select a SCALE EVAL- UATION routine. These routines define the validity of the assigned SCALE LEVEL VALUE similar to the scale type from Section 4.2.3 and determine the result of the scale. In our example, we select a from/to scale in which the result of the scale is simply the value of the scale level met by the BASE VALUE. Finally, we have to define the scale levels. For each level we have to click the CREATE icon. On the first entry you can decide whether you want to have a FROM-SCALE or a TO-SCALE.

You can also specify the units of the scale levels and the units of the scale levels' values. The INCREMENT column is irrelevant for from/to scales and is automatically set to 1. We will return to the increment later when we discuss other available evaluation routines.

In the business document, the system will now determine the base penalty depending on the copper content. The parameter value itself cannot be changed manually any longer. It is also important to know that every scale defined in a formula within the standard routines 1 of the usage tasks is evaluated prior to the BRFplus function call. Thus, the result is available there. You should note that the order of the scale evaluation is random. If a specific sequential processing is needed, because the scale base of one scale depends on the result of another, you should consider creating your own dedicated routine.

Last, note the SCALE NOT ENABLED attribute in Figure 4.55. In the figure, the actual content is the scale base. The value of 29% leads to a base penalty of -5%. This allows you to propose scales exemplified in the master data, but leave it up to the user to decide in the document if he actually wants to use it. If the attribute is set, the scale is not evaluated.

4.5.3 Customer-Specific Adaptations in CPF

With the integration of the BRFplus, the CPF provides considerable flexibility to cover a variety of requirements without programming. Nevertheless, here and there you might come to the point where even this seems to be insufficient. The CPF therefore presents some options to amend the delivered routines by your own implementations.

But before you start programming new routines, you should consider the many possibilities of BRFplus. Sometimes it may even be sufficient to extend the context data structure PRCS_PRICING_CPF_CONTEXT by an APPEND and thus provide the BRFplus with more information. When you select the field name in the APPEND structure that's identical to the field name in the communication structures KOMK and KOMP or the condition line KOMV, the content is automatically passed to the context structure.

If this does not help either, you can create your own implementations for the BAdIs described next. Please use the appropriate namespaces.

Namespaces for CPF Routines

- 0000000–0009999 (SAP standard routines)
- 0010000–0019999 (SAP routines for Industry Solutions)
- 0020000–0029999 (Partner routines)
- 0030000–0099999 (Customer routines)
- 0100000–9999999 (Not used yet)

Data Source Routines

In a data source routine, it is defined how the system retrieves the value of a parameter in the business document. Data source routines are implementations of the BAdI `BADI_PR_CPF_DATA_SOURCE`.

If you want to create your own implementation, you have to declare it in the activity by navigating to IMG • SALES AND DISTRIBUTION • BASIC FUNCTIONS • PRICING • CONFIGURABLE PARAMETERS AND FORMULAS IN PRICING • DEFINE PARTNER- OR CUSTOMER-SPECIFIC CPF ROUTINE • DEFINE CPF-ROUTINES • DEFINE DATA SOURCE ROUTINES using the NEW ENTRIES button (Figure 4.56). Otherwise, you will not be able to use the routine in the parameter catalog.

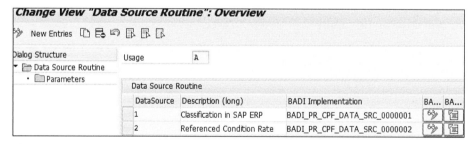

Figure 4.56 Declaration of Data Source Routines

All routines import the generic table `it_dtsrc_param`. If a data source routine is assigned to a parameter in the catalog, this table will usually contain the parameter's name and value. In the case where the parameter refers to a custom structure, however, the table does not contain the parameter's name itself but the names and values of the parameter's components or sub-parameters. The data source routine can then adjust the values of the components.

Given the very generic technical interface of the BAdI, how can we know which routine processes and parameters it needs without studying the coding? For this purpose, all routines have their explicit set of parameters declared in the customizing. You can navigate to this declaration by choosing the PARAMETERS node from the tree on the left side in Figure 4.56. If more than one parameter is listed, it is also good to define which one is actually exported by the routine and which are only imported. Export parameters are recognized by the flagged checkbox DS OUTPUT (see Figure 4.57). In the formula maintenance, parameters marked this way cannot be entered manually.

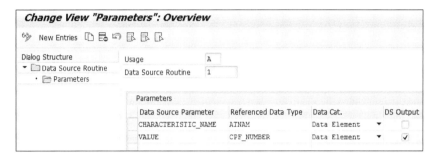

Figure 4.57 Maintenance of the Parameters of a Data Source Routine

By the way, the declaration of the parameters for a routine enables the system to check in the catalog whether a parameter and its assigned data source routine are compatible.

CPF Routines for Usage Tasks

The following BAdIs are hidden behind the usage tasks:

▶ `BADI_PR_CPF_BASE` for usage task `calculate_base` calculating a condition base value

▶ `BADI_PR_CPF_RATE` for usage task `calculate_rate` calculating a condition amount

▶ `BADI_PR_CPF_VALUE` for usage task `calculate_value` calculating a condition value

▶ `BADI_PR_CPF_DATA_RTRVL` for usage task `data_retrieval` retrieving parameter values

The namespaces mentioned here apply to all routines. You can do your implementations and interfaces from IMG • SALES AND DISTRIBUTION • BASIC FUNCTIONS • PRICING • CONFIGURABLE PARAMETERS AND FORMULAS IN PRICING • DEFINE

Partner- or Customer-Specific CPF Routine • Define CPF-Routines. A declaration of the explicit interface can be useful, but is not mandatory. When the routine is used in a formula, it allows the system to request a mapping if necessary and provide you with a F4 help.

If you want to be able to assign a BRFplus function, you need to flag the BRF enabl field (Figure 4.52).

SAP delivers the standard routine 1 for all usage tasks. Except for the data retrieval, routine 1 evaluates all scales and then executes the associated BRFplus function.

The SAP standard routine for data retrieval executes all data source routines assigned to the formula's parameters.

> **Scale Evaluation and Data Retrieval**
>
> Scale evaluation, data retrieval, and all other usage tasks are performed during each pricing call. Hence, parameter values might change if pricing data is copied from one document to another, for example, between the order and the invoice.

Routines for Scale Evaluation

Scale evaluation routines are implementations of the BAdI `BADI_CPF_SCALE_EVALUATION`. You might create your own implementations if necessary. At the moment, SAP delivers three standard implementations.

From/To Scales

The From/To-Scale in the CPF (Figure 4.58) corresponds to the From/To-Scale that you know from the maintenance of the condition type (Section 4.2.3).

Scale Type	Scale Level	Unit	Scale Level Value	Crcy	Per	Unit
From-Scale	0	%	-10		1	%
From-Scale	25	%	-5		1	%
From-Scale	30	%	-2		1	%
From-Scale	33	%	-0,5		1	%
From-Scale	35	%	0		1	%

Interval	Scale Level Value
0%-25%	-10%
25%-30%	-5%
30%-33%	-2%
33%-35%	-0,5%
35%-...%	-0%

Figure 4.58 From-Scales: The Valid Ranges Span from the Corresponding From Value to the Next From Value

Graduated Scales

The graduated scale in CPF is basically the same as the Graduated To interval scale from the condition type. However, in the CPF, the individual scale levels are not shown as separate condition lines but instead the system calculates an average overall value. The individual scale level values are therefore weighted by the portion of the overall scale base covered by their interval (see Figure 4.59).

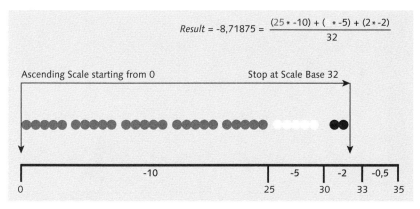

Figure 4.59 Calculation of a Simple Graduated Scale with a Given Scale Base of 32% and Scale Levels as Defined in 1.58

The CPF however provides some further options for graduated scales that we will explain by reusing our example from Section 4.5.1.

Recall that we agreed on a copper content of 35%. If the content is less, there will be a price discount. Each percentage point in the range between 35% and 33% contribute a value of -0.5%, the ones between 33% and 30% with -2%, between 30% and 25% with -5% and everything below with -10%. To get a weighted average, the sum is then divided by the overall deviation of 3%.

To achieve this, we create a scale as shown in Figure 4.60 and select the evaluation routines Graduated Scale. Two additional fields appear on the screen: Start Ascending and Start Descending. Using these fields, we can specify that our scale starts at 35% and is descending, i.e., the next scale level is always smaller than the previous one.

The system now calculates the average discount for all the intervals between 35% and the scale base if the scale base is smaller. For a scale base of 32%, this means that for the range between 35% and 33% a reduction of -0.5% is valid and for the range between 33% and 32%, a reduction of -2% (Figure 4.61). The sum will then be divided by the overall deviation of 3% to result in an average discount amount of -1% = (35 − 33) × -0.5% ÷ 3 + (33 − 32) × -2% ÷ 3. By the way, it is the increment of 1% that accounts for a reduction per 1%. If we had, for example, chosen an increment of 0.5%, the total reduction would have been -2%, because (35 − 33) ÷ 0.5 × -0.5% ÷ 3 + (33 − 32) ÷ 0.5 × -2% ÷ 3 = 2%.

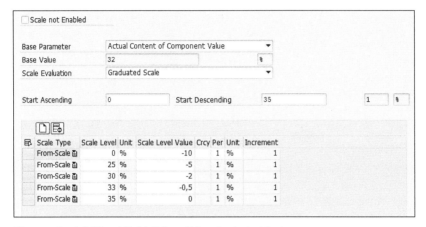

Figure 4.60 Additional Fields When Using Graduated Scales

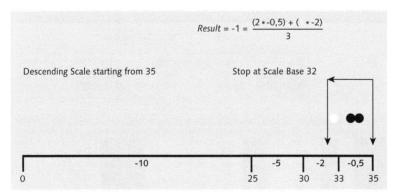

Figure 4.61 Calculation of a Descending Graduated Scale with Start Value 35% and Scale Level 32%

So far we have only used the Start Descending field. But what happens when we add a value to the Start Ascending field? Using both fields allows us to divide the scale into three separate parts—one ascending, one descending, and a neutral range in the middle. In the neutral range, the scale level value is always zero.

Consider the example in Figure 4.62. If the scale base is smaller than the starting value of the descending scales, only the scale levels between the start value and the base value will be taken into account for the calculation. If the scale base value is greater than the initial value of the ascending scale, only scale levels are considered that lie between the start of the ascending scale and the scale base. If the scale base is in between, the scale value is zero. In our example in Figure 4.62, at a scale base of 32% and an increment of 1%, the overall scale result is still calculated to be -1%. But for a scale base of 43%, the result would be (42% – 40%) ÷ 3 × 0.5% + (43% – 42%) ÷ 3 × 2% = +1%. Again we have calculated a weighted average.

Initially this looks slightly complicated, but it's useful if you want to translate deviations from an agreed value in surcharges or discounts, depending on whether the agreed value has been exceeded or undershot.

Interval	Scale Level Value
0%-25%	-10%
25%-30%	-3%
30%-33%	-2%
33%-35%	-0,5%
35%-40%	-0%

Interval	Scale Level Value
40%-42%	+0,5%
42%-45%	+2%
45%-50%	+3%
50%-100%	+10%

=

Interval	Scale Level Value
0%-25%	-10%
25%-30%	-3%
30%-33%	-2%
33%-35%	-0,5%
35%-40%	-0%
40%-42%	+0,5%
42%-45%	+2%
45%-50%	+3%
50%-100%	+10%

Figure 4.62 Scale with Ascending, Neutral, and Descending Ranges

Cumulative Graduated Scales

The cumulative graduated scales are very similar to the graduated scales. The only difference is that the individual scale levels are not added proportionally, but absolutely. That is, there is no averaging over the total deviation. For our example in Figure 4.62, a cumulative graduated scale with increment 1% would determine a value of -3% for 32% of copper and +3% for 43% copper: (35 – 33) × -0.5% + (33 – 32) × -2% = -3% and (42% – 40%) × 0.5% + (43% – 42%) × 2% = +3%, respectively.

Handling of CPF Fields on the Pricing UI

After the somewhat challenging scale evaluation routines, we can now take a breath when learning about the BAdI `BADI_PRICING_CPF_UI_FIELD`. This exit provides the possibility to control the input and output of a parameter value. You can define a `F4` help for each reference data type from the parameter catalog, check the entry, or make a conversion between the internal and external format. The reference data type serves as a filter value for the BAdI. For validation and input help, you will probably need some context data from the pricing. You can use the function module `PRICING_GET_KOMK_KOMP_XKOMV` to get the current state of the most important internal data KOMK, KOMP, and XKOMV.

4.6 Interface to Profitability Analysis

The objective of *Profitability Analysis* (CO-PA) is to show earnings on a particular profitability segment by data transfer from SAP ERP Sales and Distribution (SD). The Profitability Analysis distinguishes involves two different methods: account-based and costing-based Profitability Analysis. Both methods can be used in parallel.

When using the account-based CO-PA, only real conditions (posted in FI) are transferred to CO-PA. The only activity to acquire this information in CO-PA is to configure the relevant accounts (e.g., revenue and sales deduction accounts) as CO-related accounts.

In costing-based CO-PA, data is already passed to CO-PA for incoming sales orders. Here, a line item is generated with a CO-PA document for each order item. The same happens during billing. Again, a line item is generated for each billing item. However, a prerequisite for the analysis of the data is that the relevant quantity and value fields of the sales document be assigned to corresponding quantity and value fields of controlling.

If you use the costing-based CO-PA and bill a first order, which contains the in this chapter the newly created condition type Z501 (customer group discount), it results in an error because of this missing assignment. When you try to release the invoice to accounting, you get a qualified error message (see Figure 4.63).

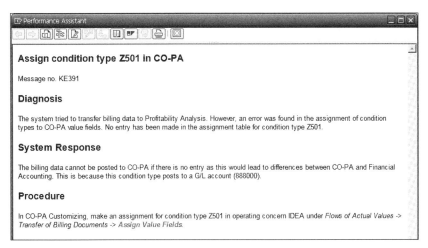

Figure 4.63 Error Message for Missing CO-PA Assignment

You can navigate directly from the error message to the relevant Customizing screen. The corresponding settings are available as well using the menu path IMG • CONTROLLING • PROFITABILITY ANALYSIS • FLOW OF ACTUAL VALUES • TRANSFER OF BILLING DOCUMENTS • ASSIGN VALUE FIELDS and IMG • CONTROLLING • PROFITABILITY ANALYSIS • FLOW OF ACTUAL VALUES • TRANSFER OF BILLING DOCUMENTS • ASSIGN VALUE FIELDS.

For example, an assignment of condition type Z501 to value field VV030 (CUSTOMER DISCOUNT) would make sense (see Figure 4.64).

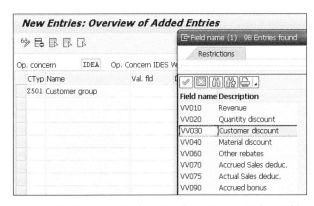

Figure 4.64 Assignment of the Condition Type to Value Field

After saving this assignment, the invoice can be released to accounting.

4.7   Summary

In this central chapter, you learned the principles of pricing configuration using an example of the implementation of a customer-specific scenario. Then we introduced the elements of pricing in detail, in order to lay the foundations for our further discussion. This included an introduction to the customer-specific adjustments that may be necessary if you have maxed out the standard customizing.

This issue is complex and requires continual learning of the technical fundamentals—enriched with tips and tricks—that we will convey in Part III of this book. Finding the optimal solution for a given task is often an iterative process that the beginner has to go through as well as the experienced consultant in order to open up new areas.

We continue now with Chapter 5, because the next step after the configuration of a pricing scenario is the provisioning of appropriate condition master data.

After discussing the tools for condition master data maintenance, we deal in this chapter with special aspects when working with condition records.

5   Working with Condition Records

Let us now deal with some issues relating to working with condition records on a daily basis. We will cover the following topics in this chapter:

▶ The (optional) release status

▶ Making mass changes using the CREATE WITH TEMPLATE function and rounding formulas

▶ Copying condition records

▶ Using the condition maintenance via area menus

▶ Other functions in condition maintenance, such as deleting condition records and tracking changes in condition records

5.1   Release Status

Release status was made available in SAP R/3 4.5 and offers you the ability to provide condition records with a status, which can be used to prevent the existing pricing from being affected by these condition records. For example, you can use this status if price changes should be approved and released by a sales manager.

To be able to use the release status for condition records, the attribute WITH RELEASE STATUS must be checked when you create the underlying condition table. Since you cannot activate this attribute retroactively for existing condition tables, the sample report SD_MOVE_A004_TO_A304 is also provided, with which you can copy the data in the database table A004 (material) into the database table A304 (material with release status) upon request. For other table combinations, the report can be copied and the coding can be adapted accordingly. In addition to condition table 304, condition tables 305 and 306 are delivered in connection with the release status. These correspond to the condition tables 004, 005, and 006 contained in the access sequence PR00 (price), and are used to configure the analog access sequence PR02 (price with release status).

Therefore, if you want to switch condition type PR00 (price) from the original access sequence PR00 (price without release status) to the newer access sequence PR02 (price with release status) in a productive environment, you would have to copy condition tables 005 and 006 to 305 and 306 using report SD_MOVE_A004_ TO_A304. In the following sections, we will look at some additional uses of the release status.

5.1.1 Available Release Statuses

For the release status, there are four predefined values:

- ▶ _ (space): RELEASED
- ▶ A: BLOCKED
- ▶ B: RELEASED FOR PRICING SIMULATION
- ▶ C: RELEASED FOR PLANNING AND PRICING SIMULATION

For pricing in the sales documents, only those condition records are used that have the release status released (space). Condition records bearing one of the other statuses will not be considered. However, the pricing analysis recognizes these statuses and displays the condition records as locked. Condition records with release status B or C can be considered in the net price list (report SDNET-PR0).

Condition records with release status C are taken into account when planning in Profitability Analysis (CO-PA).

5.1.2 Release Status in Condition Records

In order to use the release status in condition records, it is necessary to first define the *processing statuses* in Customizing for pricing, and then assign one of the four release statuses (see Figure 5.1). The corresponding settings can be accessed via the menu path IMG • SALES AND DISTRIBUTION • BASIC FUNCTIONS • PRICING • DEFINE PROCESSING STATUS.

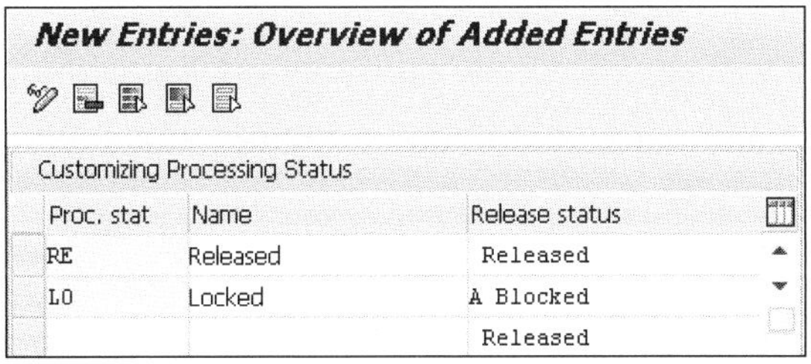

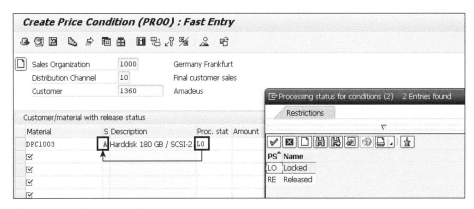

Figure 5.1 Assignment of the Processing Status to the Release Status

After being defined, these processing statuses can be used in condition maintenance. When you enter a processing status, the associated release status is automatically set in the condition record (see Figure 5.2).

Figure 5.2 Set Processing Status

In addition to the direct entry during condition maintenance, the release status can be set in connection with a sales deal.

5.1.3 Release Status in Conjunction with Agreements

The release status in the maintenance transactions for agreements, for example in Transaction VB22 (Change Sales Deal), also works for condition types that do not have the RELEASE STATUS field in the key of the condition record. The release status can be entered directly (e.g., without the detour via the processing status).

The maintenance of the release status in the sales deal takes place in the field group DEFAULT DATA. This status is set for all condition records contained in the sales deal and cannot be changed in the single condition record. A default value for the release status can be defined in Customizing of the sales deal type.

If, in the maintenance of individual condition records (e.g., via Transaction VK12 on the screen ADDITIONAL DATA), a sales deal is assigned to a condition record, the release status from the sales campaign is used for this condition record.

The release status of conditions of a sales deal can only be changed when the condition record contains the release status in the key and the sales deal has the release status released. Otherwise, the condition record always has the release status of the sales deal.

Now it gets a bit complicated: If processing statuses were defined and only assigned to exactly one release status, then (within a sales deal) the corresponding processing status is set for conditions with release status. (If more than one processing status is assigned to a release status, the condition record receives the [alphabetical] first matching entry as a processing status.) The processing status that condition records have received indirectly via the release status of a sales deal can be changed only if the sales deal is released.

In Figure 5.3, we made various states of the processing status visible under laboratory conditions.

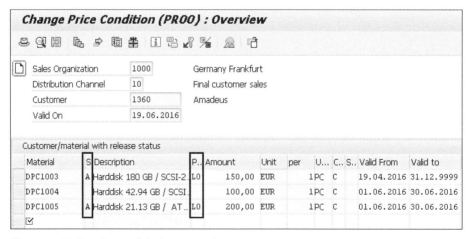

Figure 5.3 Various States of the Processing Status

In the example, the processing status of the MATERIAL DPC1003 is changeable, since this condition record is not assigned to any sales deal. The processing status of the MATERIAL DPC1004 is not assigned and cannot be changed. This condition record was assigned to a sales deal with release status blocked at a point of time when no processing statuses were yet configured, so it could therefore not be derived. The processing status of the MATERIAL DPC1005 is assigned and cannot be changed, since this condition record is assigned to a sales deal with the release status blocked.

You can check the release status set via the sales deal in the DETAILS screen consultation of the condition record (see Figure 5.4).

Figure 5.4 Release Status in Details Screen

Finally, it should be mentioned that a business transaction event 00503303 called *maintain conditions: transfers* is available, with which you can create customer-specific processing logic for changing the processing status.

Business transaction events were the enhancement technology used in SAP ERP Sales and Distribution (SD) only for SAP R/3 4.5. Although already invented and used in previous releases of SAP ERP Financials (FI), it was replaced by the method-oriented Business Add-Ins (BAdIs) as of SAP R/3 4.6. For further details about the business transaction events, see menu path IMG • SALES AND DISTRIBUTION • SYSTEM MODIFICATIONS • BUSINESS TRANSACTION EVENTS.

5.2   Mass Change/Mass Creation with Template

Condition maintenance provides the ability to perform mass changes. Nevertheless, you will change existing condition records in their current validity period only in rare cases; for example, if you want to correct a mistake. However, condition changes should only take effect starting with a specific date.

This is why, in the CREATE WITH TEMPLATE function, you first select the set of affected condition records and create a new validity period. Since there cannot be overlapping validity periods, when saving the new records, the program sets the end date of the previous validity periods to the last day before the start date of the newly created validity period. The start date of the next interval (if existing) is set to the first day after the end of the current validity period.

We will watch this process using the example of Transaction VK14 (Create with Template). In the first step, we need to select the required condition type in order to select the affected set of condition records using the offered selection parameters in the next step (see Figure 5.5).

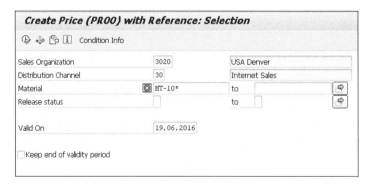

Figure 5.5 Create with Reference: Selection of Data

With the date VALID ON, the validity periods of the template data are determined. In the lower part of the selection screen, you can find the switch KEEP END OF VALIDITY PERIOD. If this switch is clicked, the validity end for the conditions is taken from the reference conditions. If the switch is not checked, then the validity end for the conditions is proposed from the Customizing of the condition type.

Next, we select the condition records found and set the validity period to the desired start and end date. In most cases, the start date will be the date of the price change and the end date will be 31.12.9999—that is, the last validity period that then always runs until further notice. We have chosen the example of a limited change in price—for example, from 01.08.2016 until 31.08.2016—in order to observe how the program-controlled validity period split takes place (see Figure 5.6).

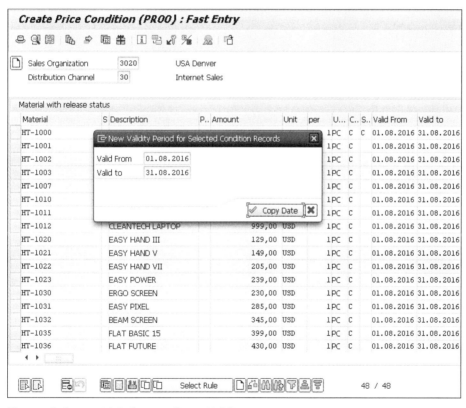

Figure 5.6 Create with Reference: Change Validity

In the next step, you can start Transaction VK12 (Change Condition Records) and set the selection parameter VALID ON, for example, to the beginning of the newly created interval in which the price change is to take place.

If we now look at the validity periods for the selected condition records, we note that—as previously described—three validity periods have been formed (see Figure 5.7).

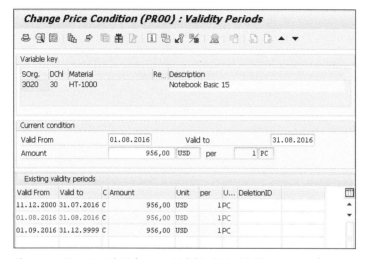

Figure 5.7 Create with Reference: Validity Period Split

If you select the set of condition records and click the 🔲 CHANGE AMOUNT button, you can specify in a subsequent popup window either PERCENTAGE or ABSOLUTE AMOUNT and optionally choose a ROUNDING RULE (see Figure 5.8). After this change, a log with the changed values will be displayed, and the changed data can be saved.

Due to the chosen situation of a limited change in price from 01.08.2016 until 31.08.2016 with the program-controlled validity period split, the situation seen Figure 5.9 is our new result.

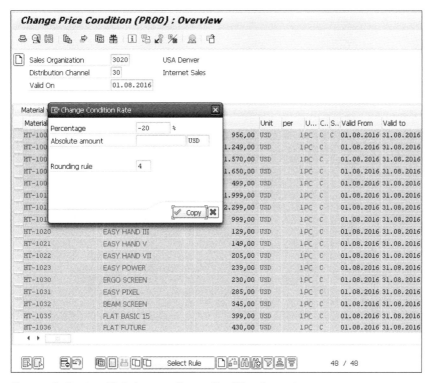

Figure 5.8 Create with Reference: Change Condition Amount

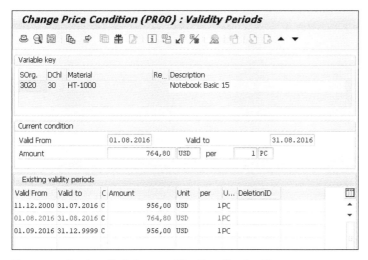

Figure 5.9 Create with Reference: Situation after the Change

The selected rounding rule 4 has ensured that the new values were set to zero in the second decimal place. In addition to rule 4, there are three other rounding rules in the standard SAP system (see Figure 5.10).

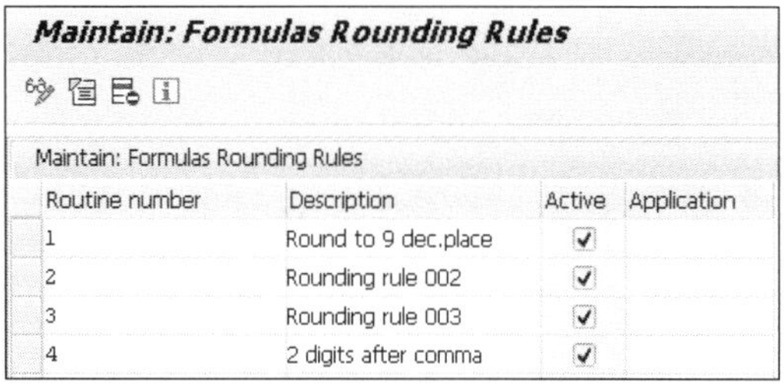

Maintain: Formulas Rounding Rules

Maintain: Formulas Rounding Rules

Routine number	Description	Active	Application
1	Round to 9 dec.place	✔	
2	Rounding rule 002	✔	
3	Rounding rule 003	✔	
4	2 digits after comma	✔	

Figure 5.10 Rounding Rules

Like most routines in SD, the rounding rules are maintained with Transaction VOFM (Maintain: Requirements and Formulas). The rounding rules can be found using menu path FORMULAS • ROUNDING RULES.

Since these are double-digit routine numbers, the customer namespace is from 50 to 99. By means of customer-specific rounding rules, the behavior when changing the condition amount can be affected in a specific way.

5.3   Copying Condition Records

The copy function enables you to copy the data of an existing condition record into another new condition record to reduce the maintenance effort. In the following sections we will look at some of the prerequisites as well as a practical example.

5.3.1   Prerequisites

The copy function is only available if, within the configuration of pricing, the appropriate copy controls for conditions is set up. The settings can be found using the menu path IMG • SALES AND DISTRIBUTION • BASIC FUNCTIONS • PRICING • COPY CONTROL FOR CONDITIONS.

An existing condition record has assigned a condition type and a condition table, referred to in the definition of the copying rules as *source condition type* and *source (condition) table*. On the Copying Rule for Condition Types screen, the possible assignment of target condition types to source condition types is performed (see Figure 5.11). In the screenshot, for example, two possible Target condit.types, K004 and K029, are assigned to the Source condit.type K004.

SC...	N..	Source condit.type	T..	Target application	TaC...	Target condit.type	
K004	01	Material	V	Sales/Distribution	K004	Material	
K004	02	Material	V	Sales/Distribution	K029	Mat.Pricing Group	
K005	01	Customer/Material	V	Sales/Distribution	K005	Customer/Material	
K007	01	Customer Discount	V	Sales/Distribution	K007	Customer Discount	
K007	02	Customer Discount	V	Sales/Distribution	K020	Price Group	
K020	01	Price Group	V	Sales/Distribution	K020	Price Group	
K020	02	Price Group	V	Sales/Distribution	K007	Customer Discount	
K029	01	Mat.Pricing Group	V	Sales/Distribution	K029	Mat.Pricing Group	
K029	02	Mat.Pricing Group	V	Sales/Distribution	K004	Material	
K030	01	Customer/Mat.Pr.Grp	V	Sales/Distribution	K030	Customer/Mat.Pr.Grp	
K032	01	Price Group/Material	V	Sales/Distribution	K032	Price Group/Material	
PR00	01	Price	V	Sales/Distribution	PR00	Price	

Figure 5.11 Copying Rule for Condition Types

The assignment of target condition tables to source condition tables is done in a second step. The following principles apply:

▸ If the condition tables of source and target condition records differ:

  ▹ Only one field may be different in the condition tables

  ▹ The condition tables must have the same number of fields

▸ If the condition types of source and targe condition record are different, the condition types must have the same calculation type, scale basis, condition class, and plus/minus sign rule.

It is possible to assign several target condition tables to one source condition table, in which case one of them is automatically marked as the proposed default rule. For example, Figure 5.12 shows that condition table 004 has assigned the condition tables 004 and 029.

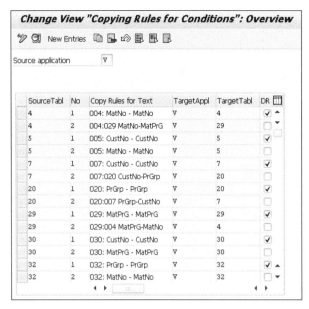

Figure 5.12 Copying Rules for Conditions (i.e., Condition Tables)

There is a detailed view (see Figure 5.13) for each entry in the overview screen.

Figure 5.13 Copying Rules for Conditions: Details Screen

Here, you assign the source and target fields. You also determine whether the expiration date of the source condition record is proposed in the target condition records. In addition, a selection report is assigned, which controls the selection screen for the selection criteria, which appears when you perform the copy function.

You can define your own selection report to use, for example, individual selection parameters. For this purpose, the standard report RV15CC01 is delivered as a template. This report also includes information for creating a new report in the customer namespace.

5.3.2   Application Example

Due to the previously presented customizing settings, the following situation arises when copying condition type K004 (material discount): Rule 1 is assigned as the proposed default rule but can be changed by clicking the SELECT RULE button (see Figure 5.14).

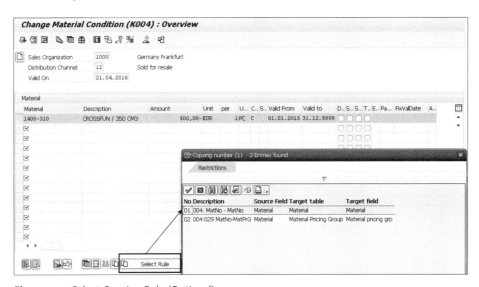

Figure 5.14 Select Copying Rule (Optional)

If you use rule 1 and click the ▭ COPY button, the associated selection screen is displayed. It will determine the number of the copied condition records (see Figure 5.15).

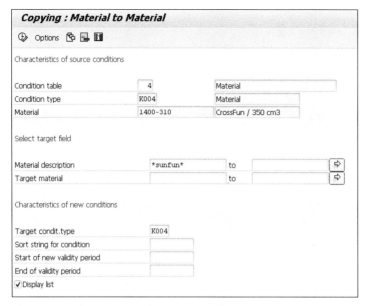

Figure 5.15 Selection Screen for Copying (Rule 1)

Due to the entry in the selection screen, all materials that have the text SUNFUN included in the short text are proposed in the results list (see Figure 5.16). For the selected entries, the corresponding condition records are then created with the values of the template condition record(s).

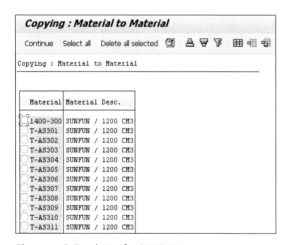

Figure 5.16 Result List for SUNFUN

In principle, copying is a very useful feature. However, if it is frequently used to copy prices of customer A to customers B and C, for example, that could be an indication that you might need to adapt your configuration. For example, you can define a new price condition type on customer group level, which is then applicable for customers A, B, and C with the commonly assigned customer group XY. That is, you then have a condition record that is valid for many customers, instead of many condition records for individual customers.

5.4 Condition Maintenance via Area Menus

As discussed in Chapter 2, Section 2.2, interesting opportunities may arise in individual cases when using special area menus. The area menus required for the following scenario cannot be maintained by the end users, but must be provided by a system administrator and be transported to the productive system.

The assignment of area menus can then be done by the user. After calling a maintenance transaction using area menus (VK31 to VK34), you can assign one or more existing area menus via menu path ENVIRONMENT • ASSIGNMENT AREA MENU. If you have assigned several area menus, you can use the NUMBER field to define the order of the resulting menu items (see Figure 5.17).

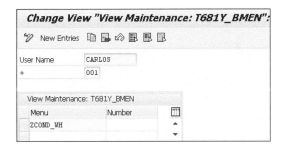

Figure 5.17 Assigment of the Area Menus

After assigning another area menu and restarting the transaction, the content of the new area menu is available and could look like Figure 5.18, for example.

If the user selects the menu item MOTO-MARKET GROUP, the underlying assigned pricing report is started in the associated variant as FILLED SELECTION SCREEN. It would make sense to hand over the maintenance of the variant (maintenance of the selection parameters, allocation of additional branches, etc.) to the department that's using it.

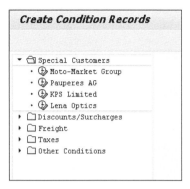

Figure 5.18 Personalized Area Menu

In addition to the assignment of area menus by the user via ENVIRONMENT • ASSIGNMENT AREA MENU, there is another, less well-known way for a centralized maintenance: Transaction SM30 (Maintain Table Views). The view is V_T681Y_ BMEN_USR. Here, the existing assignments can be displayed and maintained at the USER NAME level (see Figure 5.19).

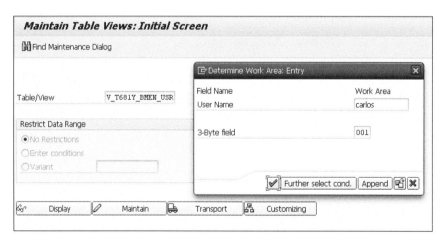

Figure 5.19 Area Menu Assignment Using Transaction SM30

In particular, for occasional users who are interested, for example, only in the prices of certain customers, such personalized area menus can be of assistance.

5.5 Other Functionalities in Condition Maintenance

In connection with condition maintenance, there are a number of issues that do not occur every day, and their solution is therefore not on the fast entry screen. Examples are questions such as, "Who changed this important price?" or "Can I enter a note with the condition record that explains why a rate of 70% is not a data entry error here?". We will discuss change documents, texts, handling of supplement conditions, and deleting conditions in this context.

5.5.1 Change Documents

As with all-important master data, changes in condition records are logged using change documents that can be evaluated if required. The change documents can be evaluated from the different maintenance transactions by choosing ENVIRONMENT • CHANGES • PER CONDITION RECORD for the selected condition record (see Figure 5.20).

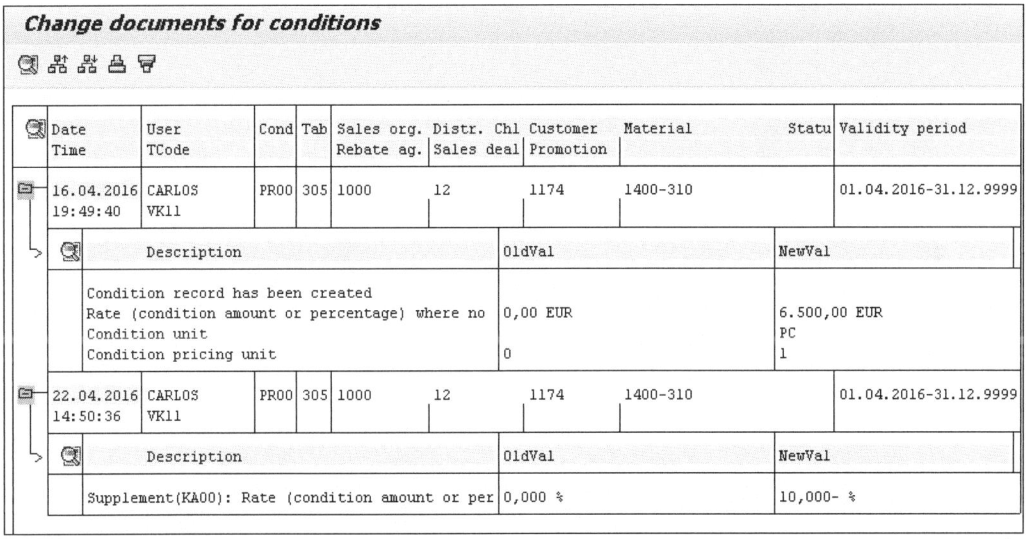

Change documents for conditions

Date Time	User TCode	Cond	Tab	Sales org. Rebate ag.	Distr. Chl Sales deal	Customer Promotion	Material	Statu	Validity period
16.04.2016 19:49:40	CARLOS VK11	PR00	305	1000	12	1174	1400-310		01.04.2016-31.12.9999

Description	OldVal	NewVal
Condition record has been created Rate (condition amount or percentage) where no Condition unit Condition pricing unit	0,00 EUR 0	6.500,00 EUR PC 1

Date Time	User TCode	Cond	Tab	Sales org. Rebate ag.	Distr. Chl Sales deal	Customer Promotion	Material	Statu	Validity period
22.04.2016 14:50:36	CARLOS VK11	PR00	305	1000	12	1174	1400-310		01.04.2016-31.12.9999

Description	OldVal	NewVal
Supplement(KA00): Rate (condition amount or per	0,000 %	10,000- %

Figure 5.20 Change Documents for Conditions

It is also possible to start a change report to track complex changes by choosing ENVIRONMENT • CHANGES • CHANGE REPORT (see Figure 5.21).

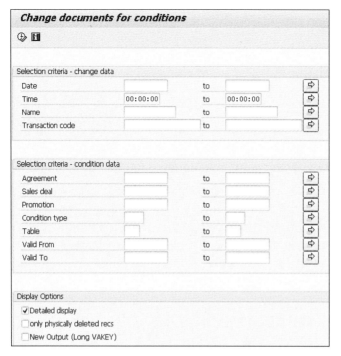

Figure 5.21 Selection Screen for Change Documents

This allows analyzing changes quickly, and you can contact the colleague who has changed the condition record in order to clarify the facts in question. Perhaps an inquiry would even be superfluous if you find an explanatory note as a text in the condition master record.

5.5.2 Texts

In condition maintenance, you can enter explanatory texts if the condition type has assigned a *text determination procedure*. The settings for configuring a text determination procedure can be found using menu path IMG • SALES AND DISTRIBUTION • BASIC FUNCTIONS • TEXT CONTROL • DEFINE AND ASSIGN TEXT DETERMINATION PROCEDURES.

A text determination procedure consists of a sequence of text types, which you can also easily create in the customer namespace. Figure 5.22 shows as an example the delivered text determination procedure for price conditions 01 (price).

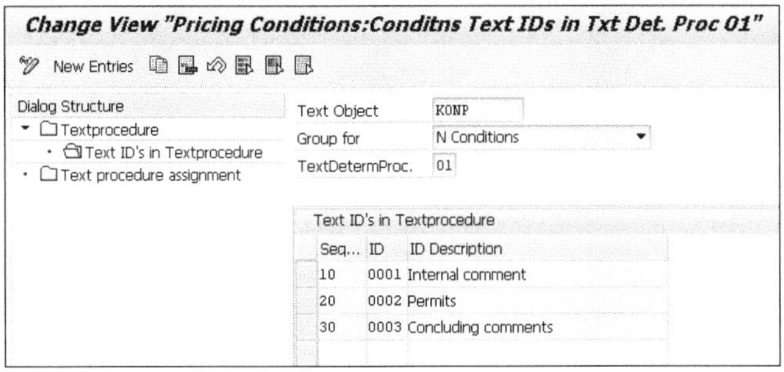

Figure 5.22 Text Procedure for Pricing Conditions 01 (Price)

The assignment of the text determination procedure to the condition type can be done in the text control Customizing, or alternatively in the configuration screen of the condition type (two views of the same data).

Together with the assignment of the text determination procedure, one of the text types contained has to be defined as a default text type for the TEXT EDIT CONTROL. For example, if we assigned the text determination procedure shown in Figure 5.22 to condition type PR00, a TEXT EDIT CONTROL subscreen will be displayed in the lower part of the DETAILS screen of the condition maintenance to allow the entry of text for the default text type (see Figure 5.23).

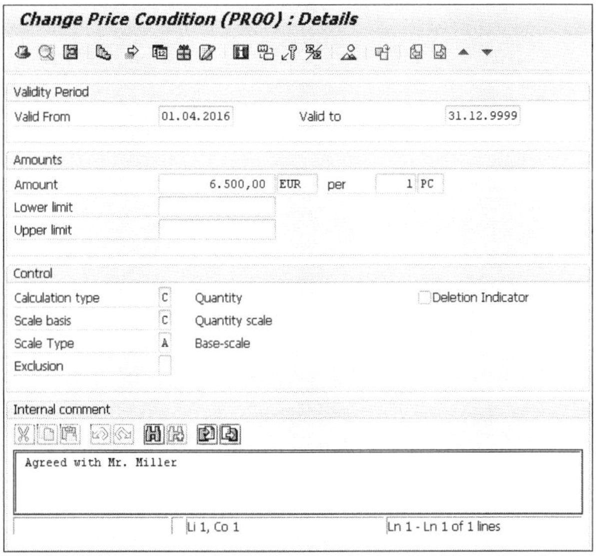

Figure 5.23 Text Maintenance in the Condition Details Screen

Out of the pricing analysis, you also have the option to display the condition records. Any existing text can provide useful information here.

5.5.3 Condition Supplements

We have already presented the prerequisites for the maintenance of condition supplements in Chapter 4, Section 4.2.3. Condition supplements do not have their own access sequence, but they are accessed together with the condition record, for which they are maintained. However, they must also be included in the pricing procedure determined for the respective sales document so that they can take effect. In pricing analysis, condition types that were found as condition supplements are specially marked as CONDITION SUPPLEMENT FOR <[CONDITION TYPE] XYZZ> (see Figure 5.24).

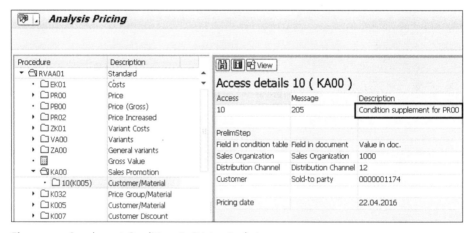

Figure 5.24 Supplement Conditions in Pricing Analysis

Finally, we would like to deal with the deletion of condition master data because, even with this issue, there are particular considerations.

5.5.4 Deletion of a Condition Record

The attribute DELETE FR. DB (delete from database) contained in the field group MASTER DATA in the configuration of the condition type, presented in Chapter 4, Section 4.2.3, controls how the system operates when deleting condition records. If the default value (blank) is configured, a deletion indicator is set so that the condition record is no longer used in pricing. The DELETION INDICATOR is displayed, for example, on the DETAILS screen of the condition maintenance (see Figure 5.25) and is stored in the LOEVM_KO field in the table KONP (see Figure 5.26).

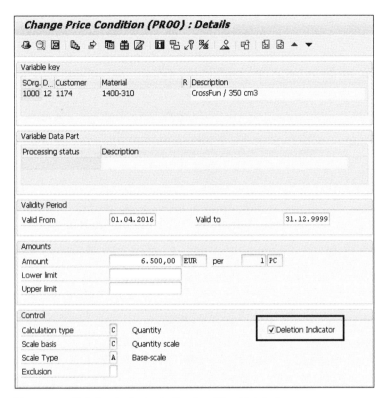

Figure 5.25 Deletion Indicator in the Condition Details Screen

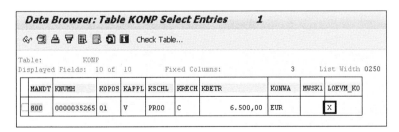

Figure 5.26 Deletion Indicator in the Database Table KONV

A condition record that was deleted under this configuration prerequisite is visible in the maintenance transactions until it is permanently removed by an archiving run.

Since SAP R/3 4.5, you can also choose the following two options for the attribute DELETE FR. DB:

- A
  You can delete the condition records from the database. You then receive a popup, asking whether the condition record should be deleted or whether the deletion indicator should simply be set.

- B
  You delete the condition records from the database. You only receive a popup if there are condition supplements available.

It should be noted that only the entry of the condition record is deleted in the corresponding A*** table. The KONP entry remains intact and bears the mark for deletion. These "invisible" components of the condition record will be deleted only with the archiving run.

5.6 Summary

Over time, the functions presented in the context of condition record maintenance have been updated and expanded because of development requests of SAP customers (for example, the *release status*), in order to meet the requirements even better. Our goal was to make you familiar with these functions, so that you can use them optimally in your environment, although they are not always found on the first look on the fast entry screen.

In the next chapter, we will build on this knowledge. We will be working intensively with the presentation and handling of the pricing results in various sales documents.

In this chapter, we discuss the representation and handling of pricing in the sales document.

6 Pricing in the Sales Document

Given the many ways to configure pricing, it is important that users understand the representation of the pricing result in order to use the possibilities of pricing successfully. Therefore, those responsible for pricing configuration must strive to provide maximum transparency, even in complex scenarios, when they develop their solutions. For example, sometimes the pricing result can be easier to understand if suitable subtotals are inserted in the pricing procedure.

Specifically, we discuss the following topics in this chapter:

- The item conditions screen
- The header conditions screen
- Predefined price elements
- Price agreements
- Pricing when creating documents with reference
- Pricing of rental and maintenance contracts (periodic billing plan)
- Pricing of fixed rate contracts (milestone billing plan)
- Pricing in resource-related billing

These various pricing scenarios are the reflection of a business complexity that requires the special characteristics of pricing presented here.

6.1 The Item Conditions Screen

In the ITEM OVERVIEW screen, there is important information available (see Figure 6.1).

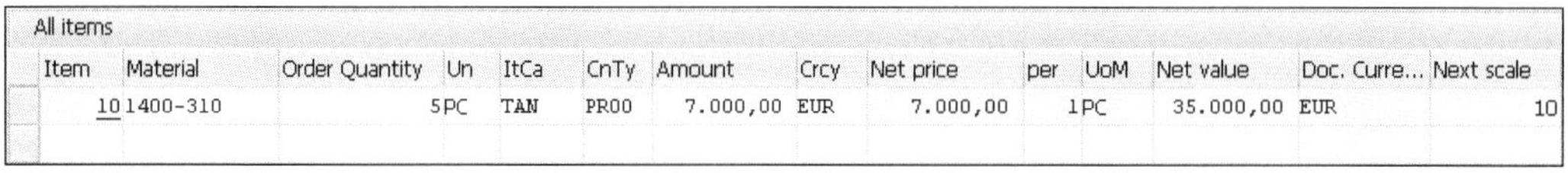

All items													
Item	Material	Order Quantity	Un	ItCa	CnTy	Amount	Crcy	Net price	per	UoM	Net value	Doc. Curre...	Next scale
10	1400-310		5 PC	TAN	PR00	7.000,00	EUR	7.000,00	1 PC		35.000,00	EUR	10

Figure 6.1 Price Information on the Overview Screen of the Sales Order

The condition type displayed in the ITEM line is specified in the respective Customizing entry for the pricing procedure determination (see Chapter 4, Section 4.1.6). This is usually the base price condition type of the pricing procedure (for example, PR00). The NET PRICE is the content of the field komp-netpr, and the calculated NET VALUE of the item. Less well known is the fact that, as additional information, the value for the NEXT SCALE can be displayed. NEXT SCALE can be used, for example, in a telephone sales order entry to point out to the customer that the price would be cheaper starting with, for example, ten pieces.

This standard information can be expanded since SAP ERP 6.0 EHP 4 after activating the business function LOG_SD_SIMP_02. By configuring the *predefined price elements*, more detailed information from the item pricing can be provided. This significantly speeds up order entry (see also Section 6.3).

However, the most important information and working tool when it comes to pricing in sales orders is the ITEM CONDITIONS screen (see Figure 6.2). You may always access this detail screen from the item overview if you are interested in reviewing more pricing details about an order item or if you need to make manual adjustments to the pricing at the item level.

On the CONDITIONS tab of the ITEM DATA screen, the details of the pricing for the current line item are shown. As long as no manual adjustments have been made, that representation is the result of the processing of the pricing procedure. The inactivity indicator in column 1 points out inactive or possibly faulty conditions.

The condition types determined automatically are ready for potential manual adjustments within the configured change options. Further information is highlighted (e.g., DISCOUNT AMOUNT) or provided (e.g., PROFIT MARGIN) by the subtotal rows. Statistical condition types complete the pricing information (e.g., CASH DISCOUNT for information about possible further sales deductions).

In Figure 6.2, the cursor is in an empty newline at the end of the ITEM CONDITIONS screen and more item conditions types can be added manually.

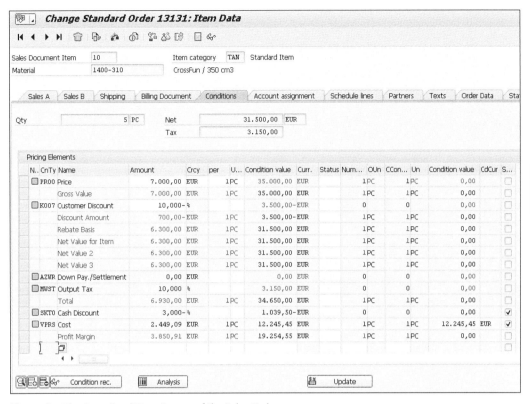

Figure 6.2 The Item Conditions Screen of the Sales Order

In the toolbar on the bottom-left of the screen, additional functions are available:

▸ CONDITION DETAIL

▸ INSERT ROW

▸ DELETE ROW

▸ MASTER DATA CONDITION RECORD

▸ ANALYSIS (PRICING LOG)

▸ UPDATE PRICES

For example, if the request would be to manually enter an agreed special price of 6,000 EUR per piece for the item, you could select the condition type PN00 (NET PRICE) using the input help. Since PN00 is another price and each item can only have one active price, all condition types preceding PN00 in the pricing procedure will automatically be set to inactive. This situation is illustrated in Figure 6.3.

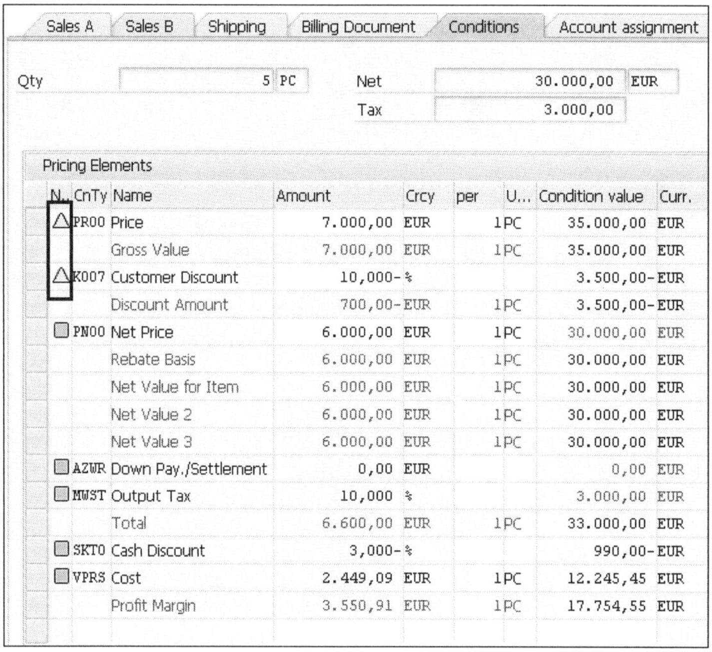

N..	CnTy	Name	Amount	Crcy	per	U...	Condition value	Curr.
⚠	PROO	Price	7.000,00	EUR		1PC	35.000,00	EUR
		Gross Value	7.000,00	EUR		1PC	35.000,00	EUR
⚠	KOO7	Customer Discount	10,000-	%			3.500,00-	EUR
		Discount Amount	700,00-	EUR		1PC	3.500,00-	EUR
☐	PN00	Net Price	6.000,00	EUR		1PC	30.000,00	EUR
		Rebate Basis	6.000,00	EUR		1PC	30.000,00	EUR
		Net Value for Item	6.000,00	EUR		1PC	30.000,00	EUR
		Net Value 2	6.000,00	EUR		1PC	30.000,00	EUR
		Net Value 3	6.000,00	EUR		1PC	30.000,00	EUR
☐	AZWR	Down Pay./Settlement	0,00	EUR			0,00	EUR
☐	MWST	Output Tax	10,000	%			3.000,00	EUR
		Total	6.600,00	EUR		1PC	33.000,00	EUR
☐	SKTO	Cash Discount	3,000-	%			990,00-	EUR
☐	VPRS	Cost	2.449,09	EUR		1PC	12.245,45	EUR
		Profit Margin	3.550,91	EUR		1PC	17.754,55	EUR

Figure 6.3 Inactivity in the Conditions Screen (See Callout Box)

This example also shows how important it is that you look for further condition details when needed, even though they may not be important during routine processing. In the example, the inactivity indicator has indeed shown that the conditions PR00 and K007 are inactive, but the exact reason—of which there may be several—is not mentioned. This and other information is provided on demand in the condition detail functionality, which we present in detail in the following section.

6.1.1 Condition Detail

As previously mentioned, complex constellations can occur because of the variety of pricing options and their interrelationship. Pricing control must keep track of these different situations. Therefore, control information such as the inactivity indicator are recorded on the condition detail level to meet these requirements.

In the previous example (see Figure 6.3), if you request the condition details for condition type PR00 (price), you will receive the information shown in Figure 6.4.

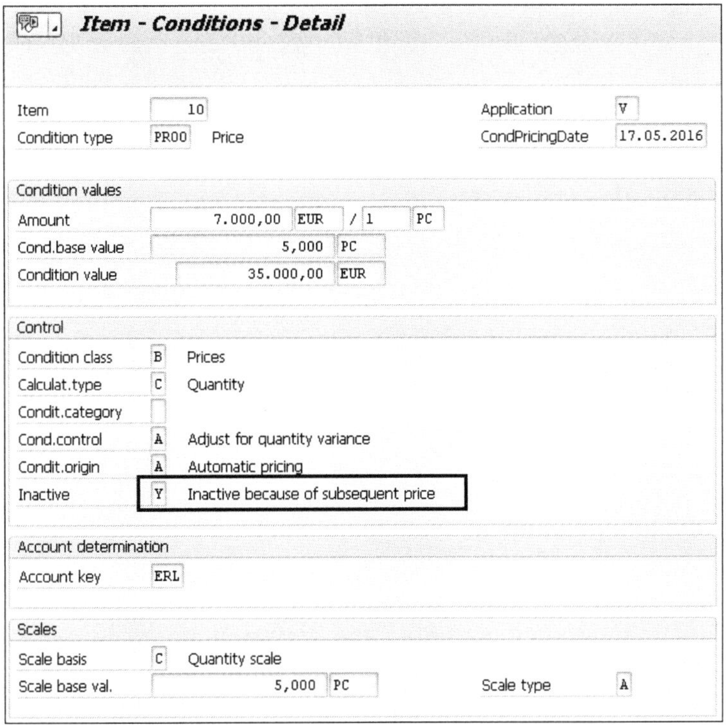

Figure 6.4 Condition Details at Item Level

In this detailed view, the condition type is inactive because of a subsequent price (inactivity control is set to Y). In addition to the already familiar information found in the CONDITION VALUES, ACCOUNT DETERMINATION, and SCALES field groups, you also see in the CONTROL field group the information on condition control (COND.CONTROL), origin of the condition (CONDIT.ORIGIN), and the INACTIVE indicator. This information is not deducted directly from the configuration attributes in Customizing, but has to do with the processing situation of the condition type in the sales document.

Condition Control

The COND.CONTROL field (xkomv-ksteu) provides information about whether the scale base, condition amount, condition basis, and condition value can be adjusted with changes in the item or whether they are fixed. It can have the following values:

- A: Adjust for quantity variance
- C: Changed manually
- D: Fixed
- E: Condition value and basis fixed
- F: Condition value fixed (billed items)
- G: Condition basis fixed
- H: Condition value fixed (cost price)

We will describe the relevance of the individual values of the condition control flag in Chapter 11, Section 11.7.

Origin of the Condition

The CONDIT.ORIGIN field can have the following values:

- A: Automatic pricing
- B: Duplicated from main item
- C: Manually entered
- D: Header condition
- E: Item total
- F: Condition supplement
- G: Original header condition
- H: Correction Rebate
- I: Cost Correction

Inactivity Indicator

The INACTIVE field can have the following values:

- A: Condition exclusion item
- K: Inactive due to calculation basis/shipping material type
- L: Condition exclusion header or inactive at header level

- ▸ M: Inactive due to manual entry
- ▸ T: Inactive at header level
- ▸ W: The document item is statistical
- ▸ X: Inactive via formula or incorrect
- ▸ Y: Inactive because of subsequent price

6.1.2 Insert Row

Using the INSERT ROW button, you can insert further item condition types that are included in the underlying pricing procedure for the document. Each condition type will be inserted exactly at the level where it is located in the pricing procedure. In the case of entering several condition types, the order of the insertion is not important, except for the special case where several condition types were placed at the same level in the pricing procedure by using the partial key counter.

6.1.3 Delete Row

Using the DELETE ROW button, all condition types whose configuration settings that allow for deletion can be deleted.

6.1.4 Master Data Condition Record

The MASTER DATA CONDITION RECORD button takes you directly to the condition master data to display any details of the condition record when needed.

6.1.5 Analysis (Pricing Log)

The analysis function allows you to trace the process of pricing for the current line item. While the ITEM CONDITIONS screen displays only the automatically found or manually added condition types, the ANALYSIS PRICING screen can help to explain a supposed malfunction of pricing. The ANALYSIS PRICING screen shows the complete path from the pricing procedure to the condition type and possibly the access sequence with the content of the fields used for accessing the condition records (see Figure 6.5). Thus, it is possible for every user with some experience to improve their understanding of how pricing works.

For some specifics of the pricing analysis, refer to Chapter 12, Section 12.2.

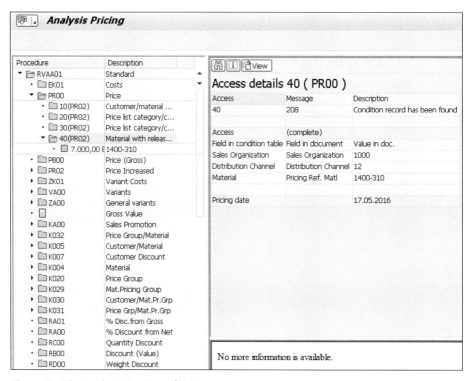

Figure 6.5 The Analysis Function of Pricing

6.1.6 Update Prices

With the UPDATE PRICES button, you can request a new pricing at the item level. Up until SAP R/3 4.0, pricing type B (carry out new pricing) was predefined for this function. Since SAP R/3 4.5, selecting the UPDATE PRICES button causes a popup window to appear which allows you to select the pricing type. Thus, all available pricing types can be selected, but pricing type B will certainly be the most frequent case.

6.1.7 Configurable User Interface for Pricing

In SAP ERP 6.0 EHP 7, comprehensive configuration options for the ITEM PRICING screen (CONDITIONS tab) have been delivered with the business functions LOG_SD_COMMODITY_02 and LOG_MM_COMMODITY_02. The basic idea is to provide users with different views on the pricing result that can be configured and assigned separately. This is especially useful if you have very complex pricing procedures, as it is often the case in the area of commodity trading. Thus, one view can include, for example, all commodity prices and another view can include only freight conditions. In the sales document, you can then choose between the different views (Figure 6.6).

Figure 6.6 Selecting the View of the Pricing Screen

Our typical CONDITIONS tab is represented by the view 1 PRICING ELEMENTS: TABLE. Another standard view is the *tree* in which all price elements are listed on the left side. Here you can easily view the corresponding details of the individual price elements on the right side. For example, the details of the configurable parameters and formulas that you learned in Chapter 4, Section 4.5, are visible in the tree details and can be maintained there.

You can find the relevant configuration settings for the configurable user interface under the menu path IMG • SALES AND DISTRIBUTION • BASIC FUNCTIONS • PRICING • CONFIGURABLE USER INTERFACE FOR PRICING.

You can also define your own views. In the simplest case, you may only want to see an excerpt of the pricing procedure, maybe even with a certain field selection. For this, you create a view of type CONFIGURED VIEW and assign the desired pricing details in the subsequent steps. Alternatively, for the view type CUSTOM VIEW, you can include your own screens and programs.

For example, in Figure 6.7 the condition type CBP1 is assigned independently of the pricing procedure to view 7501. In view 9007, the subtotal row 920 is only available when the underlying pricing procedure is CMCOP1. Thus, it is possible to grant access to sensitive information in the pricing screen like profit margin or cost access only to selected users.

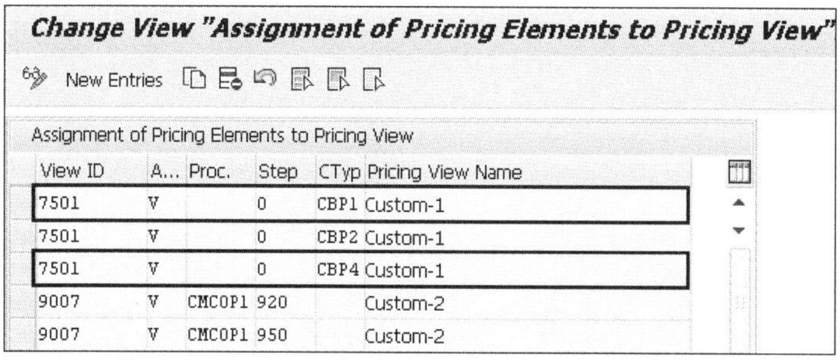

Figure 6.7 Assignment of Price Elements to Pricing Views

In addition, you can configure visibility and changeability of pricing fields per view—even dependent on the contents of other fields. You could, for example, hide individual parameters of CPF formulas.

Particularly helpful is the configuration for condition types that are determined via the Commodity Pricing Engine (CPE) and made available for pricing. Such conditions are calculated by formulas within the CPE that can contain complex rules for determining the listed stock exchange prices and a variety of other parameters.

Pricing views are assigned to one or more profiles, which you have previously defined. By the subsequent assignment of profiles to specific roles, you can specify which user group is allowed to view and edit selected price elements.

6.2 Header Conditions Screen

Pricing is performed for each pricing-relevant item. However, to enter header conditions, it is necessary to bring together the pricing data of all items in the HEADER CONDITIONS screen. You can access this screen by choosing GOTO • HEADER • CONDITIONS.

The display is similar to the item level, but shows a summary of all items (see Figure 6.8). Therefore, these accumulated item values are not changeable. However, you can manually add header conditions. When you insert such a condition type, the range of possible choices consists of a set of all condition types for the underlying pricing procedure that has been configured as a header condition (attribute HEADER CONDITION of the condition type).

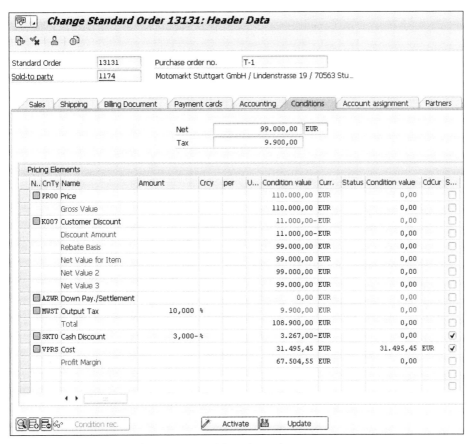

Figure 6.8 The Header Conditions Screen of the Sales Order

In the example of the pricing procedure RVAA01, this range of condition types looks like Figure 6.9. For example, it is possible to grant an agreed discount of 10% for a total sales order by entering the condition type HA00 (percentage discount) at the header level.

Header Conditions Are Distributed to the Items

Since the values of the HEADER CONDITIONS screen are available only during document processing and all header condition values entered must be distributed to the affected items, a header condition becomes part of the item and is stored accordingly on the item level. This distribution occurs when you leave the HEADER CONDITIONS screen or choose the ACTIVATE button.

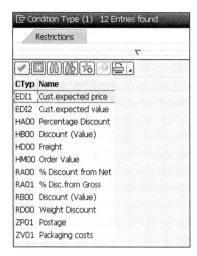

Figure 6.9 Example of a Value Range for Header Condition Types

A header discount HA00 of 10% can then be found in all affected ITEM CONDITION screens, and in turn cannot be edited there (see Figure 6.10).

Sales A	Sales B	Shipping	Billing Document	Conditions	Account assignment			

Qty		5	PC		Net		28.350,00	EUR
					Tax		2.835,00	

Pricing Elements

N..	CnTy	Name	Amount	Crcy	per	U...	Condition value	Curr.
	PR00	Price	7.000,00	EUR		1PC	35.000,00	EUR
		Gross Value	7.000,00	EUR		1PC	35.000,00	EUR
	K007	Customer Discount	10,000-	%			3.500,00-	EUR
		Discount Amount	700,00-	EUR		1PC	3.500,00-	EUR
		Rebate Basis	6.300,00	EUR		1PC	31.500,00	EUR
		Net Value for Item	6.300,00	EUR		1PC	31.500,00	EUR
	HA00	Percentage Discount	10,000-	%			3.150,00-	EUR
		Net Value 2	5.670,00	EUR		1PC	28.350,00	EUR

Figure 6.10 Representation of a Header Discount in the Item Conditions Screen

If you display the condition details for the condition type HA00, you get the screen shown in Figure 6.11.

The particular origin is tracked by condition origin D – HEADER CONDITION.

The UPDATE PRICES functionality that you already know from the item level is also available at the header level. If the function is called from the header level, all pricing-relevant items are subjected to new pricing with the selected pricing type. Note that any existing manual header conditions are not removed by this action, but are retained, possibly with adjusted values.

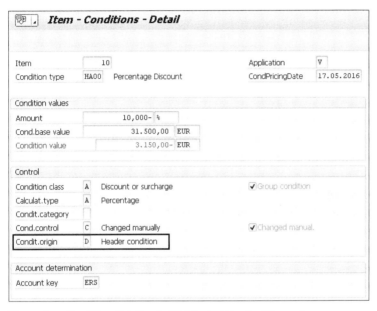

Figure 6.11 Condition Details of a Distributed Header Discount

You can also trigger this function using the menu path EDIT • NEW PRICING DOCUMENT. Then the pricing type is used that has been assigned to the pricing procedure (see Figure 6.12). If there is no pricing type assigned, pricing type B – CARRY OUT NEW PRICING is used by default.

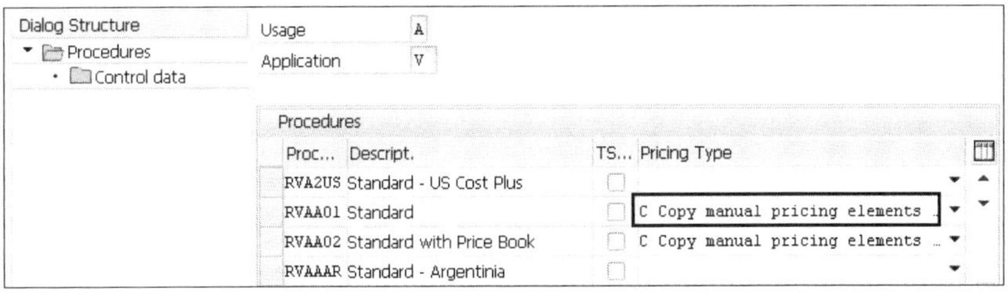

Figure 6.12 Assignment of Pricing Type on Pricing Procedure Level

6.3 Predefined Price Elements in the Item Overview Screen

Since SAP ERP 6.0 EHP 4, it is possible to enter or display *predefined price elements* in the table control of the ITEM OVERVIEW screen after the activation of the business function LOG_SD_SIMP_02 (Sales&Distribution Simplification 2 (Order-to-Cash)).

You can find the relevant configuration settings using the menu path IMG • SALES AND DISTRIBUTION • BASIC FUNCTIONS • PRICING • PREDEFINED PRICE ELEMENTS.

If, for example, the sales staff must often enter a specific discount condition manually, you can specify a predefined price element and assign this to a sales document type (e.g., to OR (Standard Order)). By doing this, the table control of the ITEM OVERVIEW screen is enhanced with this information. You can define, in addition to the condition amount, whether data such as condition currency, price unit, and condition quantity should be displayed too. For example, the condition type K007 (customer discount) configured as a predefined price element could look like that displayed in Figure 6.13.

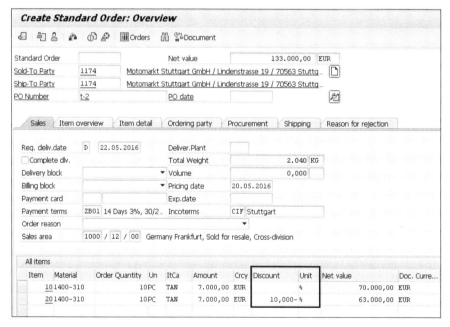

Figure 6.13 Predefined Price Elements

To illustrate the difference, in our example the same product was entered twice, wherein at item 20 a customer discount of 10% was granted—with the corresponding impact on net price and net value. It is clear that the underlying discount K007 is also displayed in the corresponding location in the ITEM CONDITIONS screen.

This procedure may result in substantial savings in processing time of the quotation or sales order in the appropriate operational environment.

6.4   Price Agreements

Using price agreements, you can create contract-specific and item-specific prices. Not only are values entered in the header or item CONDITIONS screen, but in this case new condition records are created in the background, that have in their keys, the document number that they were created, and which take effect immediately.

For service contracts, you can create the following price agreements:

▸ Condition records for the monthly service fee

▸ Condition records that offer the contract customer special prices for certain materials or material groups

One example of when you might want to use price agreements is if you want to offer a contract customer special prices for all spare parts he purchases.

6.4.1   Creating Price Agreements

You can enter a condition record for a monthly service fee for a service contract item directly in the OVERVIEW screen of the contract items. In the standard system, within the contract type SC (service and maintenance), the condition type PPSV (service price item) is provided for this purpose.

To create a condition record, select the PRICINGAGREEMENTDETAILS button (see Figure 6.14). Alternatively, choose the menu path EXTRAS • PRICE AGREEMENTS • ITEM. Price agreements at the header level are only accessible via the menu.

A maintenance screen for condition records is displayed. Here, click the OTHER CONDITION TYPE button (see Figure 6.15) before you can select the required condition.

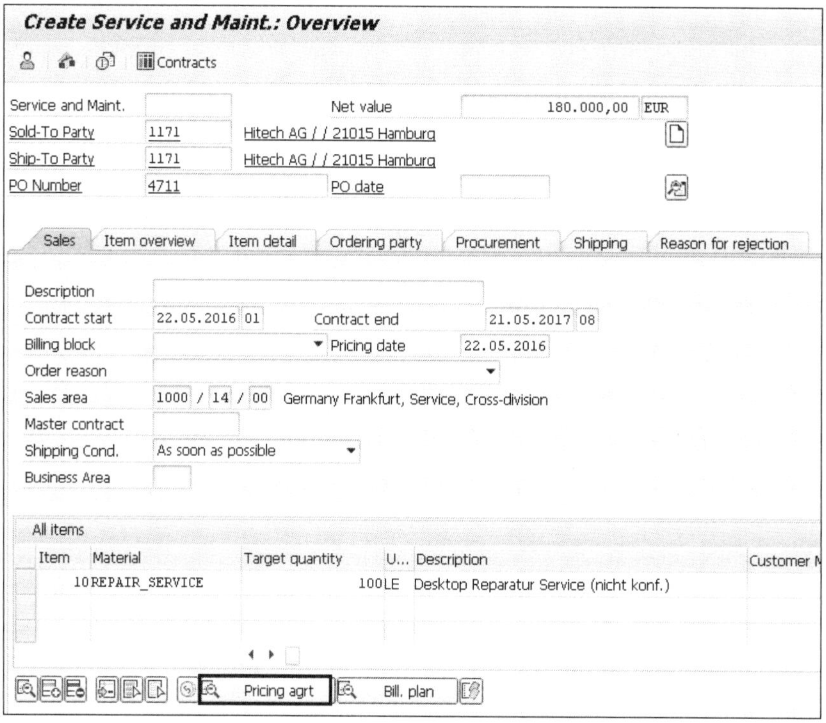

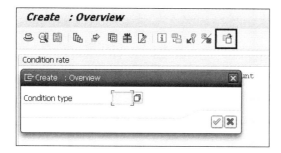

Figure 6.14 Create Price Agreement for an Item

Figure 6.15 The Other Condition Type Button

The set of allowed condition types for price agreements for contract items is determined by the pricing procedure PABR02 that is assigned in the configuration of the contract type SC in the field group CONTRACT (see Figure 6.16). However, this is not a real pricing procedure for pricing, but it is used as a grouping tool for determining the set of allowed condition types for price agreements.

Figure 6.16 Assignment of the Determination Procedures for Price Agreements

Since the contract has not yet been saved, the condition record initially contains the temporary sales document number $TEMP (see Figure 6.17).

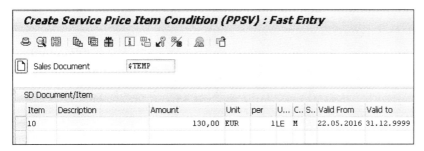

Figure 6.17 Create Price Agreement

In addition to the condition type PPSV (service price item), the standard SAP system offers additional condition types for creating contract-specific price agreements, as shown in Table 6.1.

Condition Type	Description
PPSV	Service price item
PKAR	Settlement price header
PPAG	Material group price item
PPAR	Settlement price item

Table 6.1 Condition Types for Price Agreements

The common feature of these condition types is the SALES DOCUMENT field in the key of the condition records.

6.4.2 Searching and Displaying Price Agreements Using the Condition Index

In conjunction with the price agreements, it might be useful to display existing condition records (see Figure 6.18). For this, you can use the selection via the index for sales document Transaction V/16.

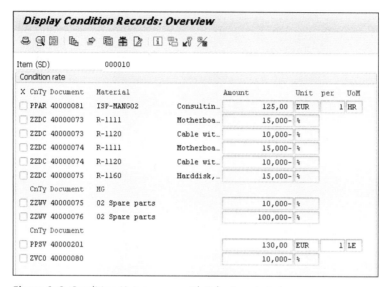

Figure 6.18 Condition Maintenance with Selection via Index

Here you can see a good example of using condition indices. With the condition index, you can efficiently find all price agreements (condition records) for sales documents.

6.5 Pricing During Creation of Documents with Reference

When creating documents with reference, pricing is determined by the pricing type. This is stored in the copying control at the item category level.

Here you have to take into account, for example, manually entered or changed conditions of the preceding document or to update the scale access to the condition record in the case of a reference with partial quantities. The desired behavior is defined by the selection of an appropriate pricing type.

For example, in the standard SAP system within the copying control of transaction type QT (quotation) to transaction type OR (standard order), pricing type A (copy price components and redetermine scales) is selected for the item category AGN (standard item) (see Figure 6.19). Thus, the demands are met.

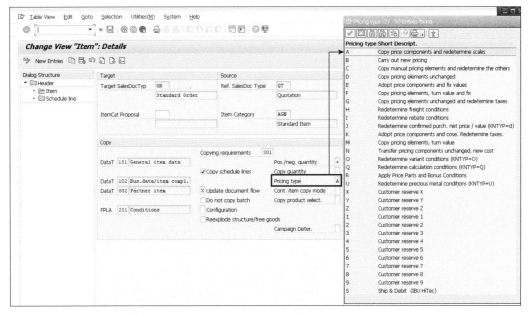

Figure 6.19 Assignment of the Pricing Type in Copying Control

For other requirements, a variety of standard pricing types is provided.

Moreover, it is possible to set up customer-specific pricing types. For this purpose, the customer-reserved naming scheme (X, Y, and Z and 1 to 9) is available. Some possible applications, such as the combination of several pricing types, are described in detail in SAP Note 24832 (pricing rules).

In Chapter 10, further technical details are described for this topic.

6.6 Pricing for Special Billing Scenarios

Rental and maintenance contracts, fixed price contracts and the resource-related billing require specific features within the pricing to provide the necessary functionality. In this section, we will have a closer look at those peculiarities.

6.6.1 Pricing in Rental and Maintenance Contracts (Periodic Billing Plan)

For rental and maintenance contracts, normally periodic billing, implemented by a *billing plan*, is used. At the item level, a detailed billing plan with multiple billing dates can be stored in the sales document instead of a single billing date.

The assignment of the billing plan type is carried out at the level of the item category. An example from the standard SAP system is item category WVN (maintenance contract item). The configuration of the item categories can be accessed via the menu path IMG • Sales and Distribution • Sales • Sales Documents • Define Item Categories (see Figure 6.20).

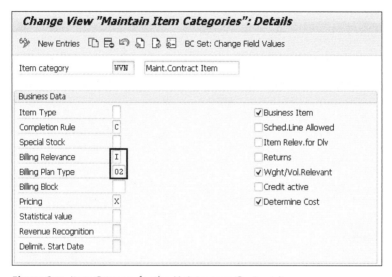

Figure 6.20 Item Category for the Maintenance Contract Item

In the configuration of item category WVN, the attribute Billing Relevance has the value I (order-relevant billing: billing plan). The associated billing plan type is 02 (Periodic Billing, see Figure 6.21).

The configuration of this billing plan can be accessed via the menu path IMG • Sales and Distribution • Billing • Billing Documents • Define Billing Plan Types.

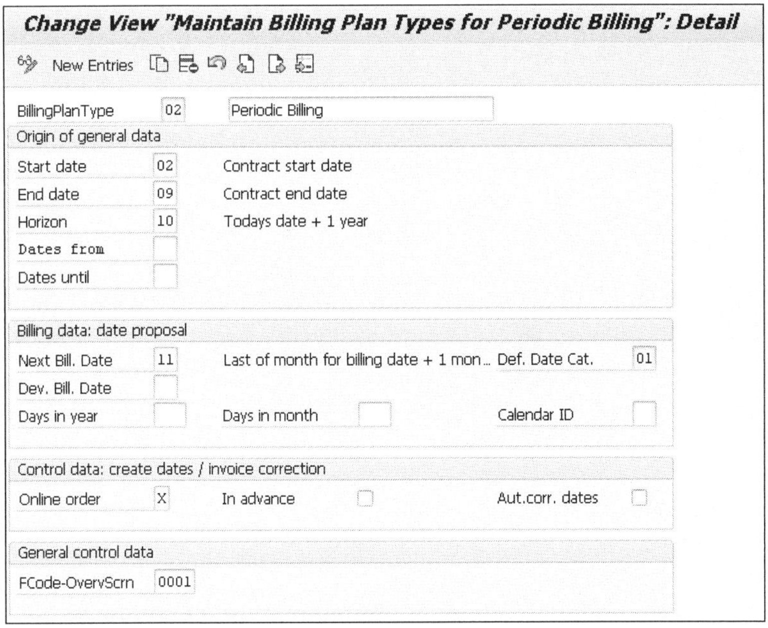

Figure 6.21 Billing Plan Type for Periodic Billing

Start and end dates define the duration of the billing plan and, if possible, are taken from the contract data. You may not set a final date, because you would like to agree on an unlimited duration. In this case, new dates can be added until reaching the *horizon*. The horizon specifies the number of billing periods that are set in the billing plan.

Let's return to the example of the maintenance contract from Section 6.4 (see Figure 6.14) and tie up the threads: In this example, we sell 100 activity units of REPAIR_SERVICE and receive the ITEM CONDITIONS screen shown in Figure 6.22. In the standard SAP system, the pricing procedure used in this scenario is PSER01 (periodic billing). For pricing procedure PSER01, see also Chapter 8, Section 8.1.4.

If we look at the billing plan for item 10, we see the situation shown in Figure 6.23, which results from the previously outlined settings for the underlying billing plan type (02). You can verify that the billing dates were created for the defined horizon TODAYS DATE + 1 YEAR and the currently valid price (condition PPSV) was used with the amount of 150.00 EUR per activity unit (LE).

Figure 6.22 Item Conditions Screen in the Maintenance Contract

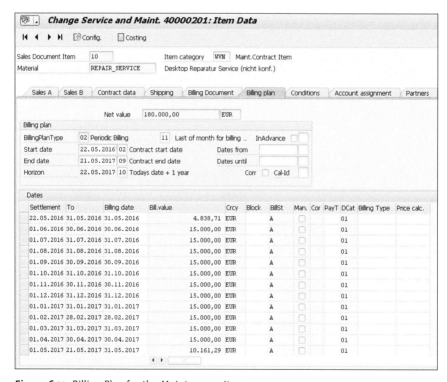

Figure 6.23 Billing Plan for the Maintenance Item

Now you can use the already featured price agreements (see Figure 6.12, Figure 6.13, Figure 6.14, and Figure 6.15) to perform a price increase effective, for example, at the VALID FROM date of 01.10.2016 (see Figure 6.24).

Change Service Price Item Condition (PPSV) : Overview

Sales Document	40000201									
Valid On										

SD Document/Item

Item	Description	Amount	Unit	per	U...	C..	S..	Valid From	Valid to
10		160,00						01.10.2016	31.12.9999

Figure 6.24 Maintenance Contract: Price Increase

After creating the price agreement, the billing plan is changed, starting with the 01.10.2016 settlement period, to use the newly created condition record with 160.00 EUR per LE (see Figure 6.25).

Dates

Settlement	To	Billing date	Bill.value	Crcy	Block	BillSt	Man.	Cor	PayT	DCat
22.05.2016	31.05.2016	31.05.2016	4.838,71	EUR		A	☐			01
01.06.2016	30.06.2016	30.06.2016	15.000,00	EUR		A	☐			01
01.07.2016	31.07.2016	31.07.2016	15.000,00	EUR		A	☐			01
01.08.2016	31.08.2016	31.08.2016	15.000,00	EUR		A	☐			01
01.09.2016	30.09.2016	30.09.2016	15.000,00	EUR		A	☐			01
01.10.2016	31.10.2016	31.10.2016	16.000,00	EUR		A	☐			01
01.11.2016	30.11.2016	30.11.2016	16.000,00	EUR		A	☐			01
01.12.2016	31.12.2016	31.12.2016	16.000,00	EUR		A	☐			01
01.01.2017	31.01.2017	31.01.2017	16.000,00	EUR		A	☐			01
01.02.2017	28.02.2017	28.02.2017	16.000,00	EUR		A	☐			01
01.03.2017	31.03.2017	31.03.2017	16.000,00	EUR		A	☐			01
01.04.2017	30.04.2017	30.04.2017	16.000,00	EUR		A	☐			01
01.05.2017	21.05.2017	31.05.2017	10.838,71	EUR		A	☐			01

Figure 6.25 Changed Billing Plan

The changed billing plan can take place before actually saving the maintenance contract and the associated price agreement, because the program has a special processing logic for this case.

As a prerequisite for this behavior, in the DATE CATEGORY (which is assigned to the billing plan type) the attribute PRICING must be set to trigger new pricing; for example, C - COPY MANUAL PRICING ELEMENTS AND PREDETERMINE THE OTHERS (see Figure 6.26).

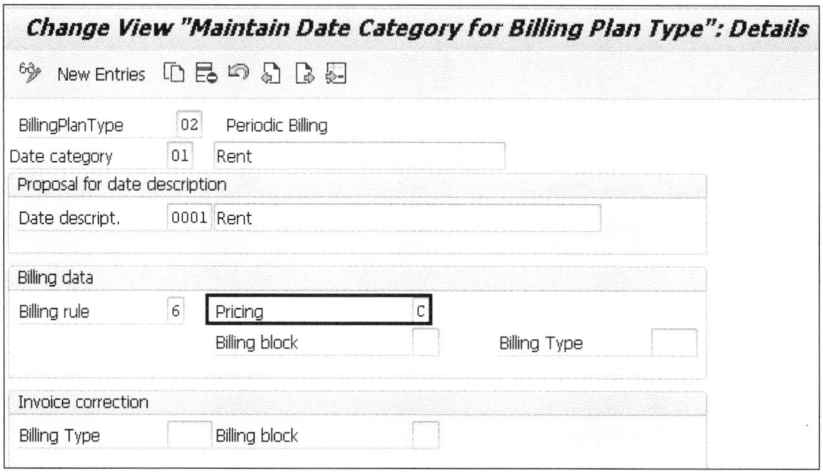

Figure 6.26 Date Category Triggering a New Pricing

In addition to the billing plans for periodic billing, there is yet another form for the processing of fixed price contracts.

6.6.2 Pricing in Fixed Price Contracts (Milestone Billing)

In fixed price contracts, which are used, for example, in plant construction, *milestone billing* is used, in which the total to be invoiced is divided according to certain rules on the individual dates of the billing plan. An example from the standard SAP system is the item category TAO (MILESTONE BILLING), as shown in Figure 6.27.

To understand the behavior of the pricing of fixed price contracts, we need to look in the configuration for billing plans.

In the configuration of the item category TAO, the attribute BILLING RELEVANCE has the value I (order-relevant billing, billing plan). The associated BILLING PLAN TYPE is 01 (MILESTONE BILLING, see Figure 6.28).

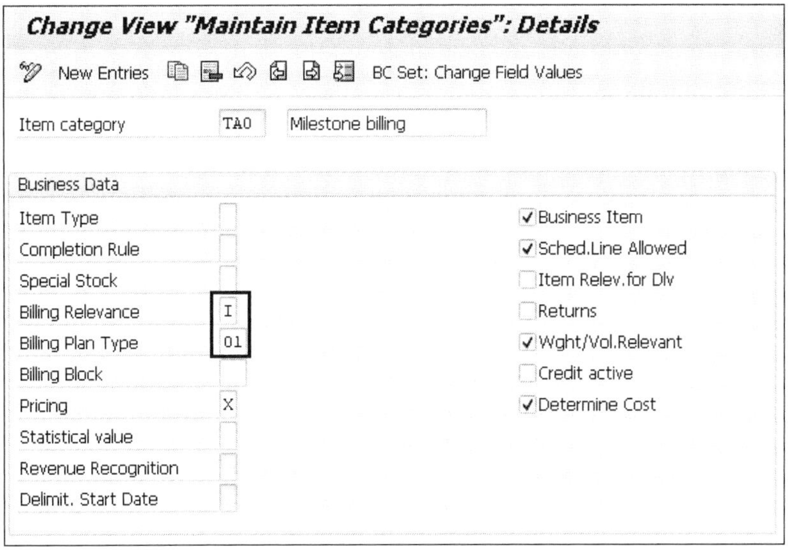

Figure 6.27 Item Category for Milestone Billing

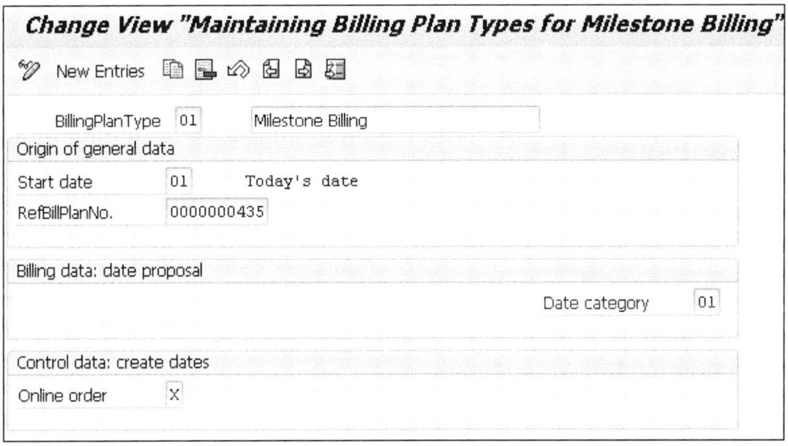

Figure 6.28 Billing Plan Type for Milestone Billing

To configure this billing plan go to IMG • SALES AND DISTRIBUTION • BILLING • BILL-ING PLAN • DEFINE BILLING PLAN TYPES.

In the ORIGIN OF GENERAL DATA field group, a standard billing plan is assigned. The system then takes over the dates of this standard billing plan as default values in the billing plan to be created. The dates are converted during the creation process according to the start date of the new billing plan.

The standard billing plan is maintained in the Customizing of the project system via the menu path IMG • PROJECT SYSTEM • REVENUE AND EARNINGS • PLANNED REVENUES • AUTOMATIC PLAN REVENUE CALCULATION • MAINTAIN BILLING PLAN SETTINGS.

Figure 6.29 shows the details of the default billing plan 435, assigned to the billing plan type 01. This billing plan type 01 in turn is assigned in the item category TAO. The dates include further controlling attributes BILLING RULE and DATE CATEGORY.

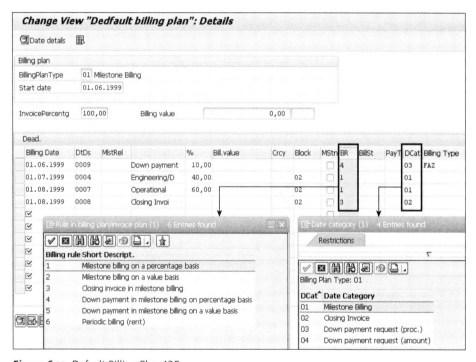

Figure 6.29 Default Billing Plan 435

If you now create a sample order with the included item category TAO (see Figure 6.30), you can observe the interaction of the settings.

Due to the default billing plan, the appropriate billing dates have been proposed based on the determined net price of 300,000 EUR.

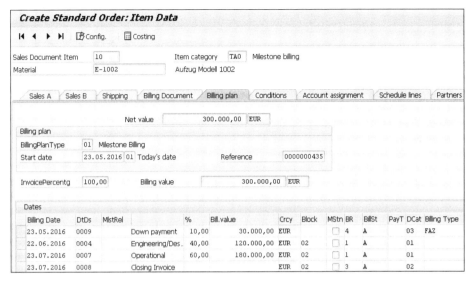

Figure 6.30 Sales Order with Milestone Billing Plan

For the first milestone, a down payment request for 30,000 EUR plus tax is created (see Figure 6.31).

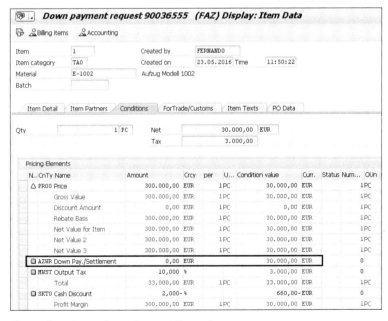

Figure 6.31 Create Down Payment Request

After receipt of the corresponding payment from the customer, the amount can be settled with the following milestone invoices. Here, the existing down payment amount is inserted as an additional billing item and can be adjusted in the ITEM CONDITIONS screen. In the example, the proposed value of EUR 30,000 was, for the first partial billing, reduced to 10,000 EUR (see Figure 6.32).

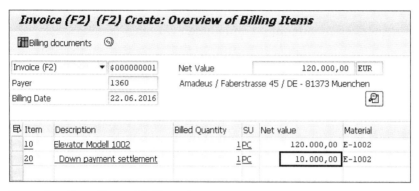

Figure 6.32 Down Payment Settlement

To make the example even more complex, we perform a subsequent price increase in the underlying sales order from 300,000 EUR to 320,000 EUR (see Figure 6.33).

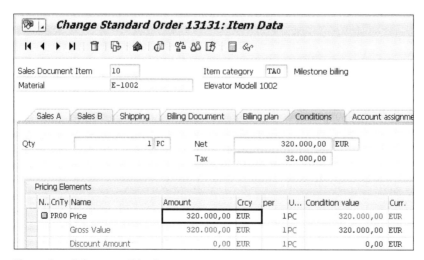

Figure 6.33 Subsequent Price Increase

Since the amounts for already billed dates cannot be changed in the billing plan, the additional 20,000 EUR is spread over the outstanding dates in the billing plan. That is, 60% of the total is added to OPERATIONAL and the rest is added to CLOSING INVOICE (see Figure 6.34).

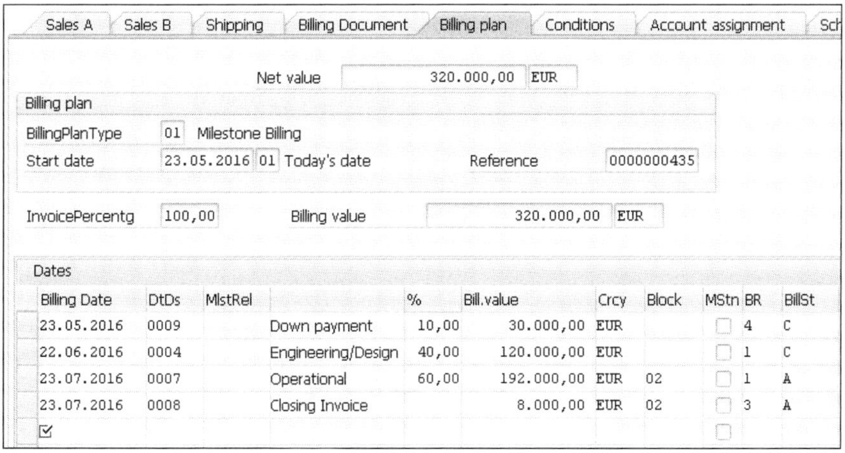

Figure 6.34 Impact of the Subsequent Price Increase on the Billing Plan

In the last milestone billing, which represents the final invoice, the untapped down payment amount of 20,000 EUR will be settled (see Figure 6.35). Thus, the sales order is fully invoiced.

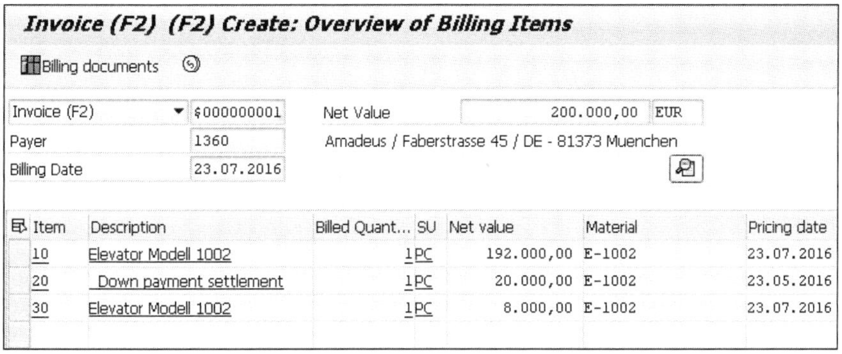

Figure 6.35 Milestone Billing: Final Invoice

During this process, the function module `PRICING_COPY` plays a central role in determining the specific billing values. We will discuss this function module in more detail in Chapter 10, Section 10.3.

6.6.3 Pricing in Resource-Related Billing

Since with service contracts not all services are generally covered by the contract, an executed service order is billed using resource-related billing.

If a service order is created with reference to a service contract, the system calculates the price for the billing request (Transaction DP90) using the price agreements in the underlying service contract (see Figure 6.36).

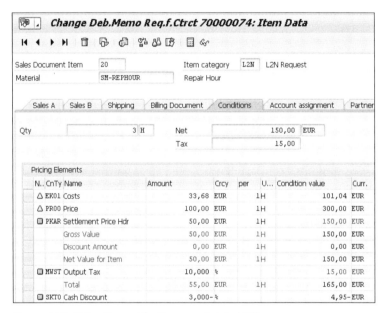

Figure 6.36 Billing Request for Resource-Related Billing

The connection is established in the respective access sequence by the field VGBEL (document number of the reference document) (see Figure 6.37).

The pricing procedure PSER02 (resource related billing) is used in the standard SAP system for this process. We will discuss this in more detail in Chapter 8, Section 8.1.5.

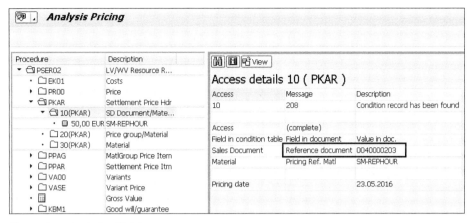

Figure 6.37 Analysis of Pricing

6.7   Summary

After reading this chapter, you should now be familiar with the representation and handling of the pricing result in several important areas. In addition, you have gained insight into related Customizing areas (e.g., billing plans) to better understand the featured functions of pricing and its context.

In the next chapter, we will deal in detail with important special functions and thereby continue moving toward an accurate overall picture of pricing.

In this chapter, we deep dive into functionalities that we touched on during the configuration of pricing. In addition, we round off the overall picture of pricing by elaborating on other important topics, e.g., tax determination.

7   Special Functions in Pricing

In addition to the condition technique and the calculation of values based on found condition records, pricing consists of many functions, the most important of which we will explore more deeply in this chapter. We will discuss about the following topics:

- ▶ Group conditions for cross-item activities
- ▶ The condition exclusion for handling dependencies between condition types
- ▶ The condition update for tracking limit values and for statistical evaluations
- ▶ The specific features of tax determination in sales and distribution
- ▶ Free goods and their effects on pricing
- ▶ The cost and contribution margin determination in a sales transaction as a basis for price negotiations
- ▶ Currencies and exchange rates and their interactions within pricing and documents
- ▶ The print formatting of the pricing result

Let's start with a topic that is one of the most challenging in pricing: the group conditions.

7.1   Group Conditions

In the configuration settings for condition types (see Chapter 4, Section 4.2.3), you can characterize a condition type as a *group condition*. If necessary, a routine number for creating a group key can be specified for condition types with scales. We will encounter group conditions a few times more in this book. This section summarizes the different options briefly; detailed information and examples appear in other chapters.

Definition: Group Conditions

Group conditions are condition types that undergo a final valuation by the `PRICING_COMPLETE` function module at the point in time "document end processing". Within this program, manual header conditions are being distributed to the document items, a rounding difference comparison is carried out, and a cross-item accumulation of the scale bases is performed. This results in an adjustment of the condition percentages and amounts.

If we look at the pricing of an order item, common condition types without the attribute GROUP CONDITION are evaluated independently of the other items in an order. However, group conditions have the property that allows the other items in the order to influence the valuation. In the following sections, we will look at the different types of group conditions.

7.1.1 Header Conditions with a Fixed Amount

Header conditions are condition types without an access sequence that are entered manually in the HEADER CONDITIONS screen of the sales order. Header conditions with the calculation type FIXED AMOUNT are distributed to the individual order items according to a freely definable distribution key. A *rounding difference comparison* is carried out and a potential rounding difference is then added to the item with the largest value. When the header conditions are distributed among the items, the requirements in the pricing procedure are checked. As a result, certain items could be excluded from the distribution. For technical reasons, header conditions are identified as group conditions since the distribution to the items is carried out together with the other group conditions in the function module `PRICING_COMPLETE`.

7.1.2 Percentage-Based Header Conditions

Header conditions with the calculation type PERCENTAGE are also distributed to the items. A rounding difference comparison is performed and a potential rounding difference is then added to the item with the largest value. The requirements are checked and, as a result, the condition could not be granted for certain items.

7.1.3 Scale-Based Conditions without Group Key

For a condition record with scales, the scale base is determined over all items in which the condition record was found. In this case, no group key routine is used.

7.1.4 Scale-Based Conditions without Group Key

If a group key routine is used for a condition record with scales, the accumulation of the scale base is performed on a level different from the level given by the key of the condition record itself. The accumulation level is determined by the group key routine. In the case of quantity scales, you must always specify the attribute UNIT OF MEASURE in the configuration of the condition type (in the field group SCALES). All item quantities must then be convertible into this unit. For example, you can accumulate the scale base for the following:

- All items in the sales document that have the same condition as the group condition currently being processed (group key routine 001, total document).
- All items in the sales document independent of which condition types have been found (group key routine 002, across all condition types).
- All items in the sales document that have the same material pricing group (group key routine 003, mat. pricing group).

The group key functionality is quite special and rarely used.

7.1.5 Percentage-Based and Fixed Amount Group Conditions with Condition Records

The condition types, which are determined automatically using condition records, are treated the same as manual header conditions with respect to the distribution mechanism and the rounding difference comparison.

Rounding Difference Comparison

A *rounding difference comparison* is performed only for percentage-based and fixed amount group conditions.

The cross-item activities presented here are performed in the function module PRICING_COMPLETE. For detailed technical information on this program, see Chapter 10, Section 10.2. A concrete example of the operation of scaled conditions with and without a group key routine is presented in Chapter 11, Section 11.4.4.

7.2   Condition Exclusion

During pricing, condition types can be found that are mutually exclusive. For example, a specially agreed customer discount should exclude discounts by a general sales campaign, or the most favorable price for a customer should be taken. In practice, there are many varieties of contradictory condition types. Most of them can certainly be implemented with the possibilities of the standard pricing configuration. When excluding conditions, three different methods can be used which are dealt with in more detail here:

▶ Simple condition exclusion using requirements (Customizing)

▶ Complex condition exclusion using exclusion groups (Customizing)

▶ Condition exclusion using formulas

The configuration for the first two methods can be found using menu path: IMG • SALES AND DISTRIBUTION • BASIC FUNCTIONS • PRICING • CONDITION EXCLUSION.

7.2.1   Simple Condition Exclusion Using Requirements

For the simple condition exclusion using requirements, in the configuration for condition types (see Chapter 4, Section 4.2.3), you can assign a default exclusion indicator to the field EXCLUSION in the field group CONTROL DATA 2. For this condition type, the field EXCLUSION will be then be filled with this indicator by default when you create a condition record. You can also enter the indicator within the condition maintenance for selected condition records. In pricing, when such a condition record is found, the exclusion indicator is transferred to the field komp-kznep in the communication structure KOMP.

Requirements in the pricing procedure can then check the field komp-kznep and, as a result, subsequent condition types may be not determined (excluded). For example, the requirement 002 (item with pricing) delivered with the standard

SAP system checks to determine if the exclusion indicator is not initial. A condition record with an exclusion indicator thus causes all subsequent condition types having requirement 002 assigned in the pricing procedure to be ignored. The source code of requirement 002 (see Listing 7.1) gives you a first impression of the operation.

```
form kobed_002.
  sy-subrc = 4.
  if komp-kposn ne 0.
    check: komp-prsfd ca 'BX'.
    check: komp-kznep = space.
  endif.
  sy-subrc = 0.
endform.
```
Listing 7.1 Exclusion Check via Requirements

You can extend the range of values for the exclusion indicator in Customizing according to personal needs, and the values 0 to 9 and Z are reserved for customers.

The advantage of this method lies in the performance. However, there are two disadvantages: the lack of transparency and it needs to be ensured that when a new pricing is performed all dependent condition types are recalculated. We therefore recommend that you use the second method—condition exclusion using exclusion groups—unless you have problems with the system performance.

7.2.2 Condition Exclusion Using Exclusion Groups

For this method, you first set up *exclusion groups* and assign condition types to these groups. In the following example, we established five exclusion groups:

▸ Z901 with the condition type PR00

▸ Z902 with the condition types K020 and K029

▸ Z903 with the condition types K031 and HI01

▸ Z904 with condition PBBS

▸ Z905 with condition Z905

In a second step, you define the exclusion procedures for your pricing procedure, as shown by the example in Figure 7.1 using the pricing procedure ZVAA01.

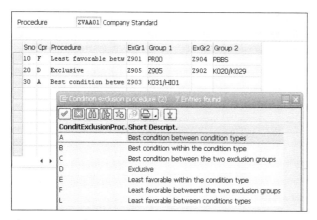

Figure 7.1 Condition Exclusion for Pricing Procedure ZVAA01 (Company Standard)

In the input help for the *condition exclusion procedure*, you will find the following values:

▶ **A, L**

All conditions found within the exclusion group are compared and the best/least favorable condition is chosen. All other conditions are deactivated.

▶ **B, E**

All conditions found for each condition type within the exclusion group are compared and the best/least favorable condition is chosen per condition type. This procedure makes sense only for condition types with additive access sequences.

▶ **C, F**

The total value of the condition records found for exclusion group 1 is compared to the total value of the condition records found for exclusion group 2. The conditions of the best/least favorable group are kept and the conditions of the other group are deactivated.

▶ **D**

Group 1 excludes group 2. If at least one condition record is found for group 1, all conditions of group 2 are deactivated.

During condition exclusion using exclusion groups, conditions are disabled by setting the INACTIVE flag to A in the affected pricing procedure steps. Note, however, that only the conditions that have a non-zero value are considered as found. Especially with surcharges, it may be desirable to include zero values in the value comparison. You can do this by assigning in the pricing procedure the condition value formula 038 (exclusion with value zero) to one of the condition types involved.

7.2.3 Condition Exclusion Using Formulas

In cases where the previous methods do not accomplish your goal, you can use formulas.

The following example is of a condition exclusion using a value formula. The request is if the discounts Z905, K007, and K004 are found simultaneously, the item is to be granted at least the value of discount RA01. This requirement corresponds to exclusion procedure C, but on the precondition that all conditions of the group occur simultaneously.

We can meet the requirement as follows:

1. We create a new value formula 901 (see Listing 7.2) and assign it to the condition type RA01 in the pricing procedure.

```
form frm_kondi_wert_901.
  check: preisfindungsart ne 'E'.
  data: zwert like komv-kwert,
        zwert2 like komv-kwert.
  if not xworkf is initial
    and not xworkg is initial
    and not xworkh is initial.
    zwert = xworkf + xworkg + xworkh.
    if zwert le xkwert.
      clear xkwert.
      xkomv-kinak = 'X'.
    else.
      zwert2 = xkwert - zwert.
      xkwert = zwert2.
    endif.
  else.
    clear xkwert.
    xkomv-kinak = 'X'.
  endif.
endform.
```

Listing 7.2 Value Formula 901 Condition Exclusion

2. Condition type Z905 is assigned in the pricing procedure SUBTOTAL = F. Thus, the value of the condition type is cached in the working variable xworkf. If the

indicator SUBTOTAL is already used for other purposes, you can set up instead the new value formula 925 (add up `xworkf`) (see Listing 7.3) and assign it to the condition type.

```
form frm_kondi_wert_925.
  add xkwert to xworkf.
endform.
```

Listing 7.3 Value Formula 925: Add Up Variable xworkf

3. Condition type K007 gets assigned SUBTOTAL = G. Alternatively, use the value formula 926 (see Listing 7.4).

```
form frm_kondi_wert_926.
  add xkwert to xworkg.
endform.
```

Listing 7.4 Value Formula 926: Add Up Variable xworkg

4. Condition type K004 gets assigned SUBTOTAL = H. Alternatively, use the value formula 927 (see Listing 7.5).

```
form frm_kondi_wert_927.
  add xkwert to xworkh.
endform.
```

Listing 7.5 Value Formula 927: Add Up Variable xworkh

Thus, the objective is achieved with minimal coding effort and good performance. How does this solution operate?

It should first be noted that this solution only works properly under one precondition: the condition type RA01, which is manipulated by formula 901, is positioned in the pricing procedure after the condition types Z905, K007 and K004. During the valuation, the condition type RA01 is thus processed as the last of the condition types involved.

You can see by the example in Figure 7.2 that the condition types Z905, K007, and K004 show a value of 3.39- EUR in total. Since RA01 calculates a 3% discount of EUR 3,60-, the routines have to make sure that this 3.60- EUR discount is granted. We achieve this with the value formula 901, which assigns to RA01 in this case the remainder of the discount totaling 0.21- EUR. Therefore, we will get a total discount of 3.60- EUR. The trick here is that we do not deactivate the excluded condition types (because we cannot change any previous condition types in value formulas), but we make sure by assigning the remainder that the condition type RA01 wins the exclusion task.

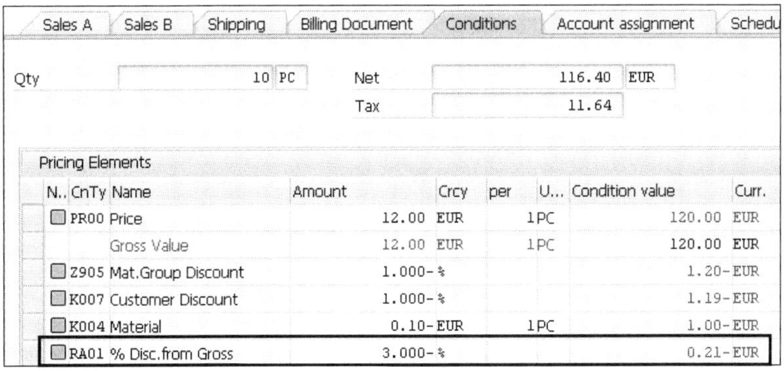

N..	CnTy	Name	Amount		Crcy	per	U...	Condition value		Curr.
	PR00	Price		12.00	EUR		1PC		120.00	EUR
		Gross Value		12.00	EUR		1PC		120.00	EUR
	Z905	Mat.Group Discount		1.000-	%				1.20-	EUR
	K007	Customer Discount		1.000-	%				1.19-	EUR
	K004	Material		0.10-	EUR		1PC		1.00-	EUR
	RA01	% Disc.from Gross		3.000-	%				0.21-	EUR

Sales A / Sales B / Shipping / Billing Document / Conditions / Account assignment / Schedu

Qty — 10 PC — Net — 116.40 EUR — Tax — 11.64

Pricing Elements

Figure 7.2 Condition Exclusion with Formula 901: RA01 Valid

In the example of Figure 7.3, RA01 has a discount of 2% corresponding to a value of EUR 2.40-, which is less than the total of Z905, K007, and K004. As a result, in this case RA01 is disabled by the value formula 901.

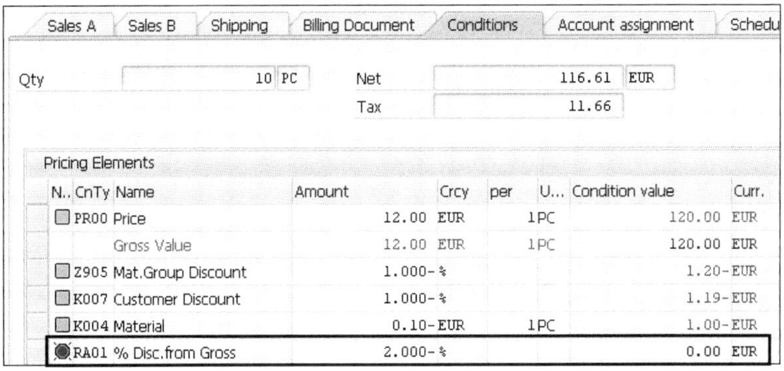

Sales A / Sales B / Shipping / Billing Document / Conditions / Account assignment / Schedu

Qty — 10 PC — Net — 116.61 EUR — Tax — 11.66

Pricing Elements

N..	CnTy	Name	Amount		Crcy	per	U...	Condition value		Curr.
	PR00	Price		12.00	EUR		1PC		120.00	EUR
		Gross Value		12.00	EUR		1PC		120.00	EUR
	Z905	Mat.Group Discount		1.000-	%				1.20-	EUR
	K007	Customer Discount		1.000-	%				1.19-	EUR
	K004	Material		0.10-	EUR		1PC		1.00-	EUR
	RA01	% Disc.from Gross		2.000-	%				0.00	EUR

Figure 7.3 Condition Exclusion with Formula 901: RA01 Inactive

We have presented in this section a meaningful example of how formulas can be used efficiently. With our next topic, the condition update, you will become familiar with another function that provides various adaptation possibilities, again of course with the use of formulas.

7.3   Condition Update

In Customizing for condition types (see Chapter 4, Section 4.2.3), the attribute CONDITION UPDATE is available in the field group MASTER DATA. This indicator can be set only if the condition type has assigned an access sequence, which means that condition records can be created for this condition type. CONDITION UPDATE consists of the following functionality:

1. For a found condition record, the statistics table S071 is updated in the case of a sales order and table S060 in case of a billing document. Detailed information can be found in Chapter 12, Section 12.1. There we show how the accumulated data can be used beyond the standard functionality to meet budgeting requirements.

2. When maintaining condition records for a condition type with condition update, three additional fields, as shown in Figure 7.5, are available in the DETAILS screen, allowing you to set limits.

   ▸ You can *limit the condition value* to be granted. For example, we want to grant a discount of 3%, but at most 1,000 EUR for the total of all affected orders.

   ▸ You can set a *maximum condition basis value*. For example, we want to grant a discount of 2.00 EUR per piece, but only for 1,000 pieces in total.

   ▸ You can set a *maximum number of orders* for which a discount is to be granted. In particular, you can define that a discount is only applied to the first order within a period.

3. In condition maintenance, the CUMULATIVE VALUES button is available (menu path is GOTO • ADDITIONAL DATA • CUMULATIVE VALUES), by means of which you can display the accumulated condition value and condition base value for orders and billing documents. In addition, you can display the first three order numbers for which the condition record was found.

In the following example, we activate the condition update for condition type K005, and then enter a condition record for customer 1360 and material DPC4000 with a discount of 50.00 EUR per piece and a maximum number of 10 pieces (see Figure 7.4 and Figure 7.5).

By choosing the ADDITIONAL DATA button (see Figure 7.4), you reach the ADDITIONAL DATA screen (see Figure 7.5), in which you can maintain the limits.

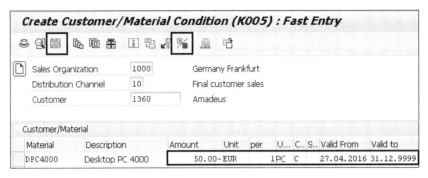

Figure 7.4 Condition Record for Condition Type K005

Limits for pricing		
Max.condition value		EUR
Max.number.of.orders		
Max.cond.base value	10	PC

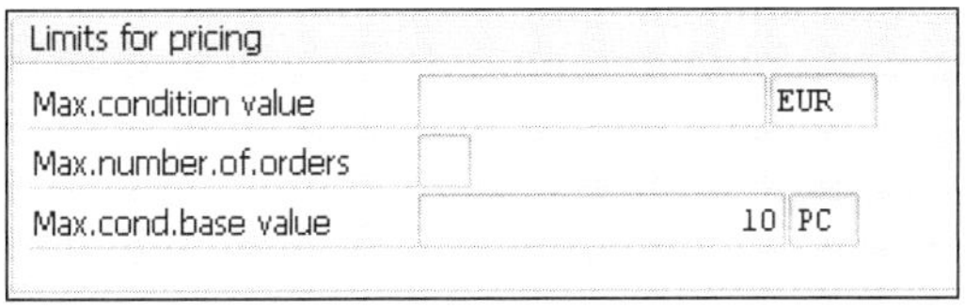

Figure 7.5 Condition Record for Condition Type K005 (Additional Data)

After creating the condition record, we create two sales orders with quantities of five and three pieces. In the condition maintenance, we now choose the CUMULATIVE VALUES button (see Figure 7.4) and check the values displayed in Figure 7.6, showing the accumulated values and quantities for sales orders per period.

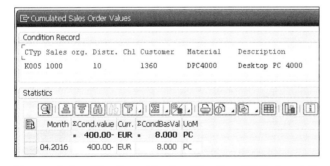

Figure 7.6 Condition Record for Condition Type K005: Cumulative Order Values

There you can click on the FIRST SALES ORDERS button and get the information presented in Figure 7.7 or you can display, by clicking the BILLING VALUES button, the accumulated values for the existing billing documents.

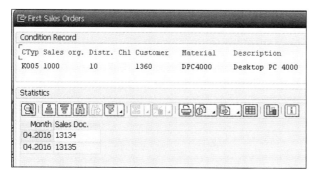

Figure 7.7 Condition Record for Condition Type K005: First Sales Orders

Now we create an additional sales order for five pieces. As we have previously sold eight pieces, only two pieces are left up to the limit of ten pieces. In the CONDITION DETAILS screen (see Figure 7.8) for condition K005 of the order item, you can see that two pieces have been identified as the condition base value. The fact that MAXIMUM BASE VALUE is set to X tells us that the condition basis value was cut off. Because as long as the limit is not reached, we have a MAXIMUM BASE VALUE = Y.

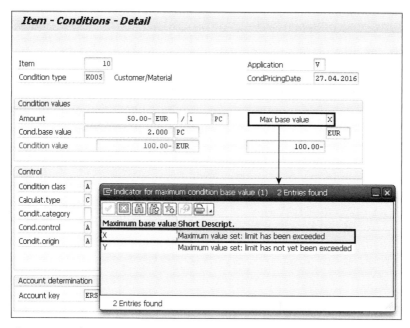

Figure 7.8 Order Item: Condition Details on Condition K005

The functionality MAXIMUM CONDITION VALUE operates analogously. In this case, a MAXIMUM VALUE field would appear in the screen of Figure 7.8, and would also use the characteristics X and Y. We will present an example in which both limits are used in Chapter 12, Section 12.1.

7.4   Tax Determination in Sales

The calculation of the tax for a sales process is an integral part of pricing. The configuration settings for the tax always start with financial accounting. There, each country is linked to the appropriate tax calculation procedure. Each country has assigned one single tax calculation procedure. These tax calculation procedures are pricing procedures for the application TX (taxes). We will describe the tax calculation for financial accounting in detail in Chapter 13, Section 13.5.

There is a close connection between the tax determination in sales orders or billing and the tax calculation in accounting. There are two variants of the tax determination in sales processes, which we describe in more detail in the following sections: the simple tax determination and the tax determination via accounting (tax trigger).

7.4.1   Simple Tax Determination

The simple tax determination method is applicable if the tax codes for a country have always assigned one single tax rate percentage in the maintenance Transaction FTXP (Maintain Tax Code), as in Germany, for example. The tax determination is called simple because only a single percentage is assigned.

In Figure 7.9, you can see the definition of the tax code AA in the country DE within Transaction FTXP. For country DE, the tax determination procedure TAXD (sales tax – Germany) was determined. All the tax codes found in the order processing must be this simple type; otherwise, the simple method is not applicable.

We now consider the pricing procedure RVAA01 from sales and distribution. Here the condition type MWST calculates the tax. The connection to the tax determination procedure from accounting is made by the relevant condition record. When creating this condition record (see Figure 7.10), which is by the way date-dependent, you enter only the tax code. The tax determination procedure is determined using the country of departure and the tax rate is determined by a pricing simulation (call function module PRICING with application TX) and stored redundantly in the MWST condition record.

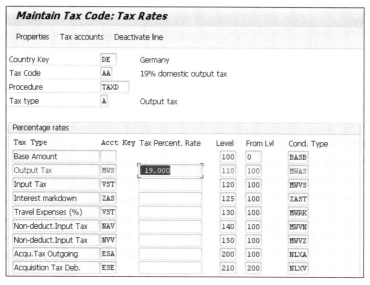

Figure 7.9 Tax Rate for Tax Code AA (Transaction FTXP)

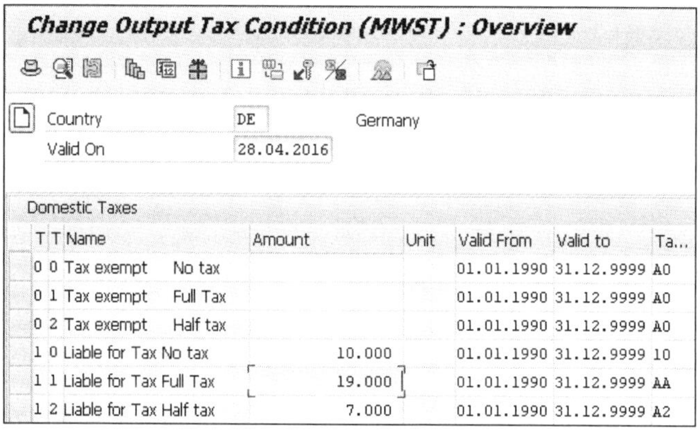

Figure 7.10 Condition Records for Condition Type MWST (Transaction VK12)

The pricing procedure RVAA01 (see Figure 7.11) contains two simple tax condition types, MWST and MW15. The condition type MWST refers to the value of goods (by condition, base value formula 16) and the percentage is determined by using the access sequence MWST based on the tax classification of the material (e.g., tax code A2 for foods with reduced rate). The second condition type MW15 refers exclusively to the condition RL00, which represents the remuneration for a service and therefore must be taxed at the full rate, irrespective of the material. This is achieved by use of the access sequence MWM1 in condition type MW15.

Step	Co...	CTyp	Description	Fro	To	Ma...	R...	St...	P	SuTot	Reqt	CalTy...	BasT...	Acc...
908	0		Net Value 3			☐	☐	☐						
910	0	PI01	Intercompany Price			☐	✓	✓	B	22				ERL
911	0	AZWR	Down Pay./Settlement			☐	☐	☐		2	48			ERL
914	0	SKTV	Cash Discount			☐	☐	✓	D	14		2		
915	0	MWST	Output Tax			☐	✓	☐		10			16	MWS
919	0	DIFF	Rounding Off			☐	✓	☐		13	16	4		ERS
920	0		Total			☐	☐	☐	A	4				
930	0	SKTO	Cash Discount			☐	☐	✓		9		11		
932	0	RL00	Factoring Discount			☐	☐	✓		23		2		ERS
933	0	MW15	Fact.Discount Tax	932		☐	✓	✓		21				MWS
935	0	GRWR	Statistical Value			☐	☐	✓	C	8		2		
940	0	VPRS	Cost			☐	☐	✓	B	4				

Procedure RVAA01 Standard — Control data — Reference Step Overview

Figure 7.11 Pricing Procedure RVAA01: Simple Tax MWST

In this way, we get order items in which two different tax codes (for example B. AA and A2) occur. This is allowed if the two taxes relate to different condition types and thus have no common base.

7.4.2 Tax Determination via Accounting (Tax Trigger)

We now consider the case of the *composite tax*. For this type of tax in Transaction FTXP, at least one tax code is assigned to more than one tax rate percentage (see Figure 7.13). We want to illustrate this process of tax determination via accounting/tax trigger by the example of the tax determination procedure TAXES for Spain (see Figure 7.12). For further details on the tax calculation in SAP ERP Financials (FI), see Chapter 13, Section 13.5.

Spain, for example, has the tax code E3. If this tax code is determined for an item in a sales transaction, the two output taxes MWAS and MWAA are to be calculated (see Figure 7.13).

Procedure			TAXES	Sales Tax - Spain											

Control Data

Reference Step Overview

Step	Co...	CTyp	Description	Fro	To	Ma...	R...	St...	P	SuTot	Reqt	CalTy...	BasT...	Acc...
100	0	BASB	Base Amount			☐	☐	☐						
110	0	MWAS	Output Tax	100		☐	☐	☐						MWS
120	0	MWVS	Input Tax	100		☐	☐	☐						VST
140	0	MWVN	Non-deduct.Input Tax	100		☐	☐	☐						NAV
150	0	MWVZ	Non-deduct.Input Tax	100		☐	☐	☐						NVV
190	0	MWAA	Clearing Tax	100		☐	☐	☐						ASB
200	0	NLXA	Acqu.Tax Outgoing	100		☐	☐	☐						ESA
210	0	NLXV	Acquisition Tax Deb.	100		☐	☐	☐						ESE

Figure 7.12 Tax Determination Procedure for Spain TAXES (Application TX)

Maintain Tax Code: Tax Rates

Properties   Tax accounts   Deactivate line

Country Key	ES	Spain
Tax Code	E3	IVA repercutido + recargo de equivalencia 16+4%
Procedure	TAXES	
Tax type	A	Output tax

Percentage rates

Tax Type	Acct Key	Tax Percent. Rate	Level	From Lvl	Cond. Type
Base Amount			100	0	BASB
Output Tax	MWS	16.000	110	100	MWAS
Input Tax	VST		120	100	MWVS
Non-deduct.Input Tax	NAV		140	100	MWVN
Non-deduct.Input Tax	NVV		150	100	MWVZ
Clearing Tax	ASB	4.000	190	100	MWAA
Acqu.Tax Outgoing	ESA		200	100	NLXA
Acquisition Tax Deb.	ESE		210	100	NLXV

Figure 7.13 Tax Rates for the Tax Determination Procedure TAXES and Tax Code E3 (Transaction FTXP)

The integration of the tax determination in the sales pricing procedure takes place using the tax trigger condition type MW01. This condition type is characterized as a tax trigger by having condition class G and being marked as statistical in the pricing procedure. In the pricing procedure that follows, note that the condition types MWAS and MWAA of the tax determination procedure are marked as manual. If these condition types are not yet available in the sales and distribution Customizing, you can create them with Transaction V/06 (without access sequence, condition class D, calculation type A).

Figure 7.14 shows a sales pricing procedure ZVAAEU (standard with tax trigger), which covers a number of European countries. A similar pricing procedure is not delivered in the standard SAP system. This pricing procedure can serve as a model, which may allow you to handle all existing tax situations in your company with a single pricing procedure.

Step	Co...	CTyp	Description	Fro	To	Ma...	R...	St...	P	SuTot	Reqt	CalTy...	BasT...	Acc...	Accr...
905	0	B005	Hierarchy rebate/mat	400			☐	☐			24			ERB	ERU
906	0	ZB07	Cust. hier./p-group	400			☐	☐			24			ERB	ERU
908	0		Net Value 3	900	907	☐	☐	☐							
910	0	PI01	Intercompany Price			☐	☑	☑	B		22			ERL	
911	0	AZWR	Down Pay./Settlement			☐	☐	☐			2	48		ERL	
914	0	SKTV	Cash Discount			☐	☐	☑	D		14		2		
915	0	MW01	Tax Trigger (RU)			☐	☐	☑			10		16	MWS	
916	0	MWAS	Output Tax			☑	☐	☐	S		10		16	MWS	
917	0	MWAA	Clearing Tax			☑	☐	☐	S		10		16	MW1	
919	0	DIFF	Rounding Off			☐	☑	☐			13	16	4	ERS	
920	0		Total			☐	☐	☐	A			4			
930	0	SKT0	Cash Discount			☐	☐	☑			9		11		

Procedure ZVAAEU Standard with Tax Trigger
Control data
Reference Step Overview

Figure 7.14 Sample Calculation Schema ZVAAEU with Tax Trigger (Transaction V/08)

The following example illustrates the use of the pricing procedure ZVAAEU with an example of a sales order with the German tax determination procedure. Figure 7.15 shows the CONDITIONS screen for an order item after you have created the condition records for MW01 for the country and have replaced the standard pricing procedure RVAA01 by the new pricing procedure ZVAAEU.

N..	CnTy	Name	Amount	Crcy	per	U...	Condition value	Curr.
		Net Value 3		295,00	EUR	1PC	295,00	EUR
☐	AZWR	Down Pay./Settlement		0,00	EUR		0,00	EUR
☐	MW01	Tax Trigger (RU)						
☐	MWAS	Output Tax		19,000	%		56,05	EUR
		Total		351,05	EUR	1PC	351,05	EUR
☐	SKT0	Cash Discount		2,000-	%		7,02-	EUR
		Profit Margin		295,00	EUR	1PC	295,00	EUR

Sales Document Item 10   Item category TAC VariantConfiguration
Material DPC4000   Desktop PC 4000

Sales A | Sales B | Shipping | Billing Document | Conditions | Account assignment | Schedu

Qty 1 PC   Net 295,00 EUR
Tax 56,05

Pricing Elements

Figure 7.15 Item Conditions Screen Based on Pricing Procedure ZVAAEU

The required condition records for tax trigger MW01 were created before, as shown in Figure 7.16.

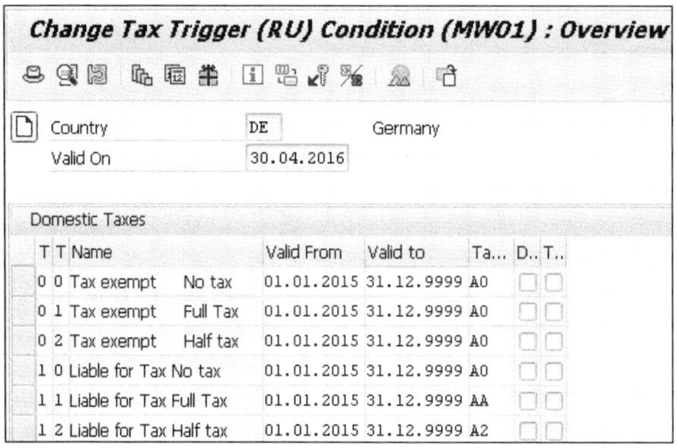

T	T	Name		Valid From	Valid to	Ta...	D..	T..
0	0	Tax exempt	No tax	01.01.2015	31.12.9999	A0		
0	1	Tax exempt	Full Tax	01.01.2015	31.12.9999	A0		
0	2	Tax exempt	Half tax	01.01.2015	31.12.9999	A0		
1	0	Liable for Tax	No tax	01.01.2015	31.12.9999	A0		
1	1	Liable for Tax	Full Tax	01.01.2015	31.12.9999	AA		
1	2	Liable for Tax	Half tax	01.01.2015	31.12.9999	A2		

Figure 7.16 Condition Records for Condition Type MW01 (Tax Trigger) for Germany (Transaction VK12)

Basically, the simple method provides better performance than the tax determination via tax trigger. However, you can also combine both methods within a pricing procedure. This means that you can also include the well-known condition type MWST in addition to the condition type MWAS. You then simply need to ensure organizationally that in one sales document only MW01 or MWST is found and never both simultaneously. You can achieve this by creating condition records for MWST only for those countries for which you will not use MW01. To be on the safe side, you could of course also use an exclusion method, which prevents condition type MW01 from being used if MWST is determined (as discussed in Section 7.2).

7.4.3 Tax Determination via External Tax Interface

In the United States, it is possible to perform the calculation of sales taxes by an external software solution (e.g., Vertex and Taxware). This has the advantage of updating the tax rate database externally, which greatly simplifies the handling of the taxes. Reporting is then also performed with this software.

In this case, the tax determination always uses the technique of the tax trigger. In accounting, the tax determination procedure TAXUSX is provided for this purpose (more information can be found in Chapter 13, Section 13.5), which cooperates with the delivered standard pricing procedure RVAXUS. Figure 7.17 shows an excerpt of a pricing procedure used to deal with the simple tax determination by MWST and the external tax interface in a single pricing procedure.

	Procedure		CF0001	CRM Claim - EU/US									
Control													
Reference Step Overview													
Step	Co...	CTyp	Description	Fro	To	Ma...	R...	St...	P	SuTot	Reqt	CalTy...	BasT...
900	0		Net value 2						3			2	
905	0	MWST	Output Tax	900							73		16
906	0	VST	Output tax	900				✓			74		16
910	0	UTXJ	Tax Jurisdict.Code	900				✓			73	300	
911	0	XR1	Tax Jur Code Level 1	900		✓					73	301	
912	0	XR2	Tax Jur Code Level 2	900		✓					73	302	
913	0	XR3	Tax Jur Code Level 3	900		✓					73	303	
914	0	XR4	Tax Jur Code Level 4	900		✓					73	304	
915	0	XR5	Tax Jur Code Level 5	900		✓					73	305	
916	0	XR6	Tax Jur Code Level 6	900		✓					73	306	

Figure 7.17 Pricing Procedure for Handling Different Tax Determination Methods (Transaction V/08)

In this scenario, the tax trigger is the statistical SD condition type UTXJ that determines the tax code using condition records. If a condition record is found, the external tax interface is called by condition value formula 300. This interface then provides the values for the "real" tax condition types XR1-XR6, which receive their values by the condition value formulas 301 to 306. The important qualifying characteristic for the settlement of U.S. taxes is the *tax jurisdiction code* (TXJCD) as an address component of the ship-to party.

7.4.4 Tax Increase

If you are not using an external tax interface, you make a change to the tax rate on a specific date by first creating a new tax code with Transaction FTXP for the country concerned and assigning the new percentages to that tax code. Thereafter, new condition records for the country and the affected tax classifications are created with Transaction VK11 or VK12 (e.g., for MWST, MW01) with this new tax code and the required valid from date.

7.5 Free Goods in Sales

In addition to direct discounts, which are deducted from each invoice, and deferred compensations (rebates), which will be settled later, there is the agreement of free goods as a sales promotion measure. The implementation of these agreements is performed in the sales order and has a direct relationship to pricing. In the SAP system, three types of free goods are available:

▶ **Inclusive free goods with item generation**
Buy x units of product A, but only pay for y units. In this variant, the order quantity of the product A is reduced to y and an additional free-of-charge order item is created with a quantity of x-y.

▶ **Exclusive free goods**
Buy x units of product A and get y units of product B for free. An additional free-of-charge subitem is generated for product B.

▶ **Inclusive free goods without item generation**
This is the same scenario as when buying x units of product A and only paying for y units. In contrast, however, no additional items are generated. The discounting is carried out exclusively by means of pricing conditions.

The free goods agreements are maintained in the form of condition records for usage N (free goods). The configuration for free goods can be found in Customizing using the menu path IMG • Sales and Distribution • Basic Functions • Free Goods.

Let's look at the operation of these three variants by example. At first, we create a free goods agreement for customer 3271 and product HT-1066 with Transaction VBN1 (see Figure 7.18).

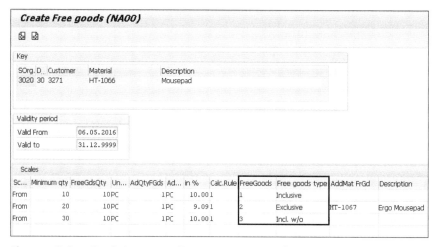

Figure 7.18 Free Goods Agreement (Transactions VBN1 and VBN2)

We combine in this example all three variants: the selection criterion for the method is the *minimum order quantity*. Specifically, from an order quantity of ten units of measure, method (discount type) 1 is used. With 20 units of measure, method 2 is selected and from 30 units of measure, method 3 is used.

We create an order with three items with the quantities shown in Figure 7.19.

All items				
Item	Material	Order Quantity	Un	Description
	HT-1066	10		
	HT-1066	20		
	HT-1066	30		

Figure 7.19 Order Items with Free Goods

After pressing ⌈Enter⌋, we obtain the situation shown in Figure 7.20. You can see the operation of the three variants.

All items								
Item	Material	Order Quantity	Un	Description	S	HL Itm	Net value	Doc. Curre...
10	HT-1066	9	PC	Mousepad	☐	0	22.50	USD
11	HT-1066	1	PC	Mousepad	☐	10	0.00	USD
20	HT-1066	20	PC	Mousepad	☐	0	50.00	USD
21	HT-1067	2	PC	Ergo Mousepad	☐	20	0.00	USD
30	HT-1066	30	PC	Mousepad	☐		67.50	USD
					☐			

Figure 7.20 Items Overview Screen after Free Goods Resolution

The generated free goods subitems 11 and 21 have the item category TANN which is configured with the attribute Pricing = B (pricing goods discount). We evaluate this characteristic of the item category in requirement 55 (pricing free goods) within pricing to activate a special condition type R100, which creates a 100% discount for this ITEM CATEGORY via the base value formula 28 (100% discount). This condition type operates without condition records. You will find it on the CONDITIONS screen for the order items 11 and 21.

For the inclusive free goods without item generation at item 30, you use the special condition type NRAB that is displayed in the CONDITIONS screen, as shown in Figure 7.21.

Net Value for Item	2.50 USD	1PC	75.00 USD
☐ NRAB Free goods	2.50-USD	1PC	7.50-USD

Figure 7.21 Condition Type NRAB for Inclusive Free Goods without Item Generation

The details of this condition are displayed in Figure 7.22.

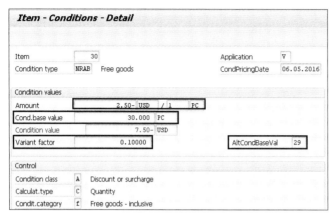

Figure 7.22 Details for the Condition NRAB

The condition type NRAB is not determined by condition records, but by the condition base value formula 29 (free goods/incl.). This formula makes the calculated net value per piece at this point (2.50 USD) negative, which, multiplied by the condition basis of 30 pieces and the free goods proportion of 0.1, results in the discount value of 7.50 USD. The free proportion can be found in the field VARIANT FACTOR. This free goods proportion is calculated before performing the pricing within the order processing using the function module NATRAB_SELECTION. It is transferred to pricing by the interface structure KOMP in the komp-nrfaktor field.

7.6   Cost of Sales

Determining the cost of a sale is very important. In the sales order or the quotation, we strive to obtain a precise idea of the actual costs that are inherently known only at a later date. Finally, we want to know what financial latitude we have in negotiating an offer, because we do not want to operate at a loss. At this stage, we speak of *planned costs*.

At the time of billing creation, we want to determine the *actual costs*. This is important, because in most processes the billing transmits this cost information to Profitability Analysis (CO-PA) to run the cost-of-sales accounting method. In this method, the revenues are compared to the actual costs.

Of course, these costs are also useful for SAP BW, controlling, and sales statistics and your own billing-related evaluations. If the actual cost at the time of billing is not yet known, there are mechanisms in the SAP system for the stock sale, drop shipment, and cost-of-sales accounting processes that transfer this cost information retrospectively to the affected billing. Thus, when looking at an invoice, you always get the best possible cost statement. Once a process is finally completed, the cost information in the billing is up to date.

Costs are handled in the pricing procedure by special statistical condition types, which vary depending on the process. It is worthwhile to read a brief overview of the various processes and their treatment of the costs:

- Stock sale (no cross-company)
- Drop shipment (third party)
- Cross-company stock sale
- Make-to-order with/without production order
- Actual-cost accounting (resource related billing)

In each of these processes, we will consider the treatment of costs in both sales orders (planned costs) and billing documents (actual costs). We will use the condition types contained in the standard pricing procedure RVAA01.

7.6.1 Stock Sale (No Cross-Company)

In the standard pricing procedure RVAA01 we use the condition type VPRS (cost) for the representation of the costs. This condition is not determined by condition records, but is triggered by the attribute CONDITION TYPE = G (cost) of the condition type within the program. In the sales order, the value of the condition is determined from the table MBEW (material valuation). The condition represents at this stage the *planned costs*. The difference between NET VALUE and planned costs is displayed in the CONDITIONS screen for the order item as PROFIT MARGIN (see Figure 7.23).

The billing document, which is usually created after a successful goods issue, transfers the value of the goods issue posting as actual costs in this condition VPRS. In the billing document, the transfer of the value of the goods issue posting to the pricing takes place with a special logic. The value is handed over via the KOMP interface in the komp-wavwr field and is stored in the VPRS condition.

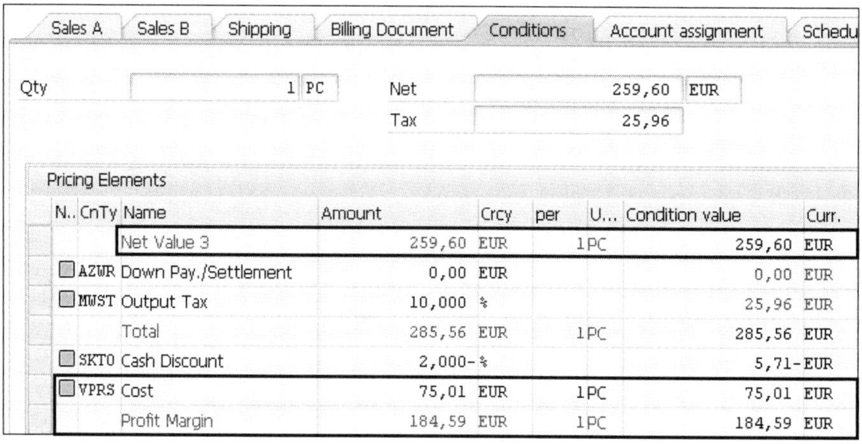

Figure 7.23 Cost and Profit Margin of the Order Item

If the billing takes place before the goods issue — this may be required for export operations — the invoices must be updated after successful goods issue. For this purpose, the SDVPRSUPDATE program is available.

7.6.2 Drop Shipment (Third Party)

For a drop shipment order, a third party supplies the goods or services. A purchase requisition is created in the purchasing module (with Materials Management) and is handled there as third-party order. The costs are represented by the condition type VPRS. Like in a stock sale, the planned costs of the sales order are determined during pricing from the table MBEW (material valuation). The billing, which usually takes place after successful vendor invoice receipt, transfers the value of the vendor invoice as actual costs in the condition VPRS. If the creation of customer billing takes place before booking the vendor invoice of the supplier, the planned costs are used. Once the vendor's invoice is posted, the VPRS condition will be updated automatically for the involved invoices, as with all subsequent costs or credits to this order.

7.6.3 Cross-Company Stock Sale

The cross-company stock sale is a variant of the drop shipment process described previously. Here the supplying company is a second company code of the client, which is handled on the same ERP system. The process is characterized by the fact that the order item is created with a delivering plant that belongs to a different company code than the selling sales organization. In contrast to the previously described drop shipment, purchasing is not involved here. Thus, there is no purchasing order to a supplying company, which simplifies the entire process significantly.

In this process, the costs in the order are not represented by the condition type VPRS, but by the internal transfer condition types PI01 or PI02. Figure 7.24 shows the CONDITIONS screen for an order item in a cross-company sales process.

| Sales A | Sales B | Shipping | Billing Document | Conditions | Account assignment |

| Qty | | 10 PC | Net | | 8,110.00 EUR |
| | | | Tax | | 0.00 |

Pricing Elements

N..	CnTy	Name	Amount	Crcy	per	U...	Condition value	Curr.
		Net Value 3	811.00	EUR		1PC	8,110.00	EUR
☐	PI01	Intercompany Price	183.00	EUR		1PC	1,830.00	EUR
☐	AZWR	Down Pay./Settlement	0.00	EUR			0.00	EUR
☐	MWST	Output Tax	0.000	%			0.00	EUR
		Total	811.00	EUR		1PC	8,110.00	EUR
☐	SKTO	Cash Discount	3.000-	%			243.30-	EUR
		Profit Margin	628.00	EUR		1PC	6,280.00	EUR

Figure 7.24 Cost (PI01) and Profit Margin in a Cross-Company Order Item

PI01/PI02 are the price agreements between the two companies. In this process, two billing documents are created:

▶ The *customer invoice* (e.g., billing type F2) is generated by the selling company code. The condition types PI01/PI02 represent the costs in this billing, as well as the respective order.

▶ The selling company code is charged by the supplying company code with an internal intercompany billing. Here the costs are supplied by the goods issue posting via condition type VPRS. Figure 7.25 shows the CONDITIONS screen for a billing item of an intercompany billing invoice.

In each scenario, the relevant condition types are determined by appropriate requirements in the pricing procedure for the condition types VPRS, PI01, and PI02.

| Item Detail | Item Partners | Conditions | ForTrade/Customs | Item Texts | PO Data |

| Qty | | 10 PC | Net | 1,830.00 | EUR |
| | | | Tax | 0.00 | |

Pricing Elements

N..	CnTy	Name	Amount	Crcy	per	U...	Condition value	Curr.
		Net value 2	811.00	EUR		1PC	8,110.00	EUR
☐	IV01	Intercompany Price	183.00	EUR		1PC	1,830.00	EUR
☐	MWST	Output Tax	0.000	%			0.00	EUR
		Total	183.00	EUR		1PC	1,830.00	EUR
☐	SKTO	Cash Discount	3.000-	%			54.90-	EUR
☐	VPRS	Cost	570.00	EUR		1PC	5,700.00	EUR
		Profit Margin	387.00-	EUR		1PC	3,870.00-	EUR

Figure 7.25 Cost (VPRS) and Profit Margin in an Intercompany Billing Invoice

7.6.4 Make-To-Order with/without Production Order

In make-to-order with/without production order, the material price from the material valuation in general does not provide suitable cost information, therefore the condition type VPRS is not useful here. In this scenario, the planned costs for an order item are either formed by a manual unit costing or taken over from the production order, if such was created. The planned costs are transferred to the condition type EK02 (calculated costs). Since these planned costs are also transferred to the billing document, we unfortunately are not able to see the *actual costs* in this scenario. For Profitability Analysis (CO-PA), that is not a handicap, because in this case the costs are not transferred from the billing into CO-PA, but by an order settlement that closes the make-to-order production order.

7.6.5 Actual-Cost Accounting

In the actual-cost accounting, also called *expense* accounting, the order item has only the function of a cost collector. Information about planned costs is at best possible with a manual unit costing. Costs relate to bookings (material withdrawals, accounts payable invoices, confirmations of working hours, account transfers, etc.) that are assigned to the order item. During the creation of billing documents for these items (Transaction DP90), the cost will be transported via the condition type EK01 into the billing document, so that in this scenario, the cost statement in the invoice is correct.

7.7   Currency Conversion in Sales

When creating condition records (e.g. for price lists), amounts are entered in a currency. Depending on the situation, currency conversions must be performed as part of the pricing. This is done in the routine `xkomv_bewerten` of the pricing program (see also Chapter 10, Section 10.1.6).

In sales orders and billing documents, we are dealing with conversions using three currency fields (and the associated exchange rates):

▶ Local currency

▶ Document currency (also known as transaction currency)

▶ Condition currency

The exchange rates are always related to a conversion date. Since we will not go into more detail later in the technical part of this book for this topic, listed here are all the fields involved in the tables in sales orders, billing documents, and conditions (see Table 7.1).

Field Name	Description
vbak-waerk	Document currency of the sales order
vbkd-kursk	Exchange rate for price determination
vbkd-kursk_dat	Associated exchange rate date
vbkd-kurrf	Exchange rate for FI postings
vbkd-kurrf_dat	Associated exchange rate date
vbrk-waerk	Document currency of the billing
vbrp-kursk	Exchange rate for price determination
vbrp-kursk_dat	Associated exchange rate date
vbrk-kurrf	Exchange rate for FI postings
vbrk-kurrf_dat	Associated exchange rate date
konv-waers	Condition currency in the document
konv-kkurs	Associated exchange rate
konv-kdatu	Associated exchange rate date
t001-waers	Local currency
konp-konwa	Currency of the condition record

Table 7.1 Currency Fields of Sales Order and Billing

7.7.1   Local Currency

The *local currency* is always required when documents or condition records exist with different currencies. The local currency is not stored in the document, but determined from the company code table T001. The company code in turn is generally determined via the sales organization.

7.7.2   Document Currency and Exchange Rates

The *document currency* in the sales order is taken from the customer master data and can be changed manually. The associated exchange rate to the local currency is calculated at the *exchange rate date*. When adding new items, the *pricing date* is used as the exchange rate date. You can find these fields in the HEADER DETAIL screen of the sales order (see Figure 7.26).

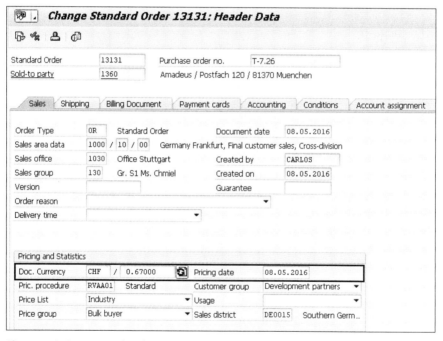

Figure 7.26 Currency and Exchange Rate in the Order Header

In the customer invoice, the document currency, the exchange rate, and the exchange rate date are adopted from the sales order. This procedure ensures that, in spite of any modified exchange rates (these are usually updated daily), the value of the billing matches the value of the order confirmation. However, this program logic can be changed in the configuration of the copying control for billing documents (Transactions VTFA and VTFL).

The exchange rate can be recalculated in the invoice if required. However, a different invoice amount in relation to the order confirmation may occur as a result.

The ITEM DETAIL screen for invoices, shown in Figure 7.27, displays the exchange rate for the billing item.

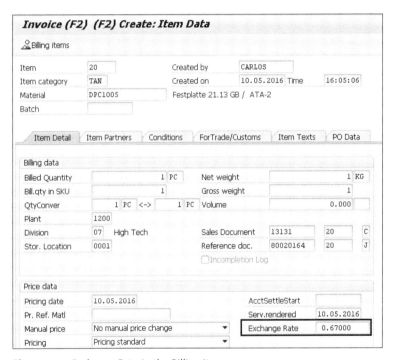

Figure 7.27 Exchange Rate in the Billing Item

7.7.3 Exchange Rate for Accounting

In addition to the exchange rate, in the sales order and billing document there is yet another rate field, called EXCH.RATE-ACCT. (exchange rate for FI posting), with the associated date fields. You will find the rate fields for sales orders and billing documents in Figure 7.28 and Figure 7.29.

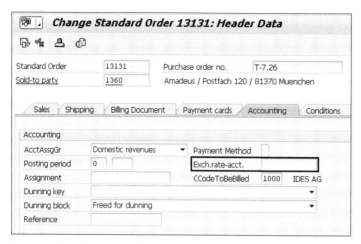

Figure 7.28 Exchange Rate for FI Postings in the Sales Order Header

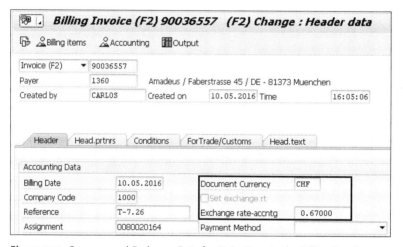

Figure 7.29 Currency and Exchange Rate for FI Postings in the Billing Header

The associated date fields are not displayed. The specification in the exchange rate is not used for pricing purposes, but it is only passed to accounting within the accounting interface of the billing. To accounting, all values are transferred exclusively in the document currency. In the accounting document, the required values in local currency are then calculated using the exchange rate for SAP ERP Financials (FI) postings. This accounting exchange rate is generally not filled in the sales order, although the exchange rate can be fixed by a manual input in this field. In the billing document, the exchange rate is either taken from the sales order or recalculated with the current date of the invoice.

Exchange Rate for Accounting in the Document Chain

The exchange rate for FI postings is automatically transferred to all documents that are created with reference to the original billing document (invoice cancellation, credit notes, debit notes, and returns). This ensures that all subsequent documents are valued at the same (historical) exchange rate. For example, a total credit will reverse the same local currency amount of the original invoice. Thus, no accounting balance in local currency is produced in the general ledger accounts.

When you create credit memo requests or returns, you should do so with reference to the billing document if possible. If they are created without reference to the billing document, the exchange rate for FI postings is recalculated for each new document. This creates a scenario where the sales documents with all the same document currency amounts result in different local currency amounts in the accounting documents.

7.7.4 Condition Currency and Exchange Rates

The currency of a condition record with a calculation type other than PERCENTAGE is transferred within pricing into the document conditions. In the routine `xkomv_kkurs_ermitteln` of the pricing program, an exchange rate is then determined. We distinguish two cases:

- If the exchange rate between the condition currency and document currency is *not* maintained, the exchange rate between the condition currency and the local currency is determined. This should be the norm, especially as the exchange rates to the local currency are usually maintained, not the relationship between any document currencies. In this situation, both conversion rates are displayed in the CONDITION DETAILS screen, as shown in the example in Figure 7.33.

- If the exchange rate between the condition currency and document currency is maintained, it will be adopted (programmatically, this situation is noted in the internal control indicator `xkomv-kbflag`). In this case, in the CONDITION DETAILS screen only *one* exchange rate is displayed.

7.7.5 Currency Customizing and Exchange Rates

Before we proceed with a currency conversion example, let's briefly look at the associated Customizing. You can find this under the menu path IMG • SAP NET-WEAVER • GENERAL SETTINGS • CURRENCIES (see Figure 7.30).

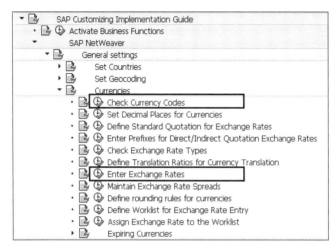

Figure 7.30 Currency Customizing

Figure 7.31 shows an excerpt of the table of exchange rates. The exchange rates are provided with a valid from date, and at any rate change, a new entry with a new valid from date is added. In the selected row, you see that in this example the value of 1 CHF (Swiss Franc) is 0.67 EUR. The FROM currency is the document currency, whereas the To currency is the local currency.

Display View "Currency Exchange Rates": Overview

ExRt	ValidFrom	Indir.quot	X	Ratio(from)	From	=	Dir.quot.	X	Ratio (to)	To
M	22.06.2004	0.00000	X		1 CHF	=	0.67000	X		1 EUR
M	21.06.2004	0.00000	X		1 CHF	=	0.66200	X		1 EUR
M	01.01.2003	0.00000	X		1 CHF	=	0.67972	X		1 EUR

Figure 7.31 Table of Currency Exchange Rates

7.7.6 Currency Conversion

The calculation logic of the currency conversion becomes clear with an example. We create a sales order with the document currency CHF (Swiss Franc) and an item with a condition PBBS (base price) with condition currency JPY (Japanese Yen). Our local currency is EUR. Figure 7.32 shows the CONDITIONS screen of the item and Figure 7.33 shows the detail screen for the condition PBBS. The calculation is normally performed in the following order:

1. Conversion from price in condition currency -> to price in local currency.

2. Conversion from price in local currency -> to price in document currency.

3. Multiplication of price in document currency with the quantity -> result: condition value in document currency.

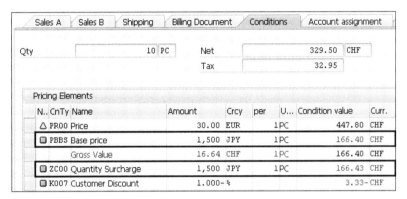

Figure 7.32 Conditions Screen of the Item

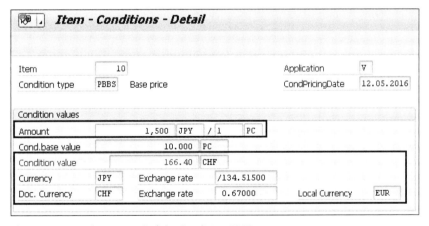

Figure 7.33 Condition Detail of the Condition PBBS

In our example of the condition PBBS, it looks like this:

1. Conversion: Price 1,500 JPY to EUR with the exchange rate 134.515 results in 11.15 EUR (price in local currency).

2. Conversion: 11.15 EUR with the exchange rate 0.67 yields 16.64 CHF (price in the document currency).

3. Multiplication: 16.64 CHF times 10 Pieces results in 166.40 CHF (condition value in document currency).

At each step, there is a commercial rounding. This procedure ensures that the calculated price per unit in the document currency is always the same.

The calculation logic for the currency conversion, described for the example of the condition PBBS, is the default method. By selecting the attribute CURRENCY CONVERSION in the configuration of the condition type, you can determine that the currency conversion is carried out only after the multiplication with the quantity. In this example, we have configured the condition type ZC00 (quantity surcharge) accordingly. In Figure 7.32, you can see the result with condition type ZC00 having a condition value of 166.43 CHF in contrast to the condition PBBS with the value of 166.40 CHF. The calculation is performed in this case, in the following order:

1. Multiplication of price in condition currency with the quantity -> result: condition value in condition currency.

2. Conversion from value in condition currency -> to value in local currency.

3. Conversion from price in local currency -> to price in document currency.

This method could be used for products with small prices, of which large quantities are sold. Due to the rounding effects of the first default method, large deviations can occur.

Currency Conversion for the Condition Type VPRS (Cost)

In the configuration of condition type VPRS, the CURRENCY CONVERSION indicator should be set. This will ensure that the values in sales order and billing will be identical as long as the material valuation price is unchanged. Due to the rounding, this is usually not the case for the delivered standard VPRS, without selected attribute CURRENCY CONVERSION.

We now come to the last topic of this chapter, output processing, where our primary interest is handling document conditions.

7.8   Print Formatting of the Pricing Result

In order processing, you must prepare documents for printing, in order to send them to the customers. In this section, we will primarily deal with the treatment of the pricing information for the issue of quotations, order confirmations, and invoices. First, however, we'll provide an overview of the functionality of output processing.

7.8.1   Functional Scope of the Output Processing

The transmission of documents (e.g. quotation, order confirmation, and invoice) to the customer can be done in three ways:

▶ In printed form using a form (SAPscript, Smart Forms, or PDF)

▶ Electronically via EDI (Electronic Data Interchange)

▶ Electronically by e-mail with a PDF attachment

Printed messages may be additionally stored for audit purposes in the optical archive.

The output processing in the documents consists of:

▶ Output determination with the condition technique for the condition usage B (output)

▶ Output processing with the dispatch times:

  ▹ Immediately when creating and saving the document.

  ▹ By the general dispatching program RSNAST00.

  ▹ By an application-specific dispatching program, if available. Transaction VF31 exists for the processing of billing print documents. There is no corresponding transaction for sales print documents. Transaction VF31 is distinguished from the RSNAST00 program by advanced selection options.

Let's discuss output processing with an example of a customer order. Here, the output determination takes place either when navigating to the output screen (EXTRAS • OUTPUT • HEADER • EDIT), as shown in Figure 7.34, or automatically when saving the document.

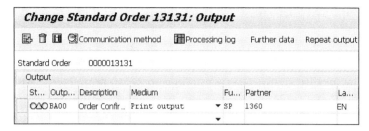

Figure 7.34 Output the Sales Order (Transaction VA02)

In the change transaction of the sales order, you can display the print document on the screen via SALES DOCUMENT • ISSUE OUTPUT TO • PRINT PREVIEW. Figure 7.35 shows the print formatting of the order confirmation in PDF format.

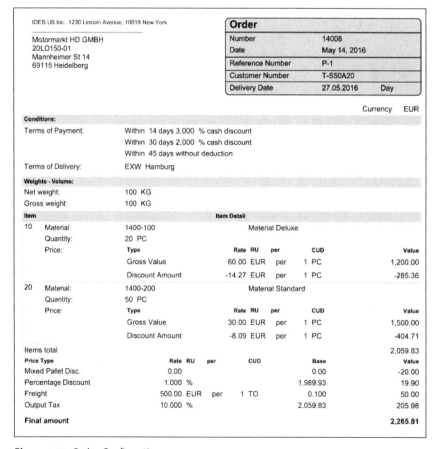

Figure 7.35 Order Confirmation

In the next section, you learn how to adjust the formatting of the values in the order confirmation.

7.8.2 Print Formatting of Order Item Values and Document Footer

We look at the associated CONDITIONS screen for the order item 10 in the order confirmation previously shown (see Figure 7.36). You can see in our special sample order confirmation that we do not print all condition types individually, but only the subtotals GROSS VALUE and DISCOUNT AMOUNT. Those lines that are printed are provided in the picture with a frame.

| Sales A | Sales B | Shipping | Billing Document | Conditions | Account assignment | Schedu |

| Qty | 20 PC | Net | 934,60 EUR |
| | | Tax | 93,46 |

Pricing Elements

N..	CnTy	Name	Amount		Crcy	per	U...	Condition value		Curr.
△	PR00	Price	80,00	EUR			1PC	1.600,00	EUR	
☐	PBBS	Base price	60,00	EUR			1PC	1.200,00	EUR	
		Gross Value	60,00	EUR			1PC	1.200,00	EUR	
☐	K007	Customer Discount	1,000-	%				12,00-	EUR	
☐	K020	Price Group	3,000-	%				35,64-	EUR	
☐	K029	Mat.Pricing Group	5,00-	EUR			1KG	200,00-	EUR	
☐	K031	Price Grp/Mat.Pr.Grp	2,000-	%				19,05-	EUR	
☐	HI01	Hierarchy	2,000-	%				18,67-	EUR	
		Discount Amount	14,27-	EUR			1PC	285,36-	EUR	
		Net Value for Item	45,73	EUR			1PC	914,64	EUR	
☐	KP02	Mixed Pallet Disc.	20,00-	EUR				9,10-	EUR	
☐	HA00	Percentage Discount	1,000	%				9,06	EUR	
☐	HD00	Freight	500,00	EUR			1TO	20,00	EUR	

Figure 7.36 Conditions Screen of the Order Item 10

Figure 7.37 shows the HEADER CONDITIONS screen; the conditions that are printed in the document footer have a callout box around them.

The representation of the values in the document item section and in the document footer are determined by settings in the pricing procedure (see Figure 7.38).

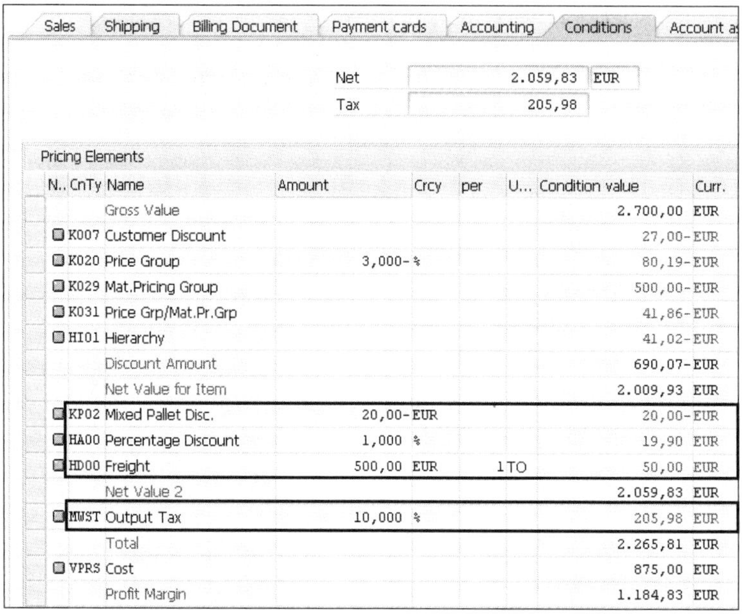

Sales | Shipping | Billing Document | Payment cards | Accounting | Conditions | Account a

Net 2.059,83 EUR
Tax 205,98

Pricing Elements

N..	CnTy	Name	Amount	Crcy	per	U...	Condition value	Curr.
		Gross Value					2.700,00	EUR
	K007	Customer Discount					27,00-	EUR
	K020	Price Group	3,000-	%			80,19-	EUR
	K029	Mat.Pricing Group					500,00-	EUR
	K031	Price Grp/Mat.Pr.Grp					41,86-	EUR
	HI01	Hierarchy					41,02-	EUR
		Discount Amount					690,07-	EUR
		Net Value for Item					2.009,93	EUR
	KP02	Mixed Pallet Disc.	20,00-	EUR			20,00-	EUR
	HA00	Percentage Discount	1,000	%			19,90	EUR
	HD00	Freight	500,00	EUR	1	TO	50,00	EUR
		Net Value 2					2.059,83	EUR
	MWST	Output Tax	10,000	%			205,98	EUR
		Total					2.265,81	EUR
	VPRS	Cost					875,00	EUR
		Profit Margin					1.184,83	EUR

Figure 7.37 Conditions Screen of the Document Header

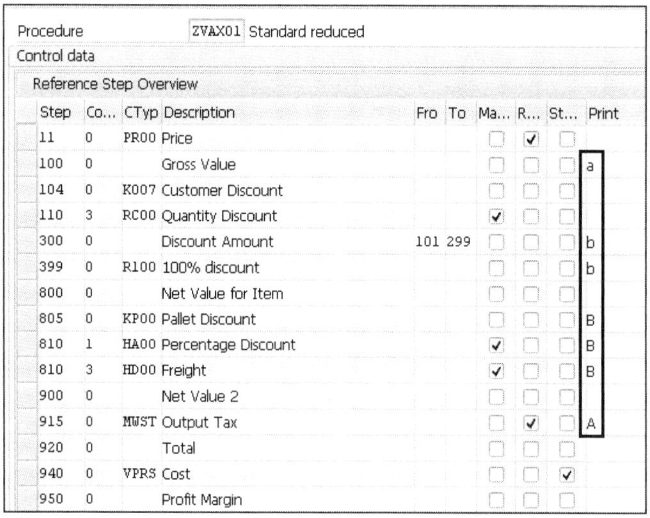

Procedure ZVAX01 Standard reduced
Control data
Reference Step Overview

Step	Co...	CTyp	Description	Fro	To	Ma...	R...	St...	Print
11	0	PR00	Price			☐	☑	☐	
100	0		Gross Value			☐	☐	☐	a
104	0	K007	Customer Discount			☐	☐	☐	
110	3	RC00	Quantity Discount			☑	☐	☐	
300	0		Discount Amount	101	299	☐	☐	☐	b
399	0	R100	100% discount			☐	☐	☐	b
800	0		Net Value for Item			☐	☐	☐	
805	0	KP00	Pallet Discount			☐	☐	☐	B
810	1	HA00	Percentage Discount			☑	☐	☐	B
810	3	HD00	Freight			☑	☐	☐	B
900	0		Net Value 2			☐	☐	☐	
915	0	MWST	Output Tax			☐	☑	☐	A
920	0		Total			☐	☐	☐	
940	0	VPRS	Cost			☐	☐	☑	
950	0		Profit Margin			☐	☐	☐	

Figure 7.38 Simple Pricing Procedure

The display of the pricing information is controlled by the printing indicator PRINT. The possible values are defined by the domain DRUKZ (see Figure 7.39).

Print	Short Descript.
	It was not printed
X	Printing at item level (previous procedure)
S	Printing at totals level (previous procedure)
A	Total: General
B	Total: if value <> zero
C	Total: if value <> previous value
D	Total: if value <> zero and value <> previous value
a	at item: General
b	at item: if value <> zero
c	at item: if value <> previous value
d	at item: if value <> zero and value <> previous value

Figure 7.39 Fixed Values of Domain DRUKZ (Printing Indicator)

The operation mode of the individual values is indicated by the description. The values X and S represent a simple method that has been refined by the introduction of the other values with SAP R/3 4.0.

What to Consider When Configuring the Print Indicator

When configuring the printing indicators, you should be aware that the various values displayed in your test documents do not automatically ensure that a consistent image will be produced for all documents. Therefore, you should set up an example for testing in which *all* condition types in the pricing procedure are contained.

The preparation of the condition data for printing or EDI output is carried out by the function modules `RV_PRICE_PRINT_ITEM` for document item information (here the conditions with printing indicators X, A, B, C, and D are processed). It is carried out by `RV_PRICE_PRINT_HEAD` for document footer information (here the conditions are incorporated with printing indicators S, A, B, C, and D). In both cases, the interface table `TKOMVD` contains those condition types for which the printing indicator is set in the pricing procedure.

You can manipulate `TKOMVD` using the pricing user exits `userexit_print_head` and `userexit_print_item`. For more information on these user exits, see Chapter 11, Section 11.8.1.

7.9 Summary

In this and the previous chapters, you were introduced to the standard customizing of pricing, along with condition maintenance and price determination. The description of this standard functionality is now complete. Before we go deep into the technology, you will be presented in the next chapter with an overview of the pricing procedures and condition types that ship with the standard SAP system. Here you will be able to reinforce what you have learned by putting these elements into a business context.

In this chapter, we present some representative pricing procedures of the sales and distribution module (SD) and the condition types used there.

8 Pricing Procedures and Condition Types in Sales and Distribution

Pricing must always be considered in the context of business processes. Depending on the scenario, you will use different pricing procedures and condition types. In practice, however, there is a tendency to use as few pricing procedures as possible—in extreme cases only a single one. On the one hand, this can simplify the maintenance and the modification effort needed to make adjustments. On the other hand, the pricing procedure may become very complex, and the fine control of the condition types must then be carried out using requirements. In some cases, you will not be able to avoid using different pricing procedures. So it probably does not make sense to merge the pricing procedures RVAA01 (standard business-to-business [B2B]) and RVAB01 (standard business-to-customer [B2C]).

Table 8.1 shows a list of selected business processes and the pricing procedures used in each case.

Process	Doc. Type	Item Category	Pricing Procedure	
Stock Sale/Drop Shipment				
Quotation	QT	AGN	RVAA01	Standard
Sales Order	OR	TAN	RVAA01	Standard
Delivery	LF	TAN		
Customer Invoice	F2	TAN	RVAA01	Standard
Internal Invoice	IV	TAN	ICAA01	Internal

Table 8.1 Business Processes and Their Pricing Procedures

Process	Doc. Type	Item Category	Pricing Procedure	
Rent Processing				
Rental Contract	QP	MVN	PSER01	Periodic
Periodic Invoice	FV	MVN	PSER01	Periodic
Service Processing				
Service Contract	QP	WVN	PSER01	Periodic
Periodic Invoice	FV	WVN	PSER01	Periodic
Cost-based Billing Request	IRC	L2N	PSER02	Service
Debit Memo	L2	L2N	PSER02	Service
Quantity Contract Processing				
Quantity Contract	QC	KMN	RVAA01	Standard
Release Order	OR	TAN	RVAA01	Standard
Delivery	LF	TAN		
Customer Invoice	F2	TAN	RVAA01	Standard
Value Contract Processing				
Value Contract (gen.)	WK1	WKN	WK0001	Value Contract
Value Contract (mat.-rel.)	WK2	WKN	WK0001	Value Contract
Milestone Invoice	FV	WKN	WK0001	Value Contract
Release Order to Value Contract (w/o Invoice)	WA	WAN	RVAA01	Standard
Delivery	LF	WAN		
Release Order to Value Contract (w. Invoice)	TA	TAN	RVAA01	Standard
Delivery	LF	TAN		
Customer Invoice	F2	TAN	RVAA01	Standard
Contract with Resource-Related Billing				
Contract	CBWV	CBVN	RVACRN	Contract
Cost-based Billing Request	CBLV	CBLN	RVACRN	Contract
Debit Memo	L2	CBLN	RVACRN	Contract

Table 8.1 Business Processes and Their Pricing Procedures (Cont.)

In the following section, we take a closer look at the most important pricing procedures of the standard SAP system. These can serve as a template when setting up your own pricing procedures. We will then take a look at the most important condition types in the standard SAP system.

8.1 Selected Pricing Procedures

The condition types contained in the pricing procedure are either determined automatically (via condition records or formulas) or entered manually during document entry on the CONDITIONS screen. Manual conditions may also have condition records. In this case, only the condition type must be entered when creating the sales document. The amount will then be determined via the condition record.

Be Careful with Changes in the Pricing Procedure in the Production System

You should be extremely careful when making changes to a productively used pricing procedure. You must consider whether the planned change can result in significant changes in the values when touching old documents. Particularly critical is the possible impact on the net value and the tax amount. The most secure method is not to change productive pricing procedures, but instead to create a new procedure and then no longer use the old pricing procedure for new sales operations.

Versioning of pricing procedures is not available in the standard SAP system.

The following are the most important pricing procedures:

- RVAA01 (standard B2B)
- RVAA02 (standard with price book)
- RVAB01 (standard B2C [tax included in price])
- PSER01 (periodic billing)
- PSER02 (resource related billing)
- ICAA01 (intercompany billing)
- WK0001 (value contract)
- RVWIA1 (plants abroad/tax treatment)
- RVACRN (contract billing)

Within the SAP industry solutions, other pricing procedures are sometimes needed that we will not cover here.

8.1.1 Pricing Procedure RVAA01 (Standard B2B)

The pricing procedure RVAA01 (see Table 8.2) is most commonly used as a template. It is applied to the common sales transactions in B2B scenarios and contains a large portion of the delivered condition types for the Sales and Distribution module (SD).

Over time, many new condition types have been created. However, they were not always integrated into the pricing procedure, but only communicated via release notes (which can be found in the menu bar under HELP • RELEASE NOTES) or SAP Notes. Therefore, the version of RVAA01 present in your system in the SAP standard client will likely vary slightly from the version presented here.

The pricing procedure is very extensive and the status shown here is an attempt to consolidate. The columns in Table 8.2 (and in the other tables throughout this chapter) have the following meanings:

► Stp: Step number
► CnTy: Condition
► From: From step number
► To: To step number
► M: Manual condition
► Rq: Requirement
► Sub: Subtotal
► S: Condition type is statistical
► Cal: Condition value formula
► Bas: Condition base formula
► Acc: Account key for revenue account determination

Stp	CnTy	Description	From	To	M	Rq	Sub	S	Cal	Bas
8	EK01	Cost			X	2	B			
11	PR00	Price				2				

Table 8.2 Pricing Procedure RVAA01 (Standard)

Stp	CnTy	Description	From	To	M	Rq	Sub	S	Cal	Bas
13	PB00	Price (Gross)			X	2				
20	VA00	Variants				2				
100		**Gross Value**					1		2	
101	KA00	Sales Promotion				2				
102	K032	Price Group/Material				2				
103	K005	Customer/Material				2				
104	K007	Customer Discount				2				
105	K004	Material				2				
106	K020	Price Group				2				
107	K029	Mat. Pricing Group				2				
108	K030	Customer/Mat.Pr. Grp				2				
109	K031	Price Grp/Mat. Pr. Grp				2				
110	RA01	% Disc. from Gross	100		X	2				
110	RA00	% Discount from Net			X	2				
110	RC00	Quantity Discount			X	2				
110	RB00	Discount (Value)			X	2				
110	RD00	Weight Discount			X	2				
111	HI01	Hierarchy				2				
112	HI02	Hierarchy/Material				2				
120	VA01	Variants %				2				
300		**Discount Amount**	**101**	**299**						
302	NETP	Price			X	2			6	3
310	PN00	Net Price			X	2			6	
320	PMIN	Minimum Price				2			15	
399	R100	100% Discount				55				28
400		**Rebate Basis**				7				
800		**Net Value for Item**				2			2	
801	NRAB	Free Goods				59				29
805	KP00	Pallet Discount				57				22
806	KP01	Incomp. Pallet Surch.				57				24

Table 8.2 Pricing Procedure RVAA01 (Standard) (Cont.)

Stp	CnTy	Description	From	To	M	Rq	Sub	S	Cal	Bas
807	KP02	Mixed Pallet Disc.				57				
808	KP03	Mixed Pallet Surch.				57				
810	HA00	Percentage Discount			X	2				
810	HB00	Discount (Value)			X	2				
810	HD00	Freight			X	57	4			
815	KF00	Freight			X	57	4			
817	AMIW	Minimum SalesOrdrVal				2	D	X		
818	AMIZ	Minimum ValueSurchrg				2			13	
820	HM00	Order Value			X	2				
900		**Net Value 2**					3		2	
901	BO01	Group Rebate	400			24				
902	BO02	Material Rebate	400			24				
903	BO03	Customer Rebate	400			24				
904	BO04	Hierarchy Rebate	400			24				
905	BO05	Hierarchy Rebate/Mat.	400			24				
908		**Net Value 3**								
909	PI02	Intercompany %				22	B	X		
910	PI01	Intercompany Price				22	B	X		
911	AZWR	Down Pay./Settlement				2			48	
914	SKTV	Cash Discount				14	D	X	2	
915	MWST	Output Tax				10			16	
919	DIFF	Rounding Off				13			16	4
920		**Total**					A		4	
921	PTVO	Voucher			X					
925		**Payment Amount**	**920**	**924**						
930	SKTO	Cash Discount				9		X	11	
932	RL00	Factoring Discount				23		X	2	
933	MW15	Fact. Discount Tax	932			21		X		
935	GRWR	Statistical Value				8	C	X	2	
940	VPRS	Cost				4	B	X		

Table 8.2 Pricing Procedure RVAA01 (Standard) (Cont.)

Stp	CnTy	Description	From	To	M	Rq	Sub	S	Cal	Bas
941	EK02	Calculated Costs			X		B	X		
942	EK03	Calculated Ship. Cost			X		B	X		
950		**Profit Margin**							**11**	
970	EDI1	Cust. Expected Price			X			X	8	
971	EDI2	Cust. Expected Value			X			X	8	

Table 8.2 Pricing Procedure RVAA01 (Standard) (Cont.)

The pricing procedure is divided into blocks and as a structuring aid subtotal rows are used (these are the lines without a condition type). These subtotals are always created dynamically during pricing and are not stored in the database table KONV. We can identify the following blocks:

▸ **Steps 001-099 (gross value)**
The possible base prices are located here. Usually, these are condition types configured as prices, with the logic that only the last price is active. The exception is the variant price VA00, which is configured as a discount/surcharge, since it may occur more than once, and so the variant prices must be accumulated.

▸ **Steps 101-299 (discounts)**
The discount condition types are listed here. These can be found automatically or entered manually.

▸ **Steps 301-399 (net conditions)**
The conditions that determine the net item value definitively are located here. You will find the following in this range:

▹ **NETP (price)**
If you enable this condition type in the pricing procedure (e.g., remove the indicator MANUAL) the previously determined net value is rounded. This is done in a way that the value represented in the line NET VALUE FOR ITEM has the property price × quantity = value (see Chapter 12, Section 12.3).

▹ **PN00 (net price)**
By this condition type, a net price can be entered manually that overrules the prices determined in the lines before.

▹ **PMIN (minimum price)**
With this condition type, a minimum price can be determined automatically.

It is configured as the discount/surcharge, causing the value to be added as a difference from the previous net value. This is achieved by the *condition value formula* 015 (minimum price). If you configure PN00 as a discount/surcharge, you can have the same effect. This procedure has the advantage that all previous condition types remain active, which usually is desired by accounting for account assignment reasons.

▹ **R100 (100% discount)**
This condition type is activated for free goods by the requirement 55 (free goods pricing) and it has no condition records. Instead, the condition value is set by the base value formula 028 to a 100% discount.

▶ **Steps 801-899 (net value 2)**
This contains some special condition types, including ones that are generally printed in the document footer. We discussed condition type NRAB in Chapter 7, Section 7.5, condition types AMIW/AMIZ in Section 8.2.5, and condition type HM00 in Section 8.2.4.

▶ **Steps 901-907 (net value 3)**
Located in this area are the conditions with condition class C ("expense reimbursement" or rather what is called a *deferred compensation*). Controlled by requirement 024, these condition types are determined only in billing documents. There, they are inserted as statistical conditions and serve to accumulate revenues in the info structures S060 and S469 for the later rebate settlement. They also serve to post accruals in accounting for the expected rebate payouts. If you want to see these condition types in the sales order, you can use requirement 002 (item with pricing) instead of requirement 024 (only in billing doc).

▶ **Steps 908-919 (total)**
These tax condition types, along with the rounding condition type DIFF and the Net Value 2, result in the final amount (total). We describe in detail the remaining condition types of this block in Section 8.2.

▶ **Steps 921-924 (payment amount)**
This section contains condition types that have the function of payments. These payments have negative values. The condition types are configured with condition category g (payment), which causes the value of the condition not to be included in the net value of the item. The outstanding item is reduced by this amount and the payment amount is instead posted in a special balance sheet account. The condition type PTVO (voucher) can be used, for example, for

booking a voucher as payment. Such condition types are used in the connection to POS systems or with sales via a web shop.

▶ **Steps 926-999 (statistical condition types)**

Here are located the statistical condition types that are serving different and usually internal purposes. Some of the condition types listed here are also discussed in detail in Section 8.2.

The condition types VPRS, EK01, EK02, PI01, and PI02 represent the cost of a sales transaction, the importance of which we have discussed in Chapter 7, Section 7.6. Also note the connection with the condition types IV01/IV02 in Section 8.1.8. All of these condition types are configured with SUBTOTAL = B, whereby the value of the condition is transferred to the field komp-wavwr (cost). The difference between the net value of the item (to find in komp-netwr) and its cost is displayed in the subtotal line 950 using the condition value formula 011 as PROFIT MARGIN.

In this presentation of the pricing procedure, we have not mentioned the attribute PRINT, because we discussed it in detail in Chapter 7, Section 7.8. In addition, we addressed the attribute SUBTOTAL only occasionally. We will discuss it in more detail in Chapter 12, Section 12.11.

8.1.2 Pricing Procedure RVAA02 (Standard with Price Book)

The previously presented pricing procedure RVAA01 contains condition type PR00 as a main condition type for determining a starting price, which provides a valid price for a process (order item) via an access sequence. In the pricing procedure RVAA02 (Table 8.3 shows the differences between it and pricing procedure RVAA01), four condition types are used to determine the starting price; the relevant condition records are created exclusively in conjunction with a sales deal. The price book is technically a sales deal. The essential difference from the condition type PR00 is that in the price book the price definition is performed in two steps:

1. Definition of prices or price-influencing characteristics within a price book (on product level). This is done using the condition type PBUD.

2. Definition of the entitled customers or customer groups. This is done with the condition type PBU.

Stp	CnTy	Description	From	To	M	Rq	Sub	S	Cal	Bas
9	PBU	Price Book: Determ.				2				
10	PBUD	Price Book: Basis				2		X		
11	PBBS	Base Price				202				
12	PBUP	Price Book: GrossPr				2				202
100		**Gross Value**					1		2	
102	PB1	SlsDeal 1: Determ.				2				
103	PB1D	Sales Deal 1				62				
300		**Discount Amount**	**101**	**299**						

Table 8.3 Pricing Procedure RVAA02 (Standard with Price Book)

The order of events during pricing and the interrelationship of the conditions types are as follows:

1. **PBU (price book determination)**
   The condition type PBU is configured as condition class H (determining sales deal). The effect of this is that the condition is only used to find the relevant sales deal (that is, the price book) and provide the sales deal number for the following condition type PBUD via the item communication structure KOMP (in field komp-knuma_ag).

2. **PBUD (price book—basis)**
   With the condition type PBUD, price-influencing parameters are determined on product or product group level for the use in the subsequent base price condition type PBBS. For example:
   - A percentage of the initial price
   - The applicable price list
   - The applicable scale

   Here the variable data fields are used, which we will describe in detail in Chapter 9, Section 9.2.

3. **PBBS (base price)**
   The condition type PBBS is the replacement for condition type PR00 (price) and determines the actual starting price. It would have been quite possible to adapt

the condition type PR00. However, since this would have meant an enhancement of the access sequence used there, it was decided to deliver a new condition type PBBS and a new access sequence PR01 (price (item price list)) instead. This access sequence first checks whether the preceding condition type PBUD has determined a deviating price list type. In addition, a possibly deviating pricing date supplied by condition type PBUD is used by the requirement 202 (price book, base price).

4. **PBUP (price book—grosspr)**
The condition type PBUP processes the information of the preceding condition types, PBUD (percentage) and PBBS (base price), for calculating the definitive starting price using the base value formula 202 (price book factor).

The two conditions types PB1 (sales deal determination) and PB1D (sales deal discount) are examples of how the same technology can be used for the processing of sales-promoting measures. Again, we use the sales deal tool, but with only two condition types:

1. **PB1 (sales deal determination)**
Like condition type PBU, condition type PB1 is configured as condition class H (determining sales deal). It is used to find the relevant sales deal and to provide the sales deal number for the subsequent condition type PB1D in the internal table XKNUMA. Contrary to condition type PBU, multiple valid sales deals can be found with condition type PB1.

2. **PB1D (sales deal discount)**
Using requirement 062 (sales deals, basis), the internal table XKOMPLOOP is loaded from XKNUMA (see Chapter 9, Section 9.3), whereby the condition records are read for all sales deals found. This means that the condition PB1D can appear repeatedly in the sales document.

It is possible to merge the pricing procedures RVAA01 and RVAA02 if you want to use both functionalities combined. You might even have to do so because, after all, you do not want to maintain the condition records for PR00 and PBBS twice. The respective price condition type must then work with a new access sequence that combines the accesses of both condition types. Perhaps it also makes sense to use the technique of referencing condition types, as we do, for example, in Section 8.2.2 with condition type MW15.

8.1.3 Pricing Procedure RVAB01 (Tax Included in Price)

The first two pricing procedures, which we described in the previous sections, have the property that the starting price (PR00, PBBS) does not include the tax. After applying discounts and surcharges to the gross value, the tax is added to the net value, resulting in the final amount. This procedure is common in B2B scenarios. However, in B2C transactions (the sales to end customers), it is necessary to define the prices including tax and to come to the final amount by applying discounts and surcharges and to finally expel the tax contained therein. For these scenarios the more complex pricing procedure RVAB02 (standard – gross prices) and the simpler pricing procedure RVAB01 (standard – gross prices (old)) are provided in the standard SAP system.

Here, we want to limit ourselves to the simpler case of the pricing procedure RVAB01 (see Table 8.4), which, in general, should be sufficient. The pricing procedure RVAB02 is an extension of RVAB01 in the way that the net value without tax is split in two amounts: the value of the starting price (for the posting in accounting as revenue) and the value of the discounts (for booking as a sales deduction).

Stp	CnTy	Description	From	To	M	Rq	Sub	S	Cal	Bas
10	PR01	Price Incl. Sales Tax				2		X		
113	K007	Customer Discount				2		X		
114	K004	Material				2		X		
116	K029	Material Pricing Grp				2		X		
210	RA00	% Discount from Net			X	2		X		
210	RC00	Quantity Discount			X	2		X		
210	RB00	Discount (Value)			X	2		X		
210	RD00	Weight Discount			X	2		X		
290	PN00	Price (Net)			X	2		X		
300		**Net Value for Item**								
310	HA00	Percentage Discount			X			X		
310	HB00	Discount (Value)			X			X		
310	HD00	Freight			X			X		
320	HM00	Order value			X			X		

Table 8.4 Pricing Procedure RVAB01 (Standard – Gross Prices)

Stp	CnTy	Description	From	To	M	Rq	Sub	S	Cal	Bas
400		**Total**					1			
410	MWSI	Output Tax	400			10				
420	NETW	Value of Goods								25
510	SKTO	Cash Discount	400			9		X		
520	VPRS	Internal price				4	B	X		
530		**Profit Margin**							11	

Table 8.4 Pricing Procedure RVAB01 (Standard – Gross Prices) (Cont.)

The characteristic feature of this pricing procedure is that all condition types, with the exception of MWSI and NETW, are flagged as statistical. Only these two are therefore relevant to accounting:

▶ **MWSI (output tax)**
The condition type is configured with calculation type H (percentage included) and referenced to the condition type MWST, which means that the condition records of condition type MWST are read.

▶ **NETW (value of goods)**
This condition type is not determined by condition records, but it is calculated by the condition value formula 025 (KZWI1 minus tax) as the difference of the final amount and the amount of tax. For this purpose, the final amount in step 400 is configured with SUBTOTAL = 1.

The pricing procedure RVAB01 has the property that only the condition types NETW and MWSI are passed to financial accounting. This means that there is no way to differentiate in the account assignment between revenues and sales deductions. This requirement is met with pricing procedure RVAB02.

8.1.4 Pricing Procedure PSER01 (Periodic Billing)

As shown in Table 8.1, the pricing procedure PSER01 (periodic billing) is used for rental and maintenance contracts. Table 8.5 shows the significant condition types. In these contracts, invoicing is triggered via a periodic billing plan. In Chapter 6, Section 6.1, we explained pricing in this context in detail.

The difference from the previously presented pricing procedures is the fact that time plays a role with periodic billing. For example, we agreed on monthly rates, but we bill quarterly. For this purpose, the condition types used in these scenarios are configured with time-dependent calculation types:

- M (monthly price)
- N (yearly price)
- O (daily price)
- P (weekly price)

Stp	CnTy	Description	From	To	M	Rq	Sub	S	Cal	Bas
10	PPSV	Service Price Item				2				
20	PPSG	Hierarchy Price Item				2				
61	VASE	Variant Price				2				
100		**Gross Value**				**1**				

Table 8.5 Pricing Procedure PSER01 (Periodic Billing Plan)

The condition types PPSV, PPSG, and VASE in Table 8.5 are configured with calculation type M. It is worth mentioning in this context the function module PRICING_DETERMINE_DATES (see Chapter 10, Section 10.6.3), which identifies the number of months, years, days, and weeks in a period.

8.1.5 Pricing Procedure PSER02 (Resource Related Billing)

The pricing procedure PSER02 (resource related billing) is used for the resource-related billing (cost-based billing; see Table 8.1) of service contracts (Table 8.6 shows the significant condition types). In this scenario, the item of the maintenance contract serves as a cost collector on which the services are collected. with Transaction DP90, billing requests are created periodically to transfer the costs incurred to customer billing. For this purpose, pricing procedure PSER02 is used. In Chapter 6, Section 6.6.3, we explained pricing in this context in detail.

Stp	CnTy	Description	From	To	M	Rq	Sub	S	Cal	Bas
8	EK01	Actual Cost			X					
11	PR00	Price				2				
20	PPAR	Settlement Price Header				2				

Table 8.6 Pricing Procedure PSER02 (Resource Related Billing)

Stp	CnTy	Description	From	To	M	Rq	Sub	S	Cal	Bas
30	PPAG	Matl Group Price Item			2					
40	PKAR	Settlement Price Item			2					
100		**Gross Value**				1	2			

Table 8.6 Pricing Procedure PSER02 (Resource Related Billing) (Cont.)

Because sales document items with values always need a material, in the cost-based billing, the services provided are recoded as service materials. The sale prices for these materials can be determined, if possible, via condition type PR00. The remaining condition types have the following properties:

▸ **EK01 (actual cost)**
By means of this condition type, the costs of the various expenses are passed to the billing request. These can be invoices from external service providers or even the value of material withdrawals. For vendor invoices, the condition type PR00 is not relevant.

▸ **Condition types PPAR, PPAG, and PKAR**
With these conditions types, special prices can be maintained for individual services or service groups. They can also be defined as contract-specific in the service contract price agreements.

8.1.6   Pricing Procedure ICAA01 (Intercompany Billing)

For sales from stock or the sale of services, the selling company and the supplying company may be different. The supplying company is determined by the plant of the order item and the selling company is determined by the sales organization. If these companies (company codes) are different, it's called intercompany sales (a *cross-company process*). In this case, in addition to the customer billing document for a delivery, an internal invoice from the delivering to the selling company is generated. This internal settlement uses the pricing procedure ICAA01 (see Table 8.7).

Stp	CnTy	Description	From	To	M	Rq	Sub	S	Cal	Bas
900		**Net value 2**				3	2			
909	IV02	Inter-company %				22	9			

Table 8.7 Pricing Procedure ICAA01 (Intercompany Billing)

Stp	CnTy	Description	From	To	M	Rq	Sub	S	Cal	Bas
910	IV01	Inter-company Price				22	9			
911	KW00	Group Valuation				22		X		
912	PC00	Profit Ctr Valuation				22		X		
914	SKTV	Cash Discount				14	D	X		2
915	MWST	Output Tax				10				16
919	DIFF	Rounding Off				13			16	4
920		**Total**					A		4	

Table 8.7 Pricing Procedure ICAA01 (Intercompany Billing) (Cont.)

The pricing procedure ICAA01 is a copy of the standard pricing procedure RVAA01 with the deviations shown in Table 8.7. The condition types IV01, IV02, KW00, and PC00 are added and the condition types PI01 and PI02 are omitted. The deviations are required because the price for the intercompany billing can be found:

▶ As the price of the customer invoice (condition types IV01/IV02 not existing)

▶ As a percentage of the price of the customer invoice (condition type IV02 exists)

▶ Regardless of the price of the customer invoice (condition type IV01 exists)

The condition types IV01 and IV02 are configured with reference to the condition types PI01 or PI02 (see Chapter 7, Section 7.6.3). The condition records must therefore be maintained exclusively for PI01/PI02. This creates the problem that the condition types in the customer billing document should be treated as costs in CO-PA, whereas in the internal transfer billing the same condition types represent revenues. This requirement is fulfilled by choosing different condition types in the two processes, since the assignments in CO-PA are made via the condition type.

KW00 and PC00 are statistical condition types that contain the value of the internal operation from the group view or from the profit center view. These values are passed to accounting.

8.1.7 Pricing Procedure WK0001 (Value Contract Procedure)

The pricing procedure for value contracts (see Table 8.8) is very simple. The value is entered manually via the condition type WK00.

Stp	CnTy	Description	From	To	M	Rq	Sub	S	Cal	Bas
50	WK00	Target Value - Value Contract			X					
100		**Net Value for Item**					1		2	
500	SKTV	Cash Discount				14	D	X		2
700	MWST	Output Tax				10				16
750	DIFF	Rounding Off				13			16	4
800	SKTO	Cash Discount				9		X		11

Table 8.8 Pricing Procedure WK0001 (Value Contract)

8.1.8 Pricing Procedure RVWIA1 (Plants Abroad/Tax Handling)

Stock transfers between plants in different countries are tax reportable, particularly in the EU area. To this end, stock transfer deliveries are invoiced with billing type WIA, which uses the pricing procedure RVWIA1 (see Table 8.9).

Stp	CnTy	Description	From	To	Rq	Sub	S	Cal	Bas	Acc
10	PR00	Prices				9				UML
20	WIA3	Output Tax Dest. Ctry								MWS
30	WIA2	Output Tax Dep. Ctry	10							MWS
40	R100	100 % Discount	10						28	UML
50	WIA1	Input Tax Dest. Ctry	40							VST
60	GRWR	Statistical Value	10		8		C	X		

Table 8.9 Pricing Procedure RVWIA1 (Plants Abroad/Tax Handling)

The final amount of this billing type has the value zero. Only the tax-relevant postings for accounting are created.

8.1.9 Pricing Procedure RVACRN (Contract Billing)

The pricing procedure RVACRN (see Table 8.10) was delivered with SAP ERP 6.0 EHP 3. It is used for special contracts, such as those found in the aerospace and defense industries, and serves to settle them resource-related, that is with Transaction DP90 (Resource-Related Billing). The pricing procedure is interesting insofar as requirements and formulas are used extensively.

Stp	CnTy	Description	From	To	M	Rq	Sub	S	Cal	Bas
9	EK01	Actual Cost			X	106	B			
10	PR00	Price				2				
11	PKAR	Settlement Price Header				2				
12	PPAR	Settlement Price Item				2				
100		Gross Value					2		2	
120	K007	Customer Discount	100			2	3			
800		Net Value for Item							2	
810	HA00	Percentage Discount			X	2	3			
815	ITD2	Previously Billed Gross Amount				106	2		112	
816	ITD3	Previously Billed Discount				106	3		112	
817	ITD4	Previously Billed ACRR				106	4		112	
820	ITD5	Previously Billed Fee				106	5		112	
850		Net Value 2							2	
851	ACRN	Budget				107	1	X	114	110
852	ACRB	ACRN Consumption				107		X	111	
853	ACRR	ACRN Delta			X	107	4		113	
854	ACRL	Limit				107		X	114	2
900		Net Value 3					7		2	
903	BO03	Customer Rebate	900			24				
908		Net Value 4	900	903						
910	PI01	Intercompany Price				22	B	X		
915	MWST	Output Tax				10				16
920		Total					A		4	
930	SKTO	Cash Discount				9		X		11
935	GRWR	Statistical Value				8	C	X		2
940	VPRS	Cost				4	B	X		

Table 8.10 Pricing Procedure RVACRN (Resource Related Billing)

Stp	CnTy	Description	From	To	M	Rq	Sub	S	Cal	Bas
941	ITDB	Previously Billed EK01				106	B	X	112	
950		Profit Margin							11	

Table 8.10 Pricing Procedure RVACRN (Resource Related Billing) (Cont.)

In addition to the usual condition types for resource-related billing from pricing procedure PSER02 (see Section 8.1.5), the following condition types are used here:

- ▶ **ACRN (budget)**
  With condition type ACRN, budgets are defined for the contracts. These budgets are then checked when billing requests are generated with Transaction DP90. For this purpose, the functionality of the condition update using the limit for maximum condition value is used. The special feature here is that the condition may occur more than once. The net value of the item is distributed by the base value formula 110 (ACRN budget) on the various budgets. The exploitation percentage is calculated by condition value formula 114 (ACRN budget) and stored in the data container xkomv-varcond for display on the screen.

- ▶ **ACRB (budget consumption)**
  By condition type ACRB the budget consumption of condition ACRN is checked with the condition value formula 111 (ACRN consumption). If the budget is exceeded, the pricing status of the item is set to error and a message is displayed.

- ▶ **ACRR (budget delta)**
  If you lack a budget, a corresponding discount can be calculated automatically by condition type ACRR. The delta is determined by the condition value formula 113 (ACRN discount).

- ▶ **ACRL (limit)**
  The condition type ACRL defines another limit using condition update with the limit for a maximum condition value. If the limit is exceeded, the item is set to error by the condition value formula 114 (ACRN budget).

- ▶ **Conditions (ITD*)**
  The profile for resource-related billing can be configured including retroactive billing. In this case, all expense items are billed, regardless of whether they might have already been billed. The already billed values are subtracted by the

condition types ITD*. The determination of these invoiced values is carried out by the condition value formula 112 (ITD-billed), which evaluates the information structure S409, in which the billing requests and billing documents for a contract are updated.

This presentation of the standard pricing procedures is intended to serve as a reference for common business processes when setting up your own pricing procedures. You should find most condition types of these pricing procedures in this chapter, unless it is an ordinary condition type, which has no special features.

8.2   Selected Condition Types of the Standard Pricing Procedures

As the conclusion to the presentation of the main standard pricing procedures, we describe some specific condition types of pricing procedure RVAA01.

8.2.1   Condition Types EDI1/EDI2 (Customer Expected Price)

With the statistical condition types EDI1/EDI2 (expected customer price), the price or value of an order item expected by the customer can be entered in the sales order. This may, for example, happen if, during the creation of sales orders in B2B scenarios via EDI (Electronic Data Interchange), one of these conditions is entered by the buyer.

The condition value Formula 008 (expected value) compares the net value determined by pricing with the transmitted value. When exceeding a tolerance limit, the order item is set incomplete by the formula (via the interface field kompcepok) and the delivery is blocked. The reason for incompleteness must be eliminated by adjusting the price or by using Transaction V.25 (Release Customer Expected Price). The tolerance limit can be adjusted to specific requirements by setting up a customer-specific condition value formula.

The comparison value is determined by positioning the condition types in the pricing procedure. If, for example, the freight conditions and the other header conditions should not be taken into account, you could place the ED1/EDI2 condition type on step 790.

8.2.2 Condition Types RL00/MW15 (Invoice List Conditions)

The condition types RL00/MW15 (invoice list conditions), flagged as *statistical* in sales orders and customer invoices, are used to handle *del credere commissions*. These are used, for example, if within the sale to members of purchasing associations, the payment of invoices is done by a central payer.

Since the payments are facilitated by this type of organization, a discount can be granted to the central payer in the form of condition type RL00. As this is a kind of service provided by the central payer, the condition type MW15 is used to calculate the tax on this commission, which is configured by a special access sequence so that the full tax rate is always applied. The condition types are configured as CONDITION CATEGORY = R. They are *invoice list conditions* and therefore are calculated in the customer billing document, but not transferred to accounting. Only within the creation of the invoice list are these condition types activated and posted in accounting as a credit.

8.2.3 Condition Types SKTV/SKTO (Cash Discount))

The statistical condition types SKTV/SKTO (cash discount) are configured as CONDITION CATEGORY = E. They are not determined by condition records, but the percentage is read via table T052 (terms of payment) instead. The difference between both condition types is that they either affect the tax base (SKTV) or they don't (SKTO).

Condition Type SKTV (Cash Discount Before Tax)

The condition type SKTV comes into play only if the company code is configured so that the cash discount reduces the tax base. This is controlled by the requirement 014 (cash discount before tax). The condition type is positioned before the tax condition MWST, so that the condition base formula 016 (net value and XWORKD) can take into account the cash discount amount.

Condition Type SKTO (Cash Discount After Tax)

The condition type SKTO uses the complementary requirement 009 (cash disc. after tax) to requirement 014. The condition type is positioned behind the tax condition type, so that the tax base is not affected. In this regard, you should know that the requirements 009 and 014 do not work if the tax is determined using tax jurisdiction codes. See the SAP Note 1080399 (Cash Discount and Tax Jurisdiction) for more information.

8.2.4 Condition Type HM00 (Order Value)

With the condition type HM00 (order value), you can manually enter a total value in the sales order. The configuration features of the condition type are:

- Condition class B (prices)
- No access sequence
- Calculation type B (fixed amount)
- Group condition
- Header condition
- Manual

The manually entered order value is distributed proportionally among the items. Since the condition type is configured as a price, all previously determined conditions types are inactive because of a subsequent price (INACTIVITY INDICATOR = Y).

This configuration has the disadvantage that a differentiated account assignment for revenues and sales deductions is not possible. For this reason, the following approach inspired by the AMIW/AMIZ process (minimum sales order value) (see Section 8.2.5) provides a reasonable alternative:

1. We configure the condition type HM00 as statistical, with SUBTOTAL = E, which means the value of the condition is temporarily stored in the working variable `xworke`.

2. We create a new condition value formula (see Listing 8.1). The variable `ykfaktor1` is only relevant in the (rather rare) combination of condition HM00 with time-dependent prices in periodic billing plans.

```
form frm_kondi_wert_913.
  data: zwert like xkomv-kwert.
  if ykfaktor1 is initial or ykrech na 'MNOP'.
    zwert = xworke.
  else.
    zwert = xworke * ykfaktor1.
  endif.
```

```
  if not zwert is initial.
    xkwert = zwert - komp-netwr.
  endif.
  if komk-vbtyp ca vbtyp_fakt and xkwert = 0.
    xkomv-kinak = 'Z'.
  endif.
  clear xworke.
endform.
```

Listing 8.1 Condition Value Formula 913 (Delta to the Order Value)

3. We create a new condition type ZM00 (delta to the order value) and position it in the pricing procedure directly after the condition type HM00. We choose the following configuration features:

   ▸ Condition class A (discount/surcharge)

   ▸ Calculation type G (formula)

   ▸ Requirement 002 (item with pricing)

   ▸ Condition value formula 913 (delta to the order value)

This solution has the slight disadvantage that the new condition type ZM00 always appears in sales orders, even if the condition type HM00 was not used (its value is then zero).

8.2.5 Condition Types AMIW/AMIZ (Minimum Sales Order Value/ Minimum Value Surcharge)

With the two condition types AMIW/AMIZ (minimum sales order value and minimum value surcharge), it is possible to activate the check against a minimum sales order value.

Condition Type AMIW (Minimum Sales Order Value)

The condition type is configured as a *statistical group condition* with calculation type B (fixed amount). For this condition type, the condition records with the desired minimum sales order values are maintained. As part of the document-end processing (PRICING_COMPLETE), the determined AMIW value is distributed proportionally among the items. By configuring SUBTOTAL = D, this value is temporarily stored in the working variable xworkd for later use in the condition type AMIZ.

Condition Type AMIZ (Minimum Value Surcharge)

The minimum sales order value is determined by the preceding condition type AMIW. If the net value of the sales order falls below this value, the difference is calculated and assigned as a surcharge by the condition type AMIZ (minimum value surcharge). AMIZ is configured as a reference to AMIW, causing the condition type to appear only if AMIW was determined before. It is not flagged as statistical or as a group condition. If the net value of the order value falls below the minimum order value (that is, komp-netwr is less than xworkd), the difference is assigned by condition value formula 013 (minimum value surcharge) to AMIZ as the condition value.

8.2.6 Condition Type AZWR (Down Payment/Settlement)

The condition type AZWR (down payment/settlement) is used in processing the down payment. This is available, for example, in a value contract (see Table 8.1) via the billing plan for milestone billing. In such a billing plan, down payment dates, dates for partial invoices, and the final invoice will be agreed. For a down payment date, a down payment request invoice is created on the due date. The value of this down payment date will be transferred to the condition type AZWR of the down payment request invoice. The condition class of AZWR is modified during billing by the function module `PRICING_COPY` from discount/surcharge to price, so that all preceding condition types are thereby deactivated. In partial billings and in the final invoice, the condition type is used in separate items to settle the advance payments. A concrete example can be found in Chapter 6, Section 6.7.

8.2.7 Condition Type GRWR (Statistical Value (Cross-Border))

The statistical condition type GRWR calculates the statistical cross-border value. This value is used in export transactions to create the necessary export documents and provide the necessary information to the authorities. The condition type is configured with Subtotal = C, whereby the value of the condition is passed to the komp-gkwrt field. Requirement 008 (export business) ensures that the condition type is determined only in export operations.

8.3   Summary

This chapter addressed all the major pricing procedures and condition types in the standard SAP system, and can serve as a reference when you're setting up your own pricing procedures. You can find more information on selected condition types in Appendix A.

With the previous chapters, you have now become acquainted with all standard configuration settings relating to condition technique, condition master data, and pricing. Perhaps you can fully implement your individual requirements for pricing using the standard configuration. Nevertheless, it is valuable to continue reading. In the next chapter, we will dive deeply into special features of the condition technique within pricing. In that chapter, you will find many ideas and examples, and we can certainly guarantee a few eye-opening revelations.

PART III
Advanced Techniques, Tips, and Tricks

In this third, "expert" part, we provide you with the detailed technical knowledge that you need to make customer-specific adaptations that are stable, efficient, and of high quality. This knowledge is required when you exhaust the possibilities of the standard configuration. We will present some typical practical demands to pricing and their solutions.

In the previous chapters, we discussed the possibilities of standard customizing. In this chapter, we lay the foundations for implementing advanced and complex pricing requirements.

9 Special Features of the Condition Technique in Pricing

The implementation of a pricing requirement is generally associated with the fact that you need to set up new condition tables, access sequences, and condition types and, where appropriate, requirements and formulas. You may want to introduce new characteristics that you want to determine in the context of pricing and reuse within pricing. Alternatively, you may want to pass these determined fields to the caller (sales order), where the information can be used further (document printing, statistics, SAP Business Warehouse [SAP BW], Profitability Analysis [CO-PA], evaluations, etc.). There are already some fields in the standard SAP system that are transferred from condition records to the document:

- Terms of payment, value days, and fixed value date (transferred to the sales order in the header fields vbkd-zterm, vbkd-valtg, and vbkd-valdt)

- Sales deal and promotion numbers (transferred to the item fields vbap-knuma_ag and vbap-knuma_pi)

Within the implementation of more complex requirements, you must observe certain rules that can have an impact on system performance. This chapter is intended to familiarize you with the internal structures of pricing and their context. Whenever you want to implement enhancements for pricing, you are faced with these internal structures.

In particular, we address the flexible functionality of *data determination* that characterizes the pricing usage compared to the other usages of the condition technique. This feature provides a number of useful applications.

Specifically, we talk about:

▶ Communication structures, internal tables, and their relationships

▶ The importance of the sequence of fields in the key of condition tables

▶ The possibility of flexible data retrieval via condition records and the use of this data

▶ The ability to map hierarchical structures entirely with the possibilities of pricing using flexible data retrieval

▶ *Multiple fields* (for example for configuration variants, customer hierarchies, and sales deals)

After reading this chapter, you will be aware of the possibilities of the condition technique in pricing beyond configuration by standard Customizing.

9.1 Interfaces, Tables, and Interrelationships

First, we want to introduce all of the structures and their significance in pricing. Once you make enhancements within pricing, you have to deal with some of these structures.

9.1.1 Interfaces to Condition Tables and Master Data Maintenance

In this section, we describe communication structures used by the transactions that create new condition tables and the transactions that maintain the condition records, as follows:

▶ **KOMG**

The structure KOMG is used to create condition tables and to maintain the condition master data. This structure provides the list of fields that can be used for creating condition tables.

▶ **KOMK, KOMP, and KOMPAZD**

The KOMK, KOMP, and KOMPAZD structures are used to create the access sequences. The access sequences play a role in the condition maintenance insofar as they specify whether a key field is mandatory or can be initial.

The structures represent the field list of all usable fields. This field list is limited per application by the respective field catalog (see Chapter 1, Section 1.6).

9.1.2 Interfaces to the Pricing Modules

In this section, we describe the interface structures of the two main function modules `PRICING` and `PRICING_COMPLETE`, which we will describe in detail in Chapter 10. They are as follows:

▶ **KOMK**

Structure of header-like fields for creating access sequences and for interfacing to item pricing (`PRICING`). Structure for the interface table `TKOMK` for pricing in the entire document (`PRICING_COMPLETE`).

▶ **KOMP**

Structure of the item fields for creating access sequences and interfacing to item pricing (`PRICING`). Structure for the interface table `TKOMK` for pricing in the entire document (`PRICING_COMPLETE`).

▶ **KOMV**

Structure for the internal table `TKOMV` of the pricing result for the entire document. The KOMV structure consists of the `KONV` table (where the pricing result is stored in the database) and the dynamic part KONVD.

To call the pricing, you simply need the KAPPL (application) and KALSM (pricing procedure) fields of the structure KOMK and the field KPOSN (condition item number) of the structure KOMP. But in order to be able to evaluate the conditions found, the WAERK (SAP ERP Sales and Distribution [SD] document currency) and PRSDT (date for pricing) fields must be filled in structure KOMK. The example program in Listing 9.1 shows the call of function module `PRICING` with a minimally filled interface.

```
REPORT  ZZHRNPRICING.
  Tables: KOMK, KOMP.
  Data: tkomv like komv occurs 5 with header line.
  clear komk.
  komk-kappl = 'V '.
  komk-kalsm = 'RVAA01'.
  komk-vkorg = '0001'.
  komk-vtweg = '01'.
  komk-prsdt = sy-datum.
  komk-waerk = 'EUR'.
  clear komp.
  komp-kposn = '000001'.
  komp-pmatn = 'HN1080'.
  komp-mgame = '20'.
  komp-vrkme = 'KI'.
  komp-meins = 'KI'.
```

```
komp-prsfd = 'X'.
call function 'PRICING'
        exporting
                comm_head_i     = komk
                comm_item_i     = komp
                calculation_type = 'B'
        importing
                comm_head_e     = komk
                comm_item_e     = komp
        tables
                tkomv           = tkomv.
```
Listing 9.1 Minimal Interface for Calling the PRICING Function Module

9.1.3 Internal Structures and Tables of the Pricing Programs

If you program requirements, formulas, and user exits, you operate within the pricing program, and so within the function group V61A (pricing). In this section, we describe all structures with which you will be working in this environment. We want to illustrate the relationship between the structures and internal tables based on Figure 9.1. In this illustration, you will find the following elements:

▸ **p1 to p4**
Item numbers of the sales order

▸ **k1 and k2**
Index of the KOMK entry belonging to the structure KOMP

▸ **s1 to s6**
Line numbers of the condition types for KOMK entry k1

▸ **s7 to s11**
Line numbers of the condition types for KOMK entry k2

▸ **z1 to z21**
Line numbers of accesses for the KOMT1 entries

Figure 9.1 shows the flow of information from the sales order to pricing (KOMK and KOMP), the way within pricing (KOMT1, KOMT2, and XKOMV) and finally the transfer of the result back to the sales order (TKOMV and KOMP).

The path from KOMT2 to XKOMV contains condition records that we have not included in Figure 9.1. In the diagram, you see those entries grayed in the internal tables that are involved in the call of pricing (function module PRICING) for the second order item (p2).

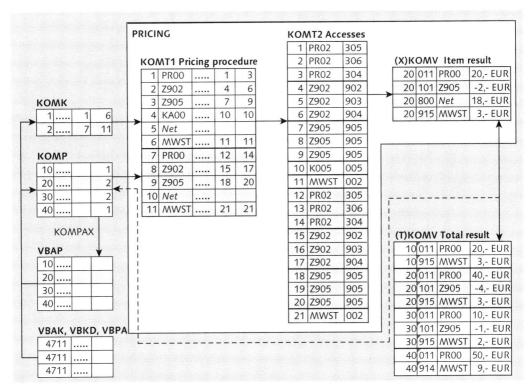

Figure 9.1 Context of the Most Important Structures in the Area of Pricing

These are the structures and internal tables involved:

▶ KOMV
  Structure of the internal table XKOMV of the pricing result of an item.

▶ KOMPAZD
  Structure of the *item-like* fields for receiving variable data fields from condition tables (VADAT). This is used within the access sequence (see Figure 9.2).

▶ KOMPLOOP
  Structure for the internal table XKOMPLOOP (see Section 9.3) of the item-like fields, to enable multiple access for one characteristic (e.g., for configuration variants).

▶ KOMPAX
  Subset of fields from the structure KOMP, which are passed to the calling line

item (e.g., sales order or billing document) as a result of pricing and are stored there (see Chapter 11, Section 11.6).

▶ STEU

Internal table of pricing types. This table is set up in routine `konditionsvorstep` (see Chapter 10, Section 10.1.2).

▶ TKSCHL

Internal table of condition types that are recalculated in pricing. You will find examples of using this internal table in Chapter 11, Section 11.2.

▶ TKSCHLEXCL

Internal table of condition types that are not recalculated in pricing. You will find examples of using this internal table in Chapter 11, Section 11.2.

▶ KOMT1

Internal table of the pricing procedure, consisting of all fields of the Customizing tables T683 (pricing procedure), T683S (pricing procedure: data), T685 (condition types), and T685A (condition types: additional price element data).

▶ KOMT2

Internal table of all accesses to the condition types in `KOMT1`.

▶ GKOMV

Internal accumulation table of group conditions, used in the overall valuation (`PRICING_COMPLETE`; see Chapter 10, Section 10.2).

▶ GKOMZ

Internal mapping table of all participating items and group conditions that have been incorporated into GKOMV (see Chapter 10, Section 10.2).

▶ KONP

Structure for the internal table `XKONP` of found condition records added to the internal table `XKOMV`. The connection between `KONP` and `XKOMV` is established by the xkomv-knumh field.

9.1.4 Field Sequence in the Condition Table

When creating a condition table, you must specify the order in which the key fields are arranged. Generally, you will be guided by how the generated condition maintenance dialog meets the demands of the users. Note, however, that header-like fields should be placed before item-like fields.

How do you recognize the header-like fields? You can identify them by the fact that all accesses within the access sequences use for this characteristic only fields of the structure KOMK or direct values.

If you want to use a new characteristic, you must think twice about whether you are inserting the field in the KOMK or KOMP structure. Technically, you should do that via an APPEND structure for the structures KOMKAZ (part of KOMK) or KOMPAZ (part of KOMP).

> **Warning**
>
> Do not append the fields as an APPEND structure directly to the structure KOMK. In Chapter 12, Section 12.2, you will find information about possible error situations that can occur if you do not adhere to this rule.
>
> If it is highly probable that the new characteristic value is the same in the items of an object (document), it should be inserted into the KOMK structure. If in doubt, you can try both variants with regard to their performance behavior in representative processes.

9.2   Data Determination via Condition Technique

As you saw in Chapter 1, Section 1.2, it's possible to include variable data fields in addition to the variable key components in the pricing conditions. The maintenance of these fields will be automatically provided as part of the generated maintenance dialog programs. The skillful use of these data fields in access sequences, requirements, and formulas offers many opportunities that again significantly increase the flexibility of pricing.

Figure 9.2 shows the different variants of this variable data. Shown here are the transport routes of the information from the condition record (Annn tables) to the target structure or table. Which method is the right one for your requirement is left to your judgment. You should always keep in mind that there are usually several possible solutions.

These are the options:

❶ Data determination in the access, use in subsequent accesses

❷ Data determination in the access, transfer to document item via requirement

❸ Transfer to document condition via formula (manipulation of the calculation)

❹ Transfer to KOMK via requirement (manipulation of the condition access)

❺ Use of data from other document conditions in formulas

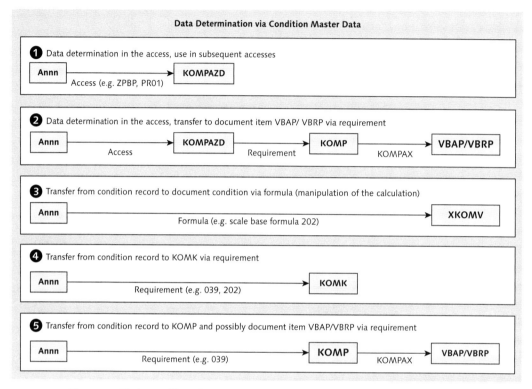

Figure 9.2 Variants of Data Determination via Condition Master Data

The next section includes some examples of these various methods of data determination via condition records.

9.2.1 Variant 1: Data Determination Within the Access: Used in Subsequent Access

This variant of data determination is based solely on the possibilities of access sequences. You can simply define it in Customizing. Requirements and formulas are not needed.

The price list type is an attribute of the customer master record and is determined *regardless of the date* during order processing from the master record of the sold-to party. The demand is now to make the assignment to the price list type date-dependent and thus changeable at any level within a given three-level hierarchy, defined by the *payer* (top level), the *sold-to party* (middle level), and the *ship-to party* (lowest level).

We can solve this task with two access sequences and respective condition types.

Action Needed at a Glance

First, we configure the access sequence ZPBP (data determination) for the standard condition table A149, as shown in Table 9.1, as an additive access sequence.

In a next step, we set up the condition type ZPBP (data determination customer) for the date-dependent determination of the different price list type. If you look at the access sequence ZPBP in Table 9.1 in more detail, you realize that the price list type is taken over from the condition record into the communication structure KOMPAZD in the field kompazd-pltyp_d. The condition type ZPBP must be configured with CONDITION CLASS = H (determining sales deal), which specifies that the condition records found only serve the data determination and are not saved as a pricing result.

As a second condition type, we use the condition type PBBS (base price) delivered with the standard SAP system. The access sequence used therein, PR01 (price, item price list), uses the different price list type in the field kompaz-pltyp that was previously provided by condition type ZPBP. You can see the in the access sequence PR01 shown in Table 9.2.

Finally, we include the two condition types ZPBP and PBBS in our pricing procedure (see Figure 9.4), maintain the required condition master data, and check the result in the sales order processing.

Condition Type ZPBP with Access Sequence ZPBP

The condition table A149 along with the access sequence ZPBP (see Table 9.1) represents the hierarchical relationship between the partner roles payer, sold-to party, and ship-to party, as illustrated in Figure 9.3.

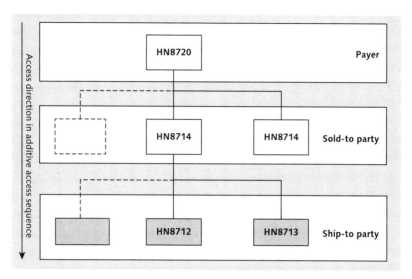

Figure 9.3 Simple Customer Hierarchy, Formed by Condition Table A149 and Access Sequence ZPBP

Acc.	Table	Condition Field		Document Field		Init	Access Type
10	A149: Payer	VKORG	=	KOMK	VKORG		
		VTWEG	=	KOMK	VTWEG		
		KUNRG	=	KOMK	KNRZE		
		KUNAG	=	KOMK	KDUMMY	X	
		KUNWE	=	KOMK	KDUMMY	X	
		PLTYP	=>	KOMPAZD	PLTYP_D		C
20	A149: Sold-to party	VKORG	=	KOMK	VKORG		
		VTWEG	=	KOMK	VTWEG		
		KUNRG	=	KOMK	KDUMMY	X	
		KUNAG	=	KOMK	KUNNR		
		KUNWE	=	KOMK	KDUMMY	X	
		PLTYP	=>	KOMPAZD	PLTYP_D		C
30	A149: Ship-to party	VKORG	=	KOMK	VKORG		
		VTWEG	=	KOMK	VTWEG		

Table 9.1 Additive Access Sequence ZPBP for Data Determination from the Condition A149 (Transaction V/07)

Acc.	Table	Condition Field		Document Field		Init	Access Type
		KUNRG	=	KOMK	KDUMMY	X	
		KUNAG	=	KOMK	KDUMMY	X	
		KUNWE	=	**KOMK**	**KUNWE**		
		PLTYP	=>	KOMPAZD	PLTYP_D		C

Table 9.1 Additive Access Sequence ZPBP for Data Determination from the Condition A149 (Transaction V/07) (Cont.)

In Table 9.1, you can see that the data field PLTYP of condition table A149, filled from a found condition record, is passed to the field kompazd-pltyp_d. The access sequence is configured additive, which causes the last entry found to be used. This is particularly useful when several data fields that are spread over different condition records need to be determined. Thus, a collection of fields is possible.

Condition Type PBBS with Access Sequence PR01

The actual price is then determined via the condition type PBBS with the second access sequence PR01 (see Table 9.2). Here, the divergent price list type cached in the field kompazd-pltyp_d is used. If no different price list type was determined, the standard price list is used.

Acc.	Table	Condition Field		Document Field	
15	A006: Differing price list type in document currency	VKORG	=	KOMK	VKORG
		VTWEG	=	KOMK	VTWEG
		PLTYP	=	**KOMPAZD**	**PLTYP_D**
		WAERK	=	KOMK	WAERK
		MATNR	=	KOMP	PMATN
16	A006: Differing price list type in local currency (requirement 003)	VKORG	=	KOMK	VKORG
		VTWEG	=	KOMK	VTWEG
		PLTYP	=	**KOMPAZD**	**PLTYP_D**
		WAERK	=	KOMK	HWAER
		MATNR	=	KOMP	PMATN

Table 9.2 Exclusive Access Sequence PR01 for Determining a Price from a Different Price List (Accesses 15 and 16)

333

Acc.	Table	Condition Field		Document Field	
20	A006: Standard price list type in document currency	VKORG	= KOMK	VKORG	
		VTWEG	= KOMK	VTWEG	
		PLTYP	= KOMK	PLTYP	
		WAERK	= KOMK	WAERK	
		MATNR	= KOMP	PMATN	
30	A006: Standard price list type in local currency (requirement 003)	VKORG	= KOMK	VKORG	
		VTWEG	= KOMK	VTWEG	
		PLTYP	= KOMK	PLTYP	
		WAERK	= KOMK	HWAER	
		MATNR	= KOMP	PMATN	
40	A004: Standard material prices	VKORG	= KOMK	VKORG	
		VTWEG	= KOMK	VTWEG	
		MATNR	= KOMP	PMATN	

Table 9.2 Exclusive Access Sequence PR01 for Determining a Price from a Different Price List (Accesses 15 and 16) (Cont.)

Enhancing the Pricing Procedure

Now you have to insert the two condition types ZPBP and PBBS into the pricing procedure (see Figure 9.4) and create the respective condition records. Then, you can check the result in the sales order.

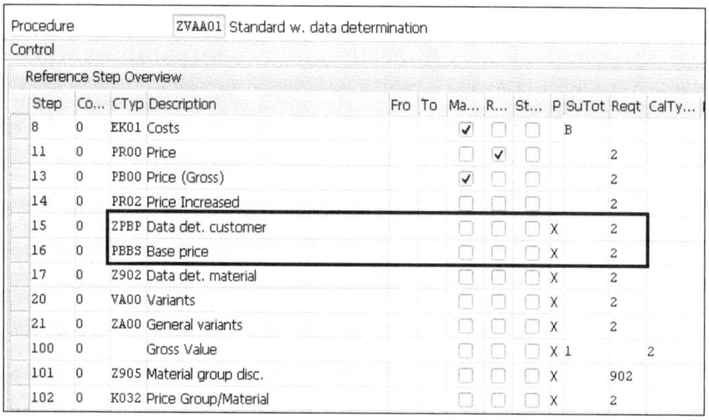

Figure 9.4 Example Pricing Procedure ZVAA01 (Transaction V/08)

Example Condition Records of Condition Type ZPBP for Variant 1

We can now set up an example and create the condition records for the data determination, as shown in Figure 9.5. For the ship-to party HN8713, the price list 02 is to be applied starting with 01.07.2016. For the PAYER HN8720, all sales orders will be based on price list 03.

Create Data det. customer Condition (ZPBP) : Fast Entry

| Sales Organization | 1000 | Germany Frankfurt |
| Distribution Channel | 10 | Final customer sales |

Customer-dependent data determination

Payer	Sold-to pt	Ship-to	Description	Price List	CondPrcgDt	C..	S..	Valid From	Valid to
HN8720				03			G	01.07.2016	31.12.9999
		HN8713	Ship-to France	02			G	01.07.2016	31.12.9999

Figure 9.5 Condition Records for Condition Type ZPBP (Data Determination Customer) Using Condition Table A149 (Transaction VK11)

Summary of Variant 1

Here again are all the necessary steps at a glance:

1. Creation of the condition type ZPBP (data determination of the price list type) with the condition table A149 and the additive access sequence ZPBP. Creation of the corresponding condition master data.

2. The second condition type PBBS (standard list price) with the condition table A006 and the exclusive access sequence PR01 is available in the standard SAP system and can be used as delivered. Creation of the corresponding condition master data.

3. Inserting the two condition types into the pricing procedure (see Figure 9.4).

4. Creation of a sales order and check of the pricing results (if necessary, using the pricing analysis functionality).

9.2.2 Variant 2: Data Determination in the Access, Transfer to Document Item via Requirement

In the previous example for data determination, we used the condition table A149. The characteristics ship-to party, sold-to party, and payer used therein represent a hierarchical relationship that is defined externally by the partner roles of the customer master data. The ship-to party is assigned to the sold-to party, and the sold-to party to the payer. The resolution of this relationship has already taken place in the sales order and the partner roles are passed to the pricing. Let's now deal with the possibility of defining and processing a hierarchical structure solely by means of pricing. We describe the solution up to the point that we can hand over the result of the data determination to the sales order.

We now will proceed step-by-step to develop the solution, starting with defining a material group hierarchy.

Definition of a Material Group Hierarchy

As elements of the material group hierarchy, we can use the fields MATERIAL GROUP 1 through 3 (MVGR1, MVGR2, and MVGR3). The possible values and the descriptions are stored in the tables TVM1 to TVM3 and maintained by the maintenance views V_TVM1 to V_TVM3. The fields can be entered in the material master and are transferred from there to the sales order item. We do not want to use this possibility, since the assignment in the material master cannot be dependent on the date.

The aim is to assign the materials to the lowest group MVGR1 and to determine therefrom the higher hierarchy nodes MVGR2 and MVGR3. The hierarchy itself can be changed depending on the date. This design has the advantage that sales orders that are created retroactively are valuated at the then valid state. If we were to use the fields from the material master records, we would have to change an assignment made directly in the material master and would therefore not be able to calculate with historical levels.

In Figure 9.6, you see the desired material group hierarchy that we can define using the condition tables A902, A903, and A904. With table A902, we can assign the materials to a certain material group MVGR1. With the tables A903 and A904, we can then determine the parent material groups MVGR2 and MVGR3.

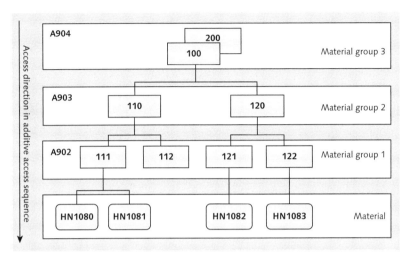

Figure 9.6 Material Group Hierarchy, Defined by the Condition Tables A902, A903, and A904 and the Access Sequence Z902

The allowed values for the groups of materials are shown in Figure 9.7, Figure 9.8, and Figure 9.9. With the definition of the material group hierarchy, we have created the prerequisite to set up a concrete hierarchy.

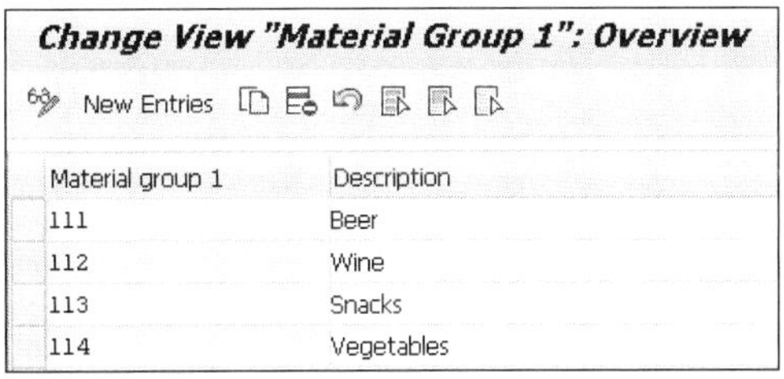

Change View "Material Group 1": Overview

New Entries

Material group 1	Description
111	Beer
112	Wine
113	Snacks
114	Vegetables

Figure 9.7 Material Group 1: The Lowest Level (SM30, V_TVM1)

Change View "Material Group 2": Overview

New Entries

Material group 2	Description
110	Beverages
120	Foodstuffs

Figure 9.8 Material Group 2: Second Level (SM30, V_TVM2)

Figure 9.9 Material Group 3: The Top Level (SM30, V_TVM3)

Action Needed at a Glance

We can solve this task with two new condition types and two new access sequences, as follows:

1. First, we set up the access sequence Z902 (data determination material), as shown in Table 9.3. With this access sequence, we determine at first the MATERIAL GROUP 1 of the material and the higher-level hierarchy levels MATERIAL GROUP 2 and MATERIAL GROUP 3.

2. Next, we configure the condition type Z902 (data determination material) for the data determination with the access sequence Z902 and CONDITION CLASS = H.

3. In the next step, we set up the second access sequence Z905 (material groups), as shown in Table 9.4. The accesses are set exclusively and determine the three hierarchical levels of the material group from bottom to top using partial keys.

4. We use this access sequence in the second condition type Z905 (material group discount), with which we provide a discount on this material group hierarchy level.

5. We can now create suitable condition master data for Z902 and Z905 (see Figure 9.10).

6. For the condition type Z905, we need a new requirement 902 (data transfer), with which we can perform the transport of the fields into the sales order item.

7. Finally, we include the two condition types Z902 and Z905 in our pricing procedure (see Figure 9.4) and can check the result in the sales order processing.

Condition Type Z902 with Access Sequence Z902

We configure the access sequence Z902 (data determination material) as displayed in Table 9.3 as an additive access sequence. We assign this access sequence to the newly set up condition type Z902.

Acc.	Table	Condition Field		Document Field/ Specific Value		Access Type
10	A902: Material	VKORG	=	**KOMK**	**VKORG**	
		MATNR	=	**KOMP**	**PMATN**	
		MVGR1	=>	KOMPAZD	ZZMVGR1	C
		KONDM	=>	KOMPAZD	ZZKONDM	C
		BONUS	=>	KOMPAZD	ZZBONUS	C
		PROVG	=>	KOMPAZD	ZZPROVG	C
20	A903: Material group 1	VKORG	=		**0001**	
		MVGR1	=	**KOMPAZD**	**ZZMVGR1**	
		MVGR2	=>	KOMPAZD	ZZMVGR2	C
30	A904: Material group 2	VKORG	=		**0001**	
		MVGR2	=	**KOMPAZD**	**ZZMVGR2**	
		MVGR3	=>	KOMPAZD	ZZMVGR3	C

Table 9.3 Additive Access Sequence Z902 for Data Determination (Transaction V/07)

With access sequence Z902, we first determine the MATERIAL GROUP 1 of the material. With the two subsequent accesses, we will find the parent hierarchy levels MATERIAL GROUP 2 and MATERIAL GROUP 3. In addition to MATERIAL GROUP 1, the data fields MATERIAL PRICING GROUP, VOLUME REBATE GROUP, and COMMISSION GROUP can be determined with table A902. However, we do not need them in our example.

We also have used *specific values* in this example. Because the accesses 20 and 30 have assigned the specific value 0001 for the access field to the sales organization, it is sufficient to maintain the material group hierarchy only for sales organization 0001.

Condition Type Z905 with Access Sequence Z905

We configure the access sequence Z905 (material group), as displayed in Table 9.4, as an exclusive access sequence. With this access sequence, we access the material group hierarchy from the bottom upward. We assign this access sequence to the newly setup condition type Z905 (material group discount), which we configure, for example, as a percentage discount.

Acc.	Table	Cond. Field		Document Field		Init
10	A905: Material group 1	VKORG	=	**KOMK**	**VKORG**	
		MVGR1	=	**KOMP**	**MVGR1**	
		MVGR2	=	KOMK	KDUMMY	X
		MVGR3	=	KOMK	KDUMMY	X
20	A905: Material group 2	VKORG	=	**KOMK**	**VKORG**	
		MVGR1	=	KOMK	KDUMMY	X
		MVGR2	=	**KOMP**	**MVGR2**	
		MVGR3	=	KOMK	KDUMMY	X
30	A905: Material group 3	VKORG	=	**KOMK**	**VKORG**	
		MVGR1	=	KOMK	KDUMMY	X
		MVGR2	=	KOMK	KDUMMY	X
		MVGR3	=	**KOMP**	**MVGR3**	

Table 9.4 Exclusive Access Sequence Z905 for Material Group Discount Z905 (Partially Qualified Access)

Example Condition Records of Condition Types Z902 and Z905

Figure 9.10 shows some example condition records for the condition types Z902 and Z905. You can also see in this figure the structure of all the condition tables involved at a glance.

Condition Type	VAKEY	DATBI	DATAB	VADAT

	KSCHL	VKORG	MATNR	DATBI	DATAB	MVGR1	KONDM	BONUS	PROVG
A902	Z902	0001	HN1080	31.12.9999	01.02.2010	111			
		0001	HN1081	31.12.9999	01.02.2010	111			
		0001	HN1082	31.12.9999	01.02.2010	121			
		0001	HN1083	31.12.9999	01.02.2010	122			

	KSCHL	VKORG	MVGR1	DATBI	DATAB	MVGR2
A903	Z902	0001	111	31.12.9999	01.02.2010	110
		0001	112	31.12.9999	01.02.2010	110
		0001	121	31.12.9999	01.02.2010	120
		0001	122	31.12.9999	01.02.2010	120

	KSCHL	VKORG	MVGR2	DATBI	DATAB	MVGR3
A904	Z902	0001	110	31.12.9999	01.02.2010	200
		0001	120	31.12.9999	01.02.2010	200

	KSCHL	VKORG	MVGR1	MVGR2	MVGR3	DATBI	DATAB	Discount
A905	Z905	0001			200	31.12.9999	01.02.2010	-1%
		0001		120		31.12.9999	01.02.2010	-2%

Figure 9.10 Condition Tables A902, A903, A904, and A905 and Sample Master Data

As a next step, we must now ensure that the data determined by condition type Z902 can be used. To this end, we set up the new requirement 902.

Requirement 902 for Data Transfer

We use the requirement 902 (data transfer) for the condition type Z905 to transfer the data fields cached in the structure KOMPAZD to KOMP. Thus, the access sequence Z905 can use the KOMP fields.

After adding the MVGR1, MVGR2, and MVGR3 fields to the structure KOMPAX (you can find more details in the action summary that follows), the contents will be automatically passed to the calling sales order and stored there in the vbap-mvgr1, vbap-mvgr2, and vbap-mvgr3 fields.

You will find the program code for requirement 902 in Listing 9.2. This requirement shows how you can transport field contents from KOMPAZD to KOMP. Here we are transferring the contents of MATERIAL GROUP 1 to MATERIAL GROUP 3. Following this template, you can add any other fields in a requirement and carry out the transport.

```
form kobed_902.
  If not kompazd-zzmvgr1 is initial.
    komp-mvgr1 = kompazd-zzmvgr1.
  endif.
  If not kompazd-zzmvgr2 is initial.
    komp-mvgr2 = kompazd-zzmvgr2.
  endif.
  If not kompazd-zzmvgr3 is initial.
    komp-mvgr3 = kompazd-zzmvgr3.
  endif.
  perform kobed_002.
endform.

* Prestep
form kobev_902.
  sy-subrc = 0.
endform.
```

Listing 9.2 Pricing Requirement 902 for Condition Type Z905

Enhancing the Pricing Procedure

Now we have to insert the two condition types Z902 and Z905 into the pricing procedure (see Figure 9.4). Then, we can create a sales order to check the result.

We can set a breakpoint in the requirement 902 and should find the state shown in Figure 9.11.

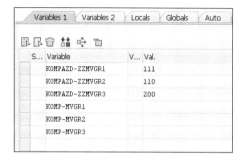

Figure 9.11 Debugger: Breakpoint in Requirement 902

Figure 9.12 shows the CONDITIONS screen of an order item. You can see here that the discount Z905 was found. You can check, using the CONDITION REC. button, whether the desired condition record was found.

N..	CnTy	Name	Amount		Crcy	per	U...	Condition value		Curr.	Status	Num...	OUn	CCon...	Un
☐	PR00	Price	12,00	EUR		1	CRT	12,00	EUR				20 PC		1 CRT
		Gross Value	12,00	EUR		1	CRT	12,00	EUR				20 PC		1 CRT
☐	Z905	Material group disc.	1,000-	%				0,12-	EUR				0		0
		Discount Amount	0,12-	EUR		1	CRT	0,12-	EUR				20 PC		1 CRT
		Rebate Basis	11,88	EUR		1	CRT	11,88	EUR				20 PC		1 CRT
		Net Value for Item	11,88	EUR		1	CRT	11,88	EUR				20 PC		1 CRT
		Net Value 2	11,88	EUR		1	CRT	11,88	EUR				20 PC		1 CRT
		Net Value 3	11,88	EUR		1	CRT	11,88	EUR				20 PC		1 CRT
☐	AZWR	Down Pay./Settlement	0,00	EUR				0,00	EUR				0		0
☐	MWST	Output Tax	10,000	%				1,19	EUR				0		0
		Total	13,07	EUR		1	CRT	13,07	EUR				20 PC		1 CRT
☐	SKTO	Cash Discount	2,000-	%				0,26-	EUR				0		0

Qty 1 CRT   Net 11,88 EUR   Tax 1,19

Pricing Elements

Condition rec.   Analysis   Update

Figure 9.12 Pricing Result in the Sales Order

Finally, we check that the determined material group hierarchy was transferred to the sales order item. You can find this information in the item detail (see Figure 9.13) on the ADDITIONAL DATA A tab.

Figure 9.13 Item Details Screen for Additional Data A: Material Group Hierarchy Determined from Condition Records

Now we have reached our goal. In the following summary, we recap the procedure.

Summary of Variant 2 and an Alternative Solution

In the method described here, the data determination is carried out within the pricing. This solution has the advantage that the data is updated when a new pricing for the document is performed, which may be required, for example, in the context of retroactive changes. The disadvantage is that you cannot handle every field this way. The method is only possible for fields that are used in the sales order exclusively for pricing or for follow-up functions such as SAP BW, CO-PA, statistics, output, etc. Furthermore, you can use this method only for document item fields (VBAP and VBRP). Fields of the header (VBAK) or of the commercial data (VBKD) cannot be determined with this method.

> **Alternative Method for the Date-Dependent Data Determination**
>
> In Chapter 12, Section 12.8, we describe a second method of date-dependent data determination that does not have these disadvantages (but has others instead).

Let's now summarize the necessary actions for variant 2 at a glance:

1. Add the fields MVGR1 to MVGR3 to the structure KOMP using an `APPEND` to the structure KOMPAZ, if these fields are not already present. Add the fields in the field catalog of allowed fields for the condition tables.

2. Add the desired variable data fields, for example ZZMVGR1 to ZZMVGR3, ZZKONDM, ZZBONUS, and ZZPROVG to the structure KOMPAZD via an `APPEND`.

3. Create the condition type Z902 (data determination) with the additive access sequence Z902 (data determination material) and create the corresponding condition master data (see Table 9.3 and Figure 9.10).

4. Create the condition type Z905 (material group discount) with exclusive access sequence Z905 (material group) and create the corresponding condition master data (see Table 9.4 and Figure 9.10).

5. Add the MVGR1 to MVGR3 fields to the structure KOMPAX by APPEND structure for the included structure KOMPAXM. Thus, the transport of the data fields from KOMP to VBAP is performed automatically by MOVE-CORRESPONDING.

6. Create the requirement 902 for condition type Z905 to transport the data fields from KOMPAZD to KOMP (see Listing 9.2).

7. Insert the two condition types in the pricing procedure (see Figure 9.4).

8. Create a sales order to check the pricing results (using the pricing analysis if necessary).

The first two variants presented here use the access sequence to process data of the variable part of the condition records. The following methods do not use this method, but rely solely on formulas and requirements.

9.2.3 Transfer from Condition Record via Formula or Requirement

In addition to the option to use data fields from condition records during the access via the KOMPAZD structure, you can access this information directly in requirements and formulas. For this purpose, two condition types are always involved. The first (PBUD) provides the data and the second (PBBS) uses this data.

One example is the price book, which is handled by the pricing procedure RVAA02 (see Figure 9.14).

For more information about the price book, refer to Chapter 8, Section 8.1.2, and Chapter 6. To summarize:

▶ Using the condition type PBU (price book determination), you determine which customers can participate in a sales deal.

▶ Using the condition type PBUD (price book, basis), you specify, per material or material group, which percentage of the base price PBBS is to be applied. In addition to this percentage, you can specify other data (pricing date, price list type, and fixed scale quantity).

▸ As a price list, the condition type PBBS (base price) provides the base price.

▸ The condition type PBUP (price book, gross price) calculates from the condition types PBBS and PBUD the final starting price.

	Step	Co...	CTyp	Description	Fro	To	Ma...	R...	St...	P	SuTot	Reqt	CalTy...	BasT...
Procedure			RVAA02	Standard with Price Book										
Control														
Reference Step Overview														
	9	0	PBU	Price book - determ.			☐	☐	☐		2			
	10	0	PBUD	Price book - Basis			☐	☑	☑		2			
	11	0	PBBS	Base price			☐	☑	☐		202			
	12	0	PBUP	Price book - GrossPr			☐	☐	☐		2		202	
	100	0		Gross Value			☐	☐	☐	X	1		2	
	101	0	K148	Product Hierarchy			☐	☐	☐	X	2			
	102	0	PB1	SlsDeal 1 - Determ.			☐	☐	☐	X	2			
	103	0	PB1D	Sales Deal 1			☐	☐	☐	X	62			
	110	1	RA01	% Disc.from Gross	100		☑	☐	☐	X	2			
	110	2	RA00	% Discount from Net			☑	☐	☐	X	2			
	110	3	RC00	Quantity Discount			☑	☐	☐	X	2			

Figure 9.14 Pricing Procedure RVAA02 (Standard with Price Book): Transaction V/08

We want to illustrate the operation using an example. With Transaction VB21 (Create Sales Deal), we create a sales deal using the sales deal type PRBU (price book) and maintain the relevant condition records. You can see this in the example sales deal 90 in Figure 9.15.

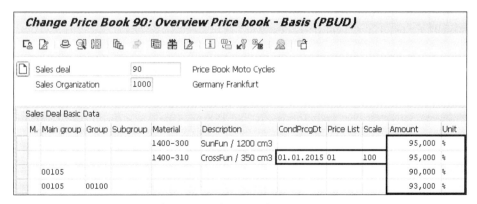

Figure 9.15 Condition Records for Sales Deal 90, Condition Type PBUD (Transactions VB12 to VB23)

345

We consider the material 1400-310, which is treated as a deviation from the normal case:

- Pricing date: 01.12.2015
- Price list type: 01
- Scale quantity: 100

Now we enter a sales order item for material 1400-310 with the order quantity of 10 pieces. Figure 9.16 shows the CONDITIONS screen for this item.

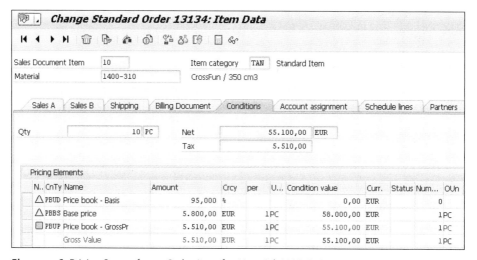

Figure 9.16 Pricing Screen for an Order Item for Material 1400-310

Now we select the CONDITIONS DETAIL screen for condition type PBBS (base price) (see Figure 9.17).

Here you can see two variants of the data transfer from the condition type PBUD determined before. On the one hand, it is taking over the different pricing date via the requirement 202 (box on the upper right), on the other hand, the fixed scale quantity is set to 100 pieces by the scale formula 202 (box on the left of Figure 9.17).

We will use the example presented here to explain the operation of the next two variants. These variants show how the variable data in the condition records can be processed with formulas and requirements.

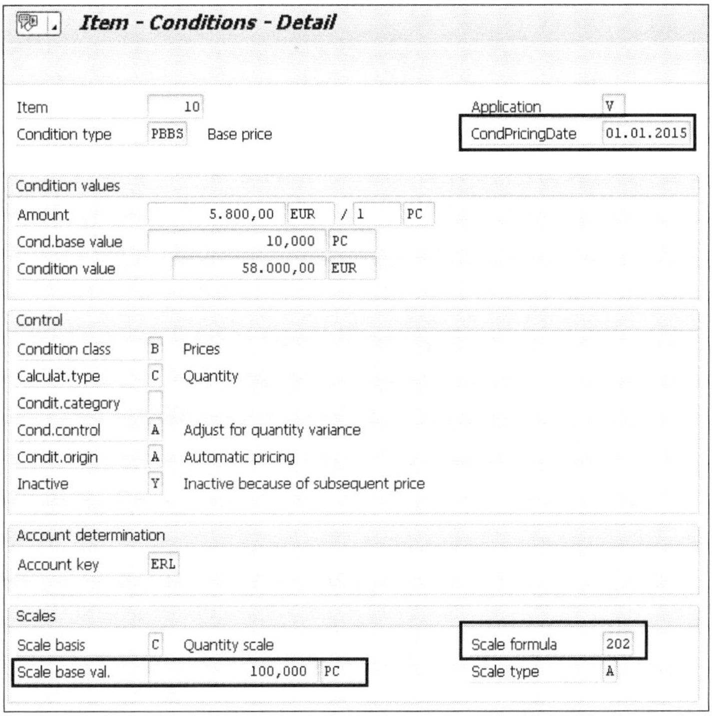

Figure 9.17 Condition Detail for the Order Item: Condition Type PBBS

9.2.4 Variant 3: Transfer to XKOMV from Condition Record via Formula

The condition type PBBS is configured with scale base formula 202 (see Listing 9.3). In our example, we transfer the fixed scale quantity 100 from rkomg-kstaf to xkwert (and further to xkomv-kstbs), whereby the scale quantity is changed from the previous 10 pieces to 100 pieces.

```
form frm_staffelbas_202.
  check: preisfindungsart ne 'E'.
  perform provide_condition_data using 'PBUD'.
  if not rkomg-kstaf is initial.
    arbfeld = rkomg-kstaf * 1000.
    if xkwert lt arbfeld.
      xkwert = arbfeld.
    endif.
  endif.
endform.
```

Listing 9.3 Scale Base Formula 202 for the Condition Type PBBS

In the structure RKOMG, we find all the fields of the variable key and the variable data fields. In addition to the scale base formulas, you can also use condition base value formulas and condition value formulas to identify and process that information. This is done according to the same pattern as in the presented scale formula. With these formulas, only the calculation of the condition values may be affected. With the next variant of the data determination presented next, the access to the condition records is manipulated.

9.2.5 Variant 4: Transfer to KOMK from Condition Record via Requirement

The condition type PBBS (base price) has assigned in the pricing procedure RVAA02 the requirement 202 (price book base price). The program code is found in Listing 9.4.

```
form kobed_202.
  sy-subrc = 4.
  if komp-kposn ne 0.
    check: komp-prsfd ca 'BX'.
    check: komp-kznep = space.
  endif.
  perform provide_condition_data using 'PBUD'.
  if not rkomg-kdatu is initial and
     rkomg-kdatu ne space.
    komk-prsdt = rkomg-kdatu.
  endif.
  sy-subrc = 0.
endform.
* Prestep
form kobev_202.
  sy-subrc = 0.
endform.
```

Listing 9.4 Pricing Requirement 202 for Condition Type PBBS

By performing the `provide_condition_data using 'PBUD'` routine, the condition PBUD is searched for in the internal table XKOMV, and the data of this entry is provided in the structure RKOMV. In addition, the associated condition master record is read and transferred to RKONP. The variable data fields are provided in the RKOMG structure.

In our example, the data field KDATU is handed over from the condition record for condition type PBUD to the komk-prsdt field. This causes the condition type PBBS to be read with the modified pricing date.

Changes to the contents of the structure KOMP within requirements are not permanent. The next condition type will reuse the original state (the initial pricing date). Note also that a possibly executed prestep will use the original state of KOMK. This means that you cannot register the relevant accesses for the condition type for *access optimization* (see Chapter 14, Section 14.2). Otherwise, inexplicable effects of missing conditions can occur, such as those described in Chapter 12, Section 12.2. The process will also not work for accesses that use KOMK fields exclusively, because in these cases, the final access to the condition tables was already carried out at the time of the prestep, using the original pricing date.

9.2.6 Variant 5: Utilization of Data of Other Document Conditions in Formula

Concluding the topic of data determination via condition technique, we want to introduce a somewhat different variant. In this method, we do not process the information from condition records, but instead use the data of other previously found condition types within formulas. The condition type PBUP (price book, gross price) in our example uses data from the previous condition types PBUD and PBBS to determine the final gross price. This can be implemented only with formulas. In the example, we use the condition base value formula 202 (see Listing 9.5). The RKOMV structure contains the data of the condition type PBUD and, in the Y-fields, the data from the last price condition type is provided (in this case, of condition type PBBS).

```
form frm_kond_basis_202.
  check: preisfindungsart NE 'E'.
  perform provide_condition_data USING 'PBUD'.
  clear xkomv-kbetr.
  if rkomv-krech ca percental.
    xkomv-kbetr = ykbetr * rkomv-kbetr / 100000.
    xkomv-krech = ykrech.
    ..
  elseif rkomv-krech ca relative.
    xkomv-kbetr = rkomv-kbetr.
```

```
    xkomv-krech = rkomv-krech.
    . .
  endif.
  . .
endform.
```
Listing 9.5 Condition Base Value Formula for the Condition Type PBUP

Finally, we want to mention once again the essential element of variants 3, 4, and 5, which is the `provide_condition_data` routine. This routine makes it possible, using formulas, to determine all the data of another previously found condition.

9.3 Fields with Multiple Values

In the standard SAP system, we have condition types that have characteristics with multiple occurrences. The task now is to perform the condition access for condition types that use such a feature several times for all specified values.

9.3.1 The KOMPLOOP Variant for Multiple Value Fields

In the standard SAP system, we have the following examples of condition types with multiple value fields:

▶ VA00: Variants (VARCOND)

▶ PB1D: Sales deal determination (KNUMA_AG)

▶ KAD0: Material costs (ADDNR) from the condition application M (purchasing)

To solve this problem, we use the Data Dictionary (DIC) structure KOMPLOOP. This structure contains the characteristics listed here as well as additional information, such as a quantity that is needed to calculate the condition (see Figure 9.18). Callout ❶ shows the component for PB1, callout ❷ the components for VA00, and callout ❸ the components for KAD0.

The structure is part of the item structure KOMP. Within the pricing program, there is a corresponding internal table called XKOMPLOOP. The access to a condition record (in the course of processing an access sequence) is performed as often as entries are contained in the XKOMPLOOP table. The fields of the KOMP structure are transferred by move-corresponding from XKOMPLOOP.

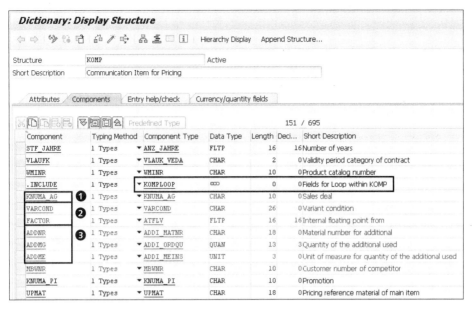

Figure 9.18 KOMPLOOP Part of the Item Structure KOMP

The setup of the internal table XKOMPLOOP is carried out as follows:

▸ **For condition type VA00 by the internal table XVCKEY**
This internal table XVCKEY is filled with the variant keys from the product configuration of a sales order item before the pricing is called. The field VARCOND varies. Besides this field, the FACTOR field is also transferred. This field represents for variable configuration characteristics the variant quantity and will be handed over later to the created document condition in the xkomv-kfaktor field.

▸ **For condition type PB1D by the requirement 062 (see Listing 9.6)**
The field KNUMA_AG varies. The internal table XKNUMA used here is provided by the preceding condition type PB1 (sales deal determination) due to its configuration with CONDITION CLASS = H. There sales deal numbers to be considered are determined.

```
form kobed_062.
  sy-subrc = 4.
   if komp-kposn ne 0.
     check: komp-prsfd ca 'BX'.
     check: komp-kznep = space.
     if not xknuma[] is initial.
```

```
        refresh xkomploop.
        clear xkomploop.
        loop at xknuma where anz_excl = 0.
          xkomploop-knuma_ag = xknuma-knuma_ag.
          append xkomploop.
        endloop.
      endif.
    endif.
    sy-subrc = 0.
  endform.
```

Listing 9.6 Pricing Requirement 062 for the Condition Type PB1D

▶ **For condition type KAD0 by the requirement 063 (see Listing 9.7)**
The field ADDNR varies. The ADDMG (quantity) field is handed over later, as in condition type VA00 into the field xkomv-kfaktor.

```
form kobed_063.
  sy-subrc = 4.
  if komp-posn ne 0.
    check: komp-prsfd ca 'BX'.
    refresh xkomploop.
    clear xkomploop.
    call function 'WTAD_ADDIS_FOR_PRICING'
          exporting
                fi_komk          = komk
                fi_komp          = komp
                fi_addicalc      = '1'    "material costs
          tables
                fet_komploop     = xkomploop
          exceptions
                addis_not_active = 1
                no_addis_found   = 2
                others           = 3.
    check sy-subrc eq 0.
  endif.
  sy-subrc = 0.
endform.
```

Listing 9.7 Pricing Requirement 063 for the Condition Type KAD0

You can use this method for customer-specific characteristics. In this case, you do not add your new characteristic as an APPEND to KOMP, but to KOMPLOOP. Then you can set up the internal table XKOMPLOOP using a customer-specific requirement, as shown in the previous examples.

9.3.2   The Repeating Field Variant for Multiple Value Fields

A second method to handle such characteristics with multiple values is to include the characteristic n-fold in KOMK or KOMP. One example of this approach is the customer hierarchy, which is represented by the fields komk-hienr01 to komk-hienr15.

The difference between the two methods is that in the KOMPLOOP case, the access sequence has a single access, whereas in this method, the access sequence can have as many accesses as there are repeating fields. In the example of the customer hierarchy, the number of accesses is therefore in the standard SAP system maximum of 15. It is thus clear that the number of accesses is limited. You need to think twice about how many multiple values can occur.

In the case of KOMK fields, these must be determined outside of the pricing and then handed over to pricing (but not in a requirement). If your characteristic is header-like (that means it is a typical KOMK candidate), you should use this method instead of the KOMPLOOP method, which is indeed only applicable on the item level. The difference lies in the performance. For KOMK fields, prestep logic is available and is described in detail in Chapter 14, Section 14.2.

9.3.3   Variant Using BAdI SD_COND_LOAD_MVA

In this third method, the multiple fields are handed over to the pricing program by method load_multivalued_attributes of BAdI SD_COND_LOAD_MVA as name/value pairs. In addition to programming the BadI, you must set in the case of multivalued attributes the indicator tkomp-use_multival_attr in the pricing preparation, so that the BAdI method is processed. The pricing program then automatically takes into account the multiple values in all affected accesses.

The advantage of this method is that you can manage a theoretically unlimited number of characteristics with multiple values without having to insert additional fields into the communication structures.

The number of values is also not limited. However, the values of the characteristics are only partially available in the rest of the pricing program, but can be recalculated, if necessary, by a second self-programmed call of the BAdI.

9.4   Summary

In this chapter, you were introduced to all the important communication structures and internal tables of the pricing program and their relationships. You will need this knowledge to successfully apply the main theme of this chapter, data determination via the condition technique, to your own pricing scenarios. In addition, you saw the importance of requirements and formulas for the solution of manifold demands. We will cover in more detail the proper use of requirements and formulas in Chapter 11. To help you understand the operation of these routines and user exits, we will introduce the most important programs of pricing next, in Chapter 10.

In this chapter, we outline the program flow of the most important pricing components. In particular, we will show where user exits, requirements, and formulas are called up.

10   Important Programs for Pricing

In this chapter, we take a close look at the main function modules of pricing. With this information, you should be able to connect your own object to pricing. The program parts are presented in simplified form, which means that the original program in general contains additional coding lines or the other coding line in addition. We have therefore cut out only the relevant parts of the original programs necessary for understanding.

Specifically, we talk about:

- The function module PRICING
- The function module PRICING_COMPLETE
- The function module PRICING_COPY
- The data storage of pricing results in table KONV
- The function module PRICING_REFRESH
- The dialog connection in SAP GUI and other interesting programs
- The relationship of the components of pricing

To perform pricing, you need the PRICING function module at the very least; the other modules are not always needed.

We recommend that you approach this chapter in an iterative way: first, read through to gain an overview of the program elements and terms. Then, gradually go deeper into the details. Within the context of specific tasks, we refer repeatedly to the same concepts and therefore give you the opportunity to increase your knowledge.

10.1   The PRICING Function Module

The PRICING function module performs pricing for an item. The caller prepares the communication structures KOMK and KOMP and passes them along with a pricing type to the function module. Listing 10.1 shows the simplified call of pricing for a sales order item in the program SAPFV45P (sales: item processing).

```
form preisfindung using preisfindungsart.
   perform preisfindung_vorbereiten using 'P'.
   call function 'PRICING'
           exporting
                comm_head_i     = tkomk
                comm_item_i     = tkomp
                calculation_type = preisfindungsart
                preliminary     = 'X'
           importing
                comm_head_e     = tkomk
                comm_item_e     = tkomp
           tables
                tkomv           = xkomv
                svbap           = uvbap.
   move-corresponding tkomp to kompax.
   move-corresponding kompax to vbap.
endform.
```
Listing 10.1 Calling the Item Pricing in the Sales Order

The particular parts of this code have the following meaning: The routine preisfindung_vorbereiten (pricing prepare) fills the communication structures (T)KOMK and (T)KOMP. We cover this routine in detail in Section 10.1.1. For more information about filling these communication structures in the various applications, see Chapter 13.

The preisfindungsart field (pricing type) must be set depending on the situation and determines which condition types should be recalculated. The possible values are stored in the domain KNPRS. The characteristics of the individual values are defined in the internal pricing table STEU, which in turn is filled in routine konditionsvorstep (see Figure 10.1). For more information on the pricing type, in particular for information about setting up customer-specific pricing types, see Chapter 11.

The internal table XKOMV contains, in the coding example shown in Figure 10.1, the determined conditions of the whole sales order. This is the name in the sales order processing. Within the `PRICING` function module, this table has the name `TKOMV`.

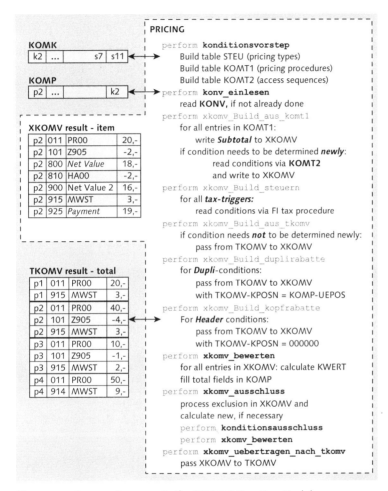

Figure 10.1 Program Sequence in the PRICING Function Module

After processing the `PRICING` function module, transporting the pricing result into the order item is performed by `move-corresponding` via the KOMPAX structure. For more details, refer to Chapter 11, Section 11.6.

Figure 10.1 provides an overview of the processing sequence of the `PRICING` function module. In the following section, we look at major routines of this function module in more detail.

10.1.1 Routine PREISFINDUNG_VORBEREITEN (Pricing Prepare)

With the `preisfindung_vorbereiten` routine, the communication structures KOMK (pricing header) and KOMP (pricing item) are set up in sales order (SAP-FV45P) and billing (SAPLV60A). The KOMK entries are stored in the internal table `TKOMK`. Initially, the structures KOMK and KOMP are filled for each line item of tables `VBAP`/`VBRP`. Then, they are checked with the key part of the structure KEY_UC KOMK to determine whether an entry with this content already exists in the internal table `TKOMK`. If it does, the item KOMP is allocated by the pointer `komp-ix_komk` to this entry. If there is no entry, a new entry is inserted in the internal table `TKOMK` and the new pricing item KOMP is allocated to this entry.

On the first call of the `PRICING` function module for a new KOMK segment, the `konditionsvorstep` (condition prestep) routine is performed and the connection to the internal table `KOMT1` is established via the pointers `komk-ix_komt1_v` and `komk-ix_komt1_b`.

Listing 10.2 shows the structure of the `preisfindung_vorbereiten` routine in the sales order.

```
form preisfindung_vorbereiten.
  * tkomk
  move-corresponding kuwev to tkomk.
  move-corresponding vbak  to tkomk.
  move-corresponding vbkd  to tkomk.
  tkomk-bukrs = tvko-bukrs.
  tkomk-hwaer = t001-waers.
  ..
  call method l_sd_sales_item_exit->item_pricing_com_h.
  perform userexit_pricing_prepare_tkomk(sapmv45a).
  read table tkomk with key tkomk-key_uc.
  if sy-subrc ne 0.
     append tkomk.
     tkomk-ix_komk = sy-tabix.
     modify tkomk index sy-tabix.
  endif.
  * tkomp
  clear tkomp.
  tkomp-ix_komk =  tkomk-ix_komk.
  move-corresponding vbak  to tkomp.
  move-corresponding vbap  to tkomp.
  move-corresponding vbapd to tkomp.
  move vbap-prodh to prodh.
  move-corresponding prodh to tkomp.
  ..
  call method l_sd_sales_item_exit->item_pricing_com_i.
```

```
    perform userexit_pricing_prepare_tkomp(sapmv45a).
endform.
```

Listing 10.2 Routine PREISFINDUNG_VORBEREITEN

The user exits provided in this routine are probably among the most frequently used ones in the SAP system.

> **Note**
>
> In the "old" `userexit_pricing_prepare_tkomp`, you could not change TKOMK fields; inexplicable pricing results could occur. The reason is that changes at this late point in time are no longer included in the `KOMK-KEY_UC` logic (see Listing 10.2).

10.1.2 Routine KONDITIONSVORSTEP (Condition Prestep)

The `konditionsvorstep` routine has two tasks. First, it sets up the internal table of pricing types STEU, and then sets up the internal tables `KOMT1` and `KOMT2` from the pricing procedure and the access sequences.

Setting Up the Internal Table STEU of Pricing Types

First, it sets up the internal table `STEU` of pricing types. Possible values are defined in the KNPRS domain as fixed values. In Figure 10.2, you can see the content of the internal table `STEU` of pricing types (obtained by debugging).

KNPRS	KNTYP [C(10)]	KOAID [C(10)]	MAUEB	STFKZ [	NOTYP	KFKIV	KVARC	PRSQU
A	f........	....		CD...	.....	.	.	
B	....	ABCDEGQWH.		CD...	JQ...	.	.	
C	....	ABCDEGQWH.	X	CD...	.....	.	.	
D	....	....		.....	.....	.	.	.
E	....	....		.....	.....	.	.	.
F	....	....		.....	.....	.	.	.
G	GLRIEfbhn.	CDEGQ.....		.....	.....	X	.	
H	BFLf......	....		CD...	.....	.	.	
I	....	C.........		.....	.....	.	.	
K	..RIE.....	CDEGQ.....		.....	.....	X	.	
M	....	....		.....	.....	.	.	.
N	G.........	....		.....	.....	.	.	
O	O.........	....	X	.....	.....	.	X	
P	....	....		.....	.....	.	.	
Q	Q.........	....		.....	.....	.	.	
U	U.........	....		.....	.....	.	.	
J	d.........	....		.....	.....	.	.	
R	GLRIEfbhn.	DEGQ......		.....	.....	X	.	
S	ij........	....		.....	.....	.	.	

Figure 10.2 Debugger: Internal Table STEU of Pricing Types

The table columns in Figure 10.2 define whether the condition type is to be newly determined or not, depending of the content of the corresponding characteristics:

▶ KNPRS: Pricing type (key of the internal table STEU)

▶ KNTYP: Recalculate condition types (maximum of ten)

▶ KOAID: Recalculate condition classes (maximum of ten)

▶ MAUEB: Keep manual changes in any case

▶ STFKZ: Scale type: Interval scales with scale type C and D have to be recalculated also in the case of item quantity changes

▶ NOTYP: Do not recalculate condition types (maximum of five)

▶ KFKIV: Recalculate intercompany billing condition types (e.g., condition type PI01)

▶ KVARC: Recalculate variant conditions (e.g., condition type VA00)

▶ PRSQU: Price source: Do not recalculate conditions that have been taken over from other applications (e.g., purchasing). The takeover of such conditions is performed by the PRICING_COPY function module. An automatic determination of such "external" conditions is generally not possible.

Within the order processing in the standard SAP system, some pricing types have a hard-coded logic programmed. This applies to the following cases and pricing types:

▶ A: In quantity change (interval scales new)

▶ C: When creating an item (all condition types are new except manual ones)

▶ G: When you change the ship-to party (taxes are new)

▶ O: When calling the variant configuration (variant conditions are new)

The userexit_pricing_rule routine is provided for configuring customer-specific pricing types (the values X, Y, and Z and 1 to 9 are reserved for customers). See Chapter 11, Section 11.8.1 for more information.

After you set up the internal table STEU of pricing types, the next step is to generate the internal tables KOMT1 (pricing procedure) and KOMT2 (access sequences) for a given instance of the KOMK structure.

Setting Up the Internal Tables KOMT1 (Pricing Procedure) and KOMT2 (Access Sequences)

You set up the internal tables only for the first item, which is processed for an instance of structure KOMK. All other subsequent items then use this information.

In the table KOMT1 the condition types from the table T683S (pricing procedure) are adopted, enriched by all the fields from tables T685 and T685A of condition types. If a requirement is assigned to the pricing procedure, the "prestep" part (kobev_nnn) is processed. If the test results in a negative outcome, the condition type is *not* included in the KOMT1 table. The connection between the KOMK structure and the internal table KOMT1 is established by the komk-ix_komt1_v and komk-ix_komt1_b pointers.

If an access sequence is assigned to the condition type, the accesses are read from table T682I and inserted in the internal table KOMT2. If an access has assigned a requirement, again the "prestep" part (kobev_nnn) is processed first. If the test returns a negative result, the access is not included in the table KOMT2. In addition, the access to the condition records is performed at this point of time to check their existence (*proofreading*). We can distinguish three situations:

- **Access includes only KOMK fields**
  If the access includes only KOMK fields, the final access to the condition table is already performed here. If a condition record was found, this is documented by filling the komt2-knumh field (a unique number of the condition record). Otherwise, the access is not included in KOMT2.

- **Access includes KOMP fields/proofreading is active**
  If the access includes KOMP fields and is marked in table T682V (optimize accesses) as CHECK IN PRESTEP, the condition table with the leading KOMK fields is performed. If no record is found, the access is not included in KOMT2. This is done by the SD_COND_ ACCESS function module if the prestep parameter is set. In this case, the komt2-knumh field remains empty.

- **Access includes KOMP fields/proofreading inactive**
  If the access includes KOMP fields and is *not marked* in table T682V as CHECK IN PRESTEP, the condition table is not proofread and the entry is added to KOMT2. In this case, the komt2-knumh field remains empty.

The connection between an entry in the internal table KOMT1 and the related condition accesses in the internal table KOMT2 is established by the pointers komt1-ix_komt2_v and komt1-ix_komt2_b. Listing 10.3 and Listing 10.4 show the program sequence of the prestep.

```
form konditionsvorstep using incl_zugriffsfolge type c.
   < read tables t001, t001k, t001w,t001r,t005,.. >
   < create internal table STEU >
   perform userexit_pricing_rule.
   loop at xt683s into t683s.
      perform kobev_nnn.
      move-corresponding t685  to komt1.
      move-corresponding t685a to komt1.
      perform komt2_aufbauen using incl_zugriffsfolge.
      move-corresponding t683s to komt1.
      append komt1.
   endloop.
endform.
```

Listing 10.3 Routine konditionsvorstep


```
form komt2_aufbauen using incl_zugriffsfolge type c.
   loop at xt682i into t682i.
      move-corresponding t682i to komt2.
      <check entry in T682V>
      perform kobev_nnn.
      call function 'SD_COND_ACCESS'
        exporting
           application                   = komk-kappl
           condition_type                = komt1-rkschl
           date                          = komk-prsdt
           header_comm_area              = komk
           position_comm_area            = komp
           prestep                       = 'X'
           read_only_one_record          = 'X'
           t682i_i                       = t682i
        importing
           condition_is_purely_header = headkz
        tables
           condition_records          = kondtab.
        komt2-knumh = kondtab-knumh.
      append komt2.
   endloop.
endform.
```

Listing 10.4 Routine komt2_aufbauen (Access Sequences)

In addition to the main task of setting up of the internal tables STEU, KOMT1, and KOMT2 from the Customizing tables T683S, T685, T685A, and T682I, in the konditionsvorstep routine are also read various Customizing tables (among others, tables T001, T001K, T001W, T001R, and T005), and the userexit_pricing_rule is called to set up customer-specific pricing types.

The internal table KOMT2 of the access sequences is set up from table T682I by the routine komt2_aufbauen. The system determines whether the "check in prestep" is enabled in table T682V. In addition, the "prestep" part of a possibly assigned requirement (kobev_nnn) is processed. Depending on the outcome of the check, the condition records are proofread with the function module SD_COND_ACCESS.

10.1.3 Routine KONV_EINLESEN (Read KONV)

The konv_einlesen routine reads the condition of a document from the database table KONV and the results are cached in the interface table TKOMV. Since the internal table TKOMV is defined with structure KOMV, the dynamic fields (KONVD) of structure TKOMV are complemented by routine xkomv_ergaenzen. There, the parameters of TKONV, which do not exist in KONV, are supplemented from the internal table KOMT1. In addition, the internal table XKONP is set up by the konp_2_xkonp routine. This table contains the data of all condition master records found in the sales document, enriched by the accumulated values from the information structures S060 and S071.

10.1.4 Routine XKOMV_AUFBAUEN_AUS_KOMT1 (Set Up XKOMV from KOMT1)

In the xkomv_aufbauen_aus_komt1 routine (see Listing 10.5), those condition types of the pricing procedure KOMT1 are determined that must be redetermined in accordance with the *pricing type*. This means that a possibly previously determined condition in the interface table TKOMV might be discarded and recalculated. The decision as to whether the condition has to be recalculated is made by the xkomv_aufbauen_pruefen routine. If a condition type must be recalculated, the final requirements are checked by kobed_nnn. The table XKOMPLOOP for multiple fields is taken into account, and finally the conditions are read via the accesses according to KOMT2 and the conditions found are added to table XKOMV (routine konditionen_lesen).

The subtotals in the pricing procedure are a special case. They are characterized by the fact that they have no condition type assigned. Subtotals are always recalculated, as they are not transferred to the interface table TKOMV.

```
form xkomv_aufbauen_aus_komt1.
   old_komk = komk.
   loop at komt1 from komk-ix_komt1_v to komk-ix_komt1_b.
      refresh xkomploop.
      <buildt xkomploop from xvckey for variant conditions>
      perform kobed_nnn.
      check sy-subrc = 0.
      perform xkomv_aufbauen_pruefen.
      check sy-subrc = 0.
      loop at xkomploop.
        move-corresponding xkomploop to komp.
        loop at komt2 from komt1-ix_komt2_v to komt1-ix_komt2_b
           perform konditionen_lesen.
        endloop.
      endloop.
   komk = old_komk.
   endloop.
endform.
```
Listing 10.5 Routine xkomv_aufbauen_aus_komt1

With the konditionen_lesen routine (see Listing 10.6), the condition records for an access from table KOMT2 (i.e., T682I) are read and added to the worktable XKOMV. Here, the possible requirement of the access is checked (kobed_nnn) and then the condition records are read with the SD_COND_ACCESS function module. Then the internal table XKONP of the condition details is set up (konp_2_xkonp) for the found condition records of the internal table KONDTAB. The XKOMV structure is filled (xkomv_fuellen) and added to the table XKOMV.

In some scenarios, the condition records are not read from the database, but from the memory using the SD_COND_READ_FROM_MEMORY function module. This is necessary when, as in the case of price agreements for contracts, the condition records are created in the same session and have not yet been stored in the database at the time of pricing (see an example in Chapter 6, Section 6.1).

```
form konditionen_lesen.
   perform kobed_nnn.
   call function 'SD_COND_ACCESS'
         EXPORTING
            application                 = komk-kappl
            condition_type              = komt1-rkschl
            date                        = komk-prsdt
```

```
            header_comm_area            = komk
            position_comm_area          = komp
            prestep                     = ' '
            t682i_i                     = t682i
         importing
            condition_is_purely_header = headkz
            condition_is_in_memory      = cond_in_memory
         tables
            condition_records           = kondtab
         changing
            position_comm_area_dynamic = kompazd.
  loop at kondtab.
     call function 'SD_COND_READ_FROM_MEMORY'
         exporting
            i_knumh                   = kondtab-knumh
         tables
            mem_konp                  = h_mem_konp
            mem_konm                  = h_mem_konm
            mem_konw                  = h_mem_konw.
     perform konp_2_xkonp using xknumh.
     read table xkonp with key xknumh binary search.
     perform xkomv_fuellen.
     if sy-subrc = 0.
        append xkomv.
     endif.
  endloop.
endform.
```

Listing 10.6 Routine konditionen_lesen

In the `xkomv_fuellen` routine (see Listing 10.7), the structure XKOMV is filled with data from KOMT1, KOMT2, and KONP (condition record). The amount for internal prices (CONDITION CATEGORY = G) and transfer prices is determined in the `xkomv_kbetr_ermitteln` routine. The exchange rate `xkomv-kkurs` for conditions in foreign currency is determined in the `xkomv_kkurs_ermitteln` routine.

Finally, the previously determined data of the XKOMV structure can be manipulated in `userexit_xkomv_fuellen` (see Chapter 11, Section 11.8.1). In addition, you can prevent the takeover of the condition by setting `returncode` to not equal zero to prohibit the acquisition in this user exit.

```
form xkomv_fuellen.
   move-corresponding komt1  to xkomv.
   move-corresponding komt2  to xkomv.
   move-corresponding konp   to xkomv.
   perform xkomv_kbetr_ermitteln.
   perform xkomv_ergaenzen_manuelle
```

```
    perform xkomv_kkurs_ermitteln.
    perform userexit_xkomv_fuellen using sy-subrc.
endif.
```
Listing 10.7 Routine XKOMV_FUELLEN

We have now introduced the most important part of pricing, the xkomv_aufbauen_aus_komt1 routine.

10.1.5   Routine XKOMV_AUFBAUEN_AUS_TKOMV (Set Up XKOMV from TKOMV)

In the xkomv_aufbauen_aus_tkomv routine, those conditions that do *not* need to be recalculated in accordance with the pricing type are taken directly to XKOMV from the TKOMV interface table. The decision is made by the xkomv_aufbauen_pruefen routine (*see* Section 10.1.4).

10.1.6   Routine XKOMV_BEWERTEN (Evaluate XKOMV)

The conditions and subtotals from XKOMV are evaluated in the xkomv_bewerten routine (*see* Listing 10.8). In particular:

▸ The condition base values are determined

▸ The condition base value formula is processed

▸ The scale basis is determined

▸ The scale base formula is processed

▸ The amounts (xkomv-kbetr) are determined from scales, where required

▸ The condition value is determined and the condition value formula is processed

▸ The values are passed as item information to KOMP

Besides the aforementioned formulas, user exits are provided at the beginning and end of the routine (*see* Chapter 11, Section 11.8.1).

```
form xkomv_bewerten.
    perform userexit_xkomv_bewerten_init.
    loop at xkomv.
        perform konditionsbasis_ermitteln.
        perform frm_kond_basis_nnn. (Konditionsbasisformel)
```

```
    perform staffelbasis_ermitteln.
    perform frm_staffelbas_nnn. (Staffelbasisformel)
    perform xkomv_kbetr_aus_staffel.
    perform xkomv_kwert_ermitteln.
    <übernehmen Werte nach KOMP-NETWR, KZWI1,..>
  endloop.
  <deactivate all condition types before the last price>
  perform userexit_xkomv_bewerten_end.
endform.
```
Listing 10.8 Routine xkomv_bewerten

Here you can see at which point in time the formulas are processed. This is important, because you can access within these formulas only information that has been previously provided. The condition value formulas, by the way, are called in the `xkomv_kwert_ermitteln` routine.

10.1.7 Routine XKOMV_AUSSCHLUSS (XKOMV Exclusion)

In the `xkomv_ausschluss` routine, the condition exclusion is performed on the worktable XKOMV in accordance with the attribute MANUAL ENTRIES of the condition type and the condition exclusion using exclusion groups (see Chapter 7, Section 7.2.2). Excluded conditions receive the indicator INACTIVE = A. If at least one condition type has been excluded, the `xkomv_bewerten` routine is called again to obtain the final valuation. Details can be found in Chapter 7, Section 7.2.

10.1.8 Routine XKOMV_UEBERTRAGEN_NACH_TKOMV (Transfer XKOMV to TKOMV)

In the `xkomv_uebertragen_nach_tkomv` routine, the pricing result XKOMV of the current item is incorporated into the interface table TKOMV of the conditions of the entire sales document. Subtotals, meaning lines from XKOMV without a condition type, are not transferred.

10.2 The PRICING_COMPLETE Function Module

The PRICING_COMPLETE function module is required, at the latest, at the time of saving the document:

- Here, the whole document is passed with all items and all conditions.
- Here, all condition types that are configured as a *group condition* are definitively valuated, including the manually entered header conditions.
- Here, the cross-item activities are carried out (e.g., determination of the scale base and rounding difference comparison).

Details about group conditions can be found in Chapter 7, Section 7.1. In the following section, we describe the four possible cases and the respective activities.

10.2.1 Types of Group Conditions

Depending on the case, different processing steps are performed.

Case 1: Percentage and Fixed Amount Group Conditions without Group Key

The first case to consider is "percentage and fixed amount group conditions without group key". It also includes the manual header conditions without condition records. Here are the processing steps:

1. First, the accumulation of the scale base (only for conditions with scales) and the condition base is carried out in the accumulation table GKOMV in the gkomv-kstbs and gkomv-kawrt fields.

2. For condition types with scales, next comes the determination of the condition amount or percentage gkomv-kbetr due to the cumulative scale base gkomv-kstbs. Previously, a possibly assigned scale base formula, with which the cumulative scale base gkomv-kstbs can be manipulated, is processed.

3. Next is the calculation of the condition value gkomv-kwert corresponding to the total condition basis gkomv-kawrt. Then a possibly assigned condition value formula is processed, with which the condition value can be manipulated.

4. In the last step, the result of the valuation on accumulation level GKOMV is distributed to the items (GKOMZ processing):

   - The amount/percentage gkomv-kbetr is transferred to the items into the tkomv-kbetr field.
   - The total value gkomv-kwert is transferred to the item conditions into the tkomv-kwert field, in the proportion given by tkomv-kawrt/gkomv-kawrt.

▷ A possible rounding difference is added to the largest item and stored in the xkomv-kdiff field.

Examples of this category of group conditions are the condition types HA00 (manual percentage header discount) and KP03 (fixed value mixed pallet surcharge with scales).

Case 2: Other Group Conditions (Not Percentage/Fixed Amount) without Group Key

The second case to consider is "other group conditions (not percentage/fixed amount) without group key" (e.g., depending on weight). This situation only occurs in conjunction with condition records with scales. Here are the processing steps:

1. First is the accumulation of the scale base in the accumulation table GKOMV in the gkomv-kstbs field.

2. Next is the determination of the condition amount or percentage gkomv-kbetr due to the cumulative scale base gkomv-kstbs. Previously, a possibly assigned scale base formula, with which the cumulative scale gkomv-kstbs base can be manipulated, was processed.

3. In the last step (GKOMZ processing), the newly determined amount gkomv-kbetr is transferred to the corresponding item conditions into the tkomv-kbetr field and the new condition value tkomv-kwert is then calculated. No rounding difference comparison is performed here.

An example of this category is the condition type Z030 (material group discount), which is discussed in Chapter 11, Section 11.4.4.

Case 3: Non-Fixed-Amount Group Conditions with Group Key

The third case to consider is "non-fixed-amount group conditions with group key". This situation occurs only in conjunction with condition records with scales. Here are the processing steps:

1. First is the accumulation of the scale base in the accumulation table GKOMV in the gkomv-kstbs field.

2. Next, a possibly assigned scale base formula, with which the cumulative scale gkomv-kstbs base can be manipulated, is processed.

3. In the last step (GKOMZ processing), the amount tkomv-kbetr is determined for the related item condition types from the respective condition records due to the cumulative scale base gkomv-kstbs. With those amounts, the new condition value tkomv-kwert is calculated. *No* rounding difference comparison is performed here.

You can check out this case using the example of the condition type Z030 from Chapter 11, Section 11.4.4, if you configure this condition type with group key routine 001 (complete document).

Case 4: Fixed Amount Group Conditions with Group Key

The fourth case to consider is "fixed amount group conditions with group key". This situation occurs only in conjunction with condition records with scales.

1. First is the accumulation of the scale base in the accumulation table CGKOMV in the cgkomv-kstbs field.

2. Next is the accumulation of the condition base in the accumulation table GKOMV in the gkomv kawrt field.

3. Then comes the takeover of the scale base gkomv-kstbs of the accumulation table GKOMV from the accumulation table CGKOMV (aggregated at a higher level) from the cgkomv-kstbs field.

4. All other steps are identical to case 1, processing steps 2, and the following steps.

An example of this category is the condition type Z031 (material group discount) in Chapter 11, Section 11.4.4.

10.2.2 Execution of Function Module PRICING_COMPLETE during Order Processing

To call the PRICING_COMPLETE function module in an object, the caller prepares the communication structures KOMK and KOMP for all items and passes them along with a pricing type to the function module. In Listing 10.9, you see the simplified section that calls the PRICING_COMPLETE function module in the sales order in program SAPMV45A:

```
form preisfindung_gesamt using preisfindungsart_kopf.
  refresh tkomp.
```

```
loop at xvbap where updkz ne updkz_delete.
  perform preisfindung_vorbereiten(sapfv45p).
  append tkomp.
endloop.
call function 'PRICING_COMPLETE'
  exporting
    calculation_type = preisfindungsart_kopf
    preliminary      = da_prelim
  tables
    tkomv            = xkomv
    tkomk            = tkomk
    tkomp            = tkomp
    svbap            = uvbap.
loop at tkomp.
    read table tkomk index tkomp-ix_komk.
    read table xvbap index tkomp-ix_vbap.
    vbap = xvbap.
    move-corresponding tkomp to kompax.
    move-corresponding kompax to vbap.
    perform vbap_bearbeiten_vorbereiten(sapfv45p).
    perform vbap_bearbeiten(sapfv45p).
  endloop.
endform.
```

Listing 10.9 Routine PREISFINDUNG_GESAMT in the Sales Order

Following are the essential steps that are processed in the preisfindung_gesamt routine:

1. First, the tables TKOMK and TKOMP are set up for all items of the sales order by the preisfindung_vorbereiten routine. The connection between the TKOMP item structure and the associated header structure TKOMK is established by the tkomp-ix_komk field. The field contains the index number (row number) of the corresponding entry in the internal table TKOMK.

2. These internal tables are passed along with a pricing type to the subsequent function module PRICING_COMPLETE, as we already know from the PRICING function module. Thus, for example, a new pricing for all items can be performed or the taxes can be recalculated.

3. After calling the PRICING_COMPLETE function module, the result is finally transferred to the sales order. The conditions of the sales order in XKOMV are already updated. Only the order items in XVBAP must be adapted (KOMPAX logic).

The respective program parts in other applications such as billing are designed to follow the same pattern.

10.2.3 Program Flow of the PRICING_COMPLETE Function Module

In Figure 10.3, you see the program flow of the `PRICING_COMPLETE` function module, which consists of three blocks recognized by a loop statement:

1. `Loop at tkomp`. Step 1 (set up `GKOMV`, `CGKOMV`, and `GKOMZ`).

2. `Loop at gkomv`. Step 2 (valuate `GKOMV`).

3. `Loop at gkomz`. Step 3 (transfer result to the items).

First, we describe the three steps briefly in order to go deeper into the details later.

Step 1: Setting Up the Internal Tables GKOMV, CGKOMV, and GKOMZ

For all group conditions (including header conditions), the `GKOMV`, `CGKOMV`, and `GKOMZ` internal tables are first set up.

Step 2: Valuation of the Accumulation Table GKOMV

Next, the table `GKOMV` is valuated. Based on the accumulated numbers, the scale amounts are possibly recalculated and stored in gkomv-kbetr. For percentage and fixed amount condition types, the condition value gkomv-kwert is then calculated based on the accumulated condition base value gkomv-kawrt (routine `gkomv_bewerten`). In this context, the scale base formulas and the condition value formulas are also processed. The condition base value gkomv-kawrt is accumulated from the item conditions and remains unchanged. The condition base value formulas are not processed here.

Step 3: Take Over the Result of the Group Valuation to the Items

In the final step, the result of this valuation of the sums is taken over to the items involved. Absolute amounts are distributed proportionally (according to condition base value xkomv-kawrt), and any rounding difference that occurs is added to the item with the highest value. This also applies for percentage condition types. This rounding difference is stored in field xkomv-kdiff. The processing in this program part is done with the special pricing type F.

This step is the most complex part of the function module. As shown in Figure 10.3, the entire PRICING block is performed for each entry in the internal table GKOMZ.

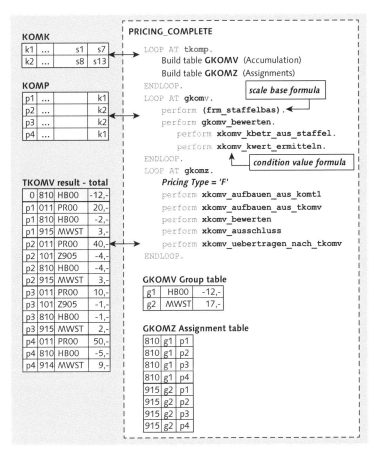

Figure 10.3 Program Flow of the PRICING_COMPLETE Function Module

The block consists of:

```
perform xkomv_aufbauen_aus_komt1
perform xkomv_aufbauen_aus_tkomv
sort xkomv by kposn stunr zaehk
perform xkomv_bewerten
```

```
perform xkomv_ausschluss
perform xkomv_uebertragen_nach_tkomv
```

In our example in Figure 10.3, we have two group conditions (HA00 and MWST) and four items, and thus the block is performed eight times. The (number of group condition types) × (number of items) = 8.

This is already an indication that the use of group conditions should be carefully considered. We now want to introduce the individual processing steps in detail.

Step 1: Setting Up the Internal Tables GKOMV, CGKOMV, and GKOMZ

We now look at the creation of the group tables GKOMV and GKOMZ in more detail (see Listing 10.10). In the case of fixed amount group conditions with group key, the internal table CGKOMV also comes into play.

```
function pricing_complete.
   ..
   loop at tkomp into komp.
      if komp-ix_komk ne komk-ix_komk.
         read table tkomk index komp-ix_komk into komk.
         perform konditionsvorstep using incl_konditionen.
         move-corresponding komk to gkomv_key.
         move-corresponding komk to gkomv.
      endif.
      move-corresponding komp to gkomv_key.
      move-corresponding komp to gkomv.

      perform konditionsvorstep using incl_konditionen.
      loop at tkomv into xkomv <all conditions of komp-kposn>.
         read table komt1 index xkomv-ix_komt1.
         move-corresponding xkomv to gkomv_key.
         if komt1-grlnr gt 0.
            perform frm_gruppenkey_nnn.
            gkomv_key-vakey = xvakey.
         endif.
         loop at gkomv <where key = gkomv_key>.
            add   xkomv-kawrt to gkomv-kawrt.
            add   xkomv-kwert to gkomv-kwert.
            add   xkomv-kwert to gkomv-sumps.
            add   xkstbs       to gkomv-kstbs.
            modify gkomv.
            perform cgkomv_aufbauen <if gkomv-rdifa = X>
            exit.
         endloop.
         if gkomv_vorhanden eq no.      "GKOMV_existing ?
            move-corresponding xkomv to gkomv.
```

```
            add   xkomv-kwert          to gkomv-sumps.
            move gkomv_key             to gkomv-key.
            append gkomv.
            perform cgkomv_aufbauen <if gkomv-rdifa = X>.
         endif.
         move-corresponding xkomv to gkomz
         append gkomz.
      endloop <tkomv>.
   endloop <tkomp>.
   ..
endfunction.
```
Listing 10.10 PRICING_COMPLETE: Set Up of GKOMV and GKOMZ

We will not look deeper into the code here, as it is largely self-explanatory.

Step 2: Valuation of the Accumulation Table GKOMV

Now let's take a closer look at the part within the `PRICING_COMPLETE` function module (see Listing 10.11), where the routine `gkomv_bewerten` (valuate GKOMV) is called, and where the routine `gkomv_bewerten` itself resides (see Listing 10.12).

```
function pricing_complete.
   ..
   loop at gkomv < for conditions with rdifa = X >.
      < read assigned entry in CGKOMV >
      gkomv-kstbs = cgkomv-kstbs.
      modify gkomv.
   endloop.
   loop at gkomv.
      move-corresponding gkomv_key to komk.
      move-corresponding gkomv     to komk.
      move-corresponding gkomv_key to komp.
      move-corresponding gkomv     to komp.
      if gkomv_key-kofrs ne 0.
         xkwert = gkomv-kstbs.
         frm_staffelbas-nr = gkomv_key-kofrs.
         perform (frm_staffelbas) in program saplv61a if found.
         gkomv-kstbs = xkwert.
      endif.
      perform gkomv_bewerten.
      modify gkomv.
   endloop.
   ..
endfunction.
```
Listing 10.11 PRICING_COMPLETE: Valuation of Table GKOMV

375

```
form gkomv_bewerten.
   gkomv_key = gkomv-key.
   check: gkomv_key-vakey = space or
          (not gkomv-key-vakey is initial and
            gkomv-key-krech = 'B').
   move-corresponding gkomv_key to xkomv.
   move-corresponding gkomv     to xkomv.
   xkomv-kdatu = gkomv-prsdt.
   if xkomv-ksteu = 'A'.
      perform xkomv_kbetr_ermitteln.
      if xkomv-kntyp = 'E'.
        perform xkomv_kbetr_ermitteln_aus_t052.
      endif.
      if xkomv-kzbzg ne space.
        xkstbs = xkomv-kstbs.
        perform xkomv_kbetr_aus_staffel.
      endif.
      gkomv-kbetr = xkomv-kbetr.
   endif.
   perform xkomv_kwert_ermitteln.
   gkomv-kwert = xkomv-kwert.
endform.
```

Listing 10.12 Routine gkomv_bewerten

You can see here that the KOMK and KOMP structures are each filled by move-corresponding from GKOMV or GKOMV_KEY. This means that only those fields are supplied in KOMK and KOMP that exist in the accumulation table GKOMV (or GKOMV_KEY). Keep this in mind when using scale base formulas and condition value formulas. The gkomv_bewerten routine performs the valuation only if one of the following two requirements is met:

▶ gkomv_key-vakey is initial, meaning that there is no group key routine assigned. This is the normal case of a group condition type. The key of the condition type in table GKOMV is in this case the condition record itself, represented by field gkomv_key-knumh.

▶ gkomv_key-krech = B and gkomv_key-vakey is filled, meaning that it is a fixed value condition type with a group key routine.

We will take a closer look at the particulars of group conditions with group key routines in Chapter 11, Section 11.4.4.

In the last step, we need to transport the result of this valuation on the accumulation level to the items.

Step 3: Take Over of the Result of the Group Valuation to the Items

The code for processing the internal table GKOMZ is shown in Listing 10.13.

```
function pricing_complete.
  ..
  sort gkomz by ix_gkomv.
  loop at gkomz.
     read table gkomv index gkomz-ix_gkomv.
     if gkomv-ix_komv ne gkomz-ix_komv.
       gkomz-ix_komv = 0.
       modify gkomz.
     endif.
  endloop.
  sort gkomz by stunr ix_gkomv ix_komv zaehk.

  loop at gkomz.
     read table gkomv index gkomz-ix_gkomv.
     tkomp_tabix = gkomz-ix_komp.
     read table tkomp into komp index gkomz-ix_komp.
     read table tkomk into komk index komp-ix_komk.
     preisfindungsart = 'F'.
     perform xkomv_aufbauen_aus_komt1.
     perform xkomv_aufbauen_aus_tkomv using yes.
     sort xkomv by kposn stunr zaehk.
     perform xkomv_bewerten.
     perform xkomv_ausschluss.
     perform xkomv_uebertragen_nach_tkomv using no.
     modify tkomp index tkomp_tabix from komp.
     modify tkomk index komp-ix_komk from komk.
  endloop.
endfunction.
```

Listing 10.13 PRICING_COMPLETE: Processing Table GKOMZ

The gkomv-ix_komv field points to the condition of the item with the highest value that receives later a possible rounding difference. By sorting table GKOMZ twice, we ensure that this item with the highest value is updated last. The result is taken over in the second loop on GKOMZ. The values are adjusted there in the routine xkomv_bewerten. The criterion used in this particular situation is the special pricing type = F. You will find additional information on this pricing type in Chapter 11, Section 11.5.

10.3   The PRICING_COPY Function Module

When creating documents with reference, the PRICING_COPY function module reads the document conditions of the reference document from the database table KONV and takes them over in the current document to XKOMV.

The given pricing type triggers a preliminary selection of the conditions to be transferred. The final decision about which condition types are taken over and which are recalculated is made in the subsequently called function module PRICING, according to the communicated pricing type. In Listing 10.14, you see the simplified call within the billing program, to which the conditions are taken over from the underlying sales order.

```
form fakturaposi_lieferbezogen.
    ..
  loop at lrefcp.
    call function 'PRICING_COPY'
            exporting
              currency_new          = vbrk-waerk
              currency_new_date     = vbrk-fkdat
              currency_new_local    = t001-waers
              currency_new_rate     = vbrk-kurrf
              currency_new_type     = vbrk-kurst
              currency_old          = lrefcp-waerk
              currency_old_local    = tvko_auft_t001-waers
              vbtyp_new             = vbrk-vbtyp
              document_number_from  = lrefcp-knumv
              document_number_to    = beleg
              item_number_from      = lrefcp-kposn
              item_number_to        = xposnr
              mode                  = lrefcp-pmode
              quantity_new          = vbrp-fklmg
              quantity_old          = lips-lgmng
              order_number          = vbak-vbeln
              source                = lrefcp-source
              check_rebate          = 'X'
            tables
              tkomv                 = xkomv.
  endloop.
  perform preisfindung using tvcpf-knprs.
    ..
endform.
```

Listing 10.14 Calling the PRICING_COPY Function Module

The pricing type is determined from the *copying control* (in this case, table TVCPF) and handed over in the mode parameter. The invoice has the property that document conditions that can be transferred not only from the sales order, but also from the delivery, the purchase order, and the freight document. The documents to be copied are stored in the table LREFCP in the form of the KONV-key field KNUMV (usually only the internal number in field the vbak-knumv field of the sales order is used). The price source is passed in the source parameter.

During a copying operation, the document currency can change. It may also be that the quantities of source item and destination item are different (partial delivery). Information about old currency, new currency, old quantity, and new quantity are handed over because certain condition values have to be adjusted in these situations. All the fixed condition values of konv-kwert are affected, which is, for example, caused by konv-ksteu = E. You will always have this situation for copied header conditions. These values are scaled proportionally to the quantity. In the case of a currency change, the respective value is converted to the target currency.

A special feature is the billing of fixed price (milestone) billing plans (partial invoice, final invoice, and down payment billing). The value of the billing plan is passed in the amount parameter (only relevant for order-related billing). In this case, all conditions are fixed, and the amount is distributed to all the condition values.

10.4   Data Storage of the Pricing Result in Clustered Table KONV

The responsibility for the pricing result of a document belongs to the calling object. For the sales order, it is program SAPM45A and for the billing document, it is the function group V60A. The pricing result is managed in the internal table XKOMV. The contents of table XKOMV are stored in the *cluster table* KONV and the update is performed by program blocks of the sales order or the billing document. For the sales order, it is the RV_SALES_DOCUMENT_UPDATE function module. The coding to update table KONV is shown in Listing 10.15.

```
form konv_bearbeiten.
  if vorgang ne 'H'.
    delete from konv where knumv = vbak-knumv.
```

```
    endif.
    loop at fxkomv.
      fxkomv-mandt = vbak-mandt.
      fxkomv-knumv = vbak-knumv.
      modify fxkomv.
    endloop.
    insert konv from table fxkomv.
    if sy-subrc ne 0.
      message a100 with 'konv' sy-subrc.
    endif.
endform.
```

Listing 10.15 Update KONV

Typically, the administration of the tables of a document is carried out by X-tables (current state after change) and Y-tables (state before the change). For example, with the tables XVBAP and YVBAP for the order items. In these tables, it can be accurately recognized via UPDKZ field (update indicator) whether a row has been added, changed, or deleted. This logic has not been implemented for table KONV. There is no table YKOMV, but only the table XKOMV, which means that UPDKZ is not used.

When a document changes, first all old KONV entries of a document are deleted from the database. Then the current state of the document is added as completely new. For simplicity, it was decided not to manage a table YKOMV, especially as there is a large amount of traffic on table XKOMV due to the constant pace of document changes.

This logic, at first glance, might seem to be unfavorable for performance. However, as the table KONV is a cluster table, no disadvantages are noted.

10.5 The PRICING_REFRESH Function Module

Each object will perform an initialization at the end and/or at the beginning of processing a document. In the example of the sales order, the beleg_initialisieren routine in the program SAPMV45A does this. There, the PRICING_REFRESH function module is called to initialize the internally used global data of the function group V61A. Since the sales order also calls modules of other integration objects (e.g., controlling) and this integration object itself also calls pricing modules, there is a challenge to accept the initialization of V61A data only from the first caller (the leading object).

In the internal table EXTR of PRICING_REFRESH, all applications existing in table KOMT1 are collected. If the application V (sales) is involved, the initialization is performed only when the refresh call comes from this application. That is, the first entry in the handed-over table TKOMK has the application KAPPL = V.

Since the table TKOMK table is managed by each caller, there is for each of these callers their own function module in their own function group. It's called to initialize the local table TKOMK. Examples are the function modules RKE_PRICING_REFRESH, PRICING_REFRESH_KA, and PRICING_REFRESH_TX.

10.6   Dialog Connection/Other Function Modules

The programs listed so far are certainly the most important, and that is why we discussed them at some length. However, you will certainly have to deal from time to time with other programs. We want to mention briefly the most important of those in the following sections.

10.6.1   Function Module PRICING_LOAD_CONDITION_TYPS

With the PRICING_LOAD_CONDITION_TYPS function module, the internal tables TKSCHL and TKSCHLEXCL can be filled. Thus, it is possible to override the logic of the pricing types that determine which condition types are to be recalculated and which are not. TKSCHL then contains those condition types that are to be recalculated in any case and TKSCHLEXCL contains the ones that must not be recalculated under any circumstances. Within order processing and billing, this function module is not used in the standard SAP system. However, if necessary you can use it in the user exit userexit_pricing_prepare_tkomp within sales order or billing. For more information, see Chapter 11, Section 11.1.

10.6.2   Dialog Connection

The dialog connection of the pricing result within SAP GUI in the sales order, delivery, billing, and purchasing order objects is implemented via the function group V69A.

There, you can also find the user exits to manipulate the field selection on the CONDITIONS screen of the documents (see Chapter 11, Section 11.8.2).

The Conditions Overview screen is the dynpro (screen) SAPLV69A 6201; the detail screen is the dynpro SAPLV69A 0640.

10.6.3 The PRICING_DETERMINE_DATES Function Module

Rental and maintenance contracts (order types MV and WV) use periodic billing plans. In this context, condition types with time-dependent calculation types for mapping yearly, monthly, weekly, and daily prices are used. To this end, the following fields are provided in the interface structure KOMP:

- ANZ_JAHRE: Number of years
- ANZ_MONAT: Number of months
- ANZ_WOCHEN: Number of weeks
- ANZ_TAG: Number of days

The determination of these *number fields* is done using the PRICING_DETERMINE_ DATES function module, based on the data of a billing plan date (tables FPGA and FPLT). In addition to these fields that describe the period of a specific billing plan date, there are these fields:

- STF_JAHRE: Number of years
- STF_MONAT: Number of months
- STF_WOCHEN: Number of weeks
- STF_TAG: Number of days

These in turn reflect the period between contract start date and the individual billing dates, which is the relative distance of an individual billing date from the start date of the contract. These fields are used in condition types with time-dependent scales.

Examples are:

- The rent is 800.00 USD per month, but the first three months are free.
- After one year, the price increases by 100.00 USD.

Of course, these types of agreements can be mapped with condition records whose valid-from date begins after three months or one year. Such condition records, however, need to be entered as contract-specific *price agreements* and cannot be maintained as general condition records, as they could then potentially be used in all contracts.

10.7 Relationship of Tables and Structures

Finally, we want to illustrate the relationship of the components of the pricing based on Figure 10.4. Here you can see all important information at a glance. The figure appears at first glance very crowded and cluttered. But now that you know the elements of pricing, this image can help you better understand the relationships of the structures, tables, and internal tables within pricing. The upper-left box lists the database tables of Customizing with the foreign key relationships. In the upper-right box, you find the condition master data and the main tables of the sales order. Outside the boxes, you find the communication structures of the pricing function modules (KOMK, KOMP, TKOMK, TKOMP, and TKOMV) and the internal tables of pricing itself (KOMT1, KOMT2, and XKOMV).

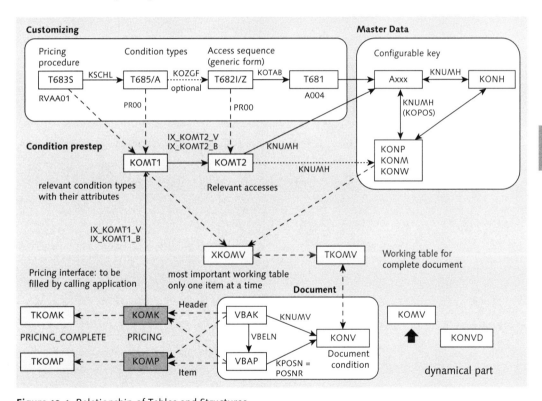

Figure 10.4 Relationship of Tables and Structures

10.8   Summary

In this chapter, you obtained an overview of the programs and their interfaces and internal structures involved in pricing. In the chapters that follow, we will repeatedly refer to these program descriptions, which certainly can contribute to a better understanding of discussed functions and solutions. Over time, you will deepen your knowledge. The next chapter contributes to this objective by discussing how to extend the functionality of pricing.

This chapter illustrates that the flexibility of the condition technique coupled with a smart use of user exits, requirements, and formulas solves almost all demands.

11 System Adaptation Using Requirements, Formulas, and User Exits

In the previous chapters, you acquired the basics and the understanding you need to assess and exploit the wealth of adaptation options. Now it's time to expand your knowledge. If you have realized that you cannot implement a pricing scenario only with the capabilities of Customizing, you will try to find a solution to the problem using requirements, formulas, or user exits. For this, you need to know the *points in time* at which the individual routines are executed, which are the input interfaces and what manipulations can be made within the respective routine. This information is the subject of this chapter. In Chapter 12, you will find some application examples.

Requirements and formulas are created using Transaction VOFM and are assigned to the respective object in Customizing. Since this is ABAP code, you are on the one hand very free, while on the other hand you need some programming skills. Since these VOFM routines are processed directly from routines in the pricing program, there is a risk that you could inflict damage. This is because these routines represent user exits in the classic style, meaning that you have access to all global data of the framework program and can manipulate those. The interfaces are not protected.

Besides these VOFM routines, there are the classic user exits with the same characteristics and risks. In some places, the user exits are provided as a Business Add-In (BAdI) implementation. If present, these are preferable to classical implementations since the interfaces are clearly defined and the implementation is located in the customer namespace.

If you have activated the LOG_SD_COMMODITY_02 or LOG_MM_COMMODITY_02 business functions, then the BAdIs of the configurable parameters and formulas (CPF) are also available. These were introduced in Chapter 4. We will demonstrate their use in a detailed example in Chapter 12.

Specifically in this chapter, we talk about:

▶ Pricing types

▶ Requirements

▶ An example of using formulas

▶ Condition base value formulas

▶ Scale base formulas

▶ Condition value formulas

▶ Group key routines used with group conditions

▶ The special logic of pricing type F

▶ The transfer of the pricing result in structure KOMP

▶ The importance of the control flag xkomv-ksteu

▶ User exits in pricing

▶ The possibility of storing information in the KONV table

▶ Performance in connection with using formulas and requirements

▶ Error messages from formulas and the general error handling within the pricing

Just like the previous chapter, this chapter is very technical. It mainly serves as a reference when you want to set up new formulas and requirements or develop adaptations based on user exits. You should read this chapter first before planning enhancements for the first time. Approach this chapter iteratively. Don't go deeply into all the details on the first read, but instead gain an overview of the various adaptation options and terms. You will then acquire the detailed knowledge in connection with specific tasks.

Before we begin describing the requirements, formulas, and user exits, we complete the previously acquired knowledge about the pricing types, which play an important role in particular in the requirements and formulas. Thus, for example, the pricing types can be overridden by requirements.

11.1   Pricing Types

A *pricing type* is used in all major interfaces. It is used primarily to determine which condition types should be recalculated on a pricing call.

The pricing types are set up in the `konditionsvorstep` routine in the internal table `STEU`. Customer-specific pricing types can be established via the `userexit_pricing_rule` (see Chapter 10, Section 10.1.2, and Section 11.8.1). This user exit is processed at a time when only the information from the interface structure KOMK is available, which may not be sufficient for a fine-tuning, since you cannot make pricing types dependent on item information such as the item categories.

If the control possibilities available using pricing types are insufficient, you can override the behavior of the pricing types via the internal tables `TKSCHL` and `TKSCHLEXCL`.

These in turn can be filled in requirements or via the `PRICING_LOAD_CONDITION_TYPS` function module (see Section 11.6.1) in the context of the preparatory work before calling the pricing in `userexit_pricing_prepare_tkomp` (see Chapter 13, Section 13.1 and Section 13.2).

Another way of oversteering is given by the two interface fields komp-kaend_typ and komp-konau_typ.

11.1.1   Control via KOMP-KAEND_TYP

In the komp-kaend_typ field (unchangeable condition categories), you can enter up to five condition categories that must not be changed within the pricing. In the billing document, for example, the condition categories G, B, and H are entered here, which prevent changes to the cost conditions and transfer pricing conditions. This is necessary because the values for these condition types are normally passed from the outside to the billing document and thus cannot be determined within the pricing.

A special role is played by the value * at the beginning of the field. If this field contains *, no condition types are recalculated, regardless of the pricing type. This function is used in sales order items that have already been billed, because in such items the change options should be strongly restricted. Within the billing process, this logic is used for cancellation documents and for billing documents that have already been transferred to accounting.

You can manipulate this field in `userexit_pricing_prepare_tkomp` of the sales order and billing document (see Chapter 13, Section 13.1 and Section 13.2).

11.1.2 Control via KOMP-KONAU_TYP

In the komp-konau_typ field (impermissible condition categories), you can enter up to five condition types that must not be determined. The manual entry of such condition types is also not possible. You can manipulate this field in `userexit_pricing_prepare_tkomp`.

11.2 Requirements

As already discussed in previous chapters, *requirements* are used in access sequences and in pricing procedures. You have learned about the differences between the check at prestep (kobev_nnn) and the final check (kobed_nnn) in Chapter 10, Section 10.2 and Section 10.1.4.

If a requirement check returns a negative outcome (`sy-subrc ne zero`), no database accesses are performed on the condition tables, or the condition type is not included in the internal table of condition types KOMT1. Thus, it is clear that it is always advantageous, if possible, to prevent database access with skillfully prepared requirements.

11.2.1 Manipulation of KOMK Fields and KOMP Fields via Requirements

In Chapter 9, Section 9.2, we discussed in detail the possibility of manipulating the KOMK and KOMP fields within requirements in order to change the basis for the condition access, and we provided examples. You also saw how you can fill the internal table `XKOMPLOOP` in order to handle multi-valued fields (see Chapter 9, Section 9.3).

11.2.2 Overriding Pricing Types via Requirements

A further possibility is to use the internal tables TKSCHL and/or TKSCHLEXCL within the requirements. These internal tables are used to override the logic of *pricing types* when their capabilities alone are not sufficient. TKSCHL then must contain those condition types that are to be recalculated in any case and TKSCHLEXCL must contain the ones that must not be recalculated under any circumstances.

11.2.3 Example 1: Using Table TKSCHLEXCL

Let's consider the condition type ITD2 of the pricing procedure RVACRN, which can be used in the context of contracts in which the services provided are billed resource-related (see Chapter 8, Section 8.1).

The billing is set up retroactively, that is all expense items are billed regardless of whether they may have already been billed. With the condition types ITD2, ITD3, and ITD4, an already invoiced value is determined using the information structure S409 and set as a negative condition value by condition value formula 112 (ITD billed). These conditions are fixed with CONDITION CONTROL (xkomv-ksteu) = E. They may only be determined when the billing request item is created and must then remain unchanged, even in the billing document.

Since the pricing types do not meet this demand, we use the requirement 106 (ITD contract) here (see Listing 11.1).

```
form kobed_106.
  sy-subrc = 4.
  if komp-kposn ne 0.
    check: komp-prsfd ca 'BX'.
  endif.
  if preisfindungsart ca 'BCDG'.
*   determine change mode
    data: changemode.
    read table tkomv with key knumv = komk-knumv
                              kposn = komp-kposn
                              binary search.
    if sy-subrc = 0 and not tkomv-zaehk is initial
                    and not tkomv-zaehk = '99'.
      changemode = yes.
    else.
      changemode = no.
    endif.
*   avoid redetermination of the condition in change mode by
*   filling exclusion table tkschlexcl
```

```
          read table tkschlexcl with key kschl = komt1-kschl
            binary search.
          case sy-subrc.
            when 0.
              if changemode = no and komk-vbtyp na vbtyp_fakt.
                delete tkschlexcl index sy-tabix.
              endif.
            when 4 or 8.
              if changemode = yes or komk-vbtyp ca vbtyp_fakt.
                tkschlexcl-kschl = komt1-kschl.
                insert tkschlexcl index sy-tabix.
              endif.
          endcase.
        else.
          refresh tkschlexcl.
          refresh tkschl.
        endif.
        sy-subrc = 0.
endform.
```

Listing 11.1 Requirement 106 for the Condition Types ITDn

In the first step, we determine whether we are in the insert or change mode of an item and store this information in the changemode variable. Since it is not easy within the pricing to determine this situation, it is worthwhile to note this program logic for other application cases.

In the second step, if we are not in the insert mode of an order item, we fill the internal table TKSCHLEXCL with our condition type.

11.2.4   Example 2: Using Tables TKSCHL and TKSCHLEXCL

Another example can be found in requirement 107 (contract ACRN) for the budget condition ACRN. In this case, the internal table TKSCHLEXCL is used to prevent recalculation of the condition type in invoices and returns or credit memo requests. TKSCHL in turn is used to enforce the determination in billing requests in insert mode.

11.2.5   Processing Time of the Prestep-Requirement (KOBEV Part)

The prestep requirement is processed at the time of the setup of the internal tables of the condition types, KOMT1, and of the access sequences, KOMT2. If this test is negative, the condition type or the access is not included in the internal table and thus the condition type or the access is not taken into account. The requirement in the pricing procedure is called in the `konditionsvorstep` routine and the requirement in the access is called in the `komt2_aufbauen` routine (see Chapter 10, Section 10.1 and Section 10.1.4).

Inbound Interface of the Prestep Requirement (kobev_nnn)

- ▶ KOMK: Communication header
- ▶ T683S: Table entry in the pricing procedure
- ▶ PREISFINDUNGSART: Interface variable (pricing type)

Outbound Interface of the Prestep Requirement

- ▶ SY-SUBRC: Return code

In the prestep requirement, only the field contents of the structure KOMK can be evaluated. Item information, meaning the fields of structure KOMP, can only be evaluated in the definite requirement. It's interesting that a negative test result in the prestep of a subsequent document causes document conditions possibly copied from the source document to be rejected in the target document. This effect does not occur in processing the definite requirement. For performance reasons, the prestep requirements are only called within billing for pricing types B and C for all condition types.

However, since SAP ERP 6.0 EHP 6, you can set the parameter `gv_pric_prelim_control` = X in the pricing preparation step and thus force a check of all prestep requirements in the billing process.

11.2.6 Processing Time of the Definite Requirement (KOBED Part)

The actual definite requirement is called in the `xkomv_aufbauen_aus_komt1` and `konditionen_lesen` routines.

Inbound Interface of the Definite Requirement (kobed_nnn)

- ▶ KOMK, KOMP, and KOMPAZD
- ▶ KOMT1: Table entry in the pricing procedure and all parameters of the condition type
- ▶ PREISFINDUNGSART: Interface variable (pricing type)

In the KOMP structure, you may use only those fields that have been passed to the pricing from the outside or fields that have been filled in requirements of preceding condition types. Fields that are filled in the xkomv_bewerten routine (the formulas are processed there, too) must not be used in any case. This is valid in particular for all the value fields (e.g., komp-netwr).

> **Outbound Interface of the Definite Requirement**
>
> ▸ SY-SUBRC: Return code
> ▸ KOMK: A change is only temporary for the current condition type
> ▸ KOMP: A change is permanent
> ▸ XKOMPLOOP

Note that the requirement check is not carried out on conditions that were taken over from a preceding document.

11.2.7 Behavior for Copied Conditions

In document chains conditions are normally transferred (at least partially) from the source document to the target document. This transfer is performed by the PRICING_COPY function module (see Chapter 10, Section 10.3). For the copied conditions, no requirement check takes place, which can, in certain circumstances, result in a new price determination in the target document that can provide a different result from that found in the source document. However, we can achieve indirectly—via the prestep-check—that the condition in the target document be discarded if it does not fulfill the requirement. This is the case when the check of the prestep requirement is negative. In this situation, the condition is not added into the internal table of the pricing procedure, KOMT1, which causes the condition type to not be processed in the xkomv_aufbauen_aus_tkomv routine. Another way to discard copied conditions is to set the indicator INACTIVE = Z by a condition value formula.

11.3 An Example Using Formulas

In this section, we present you an example of a condition type ZP03, where all the different formula types are used. This condition type is a copy of condition type KP03 (mixed pallet surcharge).

Example Condition Type ZP03 for Using Formulas

With the condition type ZP03, a surcharge of 4 EUR will be charged for the entire sales order whenever the entire order fills no whole pallets. In addition, for documents that differ from the local currency, the converted amount will be rounded in accordance with the rounding rule for the respective currency. Thus, in the case of a document in Swiss franc (CHF), the five centime rounding will take place. The amount will then be distributed to the order items in the ratio of the gross weights.

The condition type ZP03 is set as a reference to the condition type KP03, which means that the condition master records are maintained exclusively for KP03. The condition is configured with the calculation type FIXED AMOUNT, marked as a group condition. It uses a quantity scale for the assigned unit of measure PAL. A prerequisite is that all entered order items can be converted into the unit of measure PAL.

To solve this task, we use the following formulas:

▸ Scale base formula 023 (determining the partial quantity)

▸ Condition base formula 012 (setting the gross weight of the item as the condition basis): This happens in group conditions with calculation type B (Fixed Amount). The value is distributed to the items in the ratio of the gross weights.

▸ Condition value formula 017 (rounding the condition value in accordance with the rounding rule from table T001R)

To set up the example, the following steps are needed:

1. Creation of condition type ZP03 and inserting ZP03 in the pricing procedure with the settings described at the beginning of this section.

2. Creation of a condition record for the condition type KP03 (see Figure 11.1).

3. Creation of a sales order (see Figure 11.2). The materials used must be maintained with the conversion factors for the unit of measure (PAL).

4. Check of the pricing result of condition types KP03 and ZP03 at item level (see Figure 11.3 and Figure 11.4).

5. Check of the pricing result at header level (see Figure 11.5 and Figure 11.6).

The scale quantity of 0.001 pallets represents the partial quantity. That means the access to this scale does not take place with the total amount of pallets, but only with the partial quantity (Figure 11.1). A quantity of 15 pieces yields 1.5 PAL (pallets) and thus a partial quantity of 0.5 PAL. A quantity of 20 pieces yields 2.0 PAL; that is 0.0 PAL partial quantity.

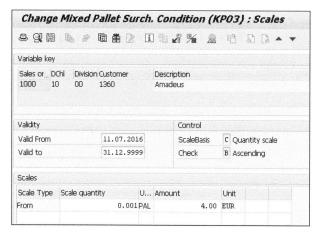

Figure 11.1 Condition Record for Condition Type ZP03 (Reference to Condition Type KP03)

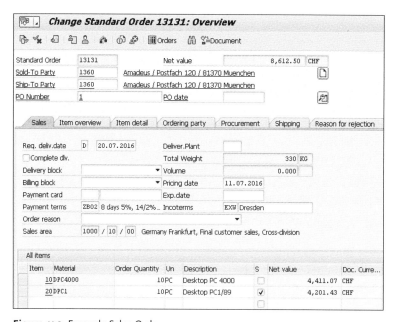

Figure 11.2 Example Sales Order

The materials used are so arranged in Figure 11.3 that for material DPC4000, 10 pieces are 1 pallet and for material DPC1, 20 pieces are 1 pallet. In our example sales order (Figure 11.2), we obtain with these conversion factors a total quantity of 1.5 PAL and thus a partial quantity of 0.5 PAL.

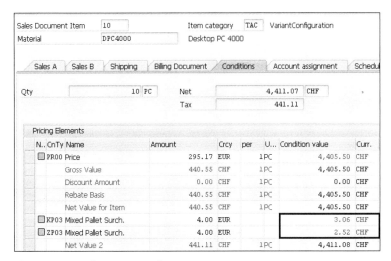

Figure 11.3 Conditions Screen for Item 20

The distribution of the condition value for condition type KP03 is done in proportion to the value; for condition type ZP03, it's done in proportion to the gross weight of the item.

As you already know, the condition basis is, depending on the calculation type, a value, a quantity, a weight, etc. The condition basis for condition types with the calculation type FIXED AMOUNT has no dimension and is neither a value nor a quantity. In our example, the condition base value is 1900 and is filled by the base value formula 012 with the gross weight of the item. For group condition types with a fixed amount, the condition base value provides the key for the distribution of the total value of the condition to the items (Figure 11.4).

The scale base formula 023 determines for the partial quantity the value of 0.5 PAL. For group conditions with a fixed amount, the scale values are only read by the PRICING_COMPLETE function module in the gkomv_bewerten routine (see Chapter 10, Section 10.2).

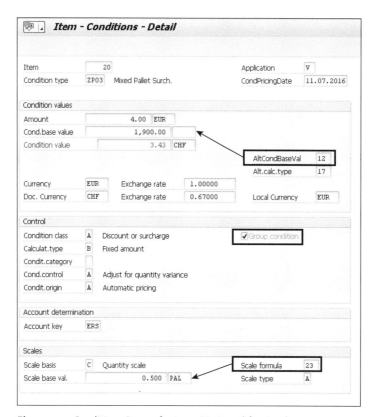

Figure 11.4 Conditions Screen for Item 20: Detail for Condition Type ZP03

For group conditions with a fixed amount, the condition value formula 017 is also processed exclusively at the point in time of `PRICING_COMPLETE` in the `gkomv_bewerten` routine. The total value of the condition type in CHF (Swiss Franc) is rounded using this value formula.

In the HEADER CONDITIONS screen (see Figure 11.5), we consider the value of the condition types KP03 and ZP03 converted to Swiss francs. The difference between the conditions types is that the condition value has been rounded for ZP03 after the currency conversion by the condition value formula 017.

In the HEADER CONDITIONS screen, we select the DETAILS screen for the condition type ZP03 (see Figure 11.6). Here you can see all the formulas used. The condition value of 5.97 CHF was rounded to 5.95 CHF during `gkomv_bewerten` by condition value formula 017.

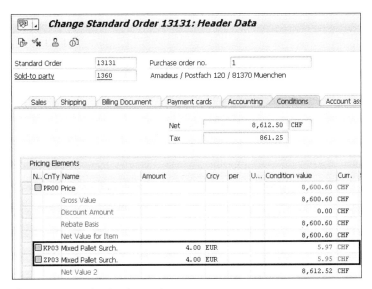

Figure 11.5 Header Conditions Screen

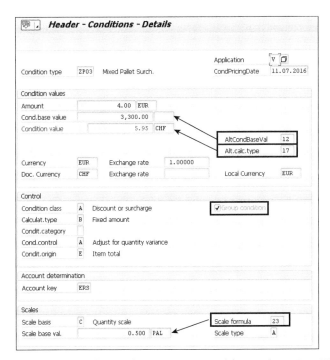

Figure 11.6 Header Conditions Screen: Detail for Condition Type ZP03

The displayed scale base of 0.5 PAL is the sum of the scale base amounts (partial quantities) of all items. Scale base formula 023 takes the decimal places and reads with this amount the scale values (see Figure 11.1). This information is only temporarily available during the runtime of `gkomv_bewerten` and will not be saved.

The CONDITION BASE VALUE represents (dimensionless) the total weight of the sales order.

11.4   Formulas for Pricing Conditions

In this section, we provide you with some important information about the use of formulas. The formulas are user exits in the form of routines that allow you to change results determined by the standard configuration. We are interested mainly in the point in time at which the routines are processed and which interfaces are available. We look at:

- Condition base formulas (also called *base formulas*)
- Scale base formulas (also called *scale formulas*)
- Condition value formulas (also called *value formulas*)
- Group key routines

11.4.1   Condition Base Value Formulas

As pointed out in Chapter 10, the condition base value xkomv-kawrt is calculated during pricing within xkomv_bewerten by the `konditionsbasis_ermitteln` routine (see Chapter 10, Section 10.1.6). Therein, depending on the calculation type, the underlying quantity, weight, value, etc., is determined and made available in the xkwert field to the base value formula, where this result can be manipulated, if necessary. The base value formula is assigned to the condition type in the pricing procedure.

Examples of Condition Base Formulas

As an introduction to the subject, you can just look at one of the following formulas of the standard SAP system with Transaction VOFM:

- 002 (Net value)

- 004 (Net value + tax)

- 008 (100% discount; used in condition type R100)

- 029 (Free goods/inclusive; used in condition type NRAB)

- 022 (Whole number; used in condition type KP00)

Processing Time and Interfaces of the Condition Base Formulas

The routine is only processed in the context of the item valuation (point in time: XKOMV_BEWERTEN) and *not* at the time of the valuation of the group table GKOMV within the PRICING_COMPLETE function block.

Inbound Interface of the Base Value Formulas

- xkwert: The condition base value determined by the standard processing (xkomv-kawrt).

- ykawrt: The condition base value (old).

- ywert: The condition value (old).

- KOMK, KOMP, and KOMPAZD: The fields komp-netwr, netpr, kmein, kpein, kumza, and kumne contain the interim status of the valuation before the current condition type.

- XKOMV: The current condition line.

- Preisfindungsart: The interface variable (pricing type).

- ykbetr, ybasis, ykrech, ykmein, ykpein, ykumza, ykumne, ywaers, ykkurs, and ykbflag: Values of the last price condition type. These determine in particular the presentation of the subtotals lines in the pricing procedure (lines without condition type).

- xworkd, xworke, xworkf, xworkg, xworkh, xworki, xworkj, xworkk, xworkl, and xworkm: These work fields can be used freely in the formulas and can also be filled from the pricing procedure via the attribute Subtotal (xkomv-kzwiw).

Outbound Interface of the Base Value Formulas

- xkwert: Changed condition base value.

- KOMP: All fields from KOMPAX except netwr, mwsbp, and wavwr.

- XKOMV: Most fields are changeable. The condition value xkomv-kwert can be set at this time only if the condition is fixed by setting xkomv-ksteu = E at the same time.

- xworkd, xworke, xworkf, xworkg, xworkh, xworki, xworkj, xworkk, xworkl, and xworkm.

The komp-netwr and komp-mwsbp fields must never be changed, because otherwise the transfer of the billing documents to accounting would fail.

11.4.2 Scale Base Formulas

For condition types with scales, the `konditionsbasis_ermitteln` routine (German for "determine condition base value") is processed during pricing within xkomv_bewerten. Therein, depending on the calculation type, the scale base value xkomv-kstbs (quantity, weight, value, etc.) is determined and made available in the xkwert field to the scale base formula, where this result can be manipulated, if necessary. The scale base formula is assigned to the condition type.

Examples of Scale Base Formulas

Scale base formulas are quite rarely used. However, they provide possibilities that sometimes can be seen only at second glance. A convincing example is the scale base formula 023 (partial quantity) for the realization of a mixed pallet surcharge with condition type KP03 (see the *condition profile* for KP03). The fact that the scales are used for this solution is a trick that you must determine first.

- **202 (price book scale)**
  Setting a fixed scale quantity in condition type PBBS. This example is explained in detail in Chapter 9, Section 9.2.

- **023 (partial quantity)**
  Setting a partial quantity in condition type KP03 for determining a mixed pallet surcharge, if necessary.

- **043 (tax license, France)**
  The total sales volume of a period is calculated for the settlement of tax exemption licenses. This formula (see Listing 11.2) is interesting, because it is only processed at the time of the document end processing `PRICING_COMPLETE` to evaluate the accumulation table `GKOMV`. At this point in time, GKOMV is generally recognized by the fact that the item number xkomv-kposn is initial. The `SD_COND_STATISTICS_READ` function module for determining the accumulation values to a condition record is, by the way, used quite often. The gkomv-kstbs field contains the sum of the scale base values of all items involved.

```
form frm_staffelbas_043.
  if xkomv-kposn is initial.
    if tkomk-vbtyp ca vbtyp_retour.
```

```
    xkwert = gkomv-kawrt.
  else.
    call function 'SD_COND_STATISTICS_READ'
        exporting
            buffer_read        = ' '
            condition_item     = gkomv_key-kopos
            condition_number   = gkomv_key-knumh
            s071_not_read      = 'X'
            s060_not_read      = ' '
        importing
            kstbs_s060         = zzkawrt
        exceptions
            others             = 1.
    xkwert = gkomv-kstbs + zzkawrt.
  endif.
 endif.
endform.
```

Listing 11.2 Scale Base Formula 043 for the Condition Type LCFR

The scale base formula 043 is a fine example of how cumulative values from statistics tables can be used.

Processing Time and Interfaces of the Scale Base Formulas

The scale base formulas and the condition value formulas are invoked at two points in time: Always during the item valuation and for *group conditions*, when the accumulation table GKOMV is evaluated within PRICING_COMPLETE.

It should be noted that the interfaces are different. The two different points in time can be distinguished by the item number field xkomv-kposn.

▶ Point in time XKOMV_BEWERTEN: xkomv-kposn is filled.

▶ Point in time GKOMV_BEWERTEN: xkomv-kposn is initial.

As you can see in the following section, the interfaces at the point in time GKOMV_BEWERTEN are significantly restricted.

Inbound Interface of the Scale Base Formula at the Point in Time XKOMV_BEWERTEN

▶ xkwert: Scale base value determined by standard processing (xkomv-kstbs)

▶ ykstbs: Scale base value (old)

▶ ykawrt: Condition base value (old)

- ywert: Condition value (old)
- KOMK and KOMP
- XKOMV: Current condition line
- Preisfindungsart: Interface variable (pricing type)
- ykbetr, ybasis, ykrech, ykmein, ykpein, ykumza, ykumne, ywaers, ykkurs, and ykbflag
- xworkd, xworke, xworkf, xworkg, xworkh, xworki, xworkj, xworkk, xworkl, and xworkm

---

Outbound Interface of the Scale Base Formula at the Point in Time XKOMV_BEWERTEN

- xkwert: Changed scale base value

Inbound Interface of the Scale Base Formula at the Point in Time GKOMV_BEWERTEN

- xkwert: Scale base value determined by the standard processing (from gkomv-kstbs).
- KOMK and KOMP significantly restricted: Only the fields that are included in the structures GKOMV and GKOMV_KEY are filled. If for the operation of your own formula another field is required, this can be optionally implemented as APPEND to these structures.
- XKOMV: Current condition line (filled from GKOMV).

Outbound Interface of the Scale Base Formula at the Point in Time GKOMV_BEWERTEN

- xkwert: Changed scale base value

As you can see, the interfaces differ significantly for the two times.

11.4.3 Condition Value Formulas

The condition value formula is probably the most widely used formula type. For all lines of the pricing procedure, the `kwert_ermitteln` routine is processed during pricing within xkomv_bewerten.

Depending on the calculation type, the condition value xkomv-kwert is determined and handed over in xkwert field to the condition value formula where this result can be manipulated. The condition value formula is assigned in the pricing procedure and particularly often used in the lines with subtotals (lines without condition type) to fill these at will.

Examples of Scale Base Formulas

There is no lack of condition value formulas in standard SAP system. We have selected three of them:

- **008 (expected value)**
  The price expected by the customer is compared to the calculated price and the item will be blocked for delivery if the difference exceeds a limit. The formula is used in the condition types EDI1 and EDI2.

- **011 (profit margin)**
  The profit margin is calculated as the difference between the fields komp-netwr and komp-wavwr. The formula is used in subtotals.

- **017 (rounding as per T001R)**
  The determined condition value is rounded according to the rounding rule the table T001R (rounding rule for each company code).

Processing Time and Interfaces of the Condition Value Formulas

Like the scale base formulas, the condition values formulas are also invoked at two points in time:

- Point in time XKOMV_BEWERTEN: xkomv-kposn is filled.

- Point in time GKOMV_BEWERTEN: xkomv-kposn is initial.

Inbound Interface of the Condition Value Formula at the Point in Time XKOMV_BEWERTEN

- xkwert: Condition value determined by the standard processing (xkomv-kwert)
- ykstbs: Scale base value (old)
- ykawrt: Condition base value (old)
- ywert: Condition value (old)
- KOMK, KOMP, and KOMPAZD
- XKOMV: Current condition line
- Preisfindungsart: Interface variable (pricing type)

- ykbetr, ybasis, ykrech, ykmein, ykpein, ykumza, ykumne, ywaers, ykkurs, and ykbflag
- xworkd, xworke, xworkf, xworkg, xworkh, xworki, xworkj, xworkk, xworkl, and xworkm

Outbound Interface of the Condition Value Formula at the Point in Time XKOMV_BEWERTEN

- xkwert: Changed condition value
- KOMP: All fields from KOMPAX except netwr, mwsbp, and wavwr
- XKOMV: Current condition line; in particular in the fields:
- xkomv-kbetr, krech, waers, kkurs, kmein, kpein, kumza, kumne, and kfaktor
- xkomv-ksteu, kherk, kinak, kstat, and fxmsg
- xkomv-kwaeh, kwert_k, and kawrt_k

Inbound Interface of the Condition Value Formula at the Point in Time GKOMV_BEWERTEN

- xkwert: Condition value determined by the standard processing (from gkomv-kwert)
- KOMK, KOMP: Significantly restricted (as described for the scale base formula)
- XKOMV: Current condition line (filled from GKOMV)

Outbound Interface of the Condition Value Formula at the Point in Time GKOMV_BEWERTEN

- xkwert: Changed condition value

Again, you can see that the interfaces differ significantly for the two times.

11.4.4 Formulas for the Structure of Group Keys (Group Key Routines)

As you saw in Section 10.2, the final valuation of the group conditions takes place in the context of the document end processing in the module PRICING_COMPLETE. In particular, the scale bases of the group conditions are accumulated across all items in tables GKOMV and optionally (for fixed amount group conditions) CGKOMV to then determine the scale values with these aggregated numbers.

The key of GKOMV is usually the condition record, represented by its uniquely identifying internal number KNUMH (gkomv-key-knumh and xkomv-knumh).

This means that the scale base for a condition record is determined precisely using those items, where this condition record was found. By using a group key routine, we can determine the scale base on a different level than the one given by the condition record.

The group key routines are processed during the setup of table GKOMV and serve to fill the variable key field gkomv-key-vakey. A filled VAKEY then replaces KNUMH as the key for GKOMV.

Inbound Interface of the Group Key Routine

- KOMK, KOMP, and KOMT1
- XKOMV: Current condition line
- GKOMV and GKOMV_KEY

Outbound Interface of the Group Key Routine

- xvakey: Group key

We want to explain at this point the operation of the group key routines by a detailed example. We consider in this example the two condition types Z030 and Z031 representing a material group discount. In Figure 11.7, you can see the condition record for the MATERIAL GROUP 02. The condition record for materials group 01 was created analogously.

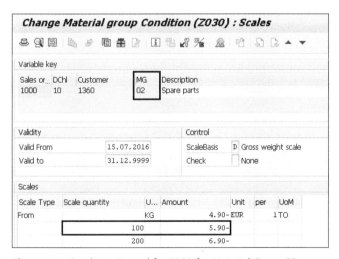

Figure 11.7 Condition Record for Z030 for Material Group 02

The condition type Z030 is configured as a weight-based group condition with weight scale and without a group key routine.

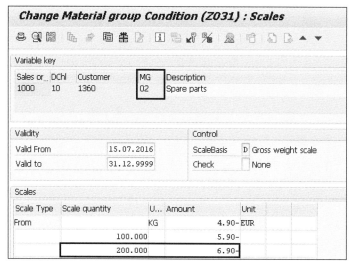

Figure 11.8 Condition Record for Z031 for Material Group 02

The condition type Z031 (see Figure 11.8) is set as a fixed amount group condition, also with weight scale, but with the group key routine 001 (see Listing 11.3). This simple routine fills xvakey with content, which causes gkomv-key-knumh to be initialized and thus the accumulation takes place at the level of the condition type and not at the level of the single condition records.

```
form frm_gruppenkey_001.
  xvakey      = '001'.
endform.
```

Listing 11.3 Group Key Routine 001 for Condition Type Z031

Consider the sample order in Figure 11.9 with four items (p1 to p4). The first two items belong to material group 01 and have a total weight of 160 kg, and the last two items belong to the material group 02 with a total weight of 144 kg.

As you can see in the HEADER CONDITIONS screen in Figure 11.10, the 100 kg scale has been applied for the condition type Z030 for both material groups. In contrast, for Z031, the 200 kg scale has been applied because of the group key routine. The following scale bases have been applied (see Table 11.1).

Material Group	Total Weight	Condition Value/Un
Z030 Material Group 01	160 kg (p1, p2)	–5,90 EUR/TO
Z030 Material Group 02	144 kg (p3, p4)	–5,90 EUR/TO
Z031 Material Group 01	304 kg (p1, p2, p3, p4)	–6,90 EUR
Z031 Material Group 02	304 kg (p1, p2, p3, p4)	–6,90 EUR

Table 11.1 Scale Base Values

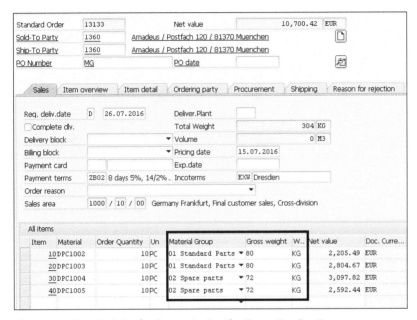

Figure 11.9 Sample Order for Demonstrating the Group Key Routines

In the HEADER CONDITIONS screen of the sales order (see Figure 11.10), you can distinguish the four condition records involved. On the associated detail screens, you can branch to the display of the condition records using menu path GO TO • CONDITION RECORD.

Restriction in the Use of Group Key Routines

When using group key routines, it is important to note that the condition type must have been found in all the items that are to be included in the scale accumulation. For example, if we do not want to grant a discount for MATERIAL GROUP 03, we still need to create a condition record for Z031 and MATERIAL GROUP 03 with the amount set to zero.

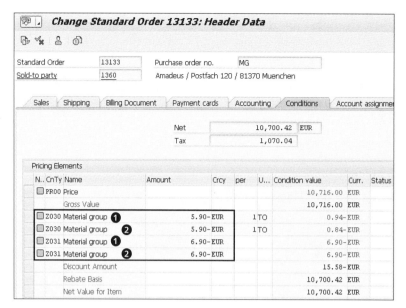

Figure 11.10 Header Conditions Screen with Condition Types Z030 and Z031

11.5 Special Logic for Pricing Type F in Routine XKOM_BEWERTEN

The update of the item conditions due to the group valuation within the PRICING_ COMPLETE function block is done by processing the internal table GKOMZ using the special pricing type F (see Chapter 10, Section 10.2). For each entry in the GKOMZ table, the xkomv_bewerten routine is called to perform this task. When the valuation of the item conditions XKOMV for a concrete item takes place, four particularly important *points in time* are to be noted in this context. For each of these points in time, special coding parts can be found in the xkomv_bewerten routine. We want to explain this with an example in which we process the marked entry in the GKOMZ table (Figure 11.11). In this figure are:

As you can see, the group condition g4 was determined in the items p3 and p4. The highlighted entry in the GKOMZ table is stating that we pass the result of the group valuation of the condition g4 (condition record Z031 for material group 02) in the item p3. This item is the last entry of the GKOMZ block for group condition g4, which means that, if necessary, for this item a rounding difference comparison is performed.

- ▸ p1 to p4: Item numbers of the sales order
- ▸ g1 to g7: Line numbers of the group condition in the GKOMZ table

CGKOMV

kschl	vakey	kstbs
Z031	001	304

GKOMV Group table

	kschl	kstbs	kawrt	kbetr	kwert	
g1	Z030	160,00	0,16	-5,90	-0,95	p1,p2
g2	Z030	144,00	0,144	-5,90	-0,85	p3,p4
g3	Z031	304,00	9221	-6,90	-6,90	p1,p2
g4	Z031	304,00	23250	-6,90	-6,90	p3,p4
g5	ZP03	0,62	304000	4,00	4,00	p1,p2,p3,p4
g6	MWST		46,92	16,00	7,51	p1,p2
g7	MWST		279,98	7,00	19,60	p3,p4

GKOMZ Assignment table

150	g1	p1
150	g1	p2
150	g2	p4
150	g2	p3
151	g3	p1
151	g3	p2
151	g4	p4
151	g4	p3
810	g5	p1
810	g5	p2
810	g5	p4
810	g5	p3
915	g6	p1
915	g6	p2
915	g7	p4
915	g7	p3

XKOMV Item conditions

p3	11	PR00	132,00
p3	101	Z905	-2,64
p3	150	Z030	-0,42
p3	151	Z031	-3,62
p3	...	...	...
p3	805	ZP03	0,95
p3	900	Net value 2	122,69
p3	915	MWST	8,59
p3	925	Paym. Amount	131,28

Point in time

```
            A
   C
          B
   D
```

Figure 11.11 Valuation of the Item Conditions for Pricing Type F

11.5.1 Point in Time "A"

At the point in time "A", all conditions *before* the group condition g4 currently being processed are handled. These are the condition types PR00, Z905, and Z030. At this time, no changes are made to the XKOMV line. Although formulas are processed, they can no longer change anything. The call is merely intended to feed KOMP fields or work variables that are filled in the formula.

11.5.2 Point in Time "B"

At the point in time "B", the group condition g4 is currently being processed and all subsequent conditions are handled. These are the condition types Z031, ZP03, and MWST. At this time, the amount/percentage xkomv-kbetr is determined from the scales (if not taken from GKOMV) and the condition value xkomv-kwert is calculated.

11.5.3   Point in Time "C"

At the point in time "C", group condition g4 currently being processed is handled exclusively, that is the condition type Z031. At this time, the amount/percentage xkomv-kbetr is transferred from gkomv-kbetr. For fixed value condition types, the condition value is calculated using the formula:

xkomv-kwert = gkomv-kwert × xkomv-kawrt ÷ gkomv-kawrt

This represents a distribution of the total value in proportion to the condition base value. For fixed value and percentage condition types, the rounding difference will be added here if appropriate.

11.5.4   Point in Time "D"

At the point in time "D", all conditions *after* the group condition g4 currently being processed are handled. These are the condition types ZP03 and MWST. At this time, the condition base value, the scale base value, and the condition value are updated.

In Figure 11.11, you can identify which condition types are affected at the time when the shaded entry of the table GKOMZ is processed.

We have covered this program logic in such detail because it can be useful, if appropriate, to react in your own formulas to these situations—not the least for reasons of performance. For example, if you programmed database accesses into your formulas, these should be carried out as infrequently as possible. In the simplest case, no database accesses are performed for pricing type F. Perhaps you can at least limit the accesses to certain points in time.

11.6   Pricing Result in KOMP

The result of the pricing is handed over to the caller by the interface table TKOMV (these are the document conditions) and the structure KOMP (pricing result at item level). We saw (in Chapter 9, Section 9.2 in the example for variant 2 of the data determination) that those fields of the structure KOMP, which are also defined in the structure KOMPAX, are transmitted to the calling order item and billing item. In addition to these fields, the komp-fxmsg field is also of interest, because you can see whether the pricing was carried out and—if applicable—

what type of error has occurred. Table 11.2 shows the fields of the structure KOMPAX, which we will now cover in more detail. The fields are divided into two blocks. This includes the KOMPAXM character fields and the KOMPAXA numeric fields.

Component	Type	Length	Short Description
.INCLUDE	**KOMPAXM**	0	**Character Fields**
PRSOK	PRSOK	1	Pricing is OK
KMEIN	KMEIN	3	Condition unit
CEPOK	CEPOK	1	Status expected price
MPROK	MPROK	1	Status manual price change
KOUPD	KOUPD	1	Condition update
AKTNR	WAKTION	10	Promotion
KNUMA_PI	KNUMA_PI	10	Promotion
KNUMA_AG	KNUMA_AG	10	Sales deal
KPEIN	KPEIN	5	Condition pricing unit
.INCLUDE	**KOMPAXA**	0	**Fields Able to be Added**
BRTWR	BRTWR_FP	15	Gross value in document currency
NETWR	NETWR	15	Net value in document Currency
MWSBP	MWSBP	13	Tax amount in document currency
NETPR	NETPR	11	Net price
WAVWR	WAVWR	13	Cost in document currency
KZWI1	KZWI1	13	Subtotal 1 from pricing procedure
KZWI2	KZWI2	13	Subtotal 2 from pricing procedure
KZWI3	KZWI3	13	Subtotal 3 from pricing procedure
KZWI4	KZWI4	13	Subtotal 4 from pricing procedure
KZWI5	KZWI5	13	Subtotal 5 from pricing procedure
KZWI6	KZWI6	13	Subtotal 6 from pricing procedure
CMPRE	CMPRE	11	Item credit price
SKFBP	SKFBT	13	Amount eligible for cash discount in document currency
BONBA	BONBA	13	Rebate basis

Table 11.2 Pricing Result: Item Fields (KOMP)

Component	Type	Length	Short Description
CMPRE_FLT	CMPRE_FLT	16	Item credit price
NRAB_VALUE	KWERT	13	Condition value (free goods)
PAYMNT	PAYMNT	15	Payment value in document currency

Table 11.2 Pricing Result: Item Fields (KOMP) (Cont.)

11.6.1 KOMP-FXMSG (Message Number)

The komp-fxmsg (message number) field indicates whether the pricing was processed completely and—if applicable—what type of error has occurred.

Here are the main messages:

▶ 801 pricing error: Mandatory condition type is missing

▶ 802 pricing error: Field overflow

▶ 803 pricing error: Exchange rate conversion

▶ 804 pricing error: Quantity conversion

▶ 805: Pricing was processed correctly

▶ 806 pricing error: Internal pricing error

▶ 807 pricing error: Factors for quantity conversion are missing

The error 806 must not occur; it can be triggered only by a program error or by an inconsistency. This type of error will be caused most likely by customer-specific modifications. All other errors are caused by an incomplete Customizing or incomplete master data (for example, missing exchange rates or missing quantity conversion factors in the material master). This last type of error can occur in the transient phase of an installation or whenever new customer or material master records are created. In all these cases, the komp-prsok field is reset and thus the order item is set to incomplete.

11.6.2 KOMP-PRSOK (Pricing Is OK)

The field komp-prsok (pricing is OK) is preset internally with X. If an error situation occurs within the pricing, komp-prsok is initialized. Moreover, in such situations the komp-fxmsg field is filled with an error number. The field can also be reset within formulas, whereby the item is set to erroneous and thus is incomplete for subsequent processing (delivery and billing).

11.6.3 KOMP-CEPOK (Status Expected Price)

The komp-cepok field (status of expected customer price) is set by the condition types EDI1 and EDI2 using the condition value formulas 008 and 009 and has the following characteristics:

- ▸ _ (Space): Not relevant
- ▸ A: Expected price OK
- ▸ B: Expected price not OK
- ▸ C: Expected price not OK but released

Once the expected price/value deviates by a defined tolerance limit in the formulas, the status is set to B. Order items with this status are incomplete and are therefore blocked for delivery or billing. Such documents can be selected, edited, and released with Transaction V.25 (Release Customer Expected Price).

This procedure is also useful for meeting additional requirements like blocking the automatic delivery of the sales order for a particular state of pricing. Thus, such orders can be monitored by an additional approval step to control, for example, budgeting requirements.

11.6.4 KOMP-MPROK (Status Manual Price Change)

The komp-mprok field (status manual price change) is always set when a manual change is made to a condition. The following values exist:

- ▸ _ (space): No manual price changes
- ▸ A: Manual price change carried out
- ▸ B: Condition manually deleted

A release procedure for such sales orders as described in the previous section for the field komp-cepok is not implemented in the standard SAP system. One possible solution is to introduce a checking condition type with a condition value formula that sets `komp-cepok = B` if komp-mprok is filled. However, we will not go deeper into this approach here.

11.6.5 KOMP-KOUPD (Condition Update)

The komp-koupd field (condition update) is always set when at least one condition type has been found for which the condition update is configured. The field may be modified for any reason.

11.6.6 KOMP-NETPR (Net Price)

The komp-netpr field contains the net price in the currency of the (single) active price condition type. A price is always accompanied by the fields komp-kmein (condition unit of measure) and komp-kpein (condition pricing unit). The conversion factors to the stock keeping unit (komp-kumza and komp-kumne) are used to calculate the quantity in the condition pricing in case there are different units of measure. The net price is determined by the net value komp-netwr of the item scaled to the condition pricing unit. For this purpose, the information of the pricing condition is available in the working variables ykmein, ykpein, ykumza, and ykumne within the routine `xkomv_bewerten` and can be used in formulas.

11.6.7 KOMP-NETWR (Net Value of the Item)

The komp-netwr field (net value of the item) is the sum of all active (xkomv-kinak = space) and non-statistical (xkomv-kstat = space) conditions that are not a tax (xkomv-koaid ≠ D). The field must not be modified under any circumstances, because the accounts receivable offsetting entry to the revenue postings in the billing documents is generated for the sum of komp-netwr and komp-mwsbp (tax amount).

11.6.8 KOMP-MWSBP (Tax Amount of the Item)

This field is the sum of all active (xkomv-kinak = space) non-statistical (xkomv-kstat = space) tax condition types (xkomv-koaid = D). The field must not be modified under any circumstances (see the note to the field komp-netwr).

11.6.9 KOMP-WAVWR (Cost of the Item)

The komp-wavwr field (cost of the item) represents the cost of an item, normally determined via the condition type VPRS. In the sales order, these are *planned costs* and, in the billing document, they are *actual costs*. As the cost of a sales transaction is determined depending on the process through different condition types, the assignment of the condition type is done by the characteristic SUBTOTAL = B (xkomv-kzwiw) in the pricing procedure (see Table 11.2 and Chapter 7, Section 7.6). Examples of conditions types that determine the cost of an item are:

▸ VPRS (stock sale, drop shipment)

▸ EK02 (make-to-order, calculation)

▸ EK01 (resource-related billing)

▸ PI01, PI02 (cross-company sales)

The field must not be modified by formulas since, especially in the case of VPRS (xkomv-kntyp = G), an update mechanism implemented in the standard SAP system would no longer work for subsequent changes of the actual cost of the billing documents. In the billing documents, it is extremely important that the internal price condition represent the actual cost.

11.6.10   KOMP–BRTWR, KZWI1–KZWI6, Etc. (Subtotals)

The komp-brtwr, kzwi1–kzwi6, etc. (subtotals) fields are filled by an assignment to the indicator SUBTOTAL (xkomv-kzwiw) (see Table 11.3). In the pricing procedure, you can assign both lines with a condition type as well as subtotal lines (lines without a condition type). In the first block, you see the indicators that serve to fill fields of the interface structure KOMP, which are passed to the caller after the pricing run and can be stored there in the document item. In the second block, you see the indicators that serve to fill working variables for use in formulas for subsequent condition types.

Fix. Val.	Short Description
1	Carry over value to KOMP-KZWI1
2	Carry over value to KOMP-KZWI2
3	Carry over value to KOMP-KZWI3
4	Carry over value to KOMP-KZWI4
5	Carry over value to KOMP-KZWI5
6	Carry over value to KOMP-KZWI6
7	Carry over value to KOMP_BONBA (rebate basis)
8	Copy values according to KOMP-PREVA (preference value)

Table 11.3 Fixed Values of Domain KZWIW

Fix. Val.	Short Description
9	Copy values to KOMP-BRTWR (gross value)
A	Carry over price to KOMP-CMPRE (credit price)
B	Carry over value to KOMP-WAVWR (cost)
C	Carry over value to KOMP-GKWRT (statistical value)
N	Value transfer to KOMP-NRAB_VALUE (free goods)
D	Copy value to XWORKD
E	Copy value to XWORKE
F	Copy value to XWORKF
G	Copy value to XWORKG
H	Copy value to XWORKH
I	Copy value to XWORKI
J	Copy value to XWORKJ
K	Copy price to XWORKK
L	Copy price to XWORKL
M	Copy price to XWORKM

Table 11.3 Fixed Values of Domain KZWIW (Cont.)

All demands that cannot be mapped by KZWIW assignments must be solved using condition formulas. The control parameter KZWIW offers, in addition to the assignment of the subtotal fields of structure KOMP, the possibility to fill the internal working variables xworkd to xworkm, which can then be used in the formulas of subsequent condition types.

11.7 Control Flag XKOMV-KSTEU

The xkomv-ksteu field is the most important control field. It provides information about whether the scale base, condition amount, condition basis, and condition value can be adjusted with changes in the item or whether they are fixed. You will find the information in the PRICING DETAIL screen for this item (see Figure 11.4). The indicator is set internally within the pricing program in certain situations but can also be changed via formulas.

Now let's take a closer look at the significance of the different values that are shown in Table 11.4.

KSTEU	Description
A	Adjust for quantity variance
B	Free
C	Changed manually
D	Fixed
E	Condition value and basis fixed
F	Condition value fixed (billed items)
G	Condition basis fixed
H	Condition value fixed (cost price)

Table 11.4 Fixed Values of the Domain KSTEU

▶ **A (adjust for quantity variance)**
This is the normal state of a condition type found automatically. In the xkomv_bewerten routine, the scale base xkomv-kstbs, the amount from scales xkomv-kbetr, the condition basis xkomv-kawrt, and the condition value xkomv-kwert are adjusted at any item changes.

▶ **C (changed manually)**
The state after a manual change of the condition type. In the xkomv_bewerten routine, only the condition basis xkomv-kawrt and the condition value xkomv-kwert are adjusted at any item changes. Scales are not updated. In this situation, the indicator xkomv-kmprs (condition changed manually) is set.

▶ **D (fixed)**
The state when creating documents with reference. The document conditions can be copied via the PRICING_COPY function module (see Chapter 10, Section 10.3). In this state, in routine xkomv_bewerten only the condition basis xkomv-kawrt and the condition value xkomv-kwert are adjusted at any item changes. Scales are not updated. When calling the PRICING_COPY function module with the pricing type A, the conditions are not fixed. Thus, the original content of xkomv-ksteu remains unchanged.

▶ **E (condition value and basis fixed)**
The state when creating documents with reference. The document conditions are copied with pricing type E, for example, for reversal billing documents. The

status E is also set for the case of a manual change of the condition value xkomv-kwert. Here, in the `xkomv_bewerten` routine, no further changes are made. The formulas are processed, but only KOMP fields and working variables can be changed. You can no longer manipulate the XKOMV fields.

▶ **F (condition value fixed (billed items))**
The state after a change of sales order items to which there exists a billing document. In the `xkomv_bewerten` routine, in this case only the condition basis xkomv-kawrt is determined, as usual, and then the new condition value is calculated by scaling with the rule *xkomv-kwert = xkomv-kwert(old) × xkomv-kawrt(new) ÷ xkomv-kawrt(old)*.

In the case of quantity changes in the sales order, the price of the item does not change after billing. The condition base formula is processed normally, but again, for the value formula a manipulation of the XKOMV fields is no longer possible.

▶ **G (condition basis fixed)**
The state after manual change of the condition basis xkomv-kawrt. In this case, only the condition value xkomv-kwert is determined in the xkomv_bewerten routine. You can't change the condition basis manually in the sales order, so that this situation can only be achieved by formulas.

▶ **H (condition value fixed (cost price))**
A special state of the transfer condition type VPRS (xkomv-kntyp = G) in the billing document. In the billing document, the actual cost of the goods issue posting (or invoice receipt posting in drop shipments) is passed to the billing document and stored in the condition type VPRS. This is documented by xkomv-ksteu = H. The same rules apply as for xkomv-ksteu = F.

11.8   User Exits

If you want to make adaptations in pricing, you will usually do this by using formulas and requirements. However, there are still a few classic user exits and BAdIs. There are situations where you cannot solve a demand alone with formulas and requirements and you need these user exits embedded in the pricing program. You will find illustrative examples in Chapter 12, Section 12.9, for handling fixed value condition types and in Listing 11.5 for recalculating the currency conversion rate.

Particularly useful are the user exits in the dialog part, where you can manipulate the appearance of the pricing result in the CONDITIONS screen of the sales documents. We will discuss the user exits within the calling objects (sales order and billing document) in connection with the pricing in Chapter 13.

11.8.1 User Exits of Function Group V61A

The function group V61A gathers the user exits of the pricing program.

Routine USEREXIT_PRICING_COPY

When creating documents with reference, the `PRICING_COPY` function module reads the document conditions from the database table `KONV` and transfers them into the new document. The user exit is processed for each `KONV` entry to be copied. Here you can fix, for example, conditions by setting konv-ksteu = D or you can prevent the handover of the condition type by setting `u15_subrc` to something other than zero. Furthermore, this user exit is often used in the context of setting up customer-specific pricing types via `userexit_pricing_rule`. Interesting in this context is the SAP Note 24832 (Pricing Rules/TVCPF).

Inbound Interface of the USEREXIT_PRICING_COPY

▶ KONV: Current condition line.
▶ The inbound interface of the function module `PRICING_COPY`. Here the parameters mode (pricing type) and `vbtyp_new` (sales document type of the target document) are particularly important.

Outbound Interface of the USEREXIT_PRICING_COPY

▶ KONV: Current condition line.
▶ u15_subrc: If this return code is not equal to zero, the condition type will not be transferred.

Routine USEREXIT_PRICING_RULE

You already know about the importance of the pricing types. In particular, you have seen in Chapter 10 that these are defined in routine `konditionsvorstep`. The `userexit_pricing_rule` routine is also located there. On the one hand, customer-specific pricing types (X, Y, Z, and 1 to 9) can be implemented with it. On the other hand, the behavior of the standard pricing types could be changed. However, we do not recommend this since otherwise, a change in the behavior of a standard pricing type by SAP will not take effect in your system.

Inbound Interface of the USEREXIT_PRICING_RULE

▸ KOMK: Structure of the pricing header

Outbound Interface of the USEREXIT_PRICING_RULE

▸ STEU: Internal table of the pricing types

Listing 11.4 shows an example of setting up the customer-specific pricing type X. This type is to be implemented so that it behaves like pricing type G, but transfer price condition types (with condition category G) should be handed over instead of being newly determined.

```
form userexit_pricing_rule.
  steu-knprs = 'x'.
  steu-kntyp = 'lriefbhn..'.
  if komk-knuma is initial.
    steu-koaid = 'cdegq.....'.
  else.
    steu-koaid = 'dg........'.
  endif.
  steu-maueb = ' '.
  steu-kfkiv = 'x'.
  append steu.
endform.
```

Listing 11.4 Routine USEREXIT_PRICING_RULE

For our example, you should copy the code for pricing type G of the routine konditionsvorstep in the function group V61A and adjust it as shown in Listing 11.4.

Routine USEREXIT_PRINT_HEAD

The `userexit_print_head` routine is called at the end of the `RV_PRICE_PRINT_HEAD` function module that processes the data required for the output of values in the message footer (order confirmation, invoice, and EDI). These condition data are provided in the interface table `TKOMVD` controlled by the printing indicator in the pricing procedure (see Chapter 7, Section 7.8). This data can be changed with the user exit.

Inbound Interface of USEREXIT_PRINT_HEAD

- ▸ KOMK: Structure of the pricing header
- ▸ Internal table TKOMVD

Outbound Interface of USEREXIT_PRINT_HEAD

- ▸ Internal table TKOMVD

Routine USEREXIT_PRINT_ITEM

The userexit_print_item routine is called at the end of the function module RV_PRICE_PRINT_ITEM that processes the data required for the output of values in the message line item. The condition data is provided in the interface table TKVD and can be modified (see Chapter 7, Section 7.8).

Inbound Interface of the USEREXIT_PRINT_ITEM

- ▸ KOMK, KOMP: Structures of the pricing header and the pricing item
- ▸ Internal table TKOMVD

Outbound Interface of the USEREXIT_PRINT_ITEM

- ▸ Internal table TKOMVD

Routine USEREXIT_XKOMV_BEWERTEN_END

The userexit_xkomv_bewerten_end routine is called at the end of the routine xkomv_bewerten. Here you can finally evaluate the pricing result, that is the internal table XKOMV, and possibly change KOMP fields within the framework of what is permissible.

Routine USEREXIT_XKOMV_BEWERTEN_INIT

The userexit_xkomv_bewerten_init routine is called at the beginning of the xkomv_bewerten routine. Here you can initialize your customer-specific fields that you added to the KOMP structure and that are processed by formulas, which in general is necessary for an error-free functioning.

Routine USEREXIT_XKOMV_ERGAENZEN

The routine `userexit_xkomv_ergaenzen` is called in the routine `xkomv_ergaenzen`. In case of changes, this routine serves first to fill the fields of the dynamic part KONVD of XKOMV (the database only stores the fields of the table KONV), and then updates information collected from the condition master records.

Inbound Interface of the USEREXIT_XKOMV_ERGAENZEN

- ▶ KOMK: Structure of the pricing header
- ▶ KOMT1: Table entry in the pricing procedure and all parameters of the condition type
- ▶ KONP: Data of the condition record
- ▶ XKOMV: Current condition line

Outbound Interface of the USEREXIT_XKOMV_ERGAENZEN

- ▶ XKOMV: Current condition line

A brief example of using this user exit: The conversion rate xkomv-kkurs for conditions in foreign currency is determined in the sales order and copied to the billing document. This ensures that sales orders and billing documents determine the same value. Now, if you want to ensure that for these copied conditions, the conversion rate is recalculated in the billing document, you can do so by implementing the user exit shown in Listing 11.5.

```
form userexit_xkomv_ergaenzen.
  if xkomv-zaehk is initial and
    preisfindungsart ca 'CG' and
    xkomv-krech na prozentual and
    komk-vbtyp ca vbtyp_fakt.
    xkomv-kdatu = komk-prsdt.
    perform xkomv_kkurs_ermitteln.
  endif.
endform.
```

Listing 11.5 Routine XKOMV_ERGAENZEN

The `xkomv-zaehk is initial` situation is given exactly when, for a copied condition, the PRICING function module is called for the first time. Compared with `userexit_pricing_copy`, this user exit has the advantage that the structure KOMK is filled and thus much more information is available.

Routine USEREXIT_XKOMV_ERGAENZEN_MANU

The `userexit_xkomv_ergaenzen_manu` routine is called at the end of the `xkomv_ergaenzen_manuelle` routine and it provides the XKOMV data for manually added condition types. In this case, the MKOMV structure contains the manual entries.

Inbound Interface of the USEREXIT_XKOMV_ERGAENZEN_MANU

- ▸ MKOMV: Manual entries
- ▸ XKOMV: New manually created condition line

Outbound Interface of the USEREXIT_XKOMV_ERGAENZEN_MANU

- ▸ XKOMV: New manually created condition line

Routine USEREXIT_XKOMV_FUELLEN

The `userexit_xkomv_fuellen` routine is called at the end of the `xkomv_fuellen` routine, which fills the structure XKOMV for a condition type for which there is a condition record. In particular, you can prevent the handover of the condition type by setting the returncode field to something other than zero.

Inbound Interface of the USEREXIT_XKOMV_FUELLEN

- ▸ KOMK, KOMP, and KOMPAZD: Structures of the pricing header and the pricing item
- ▸ KOMT1 and KOMT2: Structures of condition type and access
- ▸ KONP: Data of the condition record
- ▸ XKOMV: Condition line to be created

Outbound Interface of the USEREXIT_XKOMV_FUELLEN

- ▸ returncode: Not equal zero means "discard the condition"
- ▸ XKOMV: Condition line to be created

Routine USEREXIT_XKOMV_FUELLEN_O_KONP

The `userexit_xkomv_fuellen_o_konp` routine is called at the end of the `xkomv_fuellen_ohne_konp` routine and fills the structure XKOMV for condition types that are not determined by condition records. These are condition types without an access sequence.

Inbound Interface of the USEREXIT_XKOMV_FUELLEN_O_KONP

▸ KOMK, KOMP: Structures of the pricing header and the pricing item
▸ KOMT1, KOMT2: Structures of condition type and access
▸ XKOMV: Condition line to be created

Outbound Interface of the USEREXIT_XKOMV_FUELLEN_O_KONP

▸ XKOMV : Condition line to be created

11.8.2 User Exits of Function Group V69A

The function group V69A gathers the user exits of the dialog part of the pricing program. The routines are processed when you call the CONDITIONS screens in the sales order, billing document, and purchasing order screens in the SAP GUI.

Routine USEREXIT_CHANGE_PRICING_RULE

The user exit is called at the end of kot_ende routine and runs at the end of the DOCUMENT CONDITIONS screen to process the changes.

The processing takes place with the pricing type p_rv61a_ksteu that could be changed here.

Value E in p_rv61a_ksteu Must Not Be Changed

Note that a proposed value E in p_rv61a_ksteu must not be changed, since this value ensures that in the display mode no changes are possible.

Inbound Interface of the USEREXIT_CHANGE_PRICING_RULE

▸ KOMK, KOMP: Structures of the pricing header and the pricing item
▸ p_rv61a_ksteu: Pricing type

Outbound Interface of the USEREXIT_CHANGE_PRICING_RULE

▸ p_rv61a_ksteu: Pricing type

Routine USEREXIT_FIELD_MODIFICATION

The `userexit_field_modification` routine is called at the end of the `feldauswahl` routine (field selection) in which the SAP GUI DOCUMENT CONDITIONS screen is prepared with respect to the visibility and readiness for input of the fields. This routine is processed for all lines in the pricing procedure that contain a condition type.

Inbound Interface of the USEREXIT_FIELD_MODIFICATION

▸ KOMK, KOMP: Structures of the pricing header and the pricing item
▸ screen-name: Screen field name
▸ KOMV: Current condition line

Outbound Interface of the USEREXIT_FIELD_MODIFICATION

▸ screen-active: 0 = hidden
▸ screen-input: 0 = not ready for input; 1 = ready for input

Routine USEREXIT_FIELD_MODIFIC_KOPF

The routine `userexit_field_modific_kopf` is used to process the subtotal lines in the HEADER CONDITIONS screen. The interfaces are the same as in the `userexit_field_modification` routine.

Routine USEREXIT_FIELD_MODIFIC_KZWI

The `userexit_field_modific_kzwi` routine is used to process the subtotal lines in the ITEM CONDITIONS screen. The interfaces are the same as in the `userexit_field_modification` routine.

Routine USEREXIT_FIELD_MODIFIC_LEER

The `userexit_field_modific_leer` routine is used to process the blank lines in the HEADER and ITEM CONDITIONS screen. The interfaces are the same as in the `userexit_field_modification` routine.

Routine USEREXIT_PRICING_CHECK

The `userexit_pricing_check` routine is called at the end of the `kondition_pruefen` routine, where manual inputs in the CONDITIONS screen are checked. This is the only place where you are allowed to display error messages or warnings to prevent invalid entries.

Inbound Interface of the USEREXIT_PRICING_CHECK

- ▶ KOMK, KOMP: Structures of the pricing header and the pricing item
- ▶ *KOMV: State of the condition line before change
- ▶ KOMV: State of the condition line after change

Outbound Interface of the USEREXIT_PRICING_CHECK

- ▶ KOMV: State of the condition line after change

With this comprehensive collection, we have addressed all user exits within the pricing programs. We will cover user exits in other programs that relate to pricing in Chapter 13.

11.9 Enhancement of KONV

Sometimes there is a demand to include additional fields in the pricing result KONV (and thus also in KOMV), for example, to display additional information in the pricing screen or to print additional information in the order confirmation or in the invoice. *However, we strongly advise you not to add new fields to the* KONV *table*, not the least because it already has the most entries in a production environment. That is also why it's one of the few still delivered as a cluster table and not as a transparent database table. Nevertheless, there is the possibility of using the xkomv-varcond field as a data container. The field is used by the standard SAP system in variant condition types (xkomv-kntyp = O or xkomv-kvarc = X) and special contract condition types (the BUDGET CONDITION field in the configuration of the condition type). Within customer-specific condition types that are not of this type, you can use this field as a data container by filling it via formulas.

11.10 Performance Aspects

You saw that formulas within the `PRICING_COMPLETE` function module are processed as often as entries exist in the internal table `GKOMZ`. You also saw that there are different points in time at which the formulas are called. If you intend to use complex formulas, you should ensure that the performance-intensive part runs only as often as necessary.

This section lists again all important points in time and the respective program logic for how these points in time can be recognized (see also Figure 11.11). In particular, it is usually not necessary to perform the coding, if the pricing type E is used. This pricing type is used, for example, for displaying documents and during the print processing where no changes to the internal table `XKOMV` are made and only the subtotals are calculated.

The important points in time and the respective program logic to recognize them are as follows:

▶ **Point in time** `XKOMV_BEWERTEN`
```
if not xkomv-kposn is initial.
```

▶ **Point in time** `GKOMV_BEWERTEN`
```
if xkomv-kposn is initial.
```

▶ **Pricing type F (point in time A)**
```
if preisfindungsart = 'F'
 and not (xkomv-stunr ge gkomz-stunr and laufnr ge gkomz-zaehk).
```

At this point in time, no changes to the `XKOMV` line are made.

▶ **Point in time** `XKOMV_BEWERTEN` **or pricing type F (point in time B)**
```
if preisfindungsart ne 'E'.
  if preisfindungsart ne 'F'
  or ( xkomv-stunr ge gkomz-stunr and laufnr ge gkomz-zaehk ).
```

At this point in time, the condition amount/percentage komv-kbetr is determined from the scales and the condition values xkomv-kwert and xkomv-kwert_k are calculated.

▶ **Pricing type F (point in time C)**
```
if preisfindungsart eq 'F' and xkomv-ix_gkomv eq gkomv_tabix.
```

At this point in time, the condition amount/percentage komv-kbetr and the condition value xkomv-kwert are handed over from GKOMV or calculated based on GKOMV.

▶ **Point in time** XKOMV_BEWERTEN **or pricing type F (point in time D)**
```
if preisfindungsart ne 'E'.
    if preisfindungsart ne 'F'
        or ( xkomv-stunr ge gkomz-stunr and laufnr gt gkomz-zaehk ).
```

At this point in time, the condition base value, the scale base value, and the condition value are determined.

When implementing formulas, performance is often ignored. We therefore recommend that you generally set a breakpoint when testing complex formulas and then create a representative sales order. For simple formulas that only calculate or set working variables, there is no need to worry. However, in the case of complex formulas, you should at least consider whether you can skip the pricing type E and pricing type F (point in time A) situations, thereby reducing the number of calls of the formulas considerably.

In the next section, we discuss handling error situations. After that, you will know everything notable about user exits, formulas, and requirements.

11.11   Error Messages/Error Handling

Within the function group V61A (pricing), no dialogs in the form of error or warning messages (E or W messages) are normally triggered. Generally, it can be said that within the user exits and VOFM routines (formulas and requirements) dialogs are forbidden for customer-specific enhancements. Only S messages (S = status) are allowed. These messages produce no dialogue, but show the message in the footer of the screen at the next screen change (pending message). Dialogs are not allowed in this context because the correct subsequent processing is not guaranteed for a dialog in general. An additional consideration is that the pricing is not only called in dialog transactions, but also in batch processes (such as the batch invoicing) from ABAP reports (such as the backorder processing) as well as in the function modules for processing an object (APIs, BAPIs, and eSOA services). The only exception is the userexit_pricing_check routine in function group V69A (dialog part of pricing). Here, you may issue error and warning messages.

Error situations in function group V61A are handled in the standard SAP system in many situations by issuing an S message. The erroneous condition line is deactivated by `xkomv-kinak = X` and the error message is recorded in the fields xkomv-fxmsg and komp-fxmsg for information purposes. This can be useful for analyzing an error situation. Moreover, in such situations (depending on the severity of the error) `komp-prsok = space` is set, which tells the caller that the pricing is wrong. As a result, incompleteness is triggered in the sales order that prevents the sales order from being delivered or invoiced. You should also read the information in Section 11.6.

You must of course edit such an erroneous order to eliminate the error situation. However, the order only tells you that the pricing is incomplete, since you will not receive more information about the cause initially. To find out the nature of the fault, you must choose in the change mode of the sales order the ITEM CONDITIONS screen or possibly the HEADER CONDITIONS screen. Normally, the causative S message is triggered again, and you can pinpoint and eliminate the cause, for example, by triggering a new pricing and deleting or changing the faulty conditions.

A second way to initially block an order item for further processing is to set the field `komp-cepok = B`. An example is the value formula 008 for the condition type EDI1 that compares the result of the automatic pricing with an externally specified price (e.g., customer expected price). Again, an incompleteness is triggered that can be eliminated by correcting the cause (by adjusting the price) or by explicitly releasing the document using Transaction V.25 (Release Customer Expected Price). An interesting application example is found in Chapter 12, Section 12.1, in which we use this method to block an order item when a budget is exceeded.

11.12   Summary

You have now gained insight into all the places in the pricing where you can intervene to enhance the pricing according to your demands. In particular, you know the terms *requirement*, *scale base formula*, *base value formula*, *value formula*, and *group key routine*. Whenever you intend to use these elements, you will find in this chapter notes, what to look for, and what interfaces are available to you.

In the next chapter, you will become familiar with some typical practice demands and their solutions. There we intensively use requirements, formulas, and user exits.

Previous chapters presented the tools for adapting the pricing process. This chapter discusses typical practical case requirements for pricing and their solutions.

12 Typical Practice Demands on Pricing and Their Solutions

This chapter talks about practical questions for which there are no easy Customizing responses in the standard SAP system. We describe demands and questions to which there are already some SAP consulting notes and we make some suggestions to improve the solutions.

In addition, we developed, during the creation of this book, completely new solutions for demands, for which there was no proposed solution. These include solutions for budgeting requirements and the general date-dependent data determination using the condition technique. You might wonder what this has to do with pricing. The data determination discussed in Chapter 9 can provide information not only for pricing purposes, but also for other scenarios. We primarily use the features and flexibility of the condition technique. Of course, you could create the solutions outside of the pricing, but the advantage of using the condition technique lies in the speed with which you can provide a solution.

> **The Condition Technique for Pricing Not Only Fulfills Pricing Requirements**
>
> This chapter also serves as an inspiration to look beyond pricing and always keep an eye on whether a request outside of it can potentially be solved easier and faster with the tools of the pricing.

We give special attention to the behavior of the pricing in document chains. In this context, we repeatedly see issues and problems that are based on the fact that it is not possible for all varieties of condition types to be consistently handled, especially with quantity changes.

Here are the topics:

- Use of the condition update to fulfill budgeting requirements.
- Condition types were not found, so what do you do?
- The SAP system rounds differently than expected.
- For low-value products, prices need more than two decimal places.
- Absolute freight condition types are calculated completely in the first partial delivery so that the subsequent deliveries are carriage paid.
- Freight condition types should not be calculated for free goods items and returns items.
- Special authorizations should control which data the user is allowed to see in the CONDITIONS screen.
- The number of the freely usable subtotal fields KZWI1 to KZWI6 of the sales order and billing document items is not enough.
- Certain fields of the master data records (customer, material) should be maintained date-dependent.
- Conditions that were transferred into subsequent documents (e.g., fixed value condition types) are not automatically adjusted when there is a quantity change.
- For returns and credit memo requests created with reference to billing documents, increased prices (condition type PR02) are not transferred, but recalculated.
- For reporting purposes, key figures determined during pricing are required, with particular attention to the determination of a profit margin. How do you set the pricing procedure correctly?
- It should be possible to formulate requirements on the level of a single condition record.

The first topic, *budgeting requirements,* along with the requirements within the condition record take up most of the space in this chapter.

12.1 Budgeting Requirements

If you activate the attribute CONDIT.UPDATE in the configuration of the condition type, the condition values are accumulated for sales orders in the statistics table

S071 and for billing documents in the statistics table S060. This is possible only in condition types that are determined via condition records. The key of these tables is essentially the key of the condition record KONP consisting of the fields KNUMH and KOPOS and the usual period fields for statistics tables. You can display the cumulative value for a condition record in the condition maintenance transactions. The values of the tables to a condition record can be read using the SD_COND_STATISTICS_READ function module. Note that you set the parameters S071_NOT_READ and S060_NOT_READ as needed to avoid unnecessary reading.

12.1.1 Statistics Tables S060 and S469

The table S060 is updated for invoices. For rebate condition types (condition class C), the update is always activated automatically. If the extended rebate processing is activated, the statistics table S469 is updated too. The key of table S469 contains the key fields of table S060 as well as others, for example, the sold-to-party and material number, which are used to assign the respective revenues to the originator. This originating part (s469-vakey) is definable in Customizing and ultimately determines the granularity of the rebate payout. Rebate processing manages all required cumulative values based on these two tables. The most important values are:

- Cumulative condition value in condition currency (CC)
- Cumulative condition basis in CC
- Cumulative scale basis in CC
- Rebate: Disbursed value in local currency (LC) and CC
- Rebate: Value of accruals in LC and CC
- Rebate: Value of reversed accruals in LC and CC

An example of the use of the cumulative values in table S060 is the condition type LCFR (license – france) as a group condition for the handling of tax exemption licenses. This condition type has a value scale defining that an exemption shall be granted only up to a certain cumulative sales volume within one period. After passing that threshold, the full tax liability applies. This function is implemented by the scale base formula 043 (see Listing 12.1).

```
form frm_staffelbas_043.
  if xkomv-kposn is initial.
    if tkomk-vbtyp ca vbtyp_retour.
```

```
      xkwert = gkomv-kawrt.
   else.
     call function 'SD_COND_STATISTICS_READ'
         exporting
             buffer_read       = ' '
             condition_item    = gkomv_key-kopos
             condition_number  = gkomv_key-knumh
             s071_not_read     = 'X'
             s060_not_read     = ' '
         importing
             kstbs_s060        = zzkawrt
         exceptions
             others            = 1.
     xkwert = gkomv-kstbs + zzkawrt.
   endif.
  endif.
endform.
```

Listing 12.1 Scale Base Formula 043 for the Condition Type LCFR

By setting s071_not_read = X, only table S060 is read. KSTBS_S060 then provides the cumulative scale basis.

12.1.2 Statistics Table S071

The table S071 is updated for sales documents (e.g., sales orders). If the condition update is activated for a condition type, maximum values or quantities can be defined for a condition record. Once these limits are exceeded, the condition value or the condition base value is cut off. From this point, the condition is no longer granted. This means that it is valuated as zero.

12.1.3 Budgeting Requirements

We use this functionality of the condition update to limit the application of certain condition records to meet general budgeting requirements.

Example of a Budgeting Using the Pricing Functionality

All sales transactions to customers of the customer hierarchy node 421 should not exceed a maximum weight of 600 kg and a maximum value of EUR 1,000. Orders that are above these limits will be checked and have to be released specifically.

To this end, we set up two new condition types ZH01 and ZH02 and add them to our pricing procedure (see Figure 12.1). In addition, we need a new condition value formula called 900 for testing against the budget.

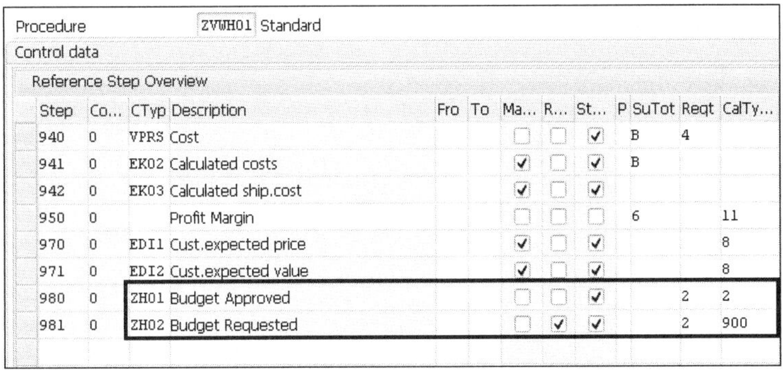

Step	Co...	CTyp	Description	Fro	To	Ma...	R...	St...	P	SuTot	Reqt	CalTy...
940	0	VPRS	Cost			☐	☐	✔	B	4		
941	0	EK02	Calculated costs			✔	☐	✔	B			
942	0	EK03	Calculated ship.cost			✔	☐	✔				
950	0		Profit Margin			☐	☐	☐		6		11
970	0	EDI1	Cust.expected price			✔	☐	✔				8
971	0	EDI2	Cust.expected value			✔	☐	✔				8
980	0	ZH01	Budget Approved			☐	☐	✔		2		2
981	0	ZH02	Budget Requested			☐	✔	✔		2		900

Procedure ZVWH01 Standard — Control data — Reference Step Overview

Figure 12.1 Pricing Procedure ZVWH01

The necessary parameters for the two required condition types and the underlying pricing procedure are:

▶ **ZH01 (budget approved)**
  ▶ Condition class: A (discount or surcharge)
  ▶ Access sequence: HI01
  ▶ Calculation type: D (Gross Weight)
  ▶ Condition category: J (customer expected price)
  ▶ Condition update: X
  ▶ Statistical condition: X
  ▶ Requirement: 002
  ▶ Cond. Value formula: 002 (net value)

▶ **ZH02 (budget requested)**
  ▶ Condition class: A (discount or surcharge)
  ▶ Access sequence: None
  ▶ Calculation type: Any (e.g., A = Percentage)
  ▶ Condition update: Not Active
  ▶ Statistical condition: X

 ▹ Cond. is mandatory: X

 ▹ Requirement: 002

 ▹ Cond. Value Formula: 900 (budget check)

The access sequence HI01 used in condition type ZH01 is only an example.

The condition value formula 900 for the condition type ZH02 (see Listing 12.2) checks whether in the condition type ZH01 the maximum condition basis or the maximum condition value is exceeded. We use the `provide_condition_data` routine to provide the data of the condition type ZH01 in the structures RKOMV and RKONP. With the `konditionsbasis_ermitteln` routine, we determine the target condition basis (here, the gross weight of the item) and compare it to the (possibly cut) condition basis of ZH01 to calculate a deviation percentage. We compare the (possibly cut) condition value of ZH01 with the net value of the item. If, in the condition type `ZH01`, a limit is exceeded (we recognize this by `rkomv-kmxaw = 'X'` or `rkomv-kmxwr = 'X'`) we set `komp-cepok = 'B'` and display the S message 780. Thus, the order item is incomplete. These orders locked for further processing can then be released or canceled using Transaction V.25 (Release Customer Expected Price).

```
form frm_kondi_wert_900.
data: workfield(16) type p decimals 2.
 xkwert = komp-netwr.
 check: komp-cepok ne 'C',
        komp-kposn ne 0,
        komk-vbtyp na vbtyp_fakt,
        Preisfindungsart ne 'E'.
 check: komp-prsfd = 'X'.
 clear rkomv.
 perform provide_condition_data using 'ZH01'.
 check: rkomv-kschl = 'ZH01'.
 xkwert = komp-netwr.
 xkomv-kawrt = 0.
 xkomv-krech = rkomv-krech.
 xkomv-kmein = rkomv-kmein.
 xkomv-kpein = rkomv-kpein.
 xkomv-waers = rkomv-waers.
 xkomv-kumza = rkomv-kumza.
 xkomv-kumne = rkomv-kumne.
 perform konditionsbasis_ermitteln.
 if rkomv-kmxaw = 'X' or rkomv-kmxwr = 'X'.
   komp-cepok = 'B'.
   if rkomv-kawrt ne xkomv-kawrt and
      rkonp-mxkbas ne 0.
```

```
      workfield = ( xkomv-kawrt - rkomv-kawrt )
                  * 10000 / rkonp-mxkbas.
    endif.
    if rkomv-kwert ne xkwert and
       rkonp-komxwrt ne 0.
      workfield = ( xkwert - rkomv-kwert )
                  * 10000 / rkonp-komxwrt.
    endif.
    message s780(VH) with workfield komp-kposn.
  endif.
* call function 'ENQUEUE_EZ_S071'
*     exporting
*        knumh          = rkomv-knumh
*     exceptions
*        foreign_lock   = 4
*        system_failure = 8.
*   if sy-subrc ne 0.
*     xkomv-kinak = 'Z'.
*     message s084(VK) with sy-msgv1.
*   endif.
endform.
```

Listing 12.2 Condition Value Formula 900 for the Condition Type ZH02

Note that the functions MAXIMUM CONDITION VALUE and MAXIMUM CONDITION BASE VALUE have the weakness that the condition record is not locked. Thus, if two users simultaneously create an order in which the same condition record is found, one of the two might unjustifiably exceed the limit. The problem occurs when the limit is initially not reached and will be exceeded only if both orders are summarized. Although this situation hardly occurs in practice, the probability depends on the generality of the condition record. If necessary, you can close this gap by creating the lock object ENQUEUE_EZ_S071 as described in SAP Note 74794 (Maximum Condition Basis In Billing Document) and activating the (commented) check at the end of formula 900 (see Listing 12.2). If the situation occurs that the condition record is locked, the condition ZH02 is deactivated by xkomv-kinak = 'Z'. Since ZH02, on the other hand, is configured as mandatory, the item is incomplete. Such orders must then be subsequently changed again (you need to trigger a new pricing in the CONDITIONS screen) to fix this issue.

Now we create the condition record for condition type ZH01 (see Figure 12.2) and maintain the fields MAX.CONDITION VALUE and MAX.COND.BASE VALUE in the additional data screen.

Figure 12.2 Budget Condition Record for Condition Type ZH01

All sales orders where this condition record is found update the accumulated values in the info structure S071. Accrued values can be found in the condition maintenance under EXTRAS • CUMULATIVE VALUES (see Figure 12.3).

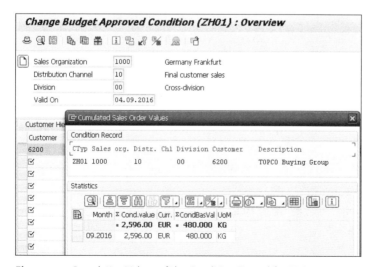

Figure 12.3 Cumulative Values of the Condition Record for ZH01

We create another sales order (see Figure 12.4) and, as soon as the limit is exceeded, we get the S message 780.

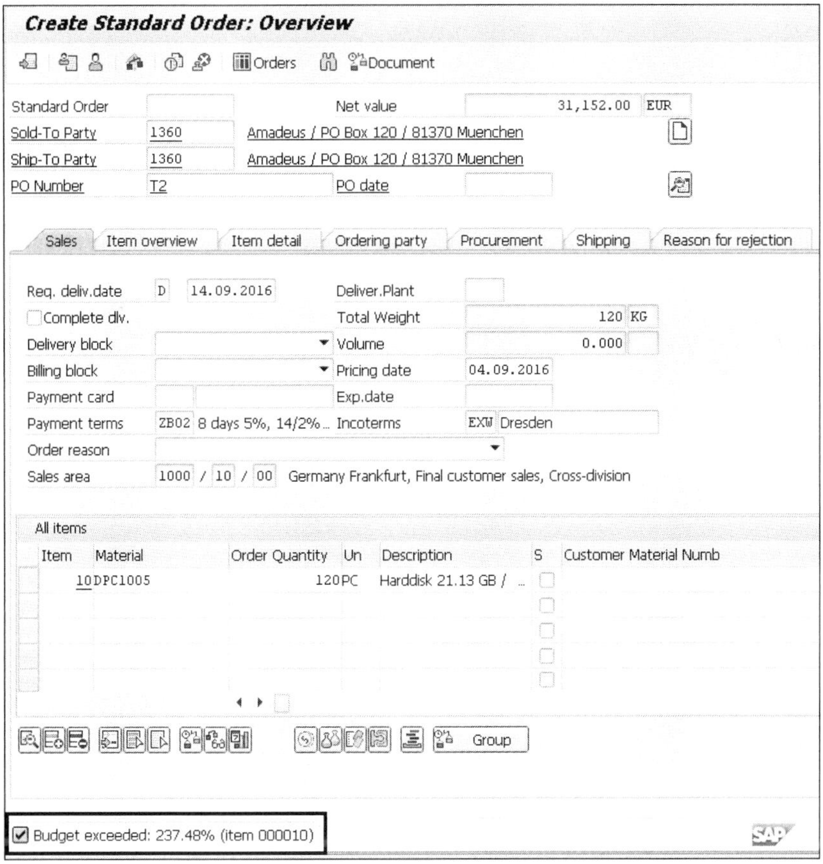

Figure 12.4 Sales Order, Budget Exceeded

We get more details in the CONDITIONS screen of the item (see Figure 12.5). Here you can see that the values of the two condition types ZH01 and ZH02 differ. This is an indication that the value limit has been exceeded.

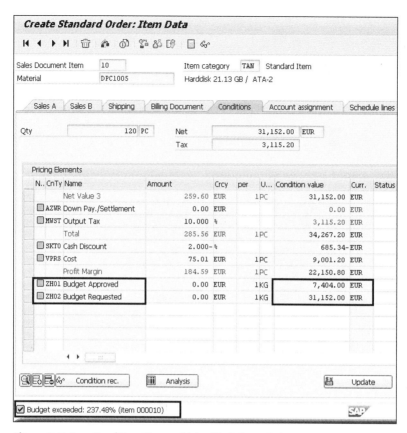

Figure 12.5 Item Conditions Screen, Value Limit Exceeded

This screen doesn't show whether the maximum condition base value has been exceeded. The information is available in the DETAIL screen of the condition type ZH01 (see Figure 12.6). On this screen, you can see the entry X in MAX BASE VALUE = X. That means that only 120 kg were still available in the additional data (600 kg − 480 kg = 120 kg) of the respective condition record for ZH01. The required condition basis (in our case, the item gross weight of 200 kg) can be displayed in the detail screen of the condition type ZH02 (see Figure 12.7).

If you later edit a sales order with an exceeded limit, it is useful to navigate to the HEADER CONDITION screen. That way, the message 780 is displayed again and you can find out in which item the limit has been exceeded.

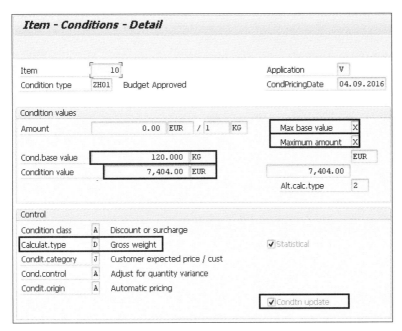

Figure 12.6 Condition Detail for the Condition Type ZH01

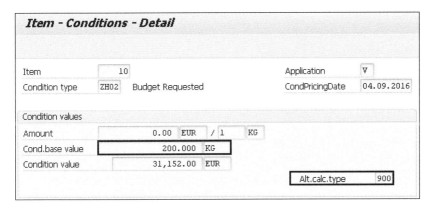

Figure 12.7 Condition Detail for the Condition Type ZH02

With Transaction V.25 (see Figure 12.8), you can select the blocked sales orders and optionally release them for further processing.

In the solution proposed, we have used the CEPOK functionality (customer expected price) to enforce a release activity when a budget limit is exceeded. This feature can of course also be used for other demands requiring a release activity. For example, you could think of another solution for the product exclusion.

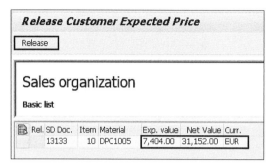

Figure 12.8 Transaction V.25 for Editing Locked Sales Orders

The delivered standard functionality for the product exclusion does not allow you to create an item with the excluded product and an error message is displayed. With a statistical condition type that determines the excluded products or groups of products and with a new formula like the presented condition value formula 900, the "CEPOK logic" could also be used here. Thus, the sales order item could be captured and would initially be incomplete. After checking the sales order, the item could be released.

12.2   Why Is the Condition Not Found?

Sometimes condition types are not found during pricing, and you might expect this due to the master data. For example, discounts that have been agreed with the customer may not have been found, so the customer complains about this discrepancy.

In these situations, you will always use the pricing analysis. You can find this in the ITEM CONDITIONS screen of the sales document (see Figure 12.9 and Figure 12.10). In the following example, you miss the condition type K031. You receive the message 108 - CONDITION RECORD EXISTS, BUT HAS NOT BEEN SET.

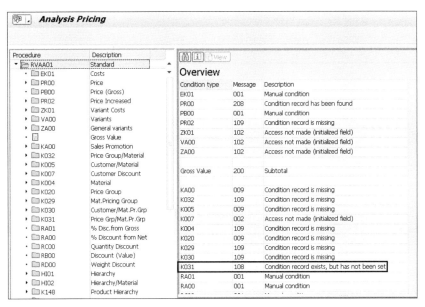

Figure 12.9 Pricing Analysis Overview, Missing Condition Type K031

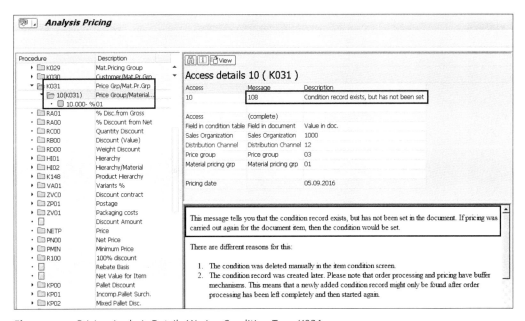

Figure 12.10 Pricing Analysis Detail, Missing Condition Type K031

The text at the bottom right shows some possible explanations for this problem. You can also consult the SAP Note 27636 (Message: Condition Exists (Removed Manually)). With this information, you should be able to analyze the problem. In most cases, the root cause will be a damage because of a modification.

Following is a list of the main situations that may cause this behavior:

▸ The condition was deleted manually on the ITEM CONDITIONS screen.

▸ The condition was deleted via a formula by setting `xkomv-kinak = 'Z'`.

▸ The condition record was created afterward.

▸ During the insertion of an item, different key fields were used to access the condition record than at the time of the change. This may also occur because a field change was made in the document, but the required recalculation is not triggered automatically.

▸ The requirement check gives different results at the time of the insertion and at the time of the change.

▸ When creating sales documents with reference, the condition was not determined in the source document and there is no recalculation in the target document.

▸ The condition type is configured with an interval scale (scale type D), but the scale quantities are not achieved.

▸ In the first order item, everything is correct. The error occurs sporadically starting with the second item. This effect can occur when a customer field is attached directly via an `APPEND` to the structure KOMK instead of to KOMKAZ.

The most common reason for errors is that the communication structures KOMK and KOMP are filled differently during the insertion of an item than at the time of the change of an item. The danger happens in particular when you use fields that are not part of the original tables. Using fields from the following tables is usually not problematic:

▸ VBAK, VBAP, VBPA, and VBKD for the sales order processing

▸ VBRK, VBRP, and VBPA for the billing processing

In the case of the billing processing, it is sometimes not taken into account that in one session several billing documents can be generated. That is, the internal tables `XVBRK`, `XVBRP`, and `XVBPA` contain data from several documents.

444

12.3 Rounding

In connection with the calculation logic of pricing, it is often the case that the correctness of the standard calculation method is under question. The problem occurs in particular in connection with the presentation of the net price on a printed order confirmation or invoice, in particular whenever hidden discounts or surcharges (more likely surcharges) are applied to the starting price, which should not be disclosed in the printed document.

The calculation logic in the standard works such that the value, and not the price, is developed. That means that starting from a gross value (given by a price condition type), a net value is determined by the application of discounts and surcharges. Bases on that value, the net price is then calculated by dividing the value by the item quantity. It's then rounded commercially.

This procedure is not SAP-specific, but in general use. So what is the problem?

The problem is which condition lines in the document are printed. The presentation is correct, if all condition types, that is, the starting price and all discounts and surcharges, are printed. However, if a hidden discount or surcharge is applied to the initial price, which is not to be disclosed to the customer, we can run into this problem. The first starting price shown in this case is a developed price with the property *price × amount ≠ value* caused by rounding effects.

In addition, the price shown is normally different depending on the item quantity, as can be seen in Table 12.1. The line *base price* represents the first price information that is printed in the output document.

For a quantity of three pieces, we get:			
	Price	135,50 USD per piece	= 406,50 USD
	Discount	9,00– %	= 36,59– USD
	Base price	123,30 USD per piece	= 369,91 USD
However, it is expected.	*123,30 USD × 3*		= *369,90 USD*
For a quantity of ten pieces, we get:			
	Price	135,50 USD per piece	= 1.355,00 USD
	Discount	9,00– %	= 121,95– USD
	Base price	123,31 USD per piece	= 1.233,05 USD
However, it is expected.	*123,31 USD × 10*		= 1.233,10 USD

Table 12.1 Rounding Effects

For suggested solutions to this problem, see SAP Note 80183 (Rounding). The three variants described therein use formulas that are not all delivered in the standard system. You must therefore set them up in the customer namespace yourself. The versions differ in the following characteristics:

- Displayed net price × quantity = displayed net value
- Displayed net price remains the same (independent of the quantity)
- Discounts and surcharges are calculated correctly

Of the three variants that have been described in the note, only the second one meets all three of these characteristics. We use this variant to display the respective pricing procedure (see Table 12.2). The characteristic *discounts and surcharges calculated correctly* means that the discounts and surcharges are calculated accurately as in the standard. In this case, the rounding difference is collected by a special condition type and can therefore be booked in accounting using a specific P&L account.

Cond. Type	Description	Req.	Value Formula	Base Value Formula	Stat.	Print
PR00	Price	2				
RA00	Discount	2	19			
NETP	Rounding difference	2	6	17		
PNTP	Net price	2	906	17	X	X

Table 12.2 Pricing Procedure for Rounding (Transaction V/08)

If you can dispense with the characteristic *displayed net price remains the same (independent from the quantity)*, the solution is much simpler. You can then only use the condition type NETP (price), as shown in the pricing procedure in Table 8.2 in Chapter 8, Section 8.1.1, which corresponds to the first variant of the note. In any case, you should study the mentioned note thoroughly.

12.4   Prices with More Than Two Decimal Places

Currencies in the SAP system have a fixed number of decimal places. For example, the USD currency has two decimal places. This means that all prices and values in this currency are always displayed with two decimal places. That is correct and necessary for the value side. However, on the price side, there is sometimes the demand to have more than two significant digits. This is especially relevant for products with low prices. The recommended solution is to use the condition unit, that is, for example, USD 1.98 per 1,000 pieces. This gives you three more significant digits. However, this procedure is sometimes not accepted because it is customary in some business areas to work with five decimal places, and it is always difficult to change habits.

In this case, you can use SAP Note 38881 (Pricing with Different Decimal Places) in which a parallel currency USD with a maximum of five decimal places is introduced. Prices in the condition records are then maintained in that currency. However, the document currency always remains USD (i.e., with two decimal places).

Our recommended solution is to use the condition unit, especially since this is a standard functionality. If the representation, for example, in the invoice printing is to take place with five decimal places, then this could be achieved by a small modification in the editing for printout via existing user exits.

12.5   Handling Freight Surcharges

Shipping costs are usually configured as fixed value condition types and often have a value scale. If the delivery takes place is in several parts, there are demands on the billing that are not met in the standard. In addition, you must clarify how these condition types are to be handled in the subsequent documents such as credits notes and returns. There is also the question of how to proceed with shipping costs for free goods items.

12.5.1   Complete Billing of Freight Surcharges with the First Delivery

For freight surcharges that are configured as group condition types with a fixed value, the condition amount is valid for the entire order. We find this same property in the manual header condition types. We know that for these condition types, the amount is distributed among the items. This means in the case of partial deliveries, that the shipping costs are calculated in proportion to each partial invoice. However, it is common to bill the total shipping cost with the first (partial) invoice and then the remaining deliveries are free.

This functionality is not provided in the standard SAP system. However, there is an SAP Note 25144 (Freight Conditions for Milestone Billing) that meets this demand via a user exit.

12.5.2 No Freight Surcharges for Free Goods and Returns

Freight conditions with a fixed value described in Section 12.5.1 are normally distributed pro rata to all items according to their individual value. In this case, no freight surcharge is calculated for free goods items because they have a net value of zero. However, this is different, if the distribution is not performed pro rata but, for example, proportionately to the weight. In this case, free goods items have freight surcharges, which is normally not desired. Even with freight conditions, whose CALCULATION TYPE is dependent on weight, the question arises as to whether a shipping cost should be calculated or not.

Another demand is that for returns items that are created with reference to a billing document with freight surcharges, these freight costs are not to be credited.

The request for the free goods items can be met by assigning to the respective condition types the requirement 057 (not for free goods) in the pricing procedure. However, with regard to the handling of returned goods, this requirement resolves only the problem of return items within a sales order. It provides no solution for return documents that are created, for example, with reference to a sales order or a billing document.

Both demands are fulfilled by the requirement 957 (not for free goods/returns) displayed in Listing 12.3, which you can create in the customer namespace using Transaction VOFM and then assign to your condition types.

```
form kobed_957.
  sy-subrc = 4.
  if komp-kposn ne 0.
    check: komk-vbtyp ca 'BCMN'.
    check: komp-prsfd ca 'X'.
    check: komp-kznep = space.
    check: komp-shkzg ne 'X'.
  endif.
  sy-subrc = 0.
endform.
* Prestep
form kobev_957.
  sy-subrc = 4.
  check: komk-vbtyp ca 'BCMN'.
```

```
  sy-subrc = 0.
endform.
```
Listing 12.3 Pricing Requirement 957 for Freight Conditions

Requirement 957 causes the condition types to be determined only within quotations, sales orders (sales document types B and C), and the associated billing documents (sales document types M and N).

If you want to credit as an exception the shipping costs in a return order or credit note, you can do this via a manual condition type (for example, by a header condition type analog to HD00 or HB00). These condition types then do not use the requirement 957 described here, but instead the standard requirements 057 or 002.

> **Removing Copied Condition Types**
>
> The prestep part of routine 957 is important. This part causes that conditions that were initially transferred by the `PRICING_COPY` function module to be rejected because they do not fulfill the requirement (see Chapter 11, Section 11.2.7).

12.6 Authorizations for the Pricing Screen

Any user who has the authorization to view or change sales orders and billing documents has unrestricted authorization in the CONDITIONS screen, too. Certain information in this screen is very sensitive, especially those components that are used to calculate a profit margin. There are condition types that represent the costs (transfer price VPRS) and condition types for internal transfer (PI01/PI02), as well as subtotal lines that use the values of these condition types (e.g., profit margin). The feature to hide information in the CONDITIONS screen depending on the user is not fully supported in the standard SAP system. It is only prepared in the form of the BAdI `PRICING_AUTHORITY_CHECK_UI` and the sample implementation `VF_PRC_AUTH_EXAMPLE`. In SAP Note 1165078 (Authorization Check for Conditions or Subtotals), you can find a description of the required steps.

12.7 Adding Subtotal Fields

In the sales order item and the billing document item (VBAP, VBRP), six freely usable subtotal fields (KZWI1 to KZWI6) are available. These value fields can be filled via the configuration of the pricing procedure by the indicator SUBTOTAL with the value of a line in the pricing procedure. If the indicator SUBTOTAL is being used for other purposes, you can fill the fields komp-kzwi1 to komp-kzwi6 via simple condition value formulas. The fields are mainly used for SAP BW or other statistical evaluations. If these six fields are not sufficient, you can add more value fields with a little effort. Simply create more data elements in the customer namespace and insert them by using an `APPEND` to the tables and VBAP VBRP and to the structures KOMPAZ and KOMPAXA. You can then fill the new KOMP fields with appropriate condition value formulas. Additionally, you should initialize these new KOMP fields in the routine `userexit_xkomv_bewerten_init` of the function group V61A. For detailed instructions, see SAP Note 155012 (Further Subtotal Fields in Pricing).

12.8   Date-Dependent Maintenance of Master Data Fields

The attributes of the master data (customer, material) are stored permanently in these objects and there is generally no way to make master data date-dependent (in the future or retroactively). Once a change is made in the master data, it is immediately valid, especially for operations that are dated in the past. Therefore, there is no way to valuate documents automatically with the historical data. You can only bring the values to the original state by manual intervention.

However, the standard SAP system enables you to maintain at least one field within the pricing condition records (and thus date-dependent). From there it is transferred to the sales order and overrides the fixed assignment from the customer master record. It is the TERMS OF PAYMENT field from the ADDITIONAL SALES DATA screen. Moreover, it is possible to provide a FIXED VALUE DATE or ADDITIONAL VALUE DAYS in this context in the condition record. The business background of this feature is that certain discounts are only granted in conjunction with a specific payment term.

In Chapter 9, Section 9.2.2, we presented a method by which we can maintain date-dependent master data attributes, determine them during the pricing, and transfer them to the calling sales order item. The positive aspect of this method is that the data determination is carried out within the pricing. This solution has the advantage that the data is updated when a new pricing for the document is performed which may be required, for example, in the context of retroactive changes. The disadvantage is that you cannot handle every field this way. The method is only possible for those fields that are used in the sales order exclusively for pricing or for follow-up functions such as SAP BW, CO-PA (Profitability Analysis), statistics, output, etc. Furthermore, you can use this method only for document item fields (VBAP, VBRP). Fields of the header (VBAK) or of the commercial data (VBKD) cannot be determined with this method.

12.8.1 Data Determination for the Sales Document Item VBAP

We now want to introduce a second general method of a data determination that does not have the aforementioned disadvantages. As an example, we again use the material group hierarchy from Chapter 9, Section 9.2.2 that we have set up with the condition type Z902 and the requirement 902 (data transfer). However, we do use them in the pricing procedure for the document pricing, but we will create a new pricing procedure that we use only for the data determination (see Figure 12.11).

Procedure	ZZVBAP Data Determination VBAP										
Control											
Reference Step Overview											
Step	Co...	CTyp	Description	Fro	To	Ma...	R...	St...	P	SuTot	Reqt
10	0	Z902	Data det. material			☐	☐	☐			
20	0		Data Transfer			☐	☐	☐			902

Figure 12.11 Pricing Procedure ZZVBAP for the Data Determination in the Document Item (Transaction V/08)

Now that we have created our new pricing procedure, we have to program the actual data determination and the INCLUDE program MV45AFZZ in the routine userexit_move_field_to_vbap, as shown in Listing 12.4. The data determination is carried out by calling the PRICING function module with the ZZVBAP pricing procedure.

```
form userexit_move_field_to_vbap.
  if vbap-matnr ne *vbap-matnr.
    perform zz_fill_vbap.
  endif.
endform.
form zz_fill_vbap.
  data: zkomp like komp,
        kond_t683s_tab like kond_t683s occurs 0
with header line,
        zkomv like komv occurs 0 with header line.
  clear tkomk.
```

```
    tkomk-kappl = 'V '.
    tkomk-kalsm = 'ZZVBAP'.
    tkomk-vkorg = vbak-vkorg.
    tkomk-vtweg = vbak-vtweg.
    tkomk-spart = vbak-spart.
    tkomk-prsdt = vbkd-prsdt.
    read table tkomk with key tkomk-key_uc.
    if sy-subrc ne 0.
      append tkomk.
      tkomk-ix_komk = sy-tabix.
      modify tkomk index sy-tabix.
    endif.
    clear zkomp.
    zkomp-ix_komk =  tkomk-ix_komk.
    zkomp-kposn = '000001'.
    zkomp-pmatn = vbap-matnr.
    call function 'PRICING'
          exporting
                comm_head_i      = tkomk
                comm_item_i      = zkomp
                calculation_type = 'B'
                preliminary      = 'X'
                no_calculation   = 'X'
          importing
                comm_head_e      = tkomk
                comm_item_e      = zkomp
          tables
                tkomv            = zkomv.
      modify tkomk index zkomp-ix_komk.
      If not zkomp-mvgr1 is initial.
        vbap-mvgr1 = zkomp-mvgr1.
      endif.
      If not zkomp-mvgr2 is initial.
        vbap-mvgr2 = zkomp-mvgr2.
      endif.
      If not zkomp-mvgr3 is initial.
        vbap-mvgr3 = zkomp-mvgr3.
      endif.
endform.
```

Listing 12.4 Coding Example for the Data Determination in the Include MV45AFZZ

You must provide all fields required for your data determination condition types in the structures TKOMK and ZKOMP. With this approach, we can achieve the same result as in our first solution. The performance is the same and we use also the prestep logic of pricing. Because of the statement `if vbap-matnr ne * vbap-matnr`, the data determination is only performed when inserting and changing the material number.

You should, as shown in this example, make the automatic update dependent on whether an affected field was changed. In the user exits of the sales order, you have the structures *VBAK, *VBKD, *VBAP, in which the state before the change is contained.

12.8.2 Data Determination for the Sales Document Header VBAK/ Business Data VBKD

If you want to determine fields of the sales document header or the business data, you must use the `userexit_move_field_to_vbkd` routine. In this user exit, you can manipulate the fields of both structures VBAK and VBKD.

For this purpose, you can set up for a new pricing procedure ZZVBKD, which is an analog to ZZVBAP. The sample requirement 902 can also be used in this case. You must only insert more field transports following the same pattern. If the determined fields are to be used for the pricing, you should remember that, for a field change, if appropriate, there must be a revaluation of the whole document. We describe how to do this in Chapter 13, Section 13.1.3.

With this method, you also have the option of replacing a characteristic value starting from a specific date or for a specified period by another value. We present an example in the following section.

12.8.3 Example: Substitution of a Customer Group (VBKD-KDGRP)

Our goal in this example is to replace the customer group 05 (field KDGRP) in the sales organization 0001 in 2017 with the customer group 06.

These are the required activities:

1. Creating a new field ZZKDGRP (new customer group) as an APPEND to the structures KOMPAZ and KOMPAZD and adding the field to the field catalog.

2. Setting up a new condition table NNN with the characteristics VKORG and KDGRP (old customer group) in the key part and with the characteristic ZZKDGRP (new customer group) in the data part.

3. Setting up a new access sequence ZXXX with the transfer of the data field ZZKDGRP into the dynamic item field kompazd-zzkdgrp.

4. Setting up a new condition type ZXXX analog to the condition type Z902 with the access sequence ZXXX.

5. Extension of the requirement 902:

```
If not kompazd-zzkdgrp is initial.
  komp-zzkdgrp = kompazd-zzkdgrp.
endif.
```

6. Programming the routine `userexit_move_field_to_vbkd` (analog, for example, as in Listing 12.4):

```
If vbkd-kdgrp ne *vbkd-kdgrp.
  Perform zz_fill_vbkd.
endif.
```

7. Programming the routine `zz_fill_vbkd` analog to routine `zz_fill_vbap` and carrying out the data transfer with these statements:

```
If not zkomp-zzkdgrp is initial.
  vbkd-kdgrp = zkomp-zzkdgr.
endif.
```

8. Setting up the new pricing procedure ZZVBKD (analog to pricing procedure ZZVBAP).

9. Creating the appropriate condition records for condition type ZXXX.

10. Checking the result in the sales order.

We have not configured this example in our test system. You can choose for the condition type ZXXX, the access sequence ZXXX and the condition table NNN as well as your own name from the customer namespace.

12.8.4 Pros and Cons of Data Determination

The advantage of the (first) method of Chapter 9, Section 9.2.2, compared to the (second) method presented here is the ability to react when a retroactive change in the condition records takes place. You can update the valuation of existing sales orders by triggering a mass processing (Transaction VA05, EDIT • MASS CHANGE • NEW PRICING).

In the second method, this retroactive change is not supported. Furthermore, there is no support of the pricing analysis for problem clarification. Another deficit is that in the case of changes of the involved VBAK fields or VBKD fields, such as the price date, the recalculation of the data for the items will not be carried out automatically (on the other hand, this may be desirable).

The advantages of the presented second method are:

▶ The method is only possible for those fields that are used in the sales order exclusively for pricing or for follow-up functions such as SAP BW, CO-PA (Profitability Analysis), statistics, output, etc.

▶ If you determine fields of the document item VBAP, you cannot just do this for those fields that are used in the sales order exclusively for pricing or for follow-up functions such as SAP BW, CO-PA (Profitability Analysis), statistics, or output, but you can determine all the fields that can be manipulated in the user-exit_move_field_to_vbap routine. You might thus be able to, for example, fill the field PLANT. This means you would have implemented a condition-based and thus date-dependent plant determination, and without any modification.

▶ If you want to fill fields of the tables VBAK or VBKD, you can achieve this only with this method.

As you can see, this second method certainly has great potential.

12.8.5 Data Determination for the Billing Documents

We described the method of data determination via user exits only for the sales order. The billing documents will usually adopt the contents of the sales order so that the characteristics in the billing document don't have to be recalculated. However, you might have to use the respective user exits in the billing process. You should then use a copying requirement for billing documents for the implementation of the data determination analog to Listing 12.4.

12.9   Copied Conditions and Subsequent Quantity Changes

There are some condition types that are problematic when you create follow-up documents. These are primarily conditions types with the calculation type B (FIXED AMOUNT), which includes the standard condition types RB00, HB00, HM00, AMIW, and AMIZ. Nevertheless, other condition types cause problems as well. In general, we can say that all those conditions types are concerned that receive in the target document the indicator Condition Control = E (xkomv-ksteu). (These are, for example, condition types in which a maximum condition basis or a maximum condition value is exceeded.). But even those conditions in which condition base formulas are used, which are to run only in the source document, are problematic (e.g., the condition types KP00 and KP01 with the condition base formulas 022 and 024).

We consider in this section the following copy operations:

▸ Creating an order with reference to a quotation

▸ Creating a billing document with reference to the delivery or an order

▸ Creating a credit memo request or return request with reference to an invoice

The condition types of the reference document are copied to the target document by the `PRICING_COPY` function module (see Chapter 10, Section 10.3). If the item quantity of the source document is different from the quantity of the target document, the value of the fixed amount condition types and of condition types, whose value is fixed, is scaled in proportion to the quantity change.

If a quantity change is made in the copied documents, the value of these condition types remains unchanged and must be adjusted manually if required. It is interesting to note that for the condition type VPRS (cost), which is of course also fixed in the billing document, the problem of a subsequent quantity change is solved in the standard SAP system. That is, the value of the condition type is scaled in proportion to the quantity change.

A general solution for all condition types is not available in the standard SAP system. We want to close this gap and have developed two possible solutions:

▸ A simple solution for fixed amount condition types under exclusive use of the routine `userexit_pricing_copy`.

▸ A general-purpose solution for all affected condition types.

12.9.1 Simple Solution for Fixed Amount Condition Types

We consider the following condition types from the standard SAP system:

▸ RB00 (manual value discount (item condition))

▸ HM00 (manual order value (header condition))

▸ HB00 (manual value discount (header condition))

▸ AMIW/AMIZ (automatic absolute amount (group condition))

One approach to automatically adjust the copied fixed amount condition types at quantity changes is the modification via a user exit in program RV61AFZA displayed in Listing 12.5.

```
form userexit_pricing_copy.
  if vbtyp_new ca vbtyp_verk and konv-ksteu ne 'A' and
     ( konv-kschl = RB00' or
       konv-kschl = 'HM00' or
       konv-kschl = 'HB00' or
       konv-kschl = 'AMIW' or
       konv-kschl = 'AMIZ' ).
       konv-ksteu = 'F'.
       konv-kherk = 'G'.
  endif.
endform.
```

Listing 12.5 Scaling Fixed Amount Condition Types at a Quantity Change

This modification causes the listed condition types by CONDITION CONTROL = F (konv-ksteu) to be fixed in a special way, in sales documents that are created with reference to a quotation or to a billing document (see Chapter 11, Section 11.7). In the case of a quantity change, the value of the condition type is now scaled in proportion to change of the condition base value.

On the other hand, the condition base value has the quality of a distribution key for the distribution of the header conditions with fixed amount to the items.

Usually, this will be the net value of the items, but there can be achieved other allocations by using a suitable condition base formula. Thus, base formulas that use the weight or the volume are unproblematic. In the case of the distribution, a header value it is generally recommended to assign at least the base value formula 002 (net value) to the affected condition types. Otherwise, potentially preceding statistical condition types can produce undesired effects.

In general, the net value of the copied items is scaled in proportion to the quantity change. Thus, the scaling of the affected condition values is indirectly also carried out in proportion to the quantity change. The statement konv-kherk = 'G' is required for the item condition type RB00.

In Chapter 14, Section 14.8, you will find test results of the example of the condition type HM00 with and without modification.

Solution 1 has the advantage that it is very easy to implement and works instantly. No adjustments in the Customizing are required. The disadvantage is that the solution is applicable only for fixed amount condition types. Moreover, no price changes may occur in copied documents; otherwise, the scaling is not carried out in proportion to the quantity change.

12.9.2 Complex Solution for Any Condition Type

With the variant presented next, we can cover the following exemplary cases:

- **Fixed amount condition types**
  These include, for example, RB00, HB00, HM00, AMIW, and AMIZ.

- **Condition types with particular base value formulas**
  These include, for example, KP00 and KP01. The problem here is that the decision whether a discount/surcharge is to be granted takes place in billing documents for partial deliveries due to the (partial) delivery quantities, which is usually not desired. The total order quantity should be used to make this decision. However, this quantity is not available in the billing document and the follow-up documents for this billing document. This means that these particular base formulas can run exclusively in the original sales order.

- **Condition types in which the maximum condition base or the maximum condition value is exceeded**
  However, you must check `userexit_pricing_copy` to determine whether it's been exceeded. This is indicated by the statement `if conv-kmxwr = 'X' or conv-kmxaw = 'X'`.

For our solution, we are digging deep into the bag of tricks. We need the following components:

- `USEREXIT_PRICING_COPY`
  Here we fix the affected condition types with `konv-ksteu = F` and prevent the standard logic of scaling the condition base value and condition value in proportion to the quantities of the source document and the target document (see Listing 12.6).

- **The condition base value formula 921**
  The code for this base value formula is found in Listing 12.7. We assign this base value formula to the pricing condition type (e.g., to PR00), because we know it is always present (PR00 should therefore be set as required in the pricing

procedure). With this base value formula, we cache the quantity old and the quantity new options in the working variables xworkl and xworkm. If you are already using these working variables, you have to use other ones.

▸ **The condition base value formula 923 (general scaling)**
The code for this base value formula is found in Listing 12.9. We use this base value formula in all condition types that have been assigned no base value formula (e.g., RB00, HB00, HM00, AMIW, and AMIZ). We scale the old condition base value ykawrt in the new one in proportion to the quantity change $xkwert = ykawrt \times xworkl \div xworkm$.

▸ **The condition base value formula 922 (scaling formula 022)**
The code for this base value formula is found in Listing 12.8. We need this base value formula to replace the base value formula 022 for the condition type KP00.

▸ **The condition base value formula 924 (scaling formula 024)**
The code for this base value formula is found in Listing 12.10. We need this base value formula to replace the base value formula 024 for the condition type KP01.

▸ **More condition base value formulas, if needed**
If you want to handle condition types that have their own base value formulas, you have to expand this formula analog to formula 922 with the scaling or create a new one.

Once we have assigned the appropriate condition base formulas in the pricing procedure for the condition types, we are done.

In `userexit_pricing_copy` (see Listing 12.6), we fix the affected condition types and prevent the standard logic of the quantitative scaling within the function module `PRICING_COPY`. The import parameters `QUANTITY_OLD` and `QUANTITY_NEW` are actually superfluous. You must include only the condition types KP00 and KP01 here, if these can be changed manually. Otherwise, the base value formulas 022 and 024 are sufficient for this type of problem.

```
form userexit_pricing_copy.
  if konv-ksteu ne 'A' and
  ( konv-kschl = 'RB00' or
    konv-kschl = 'HM00' or
    konv-kschl = 'HB00' or
    konv-kschl = 'AMIW' or
    konv-kschl = 'AMIZ' or
```

```
      konv-kschl = 'KP00' or
      konv-kschl = 'KP01' ).
   konv-ksteu = 'F'.
   clear: konv-kgrpe, konv-kmxaw, konv-kmxwr.
* Avoid quantity related scaling of values for
* conditions with ksteu = 'F'. Scaling will be done by
* apropriate condition base formulas within PRICING.
     if quantity_new ne 0.
       arbfeld = konv-kwert   * quantity_old / quantity_new.
       konv-kwert = arbfeld.
       arbfeld = konv-kwert_k * quantity_old / quantity_new.
       konv-kwert_k = arbfeld.
       arbfeld = konv-kawrt   * quantity_old / quantity_new.
       konv-kawrt   = arbfeld.
       arbfeld = konv-kawrt_k * quantity_old / quantity_new.
       konv-kawrt_k = arbfeld.
     endif.
   endif.
endform.
```

Listing 12.6 USEREXIT_PRICING_COPY, Scaling for Solution 2

With the base value formula 921 (change factor) for the condition type PR00 (Listing 12.7), we store the quantities before and after the change. We then use this information in the subsequent condition types in the base value formulas to perform the actual scaling.

```
form frm_kond_basis_921.
  xworkl = xkwert. "quantity new
  xworkm = ykawrt. "quantity old
endform.
```

Listing 12.7 Base Value Formula 921 for PR00, Caching the Quantities Old/New

The base value formula 922 (Listing 12.8) performs the base value formula 022 extended by the scaling logic.

```
form frm_kond_basis_922.
  perform frm_kond_basis_022.
  perform frm_kond_basis_923.
endform.
```

Listing 12.8 Base Value Formula 922 for Condition Type KP00

The base value formula 923 (see Listing 12.9) contains the scaling logic. It must be used in all affected condition types that so far have no base value formula assigned.

```
form frm_kond_basis_923.
  if xkomv-ksteu ca 'DF' and xkomv-kgrpe = space
                           and xworkm ne 0.
    xkomv-ksteu = 'F'.
    arbfeld = ykawrt * xworkl / xworkm.
    xkwert = arbfeld.
    if ( not xkomv-kwert_k is initial
         and xkomv-kntyp na 'GSTbhcn'
         and ykawrt ne 0 ).
      xkomv-kwert_k = xkomv-kwert_k * xkwert / ykawrt.
    endif.
  endif.
endform.
```

Listing 12.9 Base Value Formula 923 for the Condition Types RB00, HB00, HM00, AMIW, and AMIZ (General Scaling)

The base value formula 924 (Listing 12.10) finally performs the base value formula 024 extended by the scaling logic.

```
form frm_kond_basis_924.
  perform frm_kond_basis_024.
  perform frm_kond_basis_923.
endform.
```

Listing 12.10 Base Value Formula 924 for Condition Type KP01

Solution 2 has the advantage that the method is applicable to all condition types and all possible cases. The scaling is stable in the proportion of the quantity change. The disadvantage is that the Customizing has to be adapted. For all used pricing procedures, the suitable condition base value formulas must be assigned. In `userexit_pricing_copy`, there is no way to limit the process to specific pricing procedures, so it is all or nothing.

> **What You Must Observe When Activating Solution 2**
>
> You must be careful when you transport the modification to the production system. Transport the Customizing changes (formulas and calculation pricing procedures) first, without `userexit_pricing_copy` so that these formulas do nothing more (except that for the condition types KP00 and KP01, the solution already works). Only then you should transport the user exit. The user exit without simultaneous use of the new formulas would cause the affected condition types to no longer be scaled in the billing documents.

12.10 Increased Prices in Returns and Credit Notes

The condition type PR02 (price increased) is configured in the standard SAP system with scale type D (interval scale) (see Appendix A). In this situation we see, depending on the order quantity, multiple entries of the condition type. For each quantity change, a new pricing is carried out, as this may change the number of entries again. For invoices based on partial deliveries, the conditions are taken from the sales order and all values are adjusted proportionately to the partial quantity.

When we now create a return or credit memo with reference to this invoice, the condition is recalculated so that, with the reduced credit quantity, another price as in the invoice can result. Therefore, the conditions need to be copied and adjusted proportionately to the quantity.

For a possible solution to this problem, see SAP note 39774 (returns for invoices using graduated scale pricing), where a new condition type that represents the average price is introduced to solve the problem.

An alternative and much simpler solution is the new requirement 906 (copied not new) that has to be set up. You simply assign this requirement to your affected condition type. The code for this requirement can be found in Listing 12.11. You may need to copy an already assigned requirement and enhance it with the code of the requirement 906.

The new requirement is a copy of the standard requirement 002 (item with pricing) enhanced by the clever use of internal exclusion table TKSCHLEXCL (see also Chapter 11, Section 11.2).

```
form kobed_906.
  sy-subrc = 4.
  if komp-kposn ne 0.
    check: komp-prsfd ca 'BX'.
  endif.
  if preisfindungsart na 'EF'.
    read table tkomv with key knumv = komk-knumv
                              kposn = komp-kposn
                              stunr = komt1-stunr
                              binary search.
    if sy-subrc = 0 and tkomv-ksteu ca 'DEF'.
* avoid redetermination if condition is copied by
* filling exclusion table tkschlexcl
```

462

```
      read table tkschlexcl with key kschl = komt1-
   kschl binary search.
     if sy-subrc ne 0.
       tkschlexcl-kschl = komt1-kschl.
       insert tkschlexcl index sy-tabix.
     endif.
   else.
     refresh tkschlexcl.
   endif.
 endif.
 sy-subrc = 0.
endform.
form kobev_906.
 sy-subrc = 0.
endform.
```

Listing 12.11 Requirement 906, No Recalculation of Copied Conditions

By using this requirement, the fixed conditions (to be identified by the indicator CONDITION CONTROL (xkomv-ksteu) = D, E, or F), which were transferred in the subsequent document, no longer to be recalculated. The quantity scaling is then carried out for this condition types without any further action, because the interval portion of a condition line is determined by the condition factor (xkomv-kfaktor1).

12.11   Key Figures for Reporting and Analysis

SD development has left the decision of which key figures are interesting for reporting, sales statistics or SAP BW data, to the customers. Of course, the requirements differ from customer to customer. In CO-PA, this individuality is already taken into account, as there is an assignment of the condition types to the key figures, which allows a high degree of flexibility. However, this means that the condition types must have the appropriate granularity, and that is precisely the problem. We will take a closer look at this topic now.

Normally, reporting or statistics do not operate at the level of the document conditions (that would be too runtime extensive), but at the level of the document items. So we have to see which value fields we have available at the item level. There are, for example, the fields NET VALUE AND COST (NETWR and WAVWR).

The freely usable subtotal fields KZWI1 to KZWI6 are provided, if a further differentiation of the pricing result is required. If these are not sufficient, more subtotal fields can be added. We described this in Section 12.7.

The evaluations from the SD documents must provide the following key figures:

- **Key figure 1: The initial value**
  This is the value that results from a definable base price.

- **Key figure 2: The standard condition types**
  This is the sum of all the general condition types that are found automatically and that are not customer-dependent.

- **Key figure 3: The customer specific condition types**
  This is the sum of all customer-dependent condition types that are found automatically. These condition types represent individual customer contractual arrangements.

- **Key figure 4: The condition types that were entered manually in the sales document**

- **Key figure 5: The rebate condition types**
  This is the expected expense for deferred compensations that will be paid only with the rebate settlement process.

- **Key figure 6: The net value**
  This is the total of all condition types that are active, not statistical, and have no taxes.

- **Key figure 7: The cost**
  This is the cost of the sales transaction.

Basically, you can say that all values in the sales order have the character of planned values (planned revenues, planned sales deductions, and planned costs).

How do we want to implement this demand?

The key figures 6 and 7 (net value and cost) are available in the form of the fields NETWR and WAVWR, so we have nothing more to do here. We want to collect the key figures 1 to 5 in the subtotal fields KZWI1 to KZWI5. Thus we have to assign each condition type one of these subtotal indicators. This assignment is not possible for all condition types according to their current settings in the pricing procedure. We need to change the addressed granularity and will show this with the example of the condition type PR00. The assignment of the condition types to the key figures in the pricing procedure is done by the indicator SUBTOTAL.

Because of this assignment and because of the introduction of other condition types, we need to adjust the pricing procedures. This process is explained in the next section.

12.11.1 Implementation of a Consolidated Pricing Procedure

When presenting some representative pricing procedures in Chapter 8, we pointed out that it would be quite possible to combine some of them. We now take the opportunity to follow up on this idea. We want to combine the pricing procedures RVAA01 (standard), RVAA02 (standard with price book), and PSER02 (resource related billing) to a new (super) pricing procedure called ZVAA02 (standard consolidated), in which the assignment of the condition types to the key figures 1 to 5 is possible. Furthermore, we want to insert most of the newly created condition types in this book as a kind of documentation of the work done. We first present you this new pricing procedure (see Table 12.3) and then describe in detail the steps to this pricing procedure.

The columns in this table are:

- Stp = Step number
- CnT = Condition type
- From = From step number
- To = To step number
- M = Manual condition
- Rq = Requirement
- Sub = Subtotal
- S = Condition type is statistical
- Cal = Condition value formula
- Bas = Base value formula
- Ac1 = Account key for revenues
- Ac2 = Account key for accruals
- P = Printing indicator
- Obl = Condition is obligatory

Stp	CnT	Descr.	From	To	M	Rq	Sub	S	Cal	Bas	Ac1	Ac2	P	Obl
4	ZPBP	Data determination cust.				2								
5	Z902	Data determination mat.				2								
6	PBU	Price book determination				2								
7	PBUD	Price book basis				2		X						
8	EK01	Actual cost			X		B			921	ERL			
9	ZPRA	Price (general)				202				921	ERL			
10		**Base Price**				**902**	**1**		**2**					
12	ZBUP	Price book – gross price				2	1		6	202	ERL			
14	ZPRC	Price increased				906	3		906		ERL			
16	ZPRB	Price cust. specific				2	3		6		ERL			
18	ZPRD	Contract price				2	3		6		ERL			
20	VA00	Variants				2	1				ERL			
30	ZB00	Manual gross price			X	2	4		6		ERL			
100		**Gross Value**							**2**				**a**	
101	Z905	Material group discount				2	2				ERS			
102	ZC00	Quantity surcharge			X	2	4				ERS			
103	K005	Customer/material				2	3				ERS			
104	K007	Customer discount				7	3				ERS			
105	K004	Material				2	2				ERS			
106	K020	Price group				2	2				ERS			
107	K029	Mat. pricing group				2	2				ERS			
108	K030	Customer/mat. pr. grp				2	3				ERS			
109	K031	Price grp/mat. pr. grp				2	2				ERS			
110	RA01	% Disc. from gross	100		X	2	4				ERS			
110	RA00	% Discount from net			X	2	4				ERS			

Table 12.3 Consolidated Pricing Procedure ZVAA02

Stp	CnT	Descr.	From	To	M	Rq	Sub	S	Cal	Bas	Ac1	Ac2	P	Obl
110	RC00	Quantity discount			X	2	4				ERS			
110	RB00	Discount (value)			X	2	4			923	ERS			
110	RD00	Weight discount			X	2	4				ERS			
111	HI01	Hierarchy				2	3				ERS			
112	HI02	Hierarchy/material				2	3				ERS			
115	K148	Product hierarchy				2	2				ERS			
120	VA01	Variants %				2	2				ERS			
131	KA00	Sales promotion				2	3				ERS			
132	K032	Price group/material				2	2				ERS			
150	Z030	Customer/mat. grp				2	3				ERS			
151	Z031	Customer/mat. grp				2	3			923	ERS			
300		**Discount Amount**	**101**	**299**									b	
302	NETP	Price			X	2	2		6	3	ERL		b	
310	PN00	Net price			X	2	4		6		ERL		b	
320	PMIN	Minimum price				2	2		15		ERL		b	
399	R100	100% discount				55	2			28	ERS		b	
400		**Rebate Basis**				7								
701	EDI1	Customer expected price			X			X	8					
702	EDI2	Customer expected value			X			X	8					
800		**Net Value for Item**							2					
801	NRAB	Free goods				59	2			29	ERS		b	
805	KP00	Pallet discount				57	3			922	ERS		B	
806	KP01	Incomp. pallet surch.				57	3			924	ERS		B	
807	KP02	Mixed pallet disc.				957	3			923	ERS		B	
808	KP03	Mixed pallet surch.				957	3			923	ERS		B	
809	ZP03	Mixed pallet surch.				957	3		17	12	ERS		B	
810	HA00	Percentage discount	800	809	X	2	4				ERS		B	
810	HB00	Discount (value)			X	2	4			923	ERS		B	

Table 12.3 Consolidated Pricing Procedure ZVAA02 (Cont.)

Stp	CnT	Descr.	From	To	M	Rq	Sub	S	Cal	Bas	Ac1	Ac2	P	Obl
810	HD00	Freight			X	957	4				ERF		B	
817	AMIW	Minimum SalesOrdrVal				2	D	X		923				
818	AMIZ	Minimum value surch				2	2		13	923	ERS		B	
820	HM00	Order value			X	2	E	X		923				
821	ZM00	Delta to the order value				2	4		913		ERS		D	
900		**Net Value 2**							2					
901	BO01	Group rebate	400			2	5				ERB	ERU		
902	BO02	Material rebate	400			2	5				ERB	ERU		
903	BO03	Customer rebate	400			2	5				ERB	ERU		
904	BO04	Hierarchy rebate	400			2	5				ERB	ERU		
905	BO06	Sales indpndt. rebate	400			2	5				ERB	ERU		
908		**Net Value 3**	900	907										
910	PI01	Intercompany price				22	B	X			ERL			
911	AZWR	Down pay./ settlement				2			48		ERL			
914	SKTV	Cash discount				14	D	X	2					
915	MWST	Output tax				10				16	MWS		A	X
919	DIFF	Rounding off				13			16	4	ERS			X
920		**Total**							4					
921	PTVO	Voucher			X						PPG			
925		**Payment Amount**	920	924			A							
930	SKTO	Cash discount				9		X	11					
932	RL00	Factoring discount				23		X	2		ERS			
933	MW15	Fact. discount tax	932			21		X			MWS			X
935	GRWR	Statistical value				8	C	X	2					
940	VPRS	Cost				4	B	X						
941	EK02	Calculated costs			X		B	X						
942	EK03	Calculated ship. cost			X			X						

Table 12.3 Consolidated Pricing Procedure ZVAA02 (Cont.)

Stp	CnT	Descr.	From	To	M	Rq	Sub	S	Cal	Bas	Ac1	Ac2	P	Obl
943	KW00	Group price			X			X						
950		**Profit Margin**	**908**						**911**					
951		Profit margin %	908					H	918					
960	ZDB1	Minimum profit margin	908			2		X	905					
980	ZH01	Budget - approved				2		X	2					
981	ZH02	Budget - requested				2		X	900					

Table 12.3 Consolidated Pricing Procedure ZVAA02 (Cont.)

For a better orientation, we have a list of the condition types that were introduced in this book, as well as in which sections you can find them:

- ZPBP (data determination cust.) in Chapter 9, Section 9.2
- Z902 (data determination mat.) in Chapter 9, Section 9.2 and in Section 12.8
- ZPRA (price (general)) in Section 12.11.2
- ZBUP (price book – gross price) in Section 12.11.2
- ZPRC (price Increased) in Section 12.11.4
- ZPRB (price cust. specific) in Section 12.11.4
- ZPRD (contract price) in Section 12.11.4
- ZB00 (manual gross price) in Section 12.11.5
- Z905 (material group discount) in Chapter 9, Section 9.2
- ZC00 (quantity surcharge) in Chapter 7, Section 7.7.6
- Z030 and Z031 (customer/matgrp) in Chapter 11, Section 11.4.4
- ZP03 (mixed pallet surch.) in Chapter 11, Section 11.3
- ZM00 (delta to the order value) in Chapter 8, Section 8.2.4
- ZDB1 (minimum profit margin) in Section 12.11.8
- ZH01 (budget approved) in Section 12.1.3
- ZH02 (budget requested) also in Section 12.1.3

We are now developing our new pricing procedure in detail. The indicator SUBTOTAL, except for the condition types and EK01 ZPRA, carries out the assignment of the condition types to the key figures, as will be explained later. Our key figures have this property:

Sum (KZWI1 to KZWI4) = NETWR

Our new pricing procedure has only two non-statistical condition types that are configured with CONDITION CLASS = B (price): the condition type EK01 (actual cost) and the new condition type ZPRA (price (general)). One of these two condition types must always be found in pricing. All other price condition types must be configured as discount/surcharge (CONDITION CLASS = A). If these condition types were configured as price, they would deactivate all previous condition types, including the initial value. However, these condition types must have assigned the condition value formulas 006 (initial price) or 906 (initial price PR02) in order to act as a price in the end. Both formulas cause set the value of the price condition type to the difference (delta) of the previously determined net value.

12.11.2 Key Figure 1: The Initial Value (KZWI1)

We define the standard price condition type PR00 as the initial value, but only the material price and the price list. These we map in the new condition type ZPRA (price (general)). In addition, we need to "cut out" the customer-specific price from the condition type PR00 and place it in a different condition type. This is what the new condition type ZPRB (price cust. specific) is for.

The initial value must always be present, either as condition type EK01 or as condition type ZPRA. We now want to start setting up the new condition types.

Condition Type EK01 (Actual Cost)

The condition type appears in conjunction with the resource related billing, which is usually handled by the pricing procedure PSER02. Since the condition type primarily provides the actual cost, the indicator SUBTOTAL = B (cost) is assigned. As an exception, we do not transfer the value of the condition directly in the subtotal KZWI1, but we make it with the line base price in the pricing procedure with the step 10, which has the indicator SUBTOTAL = 1. The situation that in a process only the actual cost EK01 and no additional price ZPRA is found occurs when, for example, external services (supplier invoices) are billed as part of the resource related billing. The base price includes either the value of the condition type EK01 or the condition type ZPRA, if it exists.

Condition Type ZPRA (Price (General))

We first set up the new access sequence ZPRA (price (general)) as an exclusive access sequence (see Table 12.4). Then we create the new condition type ZPRA as a copy of condition type PR00, but with the access sequence ZPRA and reference condition type PR00. This means that we use the existing condition records of PR00 and do not create our own condition records for ZPRA.

Access	Table	Condition Field		Document Field	
10	A306: Requirement 003	PLTYP	=	KOMPAZD	PLTYP_D
		WAERK	=	KOMK	WAERK
		MATNR	=	KOMP	PMATN
15	A306	PLTYP	=	KOMPAZD	PLTYP_D
		WAERK	=	KOMK	HWAER
		MATNR	=	KOMP	PMATN
20	A306: Requirement 003	PLTYP	=	KOMK	PLTYP
		WAERK	=	KOMK	WAERK
		MATNR	=	KOMP	PMATN
30	A306	PLTYP	=	KOMK	PLTYP
		WAERK	=	KOMK	HWAER
		MATNR	=	KOMP	PMATN
40	A304	MATNR	=	KOMP	PMATN

Table 12.4 Access Sequence ZPRA for the Condition Type ZPRA (Price [General])

We also have taken into account the characteristics of the condition type PBBS (base price) in this access sequence for the processing of an item pricelist as used in pricing procedure RVAA02 (standard with price book). That is, the condition type PBBS is no longer needed. The value of the condition type is transferred with the line "base price" in the pricing procedure into the key figure 1 (KZWI1).

Another candidate for the key figure 1 is the condition type ZBUP.

Condition Type ZBUP (Price Book, Gross Price)

The ZBUP condition type is a copy of the PBUP condition type, but it's configured with CONDITION CLASS = A (discount/surcharge).

12.11.3 Key Figure 2: The Standard Condition Types (KZWI2)

You must assign all condition types to the key figure 2 that are determined automatically and that are not customer-dependent. You can find these in the pricing procedure assigned to the SUBTOTAL = 2. In this block, there are no special features.

12.11.4 Key Figure 3: The Customer Specific Condition Types (KZWI3)

The key figure 3 has assigned all condition types that are found automatically and that are customer-dependent in any way. These include the customer hierarchy condition types. The corresponding condition types are assigned in the pricing procedure to the SUBTOTAL = 3. In this block, we set up three new condition types: ZPRB, ZPRC, and ZPRD.

Condition Type ZPRB (Price Cust. Specific)

With the condition type ZPRB, we map the customer-dependent part from the condition type PR00. For this purpose, we create the new access sequence ZPRB (see Table 12.5) as an exclusive access sequence. Then we create the new condition type ZPRB as a copy of condition type PR00, but with access sequence ZPRB and reference condition type PR00. This means that we use the existing condition records of PR00 and do not create our own condition records for ZPRB. We also need to configure the condition type with CONDITION CLASS = A (discount/surcharge).

Access	Table	Condition Field		Document Field	
10	A305	KUNNR	=	KOMK	KUNNR
		MATNR	=	KOMP	PMATN
20	A305	KUNNR	=	KOMK	HIENR01
		MATNR	=	KOMP	PMATN

Table 12.5 Access Sequence ZPRB, Price Cust. Specific

Access	Table	Condition Field		Document Field	
30	A305	KUNNR	=	KOMK	HIENR02
		MATNR	=	KOMP	PMATN
40	A305	KUNNR	=	KOMK	HIENR03
		MATNR	=	KOMP	PMATN
50	A305	KUNNR	=	KOMK	HIENR04
		MATNR	=	KOMP	PMATN
60	A305	KUNNR	=	KOMK	HIENR05
		MATNR	=	KOMP	PMATN
70	A305	KUNNR	=	KOMK	HIENR06
		MATNR	=	KOMP	PMATN
80	A305	KUNNR	=	KOMK	HIENR07
		MATNR	=	KOMP	PMATN

Table 12.5 Access Sequence ZPRB, Price Cust. Specific (Cont.)

This configuration ensures that the customer-specific price is calculated as a difference (delta) from the initial price. In addition, we set up the access sequence so that, after the access to the customer-specific price, the customer hierarchy is also taken into account. Therefore, you can maintain the prices using condition type PR00 for all nodes of the customer hierarchy.

Condition Type ZPRC (Price Increased)

The condition type ZPRC is a copy of condition type PR02, but configured with reference condition type PR00 and set as CONDITION CLASS = A (discount/surcharge). This means that we use the existing condition records of PR02 and do not create our own condition records for ZPRC. We use the new condition value formula 906 for this condition type (see Listing 12.15).

Condition Type ZPRD (Contract Price)

With the condition type ZPRD, we replace the condition types PPAR, PPAG, and PKAR from the pricing procedure PSER02 (resource related billing). This is not a

473

one-to-one replacement, but we have combined in this condition type the document-dependent condition accesses of the three condition types. Those condition records are stored in the contract and appear in the resource related billing (the *price agreements*). In the approach chosen here, the condition records are created under the new condition type (no reference condition type is used).

We create the new access sequence ZPRD (see Table 12.6) as an exclusive access sequence. Then we create the new condition type ZPRD as a copy of condition type PPAR, but with access sequence ZPRD. We also need to configure the condition type with CONDITION CLASS = A (discount/surcharge).

Access	Table	Condition Field		Document Field	
10	A090	VBELN	=	KOMP	VGBEL
		POSNR	=	KOMP	VGPOS
		MATNR	=	KOMP	PMATN
15	A098	VBELN	=	KOMP	VGBEL
		POSNR	=	KOMP	VGPOS
		KONDM	=	KOMP	KONDM
20	A089	VBELN	=	KOMP	VGBEL
		MATNR	=	KOMP	PMATN

Table 12.6 Access Sequence ZPRD, Contract Condition Types (Price Agreements)

The other condition types assigned to key figure 3 have no special features.

12.11.5 Key Figure 4: Manual Condition Types (KZWI4)

To be able to clearly distinguish the key figures 3 and 4, you must configure for all the automatic condition types the attribute MANUAL ENTRIES = D (not possible to process manually). Manual changes can then be made only by adding condition types manually in the order processing. A change of existing, automatically determined, condition types is not possible. If this is not desired, you must combine the condition types of the key figures 3 and 4. You can find the respective manual condition types in the pricing procedure assigned to SUBTOTAL = 4.

Condition Type ZB00 (Manual Gross Price)

The condition type ZB00 is a copy of condition type PB00, but configured as CONDITION CLASS = A (discount/surcharge). The other condition types assigned to key figure 4 have no special features.

12.11.6   Key Figure 5: The Rebate Condition Types (KZWI5)

In key figure 5, all the condition types that are set as deferred compensation (CONDITION CLASS = C) are summarized. These condition types are generally statistically in the sales documents and represent an estimate value. The actual value is determined at a later point in time (rebate settlement). You can find the respective condition types in the pricing procedure assigned to SUBTOTAL = 5.

12.11.7   Key Figure 6: The Net Value (NETWR)

The NETWR field contains the sum of all condition types that are not statistically active (indicator "inactive" = Space) and have no taxes. This field is permanently programmed.

12.11.8   Key Figure 7: The Cost (WAVWR)

The cost condition types are stored in the WAVWR field. You will find the corresponding condition types assigned to SUBTOTAL = B in the pricing procedure. This key figure is used to determine a profit margin, resulting in the difference of the net value minus the cost:

   Profit margin (PM1) = NETWR – WAVWR

Of course, it is also possible to take into account the anticipated expenses for deferred compensations (rebate condition types):

   Profit margin (PM2) = NETWR + KZWI5 – WAVWR

In the pricing procedure and therefore in the CONDITIONS screen of the sales document, the profit margin is displayed in two subtotals:

▶ Step 950: Profit margin displayed as amount

▶ Step 951: Profit margin displayed as percentage

As a basis for the calculation of the profit margin, we use the reference step. We set up our new pricing procedure so that the reference step 908 is entered for two subtotals. This means that the profit margin is the value defined as PM2. Each subtotal in the pricing procedure can be used as the reference step. In order to achieve this flexibility, we had to replace the previously used condition value formulas 011 (profit margin) and 018 (profit margin %) with the two new condition value formulas, 911 (see Listing 12.12) and 918 (see Listing 12.13).

```
form frm_kondi_wert_911.
  xkwert = xkwert - komp-wavwr.
endform.
```
Listing 12.12 Condition Value Formula (Profit Margin)

```
form frm_kondi_wert_918.
  data: workfield(16) type p decimals 2.
  workfield = xkwert.
  xkomv-kawrt = xkwert.
  xkwert = xkwert - komp-wavwr.
  xkomv-krech = 'A'.
  clear xkomv-waers.
  check: workfield ne 0.
  workfield = xkwert * 100000 / workfield.
  xkomv-kbetr = workfield.
endform.
```
Listing 12.13 Condition Value Formula 918, Profit Margin Percent

In practice, there is often a demand to allow manual price changes in a sales order or a quotation only as long as a certain profit margin does not come in under goal. To achieve this objective and in order to round off the topic of the profit margin handling, we introduce another condition type ZDB1 (minimum profit margin). The condition type is configured as shown in Table 12.7.

Access sequence	K029	Material group
Condition class	A	Discount or surcharge
Calculation type	A	Percentage
Condition category	J	Customer expected price
Plus/minus sign	A	Positive
Manual entries	D	Not possible to process manually
From step number	908	Net value minus rebates

Table 12.7 Condition Type ZDB1 (Minimum Profit Margin)

Access sequence	K029	Material group
Requirement	002	Item with pricing
Statistical condition	x	
Cond. value formula	905	Profit margin check

Table 12.7 Condition Type ZDB1 (Minimum Profit Margin) (Cont.)

If you have created the condition records for this condition type and enter a sales order in which the minimum profit margin is not reached, you will get the message shown in Figure 12.12.

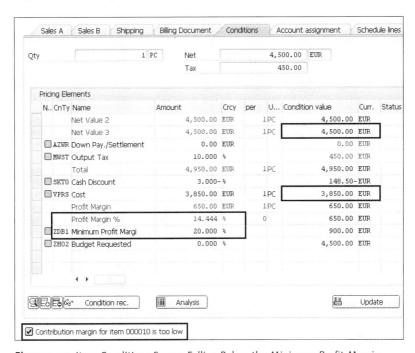

Figure 12.12 Item Conditions Screen Falling Below the Minimum Profit Margin

The information involved in the determination of the profit margin is found in Figure 12.12. The check of the profit margin is performed by the new condition value formula 905 (profit margin check) (see Listing 12.14).

```
form frm_kondi_wert_905.
  if komk-vbtyp ca vbtyp_fakt.
    xkomv-kinak = 'Z'.
  endif.
```

```
If komp-kposn ne 0
  and komk-vbtyp na vbtyp_fakt
  and xkwert gt xworkh
  and xworkh ne 0.
  message s237 with komp-kposn.
  if komp-cepok ne 'C'.
    komp-cepok = 'B'.
  endif.
endif.
clear xworkh.
endform.
```
Listing 12.14 Condition Value Formula 905 (Profit Margin Check)

At this point, for the sake of completeness, the new condition value formula 906 is listed that we set up for the condition type ZPRC (see Listing 12.15).

```
form frm_kondi_wert_906.
  data: ls_komv  like xkomv,
        lv_tabix like xkomv_tabix.
  check: preisfindungsart ne 'E'.
  lv_tabix = xkomv_tabix - 1.
  read table xkomv index lv_tabix into ls_komv
       transporting kschl knumh zaehk_ind.
  if sy-subrc ne 0 or ls_komv-kschl ne xkomv-kschl.
    xkwert = xkomv-kwert - komp-netwr - komp-mwsbp.
  endif.
endform.
```
Listing 12.15 Condition Value Formula 906 (Initial Price PR02)

The actual profit margin of the item is cached in the working variable xworkh in the preceding subtotal line with step number 951 (profit margin %) by the assignment of the indicator SUBTOTAL = H. When falling below the minimum profit margin, the order item is set to incomplete by setting the indicator CEPOK (expected price), as you already know it from the condition types EDI1 and EDI2 and the budgeting process in Section 12.1. Either the pricing of the order item is changed to the effect that the profit margin is no longer too small, or the blocked document is explicitly released by using Transaction V.25 (Release Customer Expected Price). Admittedly, the list structure of this transaction is not suitable for the profit margin situation of a percentage condition type. Thus, you can adapt the list output, but that is beyond the scope of this book.

With these considerations on the subject of profit margin, we complete our discussion about the practical demands.

12.12   Condition Record Depending Requirements

We met the configurable parameters and formulas (CPF) in Chapter 4, Section 4.5. CPF allows us to attach flexible calculation rules directly to a condition record. We will now expand the concept and link individual requirements to condition records. As an example, we will exclude several material groups from a customer discount. Of course, we could solve this requisition by adjusting our access sequence and maintaining the discount only for the entitled groups. However, this can be inconvenient if many material groups exist, especially if we only occasionally want to define exceptions. The solution to this problem is insofar exemplary that we will have to use several exits of the CPF.

To be successful, you need some basic programming skills in ABAP environment and we a couple of deeper, technical details of the CPF application. For the sake of space, we will not work out the solution in full detail. We will not take care of a proper error and exception handling. Instead, we delve deeper into the features and possibilities of CPF.

Our solution is roughly divided into two parts. First of all, we must enable the CPF to execute requirements. For that purpose, we will create a whole new usage task and call it during pricing. In the second step, we will create a formula that fulfills our very specific needs by the creative use of the CPF scale functionality.

12.12.1   Creation of a New Usage Task

Let's start with the construction of a new usage task. First you have to know that usage tasks are declared and defined in table CPFC_USAGETASK. The table provides a customer namespace so that you can define your own entries.

A usage task requires the following:

- A dedicated class and method responsible for the execution of the task. The CPF application will call the specified method if requested.

- A BAdI with one or several implementations. The implementations serve as CPF routines, among which you can choose in the CPF formula maintenance. The BAdI is called in the class method mentioned previously.

- A result parameter that defines the type of the result of the usage task. It is automatically added to all CPF formulas.

We will create these objects and then make the necessary entry in `CPFC_USAGE-TASK` table.

Creation of the New Result Parameter in the Parameter Catalog

We define the parameter `RETURNCODE` in the parameter catalog. It is of type `SYST_SUBRC` and will be the result of our new usage task. Thereby, it will automatically be added to every formula (Figure 12.13).

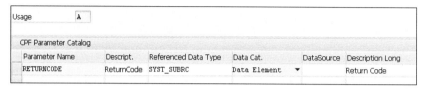

Figure 12.13 Creation of Parameter RETURNCODE in the Parameter Catalogs

Enhancement Spot and BAdI Definition

Next we create the enhancement spot `Z_ES_CPF_REQUIREMENT` (Figure 12.14) with BAdI definition `Z_BADI_CPF_REQUIREMENT` and its interface `Z_IF_CPF_REQUIREMENT` in the repository (Transaction SE80).

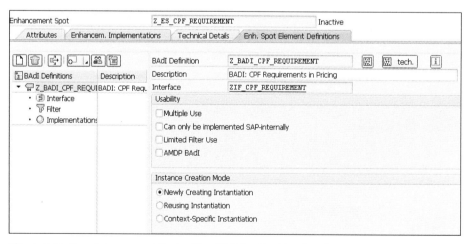

Figure 12.14 New Enhancement Spot with a BAdI for Checking Requirements; the Implementations Serve as CPF Routines

The interface offers the method CHECK_REQUIREMENT, which imports the parameters of the CPF formula at hand and returns a result parameter (Figure 12.15). To allow multiple implementations, we define a filter analog to the BAdIs of the standard tasks (Figure 12.16).

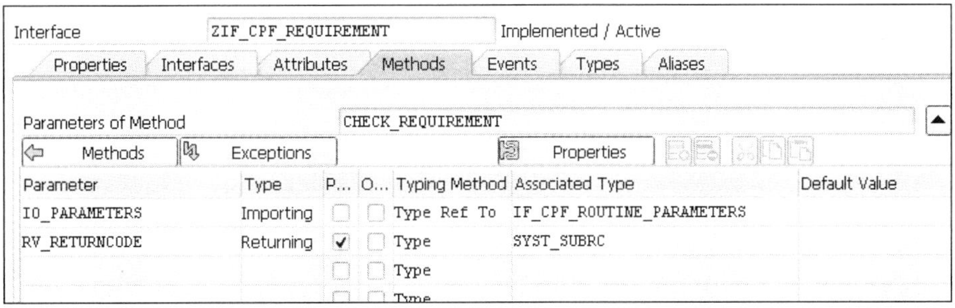

Figure 12.15 Interface of BAdI Method That Imports Parameters of Formula at Hand and Returns Result

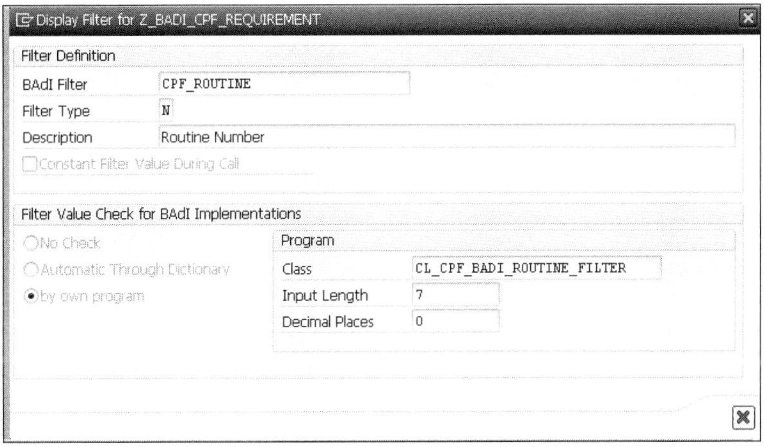

Figure 12.16 Defining the Filter of BAdI Z_BADI_CPF_REQUIREMENT

Class Executing the Usage Task

We define the class Z_CL_PRICING_REQ_CPF with the static method CHECK_REQUIREMENT to be carried out when executing our usage task. The method must have a well-defined interface, so that the CPF application can call it (Figure 12.17).

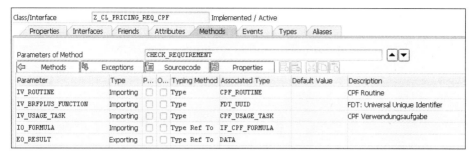

Figure 12.17 Parameter of the Method Executing the Usage Task

We copy the source code for our method almost one to one from one of the methods of standard tasks. Of course, we must call our BAdI Z_BADI_CPF_REQUIREMENT and declare the return parameter properly. The coding (without error handling) is shown in Listing 12.16.

```
METHOD check_requirement.
  DATA:
  lo_pr_requirement    TYPE REF TO z_badi_cpf_requirement,
  lo_parameters        TYPE REF TO if_cpf_parameters,
  lo_rout_parameters   TYPE REF TO if_cpf_routine_parameters,
  lv_returncode        TYPE        syst_subrc,
  lo_returncode        TYPE REF TO data,
  lo_result            TYPE REF TO data,
  lo_cx_cpf            TYPE REF TO cx_cpf,
  lo_cx_fdt            TYPE REF TO cx_fdt,
  lo_cx_root           TYPE REF TO cx_root,
  lo_cx_unknown_type   TYPE REF TO cx_sy_assign_cast_unknown_type,
  lo_cx_cast_error     TYPE REF TO cx_sy_move_cast_error,
  lo_cx_conv_no_number TYPE REF TO cx_sy_conversion_no_number,
  lo_cx_conv_overflow  TYPE REF TO cx_sy_conversion_overflow,
  lv_msg_text          TYPE        string,
  lt_bapiret2          TYPE        bapiret2_t,
  ls_cpf_context       TYPE        cpfs_context,
  lt_cpf_message       TYPE        cpft_message.

  FIELD-SYMBOLS: <fs_cpf_message> TYPE cpfs_message.

  IF iv_routine IS INITIAL.
    RAISE EXCEPTION TYPE cx_cpf_nothing_done.
  ENDIF.

  TRY.

* Prepare context for protocol
    ls_cpf_context-cpf_usage = io_formula->get_usage( ).
```

```
     ls_cpf_context-cpf_usage_task        = iv_usage_task.
     ls_cpf_context-formula_id  = io_formula->get_key( ).
     ls_cpf_context-cpf_routine             = iv_routine.
     ls_cpf_context-brfplus_function_id = iv_brfplus_function.
     ls_cpf_context-class_name   = 'Z_CL_PRICING_REQ_CPF'.

* Fill the routine parameters
     lo_rout_parameters = io_formula->build_routine_parameters(
                   iv_routine          = iv_routine
                   iv_brfplus_function = iv_brfplus_function
                   iv_task             = iv_usage_task ).

     GET BADI lo_pr_requirement
        FILTERS
          cpf_routine = iv_routine.

* call requirement check routine
     CALL BADI lo_pr_requirement->check_requirement
        EXPORTING
          io_parameters = lo_rout_parameters
        RECEIVING
          rv_returncode = lv_returncode.

     GET REFERENCE OF lv_returncode INTO lo_returncode.
          lo_result = cl_cpf_basis_helper=>copy_data_object(
                         io_data_from = lo_returncode ).

* Error Handling...
.................. . .
ENDMETHOD.
```

Listing 12.16 *Method Called for Execution of Our New Usage Task*

Now we are ready to enhance CPF with our new usage task.

Definition of a New Usage Task in CPF

We define the new task CHECK_REQUIREMENT for usage A in the CPFV_USAGETASK view using Transaction SM30. We enter our class Z_CL_PRICING_REQ_CPF, its method CHECK_REQUIREMENT, and our BAdI Z_BADI_CPF_REQUIREMENT and specify the parameter RETURNCODE as the result parameter. Because a manual override does not make sense for requirements, we leave the column for manual result parameters empty (Figure 12.18).

From now on, the usage task CHECK_REQUIREMENT, together with the parameter RETURNCODE, will be available in each CPF formula. The system knows which method must be called to perform this task and you can define CPF routines for it.

Usage A

CPF Usage Task

Usage Task	Result Parameter	Result Par. Descr.	Result Data Type	Class/Interface	Interface Component	BAdI Name	Res
CALCULATE_BASE	RESULT_BASE	Result condition base	CPFS_PRICE_BASE	CL_PRICING_CPF	CALCULATE_BASE	BADI_PR_CPF_BASE	RES
CALCULATE_RATE	RESULT_RATE	Result condition rate	CPFS_PRICE_RATE	CL_PRICING_CPF	CALCULATE_RATE	BADI_PR_CPF_RATE	RES
CALCULATE_VALUE	RESULT_VALUE	Result condition value	CPFS_AMOUNT	CL_PRICING_CPF	CALCULATE_VALUE	BADI_PR_CPF_VALUE	RES
CHECK_REQUIREMENT	RETURNCODE	Return Code	SYST_SUBRC	Z_CL_PRICING_REQ_CPF	CHECK_REQUIREMENT	Z_BADI_CPF_REQUIREMENT	
DATA_RETRIEVAL				CL_PRICING_CPF	RETRIEVE_DATA	BADI_PR_CPF_DATA_RETRIEVAL	

Figure 12.18 Create New Entry in Table CPFC_USAGETASK

Call the New Usage Task in Pricing

Finally, we need to find a suitable place for the CPF requirement check in pricing. Since we will link our requirement to a condition record, the examination must take place after the finding of the record, but before it is copied to the pricing result. After all, we do want to continue with the access sequence, if the condition record is not valid for our document. A suitable location is the user exit USEREXIT_XKOMV_FUELLEN (include RV61AFZB), in which we insert the code shown in Listing 12.17. In this code, we first check if our condition actually has a CPF formula. If it does, we call the data retrieval of the CPF to ensure that all parameters of our formula are supplied. Only then we trigger the execution of our usage task. If the requirement is not fulfilled, we set the returncode and xsubrc parameters to discard the condition record and proceed to the next step in the access sequence.

```
FORM userexit_xkomv_fuellen USING returncode.
  DATA: lo_pricing_cpf TYPE REF TO if_pricing_cpf.
  DATA: lo_result TYPE REF TO data.
  FIELD-SYMBOLS: <lv_subrc> TYPE syst_subrc.
  PERFORM get_pricing_cpf_instance USING komk-knumv
                                CHANGING lo_pricing_cpf.
  CHECK lo_pricing_cpf IS BOUND.

  TRY.
      IF NOT xkomv-cpf_guid IS INITIAL.
        PERFORM cpf_retrieve_data.
        lo_pricing_cpf->execute_task(
          EXPORTING
            iv_task        = 'CHECK_REQUIREMENT'
            iv_guid        = xkomv-cpf_guid
            iv_komk        = komk
            iv_komp        = komp
            iv_komv        = xkomv
          IMPORTING
            eo_result      = lo_result ).
        ASSIGN lo_result->* TO <lv_subrc>.
```

```
        returncode = <lv_subrc>.
        xsubrc     = <lv_subrc>.
      ENDIF.
    CATCH cx_pricing_cpf_nothing_done cx_pricing_cpf.
  ENDTRY.
ENDFORM.
```
Listing 12.17 Call of the Usage Task CHECK_REQUIREMENT in userexit_xkomv_fuellen (RV61AFZB)

We have again omitted the error handling for lack of space. Also it would be desirable to write an entry into the pricing protocol if the requirement is not fulfilled.

With this last step, we established the basis for condition record dependent requirements and can go ahead and realize the requirement for our specific use case.

12.12.2 Exclusion of Particular Material Groups in a Condition Record

If we want to work with material groups in the CPF, first of all we must make sure that we have a suitable parameter in the catalog and that it is filled properly. Hence, we need a data source routine that will do this.

We also want to be able to exclude several material groups at once. To achieve this, we will expand the scale concept of CPF and store the affected material groups in the form of scales lines. The value of the scale line will control whether the material class is valid. This requires a new scale evaluation routine.

In addition, we need an implementation of our new BAdI Z_BADI_CPF_REQUIRE-MENT to have a CPF routine. The implementation has to trigger the scale evaluation and evaluate the result.

Finally, we will create a suitable CPF formula and assign it to a condition record.

Data Source Routine Determining the Material Group MATKL

At the time of pricing, the material group is available in the KOMP structure in the field MATKL. We will get the information from there in in our new data source routine. We will express ourselves so generally so that we can reuse the routine for any KOMK and KOMP fields. You find the coding of the necessary implementation of the BAdI BADI_PR_CPF_DATASOURCE in Listing 12.18.

```
METHOD if_pr_cpf_data_source~get_value.
  DATA: ls_komk TYPE komk,
        ls_komp TYPE komp.
  FIELD-SYMBOLS:
             <fs_param> TYPE prcs_cpf_dtsrc_parameter,
             <fv_value> TYPE any,
             <fs_name>  TYPE any.

  CALL FUNCTION 'PRICING_GET_KOMK_KOMP_XKOMV'
    IMPORTING
      es_komk = ls_komk
      es_komp = ls_komp.
  LOOP AT it_dtsrc_param ASSIGNING <fs_param>.

    ASSIGN COMPONENT <fs_param>-parameter_name
      OF STRUCTURE ls_komk TO <fs_name>.
    IF <fs_name> IS ASSIGNED.
      ASSIGN <fs_param>-parameter_value->* TO <fv_value>.
      <fv_value> = <fs_name>.
    ENDIF.

    ASSIGN COMPONENT <fs_param>-parameter_name
      OF STRUCTURE ls_komp TO <fs_name>.
    IF <fs_name> IS ASSIGNED.
      ASSIGN <fs_param>-parameter_value->* TO <fv_value>.
      <fv_value> = <fs_name>.
    ENDIF.

    APPEND <fs_param> TO et_dtsrc_param.
  ENDLOOP.
ENDMETHOD.
```

Listing 12.18 Data Source Routine to Retrieve Data from KOMK or KOMP

We choose the filter value 3000001 for the implementation.

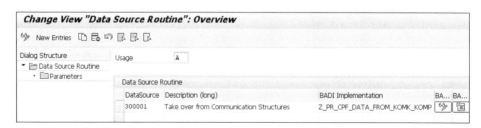

Figure 12.19 Define New Data Source Routine 300001

We declare our implementation in the IMG following the path IMG • SALES AND DISTRIBUTION • BASIC FUNCTIONS • PRICING • CONFIGURABLE PARAMETERS AND

FORMULAS IN PRICING • DEFINE PARTNER- or CUSTOMER-SPECIFIC CPF ROUTINE • DEFINE DATA SOURCE ROUTINE. We enter the material group as a data source parameter (Figure 12.19 and Figure 12.20).

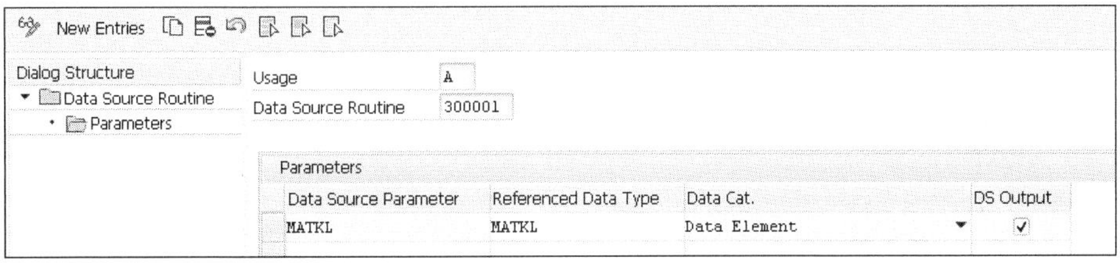

Figure 12.20 Define Material Group MATKL as Data Source Parameter

Thus, the data source routine is available in the parameter catalog.

Using CPF Scales as Decision Tables

We want to store the list of excluded material groups in the form of a scale. Each scale level corresponds to a group. The scale levels value indicates whether the group is excluded. In the document, we will then compare the current material group with the individual scale levels. We need a new scale evaluation routine that performs this comparison. You can see the necessary implementation of BAdI BADI_CPF_SCALE_EVALUATION in Listing 12.19. For the sake of convenience, we assume that the result of the scale evaluation is of type Character. It would of course be possible and certainly useful to code the routine more generally. In fact, the standard routines can deal with different types of results.

```
METHOD if_cpf_scale_evaluation~evaluate_scale.
  DATA: ls_scale_line TYPE cpfs_obj_scale_line,
        string1       TYPE string,
        string2       TYPE string,
        lv_result     TYPE cpf_text.
  FIELD-SYMBOLS: <fs_output> TYPE any.

  string2 = cl_cpf_basis_helper=>get_data_as_text(
          io_data = is_scale-scale_base_value ).

  LOOP AT is_scale-scale_lines INTO ls_scale_line.
    string1 = cl_cpf_basis_helper=>get_data_as_text(
            io_data = ls_scale_line-scale_level ).
    IF string1 = string2.
      CREATE DATA ro_output TYPE
                  (is_scale-sc_res_par_ref_data_type).
```

```
            ASSIGN ro_output->* TO <fs_output>.

*Assume that the result of the scale determination is of type CHAR
        lv_result = cl_cpf_basis_helper=>get_data_as_text(
                 io_data = ls_scale_line-scale_level_value ).
        <fs_output> = lv_result.
          EXIT.
      ENDIF.
    ENDLOOP.
  ENDMETHOD.
```

Listing 12.19 Evaluation Routine to Use Scales as Decision Tables

By the way, this approach is reusable in other scenarios. For example, you could also retrieve an alternative condition amount instead of an exclusion flag.

Implementation of a CPF Routine for the Usage Task

Last but not least, we need to create an implementation for the BAdI Z_BADI_CPF_ REQUIREMENT, to have a routine number available in the CPF formula maintenance. One could work very similarly to the delivered standard tasks with a BRFplus connection. Since in this example, we are more interested in the inner workings of the CPF, we will not do that and will formulate our requirement instead concretely. We assume that our formula always contains the parameter EXCLUDE (see Listing 12.20) and therefore assign the filter value, 1. The method first executes the scale evaluation and then returns the value of parameter EXCLUDE to the caller.

```
METHOD z_if_cpf_bedingung~check_requirement.
    DATA: lv_result type cpf_text.

    io_parameters->evaluate_scales( ).

    lv_result = io_parameters->get_parameter_value_as_text(
                           iv_parameter = 'EXCLUDE' ).
    if lv_result is initial or lv_result = '0'.
      rv_returncode = 0.
    else.
      rv_returncode = 4.
    endif.
  ENDMETHOD.
```

Listing 12.20 Implementation of a Routine for Usage Task CHECK_REQUIREMENT.

We presume the existence of a parameter EXCLUSION that is set by the scale evaluations. If the parameter is initial, the return code 4 is issued and therefore the condition record is excluded from further processing.

This implementation must also be defined in the CPF application. We use the path IMG • SALES AND DISTRIBUTION • BASIC FUNCTIONS • PRICING • CONFIGURABLE PARAMETERS AND FORMULAS IN PRICING • PARTNER- or CUSTOMER-SPECIFIC CPF-ROUTINE • DEFINE CPF-ROUTINE.

Figure 12.21 New Routine 1 for Usage Task CHECK_REQUIREMENT

As you can see in Figure 12.21, you can enter routines for the usage. By entering the BAdI name in the view CPFC_USAGETASK earlier, the system may also propose all available implementations.

It is time to briefly recap the planned program flow for the requirement check, so that you don't lose sight of the big picture:

▶ A condition record is found by the condition access and the assigned the CPF formula read in.

▶ In user exit USEREXIT_XKOMV_FUELLEN, we first call the data retrieval of the CPF. Our new data source routines fill the material group in the formula with the material group from the document item. The CPF usage task CHECK_REQUIRE-MENT is executed next.

▶ The CPF coding performs method CHECK_REQUIREMENT on our new class Z_CL_PRICING_REQ_CPF as defined in table CPFC_USAGE_TASK for the usage task CHECK_REQUIREMENT.

▶ Method CHECK_REQUIREMENT for its part calls the new BAdI Z_BADI_CPF_REQUIREMENT with the routine number from the formula as a filter value and all formula parameters.

▶ The implementation of BAdI Z_BADI_CPF_REQUIREMENT calls the scale evaluation of the formula and thus our new scale evaluation routine that derives the value of the parameter EXCLUDE from the scale. The return parameter is set accordingly and handed on to pricing, where we evaluate it in the user exit.

To create a suitable formula, we now define the necessary parameters MATKL and EXCLUDE in the parameter catalog (see Figure 12.22). The material group has the data source routine 3000001 assigned.

CPF Parameter Catalog					
Parameter Name	Descript.	Referenced Data Type	Data Cat.	DataSource	Description Long
EXCLUDE	Excluded	XFELD	Data Element ▼		Excluded
MATKL	Matl Group	MATKL	Data Element ▼	300001	Material Group
RETURNCODE	ReturnCode	SYST_SUBRC	Data Element ▼		Return Code

Figure 12.22 New Parameters EXCLUDE and MATKL in the Parameter Catalog

Creation of the CPF Formula

We define the CPF formula EXCLUDE_MATERIAL_GROUP with the parameters MATKL and EXCLUDE. For the EXCLUDE parameters, we select the checkbox SCALE so that it can be determined from scales (Figure 12.23). The task CHECK_REQUIREMENT appears automatically in the list of usage tasks. We enter routine number 1 (Figure 12.24). The DATA_RETRIEVAL task gets the standard routine number 1, too.

Dialog Structure	Usage	A			
▼ ☐ Define Formula	Formula ID	EXCLUDE_MATERIAL_GROUP			
• ☐ Assign Formula Paran					
▼ ☐ Assigned Usage Task					
• ☐ Manual Mapping	Assign Formula Parameter				
	Parameter Name	Subparameter	Scale	Result	⊞
	EXCLUDE		✓	☐	▲
	MATKL		☐	☐	▼
	RESULT_BASE		☐	✓	
	RESULT_RATE		☐	✓	
	RESULT_VALUE		☐	✓	
	RETURNCODE		☐	✓	

Figure 12.23 Creating the Formula for Excluding Material Groups; the Parameter EXCLUDE Should Be Derived from a Scale

Dialog Structure	Usage	A			
▼ ☐ Define Formula	Formula ID	EXCLUDE_MATERIAL_GROUP			
• ☐ Assign Formula Paran					
▼ ☐ Assigned Usage Task					
• ☐ Manual Mapping	Assigned Usage Task				
	Usage Task	Usage Task Descr.	CPF Routine	BRFplus Funct
	CALCULATE_BASE	Calculate condition base		
	CALCULATE_RATE	Calculate condition rate		
	CALCULATE_VALUE	Calculate condition value		
	CHECK_REQUIREMENT	Check Requirement	1	
	DATA_RETRIEVAL	Retrieve parameter values	1	

Figure 12.24 Entering Routines for the Usage Tasks

490

Assigning the Formula to a Condition Record

Now it is time. We add our formula to a condition record. (Do not forget that the condition type must be enabled for CPF in the Customizing.) In Figure 12.25, we see the result. The EXCLUDE parameter is determined via a scale, whose base is the material group. The selected scale evaluation calls to our new routine. It sets the value X for the EXCLUDE parameters if the material group corresponds to one of the scale levels. Our condition record is hence discarded if the material group has the value 02 of 03. The material group MATKL serves as a scale base.

Performance and CPF

Reading and executing CPF formulas is comparatively expensive, especially if you use many parameters in your formulas. Therefore, you should use CPF formulas sparingly if performance is a critical aspect for you.

We're done. Admittedly, this solution has required some effort, but we hope that in return you have learned a lot about the configurable parameters and formulas.

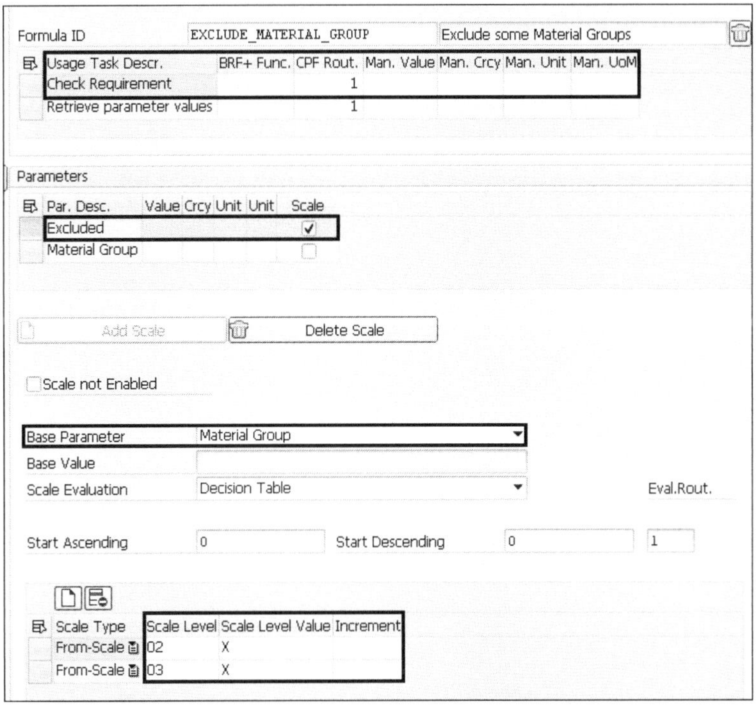

Figure 12.25 Requirement Assigned to the Condition Record

12.13 Summary

The solutions for the various demands that we have presented in this chapter show that using the pricing in connection with the condition technique offers many possibilities that go far beyond the actual task of pricing. Even if you do not have the specific issues and demands listed here, you can certainly draw valuable suggestions from these examples and in particular focus your attention on possible alternatives. You could possibly benefit from the insights that you have gained here in projects in other fields of activity in the areas of order processing and billing. You can use these methods in other application areas, especially in the purchasing process. We already have used in our examples the user exits of the sales order processing.

In the next chapter, we explain the integration of the pricing in the various applications areas more precisely. In particular, we are interested in the existing user exits in these applications and their features.

In this chapter, we look at the usage of pricing within selected applications and focus on user exits that are directly connected to the execution of pricing.

13 Pricing in Selected Applications

In the previous chapters, we have discussed the subject of pricing in the context of order processing and billing. We addressed the technical aspects of pricing and dealt with the options of adaptation within the pricing via formulas, requirements, and user exits.

In this chapter, we take a closer look at the integration of pricing in the various applications, particularly in user exits. These are primarily intended to prepare the call of the pricing program.

The topics covered here are:

- Pricing in sales orders (application V)
- Pricing in billing documents (application V)
- Pricing in purchase orders (application M)
- Pricing in accounting (applications KA and KE)
- Tax determination in accounting (application TX)
- Pricing in transport management (shipment cost calculation, application F)

By far the biggest need for adaptations is certainly in the sales order and the billing document, followed by the purchase order.

Pricing within Industry Solutions

Enhancements were made to the pricing program as part of the development of the industry solutions. However, they only have an effect if the industry solution is activated. In the simplest case, new requirements and formulas were created. In more complex cases, extensions of the interfaces in the form of new tables and structures were made. Such extensions exist particularly in the SAP's Oil & Gas industry solutions, where it is, for example, necessary to perform calculations depending on the temperature. The calculation is also strongly influenced by the components (raw materials) of the products. These industry specifics are beyond the scope of this book.

13.1 Pricing in Sales Orders

Within the sales order, the pricing is called using application V. The relevant routines are:

- `preisfindung (SAPFV45P)`: Calls the `PRICING` function module
- `preisfindung_gesamt(SAPMV45A)`: Calls the `PRICING_COMPLETE` function module
- `preisfindung_vorbereiten(SAPFV45P)`
- `userexit_pricing_prepare_tkomk (SAPMV45A)`
- `userexit_pricing_prepare_tkomp (SAPMV45A)`
- `userexit_new_pricing_vbap (SAPMV45A)`
- `userexit_new_pricing_vbkd (SAPMV45A)`

Here is a list of some important fields of TKOMK (see Table 13.1) and TKOMP (see Table 13.2) inbound interface structures.

Inbound Interface TKOMK	
KNUMV	Internal number of the document condition
KAPPL=V	Application
KALSM	Pricing procedure
KVORG	Event in condition processing
VBTYP	Document type
BUKRS	Company code
VKORG	Sales organization
WAERK	Document currency
HWAER	Local currency
PRSDT	Date for pricing and exchange rate
FBUDA	Date on which services rendered

Table 13.1 Important Fields of the Interface Structure TKOMK

Inbound Interface TKOMK	
ALAND	Departure country
LAND1	Country of destination
ZTERM	Terms of payment
KNUMA	Rebate agreement
KUNNR	Sold-to party
KUNRE	Bill-to party
KUNWE	Ship-to party
KNRZE	Payer

Table 13.1 Important Fields of the Interface Structure TKOMK (Cont.)

Inbound Interface TKOMP	
KPOSN	Condition item number
WERKS	Plant
MATNR	Material number
PMATN	Pricing reference material
VRKME	Sales unit of measure (SUN)
MGAME	Quantity (in SUN)
LAGME, MEINS	Base unit of measure (BUN)
MGLME	Quantity (in BUN)
UMVKN, UMVKZ	Divisor and factor for SUN/BUN
VOLEH	Volume unit
VOLUM	Volume of the item
GEWEI	Weight unit
BRGEW, NTGEW	Gross/net weight of the item
KAEND_TYP	Condition types that cannot be changed
KONAU_TYP	Condition categories that must be excluded
SHKZG	Reverse sign
KURSK, KURSK_DAT	Exchange rate and date
NRFAKTOR	Factor for free goods (inclusive)

Table 13.2 Important Fields of the Interface Structure TKOMP

Inbound Interface TKOMP	
Number Fields of a Period in the Periodic Billing Plan	
ANZ_TAGE	Number of days
ANZ_MONATE	Number of months
ANZ_WOCHEN	Number of weeks
ANZ_JAHRE	Number of years
Number Fields Relative to the Contract Start Date of a Period in the Periodic Billing Plan	
STF_TAGE	Number of days
STF_MONATE	Number of months
STF_WOCHEN	Number of weeks
STF_JAHRE	Number of years

Table 13.2 Important Fields of the Interface Structure TKOMP (Cont.)

The komp-shkzg field is of particular importance. It exists in the sales order and billing document item and, if it is set, indicates a return item or a credit item. However, within the pricing, the field has a different meaning. It states that the condition value for relative (for example, quantity-dependent) condition types is reversed when the indicator komp-shkzg is set. Whether the values are reversed or not depends on the "main direction" of the document type defined by the sales document category (komk-vbtyp). Thus, in a delivery order, return items have negative values but within a credit, these values are positive. If you want to determine, for example, within a formula, if the item is a return item, you have to evaluate komp-shkzg in conjunction with komk-vbtyp.

Let us now have a closer look at the provided user exits and their interfaces.

13.1.1 Routine USEREXIT_PRICING_PREPARE_TKOMK

In the `userexit_pricing_prepare_tkomk` routine, you can influence the field assignment of the interface structure TKOMK. In particular, you will fill your customer-specific fields here, if they are not anyway filled by `move-corresponding`. Some of the important fields of USEREXIT_PRICING_PREPARE_TKOMK and USEREXIT_PRICING_PREPARE_TKOMP can be seen in Table 13.3.

Inbound Interface of USEREXIT_PRICING_PREPARE_TKOMK and USEREXIT_PRICING_PREPARE_TKOMP	
VBAK	Sales Document: Header Data
VBAP	Sales Document: Item Data
VBKD	Sales Document: Business Data
VBUK	Sales Document: Header Status
VBUP	Sales Document: Item Status
KUAGV	Sold-to Party: Customer Master Record
KURGV	Payer: Customer Master Record
KUREV	Bill-to Party: Customer Master Record
KUWEV	Ship-to Party: Customer Master Record

Table 13.3 Important Structures of the Inbound Interface

Other global data (TVAK, TVKO, T001W, etc.) can also be used, but treat them with caution, as it's not ensured that this global data is always properly filled.

In this user exit, you have to make absolutely certain that the supply of the fields in the create mode and in the change mode is identical.

13.1.2 Routine USEREXIT_PRICING_PREPARE_TKOMP

In the `userexit_pricing_prepare_tkomp` routine, you can influence the field assignment of the interface structure TKOMP. The same inbound interface is available as in the user exit for TKOMK.

As with `userexit_pricing_prepare_tkomk`, you must also make sure that the supply of the fields in the create mode and in the change mode is identical. In addition, be sure to note that in `userexit_pricing_prepare_tkomp`, no TKOMK fields can be changed; otherwise, you may experience untoward effects, as described in Chapter 12, Section 12.2. You can find more information in Chapter 10, Section 10.1.1.

13.1.3 Reacting to the Changes of Document Contents

Once you make changes to a sales order, you might need to recalculate certain condition types that are affected precisely by this change. The objective would now be to identify only those condition types that are really affected by the change. Affected in this context means that the modified field is used in any of the following:

- In an involved condition table as a key field
- In a requirement
- In a formula

In the standard SAP, it will react to a couple of document changes by performing a new pricing with an adequate *pricing type* (see Table 13.4).

Examples of Document Changes and the Associated Pricing Type	
Pricing date	C: Copy manual pricing elements and recalculate the others
Material number	B: Carry out new pricing
Incoterms	F: Recalculate freights
Ship-to party	G: Recalculate taxes
Plant	G: Recalculate taxes

Table 13.4 Document Changes and Associated G Pricing Type

If you have configured customer-specific condition types and the desired recalculation is not triggered automatically by the respective document change, you can force this recalculation using the two user exits discussed in the following sections.

Routine USEREXIT_NEW_PRICING_VBAP

In the `userexit_new_pricing_vbap` routine (see Table 13.5), you can evaluate changes of item fields handing over an appropriate pricing type in the transfer parameter `NEW_PRICING`.

If in doubt, you should use the pricing type C. This may recalculate some conditions unnecessarily. However, this will do no harm, assuming you have not previously deleted a condition type. This deleted condition type would then be found again. Thus, it is always better to set the condition amount to zero instead of deleting the condition type.

Inbound Interface of USEREXIT_NEW_PRICING_VBAP	
VBAK	Header data
VBKD	Business data
*VBAP	Item data (old)
VBAP	Item data (new)

Table 13.5 Important Structures of the Inbound Interface

Routine USEREXIT_NEW_PRICING_VBKD

In the `userexit_new_pricing_vbkd` routine (see Table 13.6), you can evaluate changes in the document header or the business data.

Inbound Interface of the USEREXIT_NEW_PRICING_VBKD	
*VBAK	Header data (old)
VBAK	Header data (new)
*VBKD	Business data (old)
VBKD	Business data (new)

Table 13.6 Important Structures of the Inbound Interface

Listing 13.1 shows an example in which a new pricing for the entire document with the pricing type C is triggered when there is a change to the billing block in the order header.

```
form userexit_new_pricing_vbkd changing new_pricing.
  if vbak-faksk ne *vbak-faksk.
    new_pricing = 'C'.
  endif.
endform.
```

Listing 13.1 Trigger a New Pricing When the Billing Block Changes

13.1.4 Manual Triggering of New Pricing in the Sales Order

In the sales order processing (Transactions VA01, VA02), you can initiate a new pricing for the entire sales order via the menu path EDIT • NEW PRICING DOCU-MENT. The pricing type (usually C) used for this function is defined in the Customizing of the pricing procedure determination (maintenance view V_T683V). You can change the assigned pricing type according to your needs. In the HEADER

499

CONDITIONS screen, you have another way to trigger a new pricing for the entire document. There you can select the pricing type from a selection screen. The same possibility exists in the ITEM CONDITIONS screen, if you want to update only a selected item.

13.2   Pricing in Billing Documents

Within the billing document the pricing is also called using application V. The relevant routines in the function group V60A are:

- preisfindung: Calls the PRICING function module
- preisfindung_gesamt: Calls the PRICING_COMPLETE function module
- preisfindung_vorbereiten
- userexit_pricing_prepare_tkomk
- userexit_pricing_prepare_tkomp

> **Interfaces in Sales Order and Billing Document Must Be Generally Identical**
>
> The TKOMK and TKOMP interfaces must be filled as they were in the sales order (see Section 13.1). Otherwise, the pricing in the sales order and in the billing document can provide different results. Only if the interfaces are identical, will the result be the same. However, there are situations in which the pricing in the billing document may differ purposely from the pricing in the sales order. This is the case if, for example, information like the batch is used in pricing, which is known only in the delivery.

For the supply of the fields in the user exits, the same rules apply as in the sales order and for the use of other global data. In particular, you *must not* use the structure VBRP because it is not always filled correctly. You should only use the structure XVBRP.

A special role in the billing document plays the tkomp-wavwr field. Via this field, the actual cost of a sales transaction is transferred within pricing into the respective transfer price condition type (defined by the CONDITION TYPE = G). Some of the important fields of USEREXIT_PRICING_PREPARE_TKOMK and USEREXIT_PRICING_PREPARE_TKOMP can be seen in Table 13.7.

Inbound Interface of USEREXIT_PRICING_PREPARE_TKOMK and USEREXIT_PRICING_PREPARE_TKOMP	
XVBRK	Billing Document: Header Data
XVBRP	Billing Document: Item Data
KUAGV	Sold-to Party: Customer Master Record
KURGV	Payer: Customer Master Record
KUREV	Bill-to Party: Customer Master Record
KUWEV	Ship-to Party: Customer Master Record

Table 13.7 Important Structures of the Inbound Interface

The change options within the billing document are very limited compared to the sales order. An automatic new pricing is therefore processed only after the change of tax classifications. In this case, the pricing type G is used like in the sales order. Like in the sales order, a new pricing is possible on the conditions screens of the item and the header using an appropriate pricing type—as long as the billing is not transferred to accounting.

No User Exit to Trigger a New Pricing in the Billing Document

A user exit to trigger a new pricing after the change of certain field contents, such as available in the context of the sales order, does not exist for the billing document.

13.3   Pricing in Purchase Orders

In business-to-business (B2B) scenarios, a sales process is generally triggered when a company (the customer) places an order at another company (the supplier). This purchase order, recorded in the Purchasing module (within Materials Management), is transmitted to the vendor in printed or electronic (via Electronic Data Interchange [EDI]) form. On the supplier side, this purchase order will be entered as a sales order (manually or automatically) and will be delivered. In the end, the supplier will send an invoice to the customer for the service provided. The customer books this invoice as a vendor invoice with reference to the purchase order and pays it. Once this payment has been received and recorded on the supplier side, the process is complete.

Price agreements have been established between the two parties, which are stored as condition master data. Both components—the purchase order and the sales order—should provide the same result for an operation. The pricing will certainly take place on the selling side (that is, within the possibilities of the sales staff of the supplier), whose framework conditions are determined by the sales pricing procedure.

On the purchasing side, it is of course not possible to map the potential pricing procedures of the suppliers. For this reason, the price agreements are normally stored on the supplier side. For example, the condition type PB00 (gross price) with the condition tables A067 and A017 can be used for this purpose. Another source to store price agreements is the contract. The condition type PB00 is used here as well, but with the condition tables A068 and A016, and the respective condition records are stored at these levels. Together with the condition type PB00 and the starting price, additional discounts and surcharges can be maintained as *condition supplements* (see Chapter 5, Section 5.3). The configuration of the pricing in purchasing can be found using the menu path IMG • MATERIALS MANAGE-MENT • PURCHASING • CONDITIONS • DEFINE PRICE DETERMINATION PROCESS.

Determining the pricing procedure (in this context also called *calculation schema*) is dependent on the fields SCHEMA GROUP PURCHASING ORGANIZATION and SCHEMA GROUP VENDOR, as shown in Figure 13.1.

Schema GrpPOrg	Sch.Grp Vndr	Proc.	Description
		RM0000	Purchasing Document (Big)
	01	RM1000	Document
	EB	EBP000	Purchasing Document (Big) EBP
0001		RM1000	Document
0001	01	RM1000	Document
R001		RMISR0	Purchasing Document (Big)
R001	R1	RMISR1	Purchasing Doc. ISR Internal

Figure 13.1 Determination of the Pricing Procedure in Purchasing

Figure 13.2 shows a pricing procedure with some representative condition types.

The condition type PBXX (gross price) from Figure 13.2 is configured as a condition type without condition records and serves as an entry aid. Requirement 006 (condition exclusion ≠ X) makes sure that condition type PBXX appears only if the automatic condition type PB00 was not found before (the condition exclusion works as described in Chapter 7, Section 7.2.1).

Procedure	RM0000 Purchasing Document (Big)

Control data

Reference Step Overview

Step	Co...	CTyp	Description	Fro	To	Ma...	R...	St...	P	SuTot	Reqt	CalTy...	BasT...	Acc...	Accr...
1	1	PB00	Gross Price			☐	☐	☐	X	9					
1	2	PBXX	Gross Price			☐	☐	☐	X	9	6				
2	0	VA00	Variants/Quantity			☐	☐	☐	X						
3	0	VA01	Variants %			☐	☐	☐	X						
4	0	GAU1	Orignl Price of Gold			✔	☐	☐	X			31			
5	0	GAU2	Actual Price of Gold			☐	☐	☐	X		31	32	32		
10	1	RB00	Discount (Value)			✔	☐	☐	X						
10	2	RC00	Discount/Quantity			✔	☐	☐	X						
10	3	RA00	Discount % on Net			✔	☐	☐	X						
10	4	RA01	Discount % on Gross	1		☐	☐	☐	X						
10	5	HB00	Header Surch.(Value)			✔	☐	☐	X						
10	6	ZB00	Surcharge (Value)			✔	☐	☐	X						
10	7	ZC00	Surcharge/Quantity			✔	☐	☐	X						
10	8	ZA00	Surcharge % on Net			✔	☐	☐	X						
10	9	ZA01	Surcharge % on Gross	1		✔	☐	☐	X						
10	10	HB01	Header Disc.(Value)			✔	☐	☐	X						

Figure 13.2 Sample Pricing Procedure from Purchasing

The pricing in the purchase order is called in program SAPMM06E for the application M. The relevant program calls can be found in:

- `preisfindung(SAPMM06E)`: Calls the `PRICING` function module
- `preisfindung_complete(SAPMM06E)`: Calls the `PRICING_COMPLETE` function module
- `preisfindung_vorbereiten(SAPMM06E)`
- Function `MEPOBADI_PROCESS_KOMK`: BAdI for the KOMK interface
- Function `MEPOBADI_PROCESS_KOMP`: BAdI for the KOMP interface

Table 13.8 contains a list of some important fields of the KOMK interface and Table 13.9 of the KOMP interface.

Inbound Interface KOMK	
KNUMV	Internal number of the document condition
KAPPL=M	Application

Table 13.8 Important Fields of the Inbound Interface KOMK

Inbound Interface KOMK	
KALSM	Pricing procedure
KVORG	Event in condition processing
BUKRS	Company code
EKORG	Purchasing organization
WAERK	Document currency
HWAER	Local currency
PRSDT	Date for pricing and exchange rate
LIFNR	Vendor account number

Table 13.8 Important Fields of the Inbound Interface KOMK (Cont.)

Inbound Interface KOMP	
KPOSN	Condition item number
WERKS	Plant
MATNR	Material number
CHARG	Batch number
MATKL	Material group
EVRTN	Purchasing contract
EVRTP	Item number of purchasing contract
BSTME	Purchase order unit of measure (POU)
MGLME	Quantity (in POU)
MEINS, LAGME	Base unit of measure
VRKME	Purchase price unit (PPU)
MGAME	Quantity (in PPU)

Table 13.9 Important Fields of the Inbound Interface KOMP

Since the user exits that manipulate the interface structures KOMK and KOMP are implemented as BAdI methods, the available fields result from the interfaces of these methods.

13.4 Pricing in Accounting

In accounting, the pricing functionality is used in the following applications:

- TX: Tax determination in accounting
- KA: Cost center accounting: overhead costing
- KE: Profitability analysis: planning

We will not go into details about the KA and KE applications because there is no direct link to SAP ERP Sales and Distribution (SD) pricing and the need to exert influence via user exits does not exist there. We therefore limit the discussion to two applications of a sample pricing procedure. To maintain the condition types and pricing procedures of the KA and KE applications, special maintenance transactions have been established (OKOZ and 8KEV), which are adapted to the controlling context.

The Customizing of the pricing in the context of cost centers can be found using menu path IMG • CONTROLLING • COST CENTER ACCOUNTING • PLANNING • DEFINE PLAN OVERHEAD RATES (see Figure 13.3).

Dialog Structure							
▼ Costing sheets	Procedure	A00000 Standard0			Check		List
▼ Costing sheet rows	**Costing sheet rows**						
• Base	Row	Base	Overhe...	Description	From	To Row	Credit
• Overhead rate	10	B000		Material			
• Credit	20		C000	Material OH	10		E01
	30			Material usage......			
	40	B001		Wages			
	45	B002		Salaries			
	50		C001	Manufacturing OH	40	45	E02
	60			Wages..............	40	50	
	70			Production Costs...			
	80		C002	Administration OH			E03
	90		C003	Sales OH	70		E04
	100			Cost of goods sold...			

Figure 13.3 Pricing Procedure for Cost Center Overhead Costing (Transaction OKOZ)

The Customizing of the pricing in the context of CO-PA can be found using menu path IMG • CONTROLLING • PROFITABILITY ANALYSIS • MASTER DATA • VALUATION • SET UP CONDITIONS AND COSTING SHEETS (see Figure 13.4).

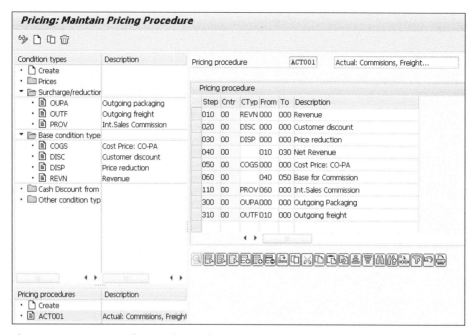

Figure 13.4 Pricing Procedure Used in Profitability Analysis (Transaction 8KEV)

In the next section, we take a closer look at the TX application, because you also need to perform a tax determination in SD processes, and thus in SD pricing.

13.5   Tax Determination in Accounting

Within the document processing in FI, a tax calculation is carried out. We go into more detail about that calculation, because there is a close connection to the SD pricing. The tax calculation in accounting is done by calling the pricing with the application TX and a specific tax code. The Customizing can be accessed using the menu path IMG • FINANCIAL ACCOUNTING • FINANCIAL ACCOUNTING GLOBAL SETTINGS • TAX ON SALES/PURCHASES • BASIC SETTINGS.

The determination of the tax calculation procedure is straightforward. It is contained in the country table T005. As a rule, a separate tax calculation procedure is created for each country. Interesting in this context is the sample tax calculation procedure TAXEUR as a collective pricing procedure for EU countries (see Figure

13.5). This procedure enables you to reduce the number of productive tax calculation procedures considerably.

Procedure	TAXEUR Collect.Proced.for Europ.Taxes

Control Data

Reference Step Overview

Step	Co...	CTyp	Description	Fro	To	Ma...	R...	St...	P	SuTot	Reqt	CalTy...	BasT...	Acc...	Accr...
100	0	BASB	Base Amount			☐	☐	☐							
110	0	MWAS	Output Tax	100		☐	☐	☐						MWS	
120	0	MWVS	Input Tax	100		☐	☐	☐						VST	
130	0	MWRK	Travel Expenses (%)	100		☐	☐	☐						VST	
140	0	MWVN	Non-deduct.Input Tax	100		☐	☐	☐						NAV	
150	0	MWVZ	Non-deduct.Input Tax	100		☐	☐	☐						NVV	
160	0	MWZU	Investment Tax Norw.	100		☐	☐	☐						ZUS	
170	0	MWZG	Offsett.Item-Inv.Tax	100		☐	☐	☐						ZUG	
180	0	MWAL	Sumptuary Tax	100		☐	☐	☐						LUX	
190	0	MWAA	Clearing Tax	110		☐	☐	☐						ASB	
200	0	NLXA	Acqu.Tax Outgoing	100		☐	☐	☐						MWS	
210	0	NLXV	Acquisition Tax Deb.	100		☐	☐	☐						VST	

Figure 13.5 Tax Calculation Procedure TAXEUR for Europe

The most important condition table is table A003 with the access sequence MWST. For certain countries, more tables are used. For example, table A053 is used for U.S. taxes with a jurisdiction code.

The Condition Tables of Accounting Are Not Date-Dependent

The condition tables used are *not* date-dependent. The date dependency of the tax determination in sales orders and billing documents is only provided by a tax condition type of the application V (MWST, MW01, and UTXJ). We dealt in detail with this connection in Chapter 7, Section 7.4.

Transaction FTXP, a separate maintenance, was created for accounting to maintain the tax rates. The maintenance starts there with the entry of a country. For this country, the associated tax calculation procedure is then determined and allows the maintenance of tax rates for a tax code in connection with the tax calculation procedure.

Figure 13.6 shows an example of the maintenance screen for the maintenance of a tax condition records for Spain (procedure TAXES) and Figure 13.7 the screen for the United States (procedure TAXUSX).

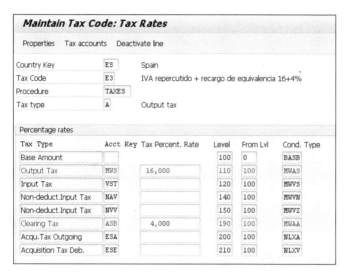

Figure 13.6 Maintenance of the Tax Condition Records for Spain (Transaction FTXP)

Figure 13.6 shows that, for the tax code E3, the two tax condition types MWAS (output tax) and MWAA (clearing tax) are maintained.

For the United States, the sample tax calculation procedures TAXUSJ and TAXUSX are delivered. Figure 13.7 shows the condition maintenance for the TAXUSX procedure. The peculiarity of this tax calculation procedure is that the determination of the final tax rates is carried out by an external tax interface. With the entry of 100%, it is determined per possible tax condition type XR1 to XR6 whether the condition type is relevant or not. The actual determination is then triggered by the condition value formula 300 directly behind the condition type BASB (base amount) by calling the external tax interface (e.g., Vertex or Taxware). The transfer of the actual percentages and values is then performed for each tax condition type XR1 to XR6 by the condition value formulas 301 to 306.

For information on the integration of the tax determination in the sales documents, see Chapter 7, Section 7.4. The call of the pricing functionality in the accounting document is carried out, for example, in the `CALCULATE_TAX_ITEM` function module. Here the interfaces KOMK and KOMP are filled and the `PRICING` function module is called.

The `PRICING_COMPLETE` function module, that is, the document-end-processing, is not used here and there are not any user exits.

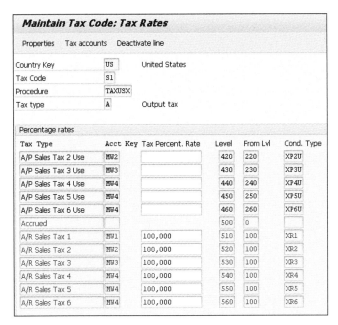

Figure 13.7 Maintenance of the Tax Condition Records for the United States

Table 13.10 and Table 13.9 list the main interface fields.

Inbound Interface TKOMK	
KNUMV	Internal number of the document condition
KAPPL = TX	Application
KALSM	Tax calculation procedure from T005
BUKRS	Company code
ALAND	Departure country
WAERK	Document currency
HWAER	Local currency
PRSDT	Date for pricing and exchange rate
TXJCD	Tax jurisdiction code
MWSKZ	Sales tax code

Table 13.10 Important Fields of the Inbound Interface TKOMK

The amount for the tax calculation is passed in the komp-wrbtr interface field. If this amount contains the tax, the komp-kzinc = X indicator field is also set. Within the pricing, this value is then reduced by the calculated tax, if applicable, and passed to the base condition type (generally BASB). These base condition types are configured with the special CONDITION CATEGORY = K (base amount excluding tax). Some important fields of the inbound interface TKOMP can be seen in Table 13.11.

Inbound Interface TKOMP	
KPOSN	Condition item number
MWSKZ	Sales tax code
KZINC	Initial amount, incl. taxes
WRBTR	Amount in document currency

Table 13.11 Important Fields of the Inbound Interface TKOMP

Initial Amount Including Tax

The normal tax calculation in a document starts with a given net value and then one or more percentage taxes are calculated. It is not necessarily the case that all the taxes relate to the same base value. The basis for a tax may also be another tax or an amount increased by the previous tax.

In the document processing in accounting (customer invoice, vendor invoice), you often need to a net value from a given invoice amount, including taxes. For a single tax that would be easy; with several taxes it is more difficult, especially when they do not relate to the same base value.

We consider only those tax calculation procedures in which the final amount E represents a linear (and continuous) function of the net value A:

$$E = f_{(A)} = mA + b$$

You can easily show that all percentage taxes, even those with different reference levels, represent linear functions. The constant b represents fixed rate taxes that are independent of the base value, provided they do not use value scales. If tax condition types that use value scales are allowed, the solution presented here will not work because the resulting function is not linear.

Examples of linear tax functions include:

1. $E = f_{(A)} = A + (A \times p1 \div 100) + (A \times p2 \div 100)$
2. $E = f_{(A)} = A + (A \times p1 \div 100) + ((A + (A \times p1 \div 100)) \times p2 \div 100)$
3. $E = f_{(A)} = A + (A \times p1 \div 100) + ((A \times p1 \div 100) \times p2 \div 100)$

In the first case, we have two taxes with the percentages p1 and p2 with the same basis. In the second case, the second tax p2 applies to the increased amount by the first tax. In the third case, p2 refers to the value of the first tax.

To solve such computational requirements, the interface structure KOMP contains a field KZINC that is filled in this situation with X. This indicator ensures that the valuation routine `xkomv_bewerten` is called within the pricing at least three times. The task is to determine the initial amount A for a given final amount E. We rely to the principle of *Newton iteration*, which is a mathematical method for the null point calculation. In this case, we are looking for a solution to A with a given value of E:

$$f_{(A)} = E$$

As our function is linear, the process is reduced to three steps.

1. **First iteration step with A0 = 0**
   The calculation is carried out with the net value of zero and determines the final amount E0 (E0 typically will be zero):

   $A0 = 0$
   $E0 = f_{(A0)}$

2. **Second iteration step with A1 = E**
   The calculation is carried out with final amount being equal to the net value and calculates the (too high) final amount E1:

   $A1 = E$
   $E1 = f_{(A1)}$

3. **Third and last iteration step**
   The last iteration uses the initial value A2 in accordance with the following relationship (see also Figure 13.8):

   $A2 = (E - E0) \times E \div (E1 - E0)$
   $E2 = f_{(A2)}$

The calculation with this initial value will meet the desired value E (with a possible rounding difference). The rounding difference E2 – E is added to the net value of A2. Finally, a valuation with the adjusted initial amount is performed, which results in:

A = A2 + (E2 – E)

The algorithm for the linear case is illustrated in Figure 13.8.

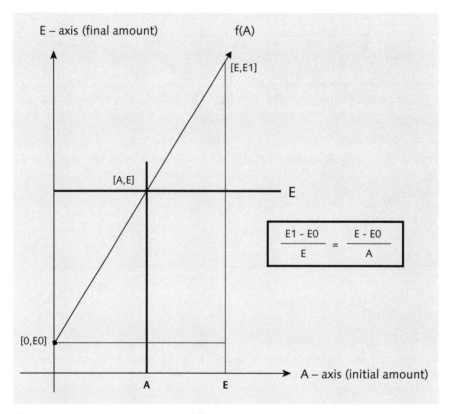

Figure 13.8 Tax as a Linear Function of the Initial Value A

In the initial phase of the SAP R/3 implementation, there were uncertainties regarding this calculation logic when customers expected an initial amount with rounding difference following their previously practiced logic of computing the simple taxes. However, these situations can occur only when the task to calculate an initial amount A for a given final amount E has no unique solution. There are no legal guidelines as to how to proceed mathematically in such cases.

13.6 Pricing in Transport Management (Shipment Cost Calculation)

Within the transport process, a shipment cost calculation is performed using the pricing functionality with the application F. The Customizing for the configuration of the pricing for transport management can be found using the menu path IMG • Logistics Execution • Transportation • Shipment Costs • Pricing • Pricing Control.

The determination of the pricing procedure depends on the transportation planning point, the freight item category, the service provider, and the shipping method. Figure 13.9 shows a representative pricing procedure.

Step	Co...	CTyp	Description	Fro	To	Ma...	R...	St...	P	SuTot	Reqt	CalTy...	BasT...
100	0	FB00	Freight Class/Weight						S	51			
100	5	ZB00	Freight weight (KM)						S	51			
100	10	ZB01	Freight weight (MI)						S	51			
105	0	FBS0	Frt class/break-wght						S	51			
110	0	FS01	Pallet (IDES)						S	51			
111	0	FS00	Container						S	51			
120	0	FV00	Insurance (IDES)						S	51			
130	0	FGT0	Weight/TZZ (IDES)						S	51			
200	0	FB10	Per diem/Flat rate			✓			S	51			
300	0												
400	0	FD00	Spread						S	51			
410	0	FD10	Absolute Margin			✓			S	51			
500	0												
600	0	FT00	Input tax						S	51		51	
950	0												

Figure 13.9 Pricing Procedure for Freight Calculation

The special feature of this application is that it only uses the `PRICING_COMPLETE` function module. Another peculiarity is that the condition records support multidimensional scales, which is customary in freight rates. Thus, for example, the freight costs can be calculated depending on distance and weight.

The shipment cost calculation is integrated in the sales order and to the billing document. In the sales order, planned freight costs can be transferred to a statistical condition type by calling a freight simulation. In the billing document, actual values from the shipment cost calculation can be passed to the billing item as statistical values, or they are billed as freight costs to the customer. At this point the field PRICE SOURCE (F = SHIPMENT COSTS) from the copying control for billing documents comes into play.

13.7 Summary

After reading this chapter, you now understand the integration of pricing in the main applications sales orders, billing documents, and purchase orders. If necessary, you can find the user exits in these applications and you know how the interfaces look. The need for adaptation of the other mentioned applications is normally limited to Customizing settings. Of course, you must also follow the rules and instructions that apply to the main applications. For example: How should the fields in the condition table be arranged? Which fields should be placed in the KOMK structure and which in KOMP?

After this little excursion into other application areas, we are approaching the end of this part. What is left? If you have made adjustments to the pricing, these should of course be stable and performant. The next chapter should help you in achieving that objective.

In productive operation, the performance of the system is always an important consideration. This chapter shows you the possibilities that exist to minimize the part that pricing consumes of the total program runtime.

14   Performance and Testing

Pricing consumes 30% or more of the resources in the sales order processing or billing process. In practice, it is not uncommon to find pricing procedures with a hundred condition types, especially in the consumer goods industry. Many times, these condition types use access sequences to scan customer and product hierarchies. If we have, for example, 50 condition types that have an access sequence with 20 accesses, we come to a maximum of 1,000 condition record accesses—and this is per item! The goal must be to carry out as few database accesses as possible. The database is the bottleneck, because there is only one per system.

Another common cause of a poor performance is the use of customer-owned condition formulas and requirements. A formula is sometimes programmed quickly, but it requires some effort to make it more performant and this is often ignored.

Therefore, it is definitely worthwhile to keep performance in mind from the beginning when setting up the pricing. It starts by considering in which order the fields should be included in the key of the condition table.

Once you have set up the pricing, you must test it intensively. This section provides you with tips on what to pay close attention to.

Here are the topics in this chapter:

▸ Using the SAP table buffer to avoid database accesses

▸ Using the prestep logic and the possibilities of access optimization

- Influencing the efficiency of the prestep logic by the right order of key fields in the condition tables
- Using requirements to avoid database accesses
- Things to note for group conditions and formulas
- Special features in the sales order and in the billing document
- Tools for the performance analysis
- Testing the pricing

14.1   SAP Table Buffering

The easiest way to keep the number of database accesses as low as possible is to use SAP table buffering. The client-server architecture is characterized by having a single database server and several application servers. For the database tables, you can specify in the Data Dictionary (DDIC) whether the table entries are to be buffered fully, partially, individually, or not at all on the application server. Other applications on the same application server, which read table entries of a buffered table, get the data directly from the buffer, if they are there. In this case, no database accesses take place.

When you create a new condition table, the buffering of this table is initially set to 100%. That is certainly correct for tables that are not too large. However, if you are using tables that will have many entries, it may be more favorable to choose partial buffering or possibly to switch it off. Finally, the size of the entire buffer area of an application server is limited. If too many buffering demands exist, other tables are removed from the buffer. When that happens frequently, the overall performance may be worse than without buffering. In most cases, the partial buffering is therefore a good alternative.

You can check the buffering settings with Transaction SE11 using the TECHNICAL SETTINGS button (see Figure 14.1).

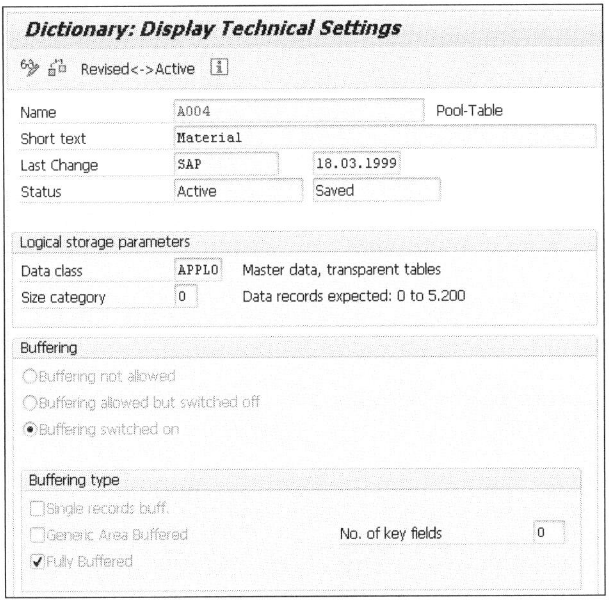

Figure 14.1 Buffering of Transparent Tables (Transaction SE11)

14.2 Prestep Conditions and Access Optimization

As mentioned, we will find pricing procedures in which possibly hundreds of accesses are to be executed on the condition tables for each item in order to ultimately achieve only a few hits. The main work is thus to determine that a particular condition record does not exist in a condition table. The solution to this challenge is the *prestep*.

This prestep is processed within the pricing on the KOMK level (routine `konditionsvorstep`). You learned that the structure KOMK should contain such fields that are identical in most items and therefore have a header-like character. In most customer orders, we will exactly find just one KOMK state. In Chapter 10, Section 10.1.2, we have accurately described this `konditionsvorstep`. The routine considers all accesses of the used access sequences and performs the following actions:

▶ **Access includes only KOMK fields**

If the access only includes KOMK fields, the final access to the condition table is already performed here. If a condition record was found, this is documented by filling the komt2-knumh field (unique number of the condition record). Otherwise, the access is not included in KOMT2. That means in general that such an access is only executed once per sales document.

▸ **Access includes KOMP fields/proofreading is active**
If the access includes KOMP fields and is marked in table T682V (optimize accesses) as check in prestep (see Figure 14.3), the condition table with the leading KOMK fields is proofread. If no record is found, the access is not included in KOMT2. This is done by the SD_COND_ACCESS function module if the prestep parameter is set. In this case, the komt2-knumh field remains empty.

▸ **Access includes KOMP fields/proofreading inactive**
If the access includes KOMP fields and is *not marked* in table T682V as check in prestep, the condition table is not proofread and the entry is added to KOMT2. In this case, the komt2-knumh field also remains empty.

In the following example of the access sequence K005 (see Figure 14.2), the proofreading is performed with the fields VKORG, VTWEG, and KUNNR to determine whether a condition record for this customer exists.

| Access | K005 | 10 | Customer/Material Discount |
| Table | 5 | | Customer/Material |

Field Overview				
Condition	I/O	Docmt Str...	Doc.field	Long field label
VKORG	⇐	KOMK	VKORG	Sales Organization
VTWEG	⇐	KOMK	VTWEG	Distribution Channel
KUNNR	⇐	KOMK	KUNNR	Sold-to party
MATNR	⇐	KOMP	PMATN	Pricing Ref. Matl

Figure 14.2 Accesses of the Access Sequence K005 (Transaction V/07)

You now have the somewhat tedious task to check all the access sequences used with regard to their suitability for the proofreading in the prestep and then enter all the interesting accesses in the Customizing. This can be found using the menu path IMG • SALES AND DISTRIBUTION • BASIC FUNCTIONS • PRICING • PRICING CONTROL • DEFINE ACCESS SEQUENCES • OPTIMIZE ACCESSES (see Figure 14.3).

You should refrain from proofreading if you can assume that the read attempt will be successful in all cases. In this situation, the proofreading loses its positive effect and, on the contrary, leads to a performance degradation, since unnecessary accesses are performed.

CTyp	Condition Type	Access sequence	A...	Access	
Change View "Proof Read at Header Level - Preliminary Step (Pricing					
	New Entries				
K005	Customer/Material	K005	10	Customer/Material	
K007	Customer Discount	K007	20	Division/Customer	
KA00	Sales Promotion	K005	10	Customer/Material	
MWSI	Output Tax	MWST	10	Domestic Taxes	
MWSI	Output Tax	MWST	20	Export Taxes	
MWST	Output Tax	MWST	10	Domestic Taxes	
MWST	Output Tax	MWST	20	Export Taxes	
PPSG	Hierarchy Price Item	PPSG	5	SD Document/Item	
PPSG	Hierarchy Price Item	PPSG	10	SD Document/Item	

Figure 14.3 Customizing of the Access Optimization (Table T682V)

Let's illustrate the decision logic using the example of the condition type PBBS (base price) with the access sequence PR01 (price [item price list]) that you can find in Table 9.2 in Chapter 9:

1. **Access 15**

   The proofreading is performed with the first successive KOMK fields, in this case with VKORG (sales org.) and VTWEG (distribution channel). This makes no sense, because this reading attempt would always be successful.

2. **Access 16**

   Here, the same as for access 15 applies.

3. **Access 20**

   The proofreading would be done with the fields VKORG, VTWEG, PLTYP, and WAERK (document currency). We assume that the price lists are maintained only in a few foreign currencies, making this access actually a candidate for proofreading. However, the access would also be executed when the document currency is equal to the local currency. We know that the price list is normally available in the local currency; hence, proofreading is not necessary. In this case, the decision will depend on how many foreign currency documents and how many local currency documents you have on average. If you are unsure, you should refrain from proofreading. This dilemma could simply be eliminated, if access 20 would receive requirement 003 (foreign currency document) instead of the next access 30. The result would be the same, but you could then activate proofreading for access 20.

4. **Access 30**

Here, the access to the price list is carried out with the local currency. Since we know that the price list in local currency exists, proofreading does not make sense.

5. **Access 40**

Again, proofreading does not make sense, since any material price is always maintained.

You can see that you should already consider these possibilities of the access optimization when setting up the access sequence.

14.3 Field Sequence in the Condition Tables

Regarding the order of the fields in the condition tables, note the remarks in Chapter 9, Section 9.1.4. You should take great care in deciding whether to add your own fields to KOMK or to KOMP. Secondly, you should carefully arrange the key fields of your condition tables in a way that you first position all KOMK fields and then the KOMP fields, which in turn positively influences the efficiency of the prestep (see Section 14.2). This is not so easy to decide when you access the condition tables with different accesses that use KOMK and KOMP fields. One example is again the access sequence PR01, which we discussed in the previous section as the decision-making factor for or against proofreading. In this access sequence, the header field komk-pltyp as well as the item field kompazd-pltyp_d are used. We have made it clear that none of the accesses was suitable for proofreading.

In retrospect, we could have done this better.

Say, for example, we created the condition table A006 with the field order VKORG, VTWEG, and WAERK and only then PLTYP and we provided accesses 15 and 20 in the access sequence with the requirement 003 (instead of the accesses 16 and 30). Under those circumstances, we would have been able to activate proofreading for the accesses 15 and 20 with the consequence of a better performance.

The Order of the Fields Affects Performance

The order of the key fields in the condition tables affects the efficiency of the prestep. You always have to consider the potential access sequences and the possibilities for access optimization when you determine the order of the key fields in a new condition table.

14.4 Usage of Requirements

We already described in detail the operation of requirements in Chapter 11. In particular, we explained there the different points in time of the check. It is generally advantageous if it is possible to prevent a database access by a requirement. We want to illustrate this with an example.

The task is to set up a discount for the MATERIAL GROUP 25. This discount will be granted depending on the customer.

We can have at least two alternative solutions:

▸ The standard approach is to set up a condition table with the key fields CUSTOMER ID and MATERIAL GROUP. We would certainly configure this access for the access optimization.

▸ A second possibility is to set up the condition table exclusively with the field CUSTOMER ID in the key and create a requirement that checks whether the item belongs to MATERIAL GROUP 25.

With the first method, there would be one database access per item for a sales order in which the discount is to be granted. The second solution would need only one single access per sales order.

Just as in this example, there are often multiple solutions to a given task. Take some time to think about the possibilities and opt for the one that is best for performance.

14.5 Group Conditions and Formulas

If you are using your own formulas, you should definitely note the hints regarding performance in Chapter 11. Carefully check your group conditions. Is it really necessary that they are configured as a group condition? New customer-specific condition types are often copied and the property as a group condition is adopted unchallenged. Incidentally, you can easily recognize the group conditions by the fact that, in the HEADER CONDITIONS screen of the sales order, the AMOUNT field is displayed for these conditions.

> **Example of a Group Condition**
>
> The statistical condition type SKTO (cash discount) is delivered in the standard SAP system as a percentage group condition, which means that during the document end processing, the rounding difference comparison is carried out. This happens in the PRICING_COMPLETE function module.

The condition type SKTO (cash discount) is set in the standard SAP as a group condition. This was done to make sure that the value of the cash discount condition type, as it can be seen in the invoice, is the same as the value that is calculated when booking the payment for the invoice in accounting. We see this exact amount on the HEADER CONDITIONS screen.

Do we really need that? If it's only for the display in the HEADER CONDITIONS screen, certainly not. We would need it if we print the condition type in the invoice footer, such as the taxes. If we do not print it, the group condition indicator can be removed. The condition type is eventually used in CO-PA (Profitability Analysis) or in statistical analysis, and there we can certainly live with the missing rounding compensation.

14.6 Peculiarities in Sales Order and Billing Document

This section discusses some peculiarities within the sales documents. Of interest are the differences when running the prestep and in the field supply of the communication structure KOMK.

14.6.1 Peculiarities in the Sales Order

The application of the prestep is controllable with the import parameter PRELIMINARY of the PRICING function module. The prestep is always performed in the sales order.

14.6.2 Peculiarities in the Billing Document

In the billing document, the prestep is performed depending on the pricing type that is set in the copy control for the billing document:

▸ For pricing type B or C: The prestep is performed for all condition types.

▸ For pricing type G: The prestep is performed for tax and rebate condition types.

▸ For all other pricing types: The prestep is performed only for rebate condition types.

This means that the item category of the first item determines the prestep logic for a KOMK state. There may be situations in which this logic is unfavorable for performance. If the first item has an item category with pricing type G and then there are (many) items with pricing type C, it is unfavorable because for most condition types the prestep is not carried out. Since SAP ERP 6.0 EHP 6, you can set the gv_pric_prelim_control = 'X' parameter in the pricing preparation and thus force a check of all prestep requirements for all pricing types. Before this release, a change in the standard behavior was possible only by a modification.

Another billing specific problem is that billing documents are often collective billing documents. That means, for example, that in a billing document all deliveries of a period are collected. In contrast to the order, we frequently have the situation that we can get many KOMK entries. Many KOMK entries indicate that the konditionsvorstep routine runs for each entry. That takes runtime.

In the following example, we consider three debit memo requests with two items that have a different pricing date and posting date (vbkd-prsdt, vbkd-fbuda). Figure 14.4 shows an example document.

Figure 14.4 Debit Memo Request (Transaction VA01)

We create a collective billing document for these three sales documents using Transaction VF01 (see Figure 14.5).

Create Billing Document
Billing due list
Billing document overview
Selection list
Default data
Billing Type
Billing Date
Serv.rendered
Pricing date
Docs to be processed
Document
Item
SD document categ.
Processing status
70000075
Debit memo request
70000076
Debit memo request
70000077
Debit memo request

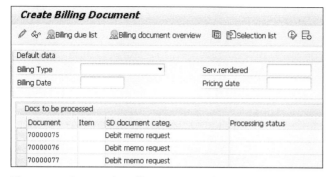

Figure 14.5 Creating the Billing Document for Three Debit Memo Requests (Transaction VF01)

After clicking the EXECUTE button, we get the billing document shown in Figure 14.6.

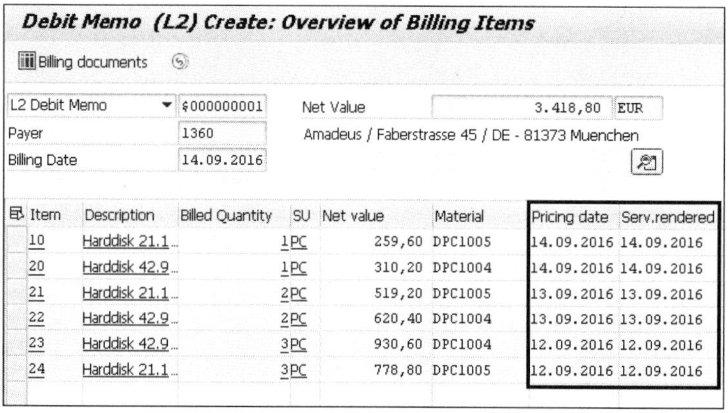

Debit Memo (L2) Create: Overview of Billing Items
Billing documents
L2 Debit Memo
$000000001
Net Value
3.418,80
EUR
Payer
1360
Amadeus / Faberstrasse 45 / DE - 81373 Muenchen
Billing Date
14.09.2016
Item
Description
Billed Quantity
SU
Net value
Material
Pricing date
Serv.rendered
10 Harddisk 21.1... 1 PC 259,60 DPC1005 14.09.2016 14.09.2016
20 Harddisk 42.9... 1 PC 310,20 DPC1004 14.09.2016 14.09.2016
21 Harddisk 21.1... 2 PC 519,20 DPC1005 13.09.2016 13.09.2016
22 Harddisk 42.9... 2 PC 620,40 DPC1004 13.09.2016 13.09.2016
23 Harddisk 42.9... 3 PC 930,60 DPC1004 12.09.2016 12.09.2016
24 Harddisk 21.1... 3 PC 778,80 DPC1005 12.09.2016 12.09.2016

Figure 14.6 Collective Billing for Three Debit Memo Requests

We set a breakpoint in the `PRICING_COMPLETE` function module and save the document. The debugger then displays the situation in Figure 14.7. We see three entries in the `TKOMK` internal table that differ only by a different pricing date (PRSDT) and the date of services rendered (FBUDA).

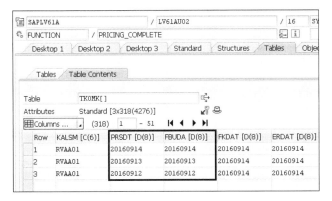

Figure 14.7 Debugger in the Billing Document/PRICING_COMPLETE

Collective billing documents are controlled by the Invoicing Dates field in the customer master data. You can specify whether a customer receives individual or monthly invoices, or is assigned another freely definable timing for billing. The effect of these billing calendars is that a billable process gets as its billing date the last day of that period. In our debit memo requests, this is last day of the month. All documents with the same billing date are combined in a collective billing document, unless other criteria prevent this. Although the pricing date and the date of services rendered are item fields in the billing document, these fields have for the pricing a header-like character and are thus part of KOMK.

If we can make the data identical for all items, we would get a single KOMK entry and would noticeably improve the runtime.

One possible solution is to equate both fields with the billing date. We achieve this with the simple data transfer routine for billing documents in Listing 14.1 that we create with Transaction VOFM and assign in the copy control of our process.

```
form daten_kopieren_902.
* Set PRSDT and FBUDA equal VBRK-FKDAT to avoid multiple
* entries in TKOMK (Performance improvement Pricing)
    vbrp-fbuda = vbrk-fkdat.
    vbrp-prsdt = vbrk-fkdat.
endform.
```

Listing 14.1 Data Transfer Routine 902 for Billing Documents

Of course, you have to consider whether this change creates other problems. You must note that the date of services rendered (FBUDA) is used to determine the taxes and the rebate conditions, and the pricing date (PRSDT) is used for the remaining condition types (apart from the configuration possibilities in the Customizing for condition types).

Under the following preconditions, the modification should be no problem:

- Your accounting periods are not longer than a month.
- The accounting periods do not extend over month boundaries.
- The valid from date of the condition records that you recalculate in the billing document (tax, rebate) is in principle the starting date of the period, for example, the first of a month.

14.6.3 Filling the Communication Structure KOMK

As you saw in the previous section, it is interesting to examine if we get multiple entries in the internal table TKOMK for a representative document (sales order and billing document). The fewer the entries, the better the performance. We check that by setting a breakpoint in the PRICING_COMPLETE function module. The procedure to reduce the number of entries of TKOMK takes place in five steps:

1. In the first step, when the breakpoint is reached, you determine which fields cause the occurrence of several TKOMK entries.

2. In the second step, you check if these fields are used in your pricing configuration. You can check by using the small analysis program in Listing 14.2, whether the field is used in any access sequences. The program determines the affected condition types and pricing procedures. If you do not use these listed pricing procedures, you can proceed.

3. In a third step, you need to ensure that the field is *not* used as a characteristic in CO-PA.

4. In the fourth step, you check whether the field is addressed in the pricing program, for example, in formulas or requirements. For this purpose, you perform with the ABAP Workbench a global search for the affected KOMK field in the SAPLV61A program.

5. If the field is not used here, you can initialize it in the fifth and last step via the userexit_pricing_prepare_tkomk routine of sales order and billing document (see Chapter 13).

```
report  zzhrnt682z.
data : begin of lt_kozgf occurs 10.
data :   kozgf like t682z-kozgf.
data : end   of lt_kozgf.
data : begin of lt_kschl occurs 10.
data :   kschl like t685-kschl.
data : end   of lt_kschl.
data : begin of lt_kalsm occurs 10.
data :   kalsm like t683s-kalsm.
data : end   of lt_kalsm.
parameters: p_field like t682z-qufna default 'WERKS'.
start-of-selection.
  write: / 'KOMK-Field: ', p_field.
  select kozgf
    into corresponding fields of table lt_kozgf
    from t682z where qustr eq 'KOMK' and
              qufna eq p_field.
  sort lt_kozgf.
  delete adjacent duplicates from lt_kozgf.
  loop at lt_kozgf.
    write: / 'Access sequence: ', lt_kozgf-kozgf.
    select kschl
      appending corresponding fields of table lt_kschl
      from t685 where kozgf eq lt_kozgf-kozgf and
              kvewe = 'A' and kappl = 'V '.
  endloop.
  sort lt_kschl.
  delete adjacent duplicates from lt_kschl.
  loop at lt_kschl.
    write: / 'Condition type: ', lt_kschl-kschl.
    select kalsm
      appending corresponding fields of table lt_kalsm
      from t683s where kschl eq lt_kschl-kschl and
              kvewe = 'A' and kappl = 'V '.
  endloop.
  sort lt_kalsm.
  delete adjacent duplicates from lt_kalsm.
  loop at lt_kalsm.
    write: / 'Pricing procedure: ', lt_kalsm-kalsm.
  endloop.
```

Listing 14.2 Analysis Report for KOMK Fields

We now demonstrate this procedure step-by-step with an example, as follows:

1. **Step 1: Determine the causative fields**
   If you enter a sales order with items for different plants, you will find (by debugging in the PRICING_COMPLETE function module) that several KOMK

entries are created. The comparison of the entries identifies the fields komk-werks and komk-wkreg as the cause.

2. **Step 2: Check whether the causative field is used in the customizing for pricing**

   You run the report, for example, for the field WERKS and get the result displayed in Figure 14.8. Of course, the result may be different in your system environment.

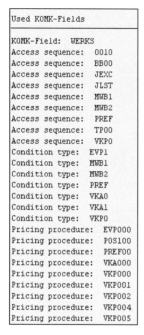

```
Used KOMK-Fields

KOMK-Field:   WERKS
Access sequence:   0010
Access sequence:   BB00
Access sequence:   JEXC
Access sequence:   JLST
Access sequence:   MWB1
Access sequence:   MWB2
Access sequence:   PREF
Access sequence:   TP00
Access sequence:   VKP0
Condition type:   EVP1
Condition type:   MWB1
Condition type:   MWB2
Condition type:   PREF
Condition type:   VKA0
Condition type:   VKA1
Condition type:   VKP0
Pricing procedure:   EVP000
Pricing procedure:   POS100
Pricing procedure:   PREF00
Pricing procedure:   VKA000
Pricing procedure:   VKP000
Pricing procedure:   VKP001
Pricing procedure:   VKP002
Pricing procedure:   VKP004
Pricing procedure:   VKP005
```

Figure 14.8 Usage of the KOMK-WERKS Field

If you are sure that you are not using the affected pricing procedures (in our example, these are mainly pricing procedures from retail), you can proceed with the next step.

3. **Step 3: Check the use as a characteristic in CO-PA**

   You must now ensure that the KOMK field is not used as a characteristic in CO-PA. For this, contact the person responsible for the income statement. If the field is actually used, you can incorporate this field into the item structure KOMP and use it in CO-PA. The WERKS field is in fact already contained in the structure KOMP and can be used instead of the KOMK field.

4. **Step 4: Check the usage in the pricing program, in formulas and requirements**

   The global search for the komk-werks field in program SAPLV61A yields in a standard SAP system only a routine of the SAP for the Oil & Gas business solution. The komk-wkreg field was not used in any access sequence. Only the condition value formula 352 for India used this field. For our example, you can perform the last step, if you do not use SAP for Oil & Gas and if you have no Indian company code in your system.

5. **Step 5: Initialize fields**

   You can now initialize the komk-werks and komk-wkreg fields in the `userexit_pricing_prepare_tkomk` routine of sales order and billing document and again test the results by debugging. You see that it is not trivial, but it might be worth it. SAP Note 43002 (Field Overflow in Pricing) describes other candidates such as the field KUNWE (ship-to-party).

14.7 Analytical Tools

After setting up the pricing, you should conduct a performance analysis by taking a representative process. With the runtime analysis, you can check whether the resource consumption of the pricing is within the limits. Figure 14.9 shows an analysis that we performed in an SAP test system for Transaction VA01 for a sales document of the order type L2 (debit note) with four items.

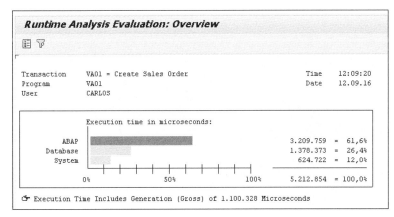

Figure 14.9 Overview of a Runtime Analysis for Transaction VA01 for a Document of the Order Type L2 with Four Items (Transaction SE30)

Choose Hɪᴛ Lɪsᴛ (see Figure 14.10) and sort the list by Cᴀʟʟ. You get a first impression by the consumption of the calls of the `pricing` and `preisfindung_gesamt` routines (German for "pricing complete").

Runtime Analysis Evaluation: Hit List

Number	Gross	=	Net	Gross (%)	Net (%)	Call
4	69.347		154	1,3	0,0	Perform PREISFINDUNG
2	51.572		485	1,0	0,0	Perform PREISFINDUNG_GESAMT

Figure 14.10 Hit List of the Runtime Analysis (Transaction SE30)

You see in this example that the pricing consumed only 2.3% of the total time. We cannot say which share of the resource consumption is appropriate for the pricing for your application, because this largely depends on your pricing procedures. If necessary, you dig deeper into the hit list by sorting it by Pʀᴏɢʀᴀᴍ and Gʀᴏss. You should especially pay attention to the SAPLV61A and SAPLV61Z programs. The sample analysis in Figure 14.11 and Figure 14.12 can serve as a reference.

No.	Gross	=	Net	Gross (%)	Net (%)	Call
501	686	=	686	0,0	0,0	Perform CONDITION_UPDATE_KAWRT
501	708	=	708	0,0	0,0	Perform CONDITION_UPDATE_KWERT
2	14	=	14	0,0	0,0	Perform FIXIEREN_KOPFKOND_KOPF
194	328	=	328	0,0	0,0	Perform FIXIEREN_KOPFKOND_POSITION
4	316		27	0,0	0,0	Perform GKOMV_BEWERTEN
74	20.221		2.147	0,4	0,0	Perform KOMT2_AUFBAUEN
192	36.941		3.759	0,7	0,1	Perform KONDITIONEN_LESEN
36	317		246	0,0	0,0	Perform KONDITIONSAUSSCHLUSS
376	1.457		989	0,0	0,0	Perform KONDITIONSBASIS_ERMITTELN
41	129	=	129	0,0	0,0	Perform KONDITIONSSTEUERUNG
41	51	=	51	0,0	0,0	Perform KONDITIONSSTEUERUNG
12	20.484		1.180	0,4	0,0	Perform KONDITIONSVORSTEP
2	3.314		643	0,1	0,0	Perform KONDITIONSVORSTEP
4	1.179		554	0,0	0,0	Perform KONDITIONSVORSTEP
8	106		89	0,0	0,0	Perform KONDITIONSVORSTEP
8	90		75	0,0	0,0	Perform KONDITIONSVORSTEP
1	35		29	0,0	0,0	Perform KONDITIONSVORSTEP
2	24		20	0,0	0,0	Perform KONDITIONSVORSTEP
7	3.624		200	0,1	0,0	Perform KONP_2_XKONP
12	23	=	23	0,0	0,0	Perform KONV_EINLESEN
2	4	=	4	0,0	0,0	Perform KONV_EINLESEN
1	2	=	2	0,0	0,0	Perform KONV_EINLESEN
268	810	=	810	0,0	0,0	Perform KSCHL_IN_TKOMV_PRUEFEN
48	228	=	228	0,0	0,0	Perform MATERIAL_UNIT_CONVERSION
37	133		107	0,0	0,0	Perform T683_LESEN

Figure 14.11 Hit List SAPLV61A (Pricing)

No.	Gross	=	Net	Gross (%)	Net (%)	Call
237	29.128		10.972	0,6	0,2	Perform SEL_KONDTAB
2	9.625	=	9.625	0,2	0,2	Open Cursor KOTE003
8	3.511	=	3.511	0,1	0,1	Open Cursor KOTE001
237	3.452		2.565	0,1	0,0	Perform T682Z_SELECT
4	579		81	0,0	0,0	Call Func. RV_T681_SELECT_AND_GENERATE
4	935		137	0,0	0,0	Call Func. SD_COND_ACCESS
4	41	=	41	0,0	0,0	Call Func. SD_COND_GET_PRIORITIES
19	1.436		637	0,0	0,0	Call Func. SD_COND_RECORD_TO_NORM_RECORD
4	5	=	5	0,0	0,0	Close Cursor A002
1	1	=	1	0,0	0,0	Close Cursor A002
8	8	=	8	0,0	0,0	Close Cursor A004
12	12	=	12	0,0	0,0	Close Cursor A005
2	2	=	2	0,0	0,0	Close Cursor A005
10	10	=	10	0,0	0,0	Close Cursor A007
3	3	=	3	0,0	0,0	Close Cursor A020

Figure 14.12 Hit List SAPLV61Z (Accesses to Condition Types)

After the runtime analysis, you can perform the SQL trace for your representative process in a second step using Transaction ST05. This will allow you to analyze the database activity. Consequences of this analysis may be, among other things, that you readjust the settings of the SAP table buffering on specific tables.

14.8 Testing

Besides the performance, it is of course important to test your configured pricing. In particular, you need to pay attention to the following:

▸ Your own formulas and requirements

▸ Condition types with the FIXED AMOUNT calculation type

▸ Condition types with scales

▸ Group conditions

At first, you test the result of the pricing with a representative sales order. If you are satisfied with the result, you need to think about the scenarios that you have in your processes. Thus, you will get an overview of the document chains that map your processes. Examples of such processes can be found in Chapter 8. Document conditions are usually copied within this document chain, and you must make sure that desired results are achieved in subsequent documents.

Figure 14.13 shows the document flow for a document chain as it could look, for example, for the process SALES FROM STOCK. You can use Table 14.1 as a model to document your own document chains and the respective test results.

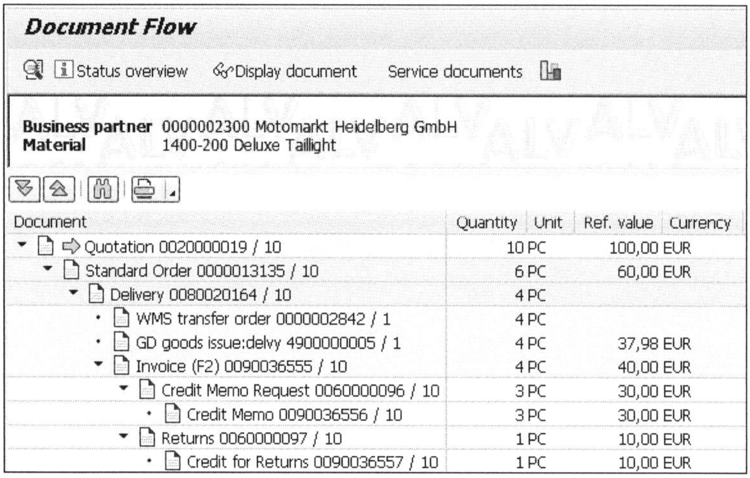

Figure 14.13 Document Flow for the Sales from Stock Process

In the example in Table 14.1, we tested the modification introduced in Chapter 12, Section 12.9, with the example of the condition type HM00 (order value). By using the `userexit_pricing_copy` routine, we have changed the behavior of the condition type HM00 in comparison to the standard SAP system. In the Before column, you see the results without the modification. Bold letters identify the situations in which the condition value is not scaled by the changed quantity. The After column shows the results after the implementation of the modification (see also Chapter 12, Section 12.9). Here the value was scaled by the changed quantity. The indicator CONDITION CONTROL (xkomv-ksteu) of the document condition type was set to the value F by the user exit in the sales documents.

The table columns have the following meanings:

- Doc: Document type (sales doc. type, delivery type, and billing type)
- ICat: Item category
- Qt: Quantity
- PType: Pricing type from the copy control
- CC: Condition Control (xkomv-ksteu)

Process	Sales from Stock				Before		After	
Condition Type HM00		Doc	ICat	Qt	PType	Value	CC	Value	CC
Quotation		QT	AGN	10		100,00	C	100,00	C
Sales order		OR	TAN	8	A	80,00	F	80,00	E
Quantity change				6		60,00	F	**80,00**	E
Delivery		LF	TAN	4					
Invoice		F2	TAN	4	G	40,00	E	**53,33**	E
Credit Memo Request		CR	G2N	3	D	30,00	F	**53,33**	E
Credit Memo		G2	G2N	3	D	30,00	E	**53,33**	E
Returns		RE	REN	1	D	10,00	F	**53,33**	E
Credit for Returns		RE	REN	1	D	10,00	E	**53,33**	E

Table 14.1 Test Documentation of Document Chains

In addition to the document chains, it is also necessary to check the potential impact of changes in the pricing in subsequent functions. Here is a brief checklist:

- Document printing and Electronic Data Interchange (EDI)
- Interfaces to SAP Business Warehouse (SAP BW) and CO-PA
- Sales statistics
- Credit management
- Customer-specific evaluation reports

Of course, this is only a rough list of the test areas. You will be limited to spot tests and there is always some residual risk that you missed something.

14.9 Summary

At the end of this chapter, we want to point out once again the importance of the performance and testing topics. In the first place, take a little time and check your settings for the access optimization with the prestep logic. This is completely harmless.

Our goal was to give you more security in assessing the possibilities and alternatives, in particular with regard to the implementation of new demands. It's important to recognize that existing solutions in practice are often reluctantly changed, since this is connected to some risk. However, the performance should always be an argument for testing existing solutions.

PART IV
Rebate Processing in Sales

In the fourth and final part of this book, we discuss rebate processing in sales. You will get to know the lifecycle of a rebate agreement, the various rebate processes, their Customizing, and the different customer-specific adaptations. You will see how rebate processing is closely related to the pricing and condition technique.

In this chapter, rebate processing in sales—which is another prominent user of the condition technique—is described in detail.

15 Rebate Processing in Sales

As you already learned in Chapter 2, Section 2.4.2, a *rebate* is a retroactively granted discount, which is granted to a rebate recipient based on purchasing a defined sales volume within a certain period. The basis of this discount can be defined arbitrarily in the form of rebate condition records within an agreement (e.g., on the level customer, customer/material, etc.). The condition records are the central objects in rebate processing. Although they belong to the usage E, they are determined and calculated in the pricing.

You might be wondering why we dedicate to rebate processing in sales such a comparatively large chapter in a book about pricing and condition technique. Rebate processing depends in such a unique way on pricing and the condition technique that a deeper understanding of it without solid pricing knowledge is not possible. In particular, only the knowledge about pricing and condition technique allows us to fully exploit the possibilities of rebate processing. Therefore, we want to take this opportunity and present rebate processing comprehensively.

15.1 Overview of Rebate Processing

Before we go into detail, we would like to explain the basic functions of rebate processing using a simple example. Our focus will be the integration with the pricing and the condition technique.

Suppose that you have negotiated with a customer that he gets reimbursed a certain percentage of his total sales after one year. To this end, in this section, you will create a rebate agreement with rebate condition records, which allows you to accumulate the revenue and pay out the agreed rebate.

15.1.1 Creating a Rebate Agreement

First, check the system if there is already an appropriate rebate condition type for this purpose. The condition type BO03 (customer rebate) allows you to grant a rebate based on the total sales of a customer and therefore meets your needs. The condition type BO03 is assigned to the *condition type group* 0003 that in turn is assigned to the *rebate agreement type* 0003. Just like in the sales deals in Chapter 2, Section 2.4.1, the condition type group defines the set of usable condition types with the respective agreement type. In addition, the rebate agreement type contains settings that define the basic characteristics of the agreement. Besides the usable condition types, these are particular the rules for payout and a set of default values. We will come back to that in detail.

We create the rebate agreement using Transaction VB01 or alternatively via the menu path SAP EASY ACCESS • LOGISTICS • SALES AND DISTRIBUTION • MASTER DATA • AGREEMENTS • REBATE AGREEMENT • CREATE and then choosing agreement type 0003.

Then we enter the sales area (see Figure 15.1) and on the next screen the *rebate recipient* (see Figure 15.2). The rebate recipient is to receive the rebate payout and therefore needs to exist with a respective account group in the accounts receivable master data as a debtor. The *payout currency*, that is the currency in which the rebate is paid, is defaulted from the customer master data. You can manually adjust it before saving if required. The validity period is derived from the Customizing of the agreement type and can be changed anytime.

Figure 15.1 Creating a Rebate Agreement: Initial Screen

Next, we specify the condition records that define the relevant sales volume. Using the CONDITIONS button (Figure 15.2), the available condition types and condition tables are displayed. We select the desired entry BO03. In the condition records, we determine by the calculation type and the condition amount how the payout value is calculated.

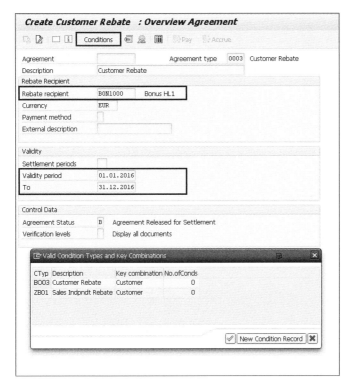

Figure 15.2 Creating a Rebate Agreement: Overview Screen of the Agreement

In our example, the total sales of the customer BON1000 in the sales area of the rebate agreement should be relevant for the rebate calculation. Therefore, the condition record contains the access fields sales organization/distribution channel/division and customer number (see Figure 15.2). Its validity period is normally equal to the one of the agreement, and may be smaller, if the agreement type allows that, but not larger.

In addition to the condition amount, which determines the payout value, you can specify the *amount for accruals* in a rebate condition (see Figure 15.3). This ensures that together with the sales documents accruals are posted in the financial accounting for the expected subsequent payments. The rebate settlement will then later reverse these accruals.

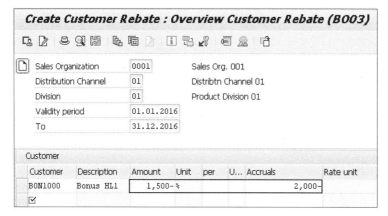

Figure 15.3 Creating a Rebate Condition with Amount and Amount for Accruals

Usually we would make the amount for accruals equal the condition amount. However, in this case, we want to reimburse a higher percentage for a higher sales volume and enter a scale (see Figure 15.4). Since we do not know which scale level will ultimately be reached, we opt for an average amount for the accruals.

Variable key				
Sales or DChl	Division	Customer	Description	
0001 01	01	BON1000	Bonus HL1	

Validity		Control		
Valid From	01.01.2016	ScaleBasis	B	Value scale
Valid to	31.12.2016	Check	A	Descending

Scales								
Scale Type	Scale value	ScCur	Amount	Unit	per	U...	Accruals	Rat...
From	10.000,00	EUR	1,500- %				2,000-	
	20.000,00		2,000-					
	30.000,00		2,500-					

Figure 15.4 Scaled Disbursement Amounts of a Rebate Condition; the Amount for Accruals Corresponds to an Average Value

Before you can save the agreement, you must specify yet the *settlement material* for the condition record. The settlement material is used in the items of the settlement documents as material and serves, *inter alia*, to determine the taxes in the settlement process.

As long as the access of a rebate condition type contains a material number, the system proposes the respective material as settlement. In our case, however, the access does not contain a material, so we need to specify one using the menu path GOTO • MATERIAL FOR SETTLEMENT (see Figure 15.5). Now we can save the agreement.

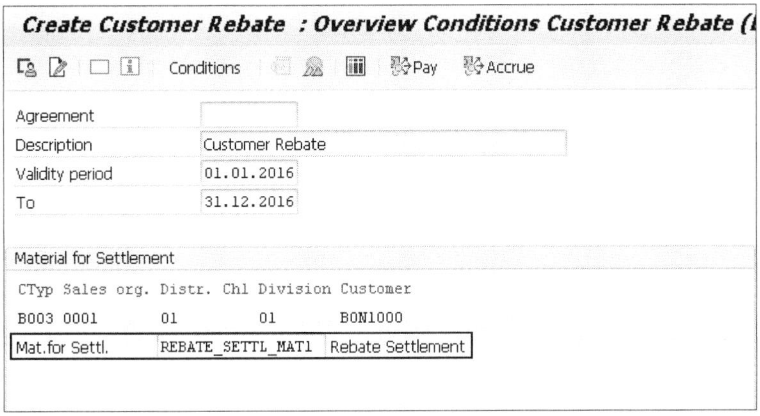

Figure 15.5 Settlement Material for a Rebate Condition Record

15.1.2 Sales Volume: Rebate Condition Types in the Sales Document

Next, we create a sales order for our customer and bill the same. In the sales order, the rebate conditions are not determined when the rebate condition types have assigned the requirement 24 (only in billing doc.) in the pricing procedure. Only billing documents are relevant to rebate processing.

Rebate Relevance of a Billing Document

The billing document type, the sales organization, and the payer must be marked as *rebate relevant* so that a billing document is to be considered in rebate processing. Otherwise, no rebate condition types are determined for the document.

During the billing of our document, all rebate conditions are recalculated. If the pricing type in the copying control does not include a recalculation, a new pricing with pricing type I, which ensures a recalculation of the rebate conditions, is carried out when the billing document is saved.

Rebate condition types are found and calculated in the document in principle much the same as normal pricing condition types. However, you need to consider a few minor features. Rebate conditions are generally only determined when the document is recognized as rebate relevant, that is, when the sales organization, the billing document type, and the payer are marked accordingly.

The value of a rebate condition in a document is calculated from the amount for the accruals and not from the condition amount. This means that the scales in the rebate condition record make no difference. This makes sense because the scale levels are relevant for the total accumulated revenues and not for a single document (see Figure 15.4 and Figure 15.6).

Pricing Elements									
N..	CnTy	Name	Amount	Crcy	per	UoM	Condition value	Curr.	Condition value	CdCur
		Net Value 2	9,46	EUR	1	CRT	9.460,00	EUR	0,00	
	B003	Customer Rebate	2,000-	%			189,20-	EUR	189,20-	EUR
		Net Value 3	9,27	EUR	1	CRT	9.270,80	EUR	0,00	

Figure 15.6 Rebate Condition in the Sales Document

When we look at the rebate conditions in detail, we find a few more special features (Figure 15.7). Rebate conditions in sales documents are always statistical and, independent of the settings in the pricing procedure, lead to accrual postings. We also see in Figure 15.7 the condition base value and the condition value twice. Both amounts are calculated in the document currency and in the *condition currency*. The condition currency corresponds to the settlement currency specified during the creation of the rebate agreement (but is technically stored separately). It determines for percentage condition types the currency in which the system accumulates the sales and the accruals. Technically, the additional values are stored in the fields KWERT_K and KAWRT_K in the condition line. This ensures that value and base are always present in all documents in the same currency and can be accumulated easily.

It is also noteworthy that the pricing program calculates a scale base even if in the agreement no scale has been maintained. It is sufficient if, in the configuration of the respective condition type, the attribute SCALE BASIS is maintained. This makes it possible to retroactively add a scale to a rebate condition without needing to recalculate the overall scale base value of all sales documents.

By the way, the validity of a rebate condition is always determined by the *date of services rendered* of the document item.

Item		10		Application	V	
Condition type	B003	Customer Rebate		CondPricingDate	19.09.2016	

Condition values

Amount		2,000- %			
Cond.base value		9.460,00	EUR	9.460,00	EUR
Condition value		189,20-	EUR	189,20-	

Control

Condition Class	C	Expense reimbursement	✓ Statistical
Calculatn Rule	A	Percentage	✓ Accruals
Condit.Category			
Cond.control	A	Adjust for quantity variance	
Condit.origin	A	Automatic pricing	

Account determination

Account key	ERB		G/L Account	884010
Accruals	ERU		Provision acc.	89000

Scales

Scale basis	B	Value scale		
Scale base val.		9.460,00	EUR	Scale type	A

Rebate

Agreement	202		
Agreemnt status	B	Agreement Released for Settlement	☐ Retroactive
Cond.Rec Status		Open	☐ Deletion Indic.

Figure 15.7 Details of a Rebate Condition in the Sales Document

Determination Date for Rebate Condition Types

Rebate condition types are determined with the date of services rendered of an item. If this is not desired, the possibility remains to influence or override the date of services rendered FBUDA in the document. However, note here that other conditions types may also use this date. Thus, you might need to assign them another determination date.

The actual accumulation of the rebate values in table S060 of the Logistics Information System (LIS) takes place with the transfer of the billing document to accounting. In the course of this, the base value and the scale base value of the condition are accumulated in condition currency. The accumulated total is the basis and scale basis for the payout. The condition value is summed up both in condition currency and in local currency, so that the system knows how many accruals need to be reversed in the settlement run. You will see the sales volume in the rebate agreement only after the update, as shown in Figure 15.8. Note that the value of the accruals and the expected payout value may vary because of the scale. Another reason for a deviation can be due to rounding.

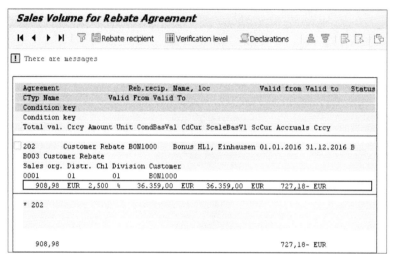

Figure 15.8 Display of the Sales Volume for a Rebate Agreement

Display of the Sales Volume in the Rebate Agreement

Sales and accruals will only be visible in the sales volume display of a rebate agreement, if you have transferred the relevant documents to accounting.

To get a more detailed overview of the sales volume, we can display the *verification level* (Figure 15.9). Depending on the SCOPE, the sales volume is listed here in a different level of detail. In Figure 15.9, we chose the itemization for each document and can therefore see exactly which business transaction delivered which sales volume.

We are leaving our example to make a short detour to fixed amount rebates. These are rebate conditions types with the calculation type B - FIXED AMOUNT. You can grant a fixed amount rebate for a service that is independent of the sales volume, for example, for the implementation of an advertising campaign. Nevertheless, you can use the calculation type B also dependent of the sales volume by linking the payout amount via a scale to the amount of sales volume. Both varieties can be distinguished in the Customizing of the rebate condition type by the REBATE PROCEDURE indicator (see Figure 15.10).

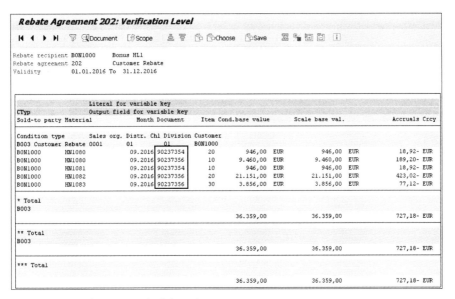

Figure 15.9 Verification Level of the Rebate Agreement

Figure 15.10 Configuration of the Rebate Procedure in the Customizing of a Rebate Condition Type

If the indicator is set, you cannot enter an accrual amount during the maintenance of the condition record. Thus, for this agreement, no accruals based on the sales volume are booked.

If the REBATE PROCEDURE is not set, you can specify for a fixed amount rebate a percentage for the accrual amount (see Figure 15.11). This makes it possible to achieve a continuous posting of the accruals throughout the validity period.

The rebate procedure has no influence on whether the rebate condition is found in the documents.

Figure 15.11 Percentage Based Accruals for Fixed Amount Rebates

In the case of rebate agreements with fixed amounts, automatic accruals are frequently disabled and accruals are booked manually within the agreement instead. You need only to click on the ACCRUE button in the agreement and enter the desired amount for the accruals. The amount has to be negative to increase the accruals (Figure 15.12).

Figure 15.12 Manual Accruals: In Order to Increase Accruals, They Must Be Negative

When you save the agreement, the system will create a credit memo request in the background that will trigger the posting of the accruals once it is billed.

15.1.3 Settlement of Rebate Agreements

If necessary, you can pay a partial amount during the duration of the agreement. To be able to do so, you must have assigned a corresponding *payment procedure* in the Customizing of the rebate agreement type. Sometimes it is part of the agreement that the payments are made on specific dates, for example, every month or every three months. In this case, you must specify in the agreement the *settlement period* in the form of a calendar. The data marked as workdays in the calendar then serve as a settlement date for the agreement.

Settlement Periods in Rebate Agreements

The allowed settlement dates in a rebate agreement are defined via a factory calendar that is stored as settlement period in the agreement. The settlement dates have to be at the end of the month, since the sales volume is always accumulated per month.

The settlement run is triggered using Transaction VB(7 or using the menu path SAP EASY ACCESS • LOGISTICS • SALES AND DISTRIBUTION • BILLING • REBATE • CARRY OUT REBATE SETTLEMENT. In the selection screen, you can restrict the agreements to be settled and specify the SETTLEMENT PERIOD and the relevant SETTLEMENT DATE (Figure 15.13).

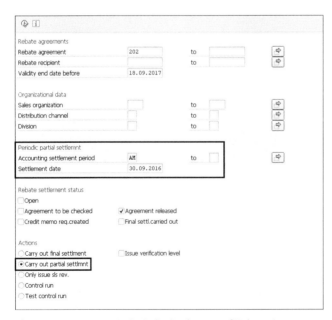

Figure 15.13 Automatic Periodic Settlement of Rebate Agreements

The settlement amount is based on the accumulated sales volume exactly up to this date. For precise deferrals and accruals, the settlement dates must lie precisely on the period limits of the accumulation of the sales volume and thus always at month-end, since the accumulation takes place in table S060 per month.

> **Periodicity of the Sales Volume Update in Rebate Processing**
>
> The sales volume in rebate processing in sales is accumulated per month. This is defined in the coding of rebate processing and must therefore not be changed for the statistics table S060.

As an alternative to automatic billing, you can also perform a manual settlement of the agreement with the PAY button or via the menu item REBATE PAYMENTS • PAY (see Figure 15.2). You can then enter the amount to be paid in the following payment screen. If you use a settlement period, you must also specify a billing date, so that the system can propose a payout amount. If you do not use a settlement period, the total sales volume determines the payout amount.

In our example, we decide to carry out a manual partial payment of 500 EUR. We enter the amount to be paid as a negative amount. As you can see in Figure 15.14, a maximum amount is proposed that we cannot exceed. You will get to know the necessary Customizing settings in Section 15.2.2.

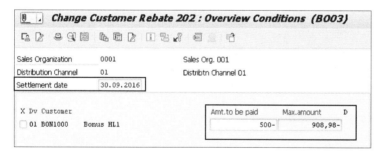

Figure 15.14 Entering the Manual Payment Data of a Rebate Agreement

If we save the agreement, the system will create a credit memo request in the background, where the rebate recipient acts as sold-to-party, payer, bill-to-party, and ship-to-party of the document.

All documents for an agreement can be displayed via the menu item REBATE PAYMENTS • REBATE DOCUMENTS. From there you can directly branch into the documents (Figure 15.15). The documents contain an item per rebate condition with the corresponding settlement material and the quantity of zero.

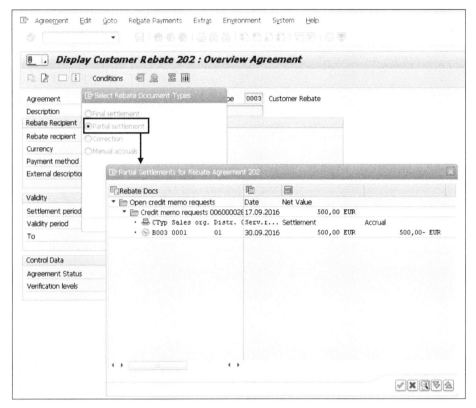

Figure 15.15 Navigation to the Payout Documents of a Rebate Agreement

Let's take a closer look at the CONDITIONS screen in Figure 15.16. As you can see, our rebate condition appears twice. The first line is not statistical and transmits the payout value; the second line is statistical and will ensure that the respective accruals are reversed. If we look at the details of the two lines, we note that both conditions are marked as entered manually and as fixed. The reason is that the two lines were not found and calculated by the pricing, but rebate processing has its values defined from the outside. In the settlement documents, no automatic determination of rebate conditions takes place.

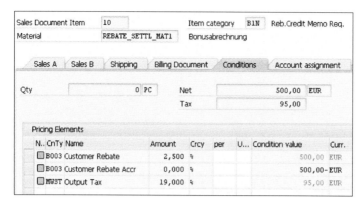

Figure 15.16 Conditions Screen of a Partial Rebate Settlement

Also notice that the pricing data in the partial settlement cannot be changed manually. This is because the rebate agreement type can provide a maximum value for a partial payout that cannot be exceeded when entering the amount. To prevent this from happening later in the credit memo request, the pricing screen is locked for manual input.

The pricing will take into account only rebate condition types and taxes from the pricing procedure. If you need more condition classes, for example for statistical purposes, you need to mark the corresponding pricing procedure in the Customizing as a *transaction-specific pricing procedure* (see also Figure 15.28 in Section 15.2.1).

We now bill our credit memo request and thus have completed the partial settlement. Incidentally, the system considers open rebate documents (payments, accruals) in the following partial payments. However, in the display of the sales volume they are visible only when the statistics update by the billing document has taken place, that is, after the transfer to accounting. The payout values and the reversed accruals are also summed up in table S060.

You can also view the payment data for a condition record via the menu item GOTO • PAYMENT DATA when you select in the condition overview the corresponding condition record. It is also possible to initiate a payment from this screen (see Figure 15.17).

Let's now assume that we have renegotiated with our customer and want to grant a rebate on the sales volume of a subsidiary. Therefore, we add a second condition record to the rebate agreement with the same validity period (Figure 15.18).

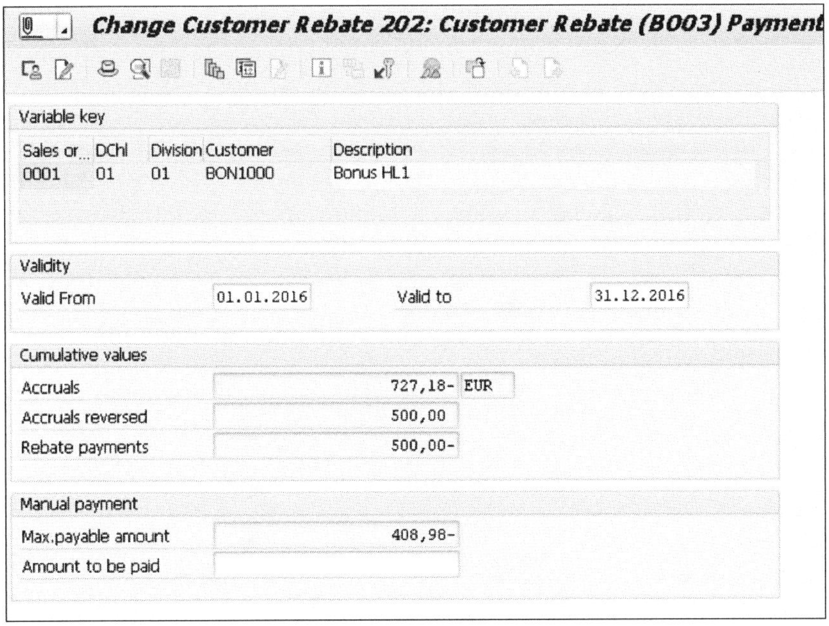

Figure 15.17 Cumulative Values and Payouts of a Rebate Condition

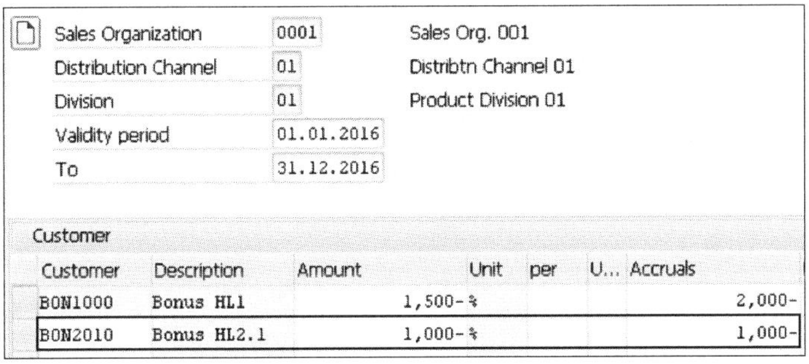

Figure 15.18 Adding Another Condition Record for a Rebate Agreement

This condition record could of course not be found so far. Therefore, we perhaps have missed some sales volume and our statistics are not up to date. We call any changes to rebate agreements that may affect the already accumulated sales volume *retroactive* changes. In the case of such a change, the system marks agreements and condition records with the appropriate indicator KSPAE as SET UP RETROACTIVELY.

To deal with retroactive changes, the rebate in SD knows two methods: the *old* and the *new rebate method*. The new rebate method is already available since SAP R/3 4.5B and is meanwhile the method most commonly used. The old method is used less and less. We will present both methods in Section 15.1.5.

The new rebate method is pursuing a strategy to keep the sales volume in the statistics up to date. If it is detected that the transactions might not be complete, all further payments are prevented until the sales volume has been updated. Therefore, we run report SDBONT06 or call Transaction VBOF or follow the menu path SAP EASY ACCESS • LOGISTICS • SALES AND DISTRIBUTION • BILLING • REBATE • UPDATE BILLING DOCUMENTS (Figure 15.19).

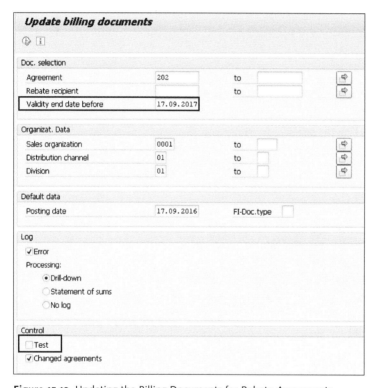

Figure 15.19 Updating the Billing Documents for Rebate Agreements

In the input screen, we specify our agreement number, enter a correct VALIDITY END DATE BEFORE, and uncheck the TEST field so that the necessary changes are actually posted.

The report will now recalculate the rebate conditions for all affected billing documents and forward the difference to statistics and financial accounting. We run the report and get a list of billing documents that were changed (see Figure 15.20).

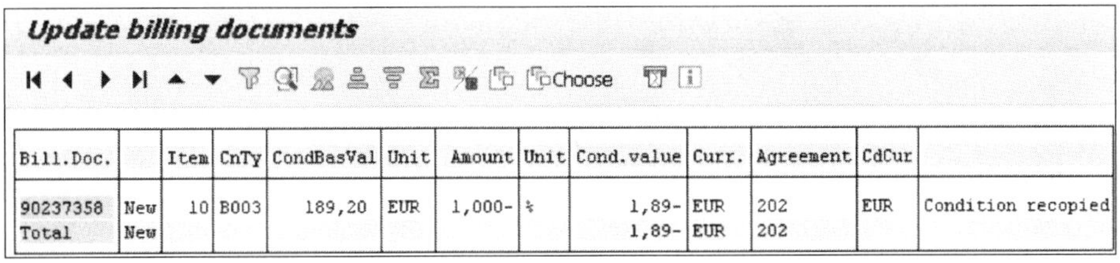

Update billing documents

Bill.Doc.		Item	CnTy	CondBasVal	Unit	Amount	Unit	Cond.value	Curr.	Agreement	CdCur	
90237358	New	10	B003	189,20	EUR	1,000-	%	1,89-	EUR	202	EUR	Condition recopied
Total	New							1,89-	EUR	202		

Figure 15.20 Result of the Update Run

The final step in the lifecycle of a rebate agreement is the *final settlement*. To do this, all previous partial payments must be billed and transferred to accounting.

We can create the final settlement either via Transaction VB(7 (Figure 15.13) or directly within the agreement via the transaction menu REBATE PAYMENTS • FINAL SETTLEMENT • AUTOMATIC or REBATE PAYMENTS • FINAL SETTLEMENT • USING PAYMENT SCREEN.

The latter corresponds to the CREATE FINAL SETTLEMENT button in the overview screen of the agreement (see Figure 15.2) and allows us to enter the payment amount manually. The proposed value is calculated as follows (Figure 15.21):

Valid condition amount × rebate base value – payments already made

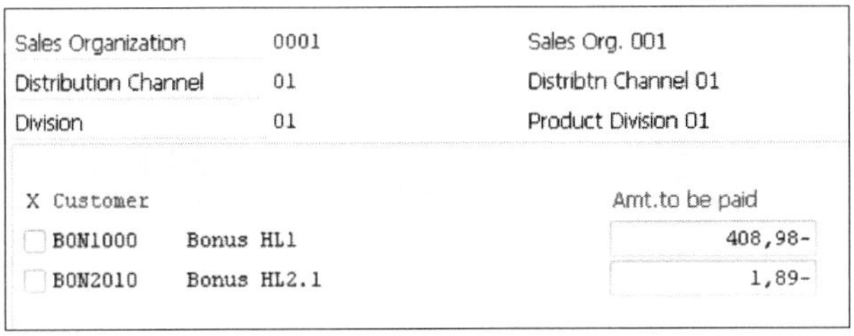

Sales Organization	0001	Sales Org. 001
Distribution Channel	01	Distribtn Channel 01
Division	01	Product Division 01

X Customer		Amt.to be paid
BON1000	Bonus HL1	408,98-
BON2010	Bonus HL2.1	1,89-

Figure 15.21 Entering a Manual Final Settlement Amount

We decide to keep the amounts proposed and save the agreement. Once again, a credit memo request is created in the background and the status of the agreement is set to C – SETTLEMENT HAS BEEN CREATED (Figure 15.22).

Figure 15.22 Status Change of an Agreement after the Creation of the Credit Memo Request for Final Settlement

---

Status of a Rebate Agreement and Pricing

Rebate conditions with the status C - SETTLEMENT HAS BEEN CREATED or D - FINAL SETTLE-MENT OF AGREEMENT ALREADY CARRIED OUT are not found by the pricing in the document anymore and are even filtered out when documents are copied. Thus, no accruals can be posted for an agreement after the final settlement.

To this point, you can open the rebate agreement again by deleting the debit memo request. However, once the debit memo request is billed, the agreement is irrevocably closed.

It is worthwhile to take a quick look at the CONDITIONS screen in the final settlement (Figure 15.23). In contrast to the partial settlement, here the condition relevant for accruals is set with the calculation type B – FIXED AMOUNT and gets assigned the accruals to be reversed as condition amount in local currency. This is done in order to ensure an accurate reversal of the accruals that is largely independent from exchange rate fluctuations. The final settlement reverses all open accruals. If you implement the SAP Note 1272817 in your system, you can reverse the accruals in the currency of the agreement.

Once the credit memo request is billed and transferred to accounting, the status of the rebate agreement is set to D - FINAL SETTLEMENT OF AGREEMENT ALREADY CARRIED OUT. With this, our example is finished.

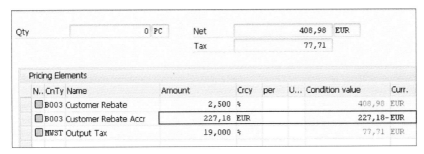

Figure 15.23 Conditions Screen of a Final Settlement

15.1.4 Deletion of Rebate Agreements

You can end a rebate agreement via the menu item AGREEMENT • DELETE. As long as there are no sales volume or payouts, the object is actually deleted from the database. Otherwise, the system creates a settlement with the payment amount zero that serves to reverse the posted accruals. If payouts exist already that you want to reclaim, you should set the amounts of the rebate conditions to zero instead of deleting the agreement and perform a final settlement. The system will then create a debit memo for the already paid sums.

15.1.5 Retroactive Changes and Rebate Index

One of the challenges in rebate processing is the handling of retroactive changes. This means any changes that could affect sales and the resulting cumulative values that have been processed before the time of the changes. An example that we have already discussed was the subsequent creation of a condition record with a validity start date in the past. Other potentially retroactive changes are, for example, deleting a condition record or changing its validity period. In the new method, the adjustment of the accruals amount is rated as retroactive. Changes to scales or the condition amount, however, are not a problem since they do not affect the sales volume.

To determine the missed sales volume, all affected documents must be identified efficiently. For this purpose, rebate processing stores for each billing document item all necessary access data in the *rebate index* table VBOX. There is, for example, a rebate access sequence that searches with the fields KNRZE (payer) and PMATN (price material) for condition records, the concatenated field content of the access fields is stored as a string VAKEY in table VBOX, together with the relevant condition tables, the document number and item number and the date of services rendered. It does not matter whether a condition record was found for this access or not. It is sufficient that a condition record could be created at a later point in time (see Figure 15.24).

Depending on the number of the defined accesses to rebate condition records and billing document items, the number of entries in the VBOX table can be enormous. You should know when exactly an index entry is to be created so that you can limit the number as much as possible.

Invoice 90237296, Item 00010:
VKORG/VTWEG/SPART = 0001/01/01
KNRZE = BON1000
PMATN = HN1080

VBOX

MANDT	KAPPL	KOTABNR	VAKEY	FBUDA	VBELN	POSNR
004	V	001	00010101BON1000 HN1080	03.01.2014	0090237296	000010

Figure 15.24 Example of the Structure of an Entry in the Rebate Index Table VBOX

An entry is created in the rebate index, regardless of whether the access B002 10 was successfully carried out on table 001 in the billing document 90237296.

For all rebate relevant billing documents, entries are generated in table VBOX for all accesses in rebate access sequences, if the following criteria are met:

- The access sequence is assigned to a rebate condition type. It is not necessary that the condition type actually be used in the pricing procedure.
- No field in the access is empty, unless the access allows this explicitly (the INITIAL VALUE ALLOWED indicator).
- The requirement in the access is met. The requirement in the pricing procedure does not matter here.

Customer-Specific Fields for the Rebate Access

If you have defined customer-specific fields in the communication structures in pricing for the rebate access, you must make sure when filling in the billing document to never use the structures VBRK or VBRP, since they are not reliably filled at the time of the VBOX setup. Instead, use the structures XVBRK or XVBRP.

The VBOX table is actually why all the rebates are searched with the same date, which is the date of services rendered. Other dates are not supported, because they are not stored in the respective data.

Now, if a rebate condition is changed retroactively, the system can identify with the rebate index those billing documents, whose field contents (the VAKEY) correspond to the key of the changed condition record.

Since SAP ERP 6.0 EHP 6 in the HANA version, the VBOX table is obsolete. The respective business functions that need to be activated are LOG_SD_REBATE_INDEX and LOG_SD_REBATE_INDEX_SBS. Although they require some additional Customizing settings, it is still advantageous, because you no longer have to worry about the size of the VBOX table, and there is no need for a reconstruction.

In the following section, we briefly introduce the two aforementioned rebate methods and their differences.

Old Rebate Method

If a retroactive change is detected in the old process, then the display of the sales volume and the calculating of the payout values are no longer based on the accumulated data of table S060, but use instead the relevant billing documents directly. For this, all documents must be identified that will contribute to the sales volume, that is, where the pricing would actually determine the corresponding condition record.

To this end, the rebate program selects all billing documents from the index that match the validity and condition keys first. Then it determines if the condition type is actually included in the pricing procedure and whether the assigned requirement and an in addition requirement 002 are met. If both are the case, the document item is taken into account for the sales volume of the rebate. After that, the system determines whether the condition is possibly already present in the pricing result. If so, the local values are transferred and summed. If the condition is not present, the system must derive the base value and the scale base value from the document data. That is relatively simple for quantity-based calculation types. The item quantity (or weight or volume) is converted in the right unit and summed to provide the sales quantity. For percentage-based rebates of value scales, the matter is more complicated. With the old method, every rebate condition type has assigned in the pricing procedure a reference-from step. This step has in turn assigned a subtotal field between 1 and 7, which thus contains the rebate base value. Since these subtotals are stored in the billing document in the VBRP table, rebate processing can directly take the condition base value and the scale base value from the document. One possible configuration is shown in Figure 15.25.

Control															
Reference Step Overview															
Step	Co...	CTyp	Description	Fro	To	Ma...	R...	St...	P	SuTot	Reqt	CalTy...	BasT...	Acc...	Accr...
399	0	R100	100% discount			☐	☐	☐	b		55		28	ERS	
400	0		Rebate Basis			☐	☐	☐		7					
800	0		Net Value for Item			☐	☐	☐	d	2		2			
801	0	NRAB	Free goods			☐	☐	☐	b		59		29	ERS	
810	3	HD00	Freight			✔	☐	☐	B	4				ERF	
815	0	KF00	Freight			✔	☐	☐	B	4				ERF	
816	0		Net Value 2			☐	☐	☐				2			
820	0	HM00	Order value			✔	☐	☐	D					ERS	
901	0	B001	Mat/Group Rebate	400			☐	☐			24			ERB	ERU
902	0	B002	Material Rebate				☐	☐			24			ERB	ERU
903	0	B003	Customer Rebate	400			☐	☐			24			ERB	ERU
904	0	B004	Hierarchy Rebate	400			☐	☐			24			ERB	ERU
905	0	B006	Sales Indpndt Rebate	400			☐	☐			24			ERB	ERU

Figure 15.25 Rebate Condition Types in the Pricing Procedure with the Old Method

The value of the reference step 400 is stored in the document via the allocation of the subtotal field 7 (BONBA, rebate base).

For the pricing, some restrictions result from the described process. For example, formulas (base, value, and scale base) are not allowed for rebate condition types in the old rebate method, as they might not be taken into account when the sales volume is determined using the VBOX table. The respective fields are therefore not ready for input, as you can see in Figure 15.25. Likewise, it is not possible to set the exclusive indicator in the access sequence. However, exclusions between rebate conditions are questionable anyway, since they would be cross-agreement, making them difficult to control.

The verification level of the rebate agreement is generated in the same manner.

The method described here has some serious disadvantages. Therefore, you can certainly imagine that for large rebate agreements, calculating the sales volume for many billing documents takes a long time and also the verification level takes time. This can lead to problems, as during the quarter-end or year-end processing, many settlements need to be processed simultaneously. SAP has therefore introduced the new rebate procedure with for SAP R/3 4.5.

New Rebate Method

The basic idea of the new method is to complete the statistics as soon as changes are performed. Thus, settlements and the display of sales volumes can always be generated based on cumulative data, which is usually much faster. If you change retroactively a condition in the new process, you will get a message the next time you edit the rebate agreement that the data is not current. A settlement of the agreement is then not allowed until the sales data has been updated. This is done with the SDBONT06 report, which you can call using Transaction VBOF or via the menu path SAP EASY ACCESS • LOGISTICS • SALES AND DISTRIBUTION • BILLING • REBATE • UPDATE BILLING DOCUMENTS. The report collects all potentially affected invoices via the rebate index table VBOX and performs a new pricing with pricing type "I" (recalculate rebate conditions). This new pricing exclusively recalculates the rebate condition types. A change to the net or tax value is prohibited. Any changes in the rebate conditions is booked. You will get to know the report SDBONT06 in more detail later in this chapter. For the moment, it is sufficient to know that it corrects the changed rebate conditions in all documents by a new pricing.

> **Performing Update Runs**
>
> You should run the document update as soon as possible after retroactive changes so that you do not need to process unnecessarily many invoices. Note, however, that the report may have a significant runtime. Therefore, you should not run the update too often.

The update itself is not faster than a determination of the rebate based via the rebate index, but you can start the program at any time, so that the individual agreements are updated at different times and the load is distributed over time on the system. Another great advantage is that even formulas for rebate conditions are now possible because of the new pricing. In addition, the accruals are booked according to the original documents, which allows for better control of the profitability of individual sales transactions.

In the new method, the VBOX table is no longer used for the verification level of the rebate agreement. Instead, the specially created statistics table S136 is used, in which each billing document enters its rebate conditions.

The new rebate method is used when you activate the updating of table S136 in Transaction OMO1. For the updating, you should choose the SYNCHRONOUS parameter.

> **Manual Changes of Rebate Conditions in the Document**
>
> Rebate conditions cannot be entered, deleted, or changed manually in the sales documents. Such a change could be retraced neither in the old nor in the new method for retroactive changes and is therefore not permitted.

15.2   Elements of Rebate Processing in Detail

In this section, we will take a closer look at the configuration of rebate processing. You will find the Customizing using the menu path IMG • SALES AND DISTRIBUTION • BILLING • REBATE PROCESSING.

15.2.1   Condition Technique for Rebate Processing

The central element of rebate processing is the rebate condition type. It has the usage E for technical reasons, but is found and evaluated within the pricing. The maintenance of the rebate condition is very similar to the one of the pricing conditions. We will therefore focus on describing the differences.

The settings for rebate conditions can be found under IMG • SALES AND DISTRIBUTION • BILLING • REBATE PROCESSING • CONDITION TECHNIQUE FOR REBATE PROCESSING.

Of course, we meet again the four basic elements of the condition technique: the condition table, access sequence, condition type, and pricing procedure.

Maintain Condition Tables for Rebate Processing

Maintaining the condition tables for rebate processing is not significantly different from that in the pricing. However, the allowed length of the table key is less.

While in the pricing keys are allowed with a total length of 100 characters, there are only 50 characters for rebate tables. This applies also to the length of the key field VAKEY in the VBOX table.

A rebate condition table is created with the name KOTE and a three-digit number, for example, KOTE999. The available field catalog is slightly reduced compared to the pricing one, but can be extended if necessary.

Maintain Access Sequences

In the access sequences, you should note that you must set the type 1 - RELEVANT FOR REBATE (see Figure 15.26). This forces the accesses rebate condition tables to be proposed in the input help. You can only set the exclusive indicator when the new rebate method is activated. However, we advise against using it.

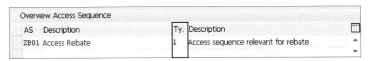

Figure 15.26 Setting the Type 1 - Relevant for Rebate for Access Sequences in Rebate Processing

Define Condition Types

A rebate condition type is characterized by the condition class C - EXPENSE REIM-BURSEMENT (the correct translation from German would be "deferred compensation"). If you choose this attribute, the field selection is significantly reduced (see Figure 15.27). However, there are also a few additional fields. So you can for fixed amount condition types, choose the REBATE PROCEDURE and thus specify whether you want to post accruals for this condition type or not. For conditions with rebate procedure A, the field for the amount of the accruals is not input-enabled in the condition record maintenance.

The second additional field is the ACCRUALS CORRECTION PROCEDURE, which allows you to specify whether the partial accruals are to be reversed for partial settlements or not.

Also worth mentioning is that you determine with the SCALE BASIS attribute the accumulation of scale basis, even if later no scale is maintained in the condition record. The unit of measure field is then used as a proposal for the unit of measure of the scale basis.

Figure 15.27 Configuration of a Rebate Condition Type

The CURRENCY CONVERSION and ACCRUALS indicators are in fact always set implicitly for rebate condition types and do therefore not appear in the configuration screen. The EXCLUSION field is only available for the new rebate method.

Maintain Pricing Procedures

For rebate condition types, there are only a few things to consider. It was already mentioned that in the old method percentage-based rebate condition types must refer to a step level in the pricing procedure that is associated with a condition subtotal. For the new method, this is no longer necessary and in addition the fields for the condition value formula and the base value formula are input-enabled here. The MANUAL indicator is not allowed in any case and therefore hidden. You should not set the STATISTICS indicator. Because in the sales documents the rebate conditions are automatically set as statistical, but in the settlement documents they should not be statistical.

Since rebate conditions trigger the posing of accruals, you must enter two account keys, one for the booking of sales deductions and the other for the accruals (see also Appendix A).

Finally, we would like to point to the TRANSACTION-SPECIFIC PRICING PROCEDURE (TSPP) indicator. You can set this flag if you want to use a pricing procedure in the rebate settlement that contains more condition types than rebates and taxes (Figure 15.28).

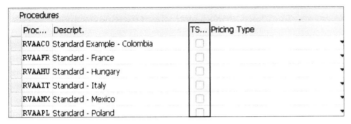

Figure 15.28 Transaction-Specific Pricing Procedure in the Maintenance of Pricing Procedures

15.2.2 Rebate Agreements

The rebate agreement is the central object of rebate processing and contains the essential data of the arrangement. Outside a rebate agreement, you cannot create rebate conditions. By means of the Customizing, you define different default data and procedures for the rebate agreements.

The condition type group defines the set of usable condition types with the respective agreement type

Each rebate agreement type has assigned to a condition type group. In the condition type group, you define the condition types and their condition tables for which the maintenance should be allowed in the agreement type. When creating a new condition type group, you must leave the CATEGORY blank so that the group can be used in rebate processing (Figure 15.29).

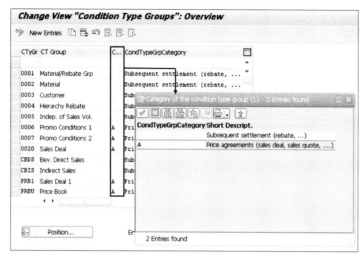

Figure 15.29 Creation of a Condition Type Group for Rebate Processing

In the second step, you assign the desired condition types and tables to the condition type group (Figure 15.30).

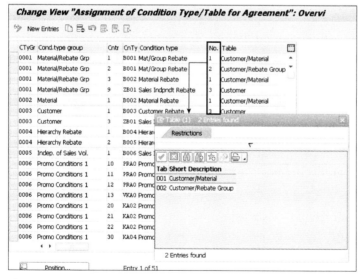

Figure 15.30 Assign Condition Types and Condition Tables to a Condition Type Group

The counter can be selected arbitrarily. The number specifies the condition table number, which is used in the assigned access sequence. In Figure 15.30, you can see, for example, that the condition type group 002 allows only the maintenance of the condition type BO02 in table KOTE001.

In the last step, you assign a condition type group to each agreement type.

The condition type group is also used by the system to find the corresponding condition records that belong to a rebate agreement. Thus, you may not remove any assignments, especially if you have open agreements for an agreement type.

Let us now have a closer look on the configuration possibilities of the agreement type. We'll start by defining the agreement type and then exploring the different field groups.

Define Agreement Types

Each agreement has an agreement type that contains important settings for the agreement. Therefore, it is worthwhile to take a closer look at its fields (Figure 15.31).

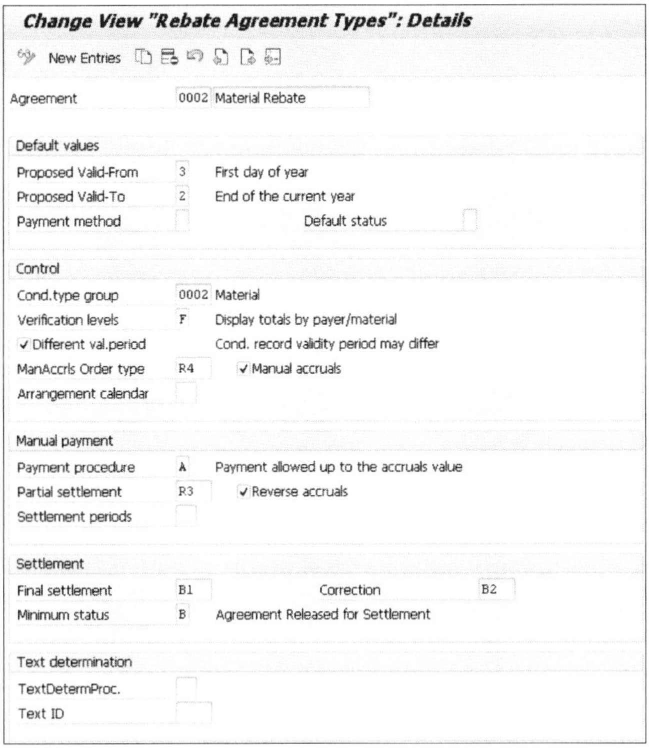

Figure 15.31 Agreement Type 0002 in Detail

The Default Values Field Group

Here you can define some default field contents for the creation of an agreement as follows:

▶ The VALID-FROM field defines the date rule for the validity start-date of the agreement. The system proposes it based on the assigned rule and the current date.

▶ The VALID-TO field specifies the date rule for the validity end-date of the agreement. The system also proposes it based on the assigned rule and the current date.

▶ With the PAYMENT METHOD you determine the method (bank transfer, check, etc.) for the execution of the rebate payout.

▶ The DEFAULT STATUS defies the status that is set during the creation of the rebate agreement. Together with the MINIMUM STATUS for the settlement, you can control whether the agreement has to be checked again before an automatic settlement.

All fields can be changed manually in the agreement.

The Control Field Group

The fields in this area can usually not be changed in the agreement. The important fields and indicators in this area are as follows:

▶ The CONDITION TYPE GROUP defines which conditions types can be maintained in the agreement.

▶ The VERIFICATION LEVELS field defines with which level of detail the verification of the sales volume is displayed for the agreement. You can change the field in the agreement.

▶ If the DIFFERENT VALIDITY PERIOD indicator is set, condition records can be created with deviating validity periods. The duration can be shorter, but not longer than defined in the rebate agreement. You can then maintain the deviating dates via the menu item GOTO • OVERVIEW OF CONDITION RECORDS in the agreement. There, select the view VALIDITY PERIODS (Figure 15.32).

▶ In the MANACCRLS ORDER TYPE field, you determine which order type is used when you want to post manual accruals.

- Select the MANUAL ACCRUALS indicator if you want to enter accruals manually for your agreements. In this case, you must also maintain an order type for the manual accruals.

- The ARRANGEMENT CALENDAR controls the extension of an agreement. *Extension* in this context means that the agreement is copied into a new agreement. The default values for the start and end of an agreement must be consistent with the chosen arrangement calendar. If you use an arrangement calendar, you must not allow a divergent validity period of the condition records.

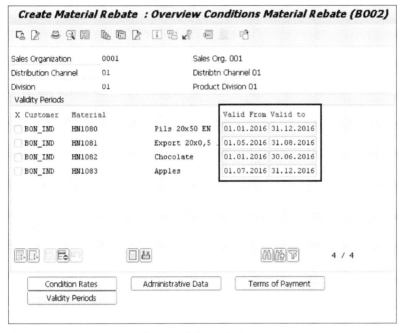

Figure 15.32 Maintaining Different Validity Periods

The Manual Payment Field Group

You control all partial settlements of the agreement—both manual and automatic. The configured parameters cannot be changed in the agreement with the exception of the calendar for the settlement periods. The characteristics combined in the manual payment field group include the PAYMENT PROCEDURE, PARTIAL SETTLEMENT, REVERSE ACCRUALS, and SETTLEMENT PERIODS. Let's explore those characteristics:

- You can specify by the PAYMENT PROCEDURE the level up to which partial settlements are allowed. You can determine, for example, that the partial payment shall not exceed the value of the already posted accruals or that the value is calculated like for a final settlement. The payment procedure not only determines the maximum value of the manual payment, but also the value for the automatic payout. You have to select the payment procedures A or B, if you want to have automatic partial settlements for your agreements.

- The PARTIAL SETTLEMENT field defines the order type used for the partial payment.

- If you set the REVERSE ACCRUALS indicator, the system will also reverse accruals for a partial settlement—namely up to the maximum payment amount or the posted accruals.

- In the SETTLEMENT PERIODS field, you can specify a calendar in which the dates for a periodic billing are maintained. You can then perform an automatic settlement of the agreement in a mass run. The working days of the calendar correspond to the settlement dates of the agreement. The dates must always coincide with the period limits of the sales volume table S060, which is always on a month-end.

The Settlement Field Group

In the FINAL SETTLEMENT field, you can specify the order type that you want to use for the final settlement of the rebate agreement.

If you enter a document type in the CORRECTION field, for the old rebate method a *correction document* is created in the final settlement, if necessary. This document corrects for retroactively changed agreements the cumulative sales volume in the statistics, so that they then meet the values provided by the rebate index table VBOX.

By the MINIMUM STATUS, you can determine the minimum status that an agreement must have before it can be finally settled.

The Text Determination Field Group

Here, a TEXT DETERMINATION PROCEDURE for the agreements can be specified. The text types contained in this text determination procedure can be used in the DETAILS screen of the agreement.

In the field Text ID, the text type can be specified from the assigned text determination procedure, which is to be proposed as a default in Details screen of the agreement.

15.2.3 Activation of Rebate Processing

To be able to create a rebate agreement in a sales organization, you must first activate rebate processing. This can be done using the menu path IMG • Sales and Distribution • Billing • Rebate Processing • Activate Rebate Processing. There you choose the activity Activate rebate processing for sales organizations. Mark the indicator Rebate proc. active for all sales organizations where you want to create rebate agreements. Since both the update of the rebate index VBOX as well as the pricing program check this indicator, you can avoid unnecessary accesses and data records, if you pay attention to set the indicator only when needed.

In the next step, select the activity under the same path Select billing documents for rebate processing and process there just the same. For performance reasons and because of the size of the VBOX table, only actually required billing documents should be marked.

To be able to grant rebates to customers, you still need to mark in the sales area data of the customer master the Rebate (relevance) flag (see Figure 15.33). If your change is to have an effect on already booked documents, you must also regenerate the VBOX table.

Figure 15.33 Mark a Customer as a Rebate Relevant

15.2.4 Document Types for Rebate Processing

We had to specify different document types in the rebate agreement type. We therefore want to take a quick look at these document types and point out the special features.

The order types for the rebate documents are normal credit memo requests. The only special feature can be found in item category. Although it is a credit item, it must not be flagged as returns in order to obtain the correct signs in the settlement conditions. Technically, the pricing program recognizes a rebate settlement document at the filled agreement number in the communication structure KOMK-KNUMA.

For the billing document types, you need to consider a few more things. In order that the accumulation in the statistics table S060 is carried out correctly, the type of the rebate document must be specified in the REBATE SETTLEMENT field (Figure 15.34).

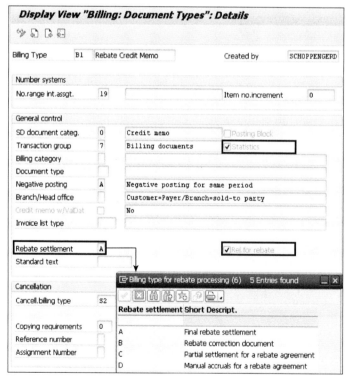

Figure 15.34 Billing Types for Rebate Settlement

Moreover, billing types for rebate settlement must be marked as statistical and relevant for rebate. Do not forget to set these indicators for the associated cancellation document type as well.

15.2.5 Activation of the New Rebate Method

The new rebate method is now the standard method and is preferred by most SAP customers. You can activate it by activating the update of the standard statistics table S136. Make sure that you set the updating to SYNCHRONOUS, and you must recreate table S136 for the existing billing documents if necessary. SAP Note 105681 (Consulting: New Rebate Procedure) contains valuable information on this topic.

15.2.6 Important Reports

In this section, we will introduce the most important reports of rebate processing.

Recalculation of Subtotals

You can call report RV15B003 using Transaction OVG1 or via the menu the path IMG • SALES AND DISTRIBUTION • BILLING • REBATE PROCESSING • RECALCULATE SUBTOTALS FOR REBATE PROCESSING. It is particularly important for the old rebate method. We remember that in the old process we needed to assign to each value-based rebate condition type a subtotal in the pricing procedure. In the case of changes to this Customizing, you can recalculate the subtotals of all billing documents.

Create Billing Index

Behind the menu path IMG • SALES AND DISTRIBUTION • BILLING • REBATE PROCESSING • CREATE BILLING INDEX hides report RV15B001 or Transaction OVB3. With this report, you can rebuild the rebate index table VBOX. For this purpose, the communication structures of the pricing are created for the affected documents and the rebate index is recreated from this data.

Recall that the rebate index is used to find all relevant billing documents in the case of retroactive changes. However, there are changes, in which the index itself is no longer complete. These changes include, for example, changes in the *rebate relevance* of customers, sales organizations, or document types, as well as the creation of new condition tables and access. Furthermore, coding changes to the setup of the pricing communication structures in the respective user exits can also require a recreation of the VBOX table.

Recreation of the Rebate Index VBOX

Check carefully whether VBOX really needs to be rebuilt, that is whether the changes actually have an impact on already booked billing documents. The recreation can have a significant runtime and will mark all open rebate agreements as RETROACTIVELY CHANGED. Thus, for the new method you need also to update all agreements. In the old method, all agreements are then settled based on the rebate index and no longer based on the statistical data, which can also lead to significantly increased runtimes.

Statistical Setup

By extending the structure of the table S060 between the releases of SAP R/3 3.1I and 4.0, it was necessary to rebuild the statistical data of the rebate when upgrading. Today it is hardly of significance, and a recreation of the S060 data should be rarely necessary, unless, for example, statistical relevance of documents is changed or errors occurred in the statistical update. In both cases, you should consider whether partly rebuilding for a specific document type is sufficient. If in doubt, you can simulate the recreation and see if it actually comes to deviations. During the recreation, the selected documents are simply booked again in the statistics. You must therefore ensure that no billing documents are counted twice in the statistics and that they are also not forgotten. For a complete new setup, it is advisable to make several packages of documents and schedule different runs. Only the first run should be started with the flag noting that the statistical data is to be initialized first, that is to be completely deleted. It is advisable to start the run for the latest billing documents first and choose a time when no new billing documents are generated during runtime.

You can then gradually process the older billing documents until the statistics are complete again. You can start the statistical setup using Transaction VFSN or via the menu path IMG • SALES AND DISTRIBUTION • BILLING • REBATE PROCESSING • SIMULATE AND EXECUTE SETUP OF STATISTICAL DATA. The report behind is SDS060RB.

Compare Rebate Basis and Correct Accruals

The report RV15B002 (Transaction VOB3, menu path IMG • SALES AND DISTRIBU-
TION • BILLING • REBATE PROCESSING • COMPARE REBATE BASIS AND CORRECT ACCRU-
ALS) compares the cumulative sales volumes with verification results (Figure
15.35). For the new method, no deviations are to be expected since the statistics
table S060 is kept up to date. For the old method, it may lead to deviations of retroactively changed agreements. In this case, the report allows you to post the
lacking accruals via the CORRECT BACKLOGS button using a correction document
(see the SETTLEMENT field group). In addition, the base and scale base value are
corrected. However, the correction is not appropriate to the period, but falls in
the current period.

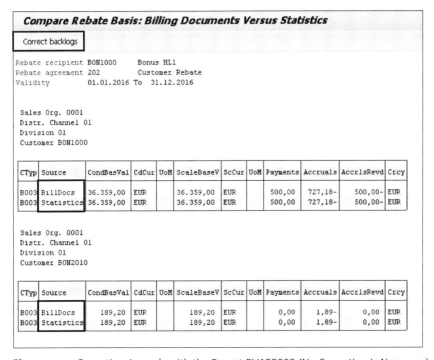

Figure 15.35 Correcting Accruals with the Report RV15B002 (No Correction Is Necessary)

Settlement of Rebate Agreements

The report RV15C001, accessible via Transaction VB(7, is one of the key reports
of rebate processing and is used specifically for the automatic settlement of rebate
agreements (Figure 15.36).

With the entries in the areas REBATE AGREEMENTS and ORGANIZATIONAL DATA, you select the agreements that are to be processed. Make sure to choose the validity end-date so that it includes the desired agreements.

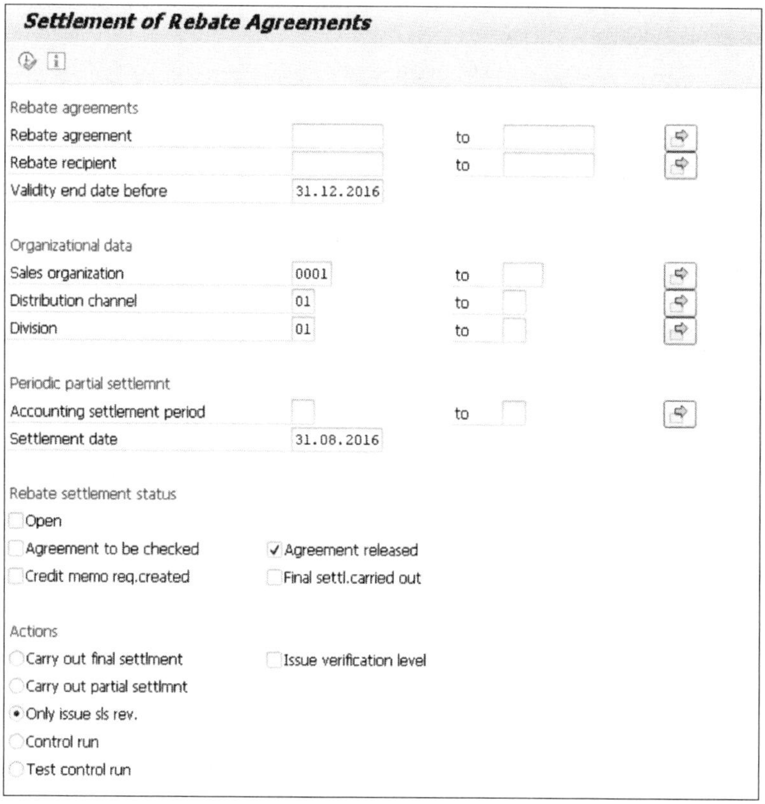

Figure 15.36 RV15C001 (Settlement of Agreements)

The PERIODIC PARTIAL SETTLEMENT area needs only to be filled in if a partial settlement is made. In this case, enter here the ACCOUNTING SETTLEMENT PERIOD and the SETTLEMENT DATE. Make sure that the date corresponds to a settlement date in the settlement period. Only those agreements will be settled that have the same settlement period. In addition, the payment procedures in the agreement types must be either A or B, since otherwise no settlement amount can be calculated. The program will then add up the total sales volume to the settlement date, and then calculate the payout amount. All existing payments are deducted from this amount.

In the REBATE SETTLEMENT STATUS area, you can further restrict the selected rebate agreements.

Finally, you specify the exact action you want to perform. You are already familiar with final and partial settlement. Nevertheless, you can also use the RV15C001 report to display a list of the sales volumes. In this case, you only get as a result a corresponding list (Figure 15.37).

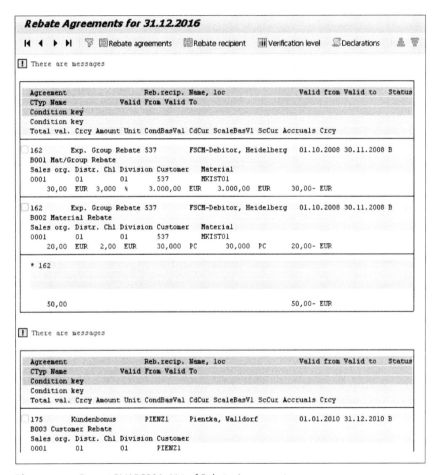

Figure 15.37 Report RV15C001: List of Rebate Agreements

From here, you can convert the status of the agreement using the transaction menu EDIT • RELEASE for all selected agreements.

Finally, we want to mention briefly the control run. For the old method, the pay-out value of finally settled agreements can be recalculated via the rebate index and differences can be settled later. One reason could be that relevant billing documents were created, transferred, or canceled only after the settlement. The new method does not support this feature, since a settlement using the rebate index VBOX table is not provided there.

Update Billing Documents

The second central report of rebate processing is SDBONT06. For the new method, the statistics are completed with this report in the case of retroactive changes of the rebate agreements. SDBONT06 is called with Transaction VBOF (Figure 15.38).

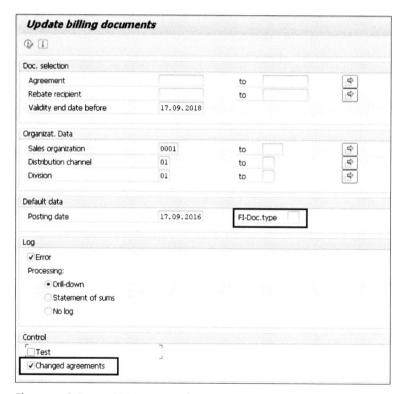

Figure 15.38 Report SDBONT06: Update Billing Documents

The report searches all potentially affected billing documents for the selected rebate agreements. Billing documents, to which changed rebate conditions must be added, are found using the rebate index. Billing documents, from which rebate conditions may need to be removed, are identified using the verification table S136. For all billing documents, a new pricing with pricing type I (recalculate rebate conditions) is performed. If the pricing result is changed, the new result is saved and the difference is reported to accounting. Changes of the net value or the taxes are not permitted. When all billing documents are processed successfully, the RETROACTIVELY CHANGED indicator is reset for the entire agreement.

Net Value and Taxable Value When Updating Billing Documents

If during operation, the pricing procedure changes or formulas are not programmed properly, the net value or the taxable value could change. In such cases, the system terminates the processing without booking the changes. The update cannot be completed. For these cases, you can find help in SAP Note 456458 (FAQ, "How Does the Report SDBONT06 Work?").

A general rule is that an update of the billing documents should be performed after a change as soon as possible so that the number of documents to be processed remains as small as possible. On the other hand, you should perhaps wait at frequent changes until the changes are completed, since the runtime at high volume of billing documents can be significant. Ultimately, you have to find a reasonable compromise for your situation.

Note that the new pricing for the documents, of course, recalculates all the rebate condition types, even those that are not part of the selected agreements. It is therefore advisable to try to combine in the selection agreements that have many common documents.

Changed rebate conditions lead to a second accounting document for the billing document. If you are using accounting document types that have an external number assignment, this can cause problems. In this case, you will need to enter a different accounting document type with internal number assignment in the DEFAULT DATA section.

Using the TEST indicator, you can perform the update without saving, and with the CHANGED AGREEMENTS indicator, you ensure that only retroactively changed agreements are selected.

Extending Rebate Agreements

With report RV15C005 or Transaction VB(D you can *extend* rebate agreements, in which you have specified an arrangement calendar. The validity of the original agreement is not adjusted, but a new agreement in the next period of arrangement calendar is created instead.

Copying Rebate Agreements

With report RV15B004, you can copy an agreement to several new agreements. Simply enter the number of the rebate agreement that is to be copied, and a list of customer numbers that should serve as rebate recipients in the new agreements. The system will also convert the customer numbers in the rebate conditions of the old agreement to rebate conditions with the new customer numbers.

Changing the Agreement Currency of Rebate Agreements

With report RV15C006 or Transaction VBOE, you can modify the agreement currency of a rebate agreement. Initially, the report was intended to replace expiring currencies within long-term rebate agreements at the introduction of the euro.

At this point, we want to take a quick look at the currencies involved in rebate processing. There is, first of all, the obvious agreement currency that determines the currency of the settlement documents and that is stored in the WAERS field in the KONA table. When creating condition records, the agreement currency is passed as condition currency (the KWAEH field in the table KONP) to the conditions. The condition currency determines the currency in which the sales values, that is the sales volume and the accruals, are accumulated. You have already seen in Section 15.1.2, that value and basis of the condition are calculated twice—in document currency and in condition currency—if needed. This ensures that the conversion of the sales volume takes place in the agreement currency at the current exchange rate and no further conversion during settlement is necessary. The accruals are also accumulated in local currency, since it is important to accurately reverse the sum booked in FI with the final settlement

If you change the agreement currency, the condition currency and thus the cumulative statistics remain unaffected. However, this also means that in the settlement, the sales volume is converted as a total into the arrangement currency with the current date. The individual point in time of the single sales revenues remains unconsidered. Therefore, fluctuations in exchange rates can have a significant impact on the final result.

Therefore, it is not recommended that you change the agreement currency when the conversion rate between the old and new currency is not fixed.

Display of Rebate Agreements

Using Transaction VB(8 or the RV15C002 report, you can display a list of rebate agreements.

Prevent Archiving of Billing Documents

Using the SDBONARCH report, you can mark billing documents that are still relevant for current agreements. These mark billing are then blocked for archiving.

Rebate Analysis Tool

The REBATE_GENERAL_ANALYZE report gives a largely complete overview of all aspects of an agreement and may be particularly helpful in finding errors.

15.2.7   Scale Base Determination Based on Grouped Condition Records

SAP ERP allows you to combine the sales volumes of different condition records for the determination of the scale level. You simply need to fill the SCALE GROUP field with any value (Figure 15.39). For all records with the same values, the scale bases are then added to determine the individual scale level. However, you have to make sure that the scale base units of the conditions involved are the same, so that the bases can be added up.

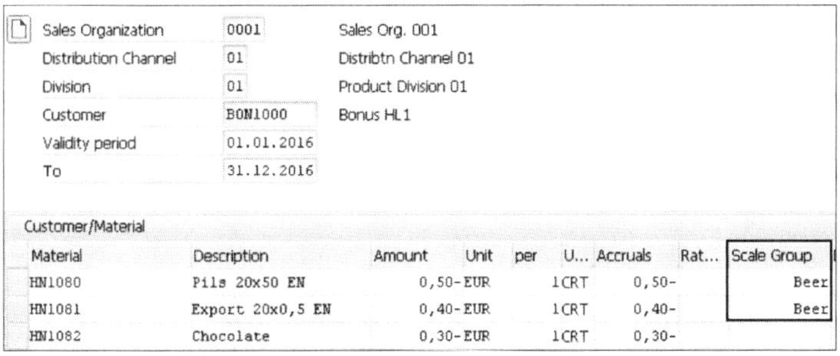

Figure 15.39 Setting the Scale Group for Collective Scale Base Determination

If you do not see in the SCALE GROUP field in your system, it can help to regenerate the maintenance screens with report RV12A001 for the usage E.

15.2.8 Replacement of the Rebate Index Table

Since SAP ERP 6.0 EHP 6, the SAP HANA version, the rebate index table `VBOX` can be dispensed. For this, you must activate either the `LOG_SD_REBATE_INDEX` or `LOG_SD_REBATE_INDEX_SBS` business functions. The system will then identify the relevant billing documents directly, without using the index. Nevertheless, some additional Customizing settings are necessary.

The `VBOX` table is set up with the fields of the communication structures KOMP and KOMK and the knowledge that the KOMK/KOMP field is part of a condition table in an access. However, if we want to find the billing documents directly, we need to know also how the KOMK/KOMP fields arise from the fields of the document.

It is this relationship that we have to define in the Customizing under the menu path IMG • SALES AND DISTRIBUTION • BILLING • REBATE PROCESSING • BILLING DOCUMENT DETERMINATION: CUSTOMER-SPECIFIC MAPPING when we deviate from the standard determination. For example, if we have enhanced KOMK or KOMP and use customer-specific fields. It is helpful in this regard to check the data under the node IMG • SALES AND DISTRIBUTION • BILLING • REBATE PROCESSING • BILLING DOCUMENT DETERMINATION: STANDARD MAPPING (Figure 15.40).

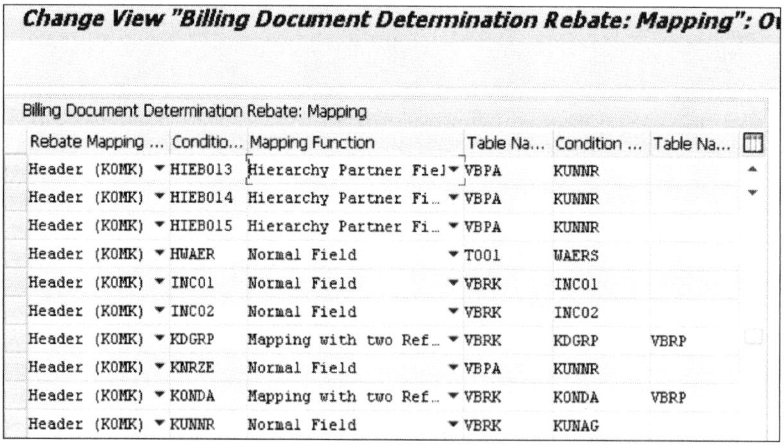

Rebate Mapping ...	Conditio...	Mapping Function	Table Na...	Condition ...	Table Na...
Header (KOMK)	HIEB013	Hierarchy Partner Fiel	VBPA	KUNNR	
Header (KOMK)	HIEB014	Hierarchy Partner Fi...	VBPA	KUNNR	
Header (KOMK)	HIEB015	Hierarchy Partner Fi...	VBPA	KUNNR	
Header (KOMK)	HWAER	Normal Field	T001	WAERS	
Header (KOMK)	INCO1	Normal Field	VBRK	INCO1	
Header (KOMK)	INCO2	Normal Field	VBRK	INCO2	
Header (KOMK)	KDGRP	Mapping with two Ref...	VBRK	KDGRP	VBRP
Header (KOMK)	KNRZE	Normal Field	VBPA	KUNNR	
Header (KOMK)	KONDA	Mapping with two Ref...	VBRK	KONDA	VBRP
Header (KOMK)	KUNNR	Normal Field	VBRK	KUNAG	

Figure 15.40 Assigning Document Fields to Fields of Pricing Communication Structures: Example of the Default Mapping

In most cases, there is a simple 1: 1 relationship between the document field and the communication field. However, there are other relationships that are characterized by a MAPPING FUNCTION and for which there are examples in the standard mapping:

► Some fields are determined from two sources (MAPPING WITH TWO REFERENCE FIELDS), wherein the second source is used if the first does not produce a result. The KONDA field is such a case. Here we need to specify both sources.

► A field specified with IGNORE FIELD is not used for the billing document determination, but only checked in the following pricing. An example of this function can be the campaign ID in the case of polyvalent or subsequent campaigns.

► If fields are used that are not stored in the document, the NONPERSISTENT FIELD mapping must be selected. Then the system will ignore this field initially and can only later restrict the selection of the billing documents with an additional pricing preparation. From a runtime point of view, such fields are of course not ideal.

► Product or partner hierarchy fields (HIERARCHY PARTNER FIELD and PRODUCT HIERARCHY FIELD) are also marked as such, as they are determined specifically.

► The function TABLE WITH ADDITIONAL CONDITION allows formulating a simple selection requirement. With that, you can use a particular partner function for searching in the VBPA table.

► Finally, the field can be also determined by a complex logic in a Business Add-In (BAdI) implementation (COMPLEX LOGIC: BAdI).

15.3 Extended Rebate Processing

If we review our example from Section 15.1, we notice that any knowledge about the composition of sales volume gets lost in the rebate settlement. For the new method, that does not matter since posting the accruals for the documents passes the corresponding information to the controlling. As long as the payment amount is equal to the amount of the reversal of the accruals, the final settlement corresponds to a zero posting. If, as in our example, scales are involved, this is no longer guaranteed. That means that the information in controlling is not complete. This could be avoided with a corresponding number of material-dependent individual postings, but of course that is quite effortful.

Then there is the restriction that a rebate agreement can only be paid to a specific rebate recipient. Especially if one uses rebates in combination with customer hierarchies, it would be desirable to be able to handle all customers of a hierarchy in one combined agreement. You could then summarize, for example, the sales volumes for the determination of the scale level.

Therefore, the *extended rebate processing* was developed for SAP R/3 4.7 Extension Set 2. In short, the extended rebate allows you to accumulate the sales volume separately for specific attributes such as the material number, and then to incorporate these attributes in the settlement. We call this rebate processing with *variable key*.

In addition, the extended rebate offers two additional functions: the handling of indirect sales, which are sales that were not transacted in the ERP system, and a slightly different calculation of periodic settlements.

15.3.1 Implementation of a First Customer-Specific Scenario

We want to familiarize you by an example with the variable key, which is the main feature of the extended rebate. Suppose that we have agreed with a parent company that the group subsidiaries get reimbursed a certain percentage of their sales volume. For the determination of scale levels, however, the total sales volume of all subsidiaries should be considered.

To be able to use the extended rebate processing, you must first activate the Enterprise Extension EA-ISE. Only then you will find the configuration settings in the IMG under the path IMG • SALES AND DISTRIBUTION • BILLING • REBATE PROCESSING • EXTENDED REBATE PROCESSING. Another precondition is the use of the new rebate method.

You can individually switch on the various functions of the extended rebate per agreement type. For this purpose, you select the relevant indicator under the menu path SETTINGS FOR AGREEMENT TYPES at the path specified. There, we choose for the arrangement type Z0E4 the characteristic W/ VAKEY (Figure 15.41).

Next, we must tell the system how we want to split the sales volume. To do this, we need to specify the variable key under the menu path SET UP VARIABLE KEY FOR

REBATE SETTLEMENT. At this point, it is helpful to better understand the operation of rebate processing.

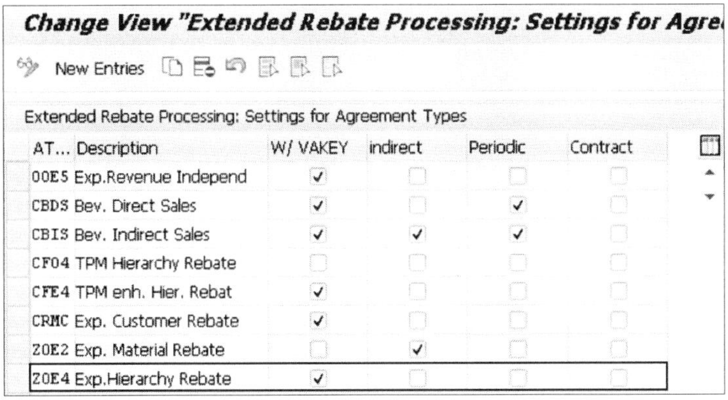

AT... Description	W/ VAKEY	indirect	Periodic	Contract	
00E5 Exp.Revenue Independ	✓	☐	☐	☐	▲
CBDS Bev. Direct Sales	✓	☐	✓	☐	▼
CBIS Bev. Indirect Sales	✓	✓	✓	☐	
CF04 TPM Hierarchy Rebate	☐	☐	☐	☐	
CFE4 TPM enh. Hier. Rebat	✓	☐	☐	☐	
CRMC Exp. Customer Rebate	✓	☐	☐	☐	
Z0E2 Exp. Material Rebate	☐	✓	☐	☐	
Z0E4 Exp.Hierarchy Rebate	✓	☐	☐	☐	

Figure 15.41 Settings for the Extended Rebate per Agreement Type

The extended rebate processing accumulates its sales volumes in the statistics table S469. The difference from table S060 is that an additional key field VAKEY has been introduced. Information from the document is to be copied in this field as a string of the length 100. All fields are available that are provided to the statistics update process. These are in particular the billing document header MCVBRK and the billing document item MCVBRP. For example, if we want that the sales volume be collected per payer and material, we take over the KUNRG field from MCVBRK and MATERIAL from MCVBRP.

In the S469 table, the sales volume is collected and there are also the payouts and the reversed accruals. It is therefore essential that the settlement document connected to a certain VAKEY produce the same VAKEY at its own statistics update so that the payout is associated in the statistics with the correct VAKEY. Therefore, we need to specify for each source field a TARGET FIELD. We can use all fields of the *general billing interface*. This means that the payer in the sales transaction must become the recipient of the rebate settlement. We also want the payer to act as sold-to party, ship-to party, and bill-to party of his settlement. Finally, we transfer the material number. The corresponding configuration is shown in Figure 15.42.

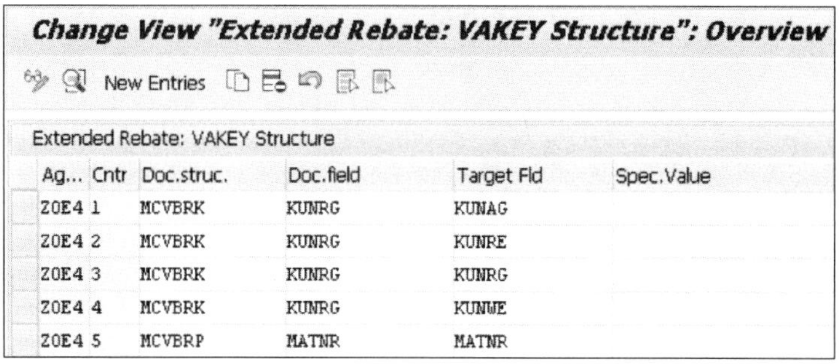

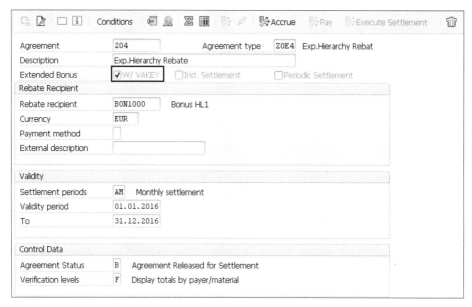

Figure 15.42 Define the Variable Key of an Agreement Type

To enable the accumulation in S469 table, we need to activate the updating of table S469 in Transaction OMO1 or under the menu path ACTIVATE EXTENDED REBATE PROCESSING. The settings must include a monthly accumulation and a synchronous updating for table S060.

Now we can create our rebate agreement. You see in the overview screen that the variable key is active (Figure 15.43).

Figure 15.43 Agreement with Activated VAKEY

We create in the agreement one a single condition record that is valid for all lower-level hierarchy nodes below our rebate recipient.

After we have created some sales transactions for this agreement, we take a look at the sales volume display (Figure 15.44). We see that the sales volume for the condition record has been split in several payer/material combinations. Each of these combinations will become a separate document item in the settlement document. If necessary, several documents are generated. In our example, we expect one document for each deviant payer, that is three documents with one, three, and two items, respectively.

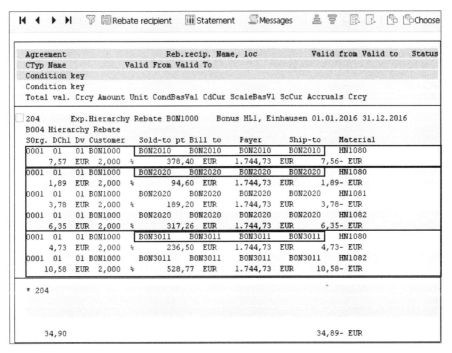

Figure 15.44 Display of the Sales Volume for an Agreement with a Variable Key

For comparison, Figure 15.45 shows the display of an identical agreement, in which the variable key has not been used.

Distribution of Fixed Amount Rebates

In the case of fixed amount condition types, the total payout amount is distributed to the variable keys in relation to the accumulated condition base values.

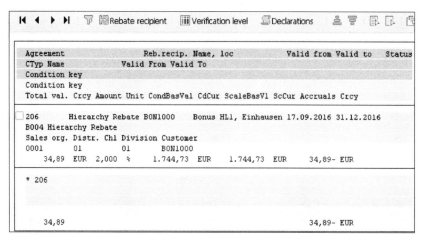

Figure 15.45 Display of the Sales Volume for an Identical Agreement without VAKEY

Finally, we want to settle the agreement. You may have noticed in Figure 15.43 that the buttons for manual payment are inactive in the agreement screen. Indeed, in extended rebate agreements with VAKEY, it is not possible to perform a payout using the payment screen. Currently, you can settle these agreements only using Transaction RBT_ENH_VB7 or via the menu path SAP EASY ACCESS • LOGISTICS • SALES AND DISTRIBUTION • BILLING • REBATE • EXTENDED REBATE PROCESSING • EXTENDED REBATE SETTLEMENT. In both ways, you run the report BON_ENH_SETTLE.

As you can see in Figure 15.46, the input screen of the extended rebate settlement is very similar to the normal rebate settlement. In the extended rebate processing, it is possible to reopen an agreement by cancelling all settlements. You would need to select the CANCEL FINAL SETTLEMENT radio button and—if the original posting period in financial accounting is already closed—specify an alternative posting date. If you make the cancellation here, the status of the agreement is reset and the agreement is marked as retroactively changed, if necessary. In our example, we simply want to process a final settlement.

After we have processed the final settlement, we will look at the generated billing documents. Figure 15.47 shows that three rebate credit memos were generated.

Settlement of Extended Rebate Agreements

Reb. agreements

Rebate Agreement	204	to		⇨
Rebate recipient	BON1000	to		⇨
Validity end date before	17.09.2017			

Organizat. Data

Sales organization	0001	to		⇨
Distribution Channel	01	to		⇨
Division	01	to		⇨

Periodic partial settlemnt

Settlement period		to		⇨
Settlement date	31.08.2016			

Rebate Settlement Status

☐ Open
☐ Release is Checked   ☑ Released
☐ Credit memo req.created   ☐ Final settl.carried out

Actions

● Carry Out Final Settlment   ☐ Issue Proof
○ Carry Out Partial Settlmnt
○ Only Issue Sls Vol.
○ Cancel Final Settlement

Cancel Final Settlement

Posting Date   [   ]

Figure 15.46 Settlement of Extended Rebate Agreements

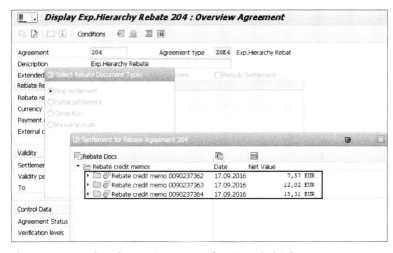

Display Exp.Hierarchy Rebate 204 : Overview Agreement

Agreement	204	Agreement type	Z0E4	Exp.Hierarchy Rebat
Description	Exp.Hierarchy Rebate			

Extended ... Select Rebate Document Types ... ment   ☐ Periodic Settlement
Rebate Re
Rebate re   ● Final settlement
Currency   ○ Partial settlement
Payment   ○ Correction
External c   ○ Manual accruals

Settlement for Rebate Agreement 204

Rebate Docs

▼ Rebate credit memos   Date   Net Value
  ▶ Rebate credit memo 0090237362   17.09.2016   7,57 EUR
  ▶ Rebate credit memo 0090237363   17.09.2016   12,02 EUR
  ▶ Rebate credit memo 0090237364   17.09.2016   15,31 EUR

Validity
Settlemer
Validity pe
To

Control Data
Agreement Status
Verification levels

Figure 15.47 Final Settlement Document of an Extended Rebate Agreement

Settlement Documents for Extended Rebate Agreements

A credit memo is created immediately during the settlement of an extended rebate agreement. A detour via a credit memo request no longer takes place. If you want to check the credit memo before the payout, you should set the posting block in the corresponding document type.

Within the settlement document, we see that the sales volume was allocated between the various materials (Figure 15.48). We have therefore produced from one rebate condition three documents with a total of six items.

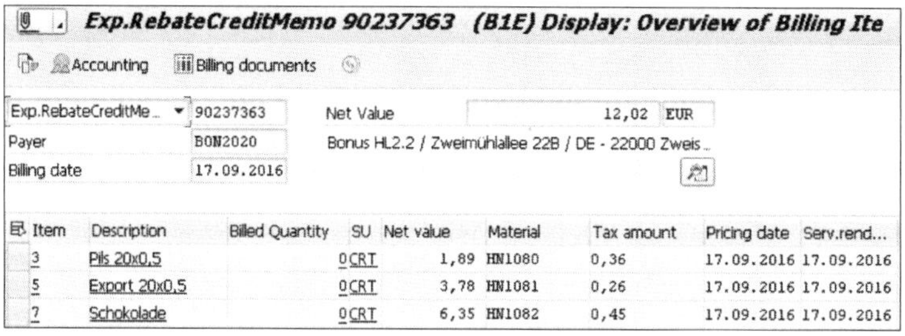

Figure 15.48 Credit Memo Request of the Settlement

With that, our example is finished. We look at the configuration of extended rebate processing in more detail in the next section.

15.3.2 Customizing the Extended Rebate Processing

You have already seen some Customizing settings of the extended rebate processing. In this chapter, we want to fill the gaps. However, we deliberately skip some details that only play a role in certain scenarios, such as, for example, the integration of the contract management or the *pendulum list* in the beverage industry. Let's now look at the configuration of the extended rebate processing in detail.

Activate Extended Rebate Processing

The activation of the extended rebate processing takes place via updating of table S469. The settings must include a monthly accumulation and synchronous updating. The relevant update program is RBT_ENH_RMCSS469.

It is recommended that you first make all other settings for the extended rebate before the update is activated.

Settings for Agreement Types

Here you can switch on the extended features individually for the different agreement types. You can then operate the standard and the extended rebate processing in parallel.

If you have selected for an agreement type one of the features, the settlement can take place only by the settlement report of the extended rebate. In addition, the settlement run creates no credit memo requests. It does create credit memos immediately, meaning billing documents. The settings are stored in the individual agreement types.

Set Up Variable Key for Rebate Settlement

Here you can define for your agreement type which data from the sales you want to use for accumulation and settlement. The fields defined here by DOCUMENT STRUCTURE and DOCUMENT FIELD are concatenated and stored as a variable key VAKEY in the S469 table. All sales transactions with the same VAKEY are accumulated. Sales transactions with different VAKEY are accumulated separately. Let's take a look at the statistics entries to our example in Figure 15.49. We defined that the payer (four times) and the material should be used to distinguish the sales volumes. The VAKEY of table S469 has been filled accordingly.

Table:		S469								
Displayed Fields:	12 of	24		Fixed Columns:			10	List Width 0250		
MANDT	KNUMH	SPMON	SPBUP	VAKEY						
004	0000061585	201609	000000	BON2010	BON2010	BON2010	BON2010	HN1080		
004	0000061585	201609	000000	BON2020	BON2020	BON2020	BON2020	HN1080		
004	0000061585	201609	000000	BON2020	BON2020	BON2020	BON2020	HN1081		
004	0000061585	201609	000000	BON2020	BON2020	BON2020	BON2020	HN1082		
004	0000061585	201609	000000	BON3011	BON3011	BON3011	BON3011	HN1080		
004	0000061585	201609	000000	BON3011	BON3011	BON3011	BON3011	HN1082		

Figure 15.49 Structure of the Field VAKEY in Table S469

The payer was written four times in the VAKEY to fill in the partner roles sold-to party, ship-to party, bill-to party, and payer.

You must also specify the field in which during the settlement to the field of the sales value is to be transferred. We have defined that the payer in the sales transaction was to be used as sold-to party, ship-to party, bill-to party, and payer in the settlement documents and that the material is reused. This ensures that payers and materials in the payment documents correspond to those in the sales transactions.

> **Use of the Target Field in the VAKEY Variable Key**
>
> It is absolutely necessary that the settlement document produces the same VAKEY as the related sales orders to make sure that the payments and the reversals of the accruals are written in the correct statistics record. Otherwise, partial settlements cannot be properly allocated and considered.

If you change the Customizing of the variable key of a rebate agreement, the new settings are ignored if postings already exist for this agreement type. This is to ensure that the sales volume data remains consistent in table S469. Only when you rebuild the contents of table S469 (see the next section) are the changed Customizing settings activated. Note, however, that existing payouts might not be correctly allocated if the VAKEY was changed.

Simulate and Execute Reorganization of Statistical Data

You can rebuild the statistics table of the extended rebate. The function corresponds to that of the rebuild of table S060 that was already presented.

Periodic Settlement

The periodic settlement differs from the known settlement in that all periods are regarded as small individual agreements. In the ordinary periodic partial settlement, the sales volume is summed up to date for all periods since the start date of the agreement and this value is used to calculate the payout amount. If the PERIODIC indicator is set in the extended rebate for the agreement type, the sales volume of the single periods is used individually to calculate the payout value per period. There are differences, especially at scales, because the scale base is also evaluated per period. Fixed amounts are payable once per period. A once settled period is no longer taken into account in future payments. The final settlement settles all outstanding periods and reverses all remaining accruals.

Extended Rebate Processing for Indirect Sales

In some industries, the rebate-relevant sales does not take place directly between rebate recipient and rebate granter, but for example by an intermediary. The rebate is therefore paid for *indirect sales*. We call this *indirect rebate*. The extended rebate processing provides some support to bring indirect sales into the system and thus to provide this sales volume to rebate processing.

These revenues must first be stored in a customer-specific table of the LIS. This part is your task. In the Customizing, you make this table known to the rebate processing. From this information, the system generates reports that create specific billing documents based on that table content. During the creation of these billing documents, a pricing is performed that determines all relevant rebate condition types and thus fills the statistics.

We will look at the process in more detail now. First, we define a table in the Sales Information System. The table should have a monthly period and two versions. Under one version, we save the planned data, which is the sales volume that we expect. Based on this date, we will post accruals. Under another version, we store the actual data, which is the actual sales volume. In Figure 15.50, you can see an example of such a table. It is important that the table contains the structure BON_ENH_S1.

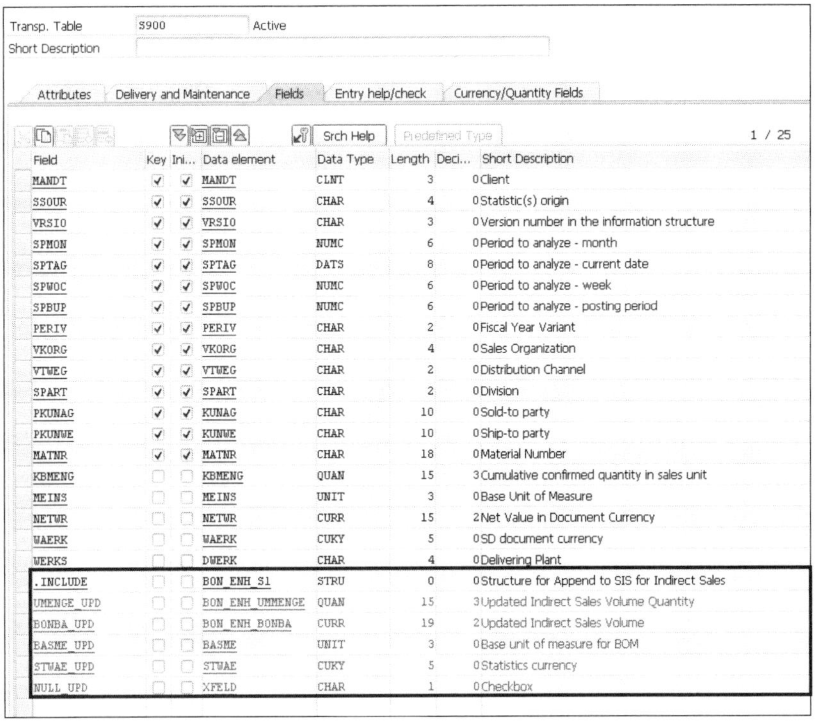

Field	Key	Ini...	Data element	Data Type	Length	Deci...	Short Description
MANDT	✓	✓	MANDT	CLNT	3	0	Client
SSOUR	✓	✓	SSOUR	CHAR	4	0	Statistic(s) origin
VRSIO	✓	✓	VRSIO	CHAR	3	0	Version number in the information structure
SPMON	✓	✓	SPMON	NUMC	6	0	Period to analyze - month
SPTAG	✓	✓	SPTAG	DATS	8	0	Period to analyze - current date
SPWOC	✓	✓	SPWOC	NUMC	6	0	Period to analyze - week
SPBUP	✓	✓	SPBUP	NUMC	6	0	Period to analyze - posting period
PERIV	✓	✓	PERIV	CHAR	2	0	Fiscal Year Variant
VKORG	✓	✓	VKORG	CHAR	4	0	Sales Organization
VTWEG	✓	✓	VTWEG	CHAR	2	0	Distribution Channel
SPART	✓	✓	SPART	CHAR	2	0	Division
PKUNAG	✓	✓	KUNAG	CHAR	10	0	Sold-to party
PKUNWE	✓	✓	KUNWE	CHAR	10	0	Ship-to party
MATNR	✓	✓	MATNR	CHAR	18	0	Material Number
KBMENG			KBMENG	QUAN	15	3	Cumulative confirmed quantity in sales unit
MEINS			MEINS	UNIT	3	0	Base Unit of Measure
NETWR			NETWR	CURR	15	2	Net Value in Document Currency
WAERK			WAERK	CUKY	5	0	SD document currency
WERKS			DWERK	CHAR	4	0	Delivering Plant
.INCLUDE			BON_ENH_S1	STRU	0	0	Structure for Append to SIS for Indirect Sales
UMENGE_UPD			BON_ENH_UMMENGE	QUAN	15	3	Updated Indirect Sales Volume Quantity
BONBA_UPD			BON_ENH_BONBA	CURR	19	2	Updated Indirect Sales Volume
BASME_UPD			BASME	UNIT	3	0	Base unit of measure for BOM
STWAE_UPD			STWAE	CUKY	5	0	Statistics currency
NULL_UPD			XFELD	CHAR	1	0	Checkbox

Figure 15.50 Example of an Update Structure for Indirect Sales

Next, we specify the billing types with which we will post the indirect sales. You can find two examples—BIND and BINP—in the standard Customizing. They both have the document pricing procedure E. Thus we can assign these billing types their own pricing procedure. We will come back to this in a minute. First, we make the necessary settings using the menu path IMG • Sales and Distribution • Billing • Rebate Processing • Extended Rebate Processing • Extended Rebate Processing for Indirect Sales • Settings to Create Indirect Billing Documents. In addition to the billing types, we need to provide the sales order types and item categories for their creation, so that the corresponding copy control can be found in the billing processing (Figure 15.51).

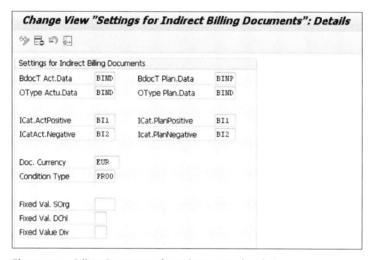

Figure 15.51 Billing Documents for Indirect Actual and Plan Data

It is also important to specify a condition type. For value-based condition types, the value is stored here. This condition type must exist in the pricing procedure found with the document pricing procedure E. In order that the billing documents get no net value, this condition type should be marked as statistical.

There is also a special feature for the rebate condition types in the pricing procedure. You need to provide all the rebate condition types with the value formula 329 (Indirect Sales Vol.). The formula will ensure that, for the planned data, only the accruals are calculated. For the actual data, the base value and scale base value are calculated and accumulated. An example pricing procedure is shown in Figure 15.52.

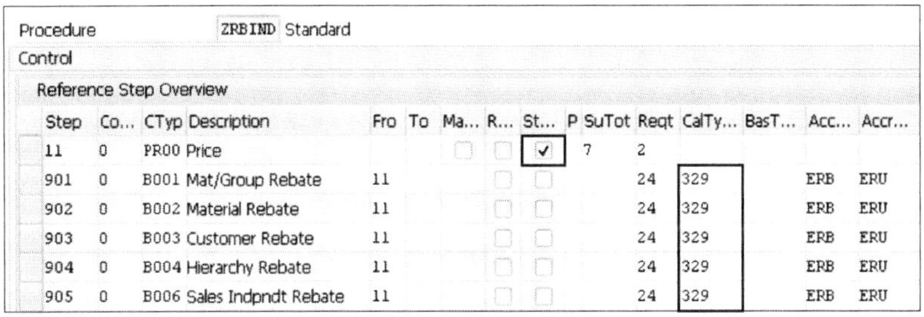

Step	Co...	CTyp	Description	Fro	To	Ma...	R...	St...	P	SuTot	Reqt	CalTy...	BasT...	Acc...	Accr...
11	0	PR00	Price			☐	☐	✓	7	2					
901	0	B001	Mat/Group Rebate	11			☐	☐			24	329		ERB	ERU
902	0	B002	Material Rebate	11			☐	☐			24	329		ERB	ERU
903	0	B003	Customer Rebate	11			☐	☐			24	329		ERB	ERU
904	0	B004	Hierarchy Rebate	11			☐	☐			24	329		ERB	ERU
905	0	B006	Sales Indpndt Rebate	11			☐	☐			24	329		ERB	ERU

Procedure ZRBIND Standard / Control / Reference Step Overview

Figure 15.52 Example Pricing Procedure for the Sales Volume Update of an Indirect Rebate

Once all the settings have been made, we can generate the needed reports. For this, the IMG activity IMG • SALES AND DISTRIBUTION • BILLING • REBATE PROCESSING • EXTENDED REBATE PROCESSING • EXTENDED REBATE PROCESSING FOR INDIRECT SALES • GENERATE UPDATE OF INDIRECT SALES is available (Figure 15.53). You still have to define in your structure the fields containing the relevant information for the billing.

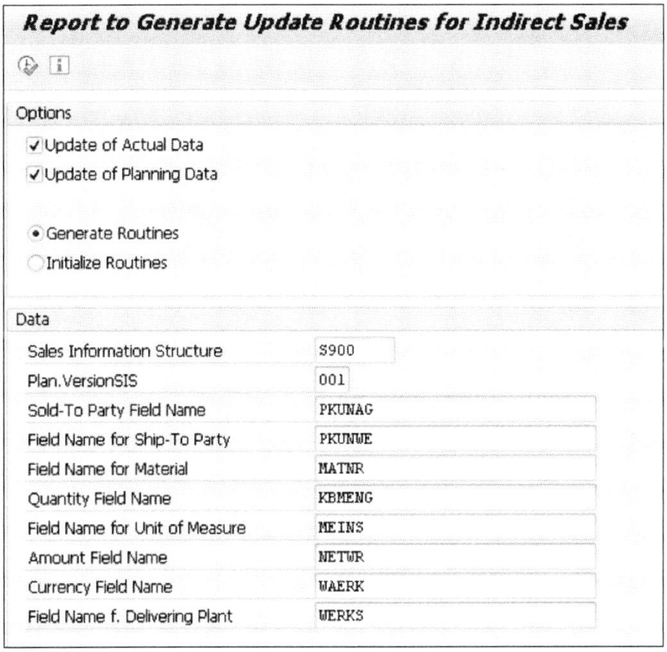

Report to Generate Update Routines for Indirect Sales

Options
- ✓ Update of Actual Data
- ✓ Update of Planning Data
- ● Generate Routines
- ○ Initialize Routines

Data

Sales Information Structure	S900
Plan.VersionSIS	001
Sold-To Party Field Name	PKUNAG
Field Name for Ship-To Party	PKUNWE
Field Name for Material	MATNR
Quantity Field Name	KBMENG
Field Name for Unit of Measure	MEINS
Amount Field Name	NETWR
Currency Field Name	WAERK
Field Name f. Delivering Plant	WERKS

Figure 15.53 Generation of the Update Routines for Indirect Sales

After the reports are generated, you can create the billing documents using the menu path SAP Easy Access • Logistics • Sales and Distribution • Billing • Rebate • Extended Rebate Processing • Update of Indirect Sales.

Of course, we will find in these billing documents rebate condition types of standard rebate agreements. So you might wonder for what purpose you set the Indirect indicator at all. Actually, this is necessary only if you use the Periodic indicator at the same time. In that case, the system will not allow the settlement of a period before the actual data is posted.

15.4 System Adaptation in Rebate Processing

If you have exploited all possibilities of the standard configuration in the Customizing, there are still some places in rebate processing where you can engage with your own code. We list these points in the following sections.

15.4.1 Business Transaction Event 00503201

The event is called immediately before the generation of the billing document in the standard rebate processing and allows last-minute changes to the input values for header, item, partner roles, and condition types of the credit memo request.

You can assign in Transaction FIBF your own function module for the 00503201 event. The function module OUTBOUND_CALL_00503201_E serves as a template for the interface. Note that payout values that have changed there are not visible in the sales volume display or in the payment screen due to processing point in time.

> **Inbound Interface of BTE 00503201**
>
> ► REBATE_AGREEMENT: Rebate agreement, table KONA.
> ► REBATE_AGREEMENT_TYPE: Rebate agreement type, table T6B1.
> ► CREDIT_NOTE_TYPE: Type of settlement (1 – Final settlement, 2 – Adjustment document, 3 – Partial settlement, 4 – Manual accruals).
> ► CONDITION: Involved condition records, table KONP.
> ► CONDITION._SCALE: Involved scales, structure CONDSCALE.
> ► CREDIT_NOTE_POSITIONS: Data for the item and payout values, structure BONUSKOM.
> ► PARTNERS: Partner table, structure VBPAKOM.

Outbound Interface of BTE 00503201

- ▸ CONDITION: Involved condition records, table KONP.
- ▸ CONDITION._SCALE: Involved scales, structure CONDSCALE.
- ▸ CREDIT_NOTE_POSITIONS: Data for the item and payout values, structure BONUSKOM.
- ▸ PARTNERS: Partner table, structure VBPAKOM.
- ▸ SALES_HEADER: Document header, structure VBAKKOM.

The event is not executed in the extended rebate, as there no credit memo requests (see Section 15.3.1).

15.4.2 BAdI BADI_SD_REBATES

The BADI_SD_REBATES BAdI was developed for the handling of multi-value fields in rebate processing. It also aims to facilitate the handling of access fields that are not stored in the billing document and that change frequently over time. You have already learned that changing master data can require a recreation of the rebate index. However, this is impracticable with frequent changes, and this BAdI can provide remedy.

Suppose you want grant a rebate to a customer on a product segment (however, you would need to expand the field catalog in rebate processing) that contains several materials. From time to time, materials are added to this segment. It is not useful for product segments to write VBOX entries when they are not reliably valid anyway. In this case, you should store, instead of the product segment, stable information from which the product segment can be reliably derived at any time (for example the material number). You do this by defining a second access that includes the relevant alternative information. You assign this access to the rebate condition type, to make sure that VBOX entries are written also for this data. Instead of the combination customer/product segment, you are updating customer/material in the VAKEY. The unwanted entries can be filtered using the REDUCE_VBOX_ENTRIES method.

When updating the billing documents, you can use the MODIFY_VBOX_READ method to redirect the actual condition key to the alternative the key. For this purpose, you must search all associated materials for the product segment in the condition record. From this data, you derive the relevant combinations customer/material and use this information to determine the billing documents. Let's take a closer look at the methods of the BAdI.

REDUCE_VBOX_ENTRIES Method

This method is performed during the VBOX update in the billing process.

Inbound Interface of the REDUCE_VBOX_ENTRIES Method

- CT_NAMEVALUE: List of the names of polyvalent access fields and their values.
- CT_T682I: List of rebate accesses.
- C_MVA_REQUESTED: Set if multi-value attributes exist and are to be updated.

Outbound Interface of the REDUCE_VBOX_ENTRIES Method

- CT_NAMEVALUE: Reduced list of the names of polyvalent access fields and their values.
- CT_T682I: Reduced list of rebate accesses that are updated.
- C_MVA_REQUESTED: May be deleted if multi-value attributes are not to be updated.

With this method, you can remove access and attributes for which you do not want to write VBOX entries, for example, for all accesses with the product segment.

MODIFY_VBOX_READ Method

The missing entries in VBOX must be reconstructed when an agreement changes. This is the purpose of the MODIFY_VBOX_READ method.

Inbound Interface of the MODIFY_VBOX_READ Method

- IS_VAKE: Variable key and other information of the condition record for which the relevant billing documents are to be found.

Outbound Interface of the MODIFY_VBOX_READ Method

- E_SKIP: When set, no billing documents for this access are sought.
- C_VAKEY: The VAKEY that's used to search in the VBOX table can be changed.
- CT_HELPTAB: Specification of additional billing documents that are to be processed.

In our example, you could determine all valid material for the product segments to find all the relevant billing documents via the VBOX entries of the alternative access and display them.

The C_VAKEY parameter can be used if the original key is converted to exactly one alternative key. For multi-value attributes, it may be desirable, for example, to reduce the number of VBOX entries. Instead of an access with other fields, you can define an alternative access, which allows an initial value for the multi-value attribute and uses the initial value (e.g., via a corresponding direct value in the access sequence). In the MODIFY_VBOX_READ method, you then redirect the actual condition key to the one with the initial value. However, you will then find and check more billing documents, as would be necessary. That means that you pay for the reduced number of VBOX entries with a loss of performance.

BUILD_INDEX_WITH_PROCEDURE Method

This method can help reduce the number of VBOX entries. If the PC_WITH_PROCEDURE_ACTIVE parameter is set, only the access sequences that are actually included in the current pricing procedure are included.

15.4.3 BAdIs of Extended Rebate Processing

The enhanced rebate offers the ways covered in the following sections to intervene in rebate processing.

BAdI RBT_ENH_BADI_SETTLE

Using the methods of this BAdI, you can influence the calculation of the payment value and the creation of the payment document.

BONUS_BASE_MODIFY Method

With this method, you can change the base value or the scale base value for the settlement of a condition record.

Inbound Interface of the BONUS_BASE_MODIFY Method

- ▸ IS_KONA: Header of the rebate agreement.
- ▸ IS_KONP: Current condition record.
- ▸ CV_TOTAL_BASE: The total condition base value calculated by the system. It is used, for example, to determine the proportionate value of fixed-amount condition types.
- ▸ CS_TURNOVER: Cumulative values for the condition record, summed over all variable keys.
- ▸ CT_TURNOVER_VAKEY: Cumulative values of the variable keys of the condition record.

Outbound Interface of the BONUS_BASE_MODIFY Method

► CV_TOTAL_BASE: Changed condition base value.

► CS_TURNOVER: Changed cumulative values for the condition record.

► CT_TURNOVER_VAKEY: Changed cumulative values to the variable keys of the condition record.

To change the values, you have to change the corresponding fields in the CS_TURNOVER and CT_TURNOVER_VAKEY structures.

BONUS_METHOD_SELECT Method

With this method, you can choose rules for the scale level determination or for the payment of fixed amounts.

Inbound Interface of the BONUS_METHOD_SELECT Method

► IS_KONA: Header of the rebate agreement.

► IT_KONP: Current condition record.

Outbound Interface of the BONUS_METHOD_SELECT Method

► E_SCALE_ON_ON_VAKEY_LEVEL: When set, the scale level is not determined by the sum of all scale bases of the various variable keys, but individually for each key.

► E_FIXED_AMOUNT_ON_VAKEY: When set, the full amount is paid for all variable keys for fixed-amount condition types.

► E_FIXED_FLAT_DISTRIBUTION: At present, no function.

BONUS_VALUE_MODIFY Method

With this method, you can adjust the payout values calculated by the system.

Inbound Interface of the BONUS_VALUE_MODIFY Method

► IS_KONA: Header of the rebate agreement.

► IS_KONP: Current condition record.

► IT_TURNOVER: Contains the sales volume information for all condition records of the agreement.

► IT_CONDITION_SCALE: Contains the scales for all conditions.

- IS_PERIOD_DATAB: Start date of the period to be settled.
- IS_PERIOD_DATBI: End date of the period to be settled.
- CT_BONUS_RECORDS: Values determined by the system that are to be used for the payment.
- CT_SETTLEMENT_VALUES: Payout information for all condition records, summed for the variable keys.
- CT_SETTLEMENT_VALUES_ENH: Payout information for all condition records for all variable keys.

Outbound Interface of the BONUS_VALUE_MODIFY Method

- CT_BONUS_RECORDS: Changed values that are to be used for the payment.
- CT_SETTLEMENT_VALUES: Changed payout information for all condition records, summed for the variable keys.
- CT_SETTLEMENT_VALUES_ENH: Changed payout information for all condition records for all variable keys.

Note that you keep the three tables CT_BONUS_RECORDS, CT_SETTLEMENT_VALUES, and CT_SETTLEMENT_VALUES_ENH consistent. It is advisable here to take a look at the documentation of the interface. Any changes you make here are visible in the sales volume display of the agreement.

BONUS_DATA_MODIFY Method

With this method, you can change the data with which the settlement document is created.

Inbound Interface of the BONUS_DATA_MODIFY Method

- IS_KONA: Header of the rebate agreement.
- IS_LINE_ITEMS: Payout values for the conditions and the variable keys.
- CS_KOMFKGN: Header and item data for the creation of the billing document.
- CT_KOMFKKO: Condition data for the creation of the billing document.

Outbound Interface of the Method BONUS_DATA_MODIFY

- CS_KOMFKGN: Header and item data for the creation of the billing document.
- CT_KOMFKKO: Condition data for the creation of the billing document.

BAdI RBT_ENH_BADI_IND

This BAdI allows you to extend the update of the indirect rebate.

15.5 Typical Practice Demands

We want to conclude the chapter on rebate processing by still discussing some typical practice demands and their possible solution.

15.5.1 Exclusion

You want to grant a rebate to a customer to its total sales volume, but to exclude specific materials. One possibility would be to create individual condition records for all enclosed products, but this is quickly quite cumbersome and costly in practice in the case of many products. Since the exemptions are to be defined per agreement, the usual exclusion methods of the pricing are also no solution. Thus, we need to dig down deep into the bag of tricks. For this purpose, we define a new rebate condition type ZEXC, (e.g., by copying BO02) and assign it to the condition maintenance group of the desired agreement type. If we now create a rebate agreement for a customer, we will create for each material to be excluded an appropriate ZEXC condition record with amount zero and accruals zero. In addition, we will insert ZEXC in our pricing procedure before the actual rebate condition type. To our actual rebate condition type, we assign a value formula, as shown in Listing 15.1. By this formula, the actual rebate condition type is removed, if for the same agreement number the condition type ZEXC was found, which means that the material was excluded from the agreement.

```
FORM frm_kondi_wert_953.
  DATA: ls_komv type komv.
  LOOP AT xkomv INTO ls_komv.
    IF sy-tabix GE xkomv_tabix AND xkomv_tabix NE 0.
      EXIT.
    ENDIF.
    IF ls_komv-kschl EQ 'ZEXC'
       AND ls_komv-knuma_bo EQ xkomv-knuma_bo.
      xkomv-kinak = 'Z'.
      EXIT.
    ENDIF.
  ENDLOOP.
ENDFORM.                         "FRM_KONDI_WERT_953
```

Listing 15.1 Condition Value Formula 953 for the Exclusion of Rebate Conditions of the Same Agreement

Finally, we still want to remove the ZEXC condition from the settlement (Listing 15.2). In the standard rebate, we can use the business transaction event from Section 15.4.1. For the extended rebate, the method BONUS_DATA_MODIFY is provided.

```
FUNCTION Z_BONUS_KOND_FILTER.
......
  DATA: ls_condition TYPE konp,
        ls_position TYPE bonuskom.

  LOOP AT condition INTO ls_condition.
    IF ls_condition-kschl = 'ZEXC'.
      DELETE condition INDEX sy-tabix.
    ENDIF.
  ENDLOOP.
  LOOP AT credit_note_positions INTO ls_position.
    IF ls_position-kschl = 'ZEXC'.
      DELETE credit_note_positions INDEX sy-tabix.
    ENDIF.
  ENDLOOP.
ENDFUNCTION.
```

Listing 15.2 Implementation of the BTE 00503201 for Filtering Conditions in the Settlement (Standard Rebate Method)

Do not worry, even if the ZEXC condition does not appear in the final settlement, its status is still set to D - FINAL SETTLEMENT OF AGREEMENT ALREADY CARRIED OUT.

15.5.2 Settlement Material and Tax Classification

For rebate conditions with settlement material, this determines, among other things, the tax classification and thus the tax amount in the settlement documents. If, however, the sales volume is composed of materials with different tax classification, this is not 100% correct. One solution is to include the tax classification in the access of the condition and to create a condition record per tax classification with an appropriate settlement material. However, it is generally desired to combine these conditions again in the determination of the scale level. For this purpose, you can use the scale group described in Section 15.2.7 or use the extended rebate and process the settlement with the original material.

15.5.3 External Control of Rebate Processing

In the context of other applications, or in-house developments, it may be necessary to read the data from rebate agreements and possibly even make postings.

For this purpose, since the release of SAP ERP, different modules in the function group V14API are available. Since their existence is not widely known, we want to list them briefly here. Their use, however, remains the domain of experts, because it requires a deeper technical understanding of the data types in rebate processing.

SD_REBATES_SALES_VOLUME Module

This module returns the sales volume of one or more rebate agreements.

SD_REBATES_GET_OPEN_AMOUNT Module

The module returns the open payment amount for a specified payment date. Unlike the module SD_REBATES_SALES_VOLUME, the amount depends on the date and considers the open partial settlement documents. In addition, the payment amount is calculated in accordance with the payment procedure of the arrangement type.

SD_REBATES_FINAL_SETTLE Module

With this module, you can process a final settlement for an agreement (standard or extended). The settlement values can be determined from outside. If you use this feature, it is advisable to call the function module twice—the first time without the ADD_SETTLE indicator to get the default values and the second time then with the adjusted payout values the ADD_SETTLE indicator set.

SD_REBATES_PARTIAL_SETTLE

Using this module, you can initiate a partial settlement. As with the final settlement, you can determine in a first call the default values and return the adjusted values in a second call.

SD_REBATES_MANUAL_ACCRUAL Module

With this module, you can book additional accruals.

SD_REBATES_CORRECTION Module

This module creates a correction document that can serve to correct the following values: base value, scale base value, accruals, and payout value. If you correct accruals, they are actually posted in FI. In contrast, if you correct base value, scale base value, or payout value, only the statistics are adjusted by the adjustment document. In particular, no actual payment is triggered. Thus, you can use this module to make payouts outside the agreement, for example, by a credit memo or a price reduction, known to the agreement.

15.6   Summary

We have now come to the end of *Pricing and Condition Technique in SAP ERP*. In this concluding chapter, you became familiar with rebate processing in sales, even if we have omitted some aspects, such as the integration with Trade Promotion Management. You have seen how closely rebate processing is interwoven with pricing and the condition technique and you learned about the possibilities that provides for you. We hope that this can give you ideas for how to tackle your demands in rebate processing.

A   Condition Type Profiles

You have seen in the course of this book that ultimately it is all about condition types. We listed many examples and we consider it helpful to provide you with an overview of the most important condition types. Here, you will find all relevant configuration settings at a glance. We mention in each case only those parameters of the condition type and the underlying pricing procedure that must be set. All others can—and some even must—remain initial.

In addition, we consider only those condition types that have a special feature, and additionally list all condition types Zxxx that we have created in the course of the book for the solution of the different requirements. These do not exist in the standard SAP system, and you must create them as described, if you want to use one or the other suggested function. The same holds true for all formulas and requirements with the key numbers greater than or equal 900 (part of the respective customer namespace). If you are looking for the coding of these routines, look in the index. The pricing procedures listed are just examples, in which the respective condition type is contained or can be used.

The condition types are listed here in alphabetical order. For each condition type, a table of configuration information will be presented.

A.1   AMIW (Minimum Sales Order Value)

With the condition types AMIW and AMIZ, a minimum order value can be established. The corresponding condition records that determine this minimum value are maintained for condition type AMIW. The access sequence K020 used in this case is an example and must in general be adapted to the company requirements. The condition itself is statistical, and the minimum order value in the sales order is active only by the complementary condition type AMIZ. Interesting here is the behavior of the condition in subsequent documents, if order quantities change. See Chapter 12, Section 12.9 for more information.

Configuration Parameter	Technical Name	Description
Access sequence	K020	Price group
Condition class	A	Discount or surcharge
Calculation type	B	Fixed amount
Group condition	x	
Manual entries	D	Not possible to process manually
Item condition	x	
Pricing procedure	RVAA01	Standard
Requirement	002	Item with pricing
Subtotal	D	Value transfer to XWORKD
Statistical condition	x	

Table A.1 Configuration of Condition Type AMIW

A.2 AMIZ (Minimum Value Surcharge)

Condition type AMIZ calculates the difference between the net value of the item at this point (komp-netwr) and the value of the preceding condition type AMIW (working variable xworkd) by the condition value formula 013.

The access sequence must be the same as for condition type AMIW. AMIZ is configured as a reference to AMIW, which means the condition type appears only if AMIW was determined previously. Note also Chapter 12, Section 12.9.

Configuration Parameter	Technical Name	Description
Access sequence	K020	Identical with AMIW
Condition class	A	Discount or surcharge
Calculation type	B	Fixed amount
Manual entries	D	Not possible to process manually
Item condition	x	
Reference condition type	AMIW	
Reference application	V	
Pricing procedure	RVAA01	Standard

Table A.2 Configuration of Condition Type AMIZ

Configuration Parameter	Technical Name	Description
Requirement	002	(Such as for AMIW)
Cond. value formula	013	Minimum value Surcharge
Account key	ERS	Sales deductions

Table A.2 Configuration of Condition Type AMIZ (Cont.)

A.3   AZWR (Down Payment/Down Payment Settlement)

The condition type AZWR is used in sales orders with (partial) billing plans. It represents:

- ▶ In down payment request invoices, the value of the payment request
- ▶ In partial and final invoices, the value of the advance payment to be settled

The value of the condition type is not determined using condition records, but within the program via the `PRICING_COPY` function module.

Configuration Parameter	Technical Name	Description
Condition class	A	Discount or surcharge
Calculation type	B	Fixed amount
Condition category	e	Down payment request/ settlement
Item condition	x	
Changes: value	x	
Pricing procedure	RVAA01	Standard
Requirement	002	Item with pricing
Cond. value formula	048	Check down payments
Account key	ERL	Sales revenues

Table A.3 Configuration of Condition Type AZWR

A.4   BOO1 (Material/Material Group Rebate)

The condition type BOO1 is representative of all rebate conditions.

These condition types are statistical in the billing documents, where they serve to trigger the posting of accruals for the later payments in the course of rebate settlement. The condition records can only be maintained within a rebate agreement. Figure A.1 shows an example condition record. In the sales orders/invoices, the accruals percentage is used to trigger the posting of accruals. The scales are taken into account during the rebate settlement because only at this point in time is the accumulated sales volume known for the entire period. Account determination for billing documents is performed using the account key for accruals. For this account key (e.g., ERU – Rebate Accruals), two general ledger accounts must be assigned: The sales deduction account and the reserve account. The account key for accruals is also used in the resolution of the booked accruals within the bonus settlement documents.

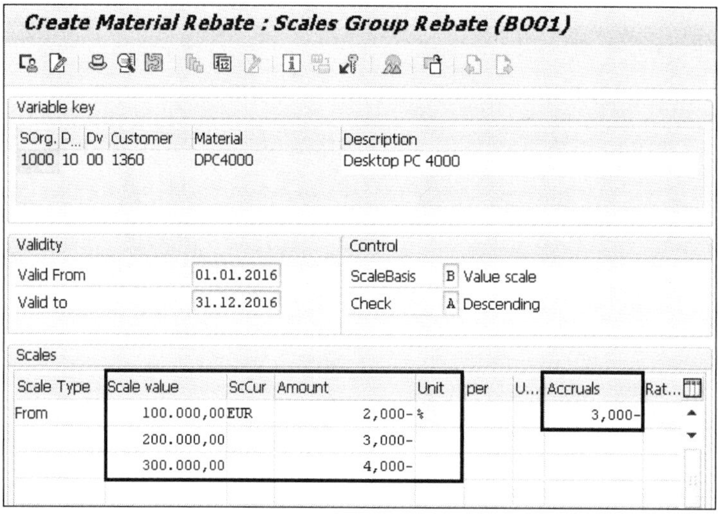

Figure A.1 Condition Record for Condition Type BO01

Configuration Parameter	Technical Name	Description
Access sequence	BO01	Material rebate/rebate group
Condition class	C	Expense reimbursement
Calculation type	A	Percentage
Plus/minus sign	x	Negative
Scale basis	B	Value scale

Table A.4 Configuration of Condition Type BO01

Configuration Parameter	Technical Name	Description
Check value	A	Descending
Pricing procedure	RVAA01	Standard
Requirement	024	Only in billing doc
Requirement (alternative)	002	In sales order and billing doc
Account key	ERB	Rebate sales deductions
Account key: accruals	ERU	Rebate accruals

Table A.4 Configuration of Condition Type BO01 (Cont.)

A.5 DIFF (Rounding of the Total)

The condition type DIFF is used to round the final amount of the pricing result of the sales document.

The value of the condition type is not determined using condition records, but by the condition value formula 016. The rounding rule is defined in the customizing table T001R. The condition type is particularly needed in Switzerland to provide the *5-centime rounding*. The value of the condition type represents the rounding difference and is usually posted in accounting to a separate account. In the pricing procedure, the condition type is located directly after the tax conditions. This differs from normal discounts/surcharges that take part in the calculation of the base amount used for tax determination, but this is no problem as long as the rounding difference is small. In the 5-centime rounding, DIFF has a maximum of 0.02 CHF. Today's standard tax rates applied to this value result in zero, so the reconciliation to accounting is not a problem.

Configuration Parameter	Technical Name	Description
Condition class	a	Discount or surcharge
Calculation type	b	Fixed amount
Condition Category	I	Generally new when copying
Group condition	x	
Manual entries	d	Not possible to process manually
Item condition	x	

Table A.5 Configuration of Condition Type DIFF

Configuration Parameter	Technical Name	Description
Pricing procedure	rvaa01	Standard
Requirement	013	Rounding as per T001R
Cond. value formula	016	Rounding the total
Base value formula	004	Net value plus tax
Account key	ERS	Sales deductions

Table A.5 Configuration of Condition Type DIFF (Cont.)

A.6 DUPL (Condition to Be Duplicated)

The condition type DUPL can be used in structured sales orders with main items and subitems. It is used to enter manual discounts or surcharges in main items. These are then copied (duplicated) to all the subitems of the respective main during pricing.

The functionality is limited to the discounts or surcharges with calculation type A, percentage.

Configuration Parameter	Technical Name	Description
Condition class	A	Discount or surcharge
Calculation type	A	Percentage
Structure condition	A	Condition to be duplicated
Item condition	x	
Pricing procedure	RVAA01	Standard
Manual condition	x	
Requirement	002	Item with pricing
Account key	ERS	Sales deductions

Table A.6 Configuration of Condition Type DUPL

A.7 EDI1 (Customer Expected Price)

With the condition type EDI1 (customer expected price), the price of an order item expected by the customer can be entered in the sales order.

The condition type can be entered manually or via an EDI process. The condition value formula 008 (expected value) compares the net value determined by the pricing to the transmitted value. When it exceeds a tolerance limit, the order item is set incomplete by the formula and a release process is launched (Transaction V.25, Release Customer Expected Price). The comparison value is determined by the positioning of the condition type in the pricing procedure. The tolerance limit can be adjusted to specific requirements by setting up a customer-specific condition value formula.

Configuration Parameter	Technical Name	Description
Condition class	B	Prices
Calculation type	C	Quantity
Condition category	J	Customer expected price
Item condition	X	
Pricing procedure	RVAA01	Standard
Manual condition	X	
Statistical condition	x	
Requirement	002	Item with pricing
Cond. value formula	008	Expected value

Table A.7 Configuration of Condition Type EDI1

A.8 EDI2 (Customer Expected Value)

In EDI2, an order item is entered into the expected value.

Configuration Parameter	Technical Name	Description
Condition class	B	Prices
Calculation type	B	Fixed amount
Condition category	J	Customer expected price
Item condition	x	
Pricing procedure	RVAA01	Standard
Manual condition	x	

Table A.8 Configuration of Condition Type EDI2

Configuration Parameter	Technical Name	Description
Statistical condition	x	
Requirement	002	Item with pricing
Cond. value formula	008	Expected value

Table A.8 Configuration of Condition Type EDI2 (Cont.)

A.9 EK01 (Actual Cost)

Within the resource-related billing (Transaction DP90), the actual cost of the services to be invoiced is passed to the billing request via condition type EK01 (see Chapter 7, Section 7.6.5).

The condition type is not statistical and therefore determines the starting price, which can possibly be overridden by a subsequent price. The value is stored in the line item (vbap/vbrp-wavwr).

Configuration Parameter	Technical Name	Description
Condition class	B	Prices
Calculation type	C	Quantity
Condition category	Q	Costing
Item condition	x	
Pricing procedure	PSER02	Resource related billing
Manual condition	x	
Subtotal	B	Value transfer to WAVWR
Requirement	002	Item with pricing
Account key	ERL	Sales revenues

Table A.9 Configuration of Condition Type EK01

A.10 EK02/EK03 (Calculated Costs)

With this condition, types in sales processes with make-to-order planned costs, which are obtained from an order calculation or a production order, are passed to the order item (see Chapter 7, Section 7.6.4).

The value is stored in the line item (vbap/vbrp-wavwr).

Configuration Parameter	Technical Name	Description
Condition class	B	Prices
Calculation type	C	Quantity
Condition category	Q	Costing
Item condition	x	
Pricing procedure	RVAA01	Standard
Manual condition	x	
Subtotal	B	Value transfer to WAVWR
Statistical condition	x	

Table A.10 Configuration of Condition Types EK02 and EK03

A.11 GRWR (Statistical Value)

The statistical condition type GRWR calculates the statistical cross-border value for export transactions (see Figure A.2).

The value is required for creating the export documents and for notification to the authorities and is stored in the line item (vbap/vbrp-gkwrt).

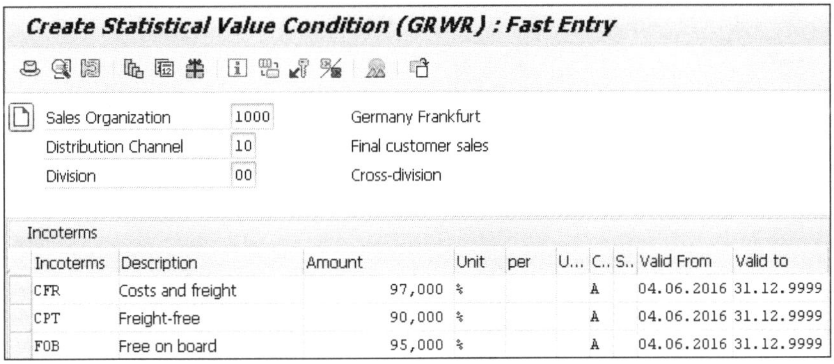

Figure A.2 Condition Record for Condition Type GRWR

Configuration Parameter	Technical Name	Description
Access sequence	K033	Incoterms 1
Condition class	B	Prices
Calculation type	A	Percentage
Condition category	L	Generally new when copying
Item condition	x	
Pricing procedure	RVAA01	Standard
Requirement	008	Export business
Subtotal	C	Value transfer to GKWRT
Statistical condition	x	
Base value formula	002	Net value

Table A.11 Configuration of Condition Type GRWR

A.12 HA00 (Percentage Discount)

With condition type HA00, a discount percentage can be entered manually in the HEADER CONDITIONS screen of the sales document, which applies to all items.

At the latest when leaving the HEADER CONDITIONS screen, the condition type is inserted in all items, if an associated requirement in the pricing procedure is fulfilled. In this context, the *rounding difference comparison* is performed (see Chapter 10, Section 10.2).

Configuration Parameter	Technical Name	Description
Condition class	A	Discount or surcharge
Calculation type	A	Percentage
Group condition	x	
Header condition	x	
Pricing procedure	RVAA01	Standard
Manual condition	x	
Requirement	002	Item with pricing
Account key	ERS	Sales deductions

Table A.12 Configuration of Condition Type HA00

A.13   HB00 (Discount (Value))

With condition type HB00, a discount amount can be entered manually in the HEADER CONDITIONS screen of the sales document, which then applies to the entire document.

The amount is distributed to all items that fulfill a possibly associated requirement. The distribution is performed in relation to the condition base value. This base value can be influenced by the use of a base value formula. If no base value formula is assigned, the current item value is taken (which can also be formed by statistical condition types). In this context, the *rounding difference comparison* is performed (see Chapter 10, Section 10.2 and Chapter 12, Section 12.9).

Configuration Parameter	Technical Name	Description
Condition class	A	Discount or surcharge
Calculation type	B	Fixed amount
Group condition	x	
Header condition	x	
Pricing procedure	RVAA01	Standard
Manual condition	x	
Requirement	002	Item with pricing
Base value formula	002	Distribution proportionally to net value
Base value formula (alternative)	012	Distribution proportionally to gross weight
Base value formula (alternative)	013	Distribution proportionally to net weight
Base value formula (alternative)	001	Distribution proportionally to volume
Account key	ERS	Sales deductions

Table A.13 Configuration of Condition Type HB00

A.14 HD00 (Freight)

The condition type HD00 is designed to enter a gross weight-dependent freight surcharge in any unit of weight in the HEADER CONDITIONS screen of the sales document.

The amount entered is inserted in all items that fulfill a possibly associated requirement. The calculation is done only at item level and no rounding difference comparison is carried out. The requirement assigned to the condition type in the pricing procedure determines in which document types the condition type will be considered. Requirement 957 (not for free goods and returns), presented in Chapter 12, Listing 12.3, can also be used here.

Configuration Parameter	Technical Name	Description
Condition class	A	Discount or surcharge
Calculation type	D	Gross weight
Condition category	F	Freight
Header condition	X	
Pricing procedure	RVAA01	Standard
Manual condition	X	
Requirement	002	Item with pricing
Requirement (alternative)	057	Not for free goods
Requirement (alternative)	957	Not for free goods/returns
Account key	ERF	Freight revenue

Table A.14 Configuration for Condition Type HD00

A.15 HI02 (Hierarchy/Material Discount)

With condition type HI02, condition records for material discounts can be established on each node of the customer hierarchy. Noteworthy in this context are the considerations in Chapter 1, Section 1.8.2, where we presented an alternative access sequence Z901, which is more general than the access sequence HI02 that's used here.

Configuration Parameter	Technical Name	Description
Access sequence	HI02	Customer hierarchy/material
Access sequence (alternative)	Z901	Customer hierarchy (generalized)
Condition class	A	Discount or surcharge
Calculation type	C	Quantity
Plus/minus sign	X	Negative
Item condition	X	
Scale basis	C	Quantity scale
Quantity conversion	X	
Pricing procedure	RVAA01	Standard
Requirement	002	Item with pricing
Account key	ERS	Sales deductions

Table A.15 Configuration for Condition Type HI02

A.16 HM00 (Order Value)

With the condition type HM00 (order value), you can manually enter a total value in the sales order.

As with condition type HB00, the entered order value is distributed proportionally among all items that fulfill a possibly associated requirement. The same distribution mechanisms apply. Interesting are the considerations for this condition type in Chapter 8, Section 8.2.4, and Chapter 12, Section 12.9.

Configuration Parameter	Technical Name	Description
Condition class	B	Prices
Calculation type	B	Fixed amount
Group condition	X	
Header condition	X	
Pricing procedure	RVAA01	Standard
Manual condition	X	
Requirement	002	Item with pricing

Table A.16 Configuration for Condition Type HM00

Configuration Parameter	Technical Name	Description
Base value formula	002	Distribution proportionally to net value
Base value formula (alternative)	012	Distribution proportionally to gross weight
Base value formula (alternative)	013	Distribution proportionally to net weight
Base value formula (alternative)	001	Distribution proportionally to volume
Account key	ERS	Sales deductions

Table A.16 Configuration for Condition Type HM00 (Cont.)

A.17 IV01 (Intercompany Price)

The condition type IV01 is used in the *cross-company sales* process within the internal intercompany billing. The condition type is configured with reference to the condition type PI01. That is, the price for internal billing between the supplying and selling company is determined by the condition records for PI01. The original condition PI01 cannot be used for reasons of value assignments in CO-PA (PI01 is *costs* and IV01 is *revenue*).

Configuration Parameter	Technical Name	Description
Access sequence	PI01	Plant/material
Condition class	B	Prices
Calculation type	C	Quantity
Item condition	X	
Reference condition type	PI01	
Reference application	V	
Condition for inter-company billing	X	
Quantity conversion	X	
Pricing procedure	ICAA01	Intercompany billing
Requirement	022	Inter-company

Table A.17 Configuration for Condition Type IV01

Configuration Parameter	Technical Name	Description
Subtotal	9	Value transfer to BRTWR
Account key	ERL	Sales revenues

Table A.17 Configuration for Condition Type IV01 (Cont.)

A.18 KP00 (Pallet Discount)

With condition type KP00, a discount can be granted for whole units of measure, such as a complete pallet (see Figure A.3). The prerequisite is that the products sold are convertible in the unit of PAL (pallet). The determined pallet quantity of an order item is converted into a whole number (integral) by base value formula 022.

You should also read the considerations in Chapter 12, Section 12.9.

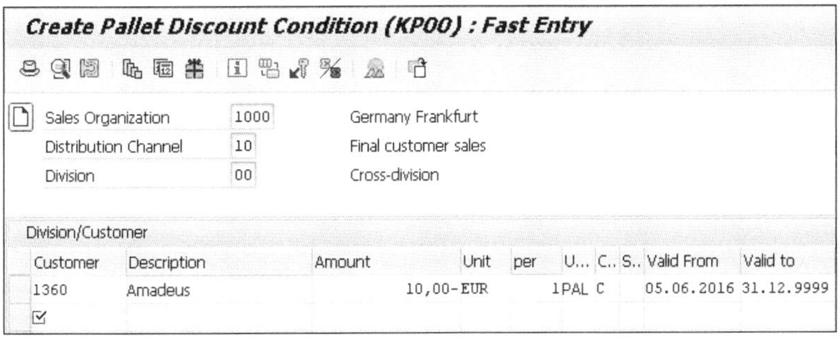

Figure A.3 Condition Record for Condition Type KP00

Configuration Parameter	Technical Name	Description
Access sequence	K307	Customer
Condition class	A	Discount or surcharge
Calculation type	C	Quantity
Plus/minus sign	x	Negative
Item condition	x	
Quantity conversion	x	
Unit of measure	PAL	Pallet

Table A.18 Configuration for Condition Type KP00

Configuration Parameter	Technical Name	Description
Pricing procedure	RVAA01	Standard
Requirement	002	Item with pricing
Requirement (alternative)	057	Not for free goods
Base value formula	022	Whole number
Account key	ERS	Sales deductions

Table A.18 Configuration for Condition Type KP00 (Cont.)

A.19 KP01 (Incomplete Pallet Surcharge)

With condition type KP01, a surcharge can be determined if the quantity of an ordered material does not correspond to a whole number of pallets (see Figure A.4). Base value formula 024 sets the condition base value 1, if the pallet quantity is not a whole number. Requirement 957 (not for free goods and returns), presented in Chapter 12, Listing 12.3, can also be used here.

You should also read the considerations in Chapter 12, Section 12.9.

Configuration Parameter	Technical Name	Description
Access sequence	K307	Customer
Condition class	A	Discount or surcharge
Calculation type	C	Quantity
Plus/minus sign	x	Negative
Item condition	x	
Quantity conversion	x	
Unit of measure	PAL	Pallet
Pricing procedure	RVAA01	Standard
Requirement	002	Item with pricing
Requirement (alternative)	057	Not for free goods
Base value formula	024	1 if partial quantity
Account key	ERS	Sales deductions

Table A.19 Configuration for Condition Type KP01

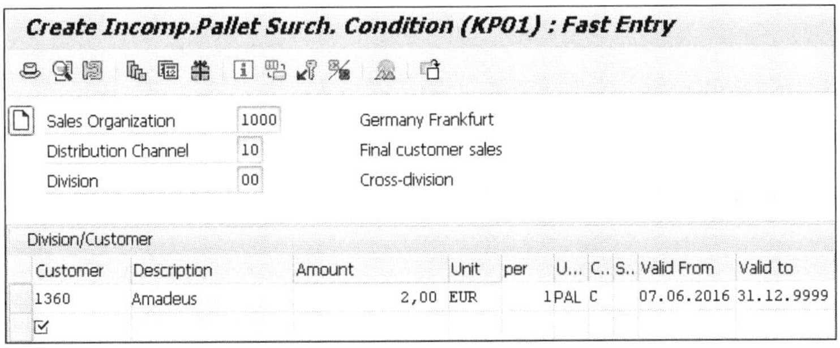

Figure A.4 Condition Record for Condition Type KP01

A.20 KP02 (Mixed Pallet Discount)

With condition type KP02, a discount can be granted if the entire order quantity fills whole pallets (see Figure A.5). Since this is a condition type with the calculation type FIXED AMOUNT, the considerations in Chapter 12, Section 12.9, could be of interest to you.

Configuration Parameter	Technical Name	Description
Access sequence	K307	Customer
Condition class	A	Discount or surcharge
Calculation type	B	Fixed amount
Plus/minus sign	x	Negative
Group condition	x	
Item condition	x	
Scale basis	C	Quantity scale
Unit of measure	PAL	Pallet
Check value	A	Descending
Pricing procedure	RVAA01	Standard
Requirement	002	Item with pricing
Requirement (alternative)	057	Not for free goods
Account key	ERS	Sales deductions

Table A.20 Configuration for Condition Type KP02

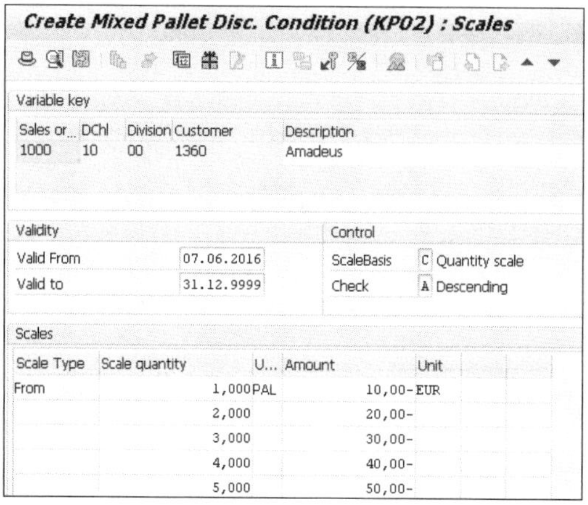

Figure A.5 Condition Record for Condition Type KP02

A.21 KP03 (Mixed Pallet Surcharge)

With condition type KP03, a surcharge can be determined if the entire order quantity does not fill whole pallets (see Figure A.6). The scale base formula 023 (partial quantity) sets the scale quantity to zero during the group processing (PRICING_COMPLETE), if the entire order quantity fills whole pallets. Since this is a condition type with the calculation type FIXED AMOUNT, the considerations in Chapter 12, Section 12.9, could be of interest to you. Furthermore, requirement 957 (not for free goods and returns), presented in Chapter 12, Listing 12.3, can also be used here.

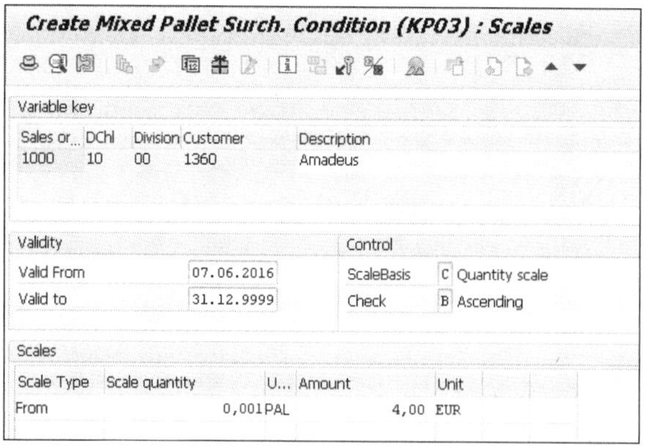

Figure A.6 Condition Record for Condition Type KP03

Configuration Parameter	Technical Name	Description
Access sequence	K307	Customer
Condition class	A	Discount or surcharge
Calculation type	B	Fixed amount
Group condition	x	
Item condition	x	
Scale basis	C	Quantity scale
Unit of measure	PAL	Pallet
Check value	B	Ascending
Scale base formula	023	Partial quantity
Pricing procedure	RVAA01	Standard
Requirement	002	Item with pricing
Requirement (alternative)	057	Not for free goods
Requirement (alternative)	957	Not for Free Goods/returns
Account key	ERS	Sales deductions

Table A.21 Configuration for Condition Type KP03

A.22 KUMU (Cumulative Condition)

The condition type KUMU can be used in structured sales orders with main items and subitems (e.g., sales BOMs) to make values of subitems visible as statistical information on the main item as a total.

The value is determined by the condition value formula 036 (cumulative condition) and the value is calculated with the net value of the current item, plus the net value of its subitems. It is possible to use a value other than the net value, for example, the internal value given by condition type VPRS. You only need to copy the source code of formula 036 into a customer-specific formula (e.g., 936) and replace the komp-NETWR field with komp-wavwr. The condition type KUMU must then of course be positioned behind the condition type VPRS. Thus, you could, for example, make the cost of the free goods subitems in the main item visible and with some skill calculate an additional profit margin with a new condition value formula.

It is possible to use several such cumulative condition types.

Configuration Parameter	Technical Name	Description
Condition class	A	Discount or surcharge
Calculation type	G	Formula
Structure condition	B	Cumulative condition
Group condition	x	
Manual entries	D	Not possible to process manually
Item condition	x	
Pricing procedure	RVAA01	Standard
Requirement	002	Item with pricing
Cond. Value formula	036	Cumulative condition
Statistical condition	x	

Table A.22 Configuration for Condition Type KUMU

A.23 KW00 (Group Valuation, Transfer Price)

In intercompany sales processes, an internal cross-company billing between the involved company codes takes place. In addition to internal prices (condition types PI01, PI02, IV01, and IV02), the valuation with group-internal prices, which can be defined by condition type KW00, plays a role.

The valuation is carried out within the program via the `TP_MATERIAL_PRICES_GET` function module.

Configuration Parameter	Technical Name	Description
Condition class	B	Prices
Calculation type	B	Fixed amount
Condition category	b	Transfer price for group valuation
Manual entries	D	Not possible to process manually
Item condition	x	
Quantity conversion	x	
Pricing procedure	ICAA01	Intercompany billing

Table A.23 Configuration for Condition Type KW00

Configuration Parameter	Technical Name	Description
Requirement	022	Intercompany
Statistical condition	x	

Table A.23 Configuration for Condition Type KW00 (Cont.)

A.24 MW01 (Tax Trigger)

Condition type MW01 triggers the tax determination via the tax determination procedure from accounting (see Figure A.7). The condition is only used to find a date-dependent tax code with which the actual tax determination is performed. For a detailed description, see Chapter 7, Section 7.4.2.

Configuration Parameter	Technical Name	Description
Access sequence	MWST	Tax on sales
Condition class	G	Tax classification
Calculation type	A	Percentage
Manual entries	D	Not possible to process manually
Item condition	x	
Pricing procedure	all	
Requirement	010	Plant is set
Statistical condition	x	

Table A.24 Configuration for Condition Type MW01

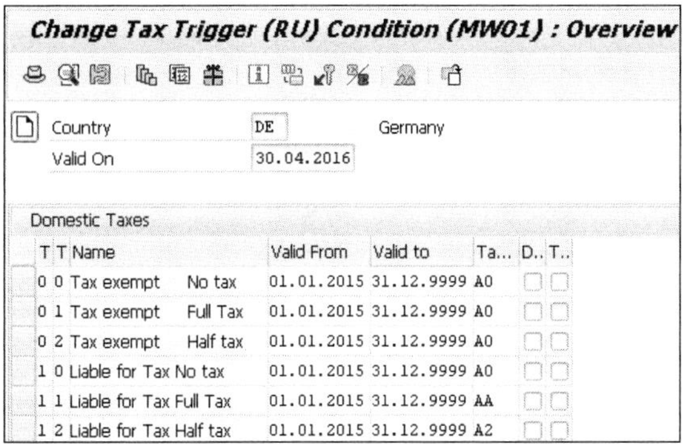

Figure A.7 Condition Records for Condition Type MW01

A.25 MW15 (Factoring Discount Tax) (Full Tax)

The condition type MW15 is used to calculate the tax for invoice list condition types (e.g., RL00, factoring discount) in invoices relevant to invoice lists.

By using the access sequence MWM1, the full tax is always applied to the invoice list conditions. Thus, the condition type MW15 will, in the sale of a product with tax classification 2 (half tax), apply the full tax rate for commissions (e.g., RL00) or freight surcharges that are, as a service, fully taxable separately. Invoice list condition types are statistically in the invoice and are only activated within the invoice list. The condition is referenced to MWST so that the condition records for condition type MWST are read.

Configuration Parameter	Technical Name	Description
Access sequence	MWM1	Tax on sales - full rate
Condition class	D	Tax
Calculation type	A	Percentage
Group condition	x	
Manual entries	D	Not possible to process manually
Item condition	x	
Reference condition type	MWST	
Reference application	V	
Condition for invoice list	x	
Pricing procedure	RVAA01	Standard
Reference step – from/to	nnn	Reference step – from/to of the invoice list condition types
Requirement	021	Invoice list control
Statistical condition	x	
Account key	MWS	Taxes on sales/purchasing

Table A.25 Configuration for Condition Type MW15

A.26   MWSI (Output Tax, Percentage Included)

The condition type MWSI serves to separate the tax in pricing procedures, where the starting price includes the tax. The condition is referenced to condition type MWST.

Configuration Parameter	Technical Name	Description
Access sequence	MWST	Tax on sales and purchasing
Condition class	D	Tax
Calculation type	H	Percentage included
Group condition	x	
Manual entries	D	Not possible to process manually
Item condition	x	
Reference condition type	MWST	
Reference application	V	
Pricing procedure	RVAB01	Tax included in price
Reference step – from	nnn	Reference step of the total
Requirement	010	Plant is set
Account key	MWS	Taxes on sales/purchasing

Table A.26 Configuration for Condition Type MWSI

A.27   NETP (Rounding Difference)

The condition type NETP can be used to change the rounding logic of the standard SAP system. The condition value is determined by formulas. For more information, see Chapter 12, Section 12.3.

Configuration Parameter	Technical Name	Description
Condition class	A	Discount or surcharge
Calculation type	C	Quantity
Manual entries	D	Not possible to process manually
Item condition	x	

Table A.27 Configuration for Condition Type NETP

Configuration Parameter	Technical Name	Description
Pricing procedure	all	
Requirement	002	Item with pricing
Cond. value formula	006	Initial price
Base value formula	003	Net price
Base value formula (alternative)	017	Net price
Account key	ERS	Sales deductions

Table A.27 Configuration for Condition Type NETP (Cont.)

A.28   NETW (Value of Goods)

The condition type NETW is used together with prices including tax in conjunction with the condition type MWSI. It represents the value of goods after deduction of tax. The value is determined by the condition value formula 025.

Configuration Parameter	Technical Name	Description
Condition class	A	Discount or surcharge
Calculation type	G	Formula
Condition category	L	Generally new when copying
Manual entries	D	Not possible to process manually
Item condition	x	
Pricing procedure	RVAB01	Tax included in price
Requirement	002	Item with pricing
Cond. value formula	025	KZWI1 minus tax
Account key	ERL	Sales revenues

Table A.28 Configuration for Condition Type NETW

A.29   NRAB (Free Goods)

The condition type NRAB is used to process a free goods agreement exclusively by means of pricing conditions as a value-based discount.

The base value formula 029 (free goods/incl.) is used to determine the values. You can find more information in Chapter 7, Section 7.5.

Configuration Parameter	Technical Name	Description
Condition class	A	Discount or surcharge
Calculation type	C	Quantity
Condition category	f	Free goods inclusive
Manual entries	D	Not possible to process manually
Item condition	x	
Quantity conversion	x	
Pricing procedure	RVAA01	Standard
Requirement	059	Free goods
Base value formula	029	Free goods/incl.
Account key	ERS	Sales deductions

Table A.29 Configuration for Condition Type NRAB

A.30 PBBS (Base Price)

The condition type PBBS provides the starting price in the price book. It uses the access sequence PR01 that first checks whether the preceding condition type PBUD has determined a deviating price list type. In addition, a possibly deviating pricing date supplied by condition type PBUD is used by the requirement 202 (price book—base price). For more information, see Chapter 8, Section 8.1.2.

Configuration Parameter	Technical Name	Description
Access sequence	PR01	Price (item price list)
Condition class	B	Prices
Calculation type	C	Quantity
Item condition	x	
Scale basis	C	Quantity scale
Scale base formula	202	Price book scale
Quantity conversion	x	

Table A.30 Configuration for Condition Type PBBS

Configuration Parameter	Technical Name	Description
Pricing procedure	RVAA02	Standard with price book
Requirement	202	Price book base price
Account key	ERL	Sales revenues

Table A.30 Configuration for Condition Type PBBS (Cont.)

A.31 PBU (Price Book Determination)

The condition type PBU is used together with the condition types PBUD, PBBS, and PBUP for pricing at sales deals of the price book type (see Figure A.8 and Figure A.9).

The condition type PBU is configured as condition class H (determining sales deal). The effect of this is that the condition is only used to find the relevant sales deal (that is the price book) and provide the sales deal number for the following condition type PBUD in the komp-knuma_ag field.

For more information, see Chapter 8, Section 8.1.2.

Figure A.8 Sales Deal of the Price Book Type with Condition Records for the Condition Types PBU and PBUD

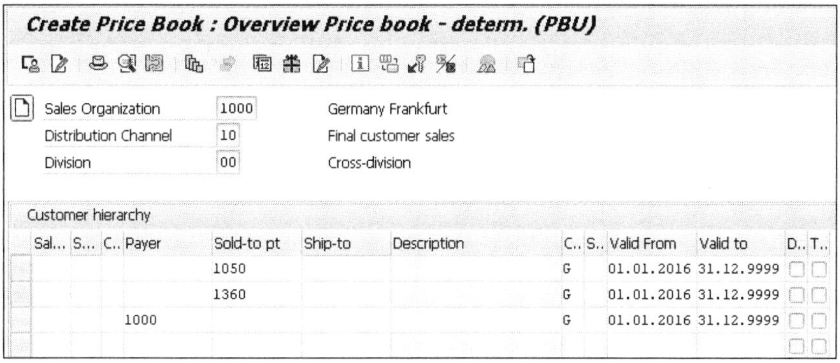

Figure A.9 Condition Records for Condition Type PBU in the Price Book

Configuration Parameter	Technical Name	Description
Access sequence	PBU	Customer data
Condition class	H	Determining sales deal
Calculation type	G	Formula
Pricing procedure	RVAA02	Standard with price book
Requirement	002	Item with pricing

Table A.31 Configuration for Condition Type PBU

A.32   PBUD (Price Book, Basis)

With the condition type PBUD, price-influencing parameters are determined on product or product group level for the use in the subsequent base price condition type PBBS (see Figure A.10). For example:

▸ A percentage of the initial price

▸ The applicable price list

▸ The applicable scale

For more information, see Chapter 8, Section 8.1.2.

Configuration Parameter	Technical Name	Description
Access sequence	PBUD	Sales deal (%/pricing)
Condition class	B	Prices
Calculation type	A	Percentage
Item condition	x	
Pricing procedure	RVAA02	Standard with price book
Requirement	002	Item with pricing
Statistical condition	x	

Table A.32 Configuration for Condition Type PBUD

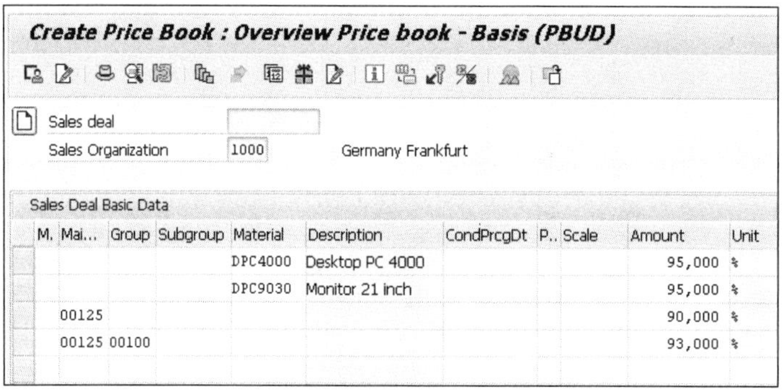

Figure A.10 Condition Records for Condition Type PBUD in the Price Book

A.33 PBUP (Price Book, Gross Price)

The condition type PBUP (without condition records) processes the information of the preceding condition types PBUD (percentage) and PBBS (base price) for calculating the definitive starting price using the base value formula 202 (price book factor).

For more information, see Chapter 8, Section 8.1.2.

Configuration Parameter	Technical Name	Description
Condition class	B	Prices
Calculation type	C	Quantity

Table A.33 Configuration for Condition Type PBUP

Configuration Parameter	Technical Name	Description
Manual entries	D	Not possible to process manually
Quantity conversion	x	
Pricing procedure	RVAA02	Standard with price book
Requirement	002	Item with pricing
Base value formula	202	Price book factor
Account key	ERL	Sales revenues

Table A.33 Configuration for Condition Type PBUP (Cont.)

A.34 PC00 (Profit Center Valuation Transfer Price)

In the cross-company sales process, an internal settlement is carried out between the company codes. In addition to the internal prices (condition types PI01, PI02, IV01, and IV02), the valuation of the internal operation from the profit center view plays a role here. These prices can be defined by condition records for condition type PC00.

Configuration Parameter	Technical Name	Description
Access sequence	PC00	Profit-center-cost valuation
Condition class	B	Prices
Calculation type	C	Quantity
Condition category	c	Transfer price for profit centers
Manual entries	D	Not possible to process manually
Item condition	x	
Quantity conversion	x	
Pricing procedure	ICAA01	Intercompany billing
Requirement	022	Intercompany
Statistical condition	x	

Table A.34 Configuration for Condition Type PC00

A.35 PI01 (Intercompany Price)

The condition type PI01 is used in the intercompany sales process (see Figure A.11). The condition records define the prices for the internal billing between the delivering company code (defined by the plant) and the selling company code (defined by the sales organization).

In this process, the costs in the sales order and the invoice are not represented by the condition type VPRS, but by the internal transfer condition types, for example PI01.

Configuration Parameter	Technical Name	Description
Access sequence	PI01	Plant/material
Condition class	B	Prices
Calculation type	C	Quantity
Item condition	x	
Intercompany billing cond.	x	
Quantity conversion	x	
Pricing procedure	RVAA01	Standard
Requirement	022	Cross company
Subtotal	B	Value transfer to WAVWR
Statistical condition	x	

Table A.35 Configuration for Condition Type PI01

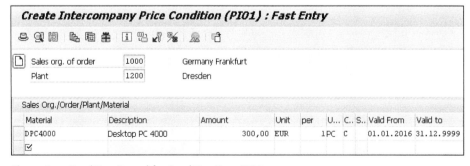

Figure A.11 Condition Record for Condition Type PI01

A.36 PMIN (Minimum Price)

With this condition type, a minimum price for each material can be set.

If the net value at this point is less than the value of the condition type PMIN, the difference is calculated by the condition value formula 015 and is assigned to PMIN as a surcharge.

Configuration Parameter	Technical Name	Description
Access sequence	K304	Material
Condition class	A	Discount or surcharge
Calculation type	C	Quantity
Item condition	x	
Quantity conversion	x	
Pricing procedure	RVAA01	Standard
Requirement	002	Item with pricing
Cond. value formula	015	Minimum price
Account key	ERS	Sales deductions

Table A.36 Configuration for Condition Type PMIN

A.37 PN00 (Net Price)

With the condition type PN00, a manual net price can be entered in the order item.

If the condition type is configured as discount/surcharge using the condition value formula 006 in the pricing procedure, the difference to present net value is calculated as a discount or surcharge.

Configuration Parameter	Technical Name	Description
Condition class	A	Discount or surcharge
Calculation type	C	Quantity
Item condition	x	
Quantity conversion	x	

Table A.37 Configuration for Condition Type PN00

Configuration Parameter	Technical Name	Description
Pricing procedure	RVAA01	Standard
Manual condition	x	
Requirement	002	Item with pricing
Cond. value formula	006	Initial price
Account key	ERS	Sales deductions

Table A.37 Configuration for Condition Type PN00 (Cont.)

A.38 PR01 (Price Incl. Sales Tax)

With condition type PR01, selling prices to end customers in the B2C scenario can be maintained. The tax is included in the price. Therefore, to determine the net value (represented by the condition type NETW), the tax must be eliminated.

Configuration Parameter	Technical Name	Description
Access sequence	PR00	Price
Condition class	B	Prices
Calculation type	C	Quantity
Item condition	x	
Quantity conversion	x	
Pricing procedure	RVAB01	Tax included in price
Requirement	002	Item with pricing
Statistical condition	x	

Table A.38 Configuration for Condition Type PR01

A.39 PR02 (Price Increased)

With condition type PR02, price intervals can be defined. In the example in Figure A.12, the first 100 units cost 120 EUR, the next 100 units cost 115 EUR, and the other units will then cost only 110 EUR within a sales order.

Depending on the situation, the condition type appears several times for each order item in the pricing screen. You should also read the considerations of using the requirement 906 in Chapter 12, Section 12.10.

Configuration Parameter	Technical Name	Description
Access sequence	K305	Customer/material
Condition class	B	Prices
Calculation type	C	Quantity
Manual entries	D	Not possible to process manually
Item condition	x	
Scale basis	C	Quantity scale
Scale type	D	Graduated to interval scale
Quantity conversion	x	
Pricing procedure	RVAA01	Standard
Requirement	002	Item with pricing
Requirement (alternative)	906	Copying in returns
Account key	ERL	Sales revenues

Table A.39 Configuration for Condition Type PR02

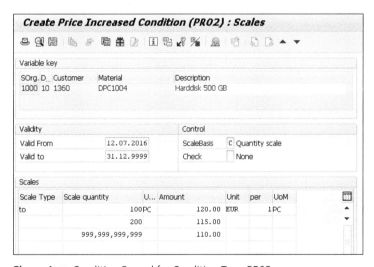

Figure A.12 Condition Record for Condition Type PR02

A.40 PTVO (Voucher)

With condition type PTVO, a manual voucher amount can be entered in the HEADER CONDITIONS screen of the sales order. This amount reduces the final amount payable and is posted in accounting to a special account.

Configuration Parameter	Technical Name	Description
Condition class	A	Discount or surcharge
Calculation type	B	Fixed amount
Condition category	g	Payment
Plus/minus sign	x	Negative
Group condition	x	
Header condition	x	
Pricing procedure	RVAA01	Standard
Manual condition	x	
Account key	PPG	Voucher

Table A.40 Configuration for Condition Type PTVO

A.41 R100 (100% Discount)

With the condition type R100 without condition records, a 100% discount will be granted for free items (free goods). The item category of these items is configured with the indicator PRICING = B (PRICING FOR FREE GOODS). The condition type is activated by requirement 055 and the value is set by the base value formula 028 to a 100% discount.

Configuration Parameter	Technical Name	Description
Condition class	A	Discount or surcharge
Calculation type	A	Percentage
Plus/minus sign	x	Negative
Manual entries	D	Not possible to process manually
Item condition	x	

Table A.41 Configuration for Condition Type R100

Configuration Parameter	Technical Name	Description
Pricing procedure	RVAA01	Standard
Requirement	055	Free goods pricing
Base value formula	028	100 % discount
Account key	ERS	Sales deductions

Table A.41 Configuration for Condition Type R100 (Cont.)

A.42   RL00 (Factoring Discount)

With condition type RL00, discounts can be granted to a central payer in connection with the use of invoice lists, since the payments are facilitated by this type of organization. The conditions are statistically in the invoice and are only activated within the creation of the invoice list and posted in accounting as a credit. The condition type generally occurs together with the associated tax condition type MW15.

Configuration Parameter	Technical Name	Description
Access sequence	RL00	Payer
Condition class	A	Discount or surcharge
Calculation type	A	Percentage
Plus/minus sign	x	Negative
Manual entries	D	Not possible to process manually
Item condition	x	
Exclusion	A	Invoice list
Condition for invoice list	x	
Pricing procedure	RVAA01	Standard
Requirement	023	Only in billing doc
Statistical condition	x	
Base value formula	002	Net value
Account key	ERS	Sales deductions

Table A.42 Configuration for Condition Type RL00

A.43 SKTO (Cash Discount After Tax)

With the condition type SKTO without condition records, the cash discount percentage of the first due date of the payment term (found in table T052) is determined as a statistical discount. The condition type must be positioned behind the tax condition type, so that the tax base is not affected. Which cash discount condition type is active (SKTO or SKTV) is controlled by the requirements 009 and 014 and depends on the company code settings.

Configuration Parameter	Technical Name	Description
Condition class	A	Discount or surcharge
Calculation type	A	Percentage
Condition category	E	Cash discount
Manual entries	D	Not possible to process manually
Group condition	x	
Item condition	x	
Pricing procedure	RVAA01	Standard
Requirement	009	Cash disc. after tax
Statistical condition	x	
Base value formula	011	Cash discount base

Table A.43 Configuration for Condition Type SKTO

A.44 SKTV (Cash Discount Before Tax)

The condition type SKTV is the counterpart to the condition type SKTO, with the difference that the condition type must be placed in the pricing procedure before the tax condition type, since it is intended to influence the tax base amount.

Configuration Parameter	Technical Name	Description
Condition class	A	Discount or surcharge
Calculation type	A	Percentage
Condition category	E	Cash discount

Table A.44 Configuration for Condition Type SKTV

Configuration Parameter	Technical Name	Description
Manual entries	D	Not possible to process manually
Group condition	x	
Item condition	x	
Pricing procedure	RVAA01	Standard
Requirement	014	Cash disc. before tax
Statistical condition	x	
Base value formula	002	Item with pricing

Table A.44 Configuration for Condition Type SKTV (Cont.)

A.45 VA00 (Variants)

With condition type VA00, the prices for the characteristics of configurable products are defined (see Figure A.13, Figure A.14, and Figure A.15). During order entry, the selected configuration characteristics are transferred via the internal table XVCKEY to the pricing program and processed with the KOMPLOOP technique. (For details, see Chapter 9, Section 9.3.)

Configuration Parameter	Technical Name	Description
Access sequence	VA00	Variants
Condition class	A	Discount or surcharge
Calculation type	C	Quantity
Item condition	x	
Condition for configuration	x	
Quantity conversion	x	
Pricing procedure	RVAA01	Standard
Requirement	002	Item with pricing
Account key	ERL	Sales revenues

Table A.45 Configuration for Condition Type VA00

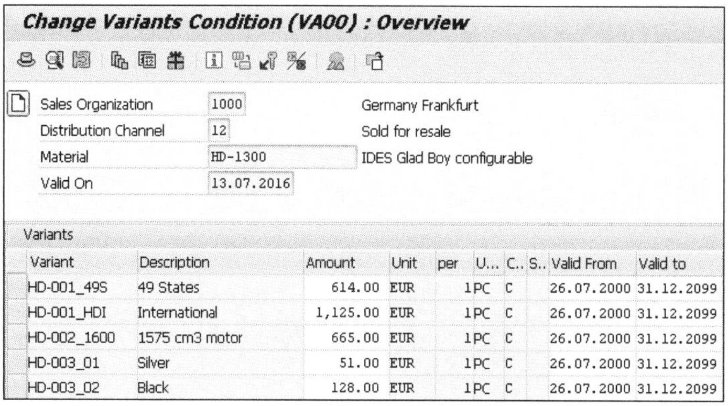

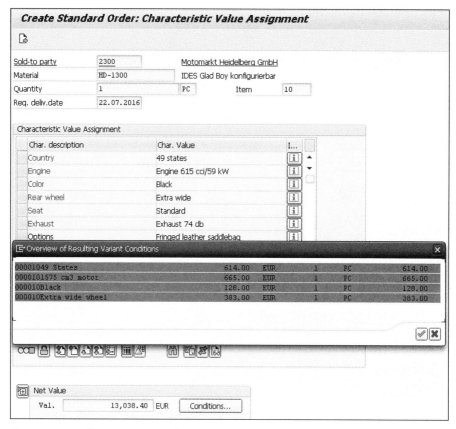

Figure A.13 Condition Records for Condition Type VA00

Figure A.14 Configuration Screen of an Order Item with Variant Configuration and Variant Conditions (the Conditions Button)

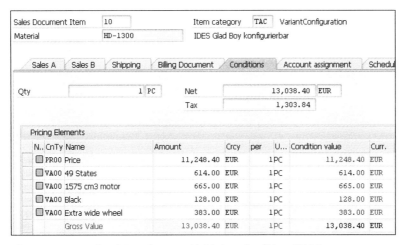

Figure A.15 Item Conditions Screen with Variant Conditions VA00

A.46 VPRS (Cost)

With condition type VPRS without condition records, the cost of the sales trans-action are determined. In the sales order, the value of the condition is determined as *planned costs* from the table MBEW (material valuation). In the billing document, these are the *actual costs* calculated from the goods issue posting (for sales from stock) or from the vendor invoice (for drop shipments). The value is stored in the document item (vbap/vbrp-wavwr).

Configuration Parameter	Technical Name	Description
Condition class	A	Discount or surcharge
Calculation type	C	Quantity
Condition category	G	Internal price
Manual entries	D	Not possible to process manually
Item condition	x	
Currency conversion	x	
Quantity conversion	x	
Pricing procedure	RVAA01	Standard
Requirement	004	Cost

Table A.46 Configuration for Condition Type VPRS

Configuration Parameter	Technical Name	Description
Subtotal	B	Value transfer to KOMP-WAVWR (cost)
Statistical condition	x	

Table A.46 Configuration for Condition Type VPRS (Cont.)

A.47   Z902 (Data Determination Material)

With condition type Z902, the attributes MATERIAL PRICING GROUP, VOLUME REBATE GROUP, COMMISSION GROUP, and MATERIAL GROUP 1 can be maintained date-dependent for a material. In addition, a parent hierarchy can be set up for the material group 1, consisting of the nodes material group 2 and material group 3. The condition type is only for the data determination for the use in subsequent condition types or for the transfer to the sales order and is not visible in the CONDITIONS screen of the sales order item (for details, see Chapter 9, Section 9.2.2). The data transmission in the calling order item is performed by the condition 902 of the condition Z905. The data transfer to the calling sales order item is carried out by requirement 902, which is assigned to the condition type Z905 in the pricing procedure.

Configuration Parameter	Technical Name	Description
Access sequence	Z902	Data determination material
Condition class	H	Determining sales deal
Calculation type	G	Formula
Pricing procedure	ZVAA02	Standard consolidated
Requirement	002	Item with pricing

Table A.47 Configuration for Condition Type Z902

A.48   Z905 (Material Group Discount)

Condition type Z905 can be used to define a discount on the level of a node of the material group hierarchy previously defined by the condition type Z902. (For details, see Chapter 9, Section 9.2.2.)

Configuration Parameter	Technical Name	Description
Access sequence	Z905	Material group
Condition class	A	Discount or surcharge
Calculation type	A	Percentage
Plus/minus sign	x	Negative
Item condition	x	
Pricing procedure	ZVAA02	Standard consolidated
Requirement	902	Data transfer
Account key	ERS	Sales deductions

Table A.48 Configuration for Condition Type Z905

A.49 ZBUP (Price Book, Gross Price)

The condition type ZBUP is a copy of the condition type PBUP, but configured as a discount/surcharge instead of as a price (see Chapter 12, Section 12.11).

Configuration Parameter	Technical Name	Description
Condition class	A	Discount or surcharge
Calculation type	C	Quantity
Manual entries	D	Not possible to process manually
Quantity conversion	x	
Pricing procedure	ZVAA02	Standard consolidated
Requirement	002	Item with pricing
Cond. value formula	006	Initial price
Base value	202	Price book factor
Account key	ERL	Sales revenues

Table A.49 Configuration for Condition Type ZBUP

A.50 ZDB1 (Minimum Profit Margin)

The condition records of condition type ZDB1 can be used to define a minimum profit margin as a percentage of any initial value. This limit is established by the exemplary use of the access sequence K029 on the material group level. The test for falling below the minimum profit margin is performed by the condition value formula 905. When falling below the minimum profit margin, the sales order item is blocked by setting the CEPOK (expected price) indicator. Details can be found in Chapter 12, Section 12.11.8.

Configuration Parameter	Technical Name	Description
Access sequence	K029	Material group
Condition class	A	Discount or surcharge
Calculation type	A	Percentage
Condition category	J	Customer expected price
Plus/minus sign	x	Positive
Manual entries	D	Not possible to process manually
Pricing procedure	ZVAA02	Standard consolidated
Requirement	002	Item with pricing
Statistical condition	x	
Cond. value formula	905	Profit margin check

Table A.50 Configuration for Condition Type ZDB1

A.51 ZM00 (Delta to the Order Value)

The automatic condition type ZM00 without condition records calculates the difference between the current net value and the preceding condition type HM00, if this is configured as a statistical price. The value is calculated by the condition value formula 913 (delta to the order value). For details, see Chapter 8, Section 8.2.4.

Configuration Parameter	Technical Name	Description
Condition class	A	Discount or surcharge
Calculation type	G	Formula
Pricing procedure	ZVAA02	Standard consolidated
Requirement	002	Item with pricing
Cond. value formula	913	Delta to the order value
Account key	ERS	Sales deductions

Table A.51 Configuration for Condition Type ZM00

A.52   ZPBP (Data Determination Customer)

The condition records of condition type ZPBP can be used to assign date-dependent different price list types to the partner roles *payer, sold-to party,* and *ship-to party.* The condition type is needed for the determination of data that is used in subsequent condition types (e.g., the condition types PBBS and ZPRA) and is not visible in the CONDITIONS screen of the sales document. (For details, see Chapter 9, Section 9.2.1, and Chapter 12, Section 12.11.)

Configuration Parameter	Technical Name	Description
Access sequence	ZPBP	Data determination customer
Condition class	H	Determining sales deal
Calculation type	G	Formula
Pricing procedure	ZVAA02	Standard consolidated
Requirement	002	Item with pricing

Table A.52 Configuration for Condition Type ZPBP

A.53   ZPRA (Price (General))

The condition type ZPRA is a copy of the condition type PR00. It is configured with reference to PR00 (and thus reads the condition records for PR00), but uses the access sequence ZPRA.

With this access sequence, only the price list price (this in addition with a differing item pricelist type, if applicable) and the material price are read. The customer-specific condition records are read by the condition type ZPRB. (For details, see Chapter 12, Section 12.11.) The condition type ZPRA replaces in the consolidated pricing procedure the condition type PBBS (Base price) used in the price book functionality (pricing procedure RVAA02).

Configuration Parameter	Technical Name	Description
Access sequence	ZPRA	Price (general)
Condition class	B	Prices
Calculation type	C	Quantity
Item condition	x	
Reference condition type	PR00	
Reference application	V	
Scale base formula	202	Price book scale
Quantity conversion	x	
Pricing procedure	ZVAA02	Standard consolidated
Requirement	202	Price book base price
Base value formula	921	Change factor
Account key	ERL	Sales revenues

Table A.53 Configuration for Condition Type ZPRA

A.54 ZPRB (Price Cust. Specific)

The condition type ZPRB is a copy of the condition type PR00. It is configured with reference to PR00 (and thus reads the condition records for PR00), but uses the access sequence ZPRB and is and set as discount/surcharge. With this access sequence, only the customer-specific condition records are read. In addition, prices may also be stored at the parent nodes of a customer hierarchy. (For details, see Chapter 12, Section 12.11.)

Configuration Parameter	Technical Name	Description
Access sequence	ZPRB	Customer-specific price
Condition class	A	Discount or surcharge
Calculation type	C	Quantity
Item condition	x	
Reference condition type	PR00	
Reference application	V	
Quantity conversion	x	
Pricing procedure	ZVAA02	Standard consolidated
Requirement	002	Item with pricing
Cond. value formula	006	Initial price
Account key	ERL	Sales revenues

Table A.54 Configuration for Condition Type ZPRB

A.55   ZPRC (Price Increased)

The condition type ZPRC is a copy of the condition type PR02. It is configured with reference to PR02 and set as discount/surcharge (see Chapter 12, Section 12.11).

Configuration Parameter	Technical Name	Description
Access sequence	K305	Customer/material
Condition class	A	Discount or surcharge
Calculation type	C	Quantity
Manual entries	D	Not possible to process manually
Item condition	x	
Reference condition type	PR02	
Reference application	V	
Scale basis	C	Quantity scale
Scale type	D	Graduated-to interval scale
Quantity conversion	x	

Table A.55 Configuration for Condition Type ZPRC

Configuration Parameter	Technical Name	Description
Pricing procedure	ZVAA02	Standard consolidated
Requirement	002	Position with pricing
Requirement (alternative)	906	Item with pricing
Cond. value formula	906	Initial price PRO2
Account key	ERL	Sales revenues

Table A.55 Configuration for Condition Type ZPRC (Cont.)

A.56 ZPRD (Contract Price)

The condition type ZPRD combines the contract dependent condition accesses of the condition types PPAR, PPAG, and PKAR by the new access sequence ZPRD and therefore can replace them (see Chapter 12, Section 12.11).

Configuration Parameter	Technical Name	Description
Access sequence	ZPRD	Contract
Condition class	A	Discount or surcharge
Calculation type	C	Quantity
Item condition	x	
Quantity conversion	x	
Pricing procedure	ZVAA02	Standard consolidated
Requirement	002	Item with pricing
Cond. value formula	006	Initial price
Account key	ERL	Sales revenues

Table A.56 Configuration for Condition Type ZPRD

A.57 ZH01 (Budget Approved)

With condition type ZH01, a weight or amount budget can be defined, for example, for a node of a customer hierarchy (see Figure A.16). For this purpose, maximum condition value and/or a maximum condition basis can be entered in the condition record. When exceeding the budget, the sales order will be blocked for delivery using the subsequent condition type ZH02 and must be explicitly released. For more information, see Chapter 12, Section 12.1.3.

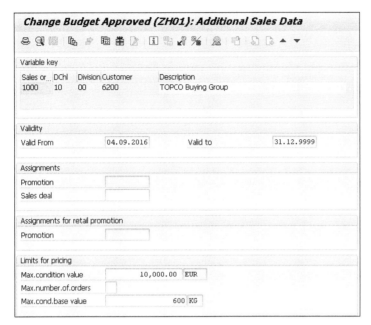

Figure A.16 Budget Condition Record for Condition Type ZH01

Configuration Parameter	Technical Name	Description
Access sequence	HI01	Customer hierarchy
Condition class	A	Discount or surcharge
Calculation type	D	Gross weight
Condition category	J	Customer expected price
Manual entries	D	Not possible to process manually
Item condition	x	
Condition update	x	
Pricing procedure	ZVAA02	Standard consolidated
Requirement	002	Item with pricing
Statistical condition	x	
Cond. value formula	002	Net value

Table A.57 Configuration for Condition Type ZH01

A.58 ZH02 (Budget Requested)

The automatic condition type ZH02 without condition records checks whether a fixed budget given by the condition type ZH01 has been exceeded. In this case, the sales order is blocked for delivery via the condition value formula 900 (budget check) and must be explicitly released. For more information, see Chapter 12, Section 12.1.3.

Configuration Parameter	Technical Name	Description
Condition class	A	Discount or surcharge
Calculation type	A	Percentage
Manual entries	D	Not possible to process manually
Item condition	x	
Condition update	x	
Pricing procedure	ZVAA02	Standard consolidated
Requirement	002	Item with pricing
Statistical condition	x	
Cond. value formula	900	Budget check

Table A.58 Configuration for Condition Type ZH02

B   The Authors

Manfred Hirn studied mathematics with a minor in business administration at the University of Würzburg. In his first job at a brewery, he was involved in the development and introduction of an order and trip management system. In 1984, he joined the SAP development and initially supervised the SAP R/2 billing program. Subsequently, he was responsible for the development of billing, the condition technique, and pricing in the new SAP R/3 system, programming the pricing and billing functionalities. Later he worked as a development manager in the area of sales, pricing, and billing.

Werner Herhuth studied mathematics and business administration with a specialization in business informatics at the University of Mannheim. He worked for 13 years as a systems analyst and head of application programming in the engineering industry and then joined SAP in 1996. He is a certified consultant in the area of order fulfillment (SAP ERP) and the author of several SAP courses.

Dr. Ursula Becker studied physics and astronomy at the University of Heidelberg. After the doctorate and two years of research, she joined SAP in 1998. In the following years, she worked in support and later in development—with a focus on pricing, billing, and rebate processing. She formerly worked in the areas of SAP Customer Relationship Management and SAP Business ByDesign, and has been the responsible development architect for the pricing functionality in SAP ERP since 2009.

Index

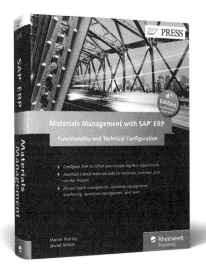

Martin Murray, Jawad Akhtar

Materials Management with SAP ERP: Functionality and Technical Configuration

▶ Configure SD based on unique
business requirements

▶ Master core SD functionality such
as sales, delivery, and billing

▶ Use reporting and analysis tools
to make sense of SD data

Ricardo Lopez, Ashish Mohapatra

Configuring Sales and Distribution in SAP ERP

How smoothly does SD data flow in your system? Learn how to tailor an SAP
ERP Sales and Distribution implementation to align with organizational processes, from quotations and sales orders to shipping and outbound delivery
documents. Get configuration guidance for sales, billing and credit management, distribution, and more. This second edition teaches the ins and outs of
configuring SD.

526 pages, 2nd edition, pub. 11/2015
E-Book: $69.99 | **Print:** $79.95 | **Bundle:** $89.99

www.sap-press.com/3903

- ▶ Explores the key sales and distribution functions and tasks

- ▶ Teaches how to use SD in daily processes, including sales, pricing, delivery, transportation, and billing

- ▶ Guides you in troubleshooting common problems and pitfalls

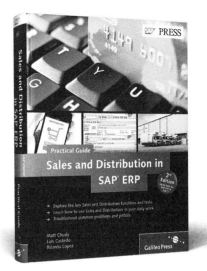

Matt Chudy, Luis Castedo, Ricardo Lopez,

Sales and Distribution in SAP ERP— Practical Guide

It's time to deconstruct your tasks in SD. In this book, you'll find the most common duties you'll need to perform in the SD component explained in a simple manner, with helpful screenshots and lists of transaction codes you'll use. Start the journey with master data setup, and then move on to explore sales, shipping, and billing tasks. Push your skills to new heights by mastering reporting and financial supply chain activities.

520 pages, 2nd edition, pub. 11/2014
E-Book: $59.99 | **Print:** $69.95 | **Bundle:** $79.99

www.sap-press.com/3672

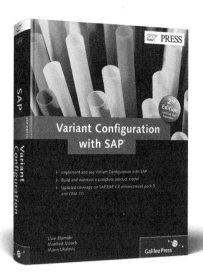

▶ Implement and use Variant Configuration with SAP

▶ Build and maintain a complete
product model

▶ Updated coverage on SAP ERP 6.0
EHP 5 and CRM 7.0

Uwe Blumöhr, Manfred Münch, Marin Ukalovic

Variant Configuration with SAP

This is your complete resource to implementing, setting up, and using
variant configuration with SAP ERP 6.0 and CRM 2007. You'll learn about
the business processes and integration issues, details of configuration in SAP
CRM, special features of industry solutions, and the selected challenges of
using variant configuration. This edition includes updated content on EHP5
and CRM 7.0, as well as extended coverage on the new PLM environment in
WebUI, Product Data Replication, iPPE, and advanced integration processes.

694 pages, 2nd edition, pub. 10/2011
E-Book: $69.99 | **Print:** $79.95 | **Bundle:** $89.99

www.sap-press.com/2889

- ▶ Explains the key financial integration points in Materials Management

- ▶ Includes best practices, real-world examples, and configuration steps for logistics, business transactions, and more

- ▶ Teaches you how to integrate procurement and financial accounting processes

Faisal Mahboob

Integrating Materials Management with Financial Accounting in SAP

Learn everything you need to know about the intersection of Materials Management with Financial Accounting. Start with an overview of SAP MM business processes and the relationship between MM and FI, and then move to the integration points between SAP MM and SAP ERP Financials. Written for ERP 6.0, Ehp 5 and 6, this edition includes details on inventory management, invoice verification, and more practical business scenarios.

508 pages, 2nd edition, pub. 08/2012
E-Book: $69.99 | **Print:** $79.95 | **Bundle:** $89.99

www.sap-press.com/3125

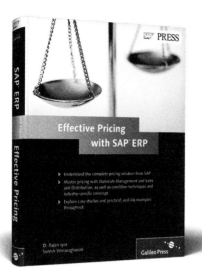

▶ Understand the complete pricing solution from SAP

▶ Master pricing with Materials Management and Sales and Distribution, as well as condition techniques and industry-specific coverage

▶ Explore case studies and practical, real-life examples throughout

D. Rajen Iyer, Suresh Veeraraghavan

Effective Pricing with SAP ERP

This is a comprehensive guide that teaches readers about the business processes and configuration of pricing in SAP ERP. The book discusses the key elements of pricing in Sales and Distribution and Materials Management, and provides complete, step-by-step instructions on how to configure pricing in SD and MM. Coverage includes condition techniques and integration points with Financial Accounting and Cost Accounting. This is a practical and complete perspective on the entire pricing process with real-world examples and practical tips to help readers master pricing.

423 pages, pub. 07/2011
E-Book: $59.99 | **Print:** $69.95 | **Bundle:** $79.99

www.sap-press.com/2543

Interested in reading more?

Please visit our website for all new
book and e-book releases from SAP PRESS.

www.sap-press.com